AEROSMITH – ON TOUR, 1973-85

JULIAN GILL

Original content copyright © 2021 by Julian Gill / AerosmithOnTour.com
Cover art by Chris Hoffman Art, LLC (www.chrishoffmanart.com) ©2020, Chris Hoffman Art.

ISBN-13: 978-1-7344412-9-1

Manuscript Revision: 03/29/2021 08:05:45 AM

No claim over the copyright of any of the original artwork or designs, or any quoted works and/or lyric excerpts, is made. Scans/photographs of artwork and/or items of collector's interest are provided for illustrative purposes only. All licensed photographs © their respective owners (see acknowledgement section for specific attributions).

Table of Contents

Introduction 5

1970–72 - The Grind 7

1973 - Aerosmith 37

1974 - Get Your Wings 75

1975 - Toys in the Attic 121

1976 - Rocks 171

1977 - Draw the Line 225

1978 - Live! Bootleg 283

1979 - Right in the Nuts 315

1980 - Let the Music Do the Talking 347

1981 - I've Got the Rock 'n' Rolls Again 381

1981 - Sharpshooter 407

1982 - Rock in a Hard Place 425

1983 - Always a Rocker 475

1984 - Back in the Saddle 521

Epilogue 555

RIAA Certifications 574

Acknowledgements 575

Introduction

Introduction

"The cleavage of men into actor and spectators is the central fact of our time. We are obsessed with heroes who live for us and whom we punish" (Morrison, Jim - "The Lords and the New Creatures").

Welcome to the 2021 printing of the unofficial & unsanctioned "Aerosmith on Tour, 1973–85." Consider this work an annual compendium. The essential reason is that historical research of this type is a process lived, never completed. So, you simply hold in your hands a point-in-time yearbook comprised of a snapshot of the point that research had reach on a particular day. The addition of new details, minutiae, clarifications, and yes, even corrections, is an ongoing and never-ending process! As a result, contributions are always welcome! Please email *archivist@aerosmithontour.com*. The aerosmithontour.com website will contain most of the material contained within this book — the two are designed to be complimentary, with the book simply being an offline hardcopy of the site.

What is this book? Foremost, it is **NOT** a biography! There's "Walk this Way," the band's official biography by Stephen Davis. Several others have also taken on the task from a third-party perspective over the years, and there is little point regurgitating or relitigating the finer points of Aerosmith's history. And some of the band members have now written their own stories adding their perspectives and memories into the mix. This book celebrates the band's history from the perspective of their life on the road, where they spent much of their time, and the place where they earned their reputation. This book is **NOT** about dirt, though some smudges inevitably will appear on the pane of glass. The compiler of this information is not an insider. Far from it! Instead, the compiled picture, jig-saw puzzle really, is built up through contemporaneous reviews and interviews, concert set lists, and other documented sources. This work DOES have an agenda: To build a view of the band on the road travelled in an if not wholly objective manner, then at least a contemporary and honest one. The desire is to rebuild the band's itinerary show-by-show to know where they were and what they were doing (musically). Concert ticket stubs, show ads, and a plethora of visual artifacts, are used to add seasoning throughout.

Music critics had a job to do, and it certainly wasn't to make fans of any particular band happy — and as a result there are some brutally negative reviews contained within these pages. If you originally read them back in the day, then one hopes you are reminded of your original emotional response back in the day. Ultimately, those reviews matter not a damn. Aerosmith built their legend over a have century of making music and entertaining their fans, with this volume celebrating their formative run 1973–85. The grammar and copy of those reviews have not been corrected, deliberately, so that the original author's voice and intent remains intact...

> **As is the nature with any documentary effort such as this, it can never be a static work considered complete or absolute. There will always be new pieces of information or details surfacing AND corrections to the existing data to be made. This edition is instead simply a current "frozen state" of a long-term project that will never cease; be it by this archivist or by others who will certainly follow...**

Structure of this work:

Not being a traditional narrative, the chapters of this book are broken down on an album-by-album basis. Each starts with a general overview of the album period covered, with U.S. major release issue dates, track listings, production, and songwriting credits, single (●) and album chart action on major U.S. charts, and sales certifications. Not attempt is made to catalogue every release issue throughout the world, and while some international chart data is provided, the work is restricted to a generally U.S. perspective due to that being more suitable for the period. A brief album focus follows, to provide an overview of the recording of an album or the period in between touring, with album review excerpts to illustrate the perception of the work at time of release, to set the stage for the main crux of the work: Aerosmith on Tour!

Usage of some terms in this work:

Other act(s) simply refers to other bands that shared the stage with Aerosmith, either as a headliner (HL) or as an opener, to try and illustrate the band's position on a bill. Sometimes, bands were switched or changed at the last minute, and frequently not all the bands performing would be mentioned in a review. Absence of a mention is a review is not proof of a band's absence from a show. And conversely, there are cases where reviewers mention incorrect bands... By the time the band's headlining status is established, the (opener) tag is generally dropped from the other acts. Generally, the other acts are listed in order of appearance on a bill (where known).

Reported audience is the attendance figure for a show gathered either from industry publications, documents, or in worst case from newspaper review estimates. Where not known, the venue capacity is provided as an alternative for measurement of show scale. Within those figures there is always scope for differences due to venue configuration or numbers of tickets offered for sale and those officially reported. If Aerosmith cancelled an appearance on a bill that still went ahead, or was replaced, then that status is noted with "Aerosmith CANCELLED." If the whole show was cancelled, postponed, or rescheduled then those are also noted. For attendances, there is scope for audience attendance to perceived differently. "Hey, that show was packed. It was a sell-out!" may make sense to the eyewitness, but it's not a factually quantitative figure! The number is simply that which was reported! Guesstimates are noted with ~ prefixed, i.e., ~12,000, or standing room only (**SRO**). Capacities provided are simple contemporary maximum capacities noted in trade references or from "like" artist show reports. For a show, the full capacity usage of a venue can be affected by staging, and many venues have a variety of scales used (i.e., half-house).

Reported gross is simply the gross total ticket sales figure reported in trades by a promoter. It is NOT what Aerosmith was paid for a particular appearance... The purpose, again, is to illustrate scale and growth along the band's career arc.

Set list is self-explanatory, perhaps! In some cases, sets are not known, but songs have been mentioned in the press as being performed. Otherwise, the sets are culled from known bootlegs. For recordings, shows recorded from the audience (**AUD**) are differentiated from soundboards (**SBD**) while videos (**VID**) are differentiated between audience and professional (**PRO**), which were generally via in-house video systems or other formats (**8MM**). In some cases, shows captured from radio broadcasts are noted (**FM**), though those can get convoluted as whether they're pre-FM reel sourced, or post-broadcast home cassette captures ☺. This work is not a bootleg guide! Regarding audio and/or video noted for shows, the quality judgment is subjective — new shows, recordings with improved quality, or alternate sources sometimes surface, leaving quality very much in the eye/ear of the beholder and whatever "version" they might have access to.

1970–72 - The Grind

Joey Kramer: "There are bands that are really terrible that are making a million dollars. There are bands that are really good that are making no money. It's all a matter of chance. No matter how good you are, you have to be lucky to a certain extent" (Boston Herald, 9/16/1973).

Clones of the Stones or heirs apparent to Jim Morrison or a neo-Dead-End Kids? It ultimately matters not a damn; a half-century of music stands testament to a Boston group that became America's band. In popular culture, the Dead-End Kids were a group of menacing New York City street kids. Punks, in other words, though that term would be appropriated for a style of music that had emerged from the garages of disaffected youths in the late-60s. Early acts wearing the label included the MC5 and Iggy and The Stooges, with the latter particularly having taken inspiration from the Stones but transformed it to the point of being nearly unrecognizable (apart from a few unfortunate physical analogues). Where the nihilism of the Velvet Underground broke from direct connections with the Warholian art seen, the emerging glitter movement of the early 70s was firmly rooted in style, performance, and attitude. Aerosmith's goals were simple: essentially to get off playing music to get people off. Though Joe also wanted to play loud, pushing the levels until he could see the sonic waves, much to the chagrin of Steve. The battles were present from the beginning, and conflict and tension would fuel the band to the heights of popularity while slowly poisoning its very soul.

At the time Aerosmith were signed to Columbia by Clive Davis in 1972, few outside of a regional diehard following would have known anything about them, or much less cared. The genre of that sort of music represented was dominated by the Rolling Stones, who had then recently released "Exile on Main St.," the zenith of a period highly acclaimed albums. While response was more mixed after the heights of "Sticky Fingers," "Let it Bleed," and "Beggars Banquet," the band was firmly entrenched in mega stardom, rivaled only by the likes of the Who and Led Zeppelin. Had the members of Aerosmith paid more attention to that album, and its successors, then they might have taken warning and had a vastly different history. Regardless, the individual influences of the band members contributed to the whole, and out of that conglomeration something special would be born. The New York Dolls tried to capture that trip, only to burn out having enjoyed more hype than substance. Aerosmith, though, did it the hard way...

Born in New York City, Steven had become something of a bohemian by the time he reached his teens and lived on the attic floor of his parent's home in Yonkers, New York during the school year while spending summers in the country. It was the best of two worlds. With his father, Victor, a musician formally trained at Julliard's Institute of Musical Art, taught at the private Foxwood school and later at Cardinal Spellman High School. Due to his father's profession and passion, music was a constant in his life. Steve recalled, "I grew up under my father's piano. I'd sit under his big Steinway and play games and pretend things while listening to him practice for two hours every day. So, I was literally immersed in Debussy, Chopin, and Liszt. That's where I got this emotional thing I have with music. My father was a schooled musician who was very much into technique. He'd play a Beethoven sonata in the living room and I'd almost stop breathing. So, I got all my emotions and feelings through music, which gives off twice the emotions and feelings of any other art form" ("Walk this Way). Music was part of Steven's DNA; his paternal grandfather was a cellist who emigrated from the Calabrian region of Italy and worked with orchestras and ballroom bands. His mother, the former Susan Blancha, taught piano. And it wasn't long before Steven was playing drums in his father's band at Trow-Rico. Located in Sunapee, NH, Trow-Rico had started out in 1935, appropriately, as music camp for children opened by his grandmother. By the 1940s it had become more of a summer getaway resort with bands entertaining those escaping the cities.

A hyper-active child, Steven was getting into trouble from the time he could walk which coupled with a bad attitude were perfect characteristics for a rock 'n roller. In his first group, with childhood friend Raymond Tabano, Steven started out on guitar and quickly switched to drums so that he could play with his father's band at Trow-Rico. His first band, the Maniacs followed. His father had already tried, unsuccessfully, to teach him piano, but it took the drumming records of Sandy Nelson to really capture Steven's attention. He was hooked and "Let There Be Drums" could almost be a theme for Steven's Green Mountain Boys. Playing waltzes and showtunes wasn't doing it for Steven, and was kryptonite to girls his age, so he soon set his eyes on something more contemporary — forming a proper band with other kids his age. Before long, Steven was playing drums in the Strangers and occasionally singing with the Dantes, which included Tabano on bass. Steven became a fulltime singer when he decided his band's singer wasn't singing badly, that he could simply do it better. Where the Strangers were more aligned with the sound of the Beatles, the Dantes was projecting a tougher image akin to the Stones.

While at Roosevelt, Steven had been drumming in the Strangers, but wanted to focus on singing. When he saw drummer Barry Shapiro at a talent show, he immediately recruited him for the band, playing their first show opening for the Byrds at the Westchester County Center on March 26, 1966. They were planning, at the time, to soon record their new song, "But I Don't Care." As one review noted, "Lead singer Steve Tallarico came on like Mick Jagger of the Stones: Bottom lip hanging, tambourine slapping against thigh. This was more like it and the audience responded" (Yonkers Herald Statesman, 3/28/1966). By April, the band had a manager, Peter Agosta, who would help take them up the local and regional ladder. They opened for the Animals at the House of Liverpool in Yonkers on May 9... Thee Strangeurs, which Steven has described as a deliberately pretentious name, evolved out of the group discovering there was already an established band in the area with the same name. In July 1966, they beat out other bands in a battle of the bands contest to win a support slot for the Beach Boys at their Iona College performance on July 24. That month the band also signed with Richard Gottehrer's Sire Productions, for a record deal. They'd start recording the following month, completing four songs in several separate sessions over a month. As Peter Stahl recalled, "'The Sun' took three weeks to record because Steven was a perfectionist and drove everybody crazy. He demanded his own mike, which no one had heard of before" ("Walk this Way"). The shape of things to come... In early October, the Strangeurs opened for the Lovin' Spoonful at Westchester's County Center. Interestingly, Aerosmith recorded an unused version of "On the Road Again" for their debut a few years later...

The Staples High School Auditorium in Westport, CT became a regular haunt for the band with them playing their own shows there and opening for the Yardbirds on October 22, 1966. Steven was a student of the Yardbirds: "As a singer, the thing I got out of the Yardbirds was that you don't have to have a great voice. It's all about attitude. Keith Relf wasn't great, but how he sang it made him a master. He was a white boy who pushed it to the max. And he was a great harmonica player. You never heard Jagger hanging out on a single note the way Keith Relf could" (Rolling Stone). More importantly, Steven had connected with a hot young concert promoter, Henry Smith, who booked that Yardbird show and regularly got the band other gigs. While Henry went to work with Jimmy on his new project in 1967, the New Yardbirds, he would later answer the call from Steven in 1973 to bring that same skillset to Aerosmith. The Strangeurs' band name didn't stick and in time, they formally become Chain Reaction in late 1966 when release of their first single on Date Records forced the issue. If competing with another band named the Strangers was a problem, then perhaps it wasn't noted that there was already a Chain Reaction band recording for Dial and Terry and The Chain Reaction on United Artists. The band continued to work with big name acts and supported the Beach Boys are Westchester County Center on April 25, 1967, along with The Buckinghams, Satan's Helpers, and other acts. Winning a battle of the bands, they also supported the band at Iona College in July. Over the next year, while they performed plenty of covers, the had also started amassing plenty of originals, including songs titled "Tomorrow's Today" and "Ordinary Girl."

(Rotated and edited from a full-page Cashbox ad, 12/1966)

By this time, Steven had been thrown out of Roosevelt High School after a drug bust. He was among 10 students arrested on a warrant for marijuana offences on the evening of March 15, 1967 and was charged with violation of 1751-A of the penal law for possession/use of the drug. He enrolled in Quintano's school for Young Professionals (also attended by future Dolls, Sylvain Sylvain, John Genzale, Billy Murcia, and Mary Weiss, Rick Derringer, and the Left Banke's Michael Brown) to finish school. The Chain Reaction had come to nothing and had ultimately broken up. The remaining songs recorded in August-September 1966 were released as a Verve Records single in August 1968. These are of more interest to Aerosmith fans now, than any ripples in the musical continuum their existence made contemporaneously, but for Steven they served part of his apprenticeship and provided more experience in the studio than the other members of a formative Aerosmith had. So too did early "session work," ending up on backing vocals on several recordings (including "Dark is the Bark") for the final Left Banke album or a very young Mark Radice's "10,000-Year-Old Blues" / "Three Cheers (for the Sad Man)" single (released in 1968). As his musical career stumbled, Steven continued to find trouble with the law. He, along with Henry Smith and two others, were busted in Miami in May 1968 for possession of marijuana...

With Chain Reaction in the past, all that Steven was left with was having had a taste... A slight taste of success, sharing the stage with some of the real stars of the day, and a couple of 45s on the Anchorage juke box back in Sunapee. It was never going to be enough. Steven knew where he wanted to get but would have trouble for the next few years trying to find the right pieces is the cosmic musical jigsaw puzzle, and he would be brutal at changing those pieces on his quest. Chain Reaction bandmate, and songwriting partner and keyboard player Don Solomon, was the only holdover for Steven's next couple of bands, the first of which, William Proud, finally reunited Steven with Raymond (on bass), with the addition guitarist Dwight "Twitty" Farren. One of the regular covers in their set, "Love Me Two Times" by the Doors, would later be covered by Aerosmith. But playing clubs in South Hampton made it clear to Steven that he was on a downward trajectory and that William Proud was going nowhere, so after he attempted to strangle Twitty for daring to yawn during a rehearsal, he hitchhiked to

Sunapee and saw Joe playing at the barn... But he didn't quite yet know that he needed a true partner in crime.

Another band followed, another link in the proverbial chain, The Chain. This band included another of Steven and Don's friends from Yonkers, Frankie Ray. This band was performing at The Barn as late as Aug. 1, 1969, before splitting. Steven, close to giving up on his dream, made another attempt at making it on his own, poaching Eddie Kistler (piano/vocals) and Peter Bover (bass), both members of the Nickel Misery (formerly the Sprites), along with Don, for Fox Chase. Steven had been making the rounds of the regional club scene scouting talent and certainly invested time and effort in his pillaging. The result was a band of exceptional quality, though one that would last just seven months even if they could play the hell out of "Pinball Wizard" and "I Want You (She's So Heavy)." The band members had attempted to live in the cabins at Trow-Rico, writing and rehearsing at the Barn, during the winter of 1969/70, but cold conditions forced them into the main house with Steven's parents. With the plan to play originals, the band performed at regional venues such as Dartmouth College which Aerosmith would use as their proving ground early during their career. The group ultimately disbanded due to what Peter described as unrelenting pressure from Steven robbing the music of fun (Brattleboro Historical Society, 7/26/2019). At the time, that perfectionism was noted by Ed Malhoit, the agent of the band (and many other acts) telling another of his bands, "They are so tight, and their arrangements are so cool and complicated. Look at this band that is the personification of rock & roll swagger" (Brattleboro Historical Society, 7/26/2019). The band opened for the Chicago Transit Authority at Endicott Junior College and were promptly banned opening further shows for them!

In 1970, Steven heard through Henry Smith that Jeff Beck was re-forming his Group and was looking for a vocalist. Without a band, which if he couldn't create one of his own, he might as well audition for someone else's, Steven recruited some musicians he knew to help him cut a rough demo of the Beatles' "I'm Down" to submit. Those musicians were Tom Hamilton, Pudge Scott, and Joe Perry. Joe recalled, "He [Steven] asked me and Tom to play on 'I'm Down' for a demo, so he could send a vocal to Jeff. We were in a club and they ran a little Wollensak tape recorder" (Guitar World, 4/1997). Afterward, Steven hopped behind the drum kit and jammed with Tom and Joe for the first real time. However, working together in a band had, at that time, not still progressed past the casual polite suggestion stage and Steven returned to mowing lawns at Trow-Rico...

What's a boy from a small town like Hopedale, MA, twenty-five miles southwest of Boston, supposed to do? While his parents may have had other aspirations for their son, the son wasn't reading from the same book. Early on, Joe idolized Jacques Cousteau, and he wanted to become a marine biologist. It was hardly surprising, with his mother a swimming instructor who also taught gym class at public schools. Activities outdoors, whether in the waters of Lake Sunapee or exploring the curiosities in the woods around his home were adventures. His father was of Portuguese descent and was a university educated accountant who had served time in the military. They were disciplined, but loving, and nurturing parents. They valued education, and all the doors that it could open — they knew firsthand its importance. And while Joe initially had lofty aspirations, he simply lacked the academic ability to translate those dreams into reality. Plagued by a learning disability (ADHD), it didn't matter how much ambition Joe had at a time when such issues weren't diagnosed or understood.

Joe's introduction to the guitar was casual. He recalled, "My uncle had a guitar he built to play folk songs on, and I thought that was cool, so I picked up on it" (Kerrang #160). It would be in his early teens that he started to take the guitar seriously. Self-taught, he recalled taking a single lesson: "I took one lesson from a guy, and then a week later when I was driving to school, I saw a hearse in front of his house. He had died — so, that was the last lesson I took... I just took it as an omen" (Guitar Player, March 1979). Initially, Joe wasn't a good enough guitarist, so he ended up as the vocalist in his first band, the Chimes of Freedom, with

Dave Meade, Bill Wright, and John Alden. Keyboard player Tony Niro joined later. Bill would later be in another band that opened for Aerosmith... Joe kept on with the guitar, improving, "I listened to Roy Orbison and played along, and then came the Beatles, and I saw how many girls they got, so I carried on" (Kerrang #160). Dave Meade recalled Joe's dedication, "He'd just sit in his room and play guitar all the time. I mean really extensively, and when he wasn't doing that, he'd be out looking at other bands" (Milford Daily News, 1/23/2005). Apart from being a friend, Dave also influenced Joe in other ways. His older brother, who's bass he often borrowed, had a music collection that they explored, moving on from the Beatles and Stones to discovering John Mayall, Eric Clapton, the Kinks and John Lee Hooker. It all contributed to Joe's musical foundations. With the cavalcade of British Invasion bands of the time, Joe was soon introduced to the Dave Clark Five and his musical vocabulary grew. But he was also inspired and influenced closer to home. The local professional band, the Wildcats, included guitarist Steve Rose who Perry soon befriended, and he did receive additional lessons from him. Joe recalled, "he just impressed on me that, the music on TV and on the radio, it was not untouchable. It's like being a baseball fan at age seven and watching a major league game on TV. It's a pretty long jump to make it there. But Steve made it seem attainable. And he helped teach me to play" (Noisecreep.com, 10/9/2012).

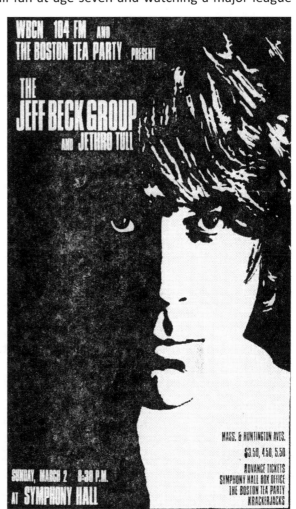

At the end of 10th grade, Joe's grades were suffering at Hopedale High School. He was shipped off to boarding school at the Vermont Academy in Saxtons River, VT, one-hundred miles to the northwest of Hopedale to repeat the grade in hopes that the change of location would spur academic growth. While he continued to play guitar, particularly getting together with friends on home visits, he also stayed active, earning his varsity letter on the school football team in 1967. He also had a prep band, Just Us, while there and the school notes another band he was purportedly involved with, The Surfing Aarjarks. The curious youth had plenty of ambition but wasn't able to translate his intellectual prowess into good grades at Vermont Academy — to the chagrin of pragmatic parents Tony and Mary. He stubbornly refused to cut his hair and dropped out of school just weeks shy of graduation, but nevertheless espoused his father's strong work ethic while toiling in a Hopedale factory and at the family's summer retreat in Sunapee. During the summers at Lake Sunapee, Joe worked the sorts of jobs many teens do. He met David "Pudge" Scott working in the kitchen of the Anchorage Restaurant and the two decided to get a band together. Pudge knew Tom Hamilton, who flipped to bass, and the Jam Band was born. The band were soon playing at the Barn, with a friend of Tom's, John McGuire, sometimes joining them on vocals and harmonica. Other line-ups included a female vocalist. During 1969, while days would be spent working a menial job, the weekends were free for music, and Joe's education continued, seeing the likes of the Jeff Beck Group at Symphony Hall or Fleetwood Mac at the Boston Tea Party. Joe recalled, "I held down a day job and had a band at night with Tom Hamilton. All we wanted was for people to see us, so we'd get another gig. It was an excuse to party and have girls around" (Kerrang #160). There was no great plan in place, though Joe did at least appease his parents by obtaining his High School equivalency.

In Hopedale, Joe played in a band named Flash at various times. It included Dave Meade on bass, and Dave booked shows for the band at the local venues Aerosmith would also later perform at, notably the Hopedale Town Hall Auditorium on June 6, 1968. Joe recalled, "I always thought it would just be a hobby. We'd play at parties when I was a kid; one guy had a garage, and we'd open up the doors so kids could come and watch. The bass player got us a gig at his brother's house, and he says: 'You'll get free beers and five dollars each,' and I said: 'what are they gonna give us money for?' It didn't occur to me that you could get paid for it" (Kerrang #160). Other band members varied depending on who was available. Back in Sunapee, for the 1969 summer Joe found Tom and Purge planning to have a Jam Band with a different guitarist, Guy Williams, that summer. Joe wasn't about to be sidelined. Tom recalled, "One day we're down at Guy's house, practicing. Joe comes over, plugs in, and proceeds to put on the most outrageous display of guitar incredibleness that I'd ever seen in my life! He had practiced his ass off all winter and had all these moves with the whammy bar and he was playing all these outrageous sounds. The rest of us stopped playing. We just stood there watching this solo performance with our mouths open, and I understood that Joe had taken a huge leap" ("Walk this Way"). That summer, on Aug. 30, 1969, the band recorded one of their shows, plus part of a rehearsal, which would be a somewhat fitting commemorative of the summer that Perry came of age. But the following summer things would change. That summer, Joe and Tom planned how they could escape the rut. The catalyst turned out to be Mark Lehman, who also happened to have a van...

Tom Hamilton was born in Colorado, the third of four children. His father was active in the U.S. Air Force during his early life, resulting in the family moving several times throughout his youth. Once his father left the force, the family settled in New London, NH where Tom's father worked as what Tom described in 1973 as an "industrial tool caster." In reality, he worked for Pine Tree Castings, a subsidiary of Sturm, Ruger & Co., Inc, a producer of parts for various firearms. Small town doesn't quite illustrate a town with a population of just 2,236 in 1970 (yes, that's more folk than who were resident at Lake Sunapee in winter). Tom started playing guitar when he was 12, picking up his older brother's Fender when he wasn't home. He'd seen his brother playing along to Elvis when they were younger but had also been given a toy organ one Christmas. Like many kids of the age, started teaching himself with some help from his brother and the "Play Guitar with the Ventures" instructional albums which included lessons to their hits including "Raunchy," "Tequila," "Pipeline," and "Walk, Don't Run." Those records also included the bass parts for players to learn. As a youth, Tom acted in his school's production of "The Skin of Our Teeth" and played on the tennis team. Tom was nearly kicked out of New London High School after an acid dropping incident that left him with a fine and curfew and labeled the town hoodlum.

Early bands included Sam Citrus and the Merciless Tangerines, which resulted in him switching to bass. His teacher for that instrument would be Bill Wyman on Rolling Stones recordings. By his sophomore year he was playing in Plastic Glass with John McGuire (guitar) and Pudge Scott (drums), with Perry sometimes also joining later on. Tom recalled, "Joe (Perry) and I used to get a band together every summer — I've known him since I was 14 or 15. We put a band together called The Pipe Dream when I was about 15. And then at the end of the summer I would go back to school; and he was a 'summer kid,' so he'd go back to Massachusetts and go back to school. The summer after that we put another band together, called Plastic Glass, and then the two summers after that, we had a band called The Jam Band" (Shark Magazine, 8/24/1989). And, more importantly, for four summers he played with Pudge and Joe in the Jam Band, playing at the Lake Sunapee Yacht club, the Barn Nightclub, the Lake Sunapee cruise boat, and house parties and colleges. Tom was inspired that he too could make it in a professional band when he watched the bass player of Spirit, Mark Andes, at a show he and Joe attended.

Making a full-time commitment to music, Joe and Tom were planning on moving to Boston to form a full-time band in the summer of 1970. Pudge wouldn't be coming — he was several years younger and intent on completing high school — but Lehman became the pair's cheerleader. Joe, borrowing money from his mother, combined with his own savings, was enough to get them started and the trio arrived in Boston September 1970. Tom had also already had experience fending for himself outside the family home, following a haircut standoff with his father. The first thing they did was rent an apartment at 1325 Commonwealth in which to live. Then they started the process of finding suitable band members...

Like Steven, Bronx born Joey had grown up in Yonkers. His father was a hardworking businessman while his mother stayed home to take care of Joey and his three siblings. Both parents were first generation Americans infused by the ethos of their parent's immigrant experience. Joey explains, "This whole immigrant experience shaped my parents and how they tried to raise me. They were all about assimilation and material gain — fitting in — and image meant everything to them and was pretty typical for parents in the fifties" ("Hit Hard"). Financial security, safety, respect, were all very important characteristics in the immigrant community, but both of Joey's parents had served in the war with his father being injured. Joey suggests that in a day when PTSD was not diagnosed, his father was likely damaged by the horrors he experienced coupled with a challenging childhood of his own. There would be many factors contributing to making Joey's upbringing anything but pleasant, filled with what Joey describes in his book as emotional and physical abuse. Not surprisingly, Joey's education was full of challenges. He acted out in school and his education suffered accordingly. As a youngster, Joey initially started out trying to learn the accordion, but soon found listening to the crooners of the day, Paul Anka or Joey Dee, captured his attention. Even with lessons, Joey just couldn't fall in love with his instrument of choice, much to his disappointment when he'd see friends passionately enraptured by their instruments and being willing to practice for hours and hours.

One Christmas, one of Joey's friends received a Slingerland kit as his present and invited Joey over to his house to check them out. The sparkle of the finish, the shine of the metal, and the feel of the stick in his hand hitting the snare was enough for Joey to finally have that emotional connection with an instrument. He recalled, "It was a rush like nothing I'd ever felt before. Right there... I was thinking, 'This is good. This feels really good'... Everything I'd experienced up to that point, all the emotions I couldn't articulate or even process or understand, I could feel being channeled through those two wooden sticks and onto the heads of those drums" ("Hit Hard"). With money saved, Joey managed to persuade his parents into letting him rent a kit of his own, a three-piece set of red sparkle Kent's. It was enough for him to get down to the business of learning and at age 13, Joey discovered one thing: He enjoyed hitting hard! And once the Beatles hit and British Invasion started, Joey knew what he wanted to be. There was no doubt! He wanted that drum throne. He wanted to be the one perched behind the other performers, with the best view of the stage and the audience. He had found his muse.

Joey started to improve his rudimentary techniques, disassembling the parts that the likes of Dave Clark, Ringo, or Dino Danelli. While the latter of these influences is better known for his work with the Rascals his background in jazz, he provided a link to the great drummers of the big band era such as Gene Krupa. If Joey saw a drummer on the television, he studied their playing. It's pretty clear that Joey had a natural talent, a good eye and ear, married to a dedication to his instrument. Getting into bands also offered the opportunity to get out of the house, so it wasn't long before Joey was playing with his first groups in 1964, named the Dynamics or shortly afterward the Medallions. As the British Invasion progressed, so did Joey's education, adding the likes of Keith Moon to his list of teachers. He had also moved on to playing with a more serious group, the King Bees, which included the talented Bobby Mayo. Unfortunately, a poor report card resulted in Joey's parents confiscating his drums. With a "battle of the bands" coming up at school, Joey was in desperate straits to not lose what he loved doing. Through a band member's brother, arrangements were made for Joey to borrow another drummer's kit for the show. That drummer? One Steven Tallarico, who even at that stage had reached levels all the amateurs could only aspire to. Steven even joined the King Bees during their performance to sing a couple of Stones songs. Ultimately, following a move to Eastchester and trouble in his new school, Joey was transferred to a private school, ended his participation with the King Bees though a new band soon followed, the Radicals. Another person Joey met in his teens was Raymond Tabano, and it would be at Ray's place that Steven introduced him to the drumming of Mitch Mitchell via Jimi Hendrix's "Electric Ladyland" album. Other bands followed, such as Strawberry Ripple and Nino's Magic Show, and Joey applied his new learning to his drumming as he evolved.

After graduating from Thornton Donovan High School in New Rochelle, the high point, literally and figuratively of Joey's summer was attending the Woodstock music festival during August 1969 with friends. While there he would unexpectedly bump into Steven Tallarico. The cosmos may have been hinting... In the fall, Joey enrolled at Chamberlayne Junior College in Boston, though he really had no interest in pursuing further education but had nothing more appealing to do at the time. By the end of his first semester there he was expelled for troublemaking, but unwelcome back at home he stayed in Boston and got a menial job. It was another fortunate situation that his boss was also involved with a R&B soul band, Chubby & The Turnpikes (who later became the Tavares). During his time working with the band that Joey became more of a "feel" player, where he learned to use the drums to communicate his emotions with the other band members and audience. Because the R&B the band performed involved dance moves, he also learned the importance of choreographed percussive enunciation — playing drum accents that complimented or enhanced the movements of the band members on stage. These would be important additions to his arsenal, in addition to the broadening of his musical vocabulary. He'd also take inspiration from the performance of James Brown, and his all-in effort, something he'd translate into his solos in a few years. Unfortunately, hard living with the soul brothers came at a steep price and Joey ended up fired from his job and hospitalized, so sick that he had to return to his parents in the middle of 1970 to recuperate.

By September 1970, Joey was back in Boston but had enrolled at the Berklee School of Music. A brief attempt to get a band together came to nothing, but Joey discovered that Raymond was living in Boston and the two reconnected. It would be he who told Joey about Joe and Tom looking for a drummer and he soon auditioned for them. He suggests in his autobiography that even at that stage, the two had secured the use of rehearsal space in the basement of 500 Commonwealth Avenue at Boston University. According to Joey's account, they initially passed on him, preferring to go with a singing drummer they knew...

Sunapee, it all went down at the barn... or maybe next to a freshly mowed lawn! By the Joe and Tom returned to Sunapee for a Labor Day party at Pudge's, they'd already auditioned a drummer for their new band. Joey Kramer wasn't sure he wanted to leave Berklee to get back into the band grind, even before they told him that they'd be going with their singing drummer. They probably should have spoken with Steven first, but seemed pretty sure that he was going to join their band in Boston even before the headed up to Sunapee. Joe recalled speaking with Steven: "He was playing with his one partner, Don Solomon, and he wasn't getting anywhere. I know he was kind of getting disillusioned with the whole thing... he said to me he was thinking about doing something else and forgetting about the music business. He was getting sick of it and at the very least wanted to take a break from it or a while. So that's when I said, 'Look, Tom and I have moved into this apartment. We're looking for a singer and a drummer and we've got a couple more bedrooms and we're looking to fill them, what do you think?'" (Rock Cellar Magazine, 11/7/2014). Steven was responsive to the idea, but adamant that he didn't want to drum. He wanted to focus all his energy into fronting the band. That didn't faze Joe, he knew that Joey with his R&B-tinged playing could add a unique seasoning to their sound, if he came on board... However, the sequence of Steven finding out about Joey, and vice-versa, it doesn't matter. Either way, Steven knew Joey and vice-versa, so things were settled. There was one problem: Steven wanted to bring in his bass player. That was a deal-breaker with Tom already being in the band and Joe was not about to dump his friend, so Steven was allowed to bring childhood friend Raymond in as a second guitarist in a trade-off. Joe was open to the idea of two guitarists in the band with other successful bands such as the Yardbirds, Stones, and Fleetwood Mac having done so. That Raymond had played bass in Steven's band previously might simply have made him both of the people Steven wanted with him. And if Steven meant Don Solomon, well Joe didn't care for him anyway...

In some ways, Raymond Tabano was the keystone to the formation of Aerosmith. He was friends with Steven Tyler and acquainted with Joey Kramer back in their youths in Yonkers and was already living in Boston at the time the others started arriving. Raymond's mother played a bit of mandolin during her youth while his father owned a bar in the Bronx where he and Steven would later casually perform, though initially Steven was the guitarist and Raymond the drummer. Steven and Raymond had been friends for years, following their first introduction: "I actually first saw Steven... just after my mother and I moved to Yonkers. I was cruising the neighborhood on my bike and some kid yelled at me and I stopped and this other kid — Steven — comes out of his house and eggs me on to kick this first kid's ass. I guess he'd been tormenting Steven or something. Then Steven kicked me out of his tree, and I had to show him who was boss. But then we became friends" ("Walk this Way"). Raymond felt they were drawn together for sharing a similarly high-octane carefree lifestyle. Tabano was playing in a rival band to Tyler while both attended Roosevelt High School, though he was a couple of years older than Steven. Where Steven's band was more Beatles-ish, Raymond's was more aligned with the Stones. Raymond survived a drug bust in July 1967, though ended up on probation.

The pair eventually joined forces in William Proud, the last band in which Steven would drum. Raymond re-entered the picture during the transitional period between the Jam Band and the formation of Aerosmith Mk.1, in a jam band consisting of Joe Perry, Steven Tyler, Tom Hamilton, and Pudge Scott on drums. He was already in Boston at the time the rest of the band members arrived, having opened a leather shop, "Yellow Cow," with his girlfriend on Newbury Street. Joe recalled, "I didn't know Steven very well at that point: I had talked with him a few times and jammed with him a few times. He said, 'I wanna bring this guy in to play guitar.' The last three years before that I'd played with a three-piece band or a band that had five or six players. I'd tried every kind of a lineup, so I was kind of flexible there. Raymond had a really cool look. He had a leather shop. He was into the American Indian kind of look and had hair down to his butt. He wore an Indian chest plate" (Rock Cellar Magazine, 11/7/2014). Being open to working with another guitarist was little different from playing with John McGuire in bands. Initially, Joe felt that Raymond was decent enough. He commented, "Raymond was a good rhythm guitar player in the classic sense. With the Beatles you had George Harrison who was the lead guitar player and John Lennon who played rhythm and there was a very clear distinction between what each cat played... Ray was really focused on playing rhythm and I was doing the leads. When the band got together Steven (Tyler) wanted someone he knew in the band and he knew Ray for a long time." (Rock Cellar Magazine, 11/7/2014).

With Joe, Tom, and Mark already living at 1325 Commonwealth, Joey soon joined them, and when Steven arrived, the Yonkers boys shared a room in the back. They got menial jobs to make ends meet, Joe working as a janitor and swept the floors at a local Brookline synagogue, Mark played taxi with his van, Steven worked in a bagel shop, and Tom worked as an orderly in a nursing home, and then creatively "managed to lie and cheat my way into a training program which paid about $2 per hour" (San Pedro News-Pilot, 12/9/1973). Joey focused on get back to 100% health following his health challenges. Initially, the band had no name, other than "Joe's new band" or "Steven's new band," discarding ideas such as Hooker or Spike Jones, before Joey suggested Aerosmith. With a name, the band's identity started to be forged in that communal apartment and the practice room at Boston University, playing hour after hour to hone their performance. The communal living bonded them together and gave Steven and Joe time to become the comfortable together. While Steven would remain the band's primary songwriter, the pair learned to work together and off each other's strengths to make the music stronger. Joe recalled the early practices: "We drilled a lot. We would pick the songs apart. I remember Tommy and Joey would drill, playing a part over and over. Sometimes the whole band would cook on one lick, just to get that pulse going" (Guitar for the Practicing Musician, 5/1986). Where Steven might have driven them crazy, especially Joey, with his perfectionism, his knowledge and experience were something that the rest of the band knew they lacked. So, they argued and snorted their way to perfection and bliss.

With a few weeks of rehearsals under their belt, Aerosmith played their first paying gig in Nipmuc Regional High School gym in Mendon on November 6. Their set consisted mostly of covers (as detailed in "Walk this Way" if memories are correct), though six of the songs performed that night later turned up on Aerosmith albums, and of course "Rattlesnake Shake" was the Peter Green Fleetwood Mac song that had gotten Steven hard for if not the quality of the playing, but at least the groove they locked into. Tom Hamilton recalled: "We set up on the floor of the gym for their big dance and we were there playing the songs that we had learned so far. We played gigs at high school because we could play the songs that we wanted. We never failed to get an audience jumping. But, after a couple of years, Steven started writing with Joe, and gradually we had our own songs" (Telegram & Gazette, 7/13/2012). They earned $50, though the show nearly didn't take place due to the band drinking and Steven liberating a Nipmuc Phys. Ed. T-shirt from a student's locker (which he wore for the show, and later). Steven and Joe had a big blow-up following the show with Joe being accused of playing too loud... It wasn't the first argument on that topic, and it certainly wasn't the last. For Tom, the band wanted to start out doing things there way: "We were not at all interested in going to clubs and playing five sets. So, we picked out songs that were fun for us to play and that people could dance to. We did Frat parties and gigs like that. So, you first create and realize your stylistic identity by the songs that you pick to cover" (Guitar for the Practicing Musician, 5/1986). Other shows in town hall auditoriums followed through the end of 1970.

Other covers the band performed during their earliest shows included the Stones' "Honky Tonk Woman" and "Live with Me," "All Your Love" (John Mayall), "Cold Turkey" (John Lennon), "Peter Gunn," and "Shapes of Things to Come." Joe recalled, "if you couldn't play a whole set of what was on the jukebox, nobody wanted you" ("Walk this Way"). But until they had enough songs of their own, they needed a musical arsenal to draw from to sprinkle their own songs in-between. As 1971 dawned, the group broadened their horizons toward the venues they had played with other bands elsewhere. Even with just six months together, by April 1971 the band was starting to look to recording demos to send in to record labels, but other than Steven, they were utter novices with few useful connections. With Mark hauling them around they were very much a cottage industry, a band paying their dues slowly trying to work their way up the proverbial ladder. However, the only thing that really changed during the summer of 1971 was the band's relationship with Raymond.

Playing with Raymond made it clear to Joe that it was not the sort of dual-guitar relationship he was looking for. That's one of the reasons I was so attracted to Fleetwood Mac and especially the Yardbirds when they had Jeff Beck and Jimmy Page in the band at the same time. They were breaking tradition with two lead guitar players in the same band. It wasn't like listening to the Shadows or the Ventures where you had one guy playing lead and one guy playing chords. I didn't have that with Ray, and I wanted that element in Aerosmith" (Rock Cellar Magazine, 11/7/2014). Furthermore, Raymond was strong-willed, independent, and argumentative. Also, not living with the rest of the band during that initial period may have left him a perpetual outsider, he was already the oldest member of the band, some eighteen months older than Steven. But for Joe, there were more important issues: "If he had continued to grow with the rest of the band he may still have been in the band. But he was kind of all over the place. He'd be late for rehearsals. Not only were we learning and getting better on our own as individuals, we were learning to find a sound and starting to develop a real musical backbone by putting our own touches on the cover songs that we were doing. That led to us finding our sound. I found there was a space there and a gap; there weren't many American bands that were doing that two-guitar blues thing" (Rock Cellar Magazine, 11/7/2014).

Raymond was aware of his musical inadequacies and external distractions but was unapologetic. Outside of the band, he was the only one who really had a life. He had a business to run, but he also intimidated other members of the band. Tom was blunt about him: "He wanted things to go his way, and his level of playing really didn't justify all the tantrums and fighting that went on as a result of his personality" (Shark Magazine, 8/24/1989). When the band returned to Sunapee to play a show with Joe Jammer at the Barn, they attended a Justin Thyme show down the lake at Sunapee Harbor. From the moment Aerosmith encountered Brad Whitford Ray's days were numbers, even though he attempted to force the other band members to choose him or Steven. He simply didn't have the musical tools to back up the confrontation and Joe was left the task of firing him, but he didn't go meekly. It took Steven's intervention prior to a booking at the Savage Beast in Ascutney, VT to make it clear that he was out of the band. Following his departure from the fledgling Aerosmith, Raymond sold up shop and headed for Mexico, and then spent time at a hippie commune in Maine. Tyler eventually urged him to return to Boston, and he became the band's marketing director. He'd design the band's original winged logo and made other valuable contributions to the organization. He stayed with the band for the rest of the decade.

Boston born Whitford started out on the piano and trumpet, which didn't last long. When his father bought a cheap acoustic guitar, Brad co-opted it, finding it more appealing. By his early teens Brad was informally attached to his guitar, preferring to learn material himself, after taking some lessons locally. Sharing a room with his older brother, he was introduced to the songs of the day — and those songs were naturally the ones he'd learn to play along with. His brother would also take him to concerts, but it was after seeing a Dave Clark Five show at Boston Garden on June 26, 1965, that Brad decided to form his own band, Symbols of Resistance. As his started to play local hotspots — school cafeterias and clubs. During high school other bands followed, Spring Rain, Teapot Dome, and later the Morlocks. At the time he graduated in 1970 was playing with Earth Incorporated. Musically, however, it would be Led Zeppelin's appearance at Framingham's Carousel Theater on August 21, 1969 that changed Brad's musical outlook towards the guitar completely. The following day he bought a Gibson Les Paul. But the other band that inspired him the most would be Humble Pie, with its two-guitar format and incredible singer.

After high school, Brad studied at Berklee College of Music for a year while playing in another band, Stray Cat. He quit, finding the snobbish attitudes of the jazz crowd contrary to his rock outlook, and he wanted to focus on playing music full time. He then joined Justin Thyme, which included Dwight "Twitty" Farren on lead a band that Farren had put together following the demise of William Proud. By 1971 the band included Brad, and they had a gig scheduled at Lake Sunapee during the summer. Members of Aerosmith turned up to check out Farren's gig, and Brad wowed them. He wowed them more the following night at The Barn when Joe Jammer jammed with Aerosmith and Perry left his guitar on stage and Brad picked it up and proceeded to rip it up with Jammer. A week after the hijinks at the barn, Joe Perry called Brad to get a feel for his interest joining Aerosmith. He invited Brad to see the band play at the Lakeview Ballroom in Mendon. Brad recalled, "They were playing Stones, Zeppelin, Lennon, all these cool covers, exactly the songs you wanted to hear but couldn't, because all the bands that played them were too big to come to your town. They had some original songs too that had a lot of promise. That's how I found the Humble Pie-type band I was looking for" ("Walk this Way"). Brad moved into 1325, with living arrangements there still cramped, but helped by Steven and Joey having moved to other nearby apartments.

Initially, Brad rehearsed with the band, with Raymond still part of the scene, and made his debut with the band during a Labor Day residency at the Savage Beast. He recalled, "My first gig was at a little club in Vermont. The name of the club was the Savage Beast (laughs), and we were playing a rock & roll club show, so it wasn't like a real high-pressure thing and we'd been rehearsing like crazy. It felt good and it worked out really well. I think we knew we were on the right road" (Glide Magazine, 7/1/2014). The autumn of 1971 continued for the band much as things had been prior to Raymond's departure. They played the same sorts of venues across Massachusetts and New Hampshire but got their first break when a club owned saw them open for the James Montgomery Band and offered them a residency at his club. That was Shaboo in Willimantic, CT. By that time, they had also upgraded Mark's van to a Ward school bus. Perry recalled, "We spent many ice-cold nights huddled in the back of the bus on the way to and from isolated gigs in rural New England, trying to keep warm around the gas stove like the crew of some B-17 lost over Germany" ("Walk this Way"). *It ain't easy livin' like a gypsy...*

The band's first big break came when the band auditioned for George Paige, who lived in an apartment with his girlfriend, and her friend who was dating Tom. He was road managing Edgar Winter at the time, and more importantly had a contact at a record label. After hearing them play he became a believer and agreed to help them, even though he thought their internal tensions would quickly end them as a band. Aerosmith recorded a demo of "One Way Street" which was duly submitted for consideration to the label, not that they had much confidence with their performance of a song that was relatively new at the time. George duly took the tape to Stephen Paley in New York City was flatly and strongly rejected. Stephen recalled, "At the time, Aerosmith did not have the song 'Dream On,' which came out several years, and several albums later. Nor did I hear anything else that sounded like something that would get played on the radio. At Epic, back then, in order to break a band, a hit single was very important. My other problem was that I felt Steven Tyler's style of singing was so derivative of Mick Jagger. For me that was the biggest problem, as I was looking for originality or a hit song. Had I heard 'Dream On' at the time, I probably would have recommended that we sign them." Funny thing was George had heard Aerosmith play "Dream On." *Dream until your dreams come true...*

Another break around this time was Aerosmith's debut in New York City, though it's debatable whether it was Tyler's glorious homecoming. The band managed to get the opening slot at the Academy of Music on a bill headlined by Humble Pie, which would have pleased Brad, and Edgar Winter's White Trash Band. With the some not being in a school cafeteria or local club, it was in essence their professional industry debut. And if it went well, it might be another step up the ladder. Promoter Steve Paul insisted that the band only perform three songs. That wasn't particularly unusual, and the crowd were bored and waiting for the bands whose names they knew to come on stage. But Steven wasn't having any of that on his homecoming and brazenly, or perhaps prophetically, opened the set with "Make It." If ever there was a song defining a band's mission, then this served emphatically as a declaration of intention. "One Way Street" and "Major Barbara" followed, perhaps representing the band's catalogue to date as broadly as possible. But after three songs, they weren't done and throwing caution to the wind ripped into "Train Kept A Rollin'" before concluding with "Walkin' The Dog." There may have been a bit of luck in getting the opening slot. British band Bell + Arc were noted on some early ads in the opener slot, then Black Oak Arkansas, so not unexpectedly there may have been some uncertainty in securing a third act. Whatever the case, Aerosmith were going to take that luck and ride it as far as possible.

Following a taste of the big time, it was back to school cafeterias for the band. Sometimes, the Gods are fickle — what is given with one hand is taken away with the other. A series of misfortunes followed the band the winter of 1971/2, some unnecessarily self-inflicted. A steady stream of bookings at the Officer's Club at the Charlestown Navy Yard were cancelled after an incident of petty theft. Not only did the band lose a good pay day, but the side benefit a hearty roast dinner thrown in would have made a nice break from peanut butter and jelly sandwiches or brown rice. Then came the departure of their original roadie, Mark Lehman, which should hardly have been unsurprising with the later admissions of how poorly they had treated him. Once his van had been superseded by the group's purchase of the school bus his days may well have been numbered anyway. Regardless, his importance to the band from their very conception can't be minimized. He made their first fourteen months of existence much easier than it might otherwise have been and did much of the heavy work that made their gigs possible. When he left, they still had the bus, but not the road manager/roadie with the experience required, even at a basic level. Gary Cabozzi filled in for the interim, to lug the band out to a gig at Marlborough High School, halfway between Boston and Worcester, but then, perhaps more critically, they had lost their rehearsal space at Boston University. And the band members still living at 1325 Commonwealth received their first eviction notice. When it rains, it pours...

Searching for a new place to rehearse, the band were advised to check out the Fenway Music Theater by a connection to the facility's assistant manager. There, Aerosmith were introduced to John O'Toole, who after trying to get them to pay for the privilege allowed them a few days free in case he liked them. Tom recalled, "We'd gone for a while without playing a gig and we were on the brink of being evicted, and we were in a local music store asking around about a place to rehearse and this guy said, 'Go ask my brother; he [works] with this manager of the Fenway Theater,' John O'Toole. Then, one day some semi-famous band was supposed to play there but they canceled out. We happened to be up in the balcony waiting for them to go on, and all of a sudden, the manager came up and said, 'Hey, you guys, I need you to play.' So, we lugged all our gear up onto the stage and played, and the audience loved it" (Shark Magazine, 8/24/1989). Fenway had been closed for much of 1971 but had reopened for a single show during the summer (June 30, for Frank Zappa the Mothers with Gross National Productions for two sold-out shows). It then reopened on a more regular basis on December 17. The plan of the owners was to showcase and audition unknown acts on Sundays. A February date had originally been booked for a T-Rex show, with that band having embarked on their first major U.S. concert tour. However, ticket sales were so poor that the show was cancelled, and the theater's manager asked Aerosmith, who'd been rehearsing there, to perform the date for what audience turned up. They played, got a good response from the audience, and the next day an impromptu audition followed. Tom recalled, "The next day John said, 'There's a manager here to see you.' We couldn't see him, the lone figure in this big theater, but we said to ourselves, 'OK, start playing, he's out there.' So, we played for about half an hour, the lights went off, the curtain closed, and he was gone But, he left behind a management contract. It was pretty exciting — that was really a scene out of some movie! So, he started to manage us" (Shark Magazine, 8/24/1989). The he was Frank Connelly...

Frank was a former U.S. Marine officer and Providence College graduate who had taken over the Carousel Theater in Framingham in 1964 — his first season opened with Janye Mansfield starring in "Gentlemen Prefer Blondes." He made a success of the venue grossing $100,000 on a week engagement featuring Tom Jones and branched out into promoting concerts for other acts. He produced the Beatles at Suffolk Downs on Aug. 18, 1966, as they played a short eleven song set for a crowd of 25,000. Another notable act he successfully promoted was the Rolling Stones for the double-header at Boston Garden on Nov. 29, 1969, days prior to Altamont, and he also brought "Jesus Christ Superstar" to Boston in early 1972. With dropping attendances at the Carousel, its property was sold for development in 1970 and the following year Frank was managing the Scarborough Fair club in Revere, while looking for new opportunities as Don Law and the Boston Tea Party filled a void he had willingly left.

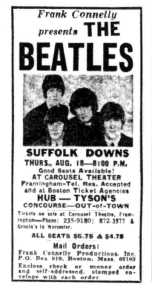

As Joe recalled, the timing couldn't have been more perfect: "We took the contracts back to our apartment, and we sat down at the kitchen table with the contracts in one hand and the eviction notice in the other. We just looked at each other and shook our heads in disbelief. That's how close it was" ("Walk this Way"). Frank had booked the "World Festival of Magic & Occult" at Fenway, March 7-19, after witnessing the large crowds at the New York run. Unfortunately, it didn't translate into sales in Boston and was cancelled at the last moment. The band doesn't appear to have been active much during March 1972, and if Joe's recollections are correct, then their first activity for Frank was to help with his production of Paul Shyre's "An Unpleasant Evening with H.L. Mencken," starring David Wayne, which was scheduled to run at the Fenway, April 11–23. Aerosmith provided the manual labor to unload staging for the show. Unfortunately, the production was cancelled, and Aerosmith continued their rehearsals at the defunct Charles Playhouse. Frank then installed them at engagements at various hotels to tighten up their performance through a grueling series of nightly sets. As he told Steven at the time, the four shows nightly weren't for his benefit (or torture), but for the benefit of the band, who simply lacked the experience Steven had. The band focused on their job — making music and writing and refining their original songs. Following this period of woodshedding, the band returned to New York City to perform a showcase at Max's Kansas City. There was no interest, though Aerosmith also opted not to enter the same glitter scene that New York Dolls were part of, venues such as the Mercer Arts Center, Kenny's Castaways, and the Popcorn Pub (Coventry). In fact, some of those places wouldn't have booked the band anyway. Popcorn Club owner Paul Sub commented, "It was a big club, around 5,000 square feet, and it held around 700 people. Everyone from KISS, The New York Dolls, The

Ramones, Blondie, Sam & Dave, The Dictators and Elephant's Memory played there. I'd put on 10 acts a week, both local and national. The only act we turned down, because we didn't want to spend $300, was Aerosmith (laughs). The New York Dolls were really the ones that kept Coventry going. They played once a month, and whenever they played, 700 people would show up" (Goldmine Magazine, 4/11/2008).

Connelly also got the band rehearsal space at Boston Garden and they were using that space when the Rolling Stones returned for a pair of shows, July 18/19. Frank also had the band rehearsing at Caesar's Monticello in Framingham. Managing a band was one thing, getting one a record deal was an entirely different proposition, and Frank knew his limitations. But Frank's skill was knowing the right people, and he was friends with a pair who had broken away from the William Morris Agency, Steve Leber and David Krebs. They had formed Contemporary Communications Corp. in early 1972, and signed John Lennon's backing group, Elephant's Memory. And in June they added the New York Dolls. During the year they'd also sign Bulldog, a rock group that included Gene Cornish (guitar) and Dino Danelli (drums), formerly of the Rascals. Frank had already promoted some of the acts that they had signed to the Agency, so it was natural that he approached them at their new firm, Leber-Krebs, with a demo from the band. Leber-Krebs were interested and setup a showcase for Columbia's Clive Davis and Atlantic's Ahmet Ertegun at Max's. Ahmet wasn't impressed with Steven's parallels with Mick Jagger, and regardless, Atlantic were already the distributors for Rolling Stones Records (via Atco). Clive, on the other hand was more than impressed, as immortalized in "No Surprize:" "I'm surely gonna make us a star / I'm gonna make you a star / Just the way you are." The $125,000 deal Leber-Krebs negotiated with Columbia was groundbreaking at the time. The artist, in this case the partnership of Aerosmith with Leber-Krebs, as 50/50 partners, would regain control of their masters after a period of 20 years. It was, if not unheard of, then highly uncommon at the time when labels generally owned their artists and controlled much of their creative output. That the band's management had signed with the label, rather than the artists themselves directly, was also not highly unusual at the time, even if it later became a problematic arrangement for both parties. But heading into the autumn of 1972, Aerosmith had inked a record deal before media darlings New York Dolls, and had the serious work to do of getting ready for the studio.

Aero Archeology - The pre-Aerosmith recordings

The Chain Reaction 7" single (1966)
Date 2-1538

A1. The Sun
(2:53) - B. Shapiro, S. Tallarico, D. Solomon, A. Strohmayer, P. Stahl
B1. When I Needed You
(1:58) - B. Shapiro, S. Tallarico, D. Solomon, A. Strohmayer, P. Stahl

Produced by Richard Gottehrer. Arranged and conducted by Dexter Foote. Released in Nov./Dec. 1966. The original June 19, 1968 copyright registration credits full band, though 1992 correction attributes B1 to Tallarico/Solomon/Stahl. The song was credited solely to Steven on "Pandora's Box." Up to six additional Chain Reaction demos are thought to have been recorded by the band and Don Solomon and Peter Stahl also registered the copyright of "The Chain Reaction Songbook I" on Feb. 2, 1968 (no titles listed). A Brazilian band, The Sunshines, released a Portuguese language cover of "When I Needed You" as "Quando Eu Precisei" on their "O Último Trem" album in 1967.

The Chain Reaction 7" single (1968)
MGM Records VK-10611

A1. You Should Have Been Here Yesterday
(2:20) - D. Sloan, P. Stahl
B1. Ever Lovin' Man
(2:25) - D. Sloan, P. Stahl

Produced by Arthur Schroeck and Gene Radice for Cloak & Dagger Productions. Released in August 1968, this single received a brief review in the trades: "Commercial rhythm item with much teen appeal for play and sales in that market. Clever arrangement and smooth group sound" (Billboard, 8/17/1968); and "This imaginative, buoyant rock date uses almost every production trick available, and adds a few of its own. Side has a compelling quality which should see lots of Top 40's going with it" (Cashbox, 8/17/1968).

The Jam Band (1969)
Unreleased

A1. Rice Pudding
Jeff Beck
A2. Shapes of Things
Jeff Beck
A3. Red House
Jimi Hendrix
A4. Let Me Love You Baby
Jeff Beck

B1. Blues Deluxe
Jeff Beck
B2. Gimmie Some Lovin'
Spencer Davis Group
B3. Ramblin' Rose
MC5
B4. Milk Cow Blues
Kinks

Track A1 recorded by Elissa Jarret at the Farm; Other tracks recorded at The Barn, Georges Mills, NH, Aug. 30, 1969 by Bob Grassmere using a Concord two-track reel-to-reel recorder and a pair of Shure microphones. The rough recording was cut to Audiodisc acetates at 33 1/3rpm. These recordings are all live or rehearsal covers attributed to the artists who inspired the young trio of Tom Hamilton, Joe Perry, and David "Pudge" Scott. None have yet been released.

Steven Tallarico: I'm Down (1970)
Unreleased

A demo recorded for his Jeff Beck Group application for the empty vocalist slot. Backing him in Sunapee were Joe Perry, Pudge Scott, and Tom Hamilton... Aerosmith finally released a cover of this important song in their history in 1987...

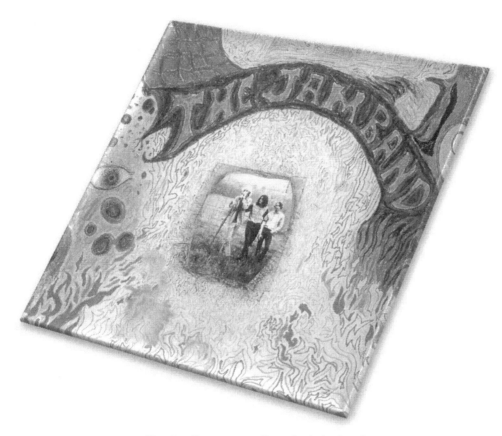

("Jam Band" acetate cover illustration by Joe Perry)

1970

October-November 1970
West Dorm Building Basement @ B.U.
Boston, MA

Notes:
- The alchemist's pit where the first attempts at magical conjuring would take place. Soon after moving to Boston, and taking up residence at 1325 Commonwealth Avenue, the band scored a rehearsal place in the basement of a dorm building at the university, under the proviso that they play some gigs for the students (they'd play outside the Student Union and occasionally in Sargent Gym for more organized Social Council events). A band name soon followed, and the original compositions started flowing as the members bonded musically. Joe recalled that Steven, with his greater musical experience, was more a teacher and the rest of the band members were his students: "He taught us order and discipline and we taught him energy and raw power" ("Walk this Way"). As a teacher, Steven was an uncompromising Sgt-Major, and the rock and roll boot camp was conducted without a velvet glove — and the lessons didn't end back at the communal apartment. While it may have been sadistic at times, the toughness contributed to building the strong foundations that would later keep the band strong musically when the metaphorical storms of performing under the adverse conditions (self-inflicted and otherwise) that ravaged them.

November 6
Nipmuc Regional High School
Mendon, MA

Promoter: Dave Meade / Nipmuc Sophomore Class
Reported audience: ~125
Set list(s): Route 66 / Rattlesnake Shake / Happenings Ten Years Time Ago / Movin' Out / Somebody / Think About It / Walkin' the Dog / Live with Me / Great Balls of Fire / Good Times Bad Times' / Train Kept A Rollin'
Notes:
- Teacher Carl Olson recalled, "Most dances back then were record hops. Having live bands was kind of an unusual thing to do. Still, a group of students convinced me to hire the group. Joe Perry (Aerosmith's guitarist) is from nearby Hopedale and the kids were friendly with him, so we convinced the principal to allow us to take 50 bucks out of the class treasury in order to pay them for the night" (Milford Daily News, 1/23/2005).
- While nominally managing Aerosmith at the time, Dave Meade was a friend of Joe's who had persuaded him to be lead singer of his band, The Witness, before Joe was shipped off to the Vermont Academy. The two continued to play together whenever Joe returned home.
- Edward Malhoit, who famously captured photographs of the band at this show, had been the agent for Steve's previous band based in VT, Fox Chase...

November 13
Town Hall Auditorium
Hopedale, MA

Promoter: Dave Meade
Notes:
- Joe's hometown. The band quickly decided to avoid the club scene so that they could perform their own material rather than get trapped into the cycle of playing covers and not developing their own songs and identity. They certainly initially learned covers, as illustrated by the set from their first show, but the inclusion of their own songs solidified their goal of becoming a concert band.

November 20
Town Hall

Uptown, MA

December 26
The Galleon
Littleton, NH
Notes:
- The band's first show outside of Massachusetts, the Galleon was a popular nightclub which Steven had previously performed at its opening night, the previous October, while a member of Fox Chase.

1971

January 15, 1971
Y.M.C.A. Gymnasium
Greenfield, MA
Promoter: Greenfield YMCA
Notes:
- This show was "open to all area students in Grades 9 and up. Dress is school clothes and teen dance identification passes are required" (Greenfield Recorder, 1/15/1971). Included with the news item was the classic Tabano lineup photo taken by Christopher Smith. The same news blurb also mentioned, "Although the members of this five-piece group hail from several different parts of the country, they are presently based in the Boston area. Two members originally played together in a very popular group from a year ago called 'Fox Chase.' Recent appearances include the Boston and New York City night club circuit as well as many college performances." As was a theme with many early Aerosmith shows, the venues were ones where he had performed previously.

February 13
Spring St. School Auditorium
Nashua, NH
Other act(s): Sanna Hey, Val-Halla, Gail Ghude, Jerry Dumas, Low Moan
Notes:
- The 6-hour "Good Children" Rock Concert featuring a Captain Video light show!

February 14
Stevens High School
Claremont, NH
Notes:
- This school hosted Senior Dances with local talent such as Gunnison Brook providing the soundtrack, usually the popular covers of the day. This show purportedly included eight acts and a lightshow as a fundraiser for the March of Dimes.

February 19
Town Hall Auditorium
Hopedale, MA
Promoter: Dave Meade
Notes:

Good Children ROCK CONCERT
SATURDAY, FEB. 13, 6 p.m. to 12
At SPRING ST. SCHOOL AUDITORIUM
WITH:
Aero Smith – Sanna Hey
Val-Halla – Gail Ghude
Jerry Dumas – Low Moan
Captain Video Light Show
Tickets $3.00 at door
$2.50 IN ADVANCE
Available at Trow Book Store, Reeds Ferry Market & Bedford Mall Book Store and Hurnum's Grunion

- For the first few months of their career, the Hopedale Town Hall, would become a near monthly booking — until late April when bookings of the hall were put on hold due to complaints of damage to the facilities and the size of the attending crowds, which forced a reassessment of safety with local police. It was a shame, since according to Meade the hall's acoustics were excellent.

February 26
Kearsarge Regional High School
North Sutton, NH

February 27
Rogers High School
Lowell, MA

March 6
Newport High School
Newport, VT

March 27
Junior High School
Claremont, NH

April 2
Y.M.C.A. Gymnasium
Greenfield, MA
Promoter: Greenfield YMCA
Notes:

Aerosmith At Y

Tonight's teen dance at the Greenfield YMCA will mark the return of a very popular five piece group from the Boston area called Aerosmith. Although members originally hail from several different parts of the country, they now appear in the Boston and New York City areas regularly. They specialize in a "showy type" act which has proven rewarding. The group has appeared at major colleges throughout the east with recent appearances at Boston College, Boston University and Harvard. They plan a deal of recording in the future. This is their second appearance at the Y dance this year. The dance is open to all area students in Grades 8 and up. Dress is school clothes. The dance will be 8 to 11 p.m. and all planning to attend must present teen dance identification passes.

- This dance was open to area students in grades 8 and above who had teen dance IDs. The local paper news item detailed, "They specialize in a 'showy type' act which has proven rewarding. The group has appeared at major colleges throughout the east with recent appearances at Boston College, Boston University, and Harvard. They plan a deal of recording in the future" (Greenfield Recorder, 4/2/71).

April 9
Town Hall Auditorium
Hopedale, MA
Promoter: Dave Meade
Notes:
- The last of the Hopedale shows booked by Meade.

April 17
Little Spruce Cafeteria
Stowe, VT

April 20
Lakeview Park Ballroom
Mendon, MA
Promoter: Dave Meade
Other act(s): The Joneses (opener)
Reported audience: 1,044
Notes:

- The Joneses were the top band in the Worcester area at the time but were unwittingly hired to open the show. Aerosmith's then manager, Dave Meade, placed an ad for the show in the Milford Daily News, the band's first for as the headliner.
- Band members were interviewed for a piece that ran in the Worcester Evening Gazette the day before the show (4/19/1971) and featured a photo of Joe.

April 23
Student Union Building @ Boston University
Boston, MA

April 24
Nashua High School
Nashua, NH

May 15
Rogers High School
Lowell, MA
Partial set list: Mama Kin / Dream On / Reefer Head Woman / Somebody / Walkin' the Dog
Notes:
- This show was recorded from the soundboard on two-track, one for the band and one for the band. The tape had been found on the same Chesterfield property where Mark Lehman's infamous van was later found abandoned but had been returned to Steven via his parents (after it was copied).

May 20 **RECORDING SESSION
Power Station
New York City, NY
Notes:
- Due to the credits in "Pandora's Box," and the attribution of the "unreleased alternate version" of "Major Barbara" to this date, it is generally considered that the band did record demos around this time. Whether that song actually dated from that time is another matter, with attributions for the Counterpart Studios recordings on the collection also clearly being incorrect. What is clear, from the April Worcester Evening Gazette feature on the band in April 1971, is that they were certainly intending on recording their first studio demos in the spring of 1971. Add to that the existence of an SBD tape from May 1971 without audience, and there may be more to the story. Finally, there's the small matter that Tony Bongiovi's Power Station Studios didn't open until 1977...

May 22
Mt. Sunapee State Park
Sunapee, NH

June 4
Kearsarge Regional High School
North Sutton, NH

June 12
Bristol, RI

June 16
Windsor High School
Windsor, VT

June 19
Newell's Casino
Whitefield, NH
Notes:
- On the shore of Forrest Lake, Newell's Casino hosted audiences of up to 1,000.

July 2 **JUSTIN THYME
Larry's Playhouse
Sunapee Harbor, NH
Notes:
- Joe and Tom attended this show to see Dwight "Twitty" Farren's new band, which he had formed with Brad Whitford following William Proud breaking up. Witnessing Brad in action came at opportune time with the relationship with Ray Tabano rapidly deteriorating.

July 3
The Barn
Lake Sunapee, NH
Other act(s): Joe Jammer
Notes:
- It would be Joe Jammer who suggested that the band should get Brad Whitford. Joe Jammer jammed with the band and Joe Perry left the stage, with Brad then then grabbing Perry's guitar to jam too ("Walk this Way").

July 16
Slope N' Shore
New London, NH

July 17
Concert on the Green
Dover, MA

July 20
Lakeview Ballroom
Mendon, MA

July 22
Lake Sunapee Yacht Club
Sunapee, NH

August 3
Lakeview Ballroom
Mendon, MA

August 7
Whitman Junior High School
Abington, MA

August 17
Lakeview Ballroom

Mendon, MA

August 19
Lake Sunapee Yacht Club
Sunapee, NH

August 20
Cole's Pond
Hardwick, VT

August 21
Newell's Casino
Whitefield, NH
Notes:
- It would be at one of the Newell shows that Steven subbed for a sick Joey on drums, presumably with the band performing as a four-piece.

August
Menlo Park
Notes:
- The last show with Ray Tabano. While he had already been voted out of the band he wasn't yet gone.

August 24-29
Savage Beast
Ascutney, VT
Notes:
- The Savage Beast was a venue located in a building owned by Louis Chabot. Operated by Joe Helie and Ole Nicolayson, the local Weathersfield Selectmen were fielding numerous complaints from residents about the volume of the music, and behavior of patrons, and other issues at the venue. During the period surrounding Labor Day the venue was the drama of the area, with the town demanding the venue install additional lighting and mitigating measures of the noise. The venue was also raided, with the town then taking legal action to revoke the venue's liquor license. Bands stayed in a cabin on the grounds when performing their usually week-long residencies.
- Prior to this show Steven made Ray's firing clear and Brad played his first show with the band.

August 31
Lakeview Ballroom
Mendon, MA

September 2
Lake Sunapee Yacht Club
Sunapee, NH

September 4
Randolph Center @ Vermont Technical College
Montpelier, VT

September 7
Keene State College

Keene, NH

October 1
Y.M.C.A. Multipurpose Room
Greenfield, MA
Promoter: Greenfield YMCA
Notes:
- Following a brief hiatus, the Greenfield "Y" restarted its Friday series of dance parties featuring local rock entertainers. Shows were moved from the gym to the newly completed second floor multipurpose room. The shows, including the likes of Atlantis and Gabriel (formerly Tracks), had become popular with 350-500 youth attending.

October 1
Barn
North Andover, MA

October 2
Dartmouth College
Hanover, NH
Notes:
- Another of the venues Steven had played at (at Kappa Sig), with Fox Chase, in November 1969.

October 8
Mendon, MA
Lakeview Ballroom

October 15
Barn
North Andover, MA

October 16
The Galleon
Littleton, NH

October 22
Merrimack College
North Andover, MA

October 23
North Reading, MA

October 30
Dartmouth College
Hanover, NH

October 27, 28
Box Club @ B.U.
Boston, MA

November 6
School Cafeteria @ Reading High School
Reading, MA
Notes:
- Brad's former high school (he graduated class of 1970), Justin Thyme had also performed at the school.

November 13
YMCA Community Center
Reading, MA

November 17, 18, 19, 20
Shaboo Inn
Willimantic, CT
Notes:
- After seeing the band open for the James Montgomery Band, the club owner offered them $700 for a four-night run. Club owner David Foster recalled, "they were doing Rolling Stones cover tunes, with a few originals. They showed up in a school bus, and they had spandex pants and shag haircuts. We watched the week build. They started on a Wednesday, and we had a couple hundred people the first night. By the end of the weekend, it was jammed" (Hartford Courant, 8/12/2007).

November 25
School Cafeteria @ Reading High School
Reading, MA
November 26
Lakeview Ballroom
Mendon, MA

December 3 **TWO SHOWS
Academy of Music
New York City, NY
Promoter: Howard Stein
Other act(s): Humble Pie (HL), Edgar Winter's White Trash
Reported gross: $62,000 **both nights, four shows
Setlist(s): Make It / One Way Street / Major Barbara / Train Kept a Rollin' / Walkin' the Dog
Notes:
- According to Robert Grasmere, in "Walk this Way," the band were only supposed to play three songs but extended their set. The band were paid $700 for the engagement.
- From an industry review: "Aerosmith, a young quintet from Boston, wore thin as the opening act, but it was difficult to determine whether nerves or lack of talent was responsible" (Variety, 12/15/1971).

December 4 **TWO SHOWS
Academy of Music

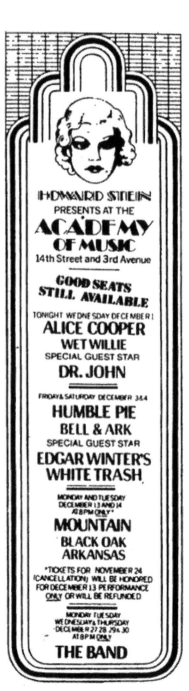

New York City, NY
Promoter: Howard Stein
Other act(s): Humble Pie (HL), Edgar Winter's White Trash
Notes:
- Often (incorrectly) detailed as taking place the following year, Humble Pie was scheduled to play with Bell + Arc, a British band, in the opening slot. However, day of show ads in the New York Times note Black Oak Arkansas. Joe Perry recalled: "We got 20 minutes. There were two shows a night, two nights in a row. Steve Paul, who managed Edgar and Johnny Winter, got us the gig because he wanted to see us. It was our first time playing on a big stage with top-level professionals. We thought, 'Holy shit, man, this is great!' At one point, mid-set, we did a song called 'Major Barbara,' where I sat down and played lap steel and Steven played harmonica. As soon as we got offstage, Steve Paul said, 'What are you doing sitting down? You only got 20 minutes to get this audience off and make them remember who you are, and you sit down? I don't care how good you are. You're a baby band!' After that we might have cut the song out of the set. The bottom line is, that show put us up against bands at the level we were shooting for. When Edgar played, Johnny came out halfway through the set and the place exploded. And then Humble Pie tore it up. It was an amazing experience, before our first record, before our first manager. It made me feel like, 'Somehow we're going to get here'" (Premier Guitar, 10/28/2014)

December 10
Sherborn Regional High School
Dover, MA

December 18
Junior High School
Claremont, NH
Notes:
- A Saturday night dance.

December
Officer's Club @ Charlestown Navy Yard
Charlestown, MA

December 31
Scarborough Fair
Revere, MA
Notes:
- The band's first of numerous New Year's shows. The Scarborough Fair had been known by various names: The Ebb Tide, the Beach Ball, Ocean's Four, and others. It had been owned by Richard Castucci, purportedly connected to the Patriarca crime family who later became infamous as an informant.

1972

January 7, 1972
Lakeview Ballroom
Mendon, MA

January 27
Church of the Good Shepherd

Waban, MA

February 4
Lakeview Ballroom
Mendon, MA

Cricket Lounge
Ashland, MA
Promoter: Fran Horne

February 26
Fenway Theater
Boston, MA
Promoter: Music Productions
Other act(s): Unknown.
Reported audience: (1,700 capacity)
Notes:
- This general story has possibly been conflated with the one told by Tom Hamilton in "Walk this Way," about Cactus being booked at the theater and cancelling due to snow preventing the band from reaching the city and Aerosmith instead being drafted to perform for the small audience.

May 8 **REHEARSAL
1325 Commonwealth Ave.
Boston, MA
Notes:
- On this night Aerosmith's rehearsal at their communal apartment was interrupted by the death of a teenaged friend of the superintendent's son, who fell from the roof of the building after huffing hair spray (as recounted, though possibly conflated, in Joe's autobiography).
- If one takes the "Pandora's Box" liner notes as gospel, then the band had also recorded a cover of the Loving Spoonful's arrangement of "On the Road Again" at Intermedia Sound Studios in Boston this day. That song had originally been recorded by the Memphis Jug Band in 1928 (credited to Jab Jones and Will Shade). The recording is described as a "pre-production rehearsal jam."

May 20
Rowes Wharf
Boston, MA

July
Galaxy Room @ Sheraton
Manchester, NH
Notes:
- Under the guidance of Frank Connelly, the band took up a two-week residency to woodshed and get tighter as a band unit and prepare for the next showcase without the distractions of being at home.

July
Max's Kansas City
New York City, NY
Notes:
- The band's first New York club performance(s) didn't generate any industry buzz.

August 1
Starlight Lounge
Peabody, MA

August
Canobie Lake Park
Salem, NH
Notes:
- Part of the RKO "Summerthing." Steven suggested this show took place in 1973 in the "Walk this Way" book.

August 5
Max's Kansas City
New York City, NY
Notes:
- Aerosmith performed what was in essence a showcase for Atlantic Record's Ahmet Ertegun and Columbia's Clive Davis.
- The day following this show, Judy Carne's eight-week run in "Cabaret," with her portraying singer Sally Bowles, at Caesar's Monticello came to an end (it had started June 13 running daily except Mondays). For those interested in Joe's story about Judy in his autobiography, Bette Midler's run at Lennie's ran June 26 - July 2.

August 6
Gunnison Manor House Party
Goshen, NH
Promoter: Gunnison Brook
Other act(s): Justin Thyme, Stop, Look & Listen, Spice, American Stone (opener)
Notes:
- Gunnison Brook's party with the bands playing off the back porch of the communal house. Aerosmith drove up on the afternoon of the party, after locating Joe, and simply were the last band to play. Following this show Joe left for Philadelphia with Judy Carne. Her run in "Cabaret" ran at Philadelphia's Playhouse in the Park, Aug. 14-19.

October 7
Max's Kansas City
New York City, NY
Notes:
- Steven suggested that this show was conducted for booking agencies and industry types, which would so some ways towards explaining the review that soon appeared below... As a result, the band signed with the International Famous Agency and met Laura Kaufman who became their first publicist.
- From a trade review: "Are you looking for that extra spurt of energy that is often missing from the new wave of 'mellow' musicians? Fear not, thy search is over. Aerosmith is bursting with rhythm and raunch, carrying on in the tradition of the Stones, but with the new rock innuendos of the 70's. The sound radiates total energy but is still dynamic enough so that this quintet managed to play tastefully in a room as contained as the upstairs at Max's. Aerosmith is into instant impact- precise licks that are direct and to the point. Even the original

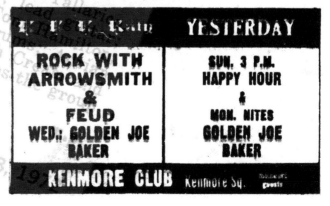

song titles reflect this concept, tunes such as 'Mama Ken' [sic], 'Make It,' 'Movin' Out,' and 'Dream On.' Group personnel is Steve Tallarico, lead singer; Joe Perry, lead guitar; Joey Kramer, guitar; Tom Hamilton, bass; Brad Whitford, drums; Adrian Barber (who worked with Cream and the Allman Bros.) produces the group on Columbia Records" (Cashbox, 11/18/1972).

October 25, 26, 27, 28, 29
K-K-K-Katy's
Boston, MA

Other act(s): Feud
Notes:
- Originally opening as a Dixieland music venue, this club borrowed its name from a World War I era song. By 1976 it had changed formats again and become a disco...
- The opener had headlined at the club, Oct. 23-24, prior to their engagement with Aerosmith. This venue was located downstairs at The Kenmore Club and held about 800 patrons for shows. One attendee at the Katy's gigs would be Charlie Farren. He later recalled, "We went to see Aerosmith at Katy's and again in Revere at a place called 'Scarborough Fair,' and thought, 'I can do this!' So, we started developing an all-original repertoire and began to really catch on. Loud and heavy! We started to try to establish ourselves as a one or two set act" (Wicked Local, 10/2/2008).

December 20, 21, 22, 23, 24
K-K-K-Katy's
Boston, MA

Other act(s): Sadbird
Notes:
- Aerosmith were advertised as "Arrowsmith" in the Boston Globe for this string of dates.

1973 - Aerosmith

U.S. Release Details:
Columbia/CBS KC/CA/PCT-32005 (Jan. 5, 1973)
Columbia/CBS CK-32847 (1987 — CD reissue)
Columbia/SME CK/CT-57361 (Sep. 7, 1993 — 20-bit SBM digital remaster)
Columbia/SME 88765486131 (Apr. 20, 2013 — 180g LP reissue)

Tracks:
A1. Make It
(3:41) — Steven Tyler
A2. Somebody
(3:45) — Steven Tyler / Steven Emspak
A3. Dream On •
(4:28) — Steven Tyler
A4. One Way Street
(7:00) — Steven Tyler

B1. Mama Kin
(4:25) — Steven Tyler
B2. Write Me
(4:11) — Steven Tyler
B3. Movin' Out
(5:03) — Steven Tyler / Joe Perry
B4. Walkin' the Dog
(3:12) — Rufus Thomas

Album Details:
Produced by Adrian Barber. Engineered by Adrian Barber and Caryl Weinstock assisted by Bob Stoughton. Recorded at Intermedia Sound, Boston, MA in October 1972. Cover design by Ed Lee and Hiroshi Morishima. Cover photograph by Robert Agriopoulos. Tracks A3 & B2 were later remixed by Ray Colcord. The original issue credited B2 as "Write Me," but some later reissues used the full "Write Me A Letter" title (which was also used on the song's copyright registration). 2013 vinyl pressing remastered by Ryan Smith At Sterling Sound, New York City, NY.

Players:
◦ Mama Kin — David Woodford on saxophone.
◦ Write Me — David Woodford on saxophone.

Chart Action:
Chart Peak (USA): #21 (4/3/1976) with 58 weeks on the Billboard charts, though it initially only reached #166 during 1973. Some sources note the album charted for 59 weeks — that number is an error. The cumulative charting weeks for the album in the Top-200 chart in the Mar. 13, 1976 issue of Billboard was incorrectly calculated. Other countries: N/A.

09/08/73	09/15/73	09/22/73	09/29/73	10/06/73	10/13/73	10/20/73
209	207	204	208	203	190	188
10/27/73	11/03/73	11/10/73	11/17/73	11/24/73	12/01/73	12/08/73
185	179	175	170	169	167	** 166 **

Second charting:

03/01/75	03/08/75	03/15/75	03/22/75	03/29/75	04/05/75	04/12/75
181	171	160	150	139	139	X

Third charting:

09/20/75	09/27/75	10/04/75	10/11/75	10/18/75	10/25/75	11/01/75
110	97	86	86	84	119	122
11/08/75	11/15/75					
171	X					

Fourth charting:

01/24/76	01/31/76	02/07/76	02/14/76	02/21/76	02/28/76	03/06/76
188	149	136	126	100	77	67
03/13/76	03/20/76	03/27/76	**04/03/76**	04/10/76	04/17/76	04/24/76
57	29	23	** 21 **	22	22	22
05/01/76	05/08/76	05/15/76	05/22/76	05/29/76	06/05/76	06/12/76
27	38	56	52	52	50	48
06/19/76	06/26/76	07/04/76	07/10/76	07/17/76	07/24/76	07/31/76
48	45	70	70	80	78	88
08/07/76	08/14/76	08/21/76	08/28/76	09/04/76	09/11/76	09/18/76
86	141	139	187	185	184	182

RIAA/Sales:

In the United States, the album was certified Gold by the RIAA on Sept. 11, 1975 and Platinum and 2X Platinum on Nov. 21, 1986. Gold by the CRIA (Canada - 50,000 units) on Nov. 1, 1976 and Platinum on May 1, 1979. During the SoundScan era, the album had sold 347,332 copies between 1991 and 2007.

Supporting Singles:

• "Dream On" (USA, 9/1973) - Chart Peak: #59 (12/1/1973) on its initial release in 1973. When reissued in Dec. 1975 the single ultimately peaked at #6 on both the Billboard and Cashbox charts. Other countries: CAN #90 (1973) and #10 (1976); ISR #12 (1976).

09/15/73	09/22/73	09/29/73	10/06/73	10/13/73	10/20/73	10/27/73
122	128	116	114	119	88	74
11/03/73	11/10/73	11/17/73	11/24/73	**12/01/73**	12/08/73	12/15/73
70	63	63	64	** 59 **	63	67

Second charting:

01/10/76	01/17/76	01/24/76	01/31/76	02/07/76	02/14/76	02/21/76
81	69	59	49	41	34	30
02/28/76	03/06/76	03/13/76	03/20/76	03/27/76	04/03/76	**04/10/76**
27	27	19	8	7	7	** 6 **
04/17/76	04/24/76	05/01/76	05/08/76	05/15/76	05/22/76	05/29/76
16	16	45	51	62	97	X

Steven: "We did it on our playing; we sold more albums in Boston than J. Geils. We never had any publicity; I can think of two ads we had in national papers and two shitty reviews. But the fact remains we're selling records" (Los Angeles Free Press, 1/25/1974).

Once Clive Davis had signed the band work began in earnest on material for the album. The band already had six definite songs, but they needed additional material and being on salary with Leber-Krebs made life easier for them. Several of the band members had girlfriends, and had moved in with them, bringing to close the time at 1325 Commonwealth. That cocoon had served its purpose, bonding the five into a unit with a collective identity — not a band of brothers (with the internal dynamics and tensions) but an Aero Force. Preproduction for the album started at a Frank's sister Mary Delmonico's vacant house in Boxborough. They were living like gypsies, backed by the support of Connelly and folks at the label such as A&R man Ray Colcord. As a freshman band they had little say in the matters of importance, such as Adrian Barber's appointment as producer. Their focus was on the music, Leber-Krebs focus was on the business side of the equation and how to grow the band from the seed that had taken root upon signing. From the band's perspective, Barber had the requisite credentials and had worked with bands whose names they recognized. They figured that his job would be to press record and turn the sounds that the band heard in their heads or on stage into a hit record. Were it only so simple ...

That the album would essentially be Steven's is hardly a surprise. With his experience and nature, he had taught the band how to rehearse, conducted those rehearsals to the point of torture, and taught them how to cook as players. He was the musical sculptor, and while all the band members would be part of what was created, it was primarily his vision being captured at this formative stage. Boston's Intermedia Studios at 331 Newbury Street was chosen for the recording of the album. Local for the band, it offered both convenience and was technically suitable for the purpose, hosting 16-track recording equipment. Managed by Dr. Gunther Weil (a psychologist), by late-1972 had become a center for national labels. Albums had been recorded for the likes of Polydor, Atlantic, Capitol, while Boston's emergence as a reputable non-hype music scene was being maintained, avoiding like a plague the gimmickry of the "Bosstown" sound. The band didn't need any gimmicks, already having an abundance of excitement and charisma, and the inherent echoes of the Rolling Stones visually and musically. That benefit wasn't lost on David Krebs: "The Dolls made the mistake of getting too heavy into the unisex trip, while Aerosmith had the good sense to go in the direction of the Rolling Stones of the Seventies, which is more difficult to pin down" (Rolling Stone #220, 8/26/1976). And more importantly, perhaps, they avoided being over-hyped, though unlike the Dolls they certainly had much more to back up their arrogance with other than image. Recording an album was the first step towards building a career, and the process for the first album took roughly three weeks.

"Make It," the album's lead-off track, would serve the critical role of being the song and sound that would introduce a new listener to the band. It had almost chosen itself as a great paean to the musical hopes and aspirations, not only of its writer, but the band and their enthusiastic manager. It was also a pretty good musical calling card that would often by used to open the set. Like the majority of the songs on the album, it was Steven's composition, one inspired by his vision of driving from New Hampshire to embark on a new dream. However, he deliberately took the perspective of how he would want to open a show with a declaration to the audience. The earliest known performance of the song dates from the band's opening slot for Humble Pie at the New York City's Academy of Music in early December 1971. For what was supposed to be a three-song slot, using it as the opener bespoke both message and belief in the song. It had likely been tested enough by then for there to be the confidence to use the song in that situation. During the sessions, a lead-in motif would be chopped from the song tightening it up and instead launching it at full-throttle (the alternate version was released on "Pandora's Box). "Somebody" also predated Aerosmith and had been written with childhood friend Steven Emspak, who came up with the music on his 12-string acoustic prior to the pair leaving for the Woodstock Music & Art Festival in mid-August 1969. While Steven was a member of William Proud at the time, he and Steven would give the song its roots at the kitchen of place they were crashing in in Tarrytown. The song would really take form in the period Aerosmith were first taking form when Steven called Emspak to remind him of the riff down the phone. The breakdown in the Rolling Stones' version of "Route 66," was referenced and rearranged, an appropriate ode to another song covered at their first show. While it may have been birthed out of a shared appreciation of the

Yardbirds and other bands of the British Invasion, lyrically it provided Steven with the belief that he could compose an exceptional song. And it was exceptional enough to have been one of the two originals performed at the very first Aerosmith gig, so perhaps rightfully takes its proper place as the second song on the album. Emspak, building on his experience in audio dating back to the Chain Reaction, would build a career in professional audio systems throughout the '70s before moving deeper into technology.

"Dream On," was Steven's baby, birthed from the subconscious influence of his father's piano expressions of great composers as he sat at a piano at Trow-Rico as a teenager, a melancholic reflection of the change of summer to autumn. With a timeless floating melody, the earnest hope of youth and promise was captured through the innocent lens of the unsullied. Well, perhaps not unsullied, but certainly undamaged, even if Tyler had never envisaged his doodle becoming a fully-fledged song. Even after the band had moved into 1325 Commonwealth, Steven would noodle along to the song, so it sank its roots into the band regardless of any intentions. He recalled, "When I wrote 'Dream On,' I went, 'Where did this come from?' I didn't question it. When I read the lyrics back now, for a guy who was stoned, stupid, and dribbling, I got something out of there" (Rolling Stone #694, 11/3/1994). Joe initially was not enthused by the song. He recalled, "Back in those days you made your mark playing live... To me a rock 'n' roll is all about energy and putting on a show... But 'Dream On' was a ballad. I didn't really appreciate the musicality of it until later, but I did know it was a great song, so we put it in our set. We also knew that if you played straight rock 'n' roll you didn't get played on the radio and if you wanted a top 40 hit the ballad was the way to go. I don't know if we really played it much live in those days, if you only had half an hour to make your mark you didn't play slow songs, it wasn't until after it became a single that we really started playing it" (Classic Rock Magazine, 11/2002).

Still, the ballad provided dynamic contrast to the rest of the material on the album, and in the set, with its irrepressible character and beauty. It also belied an understanding of music and structure that would be so central to the band's early development though their cosmic conductor. Band members recalled in Guitar World in 1997 that Brad and Joe separately followed on guitar what Steven's hands were doing on the keyboard, with Joe playing the right and Brad the left. While Steven recalled debuting the song live at the Shaboo Inn in late-1971, after Brad joined, it had been performed earlier with a version existing on a two-track soundboard found on Mark Lehman's former property. Not being able to afford an orchestra for the studio recording, Steven seasoned the song with a mellotron rented from a music store. The album was dry, and for the most part restricted to the band members and their instruments, but with the mellotron, Steven also incorporated harmonics and wood flute. David Woodford was also brought into the sessions to blow saxophone on "Mama Kin" and "Write Me."

On the early track sequence of Oct. 20, 1972, the seven minute "One Way Street" concluded the album. Like, "Make It," it had been recorded at the band's professional debut (and unofficial showcase) at the Academy of Music in late-1971. It had also served as the band's first demo that resulted in their rejection by Epic Records, but at that time had been "too new," to be a confident representation of the band. Months of refinement and development at 1325 transformed it into a confident amalgamation of influences and musical styles, with more than a few nods to the Rolling Stones' "Midnight Rambler" with its bluesy swagger and assorted soloing. In the end Brad felt that it was one of the strongest representations of his improvisational soloing style.

Another of Steven's babies was "Mama Kin," inspired by Blodwyn Pig's "See My Way," and his confidence in the song is as clear as the tattoo on his arm. That when some of the band members went to Eddy's tattoo parlor in Providence and he had the title inked onto his left bicep bespeaks his confidence in what the song represented (Classic Rock Magazine, 11/2002). Predating Aerosmith, Joe felt it was too simple when Steven presented it to the band. Yet, it is perhaps from such simplicity that its greatest strengths come. Originally closing side one, the up-tempo song works better as the lead-off track from side B on the release version rather than the originally sequenced "Movin' Out." Of the originals on the album this song was the only one co-written by a member of the band, and this composition was the first collaboration between Steven and guitarist Joe Perry. Steven recalled, "I remember being overjoyed that I had some lyrics for that, and also that we put another hole in Mark's [the long-suffering roadie] waterbed. I was sitting on the waterbed trying to write these lyrics, and the pipe was lit. We were smoking pot; dropped seeds crackling all over the place. We closed the door and I just remember a stream of consciousness came out" (Guitar World, 4/1997). An alternative take of the song was released on "Pandora's Box," featuring a looser arrangement and extended break section. While that collection may have issues in relation to the specifics attributed to the contents, another inclusion was the cover of John Sebastian's "On the Road Again," attributed to pre-production jams for the album sessions. Originally recorded by the Lovin' Spoonful for their "Do You Believe in Magic" album, Joey suggests in the liner notes that it was one of the first songs the band learned and performed during their musical development at parties and schools.

By Oct. 20, mixes for seven songs had been completed for the album. "Major Barbara" had already been discarded and replaced with the cover of "Walkin' the Dog." That song had originally been released in 1963 by Rufus Thomas, Jr., hitting #10 on the Billboard Hot 100. More appropriately, within the context of Aerosmith, the Rolling Stones included their version on their 1964 debut, though by 1973 it had also been covered by numerous artists included Mitch Ryder and the Flaming Groovies. According to Tom, Steven's "Major Barbara," also pre-dated Aerosmith, but it kept getting bumped off the album by other songs, though there may have been a concern that with "Dream On," two songs outside the more standard rock form may have been too much. That the pair shared a musical kinship having initially found form on the keyboard purchased by Steven's legendary "suitcase" money, they may have been too close. The original version of the song was later released on "Pandora's Box," while a modified version was included on "Classics Live" in 1986. It must have been a song that the band believed in at one point, having been the third of the originals performed at the Academy of Music shows in late-1971,

One of the final songs completed for the album, with a mix date of Dec. 12, was "Write Me," or "Write Me A Letter," with both titles invariably being used (the former appears on the initial pressing and on studio sheets, so it's the form used within this work). While solely credited to Steven, it was the product of unified band effort during rehearsals to thrash the arrangement into shape. According to Steven, the song was "originally 'Bite Me,' something we'd been working on for five or six months starting in the Bruins' dressing room at the Boston Garden, but just didn't make it. Then one day I said, 'Fuck this,' said something to Joey, who started playing like a can-can rhythm thing, and suddenly there it was. The intro comes from the Beatles' 'Got to Get You into My Life,' because we didn't know how to write hooks of our own yet" ("Walk this Way"). While the studio didn't turn into a period of experimentation, with neither the time nor budget, it did at least facilitate the band their first proper recording experience. While they would later bemoan the fact that the production didn't capture their energy, it certainly wasn't a reflection on the material. Their producer, Englishman Adrian Barber, had the proper sort of pedigree having worked with Cream, The Allman Brothers, Rascals, and Buffalo Springfield. Not that the band had much say in his appointment — Columbia had appointed him. The problem wasn't that the band weren't rehearsed enough. Like many debut albums, they'd had had more than enough time to perfect the material they'd record, and they'd been playing it for quite long enough in front of audiences.

The problem was them. As a collective unit, even with Steven's previous experience recording with the Chain Reaction and other bands, they were utterly green and lacked the confidence to question the process. Where the technical team pressed "record," and seemed satisfied by a take, they didn't push the band, nor did the band push themselves to do another, better. The story has often been told of the band near freezing when the red "record" light went on. They were uptight and lost the magic ingredient fluidity and spontaneity bring to the music. No more evident is the inhibition facing the band than on Steven's vocal phrasings. He didn't sound like himself and sang in a manner that he described as Kermit the Muppet singing the blues. It was forced and insecure, and with the hesitancy the material's fire was neutered. For Joe, Steven was also a problem in that his perfectionism sucked the spontaneity out of the room. As rookies, it was later easy to blame the producer as being "useless," but having no previous demoing experience the was little that could be done. Joe recalled his predicament, "Because I lacked the studio chops to prescribe a remedy, I kept quiet. It pained me, though, that my guitar was not cutting through" (Perry, Joe - "Rocks: My Life in and Out of Aerosmith").

The band also was not involved in the album's packaging and didn't see it until the product was ready for release. And then, of course, there was the unfortunate "Walking the 'Dig'" error and mediocre design with seemingly minimal effort put into the front cover. None of the issues with the album can easily be explained for a band that was purportedly signed for a decent sum of money. Even Clive Davis' firing on May 29, for allegedly misusing corporate funds (at a time when the Justice Department was investigating the label over payola), occurred months after album's release. The promotional machine certainly pushed some reviews into syndication, but the band's hopes of reading a review — positive or critical — in Rolling Stone magazine was in vain, even with their album's rear cover bio having been written by Rolling Stone/Phoenix contributor Stu Werbin (they'd have to wait until June 1974 for a mention in that tome for arbitration of pop culture acceptance). Neither Billboard nor Cashbox reviewed the album, though the reviews the album did receive were generally positive in tone. One syndicated piece, which ran in numerous papers, stated: "The music is tough, gutsy, blues-tinged rock at its best. The album is not perfect, but it consistently demonstrates such great strengths that the future of the band appears exceedingly promising" (AP, via Glens Falls Post-Star, 2/17/1973). It was a reassuringly honest appraisal. And it pegged "Dream On" for future success... By the time they had recorded a second album, that single had sold over 120,000 copies — more units than the album. With minimal support, the band had to build their reputation and following the old-fashioned way: On the road in front of audience without the benefit of hype. As Joe Perry put it, "It's one thing to have your debut criticized; it's even worse to have your debut ignored. We were pissed. But we knew that we were onto something because every time we played a new town the audience went wild. And we were always asked back... fans were digging us" (Perry, Joe - "Rocks: My Life in and Out of Aerosmith"). But it was an "us against the world" that the band would have to take.

It was an awkward situation where Columbia released both Aerosmith and Bruce Springsteen's debut albums on the same day, Jan. 5. It was clear which of the two acts they favored. And for Steven, the difference was palpable, "We feel that the album cover (of the first) really set us back. We feel the production set us back, and then they didn't help us for nine months" (Los Angeles Free Press, 1/25/1974). If the band weren't immediately satisfied to have an album out, then they were keen to prove the music to new live audiences. Aerosmith's first major tour support slot mismatched them with the jazz fusion Mahavishnu Orchestra. It is unlikely that the band opened an earlier show in New Haven on Jan. 19. It was quickly clear who the audience had come to see... The pairing didn't work. For either band or the audience, and Aerosmith were booed or, even worse, ignored and treated with contempt. Still, the opportunity provided a challenge to rise to the occasion and attempt to win over new listeners or simply perform better. According to Joe, "When you're a baby band looking to open for a more prominent act, you can't be choosy. Your hope is that their audience will become your audience. It's a way to expand your fan base. But in the instance of our first tour with a name band, that didn't happen. Our managers had us opening for the Mahavishnu Orchestra, whose sophisticated audience had no interest in what we were playing... Their audience had come to hear musical masters, not some up-and-coming garage band" (Perry, Joe - "Rocks: My Life in and Out of Aerosmith"). It was a learning experience for both band and management. According to David Krebs, "The first time I let this band out of the box I got burned. I let my booking agent talk me into having them open for the Mahavishnu Orchestra — which, on a scale from zero to a hundred, turned out to be a definite minus. But we learned to play our market so that Aerosmith opened for acts that were slightly on the downslide — bands whose audience we could cop. Even if we didn't blow them off the stage every time, we could at least count on some to buy an Aerosmith album" (Rolling Stone #220, 8/26/1976).

An industry observer opined, "The system isn't designed to spotlight the newcomer. It's built strictly for the headliner. Aerosmith was an exception. Leber and Krebs (Aerosmith's managers) beat the system. They carefully placed Aerosmith on the bill with headliners who could still draw a crowd but were on the decline. So, what happened? Aerosmith blew the headliners off the stage, night after night. They wowed the kids ... But the industry is geared against that happening. If you're the manager of a headliner, you want an opening act that is 'compatible.' That usually means 'harmless.' No one wants to be upstaged" (Los Angeles Times, 11/27/1977). Following the brief stint with Mahavishnu, the band did a series of dates with the Kinks. One would think that a British Invasion pairing would be perfect, but it wasn't. While the band may not have liked how they were treated, not being allowed to soundcheck, they at least had a more compatible audience that they had half a chance of winning over. But they had to up their game and win over the audience and nothing could be taken for granted. And show after show, their reputation started building and they were picked up by Circus, Creem, and more important regional rock mags. After a summer treading water in the high schools and local venues Aerosmith finally found a more compatible touring partner with Mott the Hoople. The band had released their "Mott" album during the summer as "Dream

On" started to rise. While in decline, the band still scored a top-40 album without the benefit of single success in the U.S. (both "All the Way from Memphis" and "Honaloochie Boogie" stiffed). But they were still a draw on the middle tier of venues, an appropriate next rung on the ladder for Aerosmith. Tom recalled, "That was early 1974, and we had our first album. But we were basically out on the road fighting for our life at that point. We had been getting on tours where we were opening for bands that were completely different than us. We were not opening for very receptive audiences... After a few tours like that we got that Mott the Hoople tour. It was great because we were on a bill that was at least in the same genre: a rock band. And we got a special guest star billing on that tour which meant we had more room on stage, and we had sound checks — now and then. We got a decent dressing room. That tour is where the band really, really made it... I had my first hotel destroying experience. We came home from the gig. And, as usual, we got together with the Mott the Hoople guys to have a party. We were actually in the lead singer of Mott the Hoople, Ian Hunter's room. He wasn't even there. Some of us and some of them got roaring high and trashed the room. Then we all left. The next morning Aerosmith flew on to the next town, but Mott the Hoople had a later flight. So, before they got to the airport, the police came over and busted poor Ian and took him to jail" (Penn Live, 4/30/2014).

"Dream On" was almost too obvious a choice for the band's first single, so many months after the album had been released. It would be lazy to describe the single version as an edit. It's more than that, a butchering of the 4:28 original with sections chopped, moved around, but most importantly it includes elemental additions that change so many of its qualities in comparison with the album version. The introduction section is reduced to the initial acoustic picking with faux orchestral backing. With the longer 24-second part being discarded, just 13 seconds remain to set the tone before the song jumps into the first verse. Bass remains prominent with Joey's percussion and Steven's haunting vocal. As the verse builds to its foot-stomping crescendo, the edit awkwardly jumps the needle to what would be the second chorus on the album version. However, additional choral vocals are layered on providing more of a soaring gospel seasoning that detracts from the guitars. The song moves into the second verse, which is followed by the same chorus as the first, though as was the case with the first use the lead guitar is muted. Instead of leading into the dual guitar picked break section, it goes straight into the chorus repetitions with electric leads that continue to the fade out. By the late summer of 1973, the single was finally lurking around the nether regions of the Billboard Hot 100 singles charts. It would bubble under prior to charting properly at #88 on Oct. 20, following which it enjoyed a brief 9-week run reaching a high of #59 on Dec. 1. It also entered Cashbox's chart at #100 on Oct. 6, charting for 11 weeks and ultimately peaking at #43. While Aerosmith's "Greatest Hits" liner notes suggest that the single had been released on June 27, contemporary trade publications suggest the single was issued in late August or early September. Whatever the case, the single (Columbia 4-45894) was backed with "Somebody" and enjoyed strong regional rotation before Columbia was able to get enough stock distributed and push airplay nationally. Like "Dream On," the single version of "Somebody" was edited, reducing the track's duration from 3:45 to 3:08. It was more than appropriate that 1973 would be capped by the band's national television debut, performing the song on Dick Clark's "American Bandstand" on Dec. 15, immediately prior to them starting work on a new album...

The eponymous album was released on Jan. 5, 1973 and paired with the success of the "Dream On" single, the album entered the Billboard Top 200 charts at #190 on Oct. 13 (having bubbled under from Sept. 8 at #209). In the United States, the album was certified Gold by the RIAA, on Sept. 11, 1975, receiving simultaneous platinum and 2X platinum on November 21, 1986. Gold by the CRIA (Canada - 50,000 units) on November 1, 1976 and Platinum on May 1, 1979. During the SoundScan era, the album sold 347,332 copies between 1991 and 2007. In the U.S., the album charted four separate times on Billboard's Top-200 for a cumulative 58-week charting. It initially enjoyed a 9-week continuous run peaking at #166 (12/08/1973) and charted on Cashbox for 8 weeks reaching #141 in early December. While not spectacular, by any means, the charting of an album released January 5 was impressive, with peak interest building right at the time the band were recording their second album. Eventually, assisted by the re-release of "Dream On," the album reached its overall high position of #21 on Apr. 3, 1976.

An evolution of album credits:

Initial versions of the album included the "Walkin' the Dig" song title error and the "punk" paragraph in the band's bio.

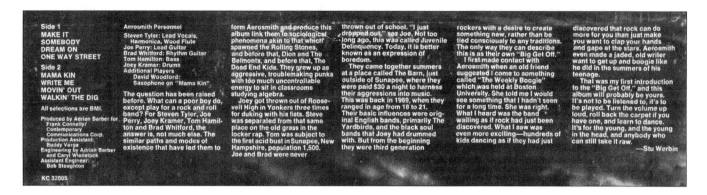

The "punk" paragraph was removed from the bio, the typo corrected, Joe was given a "backup vocal" credit, and David Woodford additionally credited on "Write Me." Also added on the bottom of the rear cover is Joyce McGregor's credit for the front cover lettering.

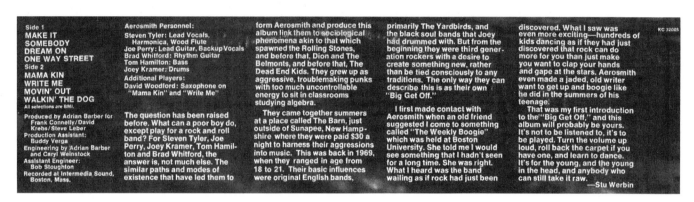

Along with the front cover being altered to wholly feature a band photo, and add "featuring 'Dream On,'" the remixing of a couple of tracks by Ray Colcord was added and the bio removed entirely.

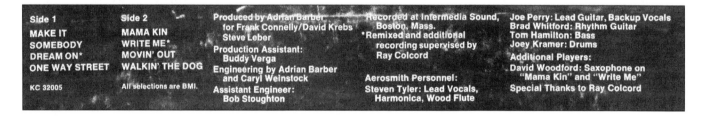

Finally, fan club information was appended to the rear credits.

A UPC code was added to this design for issues pressed in the 1980s.

The 2013 cover is a hybrid recreation based on the original version, though with the song title corrected.

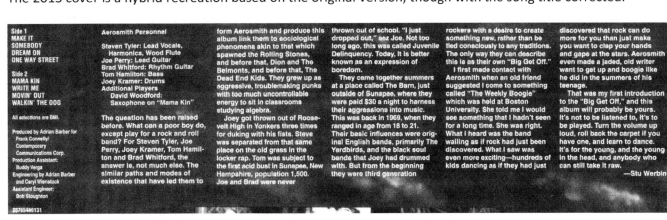

1973 - Aerosmith

Assorted review excerpts:

"Rock and roll has rarely had it as good as delivered in the best get up and dance fashion by this new East coast group headed up by lead vocalist and writer Steve Tyler. Slower, more melodic burn ignites 'Dream On,' while 'Somebody' really shakes it up" (Record World, 1/27/1973).

"With the release of its first album, (Columbia 32005), Aerosmith takes its place in the growing number of good new groups putting Boston back on the musical map. The sound is straight-on, hard driving rock featuring the vocals of Steve Tyler and the guitar of Boston-born Joe Perry" (Boston Globe, 2/2/1973).

"Aerosmith, a new band from New England, is good enough to become America 's answer to the Rolling Stones. Those who doubt that prediction, are invited to listen to their debut album, one of the best albums of hard rock by an American band in years. The music is tough, gutsy, blues-tinged at its best. The album is not perfect, but it consistently demonstrates such great strengths that the future of the band appears exceedingly promising. The music is almost all original, written primarily by lead vocalist Steve Tyler, who is good enough to hold his own with anyone. The group consists of Joe Perry and Brad Whitford on guitars, Tom Hamilton on bass, and Joey Kramer on drums. Guitar and vocals are very powerful and supporting roles of bass and drums are also excellent. The group's playing is extremely together, even though the group still has rough edges. There are several tunes in the album which could and should emerge, with 'Make It' and 'Somebody' and 'Dream On' the best. Any one could pop, particularly 'Dream On,' a beautiful rock ballad" (Glens Falls Post Star, 2/17/1973 — syndication).

"Aerosmith is a Boston-based band that's best feature is its snappiness and tightly-knit sound. Joe Perry's lead guitar is good and strong, and the whole group sounds well-practiced (that's often the case with first albums, because a group finally commits to vinyl the songs it's been doing live for a year). 'Mama Kin,' which leads off side two, is an excellent steamer, and even the slower material, such as 'Dream On,' has a quiet perseverance that makes it well worth the listening. Aerosmith really moves into its own at album's end, however, as a midnight mover called 'Movin' Out' segues into what is absolutely the best version of 'Walkin' the Dog' that's been done in the last 10 years. Everything is perfect, and the rhythm is just changed enough to keep the song from being so much recycled soul food. The group has a tendency to rip off certain Stones and Who riffs, but that's almost unavoidable when doing this type of hard rock. Aerosmith are new, and they are good" (Hartford Courant, 2/17/1973).

"This young group from Yonkers achieves all that punk-rock bands strive for but most miss. Clichéd but properly raw lyrics are growled and rasped by a fine, manic voice. The guitarist packs a Rory Gallagher wallop... 'Aerosmith' is a hearty, sensual, hip-shaking serving of hot rock" (Los Angeles Times, 2/17/1973).

"Every so often a good new group comes along, the only problem with the good new group being that it sounds like so many other good new groups. The best exceptions are the groups that suggest new directions, but that isn't what Columbia's Aerosmith does at all. If there are no new musical guideposts here, at least there is some pleasant retrospection in what they do. For here, basically, is decent rock 'n' roll, often with a John Mayall-like touch. There's something for almost everybody in these eight songs. It's the kind of record where you can listen or boogie — one that doesn't make impossible demands on your head" (Hackensack Record, 3/11/1973).

"With its first album (Columbia), Aerosmith takes its place with the growing number of good new groups putting Boston back on the musical map. The sound is a straight on, hard driving rock featuring the vocals of

Steve Tyler and the guitar of Boston-born Joe Perry. They are two-year veterans of the local club and college circuits. Seven of the album's eight cuts were written by the group, with the exception of an interesting hard rock treatment of the R&B 'Walkin' the Dog.' For a debut album, it is surprisingly devoid of weak material. 'Dream On,' the only slow tempoed number, impressed me the most with its fascinating musical themes, but the group's great appeal is in its hard, rolling-stonish rock. You'll be hearing more from this group" (Boston Globe, 3/16/1973).

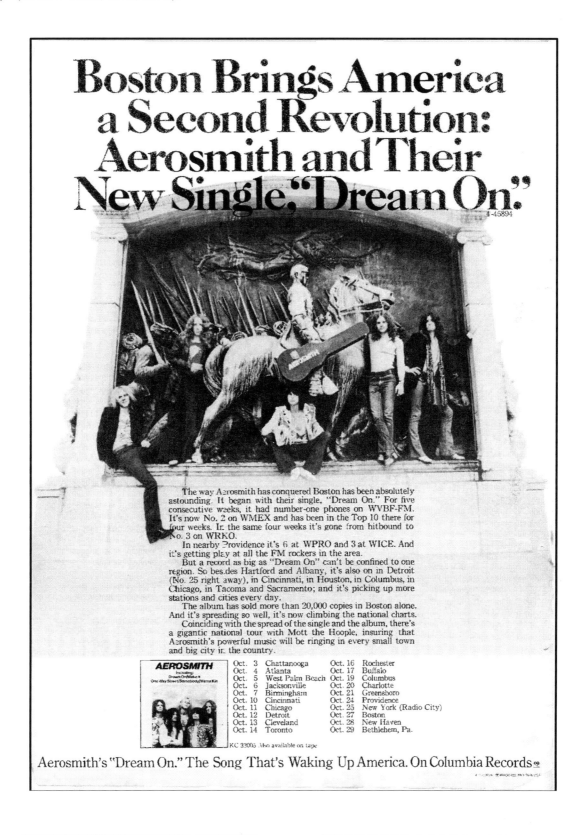

January 27, 1973
Century Theater
Buffalo, NY
Promoter: Buffalo Festival
Other act(s): Mahavishnu Orchestra (HL)
Notes:
- The pairing with John McLaughlin's Mahavishnu Orchestra was a challenging one for the young band. Mahavishnu was lauded for its musicianship, jazz infused with East Indian sounds, intense performances, and esoteric themes. The band had released their second Columbia studio album, "Birds of Fire," two days prior to the release of Aerosmith's debut. Regardless, with a studio album of their own to promote, the band were up for the sorts of challenges that they would have to face, and conquer, were they to become a successful act. The band didn't open for MVO's following night's show in Albany.

February 2
Haas Center for the Arts @ Bloomsburg State College
Bloomsburg, PA
Promoter: BSC Student Union
Other act(s): Mahavishnu Orchestra (HL)
Notes:
- From a local review: "There was a warm-up group, but they hardly merit mention. They were awful. McLaughlin and his entourage more than made up for their feeble efforts" (BSC Maroon and Gold, 4/7/1973). Ouch. Mismatched bill indeed, even if the two bands shared the same record label and both played loudly.

February 3
Civic Center
Baltimore, MD
Promoter: WKTK-FM
Other act(s): Bruce Springsteen, Eric Anderson, local talent
Notes:
- The Second Annual Exposition, which drew 18,000 to the 12-hour trade event, which included live performances by local and national bands. Traffic played a separate concert at the venue that night.

February 10
Ferris Athletic Center @ Trinity College
Hartford, CT
Promoter: Cornucopia Presentations
Other act(s): Mahavishnu Orchestra (HL)
Reported audience: ~2,500
- From a local review: "A Boston group, Aerosmith opened the evening. They played hard, blues-derived rock. Pretty nondescript, but enjoyable none the less. The lead singer bears a slight resemblance to Mick Jagger and milks it in his mannerisms and dress. During their dozen or so numbers, I could not distinguish one single word he sang. How loud and good were they? Good and loud" (Hartford Courant, 2/11/1973).
- Regardless of the tone of the concert review mention, the debut received a positive review in the same paper: "Aerosmith is a Boston-based band that's best feature is its snappiness and tightly knit sound... Aerosmith are new, and they are good" (Hartford Courant, 2/17/1973) noting standout tracks such as

"Mama Kin" and "Movin' Out," while positively salivating over the version of "Walkin' the Dog,' proclaiming it the best of the past decade.

February 14
Ford Auditorium
Detroit, MI
Promoter: Bamboo Productions
Other act(s): Mahavishnu Orchestra (HL), Jo Jo Gunne
Notes:
- The band were noted as "Arrowsmith" in ads, though the Feb. 16 Detroit Free Press review of the show omitted any mention of them. Interestingly, McLaughlin had played guitar on Miles Davis seminal jazz fusion album, "Bitches Brew" (1970), later the title of an Aerosmith song...

February 15 **POSTPONED
Western Hall @ Western Illinois University
Macomb, IL
Other act(s): Mahavishnu Orchestra (HL)
Notes:
- Two shows were scheduled. The show was postponed until Feb. 21 and was replaced with a show at the University of Toledo (at least for Mahavishnu).

February 16
Reflections
Cincinnati, OH
Promoter: Kohnen & Moorman Productions
Other act(s): Featherstitch
Notes:
- On this date, Mahavishnu Orchestra played a show at Kenyon College in Gambier, OH.
- From a trade review: "Characterized by their north-east reputation for in-person work, the group (which combine the talents of Steve Tyler as lead vocalist, Tom Hamilton on bass, Joey Kramer on drums, Brad Whitford on rhythm guitar and Joe Perry on lead guitar) wasted no time in getting into their repertoire by doing cuts such as 'Walking the Dig' [sic], Mama Kin,' 'Make It,' and others from their latest album which is titled 'Aerosmith.' Throughout the entire evening, from the time they came on stage, was there rarely a person sitting. Tyler's stage charisma was such that along with the rest of the group, it literally brought the audience away from their tables and up to the stage time after time with their 'Boston type boogie.' In all, Aerosmith is distinctively a truly good time boogieing band enhanced with R&B" (Billboard, 3/3/1973).

February 17 **Aerosmith CANCELLED
Adelbert Gym @ Case Western Reserve University

Cleveland, OH
Promoter: Belkin Productions
Other act(s): Mahavishnu Orchestra (HL)
Notes:
- Aerosmith was bumped from the bill when their equipment arrived late.

February 18
Kinetic Playground
Chicago, IL
Promoter: Howard Stein
Other act(s): Mahavishnu Orchestra (HL)
Reported audience: (500 capacity)
Notes:
- Originally booked at the Aragon, the Mahavishnu set was recorded at this show.

```
ADELBERT CLASSES &
MATHER GOV. present
Columbia Recording Artists
AEROSMITH
&
MAHAVISHNU ORCHESTRA
with John McLaughlin
SATURDAY
FEBRUARY 17, 7:30 P.M.
ADELBERT GYM
Tickets $4°° advance
      5°° at door
Tickets available at: CWRU Record Store, all Cleveland
Tux Shops, Ward's Folly & Suratorium.
```

February 21 **DOUBTFUL
Western Hall @ Western Illinois University
Macomb, IL
Other act(s): Mahavishnu Orchestra (HL)
Notes:
- Rescheduled as two shows from Feb. 15. There was no mention in the WIU Courier whether Aerosmith was also on the bill. Additionally, the Courier also calls into question whether any Mahavishnu show took place, suggesting in April that the then recent Humble Pie show had been the first rock show of 1973. Mahavishnu Orchestra were present at the NEC Convention in Cincinnati on Feb. 20 to perform a short 20-minute set for prospective show bookers. Whatever the case, Aerosmith's short run with the band had concluded around this time.

February 28
Newport High School
Newport, RI
Other act(s): Cotton Mouth

March 3
Orpheum Theater
Boston, MA
Promoter: WBCN Presents
Other act(s): Doug Sahm & Band (HL), Eric Weissberg, David Bromberg (opener)
Reported audience: (2,800 capacity)
Notes:
- Benefit concert for the Warehouse Cooperative School in Watertown.
- From a local review: "As it turned out, the highpoint of Saturday's benefit appeared early... in the form of Aerosmith. They play loud, raucous punk-rock (a sharp contrast to the other three acts) and have built an image of neo-Dead-End Kids to go along with the music. Much of their sound and on-stage style is blatantly taken from Mick Jagger and Co., but the variations and refinements of those basic are what bring Aerosmith above the level of simply Stones-rip-offs. Lead singer Steve Tyler (who sounds like the Guess Who's Burton Cummings) focuses their recorded music around his ripping vocals, and leads the band live with his Jagger-circa-'72 (complete with scarves) theatrics. Combined with guitarists Brad Whitford and Joe Perry, and the rhythm section of Joey Kramer and Tom Hamilton, they produce massive, raw doses of sizzling electricity, infused by little changes of melody. The 'Aerosmith' album is a killer, particularly numbers like 'Mama Kin,'

'Make It,' and 'Movin' Out;' on stage the power and the energy is all the more palpable. And so, it was, Saturday at the Orpheum; after Aerosmith, it was all anticlimactic" (Boston Globe, 3/6/1973).

- From another local review: "When Aerosmith took the stage everything seemed to click. The Boston-based group, which recently came out with its first album (on Columbia) stunned the crowd with a display of flash, power, and flawless execution. The lead singer had all of Mick Jagger's moves and then some and cut through the band's thick texture with searing renditions of material, which was superbly arranged, and which gave the group an opportunity to make effective use of dynamics. Perhaps the most compelling facet of the band's sound was its tight, hard-driving rhythm section. Though the bassist waxed complex at times, he was there when necessary, working with the drummer to give the band its strong kick; the drummer was simply fantastic, playing with a crisp, cutting sound, and responding to the lead singer with deep, well-timed rolls. Aerosmith is the kind of band, however, which is so collective and tightly-knit that it makes it impossible to single out any one person who is most responsible for its excellence" (Boston Herald, 3/6/1973).

March 19, 20
Paul's Mall
Boston, MA

Promoter: In-house
Set list: Make It / One Way Street / Somebody / Write Me / Mother Popcorn / I Ain't Got You / Movin' Out / Walkin' the Dog / Train Kept A Rollin' / Mama Kin
Notes:

- Paul's Mall was better known as a jazz joint but saw increased patronage when they started booking rock and pop acts such as Jesse Colin Young, Seals & Crofts, and Randy Newman.
- Aerosmith was initially scheduled to perform solely on the 19th. They were given an extra night when Tracy Nelson's run was adjusted to March 21–25. Saxophonist David Woodford, who had performed on the first album, joined the band for several songs. Steven Tyler recalled: "Joey Kramer used to play in a lot of soul bands. He was with black guys for four years before Aerosmith. And we met a guy, David Woodford, who played saxophone, and we used to jam with him every now and then. Bobby Keys, who plays with the Stones, played a show with us once. I've always had this desire to have a saxophone player in the band" (Rolling Stone #694, 11/3/1994).
- This show was originally recorded by and broadcast on WBCN-FM. "I Ain't Got You" and "Mother Popcorn" were later incorporated into Aerosmith's 1978 " Live! Bootleg" album. Due to the broadcast, the show has circulated in its entirety for decades. The date of the show has also long been debated, though Steven's flowery comment following the first song, "To the breath of spring, to energy," seems to clearly point the show being close to the spring transition of Mar. 21.

March 30
Fordham University Gymnasium
New York City, NY

Promoter: Lehman College / in-house
Other act(s): Kinks (HL)
Notes:

The Kinks were unknowingly touring in support of their "Great Lost Kinks Album" (Reprise MS2127) which had been released on Jan. 25. It would only reach #145 on the Billboard album charts. They band only discovered that the album had been released while on tour, and featured songs recorded between 1966 and 1970 as a contract

52 | Aerosmith on Tour, 1973-85

fulfillment to their label. After suing the label, the record was withdrawn from print.
- From a local review: "Aerosmith, the opening act, played loud, derivative rock, distinguished only by Steve Tyler's fawning imitation of Mick Jagger" (New York Times, 4/2/1973). Argent opened the following night's show at St. John's College in Queens.

April 1
Music Hall
Boston, MA

Promoter: Don Law
Other act(s): Kinks (HL)
Reported audience: (4,200 capacity)
Notes:
- The venue marquee listed "Kinks with Arrowsmith," which some interpreted as an April's Fools' joke...
- From a local review: "Opening the night were the local heart throbs and rock and roll stars, Aerosmith. Led by the Jagger-like Steve Tyler and his pink feathered tail, they churned out an almost nonstop, straight-ahead, steamroller, generator rock, twitching and fretting their time upon the stage. Although their material seemingly merges into one long medley, they would seem to have a future. Until that time, they'll continue to be dwarfed by such as the Kinks, but they have the talent to make it" (Boston Globe, 4/4/1973).
- From another local review: "The warm-up act, Boston's Aerosmith, looked and behaved like a teen-aged version of the Rolling Stones, even down to the eye make-up" (Boston Globe, 4/8/1973).

April 2
Elting Gymnasium @ S.U.N.Y.
New Platz, NY

Promoter: Student Union
Other act(s): Kinks (HL)
Notes:
- Albany radio station WSUA-640 was planning on broadcasting the Kinks set but were prevented from doing so at the last moment. It's not known if Aerosmith's was...
- Columbia promotion balsa airplanes with the Aerosmith name on them were distributed to the audience members, who proceeded to bombard the band with them (and abuse) during their set. Tom later recalled, "Oh yeah, New Platz. That was bad. But so were most of the other Kinks shows we did. Even worse than when we opened for the Mahavishnu Orchestra. For some reason, Kinks fans really hate us" (Miami News, 2/1/1980).

April 4
Palace Concert Theater
Providence, RI

Promoter: Concerts East
Other act(s): Kinks (HL)
Reported audience: (3,200 capacity)
Notes:
- During the show Alice Cooper's appearance at the then new Civic Center (June 7) was announced. Aerosmith didn't open the shows following: Toronto on the 5th; and Buffalo show on Apr. 6.
- From a local review: "First, let me tell you about the band that preceded the Kinks called 'Aerosmith.' If they were billed as the Rolling Stones, it would have been more appropriate 'cause they tried so hard to be a remake of them! Their lead singer, whose name I have forgotten and could care less, was a combination of David Bowie, Roger Daltrey, and of course Mick Jagger. He was dressed to kill in all fringe and glitter, and

his stage antics were completely reminiscent of the three aforementioned. The lead guitarist was a Xerox copy of Keith Richard, although he couldn't play as well as him. He was dressed in a multi-colored T-shirt and was wearing those ever-so-tight blue jeans. Perhaps the worst member of the group was the drummer, who sounded like my 5-year-old brother banging on tin cans! He had no certain rhythmic pattern and his tries at playing fancy were simply a lost cause. All in all, 'Aerosmith' wasn't a total loss as they did play a couple of good-sounding numbers. But I should have realized then that they had paved the way for the Kinks, who would prove to be just as nauseating, if not worse" (Roger Williams University Quill, 4/30/1973).

April 7
Newark State College
Union, NJ

Promoter: Monarch Entertainment Bureau
Other act(s): Kinks (HL)
Reported audience: ~350
Notes:
- The school's yearbook, the 1973 Memorabilia, included photos of Kinks' set, but alas none of Aerosmith. The show is suggested to have been poorly attended. Steven: "When Aerosmith first started, we'd go out with bands like the Kinks and the Mahavishnu Orchestra. You were a dartboard. 'Boo! We want the Kinks!' I put up with that for the longest time. And just as a guitar player combs his hair down over his face to hide behind, I would need something to hide behind too. The scarves would be my thing. And the way I tied them on to the mike, it kind of dressed it up. In the early days I used to put weights on the bottom of them, whack people in the audience with them" (Rolling Stone #694, 11/3/1994).

April 8
Alumni Gymnasium @ Rider College
Lawrenceville, NJ

Promoter: College Union Board Concerts
Other act(s): Kinks (HL)
Notes:
- From a local review: "Finally the first group, Aerosmith, walked on stage. The concert had begun... First a few comments about Aerosmith. Opening groups have one of the hardest tasks in the business: keep the natives happy while they foam at the mouth waiting for THE group. Aerosmith did a fairly good job... Aerosmith was at least entertaining even if the music wasn't too good. Aerosmith's lead singer was a carbon copy of Mick Jagger. He tied scarves to the microphone stand, went through the same gyrations, same facial expressions, and wore a belt that looked like an oversized corset. He looked like Jagger, sang like Jagger, and probably even smelled like Jagger. He danced around the stage, made advances at the lead guitarist (omigod, he's a homosexual, or is it transvestite, or homozygote?), stuck the microphone between his legs and caressed it and poured wine on the stage. He was really cute, but it's been done before and unfortunately it will be done again. What about the music? It was loud and overamplified. I've seen better, but I've seen worse. No one asked for an encore" (Rider News, 4/13/1973).
- Following this show, the Kinks headed for the West Coast.

April 13
High School Gymnasium
Dedham, MA

Promoter: Max Productions / Class of '74
Other act(s): Flite (opener)

April 14
High School Gymnasium
Millis, MA

April 23–25
Paul's Mall
Boston, MA
Promoter: In-house
Other act(s): Tufano-Giammarese (opener)
Notes:
- Carl Giammarese and Dennis Tufano had been members of the pop group, The Buckinghams, which had split in 1970. They recorded an album using several members of the group Poco as session players. Unlike many week-long residencies, there was little local press mention of this booking prior to the day before.

April 26–29 ***QUESTIONABLE
Paul's Mall
Boston, MA
Promoter: In-house
Other act(s): Tufano-Giammarese (opener)
Notes:
- It has long been suggested that Aerosmith were playing Paul's Mall in the evening, with the band performing at the Fair in Revere during the afternoon. However, later daily ads suggest that Swallow was playing Paul's Mall in place of Aerosmith, Apr. 26-29, with Tufano-Giammarese, while Aerosmith played the Fair.

April 26–28
Scarborough Fair
Revere, MA
Promoter: In-house
Other act(s): Ing (opener)

April 29 **TWO SHOWS
Scarborough Fair
Revere, MA
Promoter: In-house
Note:
- Steven's flyer from this engagement, featured in "Walk this Way," suggests that the band performed a no age limit matinee on Sunday afternoon.

May 4
B.H.S. Field House
Beverly, MA
Promoter: BHS Student Council
Other act(s): Twelve 76

May 5
Cornell Libe Slope
Ithaca, NY
Promoter: Cornell Concert Commission

Other act(s): Seatrain, New Decade, The Harvest King, Albatross
Notes:
- This concert was held as part of the school's celebrations of Spring Weekend though the band performed in Barton Hall with Joe Perry sporting a "KINKS" sticker on his guitar.

May 18
Lusk Field House @ S.U.N.Y.
Cortland, NY
Promoter: Circulating Fund Committee
Reported audience: (7,200 capacity)
Notes:
- Aerosmith were reportedly paid just $500 for this show.

June 2
Old Gym @ Phillips Exeter Academy
Exeter, NH
Other act(s): Geoff Bartley / Bob Franke
Notes:
- Opener Geoff Bartley recalled: "Bob Franke and I opened for an unknown rock band in the gym at Phillips Exeter Academy in Exeter, New Hampshire. I don't remember them yelling at Bob, but if I never hear another audience screaming, 'Get the f**k off the stage! We want Aerosmith! AEROSMITH!! AEROSMITH!!!', it'll be too soon... the rest, as they say, is history" (Geoff Bartley).

June 16
Hopedale High School
Hopedale, MA
Notes:
- Senior prom.

June 21
Arena
Worcester, MA
Promoter: MA Associates
Other act(s): Mad Angel

June 23
Cape Cod Coliseum
South Yarmouth, MA
Reported audience: ~1,500
Notes:
- The band was fined $400 for continuing to play after curfew. According to Joey, "When you walk off stage after the audience gives you three or four encores, money becomes irrelevant" (Boston Herald, 9/16/1973).

June 24
Franklin Park
Boston, MA
Notes:
- Sponsored by WBVF-FM, a 35-mile bicycle race culminated with a free Aerosmith show at the park following the award ceremony.

July **RECORDING SESSIONS

Notes:
- By July, during a break from the road, the band were in the studio with Ray Colcord (Billboard, 7/21/1973). While these sessions could well have included some pre-production for the second album, it could also have been work centered on revamping versions of "Dream On" and "Write Me," which appeared on later pressings of the debut album.

July 3
North Park
Fall River, MA

Promoter: Re-Creation '73
Other act(s): Talk of the Town, Sugarbush (opener)
Notes:
- A "Night of Togetherness" concert benefitting PolyArt's Re-Creation '73, a celebration of Boston arts, marked the opening of the event's third season.

August 1
Suffolk Downs
Boston, MA

Promoter: American Citifair Foundation, Ltd. / Odgen Promotions
Other act(s): Sha-Na-Na (HL)
Reported audience: ~35,000
Notes:
- From a local review: "The Sunset Series at Suffolk Downs concert Wednesday night was hopefully the worst concert to be seen there. The co-billing of Aerosmith and Sha-Na-Na drew a capacity crowd of rowdy, beer toting, pre-adolescents who should have been accompanied by a parent or legal guardian. As the sun set over the right side of the stage and clouds moved in from the west, Aerosmith began their set with 'Make It.' Into the third song a barrage of beer cans filled the air sending people to the ground seeking whatever shelter they could find. The show was stopped at least twice as Steve Tyler, pseudo-Mick Jagger lead singer for Aerosmith, scolded the bubbly little teens trying to make them behave. It didn't work and the show went on. Aerosmith is a local group catering to the bubble-gum set. They put out a sound that will never grow away from the AM radio top 40. The most entertaining music came during intermission. WBCN radio was piped in while the stage was prepared for Sha-Na-Na, another high school dance attraction" (Boston Globe, 8/3/1973).

August 7
High School Auditorium
Marlborough, MA

Promoter: City of Marlborough Recreation Department
Other act(s): Reddy Teddy, Cool Water Band

August 10, 11
Caesar's Monticello Theatre Restaurant
Framingham, MA

Other act(s): Reddy Teddy, Nibla
Notes:

- Nibla included Jam Band drummer David "Pudge" Scott.

August 16
Frolics Ballroom
Salisbury Beach, MA
Other act(s): The Sidewinders (opener)
Notes:
- The Sidewinders had released one album on RCA before Billy Squier joined on guitar.
- Purportedly, an AUD recording of this show exists.

August 26
North Shore Music Theater
Beverly, MA

August 30
Tower Theater
Upper Darby, PA
Promoter: Midnight Sun
Other act(s): T-Rex (HL), Estus (opener)
Reported audience: ** SOLD-OUT
Note:
- Lineup noted in Performance.

August 31 **POSTPONED
Holman Stadium
Nashua, NH
Promoter: The Greater Nashua Youth Hockey Association
Other act(s): Clayton Bod
Notes:
- This outdoor show was postponed due to rain.

Aug/Sept. **TEMP HOLD-DATE
Christian Herter Park Amphitheater
Alston, MA
Promoter: Publick Theater
Notes:
- An attempt by a promoter to book the facility for an Aerosmith show was deemed "inadvisable" and blocked by the Metropolitan District Commission on Aug. 15. Other shows requested by the promoter had been approved previously when not specifying the band...

September 1
Hotel Viking Convention Center
Newport, RI
Promoter: Dennis Dunn
Other act(s): Rock Star (opener)
Reported audience: (2,000 capacity)
Notes:

- By early September, bolstered by the performance of "Dream On," the debut album was approaching sales of 30,000 copies, primarily in the North East.

September 2 **TEMP HOLD-DATE
Cape Cod Coliseum
South Yarmouth, MA

Notes:
- Noted in Billboard (9/8/1973).

September 3
Holman Stadium
Nashua, NH

Promoter: The Greater Nashua Youth Hockey Association
Other act(s): Susan Joy, Clayton Bod
Reported audience: ~4,000
Notes:
- This benefit concert for the Nashua Youth Hockey Association was held to help raise funds for team uniforms. This outdoor show was originally scheduled for Aug. 31 but was postponed due to the weather.

September 4 **TWO SHOWS
Kenny's Castaways
New York City, NY

Notes:
- Advertised on the day of show in the New York Daily News. Two shows were scheduled, at 10p.m. and midnight.
- From an industry review: "Boston is enjoying an up period as a center of rock 'n' roll and this combo of 19-year-olds is one of the reasons. Aerosmith, with elements of glitter, have it all together in high-volume, high-energy performance. Youths have the appearance to make their mark with young femmes, and important part of a rock audience. Lead vocalist Steve Tyler, with plenty of pelvic action, is garbed in black net shirt fringed with glitter and multi-colored tights. His vocals are strong, sometimes screaming. He usually is the focus on-stage. Instrumental resources are good as the quintet goes more for unified sound than unified virtuosity. Standing out are lead guitarist Joe Perry and drummer Joey Kramer with solid assists from rhythm guitarist Brad Whitford and bass guitarist Tom Hamilton. Tyler also has good harmonica segs. Much of the material is from their current and future Columbia albums. They also toss in 'The Train Kept A-Rollin',' a tune of the Yardbirds, defunct British rock group who've strongly influenced Aerosmith" (Variety, 9/12/1973).
- From another industry review: "Columbia recording artists Aerosmith have been taking their adopted home of Boston by storm lately, and New Yorkers had a chance to see the reason why at Kenny's Castaways recently. Laying down solidly arranged R&B is this group's forte, as they espoused during a recent visit to RW's offices, and their one-night stand at Kenny's was a tribute their tight, controlled-but-uninhibited style. Led by some fine vocalizing from Jagger-esque lead singer Steve Tyler, Aerosmith deftly avoided the pitfalls that a boogying band often encounters in the confines of a small club. Tyler, along with guitarists Brad Whitford and Joe Perry (the man with the perpetual sneer), bassist Tom Hamilton and drummer Joey Kramer, apparently understand that a group can be hard, driving, and solid in a 20 by 20 room without destroying all the glassware. With their single, 'Dream On,' practically owning the Boston airwaves, a solid album also rated highly by listeners in New England, and a flair for hard-nosed, exciting live performances, Aerosmith can look towards a future that holds nothing but the best" (Record World, 9/15/1973).

September 8 **QUESTIONABLE
Cumberland County Civic Center
Portland, ME

Notes:

- Noted in Billboard (9/8/1973). On this day, the debut bubbled under on the Billboard Top-200 album charts for the first time, at #209.

September 14
The Box Club @ B.U.
Boston, MA

Set list(s): S.O.S. (Too Bad) / Somebody / Pandora's Box / Dream On / One Way Street / Walkin' the Dog / Train Kept a Rollin' / Mama Kin / Make It / Milk Cow Blues
Notes:
- Purportedly, an AUD recording of this show exists. A run of shows at this venue, Sept. 15-17, were noted in Billboard Magazine (9/8/1973).

September 21
Surf Club
Nantasket Beach, MA

September 22 **QUESTIONABLE
Michigan Concert Palace
Detroit, MI

Promoter: Leo Speer
Other act(s): New York Dolls (HL), Birtha, Radio King (opener)
Reported audience: ~4,000
Notes:
- This show marked the grand re-opening of the venue but of the opening acts, only Radio King (a revue type act) was also noted in a review of the show (Detroit Free Press, 9/30/1973), but may have been conflated with the all-female Birtha.

September 26 **RADIO SESSION
Counterpart Studios
Cheviot (Cincinnati), OH

Promoter: WKRQ Concert Series
Set list(s): Make It / Somebody / Write Me / Dream On / One Way Street / Walkin' the Dog / Pandora's Box / Rattlesnake Shake / Train Kept A Rollin' / Mama Kin
Notes:
- This studio live performance was recorded, but not broadcast. Both "Walkin' the Dog" and "Rattlesnake Shake" were included on "Pandora's Box." Interestingly, the announcer mentions that the band were heading direct to San Francisco...

September 28, 29 **Aerosmith CANCELLED
Winterland
San Francisco, CA

Promoter: Bill Graham Presents
Other act(s): Mott the Hoople (HL), Joe Walsh/Barnstorm
Notes:
- Aerosmith was added to the bill the week prior to the show but did not perform. Day of show ads excluded mention of them.

September 28
Nichols College
Dudley, MA

Other act(s): Stories (opener)
Notes:
- This show was for the school's "Homecoming." Stories had had an unexpected hit with their cover of Hot Chocolate's "Brother Louie," and had also included keyboardist Michael Brown, who had been a member of the Left Banke. By the time of this show Brown was long gone, and even guitarist Steve Love had left and been replaced by Richie Ranno (future Starz guitarist). Starz's connections to Aerosmith include touring with them later. They also chose Jack Douglas to produce their debut LP, due to Richie's love of Aerosmith's "Get Your Wings." More amusingly, Richie later replaced Joe Perry's guitar work on Gene Simmons' 1978 solo album song "Tunnel of Love." Gene and producer Sean Delaney hadn't cared for Joe's solo, so first tried to replace it with one by Jeff "Skunk" Baxter, but didn't care for that one either, so called Richie...

September 29 **TEMP HOLD-DATE
Cheshire County Fairgrounds
Swanzey, NH

Notes:
- This show was noted in Billboard (9/29/1973) but didn't take place.

September 29
McHugh Forum @ Boston College
Boston, MA

Promoter: UGBC Social Committee
Other act(s): Swallow (opener)
Reported audience: ~5,700 / 5,500 **OVER-SOLD
Notes:
- Swallow were a 10-piece local band who had released their Intermedia recorded debut, "Out of the Nest" (Warner Bros.), in May 1972. They played a mix of rock, jazz, and blues, and included David Woodford.
- Overzealous fans caused over $1,000 damage to the venue, and some 200 fans had to be turned away from the sold-out show by the Boston Tactical Force. The band were later blamed by some at the school for using radio and other advertising to bring in far more external attendees than the show would otherwise have had, resulting in the fracas. However, the social committee did may a profit of $1,800 off the show at a time when they were incurring substantial losses for entertainment. This show was still being discussed in 1976 as the university continued to try and strike a balance for the success of student union concerts.
- From a local review: "If someone had told me the morning of the concert that the Boston Tactical Force would have to be called in to help turn away more than two hundred people, I never would have believed it. With the amount of on-campus advertising (I think I saw one poster), I couldn't imagine them filling Roberts Center, let alone McHugh Forum. But they did — and with some 5,700 customers. Just ask the cops who had to carry away a number of disappointed and somewhat rowdy Aerosmith fanatics in paddy wagons. Also ask the folks who had to sweep up the pieces of broken windows from various points around the rink. Yes indeed, they really packed 'em in that Saturday night — and the reason was obvious as soon as you entered the building. What was supposedly a Boston College concert turned out to be more like a disorderly assembly at BC High. I'd wager a guess that the average age was around 15 years, though I know for a fact I saw some seven and eight-year-olds running around trying to hide their packs of Marlboros from the rent-a-cops...

I spent [the rest of the opening band's set] watching the stage crew waging a small war with a group of teen-age gatecrashers. It was great — about five guys trying to keep the backdoor from bursting through. At one point, they even had to beat the crowd back with sticks. These events ended up, as it turned out, to be even more interesting than the stage show itself. After quite a lengthy sound testing period, Aerosmith came on in full splendor. They're a five-man rock band, which released a fine album on Columbia about a year ago. Their style's rather loud and raunchy, but it's well done for a first attempt. They're finally beginning to get noticed with 'Dream On,' which has been a hit single for the past few months. The band's kingpin is a fellow named Steven Tyler, who, although he 'hates' to hear it, is a ringer for the leader of the Rolling Stones. But one simply cannot look at the heavily made-up figure prancing about the stage and teasing the girls and boys in variously familiar ways without calling to mind another individual. The costume, the movements, even the lips are all the same — there's no getting around it... Whether it's the band's music, or whether it is merely the fact that the vocalist looks like Mick, I can't say. But Aerosmith played a little over an hour set, and they almost literally brought the house down...

The majority of the night's numbers came from the first album, all of which Tyler composed with some 'help from the band.' They do some truly fine rock pieces like 'One Way Street' and 'Write Me,' which, although much better on the LP, aren't bad in concert. They create a tremendous amount of energy to say the least. They told me that their next album is going to be cut in Toronto sometime in December after a 16-date tour with Mott the Hoople. The producers? Bob Ezrin and Jack Douglas — late of Alice Cooper. They expect a lot of changes in their sound, and who knows — they might even find a cure for Tyler's current identity crisis. Whatever the result, you can be sure you haven't heard the last of Aerosmith — Boston's latest to hit the bigtime" (Boston Heights, 10/15/1973).

September 30
Gymnasium @ U.M.
Gorham, ME

Set list(s): Write Me / Downtown Baby / Somebody / S.O.S. (Too Bad) / Dream On / One Way Street/ Walkin' the Dog / Pandora's Box / Train Kept A Rollin' / Mama Kin / Make It / Rattlesnake Shake
Notes:
- "S.O.S. (Too Bad)" was introduced as "Son of Shit" from the forthcoming "Night in the Ruts" album. Things would change, and "Downtown Baby" would be revamped and recorded many many years later...
- An AUD recording circulates from this show.

October 3 **CANCELLED
Municipal Auditorium
Chattanooga, TN

Promoter: Alex Cooley, Inc.
Other act(s): Mott the Hoople (HL), New York Dolls
Notes:
- This show appears in various itineraries but seems to have either have been not booked or was cancelled. Regardless, it would have been the first date of an envisaged 25 show run by Mott through mid-November.

October 4
Municipal Auditorium
Atlanta, GA

Promoter: Alex Cooley, Inc.
Other act(s): Mott the Hoople (HL), New York Dolls
Reported audience: (5,500 capacity)
Notes:
- From a local review: "The night wasn't completely wasted though. The group, Aerosmith, opened the show and they had more talent and real crude disgust than the two mentioned above. I do not know where they are from or where they are going but they really got me off. Their stage appearance and musical qualities seem to be at a raw level still, but what they projected without the professional polish could be very promising. They had that cheap, trash appeal

mixed with an aurora of Stones' charisma. Hopefully, they will avoid the stereotyped pits of brainwashed rock 'n' roll bands" (Great Speckled Bird, 10/15/1973).

October 5
Auditorium
West Palm Beach, FL
Promoter: Howard Stein
Other act(s): Mott the Hoople (HL), New York Dolls
Reported audience: (5,000 capacity)

October 6
Coliseum
Jacksonville, FL
Other act(s): Mott the Hoople (HL), Nazareth, ZZ Top
Reported audience: (10,228 capacity)
{CB 10/6/73}

October 7 **CANCELLED
Birmingham, AL
{CB 10/6/73}

October 10
Music Hall
Cincinnati, OH
Promoter: American Concerts / Bamboo Productions
Other act(s): Mott the Hoople (HL), Marshall Tucker Band (opener)
Reported audience: (3,634 capacity)

October 11
Auditorium Theater
Chicago, IL
Other act(s): Mott the Hoople (HL), New York Dolls
Reported audience: (4,000 capacity)
Notes:
- From a local review: "Opening the show was Aerosmith, from Boston. They're a competent and inventive rock 'n' roll band, but they're a long way from headliner status. They did help make the Dolls look bad, though" (Chicago Daily News, 10/12/1973).

October 12
Masonic Temple Auditorium
Detroit, MI
Promoter: Bamboo Productions
Other act(s): Mott the Hoople (HL)
Reported audience: (4,600 capacity)

October 13
Gymnasium @ John Carroll University
Cleveland, OH
Promoter: J.C.U. Student Union / Belkin Productions
Other act(s): Mott the Hoople (HL)

Reported audience: 3,000 **SOLD-OUT

October 14
Massey Hall
Toronto, ON, Canada
Promoter: Concerts Promotion International (CPI)
Other act(s): Mott the Hoople (HL), Blue Oyster Cult
Reported audience: (2,675 capacity)
Notes:
- From a local review: "Rock 'n' roll hit rock bottom last night at the Massey Hall as three bands — Aerosmith, Blue Oyster Cult and Mott the Hoople — clearly had a contest to see which could be the worst first and stay that way longest. Aerosmith won, but against tremendous odds... In any other context, however, their playing might have been seen for what it was: a compilation of clichés disguised by an almost unbearably high degree of amplification. Aerosmith, unhappily, didn't even have the clichés to work with. Massey Hall was packed for this concert, which indicates there is still a market for loud, simple rock" (Toronto Star, 10/15/1973).

October 16
Auditorium Theater
Rochester, NY
Promoter: Concerts East
Other act(s): Mott the Hoople (HL), New York Dolls
Reported audience: (3,900 capacity)
Notes:
- There is no mention of Aerosmith in the show review printed the following day in the Rochester Democrat & Chronicle even though they are mentioned in a day of show ad and various itineraries. It is possible the band didn't perform (or simply weren't mentioned).

October 17
Kleinhans Music Hall
Buffalo, NY
Promoter: UUAB / Festivals East
Other act(s): Mott the Hoople (HL), New York Dolls
Reported audience: (2,939 capacity)
Notes:

- From a local review: "Aerosmith set the format for basic rock and roll, Mick dagger-style. No incredible moves, just rock and roll drug songs, the kind of rock you start humming after you've heard it on the radio 50,000 times... And sorrowfully, the Mick dagger look-alike appeared like seven-year-old sleepy child with stretching pants that he kept pulling down, and at the point split for the bar. Which, by the way, is Howard Johnson's among bars, with price list poster and inflated prices for poor drinks... Back in the hall, Mick dagger look-alike no. was twitching his ass and pursing his mouth for big moment. This was really getting confusing... Spirits were speaking. I had seen Aerosmith with McLaughlin last year and they were shit. Wednesday night at Kleinhans they reaffirmed my opinion, which is now probably everlasting. I saw the Dolls in New York City this summer; they were shit, too" (Spectrum, 10/19/1973).
- From another local review: "First to come on stage was Aerosmith, a unique band in that it's probably the only one in the business that reincarnates on stage. Just as they began each song with atomic blast proportions, they slowly seemed to die of radiation as it progressed — or digressed. This life-death cycle was hard to believe after listening to their fine album, simply entitled 'Aerosmith,' with which we were duly impressed. Their in-concert performance made it hard to believe we were hearing the same group. Lead singer Steve Tyler's Jagger-like movements and humping of the mike stand seemed to be lost in the shuffle

as each member of the group appeared to go off on his own tangent. All in all, Aerosmith's stage performance gave us the impression that they were very fine in-studio musicians. As Aerosmith fizzled off stage we looked forward to a big drag — the New York Dolls" (The Ascent, 11/14/1973).

October 18
Syria Mosque
Pittsburgh, PA
Promoter: Pat DiCesare
Other act(s): Mott the Hoople (HL), Spirit
Reported audience: (3,700 capacity)
Notes:
- Some print ads erroneously note the venue as the Civic Arena.

October 19
Mershon Auditorium @ O.S.U.
Columbus, OH
Promoter: O.S.U. Pop Concerts
Other act(s): Mott the Hoople (HL), Robin Trower
Reported audience: (2,500 capacity)
Notes:
- From a local review: "A capacity audience at Mershon Auditorium was treated to a dynamic concert Friday night when Mott the Hoople headlined a power-laden triple bill... Opening for Mott was a Boston-based band named Aerosmith who play heavy brand of English-style rock. With a lead singer who resembles Mick Jagger (probably by choice), the group is solid enough to rely on its music and not all the glitz and gimmicks inherent in their performance now. A decadent looking bunch of musicians, Aerosmith plays anything but decadent music. They are probably the best opening act the area has seen in ages" (Columbus Dispatch, 10/22/1973).

October 20 **TEMP HOLD-DATE
Park Center
Charlotte, NC
Reported audience: (3,000 capacity)
Notes:
- Mentioned in various itineraries, Billboard (10/13/1973) and Cashbox (10/6/1973), it was replaced by the Philadelphia shows. Instead, Kaleidoscope booked ZZ Top on Oct. 19 and a Clarence Carter / Betty Wright dance party on the 20th...

October 20 **TWO SHOWS
Shubert Theater
Philadelphia, PA
Promoter: Electric Factory Concerts
Other act(s): Mott the Hoople (HL)
Reported audience: (1,900 capacity)
Notes:

- Shows were scheduled at 8 and 11p.m. The New York Dolls had played a separate show at the venue the night prior.

October 21
Walsh Auditorium @ Seton Hall University
South Orange, NJ
Other act(s): Mott the Hoople (HL)
Notes:
- This show took place during the afternoon. According to one of the members of Mott, "It was a pretty weird gig, at 2 in the afternoon. The kids were really wild. It was a bit scary" (Minneapolis Star Tribune, 10/28/1973).

October 21 **CANCELLED
Coliseum
Greensboro, NC
Other act(s): Mott the Hoople (HL), ZZ Top
Reported audience: (5,000 capacity)
Notes:
- Mentioned in advance itineraries, this show likely didn't take place, even though it was advertised in the local press with the "ZZ Tops" opening as late as Oct. 20.

October 22
Holland Union Building @ Dickinson College
Carlisle, PA
Other act(s): Mott the Hoople (HL)

October 24
Palace Concert Theater
Providence, RI
Promoter: Concerts East
Other act(s): Mott the Hoople (HL)
Reported audience: (3,200 capacity)
Set list(s): Make It / Write Me / Somebody / S.O.S. (Too Bad) / Dream On / One Way Street / Walkin' the Dog / Pandora's Box / Train Kept A Rollin' / Mama Kin / Rattlesnake Shake
Notes:
- From a local review: "I personally know of no one else at this school who attended last Wednesday's Mott the Hoople/Aerosmith concert at the Palace, which means that virtually everyone reading this piece missed out on one of the finest rock 'n' roll experiences this hell hole of a state will ever offer. First there was Aerosmith. They're local heroes, more of less — based in Boston, they've just recently gained national attention by way of their hit single, 'Dream On' and the success of the song earned them the opening slot on Mott's current U.S. tour. To say that three weeks on the road has done wonders for the band would be a gross understatement. I saw them late in September in Maine — their last gig before the first with Mott — and they were ... good, certainly better than their appearance in April; but they still lacked a grace — a sense of how-to on the stage.

But now! I was stunned, bolted upright, and shook all over again. When I first heard the band, I ranted and raved in print 'bout how they were gonna be the best and last week's performance did much to convince me that I wasn't just babbling. Now everyone in the band asserts themselves on stage. Steven Tyler (the singer) isn't the only interesting visual thing going on. Some of their postures are amusing; but overall, they're latent monsters. Their second album will be out in mid-January to early February; a follow-up single to 'Dream On' will be released soon, a track from the upcoming album; and on the whole, they're on the

verge. To paraphrase something I've said before, there's still time to catch them on the way up" (Roger Williams University Quill, 10/30/1973).
- An AUD recording circulates from this show.

October 26 **DOUBTFUL
Radio City Music Hall
New York City, NY
Promoter: Ron Delsener
Other act(s): Mott the Hoople (HL)
Notes:
- This show was noted as being scheduled for Oct. 25 in the 10/6 issue of Cash Box. However, the concert was a midnight show so it's not clear whether Aerosmith performed, since they were scheduled to co-host on WMEX-AM in Boston with Gary DeGraide at 4p.m.

October 27
Orpheum Theater
Boston, MA
Promoter: Don Law Presents
Other act(s): Mott the Hoople (HL)
Reported audience: (2,800 capacity)
Set list(s): Make It / Write Me / Somebody / S.O.S. (Too Bad) / Dream On / One Way Street / Walkin' the Dog / Train Kept A Rollin' / Mama Kin / Pandora's Box

Notes:
- From a local review: "Many of those present came to hear their local heroes — Aerosmith. What they got was an hour's worth of extremely loud music from a group that is trying perhaps a bit too self-consciously to attain superstar status. Despite protests from the group that they are not imitating the Rolling Stones in their stage act, it all had an uncomfortable familiar ring to it. The derivative rhythm lines, the flailing gesticulations of lead singer Steve Tyler (bedecked in a silver lame jumpsuit) and the flowers tossed to the adoring crowd did little to dispel their image as imitators" (Boston Globe, 10/29/1973).
- From a local review: "One would expect England to show us what glitter is, as they once showed us what rock was. But it was a Boston band who demonstrated that night that 'all that glitters is not rock,' to flagrantly misquote a phrase. Boston's own Aerosmith, the group most people came to see that evening, did an excellent job of out rocking the Hoople. Opening with 'Make It,' the first song on the first side of their recent Columbia album, Aerosmith played a stream of fast, punchy, rocking tunes, which got the audience going as best as everyone could, under the circumstances. The tone of the evening was one of violence and apprehension, as a private security force of large black cops kept patrolling the area of the small theater, in search of drinkers and smokers. In the future, remember to do your partying prior to entering an Orpheum Concert, or else you may be hassled. Meanwhile, back to Aerosmith. Many people have compared this band to the Stones, which is difficult not to do, as lead singer Steve Tyler looks and acts so much like Mick Jagger. While the rest of the band plays, Tyler sort of struts and prances around like a rooster, sometimes picking up the mike stand and wiggling his ass in the best Stones tradition.

During the song, 'Dream On,' Tyler thanked the audience for the success of the tune, which is different from the rest of the group's music. This number brought out the talents of Joe Perry, the romping, stomping lead player of Aerosmith. The boys showed definite Yardbirds influences while performing a perfect version of the Yardbirds song 'Train Kept a-Rolling.' They encored with a new tune called 'Pandora's Box,' which will be on their second LP, due out in time for the Christmas rush... Aerosmith was the better rocker that evening, surprising everyone. Aerosmith's first album is very good and their second should also be fine — as band, they are better live than on record, which can't be said for the new version of Mott the Hoople" (Mass Media, 11/7/1973).
- An AUD recording circulates from this show.

October 28
Columbia Music Hall
West Hartford, CT
Promoter: Koplik & Finkel
Other act(s): Mott the Hoople (HL)
Reported audience: (5,000 capacity)

October 29
Johnston Hall @ Moravian College
Bethlehem, PA
Promoter: MC Social Activities Committee
Other act(s): Mott the Hoople (HL)
Notes:
- An unsubstantiated local legend holds that short of songs, Aerosmith performed "Dream On" twice at this show.

October 31 **QUESTIONABLE
Circle Theater
Indianapolis, IN
Promoter: Daydream / Showcase Productions
Other act(s): Mott the Hoople (HL), Babe Ruth, Blue
Notes:
- Aerosmith doesn't appear in any print ads.

November 1 **CANCELLED
Civic Center
St. Paul, MN
Promoter: Daydream Productions
Other act(s): Mott the Hoople (HL), Babe Ruth, Blue
Notes:
- Aerosmith wasn't listed on shows ads from as early as Oct. 21.

November 2
Fieldhouse Gym
Wayland, MA
Promoter: Student Council
Notes:
- The 1974 Wayland yearbook details: "In November (1973), a spectacular concert by Aerosmith was sponsored with much success."

November 3 **Aerosmith CANCELLED
American Theater
St. Louis, MO
Promoter: Contemporary Productions
Other act(s): Mott the Hoople (HL), Blue
Notes:
- Two shows were scheduled, at 7:30 and 11:30 p.m.

November 3
Costello Gym @ Lowell Tech
Lowell, MA

Promoter: Lowell Tech Student Union
Other act(s): Bagshot Row
Reported audience: ~2,400
Reported gross: $10,000
Partial set: Make It / Somebody / Dream On / One Way Street / Mama Kin / Walkin' the Dog
Notes:
- The Student Union earned $500 from this show. Unfortunately, Aerosmith's audience also caused damage to the canvas covered gym floor with broken glass from discarded beer bottles.

November 10
Stonehill College
Easton, MA
Promoter: Stonehill College Social Committee
Notes:
- A letter of complaint by a patron indicates that this show took place.

November 17 **Aerosmith CANCELLED
Academy of Music
New York City, NY
Promoter: Howard Stein
Other act(s): Wishbone Ash (HL), Argent
Notes:
- The bill was for the early 8pm show. The Climax Blues Band with Renaissance were scheduled to perform at the late show. Aerosmith was dropped from the lineup the week prior to the show, perhaps being too busy rehearsing in the basement of Timothy Too (formerly La Bimba/Michael's) in Framingham for their second album sessions, or having taken the opening slot at the Felt Forum...

November 21
Felt Forum
New York City, NY
Promoter: Howard Stein
Other act(s): Focus (HL), Spencer Davis Group
Reported gross: $20,979
Notes:
- Following the show Columbia Records threw a party for the band at the Penn Plaza Club. The band members posed for photos with label executives which appeared in the Dec. 29 issue of Cash Box.
- From an industry review: "Aerosmith, Boston rock quintet who opened, appeared in good form. However, the Columbia disk act's short set failed to ignite the youthful crowd" (Variety, 11/28/1973).
- From an industry review: "Columbia recording artists Aerosmith opened the show. Unfortunately, the quintet was too loud to be fully appreciated. A happening single, 'Dream On,' from their debut album was performed" (Cashbox, 12/8/1973).

November 29
Memorial Auditorium
Portland, OR
Other act(s): Flash

Notes:
- Detailed in Billboard (11/24/1973), along with the Seattle show, opening act Flash had disbanded the week prior to this show taking place. The band had included Yes' original guitarist, Peter Banks.

November 30
Paramount Theater
Seattle, WA
Other act(s): Flash

December 3, 4
Whiskey-A-Go-Go
West Hollywood, CA
Promoter: in-house
Other act(s): Raymond Louis Kennedy (opener)
Notes:
- Joe's former paramour Judy Carne attended on of these shows and hung out with Joe for a bit. It would be the last time the two had contact.
- From a local review: "Aerosmith, highly touted by several local fans whose judgment in such matters we value, turned out to fall a bit short of our expectations. Though they have said in print that the Yardbirds are one of their biggest influences (and they perform 'Train Kept a Rollin' to prove it), Aerosmith clearly owes much more to the Rolling Stones. Both the looks and sound of Aerosmith take us back a few years, to a period that the Stones themselves seem to have abandoned at least on their records. The lead guitarist, who resembles Keith Richard and holds his instrument a bit like Jimmy Page does his, has a certain amount of presence, as does the lead singer. Most of the tunes are based on boogie-riff backgrounds and don't

show a whole lot of originality or inspiration. On the other hand, they all play well and look good, and the Stones have left that hole. We'll see" (Los Angeles Free Press, 12/14/1973).

- From an industry review: "It is a rare treat indeed to have the opportunity to see a first-rate act before it is picked up and marketed like a candy bar or a laundry soap. But a recent evening at the Whisky was such an occasion. A Boston group, Aerosmith (Columbia), staged one of the best and most noteworthy performances this reviewer has seen in some time. The lead singer, Steve Tyler, came on with polish and charisma a cut above even some of the best of today's established upper echelon of rock, taking the most appealing aspects from glitter rock and from the Jaggerish mannerisms so common to many contemporary male vocalists. Tyler, however, never sank into imitation on either side. What he offered instead was a new, exciting performing style not exactly like anyone else's. Joe Perry, the group's lead guitarist, also performed admirably, with solos reminiscent of the early Stones not too long, basic, and accessible to the casual listener. As for the Aerosmith's music itself, it was well-performed rock and roll. Included in their set was their national hit 'Dream On,' a number which will probably be their follow-up, 'Woman of the World' and a boogie tune called 'Same Old Song and Dance.' A good time was had by all during the group's first, and obviously not their last, Los Angeles appearance" (Record World, 12/29/1973).

December ?? **TV FILMING
ABC Studios
Los Angeles, CA

Promoter: Dick Clark Productions / ABC-TV
Notes:
- The band's first national television appearance, where they performed "Dream On," for the teen music show, American Bandstand, hosted by Dick Clark. The episode was broadcast on Dec. 15, and presumably filmed during the band's West Coast visit earlier in the month. Also appearing on the episode was Billy Preston.

December 15
Palace Concert Theater
Providence, RI

Promoter: Frank Connelly Presents
Other act(s): Paul Pena
Reported audience: (3,200 capacity)
Notes:
- Paul Pena, a blind soul-funk-blues performer, had released one album for Capitol at the time with a second having been completed but held up due to a dispute with his label. It included his original recording of "Jet Airliner," which would become a hit for Steve Miller.

1974

January 26, 1974 **CANCELLED
Memorial Hall
Kansas City, KS

Other act(s): Brownsville Station (HL)
Notes:
- This show was widely advertised. However, Brownsville Station were scheduled to open for Slade and James Gang at the Winterland in San Francisco (a second date the night before was cancelled). Brownsville's performance was noted in the San Francisco News review on Jan. 28, so it is likely that this Kansas City show didn't take place (at least with Brownsville as the headliner).

January 30
The Brewery

East Lansing, MI
Promoter: Bill Smith / in-house
Reported audience: 750 **SOLD-OUT
Notes:
- From a local review: "Aerosmith certainly earned its wings in East Lansing. Apparently, a favorite of the Brewery management, the group has 'almost' appeared here a number of times, but due to unforeseen circumstances, has never had the chance to perform locally. When Aerosmith was finally booked, the Brewery spent a great deal of time promoting the appearance. And it all paid off — Wednesday night's show was perhaps one of the most exciting performances this area has seen in months... Their performance was a knockout. Beginning with 'Make It,' the introductory song on their debut album, Aerosmith gradually gathered momentum until full-power, hell-spawned rock and roll was delivered... There is an air of stardom about this band, one that cannot go unnoticed for long. Given a bit of time, this relatively young band will probably make it in a very big way" (State News, 2/1/1974).

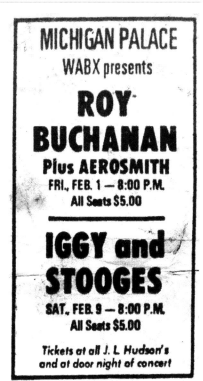

February 1
Michigan Concert Palace
Detroit, MI
Promoter: Leo Speer
Other act(s): Roy Buchanan (HL)
Reported audience: (5,000 capacity)
Set list(s): Make It / Lord of the Thighs / Somebody / Write Me / Same Old Song and Dance / Dream On / One Way Street / S.O.S. (Too Bad) / Train Kept a Rollin' / Mama Kin / Walkin' the Dog / Milk Cow Blues
Notes:
- Often attributed to Jan. 7, when the band would have still been ensconced in the studio recording the album, it would seem more likely with Steven's raps that this date is more appropriate. Steven announced during the show that the new album should be available in the middle of February while introducing "Lord of the Thighs"...
- A very good AUD recording circulates from this show.

February 3
Convention Center Arena
Indianapolis, IN
Promoter: Karma Showcase Presentations
Other act(s): Quicksilver Messenger Service (HL), Country Joe (opener)

February 9
Maritime Academy Alumni Gymnasium
Buzzards Bay, MA
Promoter: Music Unlimited Associates
Other act(s): Buck
Notes:
- Buck drummer Derek Blevins recalled Steven hitchhiking for kicks outside the venue after the show.

February 10
Gymnasium @ S.M.U.
North Dartmouth, MA

Promoter: SMU Concert Series
Other act(s): James Montgomery Band
Reported audience: **SOLD-OUT
Notes:
- From a local review: "The crowd at SMU was ready for a night of boogying. Tickets had been sold out for the concert within eight days of release — some sort of record as far as the Concert Series people are concerned. The concrete gym was packed full of college kids and teeny hoppers all with one thing in mind — get a buzz on some good music, with or without the help of the smoke that was in abundance. With a psyched crowd, the groups could do no wrong... I don't know how many people have ever seen Aerosmith in concert, but it is quite a show. The leader is a Mick Jagger type, with the ass sticking out, and the hand movements of an Eastern God. Dressed in a black fish-net top and purplish-pink lame pants so tight you could tell his muscle structure to a Bio. Major, Steve jumped, wiggled, and seduced the microphone in perfect rhythm during each song. But the time Aerosmith appeared, the crowd was even more psyched. The crowd clapped, danced, and screamed along with the band. The highlight was the hit 'Dream On,' which used special effects that would male James West smile. The perfect chords oozed out through a green smoke atmosphere. Usually, a group has two arrangements for each song: the doctored studio version, and a concert version. Aerosmith played 'Dream on' the way everyone expected to hear it — and they did it well.

After several more songs, and a few thousand perverted actions by Steve, the show ended. Aerosmith left in the same way they appeared, quietly sneaking out the back. Not to be sent home early, the crowd used the same tactics employed to get James Montgomery back. Aerosmith did a requested 'Walking my Dog,' which allowed Steve the opportunity to show the crowd how to walk a dog. After this fine educational experience, they left again — only to encore once more. The second encore number was led by Joe (I think) WHO PLAYS GUITAR FOR THE GROUP. It was alright and gave Steve someone else to sing to besides his mike, and some guy who got his kicks by taking off his shirt, throwing it in the air, and mimicking Steve's actions. After this song, Aerosmith left, and the crowd cleared, leaving only the remains of food, beer cans, and the smell of dope behind them. We left with that happy feeling a damn good concert leaves inside your head. SMU Concert Series, again, thanks for the buzz" (SMU Comment, 2/14/74).

February 14 **CANCELLED
U.N.H. Field House
Durham, NH
Promoter: Student Committee on Popular Entertainment
Notes:
- This Winter Carnival concert was cancelled due to scheduling issues: The band had purportedly been unhappy with a basketball practice session being conducted at the venue while their staging was being setup. A show at the venue was later booked in October.

February 16
Usdan Ballroom @ Brandeis University
Waltham, MA
Promoter: Brandeis Student Senate
Other act(s): Reddy Teddy
Reported audience: ~1,000 **SOLD-OUT
Notes:
- As ever, there were complaints about the number of non-student attendees at this show, which lost the student government $3,000.

**February 22
Gymnasium @ Bryant College
Smithfield, RI**
Other act(s): Free Time

1973 - Aerosmith

1974 - Get Your Wings

U.S. Release Details:
Columbia/CBS PC/PCA/PCT-32847 (Mar. 8, 1974)
Columbia/CBS PCQ/CAQ-32847 (Mar. 7, 1975 — Quadraphonic)
Columbia/CBS CK-32847 (1987 — CD reissue)
Columbia/SMEi CK/CT-57361 (Sep. 7, 1993 — 20-bit SBM digital remaster)
Columbia/SME 88765486151 (Apr. 20, 2013 — 180g LP reissue)

Tracks:
A1. Same Old Song and Dance •
(3:53) — Steven Tyler / Joe Perry
A2. Lord of the Thighs
(4:14) — Steven Tyler
A3. Spaced
(4:21) — Steven Tyler / Joe Perry
A4. Woman of the World
(5:49) — Steven Tyler / Don Solomon

B1. S.O.S. (Too Bad) •
(2:51) — Steven Tyler
B2. Train Kept A Rollin' •
(5:33) — Tiny Bradshaw / Howard Kay / Lois Mann
B3. Seasons of Wither
(5:38) — Steven Tyler
B4. Pandora's Box
(5:43) — Steven Tyler / Joey Kramer

Album Details:
Produced by Jack Douglas and Ray Colcord. Executive producer Bob Ezrin. Recorded at the Record Plant, New York City, NY, Dec. 1973–Jan. 1974. Engineered by Jay Messina, Jack Douglas, and Rod O'Brien. Mastered at the Record Plant, Jan. 27, 1974, by Jay Messina.

Players:
◦ Same Old Song and Dance — Michael Brecker, Randy Brecker, Stan Bronstein, and Jon Pearson on brass; Dick Wagner on additional guitar.
◦ Spaced — Ray Colcord on keyboards.
◦ Train Kept A Rollin' — Steve Hunter on lead guitar (1st half); Dick Wagner on lead guitar (2nd half).
◦ Seasons of Wither — Steven Tyler on acoustic guitar.
◦ Pandora's Box — Michael Brecker and Stan Bronstein on brass; Steven Tyler on piano.

Chart Action:
Chart Peak (USA): #74 (10/18/1975) with 86 weeks on the Billboard charts, though it initially only reached #100 during 1974. Other countries: N/A. The album charted for 62 weeks on Cashbox reaching #77 (5/18/1974).

03/30/74	04/06/74	04/13/74	04/20/74	04/27/74	05/04/74	05/11/74
205	193	146	133	127	103	**100**
05/18/74	05/25/74	06/01/74	06/08/74	06/15/74	06/22/74	06/29/74
109	109	117	114	117	113	129
07/06/74	07/13/74	07/20/74	07/27/74	08/03/74	08/10/74	08/17/74
131	127	134	151	144	150	162
08/24/74	08/31/74	09/07/74				
174	181	X				

Second charting:

10/19/74	10/26/74	11/02/74	11/09/74	11/16/74	11/23/74	11/30/74
187	159	148	137	124	113	110
12/07/74	12/14/74	12/21/74	12/28/74	01/04/75	01/11/75	01/18/75
108	119	157	167	183	193	185
01/25/75	02/01/75	02/08/75	02/15/75	02/22/75	03/01/75	03/08/75
182	190	187	193	183	167	150
03/15/75	03/22/75	03/29/75	04/05/75	04/12/75	04/19/75	04/25/75
140	135	177	176	184	189	X

Third charting:

09/20/75	09/27/75	10/04/75	10/11/75	10/18/75	10/25/75	11/01/75
103	91	80	76	**74**	106	106
11/08/75	11/15/75	11/22/75				
115	191	X				

Fourth charting:

01/31/76	02/07/76	02/14/76	02/21/76	02/28/76	03/06/76	03/13/76
167	157	107	102	101	98	114
03/20/76	03/27/76	04/03/76	04/10/76	04/17/76	04/24/76	05/01/76
128	128	132	141	142	138	168
05/08/76	05/15/76	05/22/76	05/29/76	06/05/76	06/12/76	06/19/76
168	169	177	170	163	163	156
06/26/76	07/04/76	07/10/76	07/17/76	07/24/76	07/31/76	08/07/76
156	154	156	160	160	174	184

RIAA/Sales:

In the United States, the album was certified Gold by the RIAA on April 18, 1975 and Platinum and 2X Platinum on November 21, 1986; and most recently, 3X platinum on February 26, 2001. Gold by the CRIA (Canada - 50,000 units) on November 1, 1976 and Platinum on May 1, 1979. During the SoundScan era, the album had sold 467,705 copies between 1991 and 2007.

Supporting Singles:

● "Same Old Song and Dance" (USA, 3/1974) — Chart Peak: Did not chart, though it did bubble under on Cashbox in April/May 1974 reaching #107.

04/13/74	04/20/74	04/27/74	05/04/74	05/11/74	05/18/74
119	113	116	106	107	X

● "Train Kept A Rollin'" (USA, 10/1974) — Chart Peak: DID NOT CHART. However, it did bubble under on Cashbox in October/November reaching #108.

10/19/74	10/26/74	11/02/74	11/09/74	11/16/74	11/21/74	11/30/74
120	116	119	112	108	116	111
12/07/74	12/14/74					
114	X					

● "S.O.S. (Too Bad)" (USA, 2/1975) — Chart Peak: DID NOT CHART.

Jack Douglas: "I made all my mistakes with the Dolls, so when it came time for Aerosmith, I knew exactly what to do."

December 1973 fittingly concluded Aerosmith's activities in support of their debut album. Their first major national television broadcast had taken place on Dick Clark's American Bandstand on Dec. 15 and soon after the band entered Record Plant Studios to start work on their sophomore album. Former CBS A&R exec Ray Colcord had been connected to the band since their performance for Clive Davis at Max's Kansas City in 1972 and had already worked with them in the studio during mid-1973. With the band not desiring to work with Englishman Adrian Barber again, the musician was well placed to contribute to the band's effort. The final show of the year took place in Providence, RI on Dec. 15, and Steven was interviewed by Stu Fine for the Providence Journal. He gave a hint to the direction the band were planning: "The head from our new music makes me feel like I'm falling in love. I'm blissful, the new stuff is much more of a group effort. Each song has a personality of its own, reflecting each one of us." Following their return from the West Coast in early December, the band had taken over Timothy's Too in Framingham to work on preproduction for the album. Some of the songs that appeared on their new album had already debuted in the band's set throughout the late-summer and fall, and the working title for the album was "Night in the Ruts" according to Steven's on-stage raps during shows leading up to the sessions. That road-testing of material was a critical part of the creative process.

Executive producer Bob Ezrin had famously heard the band perform, only to pronounce that "they're not ready." According to Steven, "Bob Ezrin heard our first album and thought we needed a lot of work. Which we did, but dig it, we're honest" (NME, 1/24/1976). If the desired effect of his pronouncement was to motivate the young band, then there is little doubt that the resulting solid slab of rock was proof enough that they'd gotten the message. If Bob didn't believe the band ready for his attentions, his colleague Jack Douglas understood the band and saw them as an American Yardbirds. Having worked with producer Todd Rundgren on the New York Dolls' debut album as an engineer, Jack had been part of the musical scene that they were part of. He recalled, "I used to go to the Mercer Arts Center; I lived in the East Village, I was part of that scene down there with Lou [Reed] and Patti [Smith]. I was a kind of a downtown connection to the band, so they put me on as a young engineer" (Best Classic Bands, 2018). During the challenged Dolls sessions Douglas proved pivotal in shepherding the project to completion. When Leber-Krebs approached Ezrin to produce another of their acts, he listened to their first album but didn't think there was much he could do, so recommended his colleague Jack for the job. After watching Aerosmith perform at a Boston high school, Douglas was hooked, and became a critical component for the band's recorded output for the much of the rest of the decade. He recalled, "I fell in love with them. They played the kind of rock that I'd been playing in bands for years — Yardbirds, Stones, that kind of raw feel. We talked about guitars and amps and pedals and backstage we got along immediately. We had so much in common. Steven [Tyler] was kind of a Bronx guy, in Yonkers, and so was [drummer] Joey [Kramer], very Bronx-Yonkers. We got along and I got the call that they wanted me to do the record" (Best Classic Bands, 2018). Ezrin retained an executive producer credit on the album.

The band were as prepared as they could be, and if Steven felt "blissful," there was also the requisite fire lit to help motivate them. The late occurring minor success of the "Dream On" single meant that the band's visibility had been raised somewhat, even though they felt that Columbia hadn't been particularly supportive of the debut. That the album had moved over 100,000 copies without benefit of a single was more than impressive, even if much of that support was regional. Regardless, there remained the threat of the band being dropped by the label if the next record didn't perform better, so the single's response was particularly fortunate happenstance. The band had rehearsed in a space under Drummer's Image on Newbury Street, shaking the walls as they sought to perfect the new material. The increased creative contributions from other members also went further in forging the band's emerging collective musical identity. A year on the road had also seasoned them further as players. For members of the band, it was all about the music and breaking away from the constraints of categorization by critics. Joe Perry: "We've been classed as a glitter band — but we ain't. We've met a lot of people who've said we're Boston's exponents of glitter and flash, but the only flash we have is the music. Music is the main selling point of the band, it always has been, and it's always been our main consideration" (Los Angeles Free Press, 1/25/1974). And all that consideration was being poured into their efforts. Perhaps most importantly, Steven found his true voice in the studio though one of the goals remained capturing the band's live sound better in the studio.

While the song writing expanded from the near total purview of Tyler on the debut, he still provided the core. And the lyrics. While only Joey and Joe were represented on the credits, the whole band played a role in crafting the arrangements of the songs. Lyrically, with one exception, the songs represented the band's image and lives they were living on the road. There was a minimum of posturing, nor was there significant preaching. Steven noted, "We're not trying to lay any heavy messages on anybody. I don't feel we can really tell anyone what to do with their lives..." (Circus Raves, 7/1974). The first of Steven's three solo compositions was originally titled "Son of Shit." It's hardly surprising that CBS executives forced the change of title of the song. Like "Pandora's Box," "S.O.S. (Too Bad)" had debuted in the band's set in August 1973, along with another song "Downtown Baby," which would not make the album (decades later it would be realized as "Love XXX"). "S.O.S.," however, became a mainstay in the band's live set throughout 1974. According to Steven, when introducing the song in Detroit in Feb. 1974, it was about a western perhaps tenuously alluded to by the "stagecoach lady" lyric. The song would also be issued as the final single from the album (Columbia 3-10105), backed with "Lord of the Thighs," when released in February 1975. It didn't chart but received a positive review in Cashbox: "A classic, moving vocal delivering and dynamite rhythm and lead work make this single a pacemaker for the days to come. Aerosmith's single will have traffic piled up for miles. Get up and dance" (Cashbox, 3/15/1975). "Lord of the Thighs," likely debuted in the band's set in January 1974, prior to the delayed release of the album. It was one of the last songs written and recorded and was more sinister than the dark and edgy material that was later written for "Rocks." Like that edgy material, it was inspired by the environs of the of the Record Plant studio, the band's lodging at the Ramada Inn on 48th St. and 8th Ave., and Steven's visceral observations of his daily life in general. Knocked together during a marathon session, it was repeatedly called out as vulgar by reviewers and critics.

The first single released coincided with the album's release, though Steven was less than impressed that the decision had been made by executives: "This is something the higher-ups told us would be a single off our new album. We told them it was a load of shit, but we've got to go with what they say, sometimes" (Detroit, 2/1974). Or he was simply deflecting until audience reaction to the new tune was known. Unlike the road-tested material he had yet to "see" the audience reaction to the song. "Same Old Song and Dance," backed with "Pandora's Box" (Columbia 4-46029), was issued on Mar. 12 (according to copyright documentation) in addition to serving as the album's opening track. That important sequencing position illustrates that someone certainly believed in the song since it would serve as the listener's introduction and set the tone for the whole of the album. Unfortunately, the single dithered around the nether regions of Cashbox's single chart, reaching a high position of #107 in early May even though that trade mag's critic had liked the song: "Boston's new premier rock and rollers deliver the mail again in the form of this top-flight hard rocker culled from their latest LP, 'Get Your Wings.' Should exceed 'Dream On' in popularity and carry this band to the heights. Definitely not the same old song" (Cashbox, 3/23/1974). Clearly the executives had it wrong, but in the long run the fans right. The second Tyler/Perry composition was "Spaced," was developed in the studio. It was something of an oddity, not being based upon reality or observations of life, and was a surprisingly endearing space-themed flight of fancy. "Woman of the World" was written by Steven and his former Chain Reaction bandmate, "Don Solomon," during that band's lifespan, but it was never used by them. Like some of the other songs, it had also debuted live in the summer of 1973. When recorded before Christmas 1973, a couple of arrangements were tried out. One version split the song into two parts, another take saw the band essentially performing it live. Those takes would be abandoned and the song was re-recorded for the form appearing on the album, though elements may have been used on the substantially different quadraphonic version released the following year.

"Train Kept A Rollin'" had been popularized by the Yardbirds in 1965. They had taken that song further from its blues roots by basing their classic arrangement on a 1956 rockabilly arrangement by Johnny Burnette and the Rock and Roll Trio, rather than the original 1951 jump blues version by the song's writer, Tiny Bradshaw. It was part of the Aerosmith's DNA, not only with the obvious connection to guitarist Beck from the Yardbirds recording (and Page's later version, reinterpreted as "Stroll On"), but it was also the only song that all the members of Aerosmith knew at the time their band came together. It's hardly surprising that it had been performed at the band's very first show at Nipmuc Regional High School in Nov. 1970. Certainly, other songs performed that night in Mendon would be also revisited during the band's career. Perry recalled, "The Yardbirds were definitely taking the blues thing — as a lot of those English guys did — and putting larger guitars on it. They had a melodic sense, you know, with Jeff Beck in the band. They were a pop band trying to incorporate some of that blues edge and still get played on the radio" (Guitar World, 4/1997). Even the 1956 version had been "heavy," utilizing what was just emerging as a musical device: the deliberately distorted guitar. While the Yardbirds may have at times been full-throttle prototypical "metal," Aerosmith managed to transcend the inspirational version, perhaps accidentally, with Joey's R&B-fusion drumming adding to the backbeat in a manner that paralleled the song's title. That, along with the band's appreciation for James Brown, added a certain "X" factor to their performance.

A further change to the song's arrangement was added to their performance in the studio, dividing it into two distinctive sections. The first part saw the song delivered in a slower manner, akin to a musical analogy of a steam train leaving the station — slowly, ponderously, and somewhat lumbering. Later, the song hits full speed, careening and nearly coming off the tracks, with full-throttle energy and enthusiasm bring the song to glorious crescendo. Going back to that analogy, one can imagine that train barreling down the tracks at full speed, on the brink of losing control. The band had wanted to record the song live, but such a methodology would have clashed when mixed with the rest of the album. As a compromise the two sections of the song were divided into "studio," and "live" with a faux audience (sourced from the "Concert for Bangladesh") added to the second half. The result? A curiously engaging hybrid that musically goes from zero to orgasm in six minutes. Sleight of hand is also part of the magician's trick book, and there would be additional "magic" added to the track with the addition of performances by two additional, albeit uncredited, guitarists: Dick Wagner and Steve Hunter. They weren't strangers. Both guitarists had been members of Lou Reed's band, with Ray Colcord, and Steve was then working with executive producer Bob Ezrin at the same in Studio A at the Record Plant while Aerosmith were ensconced in Studio C. Hunter recalled, "I had a long wait between dubs and was waiting in the lobby. Jack Douglas popped his head out of Studio C and asked 'Hey, do you feel like playing?' I said sure, so I grabbed my guitar and went in ... I had two run thru's [sic], then Jack said, 'great that's it!' That turned out to be the opening solos on 'Train Kept A Rollin'" (Detroit Rock n Roll Magazine, 2/6/2015).

Dick recalled that he had been sitting around in his apartment at the Plaza Hotel when he got a call from Jack Douglas to come over one night to record some overdubs for an Aerosmith album. For Dick, it was simply a matter that Brad and Joe weren't able to capture exactly what Jack was hearing in his head for the song, not that they weren't capable guitarists ("Not Only Women Bleed" / Bleedstreet, 8/9/2012). That the band's primary guitarists were replaced on a track was not an exceptional outlier at the time. It was simply a practice that happened. The so-called informal Wrecking Crew/Clique were an informal collective of seasoned session players who could be called on by producers to fill a specific musical role and minimize the time and takes required to capture a recording. It was simply business and necessity. A butcher edit was released as a single (Columbia 3-10034), backed with "Spaced," in early October 1974. The single edit is particularly noteworthy. At what would be the first breakdown section on the album cut, the single version instead shifts to the full-throttle section that followed Joey's drum rolls where the live audience would have kicked in, and fast forwards to the final verse. All told, over two minutes of the song fell to the single preparer's axe. However, this version of the song does not feature the overdubbed faux live audience revealing musical elements otherwise obscured. The reviewers, again at Cashbox, were positive: "If Aerosmith were given the right break, they could definitely be a premier rock 'n' roll band. Their instrumentation is heavy, and the vocals have the necessary gutsy feel to them. This new tune is a heavy solid rocker that will positively roll over your ears. Some fine lead guitar licks are complemented by heavy arrangement. Should crack them" (Cashbox, 10/5/1974). The single wouldn't chart, or "crack them," though regardless of radio airplay the song became a core classic for the band.

"Pandora's Box" provided a rare song-writing credit for drummer Joey Kramer. During the summer of 1973, as the band had started to prepare ideas for their second album, Joey had picked a guitar out of a dumpster and created the melody for this song, which Steven married with women's liberation inspired lyrics which were anything but feminist. The song had been audience tested and was included in the band's set during the fall of 1973. In the studio, Jack brought in Michael Brecker and Stan Bronstein to sweeten the performance with brass, and one of the session musicians also added the first few bars of Julie London's "I'm In the Mood for Love" on clarinet as the intro to the song. Also written on the dumpster acoustic guitar, around Halloween 1973, was Steven's melancholy "Seasons of Wither," which was purportedly inspired by the bleak Massachusetts winter. It would become one of Joe's favorite Tyler ballads. Tyler performed the acoustic guitar as part of the song's haunting beginning. Studio sheets suggest that an alternate version was also worked on for the album. There could be little accusation of "sameness" for the material on the album. It ran broad spectrum of tempos and style yet remained unified enough to work as an album. It was, simply put, the result of the band's focus on their music. It was a point all too easily missed by critics. Tom commented, "Either they put us down for being like the Stones or being glitter, but I just wish they'd recognize the music" (Los Angeles Free Press, 1/25/1974). For whatever reason, the band's singles weren't resonating on radio, but they were continuing to build their reputation as a live act, just as they'd done with the debut album the previous year. The high-energy rock 'n' roll was best captured live, in concert, and that had not yet translated onto vinyl. This was recognized in the trade magazines: "Over the last two years, Aerosmith have established a solid reputation for themselves as a high flying, solid rock and roll quintet. Well versed in that rich tradition of 60s power pop first popularized by groups like the Rolling Stones, the Yardbirds, and The Who, Aerosmith play with an all but forgotten fervor into which they add the flair of a 70s sensibility" (Cashbox, 1/18/1975).

"Get Your Wings" was released on Mar. 8, 1974 and bubbled under for a week at #205 on the Billboard Top-200 album charts before properly entering at #193 on Apr. 6. In the United States, the album was the band's first title certified Gold by the RIAA, on April 18, 1975, receiving simultaneous platinum and 2X platinum on November 21, 1986. Most recently it was recertified 3X platinum on February 26, 2001. Gold by the CRIA (Canada - 50,000 units) on November 1, 1976 and Platinum on May 1, 1979. During the SoundScan era, the album sold 467,705 copies between 1991 and 2007. In the U.S., the album charted four separate times on Billboard's Top-200 for a cumulative 86-week charting run, where it reached a peak of #100 (5/11/1974). During its third return to the chart hit its high position of #74 (10/18/1975). The album also had a pair of charting runs on Cashbox accounting for 62 weeks and a high position of #77 (5/18/1974). The quadraphonic (QL/8) version followed on Mar. 7, 1975. "Get Your Wings" mirrored the slow-burn of the debut, albeit without the benefit of any even marginally successful single. After dropping off the Billboard Top-200 in early September 1974, the album returned for a further 27 weeks in mid-October and had nearly matched its initial chart top by early December 1974. More importantly, by that point the album was selling 7,000 copies per week, setting the stage for yet another album...

Assorted review excerpts:

"Derivative they may be, but this is one band whose tough and nasty rock 'n' roll vision could well score, given the added punch of Jack Douglas and Ray Colcord's production. Leader Steve Tyler spits his vocals with studied vengeance, and guitars and rhythm section work throughout pass the heavy metal acid test. Try the raw reworking of 'Train Kept A Rollin',' crackling along behind a Yardbirds arrangement; or the dark, layered momentum of 'Seasons of Wither.' Bad taste awards may follow for 'Lord of the Thighs,' a male supremacist paean that should horrify most ladies" (Billboard, 3/23/1974).

"One of Boston's favorite bands is back again with a raucous collection worthy of its reputation as one of the punchiest hard rock bands working the big time today. Highlighted by 'Same Old Song and Dance,' the LP is geared to a heavy metal sound that's inescapably infectious. 'Lord of the Thighs,' 'Woman of the World,' 'Seasons of Wither,' 'Pandora's Box,' and a great version of a tune made popular by the Yardbirds entitled 'The Train Kept A Rollin',' give the album its soul and substance. Steve Tyler's lead vocals are spicy and to the point and the arrangements on the LP are catchy" (Cashbox, 3/23/1974).

"The musical growth of Aerosmith from their respected, yet troubled and undisciplined, debut long player to 'Get Your Wings' is startling. The guitar riffs of Joe Perry and the pushing drums of Joey Kramer pace the new professionalism of Aerosmith. For the better lead singer Steven Tyler has abandoned his Jagger-styled inflections and let loose with his own erotic rock 'n raunch vocals. The man who's brought a new-found clean and slick production sound is Jack (Alice Cooper, Guess Who, Poco) Douglas, while showcasing the sensuous best of Aerosmith, neatly waters down their youthful brand of inexperience... Song after song Tyler somehow gets absolutely the right feel the content and intent of the lyrics and music. Tyler is Boston's first glitter star. Whereas, Boston is quite serious about quality of her music, he has to be exceptional. And he is. Just as Mick is the Stones and Alice is Alice Cooper, Steven Tyler is Aerosmith. All in all, however, 'Get Your Wings,' a five-star production, lacks the elusive magical 'hit' quality of 'Dream On.' Yet, Faye Dunaway aside, this is without question Boston's best rock roll band" (Dennis Metrano, Zoo World).

"'Get Your Wings' is their second release and while I still don't consider Aerosmith one of my favorite five or six rock groups, I have altered my evaluation of their playing considerably upwards. An evident maturity has set in. This is obvious from a collection of disciplined performances, several intricately structured and ably navigated. The pivotal facet continues to be the tirelessly commanding singing of Tyler. Aerosmith's musical style is as cohesive as the best in rock, especially when lead guitarist Joe Perry is blazing the trail. I fear, however, that Aerosmith without Tyler would be like the Doors without Jim Morrison or the Stones (there you go) without Jagger. This is not written in derogation of Aerosmith, merely an observation. If tracks must be singled out for praise, then let them be the juggernauting 'Train Kept a Rollin',' the lone non-original in the album; 'Lord of the Thighs,' with focus on Perry's crisp solo and a naggingly attractive stringed staccatoing through much of the performance, and 'Woman of the World,' embellished by smartly arranged voice-and-guitar response insertions, all conveyed along on Joey Kramer's articulately unobtrusive beat. Summation: When Frank Connelly raves, you listen" (Boston Globe, 4/21/1974).

"Boston has not been a breeding-grounds for rock bands without R&B backgrounds or aspirations. Nevertheless, Boston has long been known as a 'breakout' market for English bands the likes of Led Zeppelin and the Jeff Beck Group. Aerosmith takes its cue from this array, and with this, their second album, have disproved the notion that Boston can only appreciate, not produce this brand of music. By elaborating on the fusion of blues and experimentalism originated by those patriarchs the Yardbirds, Aerosmith have staked out for themselves a style whose derivativeness can be overlooked in the face of its extreme flexibility... Tyler is a natural at writing songs which are cleverly laid out and rhythmic at no expense to their singability, yet the most that can be said for his mastery of his other responsibility is that some of his vocal affectations are more effective than others. 'Seasons of Wither' is a small masterpiece, Aerosmith's 'Stairway to Heaven,' only I wish Tyler could sing his song as well as it deserves to be sung. The rest of the material is less heady and less demanding... 'S.O.S. (Too Bad)' has a brilliantly snide, nasal guitar lead in the Jeff Beck mold. Joe Perry should be especially commended for his endlessly creative, transforming leads throughout the LP. He has a mind completely his own, and is the band's outstanding musician... Once they learn to pose for a photograph, they'll be all set" (Boston Phoenix, 5/14/1974).

"Maintaining an agile balance between Yardbirds- and Who-styled rock and Seventies heavy metal, Aerosmith's second album surges with pent-up fury yet avoids the excesses to which many of their peers succumb. The music of the five-member group contains the vital elements of economy and control — no ill-advised solo extravaganzas. The snarling chords of guitarists Joe Perry and Brad Whitford tautly propel each number, jibing neatly with the rawness of singer Steven Tyler, whose discipline is evident no matter how he shrieks, growls, or spits out the lyrics. Throughout 'Get Your Wings' the group consistently integrates their influences into their own approach. On 'Spaced,' Whitford unleashes a barrage of Townshend-inspired chords, by now an Aerosmith trademark, while the choppy rhythm and horn work of 'Pandora's Box' are a hard-rock interpretation of soul, suggesting the Stones. 'Seasons of Wither' is a surprising change of pace, a haunting arrangement that creates a rough-hewn prettiness. The group's dynamics are expert, deftly blending the hard and soft interludes. Perry makes exceptional use of feedback at the end, while Tyler's restraint reveals a Led Zeppelin influence. 'Train Kept A Rollin',' a reworking of the Yardbirds' classic, is a master demonstration of their style. Their new arrangement begins by retaining the feel of the earlier work, only to cleverly segue into what sounds like a live take, although it was recorded in the studio. They then execute a near-duplication of the Yardbirds' performance that stands remarkably well on its own. That cut proves they've absorbed yet varied the styles of their mentors, creating their own in the process. They think 1966 and play 1974 — something which a lot of groups would like to boast" (Rolling Stone, 6/6/1974).

1974 - Get Your Wings

March 8
Field House @ Plymouth State College
Plymouth, NH
Other act(s): James Montgomery Band
Notes:
- Initial touring plans did not include joining a big name on the road: "Heavy promo and appearances in Northeast, where group has particularly large following; tours other areas with 'compatible' artists" (Cashbox, 3/2/1974).

March 9 **TWO SHOWS
Orpheum Theater
Boston, MA
Promoter: Don Law Presents
Other act(s): Blue Oyster Cult
Reported audience: 5,800 **SOLD-OUT
Reported gross: $34,000
Partial set list: Make It / Write Me / Lord of the Thighs / One Way Street / Same Old Song and Dance / Dream On
Notes:

- Two separate sold-out shows (2,900 patrons) were performed by the bands (at 7 & 10p.m.). Over 1,000 fans were reported to have been turned away from the shows (Cashbox, 3/23/1974). This show would essentially have been the album's release party: "Three years ago three young musicians left the wilds of New Hampshire to seek fame and fortune in the big city, and on Saturday night the mighty Aerosmith rock 'n' roll band sold nearly 6,000 tickets to two shows in the Orpheum and could have sold another 1,000, except there are only 2,860 seats in the Orpheum. The group played several songs from its first album, which has sold 170,000 copies, 60,000 in New England, and some from its second album issued last week... The band is now getting some material together for a full-scale road trip to help promote the second album which came out last Thursday in Boston and has started doing well. 'Same Old Song and Dance' is the single from it" (Boston Globe, 3/11/1974).
- The band were interviewed by Ray Murphy of the Boston Globe between sets.
- From a local review: "The theatrics, however, were just beginning. Aerosmith, a group formed in New Hampshire introduced 'glitter rock' on the local level. A spotlight shone upon a giant backdrop; their name emblazoned in spangles. When the opening chords of 'Make It' were struck, lead singer Tyler, rose from a curled position, his back to the audience, and unfurled a bat-like cape, doubling his arm span. The cape was symbolic of their latest album, 'Get Your Wings.' The trouble with the showmanship in rock is, that with few exceptions, it is rarely unique. Aerosmith was not an exception. Tyler is a fluid, well-coordinated stage performer who has learned his lessons in choreography well. Yet his high-prancing, groin-grinding, saunters across stage (at times carrying the microphone stand with him) are reminiscent of the styles of Stewart, Cooper, and Jagger. Aerosmith is a colorful concert band" (Boston Herald, 3/11/1974).
- Joe Perry: "No one gives a damn if we sell out two shows at the Orpheum Theatre in Boston. All these other groups that aren't popular anywhere, they get all the stories..." (Circus Raves, 7/1974).

March 14
Veterans Memorial Coliseum
New Haven, CT
Promoter: Jim Koplick & Shelly Finkel
Other act(s): Deep Purple (HL)
Reported audience: 10,400 **SOLD-OUT

March 15
Butova Gym @ American International College
Springfield, MA
Promoter: Winter Carnival Committee
Other act(s): James Cotton Band (HL)

March 16
SAC Gym @ Agricultural & Technical College
Alfred, NY
Promoter: Student Activities Board
Other act(s): Chi Coltrane (opener)
Notes:
- This event was held at the gym due to the refusal of the Director of Athletics to allow concerts in the McLane Center, a result of damage caused to the floor during a concert the previous year. Rush was mentioned in some news articles following the show, but it seems unlikely that it was the famed Canadian band with whom Aerosmith would later tour.

March 17
Novak Fieldhouse @ Prince George's Community College
Largo, MD
Promoter: PGCC Student Activities Board
Other act(s): Rory Gallagher (HL)
Reported audience: 4,200 **SOLD-OUT
Notes:
- This was a free concert organized by the student activities board. The audience were purportedly still chanting for an additional Aerosmith encore during Rory's set.

March 23
IU-PU Ballroom
Fort Wayne, IN
Promoter: Student Union
Other act(s): Bull Angus
Notes:
- Tom, Steven, and David Krebs were interviewed by the University newspaper, the Communicator. The resulting feature was printed in the March 28 issue. When asked how "Get Your Wings" compared with the debut, Steve answered with a blunt, "I don't." Tom expanded: "The songs on the first album are slap happy. The kinds of songs that [people] would just pick up on and dance to. This album's a little more involved." As for the message of the band, Steven offered, "We just like to get off on music, no message."

March 24
Painter's Mill Music Fair
Owings Mill (Baltimore), MD
Promoter: Key Productions
Other act(s): Redbone, KISS (opener)
Reported audience: (2,400 capacity)
Notes:
- KISS became the opening act for this show when Badfinger purportedly pulled out and Aerosmith was promoted to the headliner slot. However, it should be noted that Badfinger had already performed at Painter's Mill on March 1 (a bootleg of that performance circulates) and had also just completed a run of dates at Alex Cooley's Electric Ballroom in Atlanta, GA on the evening of March 23. They instead performed in Little Rock, AR on March 24, allowing them an additional day for the 1,000+ miles travel/rest prior their next scheduled show: The Bayou in Georgetown, DC on March 26.

- Joe recalled, "They opened for us outside D.C... Their songs were real basic, real catchy. I think they just wore leather jackets, black jeans, and face makeup. It might've been before their [first] record came out, before they had the means to get cooler outfits. But even then, they had pyro. The audience flipped out... We were thinking, 'Holy [expletive]! What do we have to do now? Go out dressed in tutus?'" (Cleveland Plain Dealer, 8/29/2003). A couple of years after the show, Steven offered the following observation about the band that had reached a similar level of success to Aerosmith: "It must be a drag walking off stage, you take off all that clown make-up, and nobody knows who the hell you are" (Palm Beach Post, 8/1/1976).

- Steven: "It was kinda hard to see them through all the makeup, y'know? It was a comic-book thing. Then we toured with them. We must have played two or three shows before one of their road crew pulled a knife on ours. Then we said, 'sayonara.' But back then, it was all about who could blow who offstage" (Las Vegas Sun, 10/24/2003).

March 25
The Brewery
East Lansing, MI

Promoter: Bill Smith / in-house
Reported audience: 750 **SOLD-OUT
Notes:
- From a local review: "This time around they captured yet another sell-out house, but they did it the easy way — with flash masking real talent. When the band played the Brewery last January, lead singer Steve Tyler asserted himself as perhaps the best lead vocalist in America. Lead guitarist Joe Perry was the spotlight attraction, but it was rhythm guitarist Brad Whitford who did all the guitar work while Perry stole the show. The band was in the Brewery league of Bachman-Turner Overdrive, and when it is considered that most of the world's best rock bands are either Canadian or British, Aerosmith looked to be the next great American rocker. But Aerosmith has been busy since their January concert with a nationwide tour, plenty of Columbia Records hype and a second album called 'Get Your Wings.' The album was better produced than their first, but the music didn't measure up to their earlier efforts. With all the traveling, their music has suffered and been compensated with show and glitter. It's a shame because Aerosmith's strongest asset was their music.

So, when the band trouped onto the Brewery stage Monday, they were draped in satin, sequins, and distinctly feminine attire. Their speakers were louder than before, and Perry looked like a dog writhing in heat as he tried to play guitar. Tyler was still sensational on vocals and Whitford hid in the shadows doing more guitar work than before to make up for Perry. Tyler is Aerosmith. Period. How he fares, so will the band. His voice sounds stronger than ever and, if possible, he has greater range than when he last played the Brewery. Along with Whitford, poor Whitford, Tyler will take the group a long way. But Monday night Perry kept trying to upstage Tyler with his chord playing and the stage antics focusing the mostly good music on his ailing fuzz tone guitar" (Lansing State Journal, 3/30/1974).

March 26
The Rock 'N' Roll Farm
Wayne, MI

Promoter: Leo Speer
Other act(s): Punch (opener)
Reported audience: (120 capacity)
Notes:
- The bar's owner, Dr. Leo Speer, also owned Detroit's Michigan Palace.

March 27, 28, 29 **TEMP-HOLD DATES
Electric Ballroom
Atlanta, GA

Promoter: Alex Cooley, Inc.
Notes:
- While a three-night stand at the Electric Ballroom was advertised, it seems unlikely that they all took place with the confirmed shows on Mar. 26 & 31 taking place, along with the opening slot for Hawkwind, though Steven does colorfully recount adventures at the Ballroom in his autobiography.

March 27 **QUESTIONABLE
Ice Arena
Kenosha, WI

Other act(s): Pavlov's Dog

March 29
Electric Ballroom
Atlanta, GA

Promoter: Alex Cooley, Inc.
Other act(s): Hawkwind (HL)
Reported audience: (1,100 capacity)
Notes:
- Firsthand accounts recall Aerosmith opening this show for Hawkwind. They were conducting their "1999 Party," and had been scheduled to perform a midnight show at the Fox Theater (with Man opening).

March 31
Syria Mosque
Richmond, VA

Other act(s): Blue Oyster Cult (HL)
Reported audience: (3,732 capacity)
Notes:
- From a local review: "It's groups like Aerosmith that explain the 1950s musical revival. Their type of music, hard rock, has gone as far as it can. There's nothing new, nothing audibly appealing after the first musical thrust of a guitar. Aerosmith, a group that looked as young as its mostly high school-aged audience, unfortunately exhibited the minuses of hard rock at the Mosque last night. The band was loud, and in the acoustically cozy Mosque, loud is loud. Their music was repetitious, with little worth repeating. That's not to say the Aerosmith is one of the worst rock bands emerging these days. With the emphasis now on the visual rather than the auditory — especially true with 'gay rock' — a lot of new bands don't seem to know their guitars from their wardrobes. With a song like 'Same Old Song and Dance,' Aerosmith showed some traces of better music and the audience, nondiscriminatory rockers that they were, was appreciated enough to demand, and get, two encores. But even though members of Aerosmith have their standard long hair, shirts open to the waist, junior edition Mick Jagger, and microphone acrobatics, they just don't add up to a good, tight rock band" (Richmond Times Dispatch, 4/1/1974).

April 5
Albee Theater
Cincinnati, OH

Promoter: Belkin Productions
Other act(s): Foghat (HL)

Reported audience: 3,024 **SOLD-OUT
Reported gross: $15,120
Notes:
- "Get Your Wings" debuted in the Apr. 6 edition of Billboard Magazine at #193 on the Top-200 album charts. Initially, the album rose to #100 during an initial 22-week run, before dropping off charts completely. Gaining its second wind, the album re-entered the charts on Oct. 19 and hung around in the bottom half, for an additional 27-weeks, until Apr. 25, 1975, when it finally dropped out; being replaced that week by the band's then new album, "Toys in the Attic."

April 7
Michigan Palace
Detroit, MI

Promoter: Steve Glantz Productions / WABX
Other act(s): KISS, Mojo Boogie Band, Michael Fennelly
Reported audience: 5,000 **SOLD-OUT
Reported gross: $4,850
Set list: Write Me / Mama Kin / Lord of the Thighs / Woman of the World / Dream On / Pandora's Box / Same Old Song and Dance / One Way Street / Somebody / Train Kept A Rollin' / Walkin' the Dog / Milk Cow Blues
Notes:

- The WABX-FM "Kite-In and Balloon Fly" was an annual grassroots event in 1968, but quickly grew to require much larger venues that could accommodate thousands. The station broadcast both the Aerosmith and KISS sets as part of their special all-day coverage of the event, starting at noon. Paul Stanley (KISS): "Our paths crossed around 1974... My recollection is it was in Detroit. I was blown away. They really delivered the goods, both musically and in terms of their vibe onstage... I remember when their first album came out, my reaction was, 'Wow, these guys look British, a bit Stones-y.' I was really impressed" (Cleveland Plain Dealer, 8/29/2003).
- The annual "Kite-In" was cancelled due to poor weather, including rain and snow, forcing postponement of that part of the event until April 21. However, since some among the 3,000 young folk who did turn up for the event caused $2,000 damage inside the Belle Isle Casino, the local Common Council banned WABX from sponsoring any further "Kite-Ins" in Detroit parks (Detroit Free Press, 4/12/1974). Regardless, the concert raised $7,000 towards the clean-up of Belle Isle.
- As a result of being broadcast, an excellent FM recorded version has long circulated. One can hope that, like the KISS set, the pre-FM reel ultimately surfaces with a professional transfer...

April 8
Memorial Coliseum
Portland, OR

Promoter: Concerts West
Other act(s): Three Dog Night (HL)
Reported audience: ~9,000 / 11,000 (81.82%)
Notes:
- From a local review: "By comparison, opening act Aerosmith was the musical act. These five East Coast punk-rockers got their chops into some boogie tunes that thundered along nicely. However, the sound system was malfunctioning most of the group's set and the five-some was preoccupied with getting the proper sound out,

losing some of the vitality a young band like this should have. Aerosmith is a dynamic act, though, and one apparently on the move. If its stage act can be improved upon, it won't be long before the band headlines a show, instead of warming the crowd for a circus" (Oregonian, 4/9/1974).

April 10
Arena
Seattle, WA
Promoter: Concerts West
Other act(s): Three Dog Night (HL)
Reported audience: 6,500 **SOLD-OUT
Notes:
- Critic Patrick MacDonald, who had savaged KISS in a legendary review of their visit that year, deigned to not even mention Aerosmith.

April 12 **TWO SHOWS
Civic Auditorium
Santa Monica, CA
Promoter: Pacific Presentations
Other act(s): Mott the Hoople (HL)
Reported audience: (3,500 capacity)
Notes:
- Separate 8 and 11:30p.m. shows were scheduled, with the later slot being added a week prior to the date due to demand. The first show was reported as an advance sell-out (3,500). Mott's set was broadcast on local radio.
- From a local review: "By nine p.m. (after a late & lengthy sound-level check) they were ready to take off for 40 minutes of power chords, nasty snarls and pure rock and roll... Aerosmith proved themselves a band to watch, though it's a pity their development has been slowed by the woes and wherefores of the music business" (LA Voice, 4/26/1974).

April 13
Winterland
San Francisco, CA
Promoter: Bill Graham Presents
Other act(s): Mott the Hoople (HL), Bachman-Turner Overdrive
Reported audience: (5,000 capacity)
Notes:
- Tom Hamilton on band's he'd toured with (to that point) who impressed him: "Mott the Hoople. Ian Hunter sorta got a kick out of us for some reason. They kind of looked at us saying, 'Here are some kids that are in the same stage we were in years ago'" (IU-PU Communicator, 3/28/1974).
- From a local review: "Opening the show, Aerosmith generated terrific energy, which the band's material failed to justify. Lead singer Steve Tyler does a sensational Mick Jagger imitation, but the net results were destroyed by playing too loud... Aerosmith's set was abbreviated by a half-hour delay in starting, due to the later arrival of Mott the Hoople's public address system. Hoople contractually insists on using their own rig wherever they play" (San Francisco Chronicle, 4/15/1974).
-From another local review: "As rigor mortis set in with Hunter, guitarist Bender used his buttocks to pluck Hunter's guitar until it came to life with sound. Needless to say, it was gross. Surprisingly, one of the finer moments of the evening came from a supporting band from Boston, Aerosmith, Steve Tyler, a miniature

Mick Jagger, led his group through soul-stirring versions of 'The Train Kept A 'Rolling' and 'Walkin' the Dog'" (SJSU Spartan, 4/16/1974).

April 16
Ambassador Theater
St. Louis, MO
Promoter: Ron Powell Productions
Other act(s): ZZ Top (HL), Suzi Quatro
Reported audience: (3,006 capacity)
Notes:
- This was the start of a short touring run with the Texas band who had just released their "La Grange" single from their breakout "Tres Hombres" album. The bands would perform on numerous bills together over the next few years, and more extensively in 2009.
- From a local review: "Rock fans who spent more than five hours in the Ambassador Theater last night received double doses of mediocrity in the performances of Suzi Quatro and Aerosmith... the night's initial two attractions each offered some interesting guitar work, sandwiched around some terrible vocals. Suzi Quatro, her band, and Aerosmith, a heavy metal band from New England, emphasized their own sexuality, typified by Suzi Quatro's skin-tight outfit and the fishnet shirt worn by the shimmying Steven Tyler, Aerosmith's lead singer" (St. Louis Post-Dispatch, 4/17/1974).

April 18 **CANCELLED
Veterans Memorial Arena
Binghamton, NY
Promoter: Entertainment Concert Presentations
Other act(s): ZZ Top (HL)
Notes:
- This show was listed in Performance; however, no opening act was detailed locally, and the show was cancelled at the last moment, due to poor ticket sales.

April 19
International Convention Center
Niagara Falls, NY
Promoter: Entertainment Concepts Presentations
Other act(s): ZZ Top (HL)
Reported audience: (12,500 capacity)

April 20
Rockwell Cage
Cambridge, MA
Promoter: MIT Spring Concert Committee
Other act(s): Goodfoot, Fever
Reported audience: ~2,000 / 3,500 (57.14%)
Notes:
- The promoter lost some $6,000 on this 4-hour event to add insult to the ruckus caused by the influx of underage local kids to the show. Held during the school's Kaleidoscope weekend, a ticket-selling competition was blamed for the number of outsiders present. The total cost of putting the show on was $10,600, hence the urgency to recoup the expenses.

April 21
Bank Street Armory
Fall River, MA

Reported audience: (1,200 capacity)
Other act(s): Elliot Murphy
Notes:
- The Armory was an imposing venue. Constructed of granite block it looked more like a medieval castle than a welcoming house of musical debauchery.

April 22
Auditorium @ Salem State College
Salem, MA
Promoter: SSC Concerts
Notes:
- Photos from the concert were included in the school's 1974 Clipper yearbook.

April 26
Manchester, NH
Notes:
- A show on this date was listed in an itinerary in Performance.

April 27 **AFTERNOON
Ice Hockey Arena Parking Lot @ UConn
Storrs, CT
Promoter: B.O.G.
Other act(s): Fairport Convention (HL), Fat Back, Bruce Springsteen (opener)
Notes:
- This was a free show for the Spring Carnival Extravaganza. Bruce opened so that he could perform in Hartford that evening. Aerosmith also had another gig that day...

April 27 **EVENING
Brooks Concert Hall @ Holy Cross University
Worcester, MA
Promoter: 1843 Club
Other act(s): Duke & The Drivers

April 28
Veterans Memorial Auditorium
Columbus, OH
Promoter: Sunshine Promotions
Other act(s): King Crimson (HL)
Reported audience: ~3,200 / 3,964 (80.73%)
Notes:
- From a local review: "Weighty pretentiousness mixed it up with good-time rock and roll at Veterans Memorial Sunday night when King Crimson met Aerosmith. Depending on your preferences, it was a toss-up as to who won. Aerosmith, a Boston-based rockety-rollin' organization that keeps getting better and better all the time, is probably the most English-mannered of all the American boogie bands. Lead singer Steve

Tyler's penchant for aping Mick Jagger has almost become a caricature of movement and physical appearance from the glitter clothes, haircut, wide mouth, and stance — with one difference. Tyler's voice has the cutting edge of a saw-tooth shark. Strong and gritty, he comes across as androgynous as Jagger but more masculine by the power of his iron-edged voice. The music is heavy and full bore, sparing no horses. In fact, since their last appearance in Columbus six months ago, the young lads from Bean Town and points south have gotten it even more together as a cohesive performance unit supported by strong material" (Columbus Dispatch, 4/29/1974).

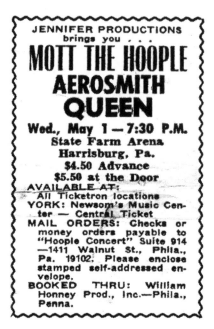

May 1 **Aerosmith CANCELLED?
State Farm Arena
Harrisburg, PA
Promoter: Jennifer Productions
Other act(s): Mott The Hoople (HL), Queen (opener)
Reported audience: ~4,700 / 8,200 (58.75%)
Notes:
- The first time Queen and Aerosmith shared a bill, with Mott headlining. Brian May and Joe Perry attacked a fifth of Jack Daniels backstage, resulting in Brian apparently playing his set blind drunk. Steven Tyler recalled in his autobiography, "We played a show one time at Harrisburg Arena in Harrisburg, Pennsylvania. Queen would not go on because we were the headliners. They refused to open for us, and the show was cancelled." Aerosmith weren't mentioned in the local Morning Call newspaper review of the show (5/2/1974), so this show may have been a case where Aerosmith cancelled (particularly if Joe was as wrecked as Brian).

May 3
Bowman Gymnasium @ Depauw University
Greencastle, IN
Promoter: Depauw Student Union Board
Other act(s): Elephant's Memory
Notes:
- This show was hosted in conjunction with the end of semester activities, and thus there was no student newspaper issue in which it was reviewed.
- Elephant's Memory are often better known as the backing band for John Lennon and Yoko Ono, notably on the "Some Time in New York City" album (1972). However, sax player Stan Bronstein also was a regular session player and performed on the studio recordings of "Same Old Song and Dance" and "Pandora's Box," and later contributed to "Draw the Line." Signed with Leber-Krebs, the band released "Angels Forever" via RCA during the year.

May 4
Memorial Auditorium
Louisville, KY
Promoter: Woodrose Presents
Other act(s): Elephant's Memory
Reported audience: (6,000 capacity)

May 5
Palace Theater
Dayton, OH
Promoter: Spectra Enterprises
Other act(s): Elephant's Memory, Blue Max (opener)
Reported audience: 1,500 **SOLD-OUT
Notes:
- From a local review: "Top billing Sunday night went to Aerosmith, a Boston-based sparkle and glitter band which has all the essential goodies to become a superstar act. First and foremost, they look and act like stars. Before a note was strummed or a vocal warbled, everyone was in awe because of their appearance. The centerpiece for this collage of the bizarre is the singer. His physical, and especially facial, appearance is a cross between Carly Simon and Mick Jagger. If this guy's voice ever fails him, he could be a top-drawer drag queen. He was effeminate and masculine all at the same time. His voice is superb, and he is a very good harmonica player, to boot. With this child of space age as a front man, the rest of the band could have been merely door mats, but it wasn't. And that's the reason this band has a good chance of becoming a superstar band. Every member has his own image and charisma, yet it is consistent with the overall personality and theme of the entire band. The boys in the band were somewhere between spacemen and space girls. They are a part of the vogue of gay rock that is sweeping both England and America. The difference between Aerosmith and the rest of the transsexual type of rockers is that when all the gold, glitter and gayness has faded away, there's a strong possibility that Aerosmith will still be on the scene, providing good sounds" (Dayton Journal Herald, 5/8/1974).

May 9
Gymnasium, Genesee Community College
Batavia, NY
Promoter: Student Activities Council
Other act(s): James Montgomery Band, Don Crawford (opener)
Notes:
- This show was emceed by comedians Edmonds & Curley.

May 10 **TEMP HOLD-DATE
Wheaton College
Norton, MA
Notes:
- Listed in an early Performance itinerary. At the time, Wheaton was an all-women liberal arts college.

May 12
Curry Hicks Cage @ UMass
Amherst, MA
Promoter: UMass SGA
Other act(s): Elliott Murphy, Chris Rhodes Band
Reported audience: ~4,000
Notes:
- From a local review: "Aerosmith brought caginess back to the Cage yesterday in the form of some of the loudest, most repelling un-music ever to have fallen on these ears. The audience — a peculiarly animalist bunch intent on reaching the highest possible state of artificially-induced euphoria — filled the place to the gills and fell at their feet... The concert, slated to be held in the Stadium, but moved due to the rain, started two hours late" (Massachusetts Daily Collegian, 5/13/1974).

May 15 **Aerosmith CANCELLED
War Memorial
Syracuse, NY

Promoter: Concerts East
Other act(s): Three Dog Night (HL)
Notes:
- Aerosmith cancelled their opening slot in favor of a show replacing Queen in Washington, DC. No replacement was booked for the band with Three Dog Night performing a 2-hour show instead.

May 15
D.A.R. Constitution Hall
Washington, DC
Promoter: Cellar Door Productions
Other act(s): Mott the Hoople (HL)
Reported audience: ~3,000 / 3,766 (79.66%)
Notes:
- From a local review: "Aerosmith (a last-minute replacement for Queen) opened the show with an overly aggressive mixture of American raunch-and-roll. Visually, the band has an emphasis on glamour, with music thrown in as an afterthought. The focus is on lead singer Steve Tyler, a soft, androgynous creature who owes his entire style to Mick Jagger. Tyler has all the moves down pat, though he overuses the arched spine and the rotate-your-rump-with-your-back-to-the-audience routines. In a terrible way, he's quite good, and if Aerosmith can develop a significant repertoire beyond what they did last night, they will go places" (Washington Evening Star, 5/16/1974).
- From another local review: "However hard Mott the Hoople tried last night, the high-powered British glitter rock outfit couldn't eclipse Aerosmith... Aerosmith's music is an outrageous copy of British heavy metal music — the kind of material pioneered by the Yardbirds... and continued with bands like Led Zeppelin, Black Sabbath and Foghat. It's frighteningly loud, built on the repeated resounding sound of basic bass and drum riffs, using two electric guitars to fill out the harmonic overtones. Last night Aerosmith didn't display the kind of instrumental fortitude that some of the better heavy British bands have. But they're certainly trying — acting on stage as if it really mattered whether they seemed like the meanest kids on the block. Their lyrics are equally menacing... Ultimately rock symbolizes some sort of contempt for traditional values, and one way to make it seems to involve flaunting whatever you've got as much as you can. With this in mind, it would seem Aerosmith has a profitable future ahead" (Washington Post, 5/16/1974).
- Queen's U.S. tour in support of their "Queen II" album had to be cancelled due to Brian May becoming ill in New York on May 12 (after a series of dates opening for Mott the Hoople at the Uris Theater). The press reported that he needed a month's recuperation from hepatitis during which time he wrote material for what became the "Sheer Heart Attack" album. Brian's battle with hepatitis was serious, and he was hospitalized and nearly lost his arm due to a dirty needle used to inoculate him prior the band's Australian tour in January 1974.

May 16 **Aerosmith CANCELLED
War Memorial
Rochester, NY
Promoter: Concerts East
Other act(s): Three Dog Night (HL)
Notes:
- While the band was noted in advertisements for the concert, Aerosmith was replaced by Jimmy Buffet on this bill.

May 17
Aragon Ballroom
Chicago, IL
Promoter: Jam Productions
Other act(s): Blue Oyster Cult (HL), Sharks
Reported audience: 4,500 / 5,000 (90%)
Reported gross: $25,000
Notes:
- From a local review: "Aerosmith, who opened, tried to communicate the same sound, and did, to a rather lesser degree. They charged around onstage with raunchy determination, dressed in skintight satin, but sound way too much like many other bands to be very remarkable" (April Olzak, Chicago Sun Times).

May 18
Kintner Gymnasium @ Stephen Decatur High School
Decatur, IL
Promoter: Crystal Ship & Gallery Music Co. / The New School
Other act(s): Unnamed second band

May 24
Palace Theater
Providence, RI
Promoter: WPRO

May 25
Cape Cod Coliseum
South Yarmouth, MA
Promoter: Rayal Productions
Other act(s): REO Speedwagon, Argent
Reported audience: 7,200 **SOLD-OUT
Notes:
- This show was considered the first true sell-out by a rock band at this venue. It seems certain that Aerosmith headlined, however, there is some debate as to whether REO Speedwagon (misnamed in on press notification as REO Speedway) or Blue Oyster Cult were the third act on the bill. With BOC having performed in Dayton on May 24 and being scheduled to perform at the State Fairgrounds in Des Moines on May 26 (cancelled on day of show due to rain), to seems more likely to have been Speedwagon (who had not yet taken over a support slot for Mott in place of Queen).

May 26
Central Maine Youth Center
Lewiston, ME
Promoter: Headlight Productions
Other act(s): REO Speedwagon, Duke & the Diggers (opener)
Reported audience: 4,000 **SOLD-OUT
Reported gross: $24,000

May 27
J.F.K. Memorial Coliseum
Manchester, NH
Promoter: Headlight Productions
Other act(s): REO Speedwagon, Duke & the Diggers (opener)
Reported audience: 4,200 **SOLD-OUT
Reported gross: $21,000
Notes:
- 2,000 patrons were reportedly turned away from this show, some of whom "went on a rampage, trashing the coliseum windows and numerous cars in the parking lot" (Performance).

May 29 **TWO SHOWS
Tower Theater
Upper Darby, PA
Promoter: Midnight Sun
Other act(s): Ken Lyon & Tombstone (opener)
Reported audience: 3,022 **SOLD-OUT
Reported gross: $5,681.36 **both shows
Notes:
- Tickets were sold for a promotional price of 0.94c.

May 31
Felt Forum
New York City, NY
Promoter: Howard Stein Presents
Other act(s): Slade (HL)
Reported audience: 4,500 **SOLD-OUT
Reported gross: $29,000
Set list: Write Me / S.O.S. (Too Bad) / Lord of the Thighs / Dream On / Same Old Song and Dance / Woman of the World / Train Kept A Rollin' / Milk Cow Blues
Notes:
- From a mainstream review: "It was a fight for the decibel and Slade won. Opening act Aerosmith's mighty sound paled in comparison to the power and energy from Slade's four members" (Rolling Stone #164, 7/4/1974).
- From an industry review: "The audience included many on their feet as the concert began with Aerosmith, Columbia disk act from Boston, who had one of their best vocal turns, especially lead vocalist Steven Tyler and lead guitarist Joe Perry. Aisles were quickly clogged, never to be cleared" (Cashbox, 6/5/1974).
- From another industry review: "Aerosmith opened the bill with another relatively loud set (almost mild by comparison to Slade) but the rock did have a certain finesse that shows distinctively that Aerosmith is a band of the future with greater success on the way. Their latest Columbia LP, 'Get Your Wings' is where much of their performance material originated" (Cashbox, 6/29/1974).
- An AUD recording circulates from this show.

June 1
Allen Theater

Cleveland, OH
Promoter: Belkin Productions
Other act(s): Blue Oyster Cult (HL)
Reported audience: (3,000 capacity)

June 2
Gardens
Cincinnati, OH
Promoter: Belkin Productions
Other act(s): Blue Oyster Cult (HL)
Reported audience: 3,000 / 3,500 (85.71%)
Notes:
- This show was the first at the Gardens to utilize a 1/3 house set up "to improve sight and sound for smaller concert audiences. The stage will be moved forward, past the center of the arena, toward the west end. A curtain will be hung behind the stage and across the arena floor" (Hamilton Journal News, 5/21/1974).

June 7
Dave Finkelman Auditorium @ Miami University
Middletown, OH
Promoter: MUM Pops Concerts Committee
Reported audience: (670 capacity)

June 9
Mid-South Coliseum
Memphis, TN
Promoter: Sunshine Productions
Other act(s): Rare Earth (HL), Soul Children (opener)
Reported audience: ~2,500 / 12,500 (20%)
Reported gross: $13,200
Notes:
- Steven was arrested for allegedly yelling obscenities from the stage during the show.

June 14
Sports Arena
Toledo, OH
Promoter: Sunshine Promotions
Other act(s): Rare Earth (HL)
Reported audience: (7,500 capacity)
Notes:
- Following this performance, the band flew to California to film their "Midnight Special" TV appearance in Burbank.

June 15 **TV FILMING
NBC Studios
Burbank, CA
Promoter: Burt Sugarman Productions / NBC
Set list: Dream On / Train Kept A Rollin'
Notes:

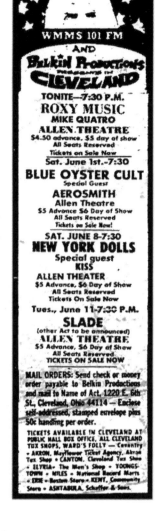

- The band's performances aired nationally on Aug. 16. "Train Kept A Rollin'" was included on the 2006 "But Sugarman's Midnight Special" DVD set.

June 18
City Auditorium Arena
Omaha, NE
Promoter:
Other act(s): ZZ Top (HL), Dr. Hook & the Medicine Show
Reported audience: 5,124 / 9,000 (56.93%)
Notes:
- From a local review: "Rolling Stone imitators Aerosmith were first on the bill, offering such innovations as shaggy hair, faded jeans, and open vests. The lead singer tried hard to be Mick Jagger, singing about worldly women with a sinister arrogance, but falling far short of the real McCoy. In between times, he took the opportunity to plug the group's albums repeatedly. All in all, Aerosmith is one of the dumber groups to play Omaha lately. But the young audience of 5,124, the official auditorium count, loved them, saluting the group with lighted matches, the latest rock 'n' roll equivalent to the standing ovation" (Omaha World-Herald, 6/19/1974).

June 19
R.K.O. Orpheum Theater
Davenport, IA
Promoter: Celebration Concerts
Other act(s): Lynyrd Skynyrd (HL)
Reported audience: (2,997 capacity)

June 20 **Aerosmith CANCELLED
University Union Auditorium
Normal, IL
Notes:
- Aerosmith, blacked out, was included on tickets printed for the event.

June 20
Veterans Memorial Coliseum
Cedar Rapids, IA
Promoter: Celebration Concerts
Other act(s): Lynyrd Skynyrd (HL), Charlie Daniels Band (opener)

June 21
Michigan Concert Palace
Detroit, MI
Promoter: Michigan Concert Palace, Inc.
Other act(s): Cactus, Elephant's Memory (opener)
Reported audience: 5,000 **SOLD-OUT
Reported gross: $28,000
Notes:

- Reported as the first advance sell-out in the venue's history.

June 22
Convention Center Arena
Indianapolis, IN
Promoter: Sunshine Promotions
Other act(s): REO Speedwagon (HL), Strawbs (opener), Locomotiv-GT (opener)
Reported audience: (capacity 12,000)
Reported gross: $55,200

July 2
My Father's Place
Roslyn, NY
Promoter: in-house
Other act(s): Elephant's Memory
Set list(s): Write Me / S.O.S. (Too Bad) / Lord of the Thighs / Dream On / Same Old Song and Dance / Woman of the World / Train Kept A Rollin' / Walkin' the Dog
Notes:
- This show was broadcast on WLIR-FM.

July 5
Casino Arena
Asbury Park, NJ
Promoter: John Scher
Other act(s): Blue Oyster Cult (HL)
Reported audience: 1,748 / 4,000 (43.7%)
Reported gross: $7,648

July 6
Stepping Stone Ranch
West Greenwich, RI
Promoter: Concerts New England, Inc.
Other act(s): Sha-Na-Na (HL), Mahavishnu Orchestra, Brownsville Station, Refugee, Wendy Waldon (opener)
Reported audience: ~20,000
Notes:
- From a local review: "A crowd of about 20,000 young people turned out during the weekend of a 12-hour 'Freedom Jam' rock concert at Stepping Stone Ranch here. Police said seven youths were treated at Kent County Memorial Hospital for drug overdoses. Four persons were arrested and charged with breaking into a vacant house near the festival site... No other incidents were reported, except for traffic tie-ups along Escoheag Hill Road. Featured among the seven performing groups were Sha-Na-Na and Aerosmith. Concert Promoter Henry W. Davis said Sunday he made money on the festival and will try to sponsor another one. Davis did not have a precise profit estimate" (Newport Daily News, 7/8/1974).

July 7
Cousens Auditorium @ Tufts University
Medford, MA
Notes:
- Listed in an early Performance itinerary.

July 9, 10
Electric Ballroom
Atlanta, GA
Promoter: Alex Cooley, Inc.
Other act(s): Kansas

July 10 **POSTPONED
Auditorium
Sioux City, IA
Promoter: Schon Productions
Other act(s): Santana (HL)
Notes:
- The Santana shows were postponed when their drummer, Michael Shrieve, was "hospitalized" in San Francisco following complications with kidney stones. However, he had departed the band — disappearing off to a health spa for a month — and by the time the band returned to the Winterland in September, had been replaced by Leon "Ndugu" Chancler.
- This show was initially rescheduled for July 17.

July 13
Civic Arena
Allen Park, MI
Promoter: Paul Stanley / Elliot Ness Productions
Other act(s): Tim Buckley
Notes:
- REO Speedwagon is also noted on some ads as opening.

July 14 **CANCELLED
Pine Knob Music Theater
Clarkston (Detroit), MI
Promoter: Nederlander Productions
Other act(s): Santana (HL)
Notes:
- This show was postponed on July 12.

July 14
Union Auditorium @ I.S.U.
Normal, IL
Promoter: Hard Times Productions
Other act(s): Harvey Mandel
Notes:
- This last-minute show took place — or at least Harvey Mandel performed — though the Entertainment Committee had decided a week earlier to not book summer entertainment following poor attendance of shows the previous academic year.

July 15
Pershing Auditorium
Lincoln, NE
Notes:

- Listed in early Performance and Billboard itineraries, this was the only rock concert held at the venue during the summer (Lincoln Star, 8/14/1974). However, the local paper's article about poor year the venue had endured noted the date of show as July 21.

July 17 **CANCELLED
Auditorium
Sioux City, IA
Promoter: Schon Productions
Other act(s): Santana (HL)

July 19 **CANCELLED
Civic Center
St. Paul, MN
Promoter: Schon Productions
Other act(s): Santana (HL), Poco, Mountain (opener)
Notes:
- This festival was named "Fillmore's Finest" as part of Minneapolis Aquatennial celebrations.

July 20
State Fairgrounds
Sedalia, MO
Promoter: Music Productions, Inc.
Other act(s): Tower of Power, Amboy Dukes
Reported audience: ~100,000
Notes:

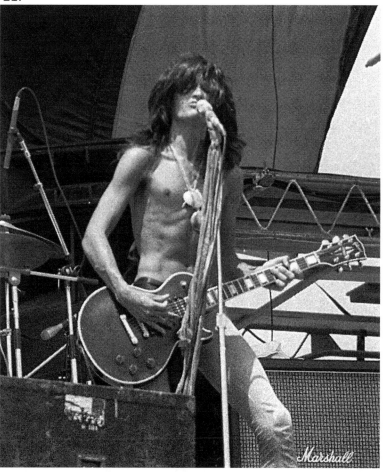

- The Ozark Music Festival, with some attendance figures ranging as high as 160,000 for the event, during which there was one death, 1,000 patrons requiring medical intervention, and an estimated $100,000 damage to the site. Various FM stations later broadcast 12 hours of rock music recorded during the event. The festival ran July 19–21.
- "Write Me," "S.O.S. (Too Bad)," and "Dream On" were broadcast on the radio. Photos © Richard Galbraith.

July 26 **TEMP HOLD-DATE
Suffolk Downs
Boston, MA
Notes:
- Listed in an early Performance and Billboard itineraries.

July 27 **Aerosmith CANCELLED
Marion County International Raceway
LaRue, OH
Promoter: William & Thomas Guthery
Other act(s): Blue Oyster Cult (HL), New York Dolls
Reported audience: ~2,335 / 4,000 (58.38%)
Notes:
- The Dudley Creek Outdoor Rock Concert. The show's attendance was affected by a local sheriff's attempt to obtain an injunction preventing the concert from going ahead. The PA blew out towards the end of the Dolls' set and Aerosmith bailed. Blue Oyster Cult played their set before PA issues again cut it short.

July 28
Thunderoad Raceway
Cass City, MI
Other act(s): Babe Ruth, Fresh Start (opener)
Notes:
- The grand opening of the Michigan Motorcycle Association raceway.

August 8 **POSTPONED
Auditorium
Bangor, ME
Promoter: Concerts East
Notes:
- This concert was postponed until Sept. 5, due to one of the band members being ill on the day of show.

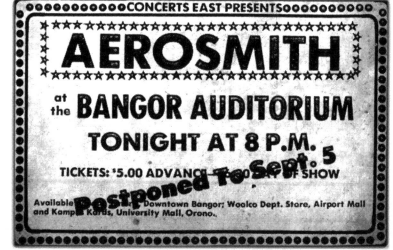

August 10
International Convention Center
Niagara Falls, NY
Promoter: Entertainment Concepts
Other act(s): Uriah Heep (HL), Manfred Mann
Reported audience: (10,428 capacity)
Notes:
- Listed in assorted early itineraries.

August 14
Memorial Coliseum
Fort Wayne, IN
Promoter: Sunshine Promotions
Other act(s): Black Oak Arkansas (HL)
Reported gross: $41,500

August 15
I.M.A. Auditorium
Flint, MI
Promoter: Standback Productions
Other act(s): James Gang (HL)
Reported audience: 5,300 **SOLD-OUT
Reported gross: $32,000
Notes:
- The night following this show, the band's appearance on the Midnight Special was broadcast on NBC. Hosted by Little Richard, the band performed "Dream On" and "Train Kept A Rollin'." Other guests included Kool & the Gang, Eddie Kendricks, David Clayton-Thomas, and Golden Earring.

August 18
Westboro Speedway
Westboro, MA
Promoter: R&T Productions
Other act(s): Mad Angel, Duke & The Drivers
Reported audience: ~15,000
Notes:
- Mad Angel included Joe and Jimmy D'Angelo who had been members of The Joneses. Aerosmith were not the first choice as the headliner for the event. According to one of the promoters of the event, "I was trying to get J. Geils, because they had a lot of local guys... We talked to the J. Geils Band and we talked to Aerosmith and, believe it or not, Aerosmith, at the time, was a little less money. So, we went with Aerosmith" (Telegram & Gazette, 7/13/12).
- Tom Hamilton recalled, "That was awesome. That was a blast. That was a big show for us. We were headlining a big outdoor venue. It was really exciting. It was one of the

biggest crowds that we ever played for. In our minds, in our imagination, it was like a mini-Woodstock. And, yes, I still come across people all the time who were at that show. That gig was really in the heart of Aerosmith country... The Joneses, we used to love them. They were the best band around, next to us. That's how we thought of it. We thought these guys are going all the way. And we were very surprised when that didn't happen" (Worcester Telegram & Gazette, 7/13/2012).

August 23
Parthenon Theater
Hammond, IN
Promoter: in-house
Other act(s): Hyway (opener)
Reported audience: (2,500 capacity)

August 24
Sports Arena
Toledo, OH
Promoter: Sports Arena, Inc.

Other act(s): Cactus
Reported audience: (7,500 capacity)
Notes:
- Tickets were misprinted with "Arrow Smith" as the band's name.

August 25 **CANCELLED
Fans Field
Decatur, IL
Promoter: Hard Times Productions
Other act(s): REO Speedwagon (HL), Climax Blues Band, Electric Flag, Renaissance, New York Dolls, Flock (opener)
Reported audience: (7,000 capacity)
Notes:
- The "Good Times Sunday" festival. Decatur Baseball, Inc. (who held exclusive rights to the field's usage), filed for an injunction against this concert, citing vandalism and drug use during a previous concert held there (a July 21 Ted Nugent concert attended by 2,000). However, even at that time the venue was struggling to stay open as a viable minor league facility, though the baseball team even went so far as to request a city inspection of the facility that put it at risk of condemnation due to possibly unsafe conditions. At a public hearing, many local residents expressed their opposition due to fears of the repeat of violence and disruption. Ultimately an injunction was granted, and the promoter moved the event to the I.S.U. Auditorium in Normal, though not all the scheduled acts would perform.

August 25 **Aerosmith CANCELLED
I.S.U. Auditorium
Normal, IL
Promoter: Hard Times Productions
Other act(s): Climax Blues Band, Electric Flag, Renaissance
Reported audience: 1,572 / 3,400 (46.25%)
Notes:
- Due to the legal and social issues affecting the concert's planned location in Decatur, many patrons opted for refunds rather than attend in Normal. Aerosmith and three other bands did not perform at the relocated show.

August 26
Dillon Stadium
Hartford, CT
Promoter: Jim Koplick & Shelly Finkel
Other act(s): Deep Purple (HL), Elf (opener)
Reported audience: ~8,000 / 20,000 (40%)
Notes:
- Members of the future Rainbow sandwiched Aerosmith this day.

September 1
Cape Cod Coliseum
South Yarmouth, MA
Promoter: Don Law Presents
Other act(s): Blue Oyster Cult (HL), Lynyrd Skynyrd
Reported audience: 7,200 **SOLD-OUT
Reported gross: $44,000

September 3
Athletic Center @ St. John Fisher College

Rochester, NY

Promoter: St. John Fisher Student Council
Notes:
- It cost the Student Council $7,500 to bring Aerosmith to this freshman orientation weekend performance.

September 5 **CANCELLED
Tower Theater
Upper Darby, PA

Promoter: Midnight Sun
Notes:
- This show, with the same bill as that which performed in Bangor, was cancelled.

September 5
Municipal Auditorium
Bangor, ME

Promoter: Concerts East
Other act(s): Lynyrd Skynyrd
Reported audience: (capacity 6,000)
Reported gross: $19,600
Notes:
- A fire purportedly broke out during the band's set: "First reports of the incident indicated everything from an exhibition of harmless slapstick on up to a major holocaust" (Bangor Daily News, 9/6/1974).

September 7 **TEMP-HOLD DATE
Baltimore, MD

September 7
Wollman Rink in Central Park
New York City, NY

Promoter: Schaefer Music Festival
Other act(s): Rory Gallagher (opener)
Reported gross: $11,070
Set list(s): Lord of the Thighs / Woman of the World / Movin' Out / Woman of The World (concludes) / Dream On / One Way Street / Same Old Song and Dance / Train Kept A Rollin'
Notes:
- Final concert of the Schaefer Music Festival concert season at the Wollman Skating Rink. Aerosmith was a replacement for Savoy Brown. Rory was initially billed as the headliner but ended up opening the show.
- From a local review: "Aerosmith, a group from Boston, showed that rock fans have short attention spans, however, wasting no time in carving out its own niche in the evening. It was a group that musically had no frills — the second number was an old classic, 'Walking the Dog' — and Aerosmith provided a contrast to Mr. Gallagher by stressing the vocal side. In essence, flashes of virtuosity apart, the evening was another exploration of musical paths already travelled" (New York Times, 9/9/1974).

- From an industry review: "The 1974 Schaefer Music Festival season closed (or came to a screeching halt) Saturday night (7), as a horde of knuckleheads extraordinaire descended upon the Wollman Rink and nullified the pleasant effects of an excellent set by Rory Gallagher (Polydor) and kept bad vibes aloft during an inconsistent set Aerosmith (Columbia)... When Gallagher didn't return for an encore, many in the audience showered the stage with beer cans. The roadies were switching equipment when the barrage became heavier and deadlier: Liquor bottles had been added to the arsenal... Try though they did, Aerosmith hardly won the affection of the pro-Gallagher audience.

But the audience's antics could not obfuscate some good material, notably 'Too Bad' [sic] and 'Lord of the Flies' [sic]. The Boston glitter rockers also displayed a deft touch on two oldies, 'Walkin' the Dog,' and 'Train Kept A Rollin',' the latter being their finest musical moment of the night. Altogether it was a gallant effort by the beleaguered band. Fittingly enough, a fight erupted near the press gate as people filed out of the rink. The crowd moved *en masse* away from the two fighters, and at least a dozen people were in immediate danger of falling underfoot or being hit by an errant punch. A policeman stood off to one side, immobile, with eyes wide open. Aerosmith did not return for an encore" (Record World, 9/21/1974).
- A partial AUD recording circulates from this show which is missing the presumed start of the show.

September 10
Kellogg Arena
Battle Creek, MI
Promoter: Sunshine Promotions
Other act(s): Kansas
Reported audience: 2,441 **SOLD-OUT
Reported gross: $12,247

September 12
Veterans Memorial Auditorium
Columbus, OH
Promoter: Sunshine Promotions
Other act(s): Kansas
Reported audience: 3,249 / 3,900 (83.31%)
Reported gross: $16,917

September 13
Pine Knob Music Theater
Clarkston (Detroit), MI
Promoter: Nederlander Productions
Reported audience: (15,920 capacity)
Notes:
- Reported as virtually sold-out in the Sept. 4 issue of the Ann Arbor Sun.

September 14
Roberts Municipal Stadium
Evansville, IN
Promoter: Sunshine Promotions
Other act(s): Bachman-Turner Overdrive (HL), Neil Merryweather & The Space Rangers (opener)
Reported audience: 10,244 / 13,600 (75.32%)

September 15
Convention Center Arena
Indianapolis, IN
Promoter: Sunshine Promotions

Other act(s): Bachman-Turner Overdrive (HL), Bob Seger (opener)
Reported audience: 13,500 / 18,500 (72.97%)
Reported gross: $74,430
Notes:
- Neil Merryweather & The Space Rangers were noted on ads as the opener.

September 20
Expo Hall
Tampa, FL

September 21
Sports Stadium
Orlando, FL

September 22
The Sportatorium
Hollywood, FL
Notes:
- Dates Sept. 20–22 were listed in early Performance and Billboard itineraries but may have been temp hold-dates, since there is currently no evidence of any Aerosmith shows, or other acts, on those dates. Additionally, some itineraries note the Orange County Civic Center in Orlando, though that venue wouldn't open until 1983...

September 22 **TEMP HOLD-DATE
Hampton Roads Coliseum
Hampton, VA
Notes:
- Listed in an early Performance itinerary, after the FL dates Sept. 20-22 had been changed. No Aerosmith show was booked, and Joe Cocker headlined a show instead (with the Cock & Bull Band and Little Feat).

September 24
Keystone Hall @ Kutztown State College
Kutztown, PA
Promoter: UAA

September 26, 27
Electric Ballroom
Atlanta, GA
Promoter: Alex Cooley, Inc.
Other act(s): Mother's Finest, Muscadine Blues Band (opener)
Notes:
- An initial itinerary date noted in Performance was scheduled at the larger Fox Theater.

September 28
Hulman Center @ I.S.U.
Terra Haute, IL
Promoter: National Shows

Other act(s): REO Speedwagon (HL), Mahogany Rush (opener)
Reported audience: 7,500 **SOLD-OUT
Reported gross: $31,500
Notes:
- Montrose was also reported in the opening slot for this "Fall Jam '74."

September 30
The Brewery
East Lansing, MI
Promoter: Bill Smith / in-house
Reported audience: 750 **SOLD-OUT
Notes:
- Name in ad misspelt "Arrow Smith." This show opened the venue's fall concert lineup, following a summer where patron trouble resulting in the injury to police had led to an effort to revoke the venue's liquor license.

October ??
Hamburg Field House
Pittsburgh, PA
Notes:
- An ad for this show ran Sept. 26, in various local papers, but didn't detail the specific date.

October 4 **TWO SHOWS
Palace Theater
Providence, RI
Promoter: Concerts East
Other act(s): Elephant's Memory
Reported audience: **SOLD-OUT
Reported gross: $31,600 **both shows

October 5
U.N.H. Field House Gym
Durham, NH
Promoter: Student Committee on Popular Entertainment
Other act(s): Elephant's Memory
Notes:

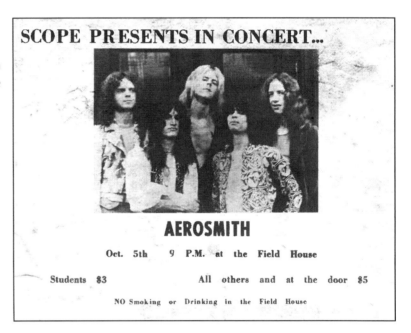

- This show was rescheduled from a Feb. date that had been cancelled due to scheduling issues... Police arrested 4 patrons during the show.
- From a local feature: "An accident occurred around quarter of six which almost ended the show. A rear-stage light tower fell over, knocking over the front tower and crashing into the stack of speakers and horns on the speaker platform. Luckily, no one was injured. But some equipment was damaged... About 10 minutes after the accident, Tyler came upstairs. He looked around and asked what happened. When the roadies told him that the sound and lighting would be normal, he appeared relieved. Then, someone pointed up to the balcony, and said, 'Hey Steve, look.' Tyler looked up, saw the trampoline, said, 'No shit!' in his raspy, Brando-like voice, and ran up. He worked out on it for about 10 minutes, with the group's drummer giving him a circus-like accompaniment, playing drum rolls before each flip, and hitting his toms and bass with each landing. After his workout, Tyler conducted the sound check himself. He seemed to be quite knowledgeable about the technical aspects of the concert. He shouted out directions to the drummer and the soundmen" (The New Hampshire, 10/8/1974).

- From a local review: " Aerosmith is not a capable band, that is, they lack talent and creativity. Their guitarist, Brad Whitford, plays frantically, but without imagination. Harsh guitar work, joined by stomach-churning bass, and ear-pounding drums, assault the audience. The material often seems like a distant echo of a song they had written before, and reworked in order to sound somewhat different, or other bands' styles. To cover for this lackluster production, gimmickry and subjects of twisted taste are played up. Steve Tyler, the singer (or is it screamer?), moves on the stage in a series of hyperactive motions, giving a poor imitation of Mick Jagger. Their clothes follow recent trends of glitter and flash. And songs like 'Lord of the Thighs,' dedicated Saturday night to all the pimps for the fine work they do, are exemplary of Aerosmith's 'message.' But they still draw a crowd. The style and sound of the band hasn't undergone any major changes since the group was playing at high school dances — just three years ago — but they are now inexplicably one of the most commercially successful bands in New England. There must be reasons" (The New Hampshire, 10/8/1974).

October 6
Northampton Co. Area Community College
Bethlehem, PA
Promoter: N.C.A.C.C. Student Senate
Other act(s): Good Rats

October 9
Joint in the Woods
Parsippany, NJ
Promoter: in-house
Reported audience: (1,500 capacity)
Set list(s): S.O.S. (Too Bad) / Somebody / Lord of the Thighs / Woman of the World / Seasons of Wither / Same Old Song and Dance / Walking the Dog / Train Kept A Rollin' / Dream On / Mama Kin
Notes:
- From a local review: "The show began with an instrumental as the group got into their music and Steven Tyler dances with his microphone with the long sash tied to it... Unfortunately, he had been struck with laryngitis, but his voice did not suffer too much from it... Joe Perry is one of the fastest and most fluid lead guitarists of today and his style is well-matched to Aerosmith's music. As Joe said, 'It's all in the music...' The drums of Joey, rhythm of Brad Whitford, bass of Tom Hamilton, and lead guitar of Joe were all demonstrated to their maximum proficiency. Then Tyler showed the audience how people walk their dogs down Comm. Ave. in Boston while he sang, 'Walkin' the Dog.' Joe Perry's guitar simulates the sound of a train with the commencement of 'Train Kept A Rollin',' a song recorded in the early sixties by the Yardbirds that Aerosmith improves upon. The song simmers out as everyone, except for Kramer on drums, walks off stage. Joey continues with the drums, throws his drumsticks to the audience, continues teasing his views using his hands on the drums, gets another pair of sticks, and starts in as the group walks on stage to finish the song. And that ended the night — almost. The encore started with their smash hit, 'Dream On,' as Tyler's seductively raunchy vocals again make this work... Aerosmith is now on tour to demonstrate to the rest of the country how fantastic there are" (Farleigh Dickinson University Metropolitan, 10/16/1974).

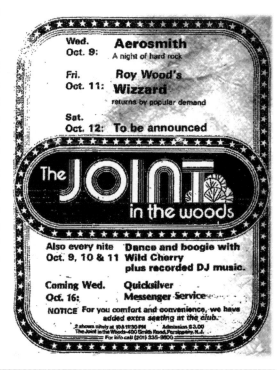

October 10
Public Hall

Cleveland, OH
Promoter: Belkin Productions
Other act(s): Bachman-Turner Overdrive (HL)

October 12 **TEMP HOLD-DATE
Civic Center
Providence, RI
Notes:
- Listed in an early Performance itinerary.

October 12
B.G.S.U. Memorial Hall
Bowling Green, OH
Promoter: BGSU Union Activities Organization
Other act(s): Mahogany Rush
Reported audience: 5,300**SOLD-OUT
Notes:
- The concert was later criticized for only selling 1,300 tickets to students and numerous teen students present being wasted. The issue led to a change in process in which tickets would only be sold to the public if a large loss would be incurred otherwise.
- From a local review: "Aerosmith is a band from Boston that looks, sounds, and acts like the best of England's mid-60s rock powerhouses. Its five members have discovered nothing new about rock music. When examined closely, they seem to be playing with the same simple taste and economy that has characterized every competent band from the Rolling Stones to the favorite Bowling Green bar band. No more, no less. There is a magic ingredient in Aerosmith, however, that sparks the band's general competence and relatively average stage show. It could be the reverence the band obviously holds for its English roots. It could be flamboyant lead singer Steven Tyler, who captures enough of Mick Jagger's voice and manner to be exciting but has enough of his own style to be much more than an imitator. Or it could be the ability of the band to write material that is distinctively its own while it echoes the best rock of the past. Whatever the ingredient is, it has affected rock fans ranging from jaded critics to enthusiastic concertgoers...

Bowling Green's Memorial Hall was sold out last Saturday evening when they performed. Aerosmith's performance did not disappoint its fans. The band put on a show that had all the fire and musical energy one could expect from a band that has the potential to become one of the most important rock ensembles of the 70s. The concert set consisted of material liberally drawn from both of Aerosmith's albums. It opened with a raucous and spirited performance of 'SOS (Too Bad)' ... The only significant departure from the high-powered rock attack was Aerosmith's performance of the mesmerizing 'Dream On,' a song from the first album that is getting a surprising amount of airplay these days. Interestingly enough, this was probably the strongest and best-received song of the set. Aerosmith closed its set with an old favorite from the early days of the English invasion, 'Train Kept a Rollin.' This song not only gave the band a chance to celebrate its roots but gave drummer Joey Kramer the chance to play one of the best drum solos done by a rock drummer" (BG News, 10/15/1974).

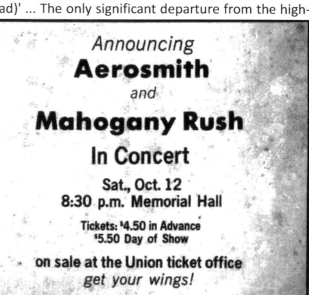

October 17
Riverside Theater
Milwaukee, WI
Promoter: Daydream Productions
Other act(s): Golden Earring (HL), Gentle Giant (opener)
Reported audience: ~2,400 / 2,450 (97.96%)
Notes:
- From a local review: "Rock music can be so much, played well, but rock without the music is next to nothing. An English group, one from Holland, and another from Boston made that very clear ... Arrowsmith [sic], a band from Boston that is loud and uninspired, provided the contrast... on the other hand, was loud and little else" (Milwaukee Sentinel, 10/18/1974).

October 18
Aragon Ballroom
Chicago, IL
Promoter: Jam Productions
Other act(s): Mahogany Rush
Reported audience: (5,000 capacity)

October 19
Municipal Auditorium
Sioux City, IA
Promoter: Schon Productions
Other act(s): Kansas
Reported audience: (5,200 capacity)

October 20
Morris Civic Auditorium
South Bend, IN
Promoter: Sunshine Promotions
Other act(s): Mahogany Rush
Reported audience: (2,483 capacity)
Set list: Woman of the World / Dream On / Milk Cow Blues / Somebody / Same Old Song and Dance / Walkin' the Dog / Train Kept A Rollin' / Mama Kin
Notes:
- An AUD recording circulates from this show.

October 22
McMorran Place Arena
Port Huron, MI
Promoter: St. Clair County Community College / S.G. Fatso
Other act(s): Focus, Mike Quatro (opener)
Reported audience: ~4,000 **SOLD-OUT
Notes:
- Aerosmith's contract rider called for: "Cadillac limousine service from Detroit to Port Huron and back; two cases of Heineken's; one case of Budweiser; two fifth of Jack Daniels; on fifth of Smirnoff's Vodka; one fifth of Kahlua; orange juice; apple juice; milk; roast beef and ham sandwiches for 30 people; and a complete roast turkey dinner" (Port Huron Times-Herald, 10/25/1974).
- From a local review: "The group had the audience on their feet for the entirety of their set and three callbacks, of which two were answered. Aerosmith featured a 'heavy rock' sound which at most times had the audience clapping along with the music. Good showmanship was the key to the Aerosmith set, with the

male lead singer in a dress with half a see-through nylon suit. Other special effects included smoke bombs and a microphone with material streamers hanging off of it. The lead singer for Aerosmith was nothing short of fantastic with antics that shadowed those of Mick Jagger and Alice Cooper. The concert was a wonderful breath of fresh air to rock fans in the Port Huron area" (Port Huron Times-Herald, 10/24/1974).

October 23
Civic Center
Charleston, WV

Promoter: National Shows
Other act(s): Santana (HL)
Reported audience: (10,195 capacity)
Notes:
- From a local review: "The level of musical proficiency at Wednesday evening's Santana concert was outstanding. First there was Aerosmith, a very solid rock group that played rough and ragged rock the way the best bands do, and then there was Carlos Santana and crew who created some incredibly beautiful music. Aerosmith is a relatively new performing entity, and it is fine. The band is musically solid with two fine guitarists and an expert drummer. But Aerosmith's strongest point is singer Steve Tyler. Tyler's body is tuned to the beat of the music finer than practically any other singers. His voice has just the pitch of frenzy, just the taste of gravel, and his gyrations across the stage keep the eyes busy while the sound fills the ears. His harmonica playing, too, is strong. In a very good set, 'The Train Kept a Rollin'' was the standout. It is the band's new single" (Charleston Gazette, 10/25/1974).

October 26
Grand Valley State College Fieldhouse
Allendale, MI

Promoter: Dome Productions
Other act(s): Mike Quatro Band (opener)
Reported audience: (5,900 capacity)

October 27
Renziehausen Park
McKeesport, PA

Promoter: WKQT 13Q
Other act(s): Brownsville Station (HL), Diamond REO
Set list(s): S.O.S. (Too Bad) / Somebody / Lord of the Thighs / Woman of the World / Pandora's Box / Dream On / Same Old Song and Dance / Walking the Dog / Train Kept A Rollin'
Notes:
- This was a free concert which wasn't clear was going to take place until the day prior. The Station was originally scheduled at Cedar Creek Park in Rostraver Township (south of Pittsburgh), was then cancelled, and then moved, with some 75,000 being expected to attend. Aerosmith was listed as performing in a Performance itinerary, and some attendees recount them arriving by helicopter and performing first.
- A decent AUD recording circulates from this show.

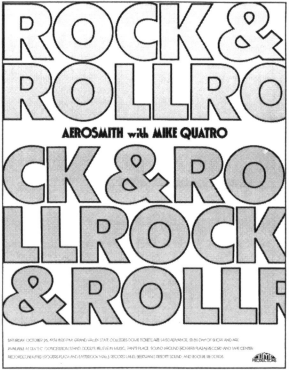

November 2 **TEMP-HOLD DATE
Tower Theater
Philadelphia, PA
Notes:
- Listed in an early Performance itinerary.

November 2
Academy of Music
New York City, NY
Promoter: Howard Stein Presents
Other act(s): Mahogany Rush, James Montgomery Band (opener)
Reported audience: (3,400 capacity)
Set list(s): S.O.S. (Too Bad) / Somebody / Lord of the Thighs / Woman of the World / Dream On / Same Old Song and Dance / Walkin' the Dog / Train Kept a Rollin'
Notes:
- Aerosmith was scheduled to play the 8pm show slot with Hawkwind performing at a separate 11:30pm show. Silent movies were played during band changeovers. This show is sometimes misidentified as taking place Feb. 11.

- From a local review: "Rock 'n' Roll is not dead. If these three bands have anything to say about it, the form will be alive and well for many years to come. It was loud, pulsating, contagious and damn good music. The Academy of Music in New York City is a dump. This concert was the first one I went to in 3 1/2 years at this theatre. The sound is excellent, but the facilities are not. In the back the bathrooms and lobbies are falling apart. It makes one wonder about the state of Rock Concerts. I know that I can remember back to the days of the Filmore when tickets were cheaper, and bands played to make music not money. Now the talent is into the star ego trip. That's what made this concert such a delight. These three bands were into making music and playing for the audience and not for themselves. It was like a throwback... Nowadays it is very unusual for the main act to be unknowns that have only two albums out. They played some good shit-kicking Rock and Roll. It was the type that makes you think that 'Heavy Rock' still has a chance. They went back to the basics, 2 guitars, bass, and drums. The only thing that rubbed me the wrong way was the glitter trappings on the band. Still, the music was outrageous. This concert was worth the $4.50 and probably more" (Potsdam Raquette, 11/14/1974).
- An average AUD recording circulates from this show.

November 3
Civic Center
Springfield, MA
Promoter: Don Law Presents
Other acts: Blue Oyster Cult, Hydra (opener)
Reported audience: (10,000 capacity)
Notes:
- Hydra's bassist Orville Davis later recounted a power struggle between BOC and Aerosmith at this show. While Aerosmith usually opened, the popularity of "Get Your Wings" was such that Aerosmith was the headliner, much to the chagrin of BOC. Power got pulled during the Cult's set, who purportedly retaliated by doing the same to Aerosmith during the climax of their set (Rising Up Angry, 11/24/1974).

November 8 **CANCELLED
Fox Theater
Atlanta, CA
Promoter: Alex Cooley, Inc.

Other act(s): Focus (opener)
Notes:
- This show was cancelled Nov. 3 without further details.

November 9
Memorial Field House
Charleston, WV

Promoter: National Shows
Other act(s): Mountain (HL), Duke Williams & The Extremes (opener)
Reported audience: (10,195 capacity)

November 10
I.U. Assembly Hall
Bloomington, IN

Promoter: Sunshine Promotions
Other act(s): Blue Oyster Cult, Wet Willie (opener)
Reported audience: (17,222 capacity)

November 14
Hara Arena
Dayton, OH

Promoter: Palace Productions
Other act(s): Wet Willie, Bob Seger (opener)
Reported audience: ~6,000 / 13,170 (45.56%)
Notes:
- From a local review: "Aerosmith — those slick hard rockers — returned to Dayton Thursday night, but instead of playing to a packed Palace Theater (capacity about 1,200), they performed for about 6,000 fur-bearing friendlies at Hara Arena. Just eight months ago, Aerosmith played the Palace, which was

quite adequate for a semi-known hard rock group. But at the time, it was easy to see Aerosmith would go much further up the ladder of fame and success. And near capacity filled Hara was proof Aero's star is rising... Aerosmith came on, and it was instantaneously obvious they were the stars and deserved their top billing. They look like maniacs, which is always a big help. Lead singer Steve Tyler affected a bi-sexual look, dressed in a see-through nylon body suit (obviously brought at Fredrick's of Hollywood), which was covered by a red velvet suit with huge strategic cut-out areas that added to his Mick Jagger-Carly Simon image. Tyler flies around the stage like a half-crazed hustler and somehow projects masculinity and femininity at the same time. How can he lose with that combination? On top of all that, his voice is unique, he's a great singer and he writes all the songs — which is the real key to Aero's success. Their material is sensational. It is super-commercial, yet it has taste, depth, creativity, and most important of all, it has salability. That means Aerosmith becomes famous, buys Park Place and Boardwalk, passes Go, collects $1 million and retires at 30" (Dayton Journal Herald, 11/16/1974).

November 15
Firestone High School Auditorium
Akron, OH

Promoter: Jer-Mar Productions
Other act(s): Cactus, Joe Vitale Band (opener)
Reported audience: ~3,000
Notes:
- From a local review: "The teen world's facsimile of the Rolling Stones fit into the atmosphere of Firestone gymnasium like a glove. The audience, made up largely of teenagers, loved every minute of Aerosmith's heavy metal set. They were prepared to boogie, and they got a full dose of it. Lead singer and Boston's Mick Jagger look-alike contest winner Steve Tyler strutted around the stage swinging his microphone stand, rubbing backs with the rest of the band and attempted to sing. Yeah, there were times when he sounded like Mick Jagger, but so what: there were also times... that his voice actually sounded good. But it didn't matter if the vocals were good or bad, the packed gym wanted to hear loud chords and hard drumming and some fancy stage play. Aerosmith gave them what they wanted. The band kept up with Tyler beautifully. I think there were even times when the two guitarists played together, but I could be mistaken. Unfortunately, drummer Joey Kramer wasn't quite able to keep up with the rest of the band. His unembellished, rather forceless drumming did little to add to the heavy rhythm. In that sense, he was the band's weakest point" (Cleveland Scene, 11/21/1974).

November 16
Capitol Theater
Passaic, NJ

Promoter: John Scher Presents
Other act(s): Climax Blues Band (HL)
Reported audience: (3,200 capacity)
Notes:
- This was the late show, with Donovan performing separately at the venue for an 8pm concert. The Climax Blues Band had originally been scheduled to open for Golden Earring on Oct. 25, but that show was postponed due to travel issues for the headliner.

November 17
Civic Center
Baltimore, MD

Promoter: Entertainment Concept Corporation
Other act(s): Steppenwolf (HL), Blue Oyster Cult, P.F.M., Ruth Copeland (opener)

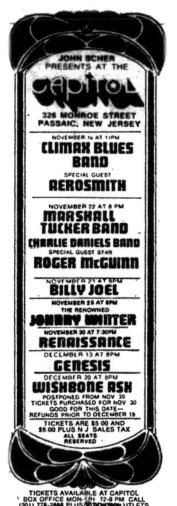

Reported audience: ~12,500
Notes:
- Attendance would be close to sell-out for the capacity of the venue.
- From a local review: "Many in the audience came primarily to see Blue Oyster Cult, from New York, or Aerosmith, from Boston, both groups relying in no small part on dry ice, strobe lights and flash powder... Aerosmith is a usually boring, occasionally bright poor man's Rolling Stones, clinging to what Thinking Man would hope is in the death throes of glitter-glam-drag rock" (Baltimore Sun, 11/19/1974).

November 21
I.M.A. Auditorium
Flint, MI

Promoter: Standback Productions
Other act(s): Salem Witchcraft
Reported audience: ~4,500 / 5,400 (83.33%)
Notes:

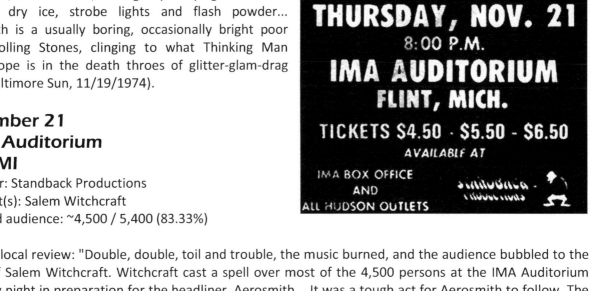

- From a local review: "Double, double, toil and trouble, the music burned, and the audience bubbled to the sound of Salem Witchcraft. Witchcraft cast a spell over most of the 4,500 persons at the IMA Auditorium Thursday night in preparation for the headliner, Aerosmith... It was a tough act for Aerosmith to follow. The colorfully costumed band was well received by the audience — most of the youths on the main floor and many in the balconies stood up and danced for Aerosmith's set. Aerosmith is a hard-working band that plays straight forward rock 'n' roll. The band's sound features a heavy beat; screeching guitars — the guitarists play nice leads together — and screaming vocals. This combination made for wild music that excited the audience; hardly a foot was not tapping or body not wiggling. But the music was not as impressive as it was the last time Aerosmith played here — as a warm-up band" (Flint Journal, 11/22/1974).

November 22
Crisler Arena
Ann Arbor, MI

Promoter: UAC Concert Co-op / Steve Glantz
Other act(s): Mahogany Rush, Joe Vitale's Madman (opener)
Reported audience: (14,343 capacity)
Notes:
- From a local review: "For all of you died-in-the-wool rock and roll fans who missed Friday night's Aerosmith (and Friends) concert in the Crisler Arena, you ought to kick yourself in the pants and promise yourself that you'll see them the next time they come around. Aerosmith and Friends, Madmen and Mahogany Rush, all put on an amazing show that will long be remembered by those who witnessed it. And rightly so — Aerosmith recorded their hit song, 'Train Kept A Rollin,' live for their next album. Not only that but they performed for nearly two hours putting everything they had into the show. It was total, uncompromising energy... Aerosmith is synonymous with rock and roll. They play the kind of music that comes at you like a Mack truck, and keeps on going once it runs you over. But they make no pretentions whatsoever" (Michigan Daily, 11/27/1974).
- From another local review: "Imitation is not only the sincerest form of flattery, but the key to financial success in, as well, as a prime cause of, the ever-increasing stagnation of rock... Aerosmith was there to shake their moneymaker, and I have no quarrel with their particular brand of high-power rock and roll. The thing is, when you get down to the basics, they only have one song in their repertoire, and they just play it over and over again under different titles. They opened with Lennon's Manson-inspired 'Helter Skelter,' and went on to play numbers from the first two album and the forthcoming third which will feature, we are told, their Crisler rendition of 'Train Kept a-Rollin.' Personally, I won't hold my breath for it. The antics of

Steve Tyler, androgyne cum vocalist, left me unimpressed after the second number. He may be a lover, but he ain't no dancer... Tyler must have seen every Stones movie five times; he even moves like Jagger. The rest of the band stumbled around the stage for two hours. Just the same old song & dance, children" (Ann Arbor Sun, 12/6-13/1974).

November 27
Cobo Hall
Detroit, MI

Other act(s): Montrose (opener)
Reported audience: 12,000 **SOLD-OUT
Notes:
- From a local review: "Last Wednesday night Cobo Hall's stage provided the setting for a performance that may very well have lessened the life span of the building by ten years... Aerosmith hit the stage like a Pacific hurricane and literally just blew people's minds away. Picture a giant Aerosmith backdrop coming up behind the stage like a prairie sunrise, two flashing strobe lights mounted on revolving podiums and a familiar sounding hard hitting drumbeat. 'S.O.S. (Too Bad)' put me on the edge of my seat and besides the times I was hanging from the ceiling that's where I was transfixed for the night. In 'Lord of the Thighs' and 'Seasons of Wither,' as in all of the arrangements they did, Aerosmith utilized the sound energy available exceptionally well.

'Same Old Song and Dance' sent a frenzied mass of rock aficionados into hysterics. Just 'Walkin' the Dog' was an interesting version an old classic... All night long the crowd screamed out and the tune we'd all been waiting for came pounding down like a hammer on hard steel. 'Train Kept A Rollin'' featured one of the most phenomenal drum solos I've seen since Jethro Tull. You'd be surprised how various parts of the body can be used to make the tightened skins rumble. Detroit went completely crazy. Dry ice engulfed the stage with fog and thousands of balloons released from the ceiling created an atmosphere of musical madness. No group gets out of an auditorium after a set like that and they returned when seismograph readings went into the red and did a superb rendition of 'Dream On...' They closed with one of my favourite songs, 'Mama Kin.' My mind was overcome by such delirious excitement I could no longer see the stage. Aerosmith was one of those concerts where when you get up in the morning even your eyelids are stiff. They infected my body with a dose of rock I'll never forget" (University of Windsor Lance, 12/6/1974).

November 29 ???QUESTIONABLE
International Convention Center
Niagara Falls, NY

Promoter: Entertainment Concepts / Concerts East
Other act(s): Johnny Winter (HL)
Reported audience: (10,428 capacity)
Notes:
- The details of this show come from a very partial AUD bootleg title (essentially only "Train" and Joey's drum solo). This date, for the recording and Aerosmith opening for Johnny is questionable since Joe later only recalled meeting Johnny decades later and only opening for him in 1971. He recalled, "I've been influenced by Johnny probably since I was about seventeen or eighteen. I've always loved his music... " (Louder Sound, 12/19/2014). He'd later perform with Johnny on a cover of a Lightnin' Hopkins' song, "Mojo Hand," released on Johnny's "Step Back" album in 2014. In PR for that album Joe noted, "If it wasn't for Johnny, I'd never have picked up the guitar."

December 5
Music Hall
Boston, MA

Promoter: Don Law
Other act(s): Mahogany Rush (opener)
Reported audience: ~4,200 **SOLD-OUT

Notes:
- From a local review: "Aerosmith, you see, is a local group with lofty ambitions not yet completely realized after two years of steady touring and a pair of raunchy rock albums on Columbia. On their own turf, however, they can do no wrong. The concert itself was predictable: loud, relentless, aggressive, piercing pile-driving rock & roll. Just what the sellout house had come to hear. Lead singer Steve Tyler, his long and layered locks framing that Anglo-punk face and puffy, pouting lips, was decked out in a lacey black jump suit that accentuated his already androgynous appearance. Sensing what the home folks craved, most of the material the group played was culled from 'Get Your Wings,' with a few surprises thrown in, including a sensational Beatles' 'Helter Skelter.' No quite so outrageous as the New York Dolls, a group to whom they've often been compared, Aerosmith plays with a great deal more polish that those Gotham boys. But one wonders what direction they will now take. With glitter rock seemingly entering its death throes (even David Bowie has discarded his mascara), Aerosmith might yet outgrow this fad and generate some enthusiasm outside of New England" (Boston Globe, 12/8/1974).

December 6
Music Hall
Boston, MA
Promoter: Don Law Presents
Other act(s): Two unknown openers
Reported audience: (4,200 capacity)
Notes:
- From the same review above: "Opening the first show (there were two more last night) was a Canadian trio called Mahogany Rush" (Boston Globe, 12/8/1974).

December 8
Winterland
San Francisco, CA
Promoter: Bill Graham Presents
Other act(s): Kinks (HL), Climax Blues Band
Reported audience: (5,000 capacity)
Notes:
- Originally, Aerosmith was advertised as opening this bill. By the week of the show the lineup had erroneously been changed to the Eric Burdon Band and Triumvirate supporting the Kinks — both had just opened for Fleetwood Mac (the real one) at their show at the venue on Dec. 3, making a second appearance five days later highly improbable.

December 11
Convention Center
Fresno, CA
Promoter:
Other act(s): Guess Who (HL), Wet Willie
Reported audience: (7,410 capacity)

December 13
Convention Center Arena
Anaheim, CA
Promoter: Concert Associates
Other act(s): Guess Who (HL)

Reported audience: (7,500 capacity)
Notes:
- From a local review: "Opening the show was Aerosmith, alias the Boston Dolls" (Los Angeles Times, 12/16/1974).

December 15
Honolulu International Center Arena
Honolulu, HI
Promoter: Papa Productions / JFP Concerts
Other act(s): Guess Who (HL)
Reported audience: (8,000 capacity)
Notes:
- Emceed by Wolfman Jack.

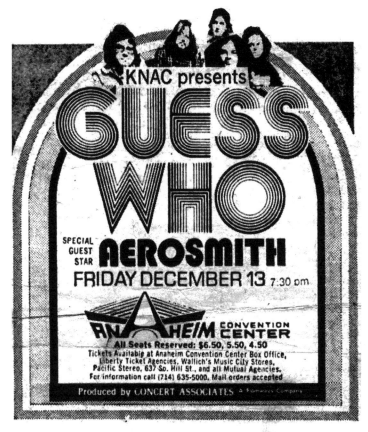

1975

January 30, 1975
Fairmont Hotel
Atlanta, GA
Promoter: CBS Records
Other act(s): The Manhattans, Honk
Notes:
- The CBS Spotlight Meeting which comedian Robert Klein hosted as master of ceremonies. After an extraordinarily successful 1974, which Aerosmith contributed to, 400 CBS staffers attended four days of meetings to communicate their strategy for 1975. Aerosmith were one of several acts reported as performing showcases for the assembled national promotion reps on whom they'd rely on to promote their product.

1974 - Get Your Wings

1975 - Toys in the Attic

U.S. Release Details:
Columbia/CBS PC/PCA/PCT-33479 (Apr. 4, 1975)
Columbia/CBS PCQ/CAQ-33479 (June 6, 1975 — Quadraphonic)
Columbia/CBS CK-33479 (1987 — CD reissue)
Columbia/SMEi CK/CT-52857 (Sep. 7, 1993 — 20-bit SBM digital remaster)
Columbia/SME 88765486191 (Apr. 20, 2013 — 180g LP reissue)

Tracks:
A1. Toys in the Attic
(3:07) — Steven Tyler / Joe Perry
A2. Uncle Salty
(4:09) — Steven Tyler / Tom Hamilton
A3. Adam's Apple
(4:33) — Steven Tyler
A4. Walk this Way •
(3:40) — Steven Tyler / Joe Perry
A5. Big Ten Inch Record
(2:16) — Fred Weismantel

B1. Sweet Emotion •
(4:34) — Steven Tyler / Tom Hamilton
B2. No More No More
(4:34) — Steven Tyler / Joe Perry
B3. Round and Round
(5:03) — Steven Tyler / Brad Whitford
B4. You See Me Crying •
(5:12) — Steven Tyler / Don Solomon

Album Details:
Produced by Jack Douglas. Arranged by Jack Douglas and Aerosmith except tracks A3 & B4 arranged by Steven Tyler. Orchestra arranged and conducted by Michael Mainieri. Engineered by Jay Messina assisted by Rod O'Brien, Corky Stasiak and Dave Thoener. Recorded and mixed at the Record Plant, New York City, NY. Mastered at the Mastering Lab, Los Angeles, CA, by Doug Sax. Album design and packaging by Pacific Eye and Ear. Cover illustration by Ingrid Haenke. Rear cover photo by Bob Belott.

Players:
◦ Uncle Salty — Tom Hamilton on rhythm guitar.
◦ Big Ten Inch Record — Scott Cushnie on piano.
◦ Sweet Emotion — Jay Messina on bass marimba.
◦ No More No More — Scott Cushnie on piano.
◦ You See Me Crying — Orchestral arrangement and conducting by Michael Mainieri.

Chart Action:
Chart Peak (USA): #11 (9/13/1975) with 128 weeks on the Billboard charts. Other countries: AUZ #79; CAN #7.

04/26/75	05/03/75	05/10/75	05/17/75	05/24/75	05/31/75	06/07/75
160	88	68	54	44	40	32
06/14/75	06/21/75	06/28/75	07/05/75	07/12/75	07/19/75	07/26/75
26	26	33	41	35	29	23
08/02/75	08/09/75	08/16/75	08/23/75	08/30/75	09/06/75	**09/13/75**
21	20	16	14	14	12	**** 11 ****
09/20/75	09/27/75	10/04/75	10/11/75	10/18/75	10/25/75	11/01/75
16	25	40	38	38	69	69
11/08/75	11/15/75	11/22/75	11/29/75	12/06/75	12/13/75	12/20/75
77	66	55	55	54	53	53
12/27/75	01/03/76	01/10/76	01/17/76	01/24/76	01/31/76	02/07/76
58	56	51	41	31	41	23
02/14/76	02/21/76	02/28/76	03/06/76	03/13/76	03/20/76	03/27/76
21	20	19	18	19	22	41
04/03/76	04/10/76	04/17/76	04/24/76	05/01/76	05/08/76	05/15/76
41	83	83	97	96	109	105
05/22/76	05/29/76	06/05/76	06/12/76	06/19/76	06/26/76	07/04/76
110	99	88	78	66	62	87
07/10/76	07/17/76	07/24/76	07/31/76	08/07/76	08/14/76	08/21/76
88	81	70	70	71	71	71
08/28/76	09/04/76	09/11/76	09/18/76	09/25/76	10/02/76	10/09/76
110	160	154	199	190	186	186
10/16/76	10/23/76	10/30/76	11/06/76	11/13/76	11/20/76	
185	185	185	185	185	X	

Second charting:

12/04/76	12/11/76	12/18/76	12/25/76	01/01/77	01/08/77	01/15/77
162	152	142	122	122	106	80
01/22/77	01/29/77	02/05/77	02/12/77	02/19/77	02/26/77	03/05/77
70	60	54	56	46	43	42
03/12/77	03/19/77	03/26/77	04/02/77	04/09/77	04/16/77	04/23/77
40	41	48	64	59	59	65
04/30/77	05/07/77	05/14/77	05/21/77	05/28/77	06/04/77	06/11/77
72	90	103	142	142	142	138
06/18/77	06/25/77	07/02/77	07/09/77	07/16/77	07/23/77	07/30/77
134	132	144	144	144	142	140
08/06/77	08/13/77	08/20/77	08/27/77	09/03/77	09/10/77	09/17/77
138	149	144	153	161	191	188
09/24/77	10/01/77	10/08/77	10/15/77	10/22/77		
185	178	176	177	X		

RIAA/Sales:

In the United States, the album was certified Gold by the RIAA on August 11, 1975 and Platinum and 4X Platinum on November 21, 1986; 5X Platinum followed on December 21, 1988; 6X on October 28, 1994; and most recently 8X on June 4, 2002. Gold by the CRIA (Canada - 50,000 units) on April 1, 1977 and Platinum on December 1, 1978. During the SoundScan era, the album had sold 1,279,992 copies between 1991 and 2007.

Supporting Singles:

• Sweet Emotion (USA, 5/1975) - Chart Peak: #36 (8/7/1975) with 8 weeks on the Billboard charts. Other countries: CAN #56.

06/14/75	06/21/75	06/28/75	07/05/75	07/12/75	**07/19/75**	07/26/75
83	73	61	50	40	** 36 **	36
08/02/75	08/09/75					
63	X					

- Walk this Way (USA, 8/1975) - Chart Peak: DID NOT CHART (during original release period). Reissued in Nov. 1976: Chart Peak (USA): #10 (1/29/1977) with 17 weeks on the Billboard charts. Other countries: N/A.

11/20/76	11/27/76	12/04/76	12/11/76	12/18/76	12/25/76	01/01/77
90	65	55	45	38	28	28
01/08/77	01/15/77	01/22/77	**01/29/77**	02/05/77	02/12/77	02/19/77
20	14	12	** 10 **	10	18	26
02/26/77	03/05/77	03/12/77	03/19/77			
35	54	74	X			

- You See Me Crying (USA, 11/1975) - Chart Peak: DID NOT CHART.

1975 - Toys in the Attic

Joe Perry (1975): "I'd rather have a number 30 album, and have it stay on the charts for a year, than have a number 1 album that lasts for 2 weeks" (Rock Scene, 9/1979).

For all intents, Aerosmith were in something of a state of limbo, with both their label and the public at large, as 1974 waned. The singles being released weren't setting the airwaves alight, and while the first album's performance had been middling at best — it was more of a select market success rather than breakout phenom — "Get Your Wings" had dialed in enough success to keep Columbia marginally behind the band. Aerosmith still weren't the label's darlings or focus, but their third album provided an opportunity that they knew they would have to capitalize on. While they had not yet broken commercially, the performance of "Get Your Wings" had been solid enough to be deemed respectable. It had charted March–September, and then returned to the lower reaches of the Billboard Top-200 from late-October onwards, as their touring wound down for the year and they turned their gaze to 1975 and work on a new album. By that time, the first two studio albums were "selling at the rate of almost 15,000 copies per week" (Cashbox, 4/12/1975). Both the band and their fortunes were fully primed, from their ceaseless grind from stage to stage, and the populist buzz surrounding the band was starting to build. All without the benefit of hit singles or many major national television appearances. They were about as far away from "hype" as one could get.

During January 1975, initial musical rehearsals took place at Aengus Studios in Fayville (Southborough), MA. The 16-track studio, owned by Jon Cole and Bill Riseman and built in a converted barn, is sometimes noted as being in nearby Ashland. The facility was extensively used by Columbia for other recording projects and was conveniently located to serve the function Jack Douglas and the band required. This period of pre-production saw the band members working out the riffs and rough ideas that had been brought in from the road. The year had been a true grind for the band with them having successfully made the jump to headliners in some markets, but remaining openers in others. The near unending slog had benefitted the band members, collectively and individually, making them more consistent and stronger players, even though there had seldom been the time dedicated to working on new material. That's not to say that many of the ideas that became songs on "Toys in the Attic" weren't born on the road, band members had noodled around in hotel rooms planting the proverbial sonic seeds. According to Joe, it was at the sound-check for the last date of the "Get Your Wings" tour in Hawaii (Dec. 15, 1974), that the riff for "Walk this Way" was written. No doubt it was a similar case for some of the other ideas, even if they were only licks or phrasings... Jack recalled, "Toys was the first time the band came off a tour prepared to record. They had a lot of energy, road energy, and they didn't have to go on sabbatical or take time out to play with their new toys. They wanted to get into making a record" ("Walk this Way").

Recording for the band's third studio album was noted in a Performance schedule, Feb. 10 – Mar. 6. The album's working title was "Teddy Bear's Funeral," though "Love at First Bite" was also considered; alluding to a pair of songs recorded early during the sessions. No amount of time spent woodshedding ideas can craft the indelible attitude some music seems to naturally exude. There's a fine line between confidence and arrogance, and the band had an abundance of both. "Toys in the Attic" provided a plethora of the sort of raunch the band were noted to present during their live performances; and which was in their DNA. Some of that grit was likely due to the bleak environs of New York City's 44th Street Record Plant studios and Steven's conversations with hookers and street toughs. He was constantly absorbing the colors of his surroundings that would eventually be painted into the lyrics of the songs. Located in Midtown Manhattan, Joe painted a picture of gritty urban darkness while recording at the Record Plant: "I can remember walking back to the Ramada Inn from the Record Plant, literally in the middle of the street... I only had a couple guitars back then, and I always carried my favorite one with me, a fifty-nine Les Paul. We would walk down the middle of the street at four or five in the morning, because it was the safest place. We didn't want to get too close to the dark alleys" (Classic Rock). That Les Paul alludes to the huge Jimmy Page inspired riffs that found in abundance on the album married to the swagger of the Rolling Stones that the band loved so much.

If the road had made the member's crafts stronger, their individual and collective growth and increasing musical maturity was well represented by the material being created in the studio under the guidance of Douglas. For the band, everything seemed to be clicking as their career seemed to advance step by step, with modest increments towards their goal of stardom. A solid foundation had been established with Jack Douglas in the studio during the previous album's creation, and he in turn was tuned into the members and knew how to maximize both their contributions and performance. There was synergy in the combination. As Joey Kramer told Red Beard on "In the Studio," even mistakes in the studio would be filed away for later analysis to determine whether an idea had been presented that could be developed into a song. It wasn't so much a matter of "waste-not-want-not," but a core understanding that valid musical ideas could easily be missed, even if they weren't immediately acted on or developed. Jack also encouraged ideas, fostered an environment of fun, and the band members did their part with attention to their roles in the process; even if there were supplements of the chemical type added to the equation. At that point, the scales of harmony had not fallen out of balance.

Engineer Jay Messina, who was behind the 16-track console during the sessions, recalled the basics of the sessions, "My basic approach was to capture the energy of Aerosmith... Getting the right moment on tape is far more important than any recording techniques. And with Steven's vocals it was always easy. He always had that edge that was just naturally there, so you wouldn't have to do anything extra to help him. His voice cut through. He had attitude, great phrasing, and pitch. We would record a few takes, then he and Jack would comp the best lines and bounce it to one track. But all the takes were usually great" (Classic Rock #210, 11/2016). Mastering was completed on Mar. 22, after the band had hit the road (a point that Steven would later bemoan, in that the band had left before the process was complete).

Appropriately enough, the album blasts off with its seminal title track, a studio written creation that made Joe appreciate the difference between being a studio band and simply writing songs that were then recorded. "Toys in the Attic" was a result of that new ethos, building upon a riff until it became a fully realized song. But there was also a certain amount of nonchalance towards the authenticity of these recordings, which feature some unplanned sonic "artifacts" (similar occurred during the sessions for the subsequent studio album). According to Perry, "We put some amplifiers down where the dumpsters were on the street, and there's some parts where you can actually hear the traffic... We left it on there" (Spin, 5/2015). Stylistically, the influences of the stadium bands of the early 1970's, be it Led Zeppelin or Deep Purple, are self-evident. Riffs such as the one this song is based on quickly blossomed with the creative input of the other band members and the tutelage of Douglas, while there was no rule book to follow, and creative whims could be followed as the ideas flowed. Brad illustrated the creative process at the time perfectly: "It's very organic. [Joe] would write these ideas in his home studio, then we'd play it and suddenly another part would spill out of it and another would spill out of that. He would just come up with these amazing, amazing riffs. We would just play it because it was fun, and then it would turn into a song" (Spin, 5/2015). And then another band member would present an idea and the process would be repeated.

Where Perry had been inspired by the rocking funk of the Sly and The Family Stone or New Orleans' funk group The Meters, both popular at the time, all the band members contributed to developing "Walk this Way." By the time they reached the Record Plant, Steven had a melody for the piece, but they were stuck with what direction to take the song from there. It took the inspiration of Marty Feldman's portrayal of Igor, during the train station scene in the popular Mel Brooks "Young Frankenstein" movie, to provide the catalyst for both song title and lyrics. Tom recalled, "We told Steven, you've got to call the song 'Walk this Way.' Steven was like, 'You can't tell me what to call the song, I haven't even written the lyrics yet!' But we told him he had to do it. So, he did" (Spin, 5/2015). As Joe recounted, once they had that Three Stooges-esque basis, it only took Steven a few hours to write the lyrics. Whether it was in the studio during the session or the night before, with Steven's original lyrics left in a taxi, are irrelevant to the end result — a danceable epically raunchy track for the ages was born. A slightly edited version of the song, backed with "Round and Round" (Columbia 3-10206), was released as the second single from the album in late August. While it failed to chart, it generated positive reviews: "Culled from the 'Toys in the Attic' LP, this band shows Aerosmith is coming of age as a rock 'n' roll entity. Steve Tyler's vocal is aggressive, gritty, and right on, as he literally spits out a slew of lyrics while never losing clarity. The music itself is hardboiled rock — just the way the AM programmers want it" (Cashbox, 9/13/1975). But on the charts in 1975, it seems that much of the American public weren't yet ready to walk Aerosmith's way quite yet...

Studio documentation suggests that "No More No More," the third of the Tyler/Perry compositions, was comprised of a single take (#8) mixed March 13. Steven recalled that the lyrics came from his typical verbal diarrhea, and were "a mishmash that I made up..." He "eventually changed the lyrics to something cool... about life on the road: boredom, disillusion, Holiday Inns, stalemate, jailbait" ("Walk this Way"). In other words, a reflection of the life he was living at the time. Joe loved the lyrics, recalling, "I still love the song because of Steven's lyrics. It's not one of those stupid, generic 'I love rock n' roll songs' that some bands do. It's a real song about the rock n' roll lifestyle, or our rock n' roll lifestyle. I don't know if it's the definitive song about life on the road, and I don't even care. It's like a page from our diary" ("Pandora's Box" liner notes). "Uncle Salty," the second song on the album that saw Tom Hamilton flexing his musical muscles, was a bleak anti-child abuse song. Steven crafted the disconcerting lyrics based around a lecherous foster home custodian who wanted to molest the children. He recalled, "Just a fantasy I had of being a madame, the boss of a bordello: work with the girls, hire and fire, keep things running. Salty worked in a home for lost children and had his way with this little girl. That's what it's about. I'm the little girl, the orphaned boy. I put myself in that place. I'm Uncle Salty too" ("Walk this Way"). Tom also got to contribute rhythm guitar to the recording. Clearly, the subject matter was similar to that investigated was later made much less cerebral and direct with "Janie's Got a Gun."

The first single released to support the album was "Sweet Emotion." The song had started with a jam session bass riff that Tom had played for a long time, married to a bastardized "Rice Pudding" (Jeff Beck) guitar pattern. During the pre-production sessions focus was finally placed on the initial melodic seed which rapidly grew into a full-formed song. According to Tom, "Jack [Douglas] was into refereeing and making sure any ideas that came up got tried out. That's how we ended up with a song like 'Sweet Emotion' on there... It was at the end of the recording and Jack said, 'Tomorrow's jam day, if anybody's got a stray riff hanging around.' I said, 'Yeah, I do.' So, I spent the day showing everybody everything and we took it from there, refining it into what it is. Steven had the idea of taking that intro riff, which became the chorus bass line under the 'sweet emotion' part, and transposing it into the key of E, and making it a really heavy Zeppelinesque thing" (Guitar World, 4/1997). The song also gave Joe his first opportunity to experiment with the talk-box effect popularized by the likes of Stevie Wonder and used by Jeff Beck. Lyrically, the song was more of a veiled rant by Steven about the increasing role of Elyssa in Perry's life and Steven's frustrations with the guitarist. Released as a single in late-May 1975 (Columbia 3-10155), backed with "Uncle Salty," the song provided the band with their first top-40 appearance on the Billboard's Hot-100 singles chart. While the single peaked at #36 and only charted for eight weeks, it was a marked improvement on the performance of previous singles. It also resonated with many reviewers as a "real gem" on the album. Others, such as Cashbox noted, that the Hamilton/Tyler composition "explodes with inspired harmony, virtuosity in some searing guitar licks, and powerful production by Jack Douglas. Should figure heavily in this important group's growth" (Cashbox, 5/31/1975). Unfortunately, the price for success of the single meant that the song's original 4:34 duration was reduced to just the essential melodic elements to fit radio's preferred 3:00 format at the time. It may have been akin to taking an axe to a beautiful tree.

Fred Weismantel's "Big Ten Inch Record" was originally recorded by Bull Moose Jackson in 1952 and released late that year. The band's story, presented in their "Walk this Way" autobiography, detailed that they had been passed the song by Zunk Bunker after he had heard the song on Dr. Demento's KLOS radio show. That Moose had already recorded a dirty blues version of the song appealed to the band, and Jack, so it was recorded with blind pianist Scott "Professor Piano" Cushnie recruited to give it a suitable boogie-woogie feel. Such was his contribution that he also seasoned "No More No More" in the studio. He also went on the road with the band that year to enhance their live sound. Scott recalled, "It was a riot. I went from Volkswagens to Cadillac limousines. They played their own brand of hard rock and I played boogie-woogie along with it in the same key" (Ottawa Journal, 3/21/1980). "Big Ten Inch Record" was completed with some big brass seasonings added by uncredited Michael and Randy Brecker and saxophonist Stan Bronstein (though the addition of the brass wasn't new to the song as it had been present on the original recording). For Joey, Cushnie's performance made the song more than memorable. He recalled, "Not only was it something we had never tackled before, that genre, but it was a fun song to begin with, and we put our little spin on it. Scott Cushnie was in a band called the Hawks, who eventually became the Band, Bob Dylan's band. He was older than all of us, but he had a lot of experience, and one of the things I really remember getting off on was him playing honky-tonk piano on our track. That was probably the funnest song to record" (Spin, 5/2015).

Steven's solo composition, "Adam's Apple," allowed him full control of the song, while the slide guitar performance allowed Joe to shine musically. Reviewers were mixed with some believing the song to be little more than "punk doublespeak." Still, many others noted the song as one of the standouts on the album, and it one of the six core songs performed live from the album during the tour. Written by Steven and Brad, the album version of "Round and Round" was constructed from takes 7 & 10 and mixed on March 15. Brad, who had brought in the riff, performed the lead guitar on the track, with Joe relegated to rhythm. By far, the most complex and demanding song on the album (being comped from takes 12, 14 & 15, mixed on March 20) was Steven's collaboration with pre-Aerosmith writing partner Don Solomon, "You See Me Crying." Keyboardist Don had met Steven in junior high school, and had been in a band, the New York Rockers with him (the band was renamed the Strangeurs and ultimately became the Chain Reaction). He'd also taken lessons from Steven's father. For the recording Brad took the melodic first and coda solos on the song; Joe provided the second. Mike Mainieri conducted the orchestra providing the full embellishment required. As had been the case with "Sweet Emotion," a butcher edit of the song was provided for release as the album's final single (Columbia 3-10253) in November. More than two minutes of the song was axed to whittle the ballad down to a three-minute single for radio. However, even positive trade reviews couldn't help the song's chart performance on the chart. It was almost a second attempt at writing a radio friendly ballad, in the vein of the almost-a-hit "Dream On" (at the time). Some reviews were less than kind: "Steve Tyler, who sounds as if he's been gargling paint thinner, coughs up a rock ballad sure to raise nodules on your turntable. Heavy metal enthusiasts will appreciate the large-scale production as Aerosmith sounds like five major symphony orchestras all playing different songs. Don't knock it — this stuff draws the kids like moths to the flame" (Cashbox, 11/22/1975).

Following its release, "Toys in the Attic" took over four months to reach its Billboard album chart high position of #11. By any definition, particularly without benefit of a hit single, the album was a slow burn — albeit a long steady one considering the initial 82-week chart run the album enjoyed (through Nov. 1976). In December, a Los Angeles Times' concert review was titled "Aerosmith Steps Up on Treadmill." Perhaps that last word ought to have been replaced with "Escalator." The band was clearly starting a rapid ascent. With the noted "persistence" and "supercharged Yardbirds-derived boogie" the band had seen their fortunes at the forefront of America's rock scene transformed throughout the year. They were primed for superstardom, having fully transitioned from opening act, or bill partner, to solidified headliner. While starting out in smaller venues, a step up from music halls, the band quickly started to have concerts booked at the larger venues in many markets. But they'd still be playing gyms now and then and took opening slots for established megastars in major markets, as necessary. An interesting contrast in metrics saw the band playing to 17,522 opening for ZZ Top at the Forum in June, and then selling it out (18,149) as headliners in December. That single example illustrates the band's continued growth during the year nicely. The band also headlined a stadium festival show, playing to over 30,000 at the U.C. Nippert Stadium, in early August. They were also on the bill for over 60,000 at the Faces' Cleveland Stadium show weeks later. As the year closed, Aerosmith found themselves in a similar situation to the previous December, except one step higher up on the ladder towards the top of the rock heap. They were ready to rinse and repeat the record-tour cycle with the added pressure of continuing to build on what they had accomplished in 1975.

"Toys in the Attic" was released on Apr. 4, 1975 and entered the Billboard album charts at a less than spectacular #160 on Apr. 27. A quadraphonic (QL/8) version followed on June 6. In the United States, the album was certified Gold by the RIAA on August 11, 1975 and Platinum and 4X Platinum on November 21, 1986; 5X Platinum followed on December 21, 1988; 6X on October 28, 1994; and most recently 8X on June 4, 2002. Gold by the CRIA (Canada - 50,000 units) on April 1, 1977 and Platinum on December 1, 1978. During the SoundScan era, the album had sold 1,279,992 copies between 1991 and 2007. In the U.S., the album reached #11 on the Billboard Top-200 charts 9/13/1975) during a noncontinuous 128-week run, and #14 on Cashbox (6/21/1976) during a solid 122-week residency. Internationally, the album reached #7 in Canada, and #79 in Australia. The full charting period of the album, Apr. 1975 through Sept. 1977, essentially encompasses the band's original golden era.

Assorted review excerpts:

"Aerosmith, attaining great success with two previous albums 'Aerosmith,' and 'Get Your Wings,' have really pulled out all the stops with their 3rd LP on Columbia, 'Toys in the Attic.' Hard drivin' rock and lyrics that make sense, make these five guys from Boston almost an unstoppable combination. This will burn the FM playlist and any track on the album could break on AM as well. Our favorites are 'Uncle Salty,' 'Sweet Emotion,' 'No More No More,' and the title track" (Cashbox, 4/19/1975).

"Aerosmith specializes in straight ahead rock with few frills, and while they somehow seem to be neglected when people begin discussing major groups, they are one of rock's steadiest LP sellers. Music here, as always, is basic with rough and raucous vocals. No great change from previous efforts, which is welcome news for fans. Set is full of tasty, reasonably short guitar solos, with the double leads working particularly well. A softer cut or two is included, but it is the familiar rock that should get most attention. Best cuts: 'Uncle Salty,' 'Big Ten Inch Record,' 'No More No More,' 'You See Me Crying.' Dealers: As mentioned, group sells on a steady basis in good numbers and tours consistently. Sicko cover sure to attract attention" (Billboard, 4/26/1975).

"Almost entirely on the basis of its Eastern following, Aerosmith's second album, 'Get Your Wings,' has attained gold record status, and its sales recently influenced Columbia to re-release their first album, 'Aerosmith,' in a new cover. 'Toys in the Attic,' simply because it is the equal of the previous albums, will surely spread the word west — the word being that Aerosmith is the best hard rock group in the United States, fulfilling all that the Dolls and their ilk promised and never delivered. The power and sweep of Steve Tyler's voice is unmatched today by anyone except Paul Rodgers; the raw attack of the band evokes the Yardbirds, Stones or Alice Cooper at their peak" (Los Angeles Times, 6/1/1975).

"Aerosmith bring hope from America. They're not a new Steely Dan, or even yet another variation on the Doobie Brothers. Yet they are most people's idea of what a good rocking band should be, probably the key to their growing success. They're not attempting to lay anything on us, but have an energetic, refreshing approach to music-making, with their roots in the British group sound of the '60s, but with modern refinements. Listen to the contrasting beats and heavy rock of the tongue-twisting 'Walk this Way', where new star vocalist Steve Tyler chicken-walks against the howling guitars of Joe Perry and Brad Whitford.

Aerosmith know just how much to give away, so that as Joe and Brad begin to heat up their solos, the engineering department cheerfully fades them out. But to begin, though, there is no denying the similarity between opening track 'Toys in the Attic' and a certain Led Zeppelin riff — the day bands stop copping licks from each other the Pyramids will reveal their secrets. 'Toys' is a fast, jumping tune with Steve employing one of his favourite devices, unison singing with Joe Perry's lead. And Joey Kramer's drums have a simple bounce, all cymbal and clipped snare drum, that typified British rock drumming before the age of super heaviness" (Melody Maker, 7/12/1975).

"'Toys in the Attic' is Aerosmith's third record. No one here knows that much about Aerosmith, except that they're a straight-ahead Eastern seaboard band with roots in New Hampshire, Boston and Manhattan who concentrate on emulating the R&B raunch of the 60's allied to the supposed improvements of today. That's what it says here, anyway. Their strength (derivative simplicity) may well turn out to be their downfall as far as sustained success goes because, though Toys is rifling high in the U.S. charts, we've already heard this brand of hard rock more than enough — to wit the recent inroads made by the likes of Queen and Golden Earring. The title track bursts right in as if it had been playing for several minutes. A clever touch with plenty of The Who in there. Lead singer Steve Tyler looks remarkably similar to the dreadful Freddy Mercury, but he sings O.K. so we'll let him off. Anyway, Aerosmith keep the influences nice and obvious at first until you realize that what you're experiencing is actually incestuous déjà vu... Jack Douglas has produced a thick, strong mix around sophisticated material but, as a whole, the experience is immediately expendable. There's not enough deviation from a predictable norm. So: 'Walk this Way' and 'Adam's Apple' are interchangeable. Pleasant slide creations and uncomfortably fast sound level — odd bursts of high octane in all the right places. Text-book rock and wasted energy... Maybe as a first album this would be a commendable offering but, as it's their third, Aerosmith haven't got a lot to shout about. Their claims that 'our music is rough and raunchy R&B with a lot of refinement', and claims made for them that 'they capture the tradition of the Stones' aren't borne out here. The Stones were originals of a sort. By the time you get to third-generation bands it's reasonable to hope for slightly more than the basics — even if they are well done" (New Musical Express, 7/26/1975).

"Aerosmith, a five-piece Boston hard-rock band with almost unlimited potential, can't seem to hurdle the last boulder separating it from complete success. Like 'Toys in the Attic,' their two previous LPs have had several stellar moments which were weakened by other instances of directionless meandering and downright weak material. That these albums stood the test of time is testimony to the band's raw abilities and some outstanding production on the part of Jack Douglas — 'Toys in the Attic,' I'm afraid, can't claim the latter. What's really important to bands of this sort is initial impact — the production must explode, enveloping the listener with a rampaging barrage of sound. The ideal mix is hot and spacious, with each instrument well defined and immediately intimate. A mix, in fact, not at all unlike that of the band's previous LP, 'Get Your Wings.' On 'Toys,' Aerosmith is given a more compact, jumbled mix that gives more of a 'group' feel but robs them of that explosive ambience. Hence, it's much harder to get involved with the music at first exposure to it. The material here follows the familiar patterns — some good moments, some nondescript ones. With their aggressive, ambisexual stance, reliance on bristling open chording and admitted mid-Sixties English rock roots, Aerosmith can be very good when they're on, and material like 'Walk this Way,' 'Sweet Emotion' and the title cut adequately proves this once you're past the generally oppressive production. 'Big Ten-Inch Record,' 'Uncle Salty' and 'You See Me Crying,' though, are poor choices, changes of pace which deny the band the use of their strongest asset — hard-nosed, aggressive raunch. If Aerosmith can avoid the sloppiness that's plagued their recent live performances, if they return to the production that made parts of 'Get Your Wings' so memorable, and most importantly, if they avoid tepid, trite material, then their potential is extremely high" (Rolling Stone, 7/31/1975).

"About a year ago Aerosmith got me to do the impossible — go to a Band concert. Due to a last-minute mix-up, they ended up second on the bill and all the people who came to see the Band didn't like it one bit. 'Go away' and worse cried most of the crowd, seemingly unaware that they were witnessing what would undoubtably be the most energetic happening of the evening. 'This is uncivilized savagery,' moaned someone near me, and soon afterwards the more 'civilized' elements of the crowd rained down firecrackers, etc. in the general direction of the stage. Things were getting nasty for our heroes — indeed for everyone present — when suddenly lead guitarist Joe Perry decided that he'd had enough. At the end of a number, he mumbled something on the order of 'motherfuckers' into the mike, turned his guitar up to ten and turned around in front of a full bank of Marshall amps!

I left a little more of my ear drums on the concert floor that night, so maybe I'm not hearing this newest Aerosmith offering properly. In a few words, it sounds decidedly weaker than its two predecessors — the songs less well-structured, the overall sound a bit tinnier, some of the songs somewhat ill-conceived. The 'guidance' of Jack Douglas seems most at fault — I think he had something a bit more commercially-oriented in mind this time, only it didn't work out too well. He failed to capture the hard-charging essence of Aerosmith as fully as he had before — much as had been the case with the now-defunct Foxie's 'Close Enough to Rock & Roll,' the album doesn't sound that much like the band in concert at all. In fact, two songs ('Big Ten Inch Record' and 'You See Me Crying') neither bear any even abstract relation to previous Aerosmith efforts nor succeed on their own merits. Poor Steven Tyler really makes a fool out of himself on the latter — a crooner he's not. A good band, a weak record—Aerosmith's gonna have to make it on the strength of their live appearances I'm afraid. But I'm certain they'll ultimately be able to do it. That Joe Perry boy is really a good little rock and roll guitarist — you know that" (Circus Raves, 8/1975).

130 | Aerosmith on Tour, 1973-85

1975 - Toys in the Attic

March 13 **CANCELLED
Tiger Gym
Biddeford, ME

Promoter: St. Francis College Student Senate
Notes:
- Due to complaints by the public, particularly about a high school facility being used for an open concert, the Student Senate cancelled the event on Mar. 2. Local police and fire were also concerned about the number of prospective attendees and the behavior of youth at such events.

March 14
Field House @ Plymouth State College
Plymouth, NH

Promoter: Cedric Kushner Productions
Notes:
- It's not clear if this show, listed in Performance, took place or was simply a temp-hold, but it seems likely that the band did perform some warm-ups gigs prior to the tour commencing properly, though they would have been actively still recording/mixing at the time of both of these mid-March shows.

March 18
Morris Civic Auditorium
South Bend, IN

Promoter: Sunshine Promotions
Other act(s): Rush, Leo Sayer (opener)
Reported audience: 2,500 **SOLD-OUT
Reported gross: $13,785
Note:
- Official opening night of the "Toys in the Attic" tour. Canadian act, Rush, had then recently released their second studio album, "Fly by Night," their first with new drummer (and chief lyricist) Neil Peart. Neil recalled: "We opened for Aerosmith like 40 times and never got a sound check... If you name any band from kind of the mid '70s, we probably opened for them, because we were an opening act. And then we'd start headlining small halls and still be opening shows in between" (The Hour, 9/4/2012). Joe Perry later responded to the suggestion of friction between the bands, and the suggestion that when the Project later opened for Rush, he'd apologized for the behavior of Aerosmith towards them: "Frankly, I don't remember playing with Rush... The competition between bands was stiff, the competition between crews even stiffer, so I don't doubt Geddy's word" (Rolling Stone, 6/16/2015).

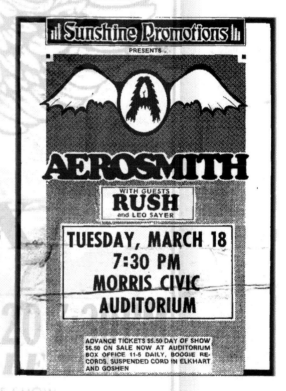

March 20
Hulman Center @ I.S.U.
Terre Haute, IN

Promoter: National Shows / Sycamore Showcase Committee
Other act(s): Styx, Rush (opener)
Reported audience: 7,508 / 10,200 (73.61%)
Notes:
- Tickets were initially issued printed with March 21 as the show's date.

March 22
Schmidt Memorial Field House @ Xavier University

Cincinnati, OH
Promoter: Belkin Productions / X.U. Concert Committee
Other act(s): Styx, Rush (opener)
Reported audience: (3,000 capacity)
Notes:
- From a local review: "The score stood two to nothing, with but one band left to play on the evening of March 22 — two altogether atrocious 'music' groups had performed at Schmidt Fieldhouse. Then Aerosmith came on, to save the day for those who prefer quality to volume. All this reviewer can say is: 'praise the Lord and pass the earplugs.' The leadoff group, Rush, was worse than terrible. They were loud and terrible, producing a severe headache for the reviewer and little music of quality... Styx was not much better. Once again, most of the vocals of this group were unintelligible yells and grunts, with the exception of their slower-paced selections... Aerosmith was, to understate, excellent. (Up to that point, the best music all night had been during the first intermission — a tape of side one, 'Sergeant Pepper's Lonely Hearts Club Band'.)

The audience loved Aerosmith's first four numbers, which were played without a break. The solos were played properly — one person playing with the others quiet. They played several numbers from their new album, 'Toys in the Attic,' which the audience (mob) was not pleased with, but which were musically quite good. No doubt, this was due to their impatience and desire to hear the best-known past singles; their reaction to 'Dream On' and 'Same Old Story' proved it. Despite some amateur theatrics, 'Train Kept on Rollin'' was excellent, especially the drum solo. Two loudly demanded encores were given, to conclude an outstanding segment of an otherwise abysmal concert. The reviewer left with a severe headache, a poor opinion of two amateurish groups, an appreciation for Aerosmith, and neutral thoughts on the unique acoustic qualities of our beloved Fieldhouse" (Xavier University News, April 1975).

March 24
Wendler Arena
Saginaw, MI
Other act(s): Rush (opener)
Reported audience: ~7,000 **SOLD-OUT

March 26
Allen County War Memorial
Fort Wayne, IN
Other act(s): James Gang, Rush (opener)
Reported audience: (10,000 capacity)

March 28
Aragon Ballroom
Chicago, IL
Promoter: Jam Productions
Other act(s): Rush, Pavlov's Dog (opener)
Reported audience: (4,500 capacity)
Notes:

- Les Variations were listed as the opener in some ads in place of Pavlov's Dog.

March 29
The Omni 41
Schererville, IN
Other act(s): Rush (opener)
Reported audience: (6,000 capacity)
Notes:
- This venue was an ice rink.

March 31
Metro Ice Arena
Lansing, MI
Promoter: Paul Stanley Productions
Other act(s): Ted Nugent, Rush (opener)
Reported audience: (4,600 capacity)
Notes:

- Ted Nugent had then recently signed with Leber-Krebs but was highly suspicious and distrustful of managers in general. They allowed him to stay with his old booking agent, DMA, and took the lowest commission they'd ever agreed to. But they played a trump card by pairing him with Aerosmith, and it wasn't for Aerosmith's benefit. The move was specifically designed to help break Ted as a solo act. When his first solo album was released in September 1975, he was perfectly poised to benefit from the coordinated effort made on his behalf.
- From a local review: "Thousands of hard-rock addicts assembled for a ritualistic appreciation of the electronic excesses of three bands — Rush, The Amboy Dukes, and Arrowsmith [sic]. The concert was presented by Paul Stanley, erstwhile prime mover of ASMSU pop entertainment, who promises more of the same in the future. The people responsible for setting up the lighting and sound systems did their work with commendable skill. The large open floor of the arena gave everyone ample room to mingle and air to breathe. The evening moved through a familiar rhythm. Security guards casually confiscated pints of whiskey, downer freaks stumbled through the haze, juicers belched and messed their shoes and aren't the '50s fun, Buffalo Bob? Ecology buffs grooved on the strange atmospheric phenomenon of a fog that rolled across the audience and prevented anyone from seeing clearly from one side of the room to another... All in all, people got their monies worth and will have another opportunity to do the same when Blue Oyster Cult plays in the arena on April 14" (Michigan State News, 4/2/1975).

April 2
Veterans Memorial Auditorium
Columbus, OH
Promoter: Sunshine Promotions
Other act(s): Rush (opener)
Reported audience: 3,963 **SOLD-OUT
Reported gross: $19,574

April 4 **Aerosmith POSTPONED
New Century Theater
Buffalo, NY
Promoter: Harvey & Corky Inc.
Other act(s): Les Variations, Rush (opener)
Reported audience: (3,076 capacity)
Notes:

- Billed as a "New Year's Eve in April" party, Joe falls off stage injuring himself (per the following night's show University paper piece). Variety, however, reported that the band had been stranded in Boston due to a storm with the other two acts performing without the headliner (there was a large storm in New England resulting in high wind and heavy rain in the Boston area). Aerosmith's performance was rescheduled for May 7.

April 5 **POSTPONED
Beeghly Center Auditorium @ Y.S.U
Youngstown, OH

Promoter: Y.S.U. Major Events
Other act(s): REO Speedwagon, Rush (opener)
Reported audience: (6,000 capacity)
Notes:
- Brownsville Station was initially booked in place of REO Speedwagon. This show was rescheduled for Apr. 13. According to Jonathan Bird, Major Events spokesman, "Late Friday afternoon Major Events was informed that Aerosmith couldn't make the concert. It seems that the lead guitarist had an unfortunate accident. It's rumored that he had fallen off a stage during a performance and injured his face. The road manager then informed us that they couldn't make the date" (The Jambar, 4/8/1975).

April 8
Finch Fieldhouse
Mt. Pleasant, MI

Promoter: Steve Glantz Productions / Program Board
Other act(s): Ted Nugent
Reported audience: 4,000 **SOLD-OUT
Reported gross: $19,000
Notes:
- Reportedly, the scheduled opener, Baker-Gurvitz Army's truck broke down en route from Florida. This show was initially scheduled for Apr. 9.
- From a local review: "Aerosmith brought its

high energy show to Finch Fieldhouse Tuesday night and easily proved it is one of the top rock bands in the country today. An appearance by Ted Nugent and the Amboy Dukes, who replaced the scheduled Baker-Gurvitz Army, opened the evening on time... Aerosmith brought a complete evening of entertainment to the Central crowd. After a Beatles tune 'Helter Skelter,' the band broke into 'Too Bad' and the crowd excitement accelerated as the backdrop reading 'Aerosmith' topped by a bank of lights made its way toward the ceiling. 'Somebody' was followed by two new tunes from a coming album. The band did a good job of mixing oldies with the new stuff by alternating the material. The general sound of the show was less than desirable but it was not the band's fault. The acoustics of Finch Fieldhouse distorted the music as contrasted to the instrumental clarity of Aerosmith's studio work.

The audience behavior was less than admirable to say the least. The band was plagued by flying objects throughout the show. The lead guitarist, Joe Perry was hit by what appeared to be a beer can. It became obvious the band avoided the crowd by withdrawing from front stage until later in the show. The introduction into 'Dream On' saw the stage filled with the fog and a bank of floor lights creating a unique effect. After more new material, Steve Tyler complemented his excellent vocals with his harmonica on 'One Way Street.' Tyler was the most theatrical member of the band with his use of the microphone stand, and his costume, a tight-fitting black caped outfit. 'Same Old Song and Dance' brought the crowd to its feet before an extended version of 'Train Kept on Rollin'' captivated them. Tyler even thrusted his microphone in the front rows of people to get them to sing along... Aside from the initial audience harassment with the flying objects, the concert was an excellent rock and roll experience which probably won't be topped around here for quite a while" (CM-Life, 4/12/1975).

April 9 **TEMP HOLD-DATE
Ada, OH
Notes:
- Listed in early Performance itinerary, several dates were juggled or not booked around this time.

April 9 **TEMP HOLD-DATE
Pittsburgh, PA
Notes:
- Listed in early itineraries, this date appears not to have been booked with it instead being used to facilitate a second Toledo show.

April 9
Sports Arena
Toledo, OH
Promoter: Steve Glantz Productions
Other act(s): Michael Quatro Band
Reported audience: (7,500 capacity)
Notes:
- The Baker-Gurvitz Army were the originally announced opening act.
- The original Apr. 11 show quickly sold out, so this additional date was booked by the promoters.

April 11
Sports Arena
Toledo, OH
Promoter: Steve Glantz Productions
Other act(s): Michael Quatro Band
Reported audience: 7,500 **SOLD-OUT
Reported gross: $38,000

April 12
C.S.U. Woodling Gym
Cleveland, OH
Promoter: Belkin Productions
Other act(s): Pavlov's Dog (opener)
Reported audience: (3,000 capacity)
Notes:
- From a local review: "The capacity crowd's spirits were rekindled by the high-energy rock of Aerosmith. Direct from the Stones/Yardbirds' mold, Aerosmith features churning guitars and blues-bases lyrics buried under layers of pounding rhythm. Opening with the Beatles 'Helter Skelter,' Aerosmith rocked through selections from their three albums, skillfully blending the newer material with the familiar favorites. Lead singer (and songwriter) Steve Tyler was his usual frenetic self, guiding the band through 'Dream On,' 'Same Old Song and Dance,' and the showstopper, 'Train Kept A Rollin'.' The bulk of the new album was played including, notably, 'Adam's Apple,' and 'Sweet Emotion.' Augmenting the sound was an effect from the pre-synthesizer era, deliberate microphone feedback. Aerosmith's faults are a PA that cannot handle the eccentricities of Tyler's voice, and a failure to incorporate subtle melodics, leading to a droning sameness" (Cleveland Scene, Apr.17-23, 1975).

April 13
Beeghly Center Auditorium @ Y.S.U
Youngstown, OH
Promoter: Y.S.U. Major Events
Other act(s): Pavlov's Dog, Blush Ash
Reported audience: (6,000 capacity)
Notes:
- Rescheduled date from Apr. 5 without Rush, who were performing elsewhere. Steven, Joe, and Brad were briefly interviewed for the Jambar, the student newspaper. Steven: "I enjoy studio recording but I like live performances better, because you have the magic of the crowd. I guess it's like one hand washing the other. You record an album, people listen to it, and when they see you in concert, they can relate to it. You can see them mouthing the words when you're playing" (The Jambar, 4/15/1975).
- This show lost $300-700 for the school's Major Events Committee.

April 18
Boston Garden
Boston, MA
Promoter: Don Law
Other act(s): Foghat, Barnaby Bye (opener)
Reported audience: 15,000 **SOLD-OUT
Reported gross: $191,000 **both nights
Notes:
- Following this show Columbia hosted a reception for the band where they were presented with their RIAA Gold record awards for "Get Your Wings." Local ads advertised Barnaby Bye as the opening

act, while Performance reported Angels with Dirty Faces (the Connecticut band then formerly known as White Chocolate; and later Dirty Angels).
- From a local opinion piece: "Aerosmith is an interesting phenomenon though. A few weeks ago, I noticed that they were playing in Boston again. It was only about two years ago that they were hitting the colleges big, and a mere six months ago that they played The Orpheum in Boston which holds about 2,500. I was absolutely astonished when I saw that Don Law had booked them into the Boston Garden... The concert was general admission, meaning it would be a zoo, and the price per ticket was $7.00!! Why $7.00 is more than anyone has gotten at the Boston Garden with the exception of Elvis, and George Harrison, and both those guys have a little more history and talent to them than Aerosmith. While Don Law might be tough to work with, he is a smart cookie, smarter than me anyway. You can imagine my surprise when I returned home to find that the concert had sold out and a second show was added. Aerosmith selling out the Garden at $7.00 bucks a head? I could not comprehend. I still cannot understand what would motivate anyone to spend that much cash for what is sure to be an acoustically poor concert. Maybe I was just completely ignorant to how popular Aerosmith was. I can guarantee that nothing like this would ever happen outside the state and possibly outside of Boston. Since the original billing, Wishbone Ash and Foghat have been added to the show. While this certainly makes the $7.00 better spent, it is an injustice to have two talented groups like Wishbone and Foghat, play second fiddle to a mere beginner. While I enjoy Aerosmith, I can't help but feel there's an injustice in their ticket price. 15,000 tickets were sold prior to the official release of their new album" (Springfield Student, 4/17/1975).

- From an industry review: "Fresh from the news that its second LP, 'Get Your Wings,' was certified gold, the five-man group Aerosmith displayed a homogenous brand of rock to a sellout crowd April 18. While the Columbia group has attained a modicum of success on the recording side, a healthy stretch of the road lies ahead before any additional success translates over into their stage act. Fortunately, though, they were on home turf here and audience reaction was balanced between what seemed like calm indifference to sporadic bursts of enthusiasm. The group isn't all that bad, it's just that they are not exceptionally good. Lead singer Steven Tyler handles his role well, and the stage and musical interplay between band members Tom Hamilton, Joe Perry, Joey Kramer, and Brad Whitford is up to par. Unfortunately, nothing new is involved. You can't help getting the feeling that you've seen it all before-at least a dozen times. As for material, the group leaves a lot to be desired. They come out on one level, both decibel and content wise, and remain there through- out most of their set. Color it boring. One stand-out selection for the evening, though, was their handling of 'One Way Street.' Additional selections used came from their latest album 'Toys in the Attic,' as well as from their first venture, 'Aerosmith.' In all, an average night in rock 'n' roll land, no real ups, and no real downs" (Billboard, 5/24/1975).

AEROSMITH GOLD—Following SRO Boston Garden concert for Aerosmith, Columbia held reception at which group got first gold disks for its second LP, "Get Your Wings." From left are Brad Whitford, guitars; Max Ann, WBCN-FM; David Krebs, Leber-Krebs Mgmt.; Steven Tyler, lead vocals; Ed Hunes, Col local promo manager; Joe Kramer, drums; Tom Hamilton, bass; Joe Perry, guitars; Al Perry, WBCN-FM; Sal Ingeme, Col regional promo mgr.

- From another industry review: "For the past year, Aerosmith have put most of their energies into live performances — touring dutifully across the country and earning a reputation as a solid hard rocking band. The group recently returned home to Boston with a gold record for their 'Get Your Wings' LP to show for their effort, and promptly sold out two nights at the biggest concert hall in the city. Combining a keen sense of showmanship with some well-paced rock and roll songs, the Columbia group played under optimal conditions for their hard-hitting brand of rock. From the first chords of the group's opening number, 'Helter Skelter,' it became immediately apparent that Aerosmith could do no wrong in front of the hometown crowd. Following with selections from all three of their albums, the group, fronted by lead singer Steven Tyler and propelled by guitarists Joe Perry and Brad Whitford, had the crowd surging toward the stage most of the night. Playing off the audience's enthusiasm, Aerosmith proudly displayed both power and dynamism throughout their set. The rhythms were fast and pulsated under the urgings of Tyler's extroverted stage mannerisms. Boasting several exceptionally strong original numbers such as 'S.O.S.,' 'No More Song and Dance' [sic], and 'Toys in the Attic,' in addition to a rousing version of the Yardbirds' 'The Train Kept A Rollin',' Aerosmith took the bicentennial city by storm and stand posed to repeat their success on a grander scale" (Cashbox, 5/31/1975).

April 19
Boston Garden
Boston, MA
Promoter: Don Law
Other act(s): Foghat (opener)

Set list: Toys in the Attic / S.O.S. (Too Bad) / Somebody / Adam's Apple / Lord of the Thighs / Sweet Emotion / Dream On / Walk this Way / No More No More / Write Me / Same Old Song and Dance / Train Kept A Rollin' / Make It / Big Ten Inch Record / Mama Kin / Walkin' the Dog

Notes:

- At a reception following one of these shows the band were presented with their RIAA "Gold" awards for the "Get Your Wings" album, their first. During the brief break that followed this show, Joe attended Muddy Water's show at Paul's Mall on Apr. 22 and sat in with the legend. Others present included James Montgomery, Peter Wolf, and Jeff Beck... A review of the album appeared in this date's Billboard issue: "Aerosmith specializes in straight ahead rock with few frills, and while they somehow seem to be neglected when people begin discussing major groups, they are one of rock's steadiest LP sellers. Music here, as always, is basic with rough and raucous vocals. No great change from previous efforts, which is welcome news for fans. Set is full of tasty, reasonably short guitar solos, with the double leads working particularly well. A softer cut or two is included, but it is the familiar rock that should get most attention" (Billboard, 4/26/1975).
- A lower quality AUD recording circulates from this show.

April 25
Civic Center
Springfield, MA

Promoter: Don Law
Other act(s): Atlantis
Reported audience: ~6,500 / 10,000 (65%)
Reported gross: $40,000
Notes:

- From a local review: "Two minutes before the hard rock group Aerosmith Center Friday night, lead singer Steven Tyler called a youth hospitalized at the Medical Center of Western Massachusetts. Tyler called Dan Lee, 22, from the Springfield area who had tickets to the concert that he never made. 'Somebody brought this to Steve's attention and Steven figured it would be a nice thing to do, to give him a call,' said Robert Kelleher, tour director for the five-man group. Aerosmith played to a crowd of about 6,500 fans whose ages ranged from their early teens to mid-20s. They greeted their group with sparklers held high in the air, lit matches, clapping and cheering. Banks of multi-colored spotlights cut through the smoke-filled arena and flashed as the group segued through songs including 'No More No More' and 'Toys in the Attic,' the title song of their third and most recent album. Their last two albums were gold, selling $1 million worth of records. The group included two guitarists, a drummer, a bass, and vocalist Steven Tyler, who has a Mick Jagger-Rolling Stone image in the rock world. The mostly-peaceful but mobile crowd, switching seats and walking back and forth across the aisles while the concert was playing, threw Frisbees to keep themselves entertained during the intermission" (Springfield Union, 4/26/1975).

April 27 ???QUESTIONABLE
Onondaga War Memorial Auditorium
Syracuse, NY

April 28
War Memorial
Rochester, NY

Promoter: RH Productions
Other act(s): Atlantis

Reported audience: (11,000 capacity)
Set list: Toys in the Attic / S.O.S. (Too Bad) / Somebody / Adam's Apple / Lord of the Thighs / Sweet Emotion / Dream On / Walk this Way / No More No More / Write Me / Same Old Song and Dance / Train Kept A Rollin' / Big Ten Inch Record / Mama Kin
Notes:
- A below average AUD recording circulates from this show.

April 30
County Fieldhouse
Erie, PA
Promoter: Belkin Productions
Other act(s): Atlantis
Reported audience: (5,250 capacity)
Notes:
- From a local review: "The singing is kept a few decibels above a shout, the guitars are relentless, the drumming emphatic and deliberate. Each song is impressive in itself, featuring guitar playing that is effectively berserk in style, providing the impetus for the group's sound. Once it's joined with that powerful vocalizing and drumming, one thing is definite about Aerosmith: They are a tremendously hard-working band. After about the first 20 minutes of their set, after my senses had taken a thorough beating, I expected the group to mellow out briefly and, if nothing else, let the audience appreciate how loud 'loud' really is. But they just kept driving hard... Aerosmith does more than let their music speak for them. They also put on an entertaining stage show highlighted by an oftentimes dazzling light display that flashed in time with the music" (Erie Times-News, 5/1/1975).

May 3
Civic Center
Providence, RI
Promoter: Concerts East
Other act(s): Journey
Reported audience: (14,000 capacity)

May 4
Hill Gymnasium @ UMPG
Gorham, ME
Promoter: UMPG Concert Committee
Other act(s): Acme Rhythm and Blues Band
Notes:
- Band members drove up from Boston, Steven in a limo, and other members in their personal Corvettes or Porsches (Biddeford Saco Journal).

May 5
Civic Center
Augusta, ME
Other act(s): Atlantis
Reported audience: (6,500 capacity)

May 6
Auditorium
Bangor, ME
Reported audience: (6,800 capacity)

May 7
New Century Theater
Buffalo, NY
Promoter: Harvey & Corky Inc.
Reported audience: (capacity 3,076)
Notes:
- Billed as a "New Year's Eve in May" party, this show was a make-up for the postponed April 4 date.

May 9
Spectrum
Philadelphia, PA
Promoter: Electric Factory Concerts
Other act(s): Hunter-Ronson (HL), Journey (opener)
Reported audience: (19,500 capacity)
Notes:
- From a local review: "With music so metallic is sounds like an erector set gone mad, Aerosmith showcased their latest album, 'Toys in the Attic,' at the Spectrum on Friday evening. The music, however, was not the only show — Steven Tyler, the group's lead singer, was a trip in himself. To watch Tyler gyrate around, across and over the stage like a crazed Rumpelstiltskin, an observer can't help but think the singer keeps the guardian angel of the week and feeble-minded working overtime. Tyler is a kind of crazy marriage between Freddy of Freddy and the Dreamers and Mick Jagger (although none of Jagger's stage malevolence really surfaces). Instead, only a lot of copies — second time-around characterizations are left. But that seems to be the story of the group itself as few of their onstage antics are original. Tyler sounds alternatively like Jagger, Alice Cooper, Robert Plant, and a few other lead singers, while the rest of the group goes in for such dog-eared visuals as dry ice wafting over the stage at strategic points during certain songs — a trick used by the Who very early in their career. And back to Tyler, who has numerous uses for the microphone — aside from singing" (Bucks Country Courier Times, 5/14/1975).

May 10
State Farm Show Arena
Harrisburg, PA
Promoter: Jennifer Productions
Other act(s): Rush, Atlantis (opener)
Reported audience: (8,200 capacity)

May 11
Civic Center
Baltimore, MD
Promoter: Creative Promotions, Inc.
Other act(s): Brian Auger's Oblivion Express (opener)
Reported audience: (12,500 capacity)

May 13
D.A.R. Constitution Hall
Washington, DC
Promoter: Cellar Door Concerts

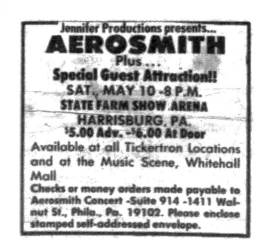

Other act(s): Richard Torrance, Eureka (opener)
Reported audience: 4,000 **SOLD-OUT
Reported gross: $21,053
Notes:
- Prior to the booking, the promoter expressed concerns that Aerosmith was going to be too loud for the venue.
- From a local review: "Last year I was impressed with Aerosmith. As a stand-in for Queen, it easily upstaged Mott the Hoople. But last night's Constitution Hall appearance firmly entrenches this Boston band as an advocate of the musical overkill that justifies criticism of heavy metal as rock's least durable, most non-evolutionary school. Like too many groups, it insists on outplaying the acoustic capabilities of the concert hall and the result is a muddled ménage of thunderous low-end power chords and screaming lead guitar. Guitarists Joe Perry and Brad Whitford could demonstrate more facility and flash if their love of volume didn't obscure their best playing.

Tyler approximates that mythic creature, the rock star, as well as many do. His vocals are clear and brutal, and his occasional lewd gestures coupled with the convulsive beat of the music bring flurries of applause. But even the energetic Tyler succumbs to repetition — his gestures become contrived mannerisms that even the ever-popular smoke machine hides. Two songs which express Aerosmith best are 'No More No More,' a testament to the ennui and weariness that rock 'n' roll life inspires and 'Same Old Song and Dance,' an accurate description of the group's music. During 'Train Kept A Rollin',' the old Yardbirds' favorite, drummer Joey Kramer delivered three superfluous drum solos, finishing with a barehanded attack that left the fans raving. The obligatory, lame encore proved that metal is like real metal — if you keep hitting on it, it eventually wears thin" (Evening Star, 5/14/1975).

May 18 **TEMP HOLD-DATE
Baltimore, MD

May 20
Convention Center Arena
Indianapolis, IN
Promoter: Sunshine Promotions
Other act(s): Wet Willie, Les Variations
Reported audience: 9,506 / 12,000 (79.22%)
Reported gross: $54,070
Notes:
- Initially scheduled for June 3.

May 21 **TEMP HOLD-DATE
L.C. Walker Arena
Muskegon, MI
Reported audience: (6,000 capacity)
Notes:
- Listed in an early Performance itinerary.

May 23 **TEMP HOLD-DATE

Grand Rapids, MI
Notes:
- Listed in an early Performance itinerary. The Kalamazoo Index also suggested a date with Kansas at Wings Stadium on this date.

May 24
Hara Arena
Dayton, OH

Promoter: Windy City Productions
Other act(s): Ted Nugent
Reported audience: (13,170 capacity)
Set list: Toys in the Attic / S.O.S. (Too Bad) / Somebody / Sweet Emotion / Lord of the Thighs / Dream On / Walk this Way / No More No More / Write Me / Same Old Song and Dance / Train Kept A Rollin'
Notes:
- A partial AUD recording circulates from this show.

May 27, 28
Cobo Arena
Detroit, MI
Promoter: Steve Glantz Productions
Other act(s): Wishbone Ash (HL)
Reported audience: (capacity 10,700)
Notes:
- From a local review: "Given that one decides, for some reason, to attend an Aerosmith concert, he is face immediately with a thorny problem: Should the Aerosmith fan buy a ticket near the stage so he can watch lead singer Steven Tyler in the full bloom of depravity, or should he sit back a bit, letting Tyler's Jagger-like face fade into a fleshy haze but also saving the fan's hearing. The kids chose both alternatives at Aerosmith's Cobo Arena concerts Tuesday and Wednesday, but up front or way back in the balcony, they all got a rare combination of rough-tough rock and polished musicianship... It is luridness that powers this band, from Tyler's lolling tongue to lyrics that are too explicit to be sensuous. Whether one digs Aerosmith depends, to a large degree, on how loud and strident he likes his rock. The band serves it up powerfully on both counts, and the fan who gets too near the stage risks morning-after buzzing ears" (Detroit Free Press, 5/29/1975).
- Following the second show Steven and Tom attended a Columbia Records reception at the Playboy Club.

May 30
SIU-E
Edwardsville, IL
Promoter: SIU-E University Center Board
Other act(s): Wishbone Ash (HL), Head East (opener)
Reported audience: ~9,200
Notes:
- Mississippi River Festival.
- From a local review: "The SIUE University Center Board held a spring concert Friday night featuring two second-rate rock acts and one even lesser-rate attraction. Wishbone Ash, has-been English rockers, teamed with Aerosmith, a Boston hasn't-been outfit, for an evening of over-modulated rock before some 9,200 paying customers who would apparently applaud anything. The real show was backstage, where the two groups argued over who would get top billing. In spite of it all, most everyone seemed to have a good time although the rock music filled the site so well that many people left to make room for it" (Alton Telegraph, 5/31/1975).

May 31
Convention Center
Louisville, KY
Promoter: Sunshine Promotions
Other act(s): Wishbone Ash (HL), Bob Seger (opener)
Reported audience: (6,000 capacity)
Notes:
- Bob Seger replaced previously announced opener Kansas.

June 1
Roberts Stadium
Evansville, IN
Promoter: Sunshine Promotions / Aiken Productions
Other act(s): Wishbone Ash, Kansas (opener)
Reported audience: (13,600 capacity)

June 3 **TEMP HOLD-DATE
Convention Center Arena
Indianapolis, IN
Notes:
- Listed in an early Performance itinerary, this show was ultimately booked for May 20.

June 5
Brown County Arena
Green Bay, WI
Promoter: Brass Ring Productions
Other act(s): Wishbone Ash, Kansas (opener)
Reported audience: ~2,700 / 10,000 (27%)
Notes:
- During 22 concerts police arrested 77 patrons for various offences. 31 of those arrests were made at this one concert...
- From a local review: "Thursday night at Brown County Veterans Memorial Arena, a crowd of 2,700 got a look at the latest rock permutation, punk rock, in the form of Aerosmith. Punk rock is distinguished by a youthful audacity that harps on current clichés, a tough flaunting of sexuality, usually male, and a sound level that's cranked up to around 125 decibels. (130 is considered pain.) That is how Aerosmith comes across. There are no new twists to the songs. They all have the mandatory beginning, with the lead singer singing (singing?) the first two verses, the standard middle, where the lead guitarist often shows an appalling lack of imagination and even less knowledge of his instrument, and a ho-hum ending as everybody gets together and sweats a lot. Then it starts all over again. Boston seems to breed bands like that. The J. Geils Band started out that way until it realized it wasn't getting anywhere and started writing some good tunes. Now we have Aerosmith, among others, to contend with. Aerosmith built its reputation on all the things that make a band big, for about a year, then it's off to the scrap heap. It may be fun while it lasts, but it doesn't last long" (Green Bay Press Gazette, 6/6/1975).

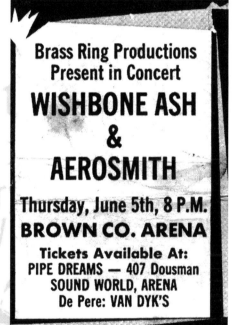

June 6
Arena
Duluth, MN
Other act(s): Wishbone Ash (HL)
Reported audience: (7,765 capacity)

144 | Aerosmith on Tour, 1973-85

June 7 **TEMP HOLD-DATE
Kenosha, WI
Notes:
- Appearing in various early Performance itineraries, this show was not booked with other dates being moved around.

June 7
Civic Center Auditorium
St. Paul, MN
Promoter: Schon Productions
Other act(s): Wishbone Ash (HL), Kansas (opener)
Reported audience: (12,000 capacity)

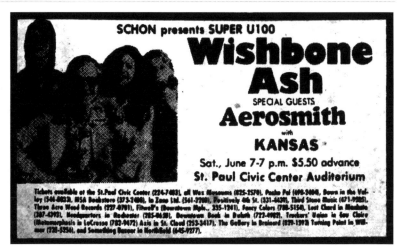

June 8 **Aerosmith CANCELLED
Winnipeg Arena
Winnipeg, MB, Canada
Other act(s): Wishbone Ash (HL), Bounty (opener)
Reported audience: ~5,000
Notes:
- Aerosmith cancelled, citing illness, but purportedly "decided they would rather catch the Rolling Stones' attendance-shattering gig in Milwaukee, Wisconsin the same night" (Winnipeg Free Press, 6/11/1975). The show still went ahead, with a replacement local band being found in place of Aerosmith. During the intermission, fans who had come specifically to see Aerosmith were offered refunds. The task of MC'ing the event fell to CKRC DJ Gary Roberts. Free Press "Youthscene" writer Andy Mellen was offended by the band's no-show at the concert, having heard glowing reviews from friends who'd attended the shows in Duluth and St. Paul...

June 10 **TEMP HOLD-DATE
Fargo, ND

June 13
St. Louis, MO
Notes:
- Several dates listed in an early Performance itinerary appear to have not been booked.

June 14
Municipal Auditorium
Sioux City, IA
Other act(s): Ted Nugent, Outer Space (opener)
Reported audience: (5,200 capacity)
Notes:
- This show was scheduled for June 11 on some early itineraries.

June 15
Pershing Auditorium
Lincoln, NE
Promoter: Sundown Associates

1975 - Toys in the Attic

Other act(s): Ted Nugent
Reported audience: (8,400 capacity)

June 17 **TEMP HOLD-DATE
Denver, CO
Notes:
- Appearing on an early itinerary

June 19
The Forum
Inglewood (Los Angeles), CA
Promoter: Concerts West
Other act(s): ZZ Top (HL)
Reported audience: 17,522 / 18,679 (93.81%)
Reported gross: $100,765
Notes:
- From a trade review: "Opening the show was Columbia's answer to how fast can you run amuck; Aerosmith. Aerosmith proved enthusiasm unchained as they combined the less disciplined aspects of Led Zeppelin with a steady stream of riff-infested rockers that were as mana from heaven to the Forum crowd" (Cashbox, 7/5/1975).
- From a mainstream review: "Ten years after the beginning of the British Invasion there exists a crowd of anxious young bands whose roots are secondhand. These are groups who can function perfectly well while believing that the Stones had the definitive version of 'Walking the Dog' and that Jeff Beck invented the electric guitar. And if the musicians themselves aren't quite that naive, a large, even younger portion of their audience is. Two such bands, both American, are Z.Z. Top and Aerosmith. Each has come to prominence within the last three years and though neither regards Los Angeles as one of their especially popular bases, they were able to nearly fill the Forum on a Thursday night during a week when Alice Cooper and Bad Company were playing the same hall.

Aerosmith, which opened the show, takes itself very seriously onstage — even though its act has been lifted in equal parts from the Rolling Stones and the Yardbirds. It has the same instrumental lineup (two guitars, bass, drums, and lead singer), a look that's strictly Mick and Keith, dazzling guitar work that's as complex as Clapton's, Beck's and Page's and a prancing, pouty lead singer (Steve Tyler) who looks as though he spends hours before each show standing in front of a mirror sucking in his cheeks. The staging is tight and carefully planned and the lighting and sound are excellent. But tonight's material, with the exception of the excellent ballad 'Dream On', wasn't exactly memorable. Still, audience response was unusually strong for an opening act, and the boys — especially Tyler — seemed particularly popular with the ladies" (Rolling Stone, 7/31/1975).

June 20
Sports Arena
San Diego, CA
Promoter: California Concerts Productions
Other act(s): ZZ Top (HL)
Reported audience: 14,250 / 15,000 (95%)
Notes:
- From a local review: "It should be remembered, though, that the opening act, Aerosmith, didn't come on-stage until 50 minutes after the announced starting time, and the intermission between bands lasted another 50 minutes. Together, the delays added up to a dismal lack of professionalism... Aerosmith transmitted a remarkable measure of energy, but its attributes stopped there. Its members played competently but suffered from an utter lack of originality. Vocalist Steven Tyler apparently has spent countless hours watching films of Mick Jagger in action, and has his impersonation down pat. Other hokey

bits by Aerosmith include a fist-pounding drum solo by Joey Kramer, swirling smoke across the stage and a guitar solo with the instrument held behind the head" (San Diego Union, 6/22/1975).

June 21
Tempe Stadium
Tempe, AZ
Promoter: Beaver Productions
Other act(s): ZZ Top (HL), REO Speedwagon, Nitty Gritty Dirt Band, Johnny Winter
Reported audience: (25,000 capacity)
Reported gross: $142,000
Notes:
- Summer Festival of Rock.

June 26
Selland Arena
Fresno, CA
Promoter: Pacific Presentations
Other act(s): Dr. Hook
Reported audience: (7,500 capacity)

July 3
Center Arena
Seattle, WA
Promoter: John Bauer Concert Company
Other act(s): Richard Torrance, Eureka (opener)
Reported audience: 6,400 **SOLD-OUT
Notes:
- From a local review: "Aerosmith has had a couple of AM hits, including the current climber 'Sweet Emotion,' but nothing giant and I was quite surprised to find the house sold and scalpers hawking tickets outside. Maybe it was the night, but it might just be that a lot of people are really hip to the band. The group certainly put on a dynamite rock 'n' roll show, quantum jumps better than the previous shows they've done here. The set started hot with a rocking version of 'Walkin' the Dog,' with lead singer Steve Tyler doing the walking. He was wearing something that had long sleeves and pieces of fabric hanging from it and all of it swayed around as he jumped, danced, and strutted. Aerosmith is a hard rock band, and their show is powerful and frankly sexual. Tyler is borrowing a lot of tricks from Jagger this time out, including the eye makeup and constant excited movement. He already has the same inordinately large mouth and full lips of Jagger and uses them in much the same way.

He doesn't suffer from the comparison, though, he still maintains an individual style and unique sense of movement and one's attention can't help but be riveted on him. But it isn't just Tyler who makes the band unique. Aerosmith would be just another rock 'n' roll band if it weren't for Joe Perry and Brad Whitford, two excellent rock guitarists. Most heavy rock bands can't see beyond simple chords, but these two guys add all kinds of textures to the basic rock beat of the band. The band's tunes are all pretty derivative and generally based on recognizable rock patterns, but they embellish them, expand them, improve them — have a lot of fun doing it. Their show is geared to heighten the excitement already caused by the music and it does just that... The show was timed just right, one tune following closely after another, with variety in each tune, including a comparatively slow one occasionally. Their sound system was excellent, you could hear every word of the vocals and the nuances of the electric guitars" (Seattle Daily Times, 7/4/1975).

July 5
International Raceway
Portland, OR

Promoter: Albatross Productions
Other act(s): Bachman-Turner Overdrive (HL), Journey, Mojo Hand (opener)
Reported audience: ~25,000
Notes:
- From a local review: "Aerosmith played next, performing nearly an hour to the sea of milling fans who greeted the finale by the quintet with enough enthusiasm that an encore, 'Toys in the Attic,' an up-tempo rocker that burned its way over the massive speaker system, keeping the crowd on its feet and yelling for more. BTO closed the night of music and proved why its popularity has been increasing by giant steps the past two years. It's a muscular, gutsy quartet that is steeped in lowdown rock and roll, the kind with equal parts of punkness, grace, volume, and heavy rhythm. It would be a toss-up, though, which band, Aerosmith or BTO, was the better. Aerosmith has been also tapping the underground for two years, rounding up a legion of fans while getting little air play. The tide of enthusiasm when the band was introduced was not as large as for BTO, but Aerosmith showed definitely it was no longer in the opening act category" (Oregonian, 6/6/1975).

July 6 **Aerosmith CANCELLED
Interstate Fairgrounds
Spokane, WA

Promoter: Albatross Productions
Other act(s): Bachman-Turner Overdrive (HL), Journey (opener)
Reported audience: ~11,000
Notes:
- Aerosmith cancelled and did not perform at this show. There was a two-hour delay between the gates opening and Journey taking the stage (due to the cancelled local opening acts). A further hour delay took place before BTO took the stage following Journey, having been swapped in performance order due to adverse weather threatening the venue. The promoter felt that the audience would prefer to see the performance of the billed headliner in case the concert had to be ended earlier due to the weather. They were to be followed by Aerosmith. Unfortunately, Aerosmith reportedly did not like the changes — particularly the dangers of being rained on while performing on the uncovered stage — and left the venue (with their $5,000 guarantee). One of the cancelled local openers, Mojo Hand (the other was Child), was left to perform in their place. Initial reviews of the show incorrectly suggested that Aerosmith had played, though with a highly non-specific description limited to "Aerosmith came much later yet to round out the program with some more heavy metal music of the 70s" (Spokesman-Review, 7/7/1975). They certainly did not. Promoter Ken Kainnear told the local paper, "I can understand why people were upset about the delays and

Aerosmith not playing. I was upset, too. I paid them $5,000 to play and they walked out" (Spokesman-Review, 7/8/1975).

July 13
H.I.C. Arena
Honolulu, HI
Promoter: Ken Rosene
Other act(s): Sassafras
Reported audience: 8,000 **SOLD-OUT

July 19 **TEMP HOLD-DATE
Long Beach Arena
Long Beach, CA
Notes:
- This date was moved to July 20 and the date in San Jose not booked. Several dates July 19-August 29, appeared in a trade ad (Billboard, 7/29/1975 & Cashbox 7/19/1975).

July 20 **TEMP HOLD-DATE
The Grove @ Fairyland Park
Kansas City, MO
Promoter: Chris Fritz
Other act(s): Electric Light Orchestra (HL), Henry Gross, Trapeze, Pavlov's Dog
Reported audience: (10,000 capacity)
Notes:
- What was intended to be the lineup for the third concert of the "Carney Rock III" summer series of shows. It was initially planned for there to be four shows during the summer.

July 20 **TEMP HOLD-DATE
San Jose, CA
Notes:
- This date was noted in early itineraries but was not booked.

July 20
Arena
Long Beach, CA
Promoter: Wolf & Rissmiller Concerts
Other act(s): Mahogany Rush, Status Quo
Reported audience: (13,000 capacity)
Set list: Walkin' the Dog / S.O.S. (Too Bad) / Somebody / Sweet Emotion / Lord of the Thighs / Dream On / Walk this Way / No More No More / Same Old Song and Dance / Train Kept A Rollin' / Big Ten Inch Record / Toys in the Attic
Notes:
- From a local review: "Once the mollifying disclaimer — that Aerosmith works hard, conducts a tight, professional presentation, and so probably gives its fans what they consider to be their money's worth—is made, kindness must give way to the inevitable conclusion that it's really a bunch of garbage. The six-piece from Boston is another example of the perseverance syndrome, i.e., if you show up often enough people are going to think you've got something whether you do or not. It has brought Aerosmith to headline status at the Long Beach Arena, where on Sunday it topped a miserable bill that was saved only by the crisp, compact boogie of Quo (whose status slot after all these years and all those tours is a shocking reversal of the perseverance syndrome). Aerosmith's angle is flash-boogie, American metal riffing descended from the Stones and Yardbirds, delivered with punch but no passion. The songs and playing are both basic and competent, but hotshot lead singer Steve Tyler has a voice that picks up where Alice Cooper's leaves off and

the stays there. As the visual centerpiece, Tyler has the equipment but little inclination to do anything interesting with it. Sporting the decadent look of the Dolls and other wan New York sorts, he alternates between a pout and a crazed glare, neither of which emanates much charisma. The combination of Tyler and band adds up to bloated, retread rock, a catalogue of clichés and proven devices packed in punk wrapping, so contrived that there is no room for spontaneity, too derivative to be striking. The only thing that made the group even slightly refreshing was the set of obnoxious, pointless Hendrix imitations offered beforehand by Mahogany Rush" (Los Angeles Times, 7/22/1975).

- From an industry review: "There's a hell of a lot more to rock and roll than meets the eye. Beyond the basic drive and excitement that the music generates there are subtle shadings and changes in progressions that subdivide the music into 'rock,' 'boogie,' and 'heavy metal.' The recent appearance of Aerosmith, Mahogany Rush and Status Quo at the Long Beach Arena showed the intricate inner workings of each level. Top lined Aerosmith (Columbia) proved an exercise in metaloid overkill as the power unit from Boston laid down riff upon riff of raw musical power. No subtleties and no excess fat. The perfect quotient for head on excursions into abrasive rock and roll. A major factor in Aerosmith's rising above the glut of asphalt rending bands is the band's playoff of music and sound. Neither got the overriding edge during the course of the band's set and the resultant sound balance provided the stance necessary for this branch of the rock and roll beast... This night the Long Beach Arena was as a foundry, spewing forth a continuous stream of musical sheet metal" (Cashbox, 8/2/1975).

- A decent AUD recording circulates from this show.

July 24
Music Hall
Houston, TX
Promoter: Michael Dunham
Other act(s): White Lightning
Reported audience: 2,840 / 3,000 (94.67%)
Reported gross: $14,100

July 25
Municipal Auditorium
San Antonio, TX
Promoter: Stone City Attractions
Other act(s): Too Smooth
Reported audience: 6,000
Reported gross: $35,000
Notes:
- The reported audience figure would have placed it at or close to sellout, without being specified such.

July 26
City Park Stadium
New Orleans, LA
Promoter: Beaver Productions
Other act(s): ZZ Top (HL), Jeff Beck, Fleetwood Mac, Trouper, Jay Boy Adams
Reported audience: ~30,000
Reported gross: $311,000
Set list: Walkin' the Dog / S.O.S (Too Bad) / Sweet Emotion / Walk this Way / No More No More / Same Old Song and Dance / Train Kept A Rollin' / Toys in the Attic
Notes:
- This was purportedly the largest ever (at that time) audience at a music event in the city, beating a previous record set by Led Zeppelin. Aerosmith performed after Trouper.
- An AUD recording circulates from this show.

July 27
Tulsa Fairgrounds Pavilion
Tulsa, OK
Other act(s): Status Quo
Reported audience: (6,500 capacity)
Notes:
- Some online itineraries the headliner noted for this show was ZZ Top. However, that band had grossed $183,000 at the venue on Jul. 3 with Johnny Winter, J. Geils, and Jay Boy Adams.

July 28
Memorial Hall
Kansas City, MO
Promoter: Continental Entertainment
Other act(s): Kansas, Head East (opener)
Reported audience: 3,500 **SOLD-OUT
Reported gross: $20,500

July 31
Texas Hall @ U.T.A.
Arlington, TX
Promoter: Zoo Productions
Other act(s): Kansas
Reported audience: (3,000 capacity)

August 3
U.C. Nippert Stadium
Cincinnati, OH
Promoter: Lombardo Productions
Other act(s): Black Oak Arkansas, Foghat, Blue Oyster Cult, Nitty Gritty Dirt Band, Bobby Womack, Mahogany Rush, Status Quo, Styx, The Outlaws
Reported audience: 32,824 / 40,000 (82.06%)
Reported gross: $299,000
Notes:

- Ohio River Music Festival. REO Speedwagon and Foghat were also on the bill, but apparently did not perform.
- From a local review: "Aerosmith, the headliner, closed the Festival. Aerosmith, an inordinately mediocre band, mixed the mike-stand swinging histrionics of its vocalist, Steven Tyler with the band solos of drummer Joey Kramer and guitarist Brad Whitford to cause the audience to demand an encore. Aerosmith responded with an appropriately-named finale, 'Toys in the Attic'" (Cincinnati Enquirer, 8/5/1975).
- Following this show the band took a break long-enough for Joe to marry Elyssa in Boston on Aug. 5, before heading back out on the road. During the break "Toys in the Attic" was certified Gold by the RIAA (Aug. 11), becoming the band's second U.S. sales certification...

August 23
Cleveland Stadium
Cleveland, OH
Promoter: Belkin Productions
Other act(s): Rod Stewart and Faces (HL), Uriah Heep, Blue Oyster Cult, Mahogany Rush
Reported audience: 60,900 / 80,100 (76.03%)
Reported gross: $615,000

Set list: Walkin' the Dog / S.O.S. (Too Bad) / Somebody / Big Ten Inch Record / Sweet Emotion / Dream On / Write Me / Walk this Way / Same Old Song and Dance / Mama Kin / Train Kept A Rollin' / Toys in the Attic

Notes:
- Aerosmith performed in between Heep and BOC.
- The fourth World Series of Rock. Attendee Eric Singer, later drummer for Black Sabbath, Alice Cooper, and KISS, recalled: "In 9th grade I started playing in my father's band and so I had to play gigs every weekend with my dad when most of my friends were going to concerts... I remember they played a high school with Blue Oyster Cult, but I couldn't go to that one... I loved them, I just couldn't get to see them as often as my friends, as I would literally have to pick and choose what concert I really wanted to go and see mainly because I always had to work. It was frustrating, all through high school I was working nearly every weekend... They did those 'World Series of Rock' for a few years, but these had a theme, and sometimes they'd do three or four of them during the summer. Aerosmith went on, but Steven was a great front man, and how he works the stage, and his stage presence was always really great. I saw them the next year playing Richfield Coliseum and Joey Kramer was playing a clear acrylic flexi Fibes brand set of drums and he did the drum solo with his hands." Eric's solo project, ESP, later recorded a cover of "S.O.S. (Too Bad)." Eric recalled why that song: "It was John Corabi and I. John was a big Steven Tyler fan, and influenced by him, and I loved the song because it's on my favorite Aerosmith album. The ESP album was supposed to be songs by bands we were really influenced by." He also recorded "Round and Round" for the 2001 Bob Kulick produced "Let the Tribute Do the Talkin'," recalling: "That song is a really heavy tune. It's got serious attitude to it, so that's why I dug getting to play that song. Doing those tribute albums was a lot of fun because you got to cover some of the songs you'd really loved..."
- An average AUD recording circulates from this show.

August 24
State Fairgrounds
Trenton, NJ

Promoter: Hollow Moon Concerts
Other act(s): Kingfish, Poco, Slade, Nils Lofgren, Mahogany Rush, Hootchie Kootchie Blues Band
Reported audience: 27,000 / 30,000 (90%)
Notes:
- Kingfish included Bob Weir and Dave Torbert. This event was afflicted by ticketless fans attempted to storm the fences to gatecrash the event, which had attempted to cap tickets at 8,000. Because of the violence at this even, Hamilton Township banned future rock concerts at the fairgrounds and within the township. The local fairground operator blamed the newspapers for blowing the incident out of proportion, while the promoter and town officials exchanged arguments regarding blame for the incident.
- From a local review: "But as Lofgren croons his tunes, the Hollow Moon Afternoon goons moved too soon and with baseball bats hastened to drive the concert-crashers back. Beer cans and bottles flew freely through the air as the Hollow Moon security swung their bats just as freely. But the fence-busters were too much as they bust through as if a prison-

break were in effect. The concert became a free one when Hollow Moon finally decided to let everyone in for nothing — something the producers should have realized was bound to happen. It always does. Crowd estimates put the figure over 14,000 who attended, but no one really knows how many actually paid. The more fortunate members of the audience sat and listened or wandered around in bleary-eyed stupors. But at least eight persons were hospitalized for drug overdoses" (Bucks County Courier Times, 8/25/1975). Trades reported a significantly higher attendance figure.

August 27
Coliseum
Richmond, VA

Promoter: Cellar Door Productions
Other act(s): REO Speedwagon, Slade
Reported audience: 5,304 / 11,800 (44.95%)
Notes:
- From a local review: "Just like last time, Speedwagon upstaged the top-billed act. This time, the victim was Aerosmith, a Boston band whose style falls somewhere between Slade and Speedwagon. Like its predecessor... the group's performance was top-heavy with fast-paced, loud rockers. By the third number, the Coliseum crowd was properly whipped up, but Aerosmith had to depend on flashier lighting and its dancing, shouting lead singer to draw the response Speedwagon earned with pure music" (Richmond Times Dispatch, 8/27/1975).

August 28
Capital Centre
Landover (Largo), MD

Promoter: Cellar Door Productions
Other act(s): REO Speedwagon, Slade
Reported audience: ~19,000
Notes:

- From a local review: "Aerosmith's music is intended to create excitement and even frenzy. Though last night's show was their first appearance as a headliner at the Capital Center, they are one of the fastest rising groups in the United States, thanks to a sound that emulates older and more established bands, particularly those from Britain. Aerosmith is originally from Boston, but they try their hardest to look and act like the Rolling Stones, and musically they bear an uncanny resemblance to the Yardbirds. From the moment Aerosmith began with 'Walking the Dog,' a song closely associated with the Stones, it was apparent that for their adoring fans they could do no wrong. The. Yardbirds' 'Train Kept a 'Rolling' was especially well received, and though guitar riffs in this, and other numbers, tended to be overly simple and repetitive, the music had a power and drive that transcended its individual components" (Washington Post, 8/29/1975).

August 29
Central Park
New York City, NY

Promoter: Schaefer Music Festival
Other act(s): Ted Nugent

Set list: Walkin' the Dog / S.O.S. (Too Bad) / Somebody / Big Ten Inch Record / Sweet Emotion / Dream On / Write Me / Walk this Way / No More No More / Same Old Song and Dance / Train Kept A Rollin' / Toys in the Attic
Notes:
- 10th Anniversary of the Schaefer Music Festival at the Wollman Skating Rink.
- From a local review: "Raunch has always been a favorite descriptive word in rock 'n' roll over the last two decades, signifying a tough, insolent, perhaps sleazy approach to the art form. Aerosmith, a group from Boston, is the latest in a seemingly endless line of groups to use raunch as a way of rock, working well, and well within the limits of early rock aided (and at times hampered) by modern technology in the amplification department. Aerosmith headlined a concert at the Schafer Music Festival in Central Park on Friday. Steve Tyler is the lead singer of this group, which is now showing the benefit of years of touring in its togetherness. He has his vocal and, it must be admitted, visual roots in Rod Stewart and Mick Jagger, with a lot of posturing, microphone twirling, and a coat of many colors. But he gets the job done cleanly and efficiently, in line with the rest of Aerosmith, who play straightforward rock-boogie that is quite satisfying, if elemental" (New York Times, 8/31/1975).
- From an industry review: "Aerosmith takes reverberating rock and roll and shoves it down your throat so that you're are forced to swallow, or choke. And there are ample fans across the nation who are lapping it right up, swallowing, and begging for another portion. Thus, this group has been earning huge popularity with the bumpers and grinders of today's rock generation. At Central Park August 29, Aerosmith displayed a basic 2/4 beat, combined with a batch of good-looking musicians and more than enough pelvic and facial contortions to drive little girls wild and add some entertainment where the music leaves off. Though the tunes themselves are catchy at the time of the performance, there is not one concrete enough to plant itself and shackle the memory cells... Aerosmith exudes a tremendous amount of controlled energy and leaves its fans exhausted" (Performance).
- An AUD recording circulates from this show. The show was also the band's first King Biscuit Flower Hour appearance, being broadcast on Sept. 28 (paired with a set from Gentle Giant), though it didn't include the full set (which was later more fully re-broadcast as part of "Best of the Biscuit").

September 2
Massey Hall
Toronto, ON, Canada
Other act(s): Thundermug
Reported audience: (2,675 capacity)
Notes:
- From a local review: "Aerosmith? Isn't that a novel about a doctor by Sinclair Lewis? Almost (different spelling), but in this case we're talking about a five-piece band and if you like your rock hard, abrasive, and unrelenting, then this group will be good for your ears. Boston-based Aerosmith didn't fill Massey Hall last night on its first Toronto appearance, but the house was respectable, and I'll wager that it will sell out the next time through on the basis of its stage act alone, never mind its music, of which more later. Aerosmith really looks like a rock band. The players are all young and arrogant looking, skinny, shaggy, and swaggering. They know what they're supposed to do on stage, but they accomplish it with an insolent offhandedness that is refreshing and arresting. They also look somewhat like the Rolling Stones. It's a resemblance which lead singer Steven Tyler rejects, claiming that it is purely coincidental. It surely can't hurt them, however, as long as their music is good, and it is. Tyler had Mick Jagger's marionette-without-strings appearance as he flung himself around the stage while his arms and legs seemed to move in eight directions at once.

Lead guitarist Joe Perry has a black mane and staggered around the stage in a manner reminiscent of the Stones' lead guitarist, Keith Richard. Tom Hamilton has a blond pageboy haircut that looks like the late Brian Jones', but Hamilton plays bass guitar whereas Jones played rhythm guitar. There was even a ghostly sixth semi-member, Scott Cushnie, on piano, like the Stones' Ian Stewart. It is an indication of how far rock show presentation has advanced to compare the show Aerosmith put on last night with an early Stones concert. Aerosmith had a sophisticated lighting system, special effects like flash bombs and dry ice machines to produce mist, and a sound board that filtered the sound of Joey Kramer's drums as he played them. The Stones had none of this when they were as unknown as Aerosmith still is. It takes a lot more to break in a group these days as a stage act. Aerosmith has the makings. It also requires music. As Tyler has pointed out. Aerosmith doesn't sound like the Stones. It does, however, sound like a band that has listened to the Stones and assimilated them along with many other influences. The result is pure American hard rock. There's very little feeling of specific influences like blues, boogie, rhythm 'n' blues or even the extreme heavy-metal brand of hard rock as purveyed by Uriah Heep and Black Sabbath. Everything has been blended. If there's such a thing as a middle of the road in hard rock, Aerosmith is walking down the white line. But enough of definition. The band is energetic, engaging, and entertaining. It made a lot of people want to dance and what more can we ask?" (Toronto Globe & Mail, 9/2/1975).

September 10
New Century Theater
Buffalo, NY

Promoter: Harvey & Corky Productions
Other act(s): Les Variations, Hydra
Reported audience: (3,076 capacity)
Notes:
- The day following this show, the debut album was certified Gold by the RIAA. It would be the band's third and final album sales award of the year.

September 13
Grand Valley State College Fieldhouse
Allendale, MI

Promoter: Dome Productions

September 14
U.I. Stadium
Bloomington, IN

Promoter: Lombardo Productions
Other act(s): Blue Oyster Cult, Slade, Chris Hillman Band, Savoy Brown, L.T.D., Atlanta Rhythm Section
Reported audience: ~12,000 / 30,000 (40%)
Notes:
- Jordan River Music Festival.
- From an industry review: "Despite the cancellation of five acts and unseasonably cold weather, the Jordan River Music Festival on the Indiana Univ. campus here set a

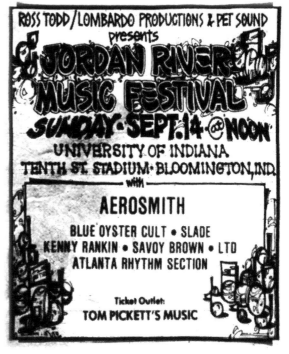

crowd dancing Sept. 14. Chris Hillman, who made an appearance with his band, was quoted as saying, 'This is a '68 acid rock festival...' Advertising for the outdoor concert was spread across a four-state area — Indiana, Illinois, Kentucky and Ohio, with 35 ticket locations, something new for I.U.'s yearly outdoor concerts. The major portion of the $25,000-$30,000 budget went into radio spots in all major market areas, including Louisville, Indianapolis, Chicago, South Bend, Terre Haute, Fort Wayne and Evansville, Ind. IUSA concert director John Browning estimates that about half the concertgoers were from out-of-town. The changing roster of attractions necessitated changes in advertising, posters, and leaflets, but Browning says the final schedule 'had something for everyone jazz, rock and soul.' The stadium where the concert was held has a 30,000-seat capacity, but Browning says the biggest outdoor show at I.U. has only drawn about 18,000. George Andria, a promoter with Pet Sounds, blamed the weather for the relatively light attendance, calling the rainfall on the previous Thursday a 'monsoon which discouraged ticket sales'" (Billboard, 10/4/1975).

September 16
Horton Fieldhouse @ I.S.U.
Peoria, IL

Promoter: I.S.U. Entertainment Committee
Other act(s): Ted Nugent
Reported audience: ~10,000
Notes:
- The band were reportedly paid a $10,000 fee for this show. Opener, Ted Nugent, had then recently released his debut solo album via Columbia.
- Three patrons were arrested during the show, and 43 ejected, for drugs and behavior related offences.
- From a local review: "Aerosmith seemed somewhere else. It felt like a side show more than a rock concert of a group that is supposed to be the hottest thing around these days. Lead singer Steve Tyler has gone from rags to regalia, as he has certainly changed with the coming of the third album, 'Toys in the Attic.' He resembled a wild dancing scarecrow complete with simulated prairie wind trying to keep his band afloat amidst a flailing beat and technical problems which shadowed the talents of lead guitarist Perry. Tyler's habitual phallic gestures bordered on a poor example of Jim Dandy (is there ever a good one?) and a case of the crabs. The band didn't seem to have the same punch they had a year ago. Renditions of their older material didn't seem to have the same smooth flow anymore. 'Train Kept a-Rollin',' was overdone, especially the Grand Funk-ish drum solo which took an unnecessary 15 minutes of the song. Aerosmith only played a paltry hour and one-half set which included mostly new material. 'Toys in the Attic' is not a bad studio album, and the group is actually very interesting to watch. Tyler's prancing around is really OK, when he isn't fondling himself as he did periodically throughout Tuesday's set. To say that Aerosmith got me going, however, would be an unfortunate lie" (The Vidette, 9/18/1975).

September 18
Ambassador Theater
St. Louis, MO
Promoter: Contemporary Productions
Other act(s): Ted Nugent
Reported audience: ~3,000
Set list: Walkin' the Dog / S.O.S. (Too Bad) / Somebody / Big Ten Inch Record / Sweet Emotion / Dream On / Write Me / Walk this Way / No More No More / Same Old Song and Dance / Train Kept A Rollin' / Toys in the Attic
Notes:
- From a local review: "Last night's concert at the Ambassador Theater left no room for anything close to soft and smooth music... Aerosmith had some great moments playing in basically the same vein as the Nugent group but failed to generate much momentum. The five-man band had no apparent weaknesses and could be on the verge of something great if it could find its own sound. It probably will. Much of the music was dominated by the singing of Steven Tyler whose raspy voice had surprisingly good range. Tyler moves around the stage like a pro and manipulates his microphone stand like a war lance. The band was loud, but the volume was a necessary part of its show and was never offensive" (St. Louis Post-Dispatch, 9/19/1975).
- A partial SBD circulates from this show. It's missing the final song (if the assumed encore was performed).

September 19
Amphitheater

Chicago, IL
Promoter: Windy City Productions
Other act(s): Ted Nugent
Reported audience: 11,000 **SOLD-OUT
Reported gross: $80,000

September 20
St. John Arena @ O.S.U.
Columbus, OH
Promoter: Sunshine Promotions
Other act(s): Ted Nugent
Reported audience: **SOLD-OUT
Reported gross: $52,750
Notes:
- Fans purportedly caused $1,500 worth of damage to the venue during the show.
- From a local review: "Making their second Ohio appearance within a month, Aerosmith proved why they are the fastest-rising group in America today. Coming off a Cleveland Stadium appearance that had been fraught with mechanical difficulties, Saturday's attempt was a much better indication of just how good a band they can be... In the prevailing atmosphere, songs like 'Walking the Dog,' 'Big Ten-Inch Record' and 'Walk this Way' needed that terrific punch to get across. That punch was provided by the co-mayors of Feedback City, Joe Perry, and Brad Whitford, who's powerful made a perfect backdrop for the flamboyant vocals of Steven Tyler. Honorable mention must also go to Tom Hamilton (bass) and Joey Kramer, one of rock's primo percussionists. Anyone who attempts a drum solo in an age where drum solos have long been dead and buried had better be more than good. He's gotta be excellent. Joey Kramer is. In fact, it's his percussioning, as much as anyone else's contributions, that made 'Train Kept A Rollin'' the Aerosmith trademark" (Cleveland Scene, Sept. 25-Oct. 1, 1975).
- From another local review: "The dream come true almost became a nightmare for Aerosmith fans at St. John Arena Saturday when an unruly and uncooperative crowd took 20 minutes to clear the center and front aisles of the main floor, almost preventing the concert from starting. The crowd was asked several times to clear the aisles for fire safety reasons and were told repeatedly the concert would not begin until they obeyed... After the equipment was set up for Aerosmith the crowd was told to clear the aisles. They stood their ground and were again told to move, or the concert would not begin. After 20 minutes, the aisle-blockers began to move, seating themselves as close to the stage as possible. The lights went out and Aerosmith was on stage. The response was wild cheering and lighted matches. The lights came on again. The crowd had been warned about lighting matches. Steven Tyler, lead vocalist of the group, demanded that the lights be turned off. The opening numbers formed a collage of hard rock. Tyler, dressed in bright green and black shining satin, brought the crowd back to their feet with a burning 'Walking the Dog' and 'Too Bad, You Can't Get Your Money Back' [sic].

The crowd was making an effort to attain concert hysteria. The crowd could not come together, and people were still a little hostile. An excellent version of 'Sweet Emotions' re-ignited the flicker of excitement. Some of Tyler's fine vocals were lost in the loud music. Joe Perry played a strong lead rhythm guitar and Tom Hamilton backed him with a wall of brass playing Tyler and Perry's 'Walk this Way.' A cloud of smoke enveloped the stage and the very familiar opening notes of 'Dream On' filled the arena. A red spotlight shone on Tyler's wet hair; his green satin soaked with sweat. Aerosmith has matured and their now-legendary version of 'Dream On' has come a long way. The audience appeared hypnotized. Tyler worked at holding the crowd together, but things wouldn't jell. 'Same Old Song and Dance' and 'No More No More' didn't excite anyone. Brad Whitford turned in a good performance on lead guitar during 'Train Kept A 'Rollin'' and a drum solo by Joey Kramer proved that he could well be described 'the greatest drummer in the United States.' The main lights went up. The concert was over, but the crowd continued to cheer.

Aerosmith returned to the stage. The lights went down, and a brilliant flash exploded on the stage. Tyler launched into 'Toys in the Attic.' Then it was over. Aerosmith left and finally so did everyone else. A good concert that could have been excellent is a sad loss to the entertainers as well as the crowd. Hopefully, Aerosmith won't remember this unfortunate event and will return to Columbus" (Ohio State Lantern, 9/22/1975).

September 23
Stanley Theatre
Pittsburgh, PA
Promoter: DiCesare-Engler Productions
Other act(s): Ted Nugent
Reported audience: 4,000 **SOLD-OUT
Reported gross: $24,000

September 24
Keystone Hall @ Kutztown State College
Kutztown, PA
Promoter: DiCesare-Engler Productions
Other act(s): Ted Nugent, Point Blank
Reported audience: 4,500 **SOLD-OUT
Reported gross: $24,750

September 26
Civic Center
Charleston, WV
Promoter: Entam, Ltd.
Other act(s): Ted Nugent, Point Blank, REO Speedwagon
Reported audience: 6,750 / 8,000 (84.38%)
Reported gross: $40,000

September 27
Scope Convention Hall
Norfolk, VA
Promoter: Entam, Ltd.
Other act(s): Ted Nugent, REO Speedwagon
Reported audience: 12,000 **SOLD-OUT
Reported gross: $72,000
Notes:
- On the following night Aerosmith was broadcast on the King Biscuit Flower Hour (on a show shared with Gentle Giant). Aerosmith's set had been recorded during their Shaeffer Music Festival set the previous month.

October 1 **POSTPONED
Freedom Hall
Johnson City, TN
Promoter: Entam, Ltd.
Other act(s): Ted Nugent
Notes:
- This show was rescheduled, at the last moment, for Oct. 13, due to a band member's "illness" leaving them unable to depart Boston for the show.

October 2
Coliseum
Knoxville, TN
Promoter: Entam, Ltd.
Other act(s): REO Speedwagon, Ted Nugent
Reported audience: 4,166 / 6,500 (64.09%)

October 4
Coliseum
Greensboro, NC
Promoter: Entam, Ltd.
Other act(s): REO Speedwagon, Ted Nugent
Reported audience: 8,000 / 10,000 (80%)
Reported gross: $48,000
Notes:
- From a local review: "Last Saturday, before a crowd I estimated at 8,000, Aerosmith tossed and turned to the delight of the audience. The crowd gawked at the lead singer as he straddled the streamer-wrapped microphone stand and roared with admiration as he shoveled out the words of his opening song. The second number, 'S.O.S. (Too Bad)' seemed to sink like a lead weight in a pail of water. The number was rough and out-of-balance, and the singer, Steven Tyler, appeared to suffer a memory lapse, for I noticed he forgot some of the words. In 'Train

Kept A-Rollin',' which I particularly looked forward to hearing, it was obvious Tyler's efforts were only half-hearted. It seemed to me that he didn't care what happened or what it sounded like. He was just there, only existing... Aerosmith did come out to a responsive crowd, and even when Tyler made mistakes (in 'Same Old Song and Dance' he completely left out some words), he received a solid round of applause, punctuated by yells and screams. Personally, however, I got nothing from the overpowering music but a splitting headache. 'Train Kept A-Rollin'' was so slow and uninspiring that I could have gone to sleep without missing a thing. The number's best feature was Joey Kramer's drum solo, which lasted approximately 15 minutes. About three-quarters of the way through his solo, he threw his drumsticks into the audience, and finished by using his hands and his head. He actually would hit one drum with his left hand, and another with his right, winding up by striking a third with his head or forehead. As the other band members returned to the stage, they climaxed the show's stupidity by striking up the theme from 'Batman,' progressing to the Burger King commercial 'Have It Your Way.' After they completed the 'special orders don't upset us' portion of the 'song,' they finally, much to my relief, wrapped up 'Train Kept A-Rollin.'

During a slow song, Aerosmith tried to achieve an eerie effect with smoke, but that was just another gimmick, as far as I was concerned. It all seemed very poorly done. With practice and hard work, Tyler might be able to imitate Mick Jagger, but unless he improves his disinterested attitude, he won't ever get past his own shadow. The group's live performance completely contradicts the impression they convey on records. Aerosmith's recordings are excellent, and I can't listen to them often enough, but I would not care to sit through another live performance. The band had a chance to redeem itself with an encore but displayed great arrogance by taking much too long to return to the stage. After such a poor performance, I felt they should be grateful for the chance to make it up. I should have been grateful to let than be, instead of having them play again, but after paying $6.50 for a piece of trash, I felt that I could stick it out. Obviously, the performance struck me as very disappointing. The admission price was high, and should have guaranteed a good show, but the set was (about one hour) as well as low in quality. The band just didn't care, and it showed" (Statesville Record & Landmark, 10/11/1975).

October 5
Spectrum
Philadelphia, PA
Promoter: Electric Factory Concerts
Other act(s): REO Speedwagon, Ted Nugent
Reported audience: ~19,000 SRO
Notes:
- Steppenwolf was the initially announced opening act.
- From a local review: "Sunday's concert (a very charitable description), at the Spectrum proved to be a sad and disturbing evening for those who view rock 'n' roll as a viable art form. The headlining group, Aerosmith, along with two supporting rock acts, REO Speedwagon and Ted Nugent, put on one of the least musical spectacles seen at the hail in recent memory. While the SRO crowd seemed to be caught up in the hysteria of the moment, little real entertainment could be discerned. Aerosmith, the new masters of American 'schlock' rock, have just recently come into their own with constant SRO concerts and tremendous sales of their three albums despite the continued disfavor of the critics. A Boston based 'boogie' band; the group pounds out simple four-four rock 'n' roll in a manner not for the faint-hearted. Unfortunately, almost every song sounds alike, with the same chord progressions matched with slight variations in rhythm.

The group's main attraction is Steven Tyler, who generates crowd excitement with the usual time-worn tricks of the trade. While visually adequate, musically Tyler comes off as an ineffectual copy of Mick Jagger, using screams, tantrums, and volume, to make up for his lack of vocal abilities. While tunes such as 'Dream On' and 'Sweet Emotion' are a cut above many songs of the same genre, Aerosmith seems unable to present them in any listenable context, possibly setting a record for the loudest and most unintelligible band ever to appear at the Spectrum. Aerosmith, the present darlings of the young mass market, are hopefully soon to be forgotten — and the sooner the better" (Philadelphia Inquirer, 10/7/1975). Amusingly (or not), the aforementioned review was written by one John Kalodner...

October 8 **CANCELLED
Louisville Gardens
Louisville, KY
Promoter: Sunshine Promotions
Notes:
- This show was cancelled 10 days prior without explanation. No opening act had been announced.

October 10 **TEMP HOLD-DATE
Civic Center
Philadelphia, PA
Promoter: Midnight Sun Co.
Notes:
- Booked in early September, the show was relocated to the larger Spectrum.

October 11 **TEMP HOLD-DATE
Island Music Center

Long Island, NY

October 13
Freedom Hall
Johnson City, TN
Promoter: Entam, Ltd.
Other act(s): Ted Nugent, Rush
Reported audience: (7,500 capacity)
Notes:
- Rescheduled from Oct. 1.

October 15 **POSTPONED
Civic Center
Lakeland, FL
Promoter: Beach Club / Pacific Presentations
Other act(s): Rod Stewart and Faces (HL), Jeff Beck
Notes:
- Rod Stewart cancelled shortly before the concert was due to start, purportedly due to laryngitis, and the show was rescheduled for Oct. 17.

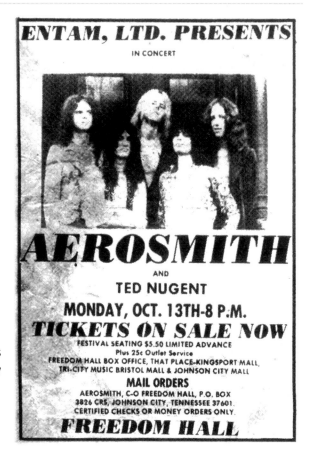

October 16
Civic Center
Lakeland, FL
Promoter: Beach Club / Pacific Presentations
Other act(s): Jeff Beck, Bryan Bowers (opener)
Reported audience: (10,000 capacity)
Set list: Walkin' the Dog / S.O.S. (Too Bad) / Somebody / Big Ten Inch Record / Walk this Way / Dream On / Lord of the Thighs / Sweet Emotion / Adam's Apple / Same Old Song and Dance / Train Kept A Rollin' / Toys in the Attic
Notes:
- Rod cancelled again, both this night's show and the following night's scheduled make-up date. However, the other groups opted to perform. Regardless, some fans rampaged causing $800 in damage to the area surrounding the civic center.
- A poor AUD recording circulates from this show. It's missing the last two songs.

October 17
Civic Center
Lakeland, FL
Promoter: Beach Club / Pacific Presentations
Other act(s): Rod Stewart and Faces (HL), Jeff Beck, Bryan Bowers (opener)
Reported audience: (10,000 capacity)
Notes:
- Rod changed his mind about cancelling at the last moment and performed at this show. Many fans didn't turn up, thinking he wouldn't perform, and refunds were offered. Later that night the Faces were accused of causing $3,500 in damage to the Holiday Inn South, by tearing up their rooms after being thrown out of the hotel bar at 2am. Citing this behavior Civic Center Director Neal Gunn planned to never invite the band back to the venue.

October 18 **Aerosmith CANCELLED
Gulfstream Raceway
Ft. Lauderdale, FL

Promoter: Cellar Door Concerts
Other act(s): Rod Stewart and Faces (HL), Jeff Beck, Bryan Bowers (opener)
Reported audience: ~11,000
Notes:
- A rainstorm forced the cancellation of both Bryan Bowers and Aerosmith, due to there being a 6p.m. curfew for the conclusion of the show, which had then already been afflicted by other delays and backstage problems. Funnily enough the venue had imported and installed an Auto-Tile canopy to protect the performers should it rain... A $1 parking fee was charged to raise money for the Pediatric Care Center. The promoter intended to book the band for a return visit to Miami as soon as was possible.

October 19
Omni
Atlanta, GA

Promoter: Alex Cooley, Inc.
Other act(s): Rod Stewart and Faces (HL), Jeff Beck
Reported audience: 16,000 **SOLD-OUT
Notes:
- From a local review: "Aerosmith, a brash Boston group, opened with an exuberant set... A Beantown band with three Columbia albums under their belts. Aerosmith may well represent the last bastion of American punk rock (especially With the New York Dolls now Just a brief, pleasant memory). Aerosmith, a local favorite due to a smashing stint at Alex Cooley's Electric Ballroom, play get-down, no-holds-barred rock 'n roll. Singer Steven Tyler, who is visually a cross between Mick Jagger and Carly Simon personifies the punkitude [sic] of Aerosmith's music; wearing a striped pajama suit (*tres chic*, these days), he taunted and teased the ringside ladies as he strutted and posed.

Not surprisingly, Aerosmith's love for basics is both their strong suit and weakness. Their 45-minute set leaned heavily on material from their first two albums ('Dream On,' 'Somebody,' 'Lord of the Thighs'), and their opening and pseudo-closing numbers were well-worn rock warhorses: 'Walking the Dog' and 'Train Kept A Rollin'.' Fact is, I can't knock them: they were tight and to the point. I just hope Aerosmith doesn't become the Black Oak Arkansas of the north. And I think they're smart enough not to" (Huntsville Times, 10/24/1975).

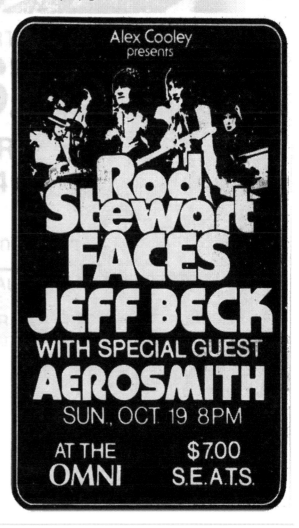

October 24 **POSTPONED
Dome Arena
Henrietta, NY

Promoter: Concerts East
Other act(s): Slade, Mott
Notes:
- This show was postponed until Oct. 31.

October 25 **POSTPONED
War Memorial

Syracuse, NY
Promoter: Concerts East
Other act(s): Slade, Mott
Notes:
- This show was rescheduled for Oct. 29.

October 27
Civic Center
Providence, RI
Promoter: Concerts East
Other act(s): Slade, Mott
Reported audience: 13,000 **SOLD-OUT
Reported gross: $73,000
Notes:
- Following the rapid sell-out of this show a second date was added the following night.

October 28
Civic Center
Providence, RI
Promoter: Concerts East
Other act(s): Slade, Mott
Reported audience: ~10,500 / 13,000 (80.77%)
Reported gross: $60,000

October 29 **POSTPONED
War Memorial
Syracuse, NY
Promoter: Concerts East
Other act(s): Mott
Notes:
- This show was rescheduled for Nov. 23 and tickets were required to be exchanged for the new date. No reason was provided for the second postponement.

October 31
Dome Arena
Henrietta, NY
Promoter: Concerts East
Other act(s): Slade, Mott
Reported audience: 5,600 **SOLD-OUT
Reported gross: $30,800
Notes:
- Around this time the band performed privately for the opening party of their newly acquired Wherehouse in Waltham, MA.

November 11
Auditorium
Milwaukee, WI
Promoter: Daydream Productions
Other act(s): Edgar Winter (HL)
Reported audience: 6,200
Notes:

- The band barely received any mention in the show review printed in the Journal review on Nov. 12, but Edgar Winter apparently went down well with the crowd.

November 12
R.K.O. Orpheum Theater
Davenport, IA
Promoter: Windy City Productions
Other act(s): Climax Blues Band
Reported audience: 2,708 **SOLD-OUT
Reported gross: $19,500
Notes:
- From a local review: "After a false start to tease the fans, Aerosmith finally comes to Davenport and announces its presence with a hard-driving version of 'Too Bad.' A rock music concert assaults all the senses. Besides the heavy music, there is a light show to dazzle the eyes, and the pungent aroma of marijuana tickles your nostrils, even though smoking is supposedly banned in the auditorium. Twirling his microphone like a baton, Tyler races across the stage beneath a rainbow of spotlights that pierce alternating colors through the smokey fog in perfect timing to the beat of the band. With a microphone festooned with streamers, Tyler seems to be jousting imaginary knights in armor on stage as he waves it at the audience. His face is heavily made up, and he wears a brilliant red costume made especially for him by his wardrobe designer. Tyler alternates his acrobatics with saucy, strutting movements like those he puts on while the crowd roars to his 'Walkin' the Dog'" (Quad City Times, 11/23/1975).

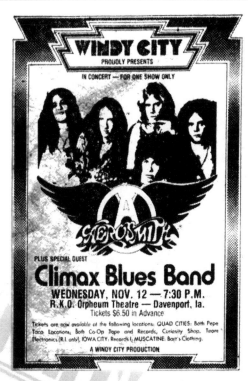

November 14
Civic Center Arena
St. Paul, MN
Promoter: Schon Productions
Other act(s): Edgar Winter (HL), Sensational Alex Harvey Band (opener)

November 15
Drake University Fieldhouse
Des Moines, IA
Promoter: Windy City Productions
Other act(s): Ted Nugent
Reported audience: 4,500 **SOLD-OUT
Reported gross: $26,500
Notes:
- From a local review: "Saturday night, Drake's MAC helped Windy City Productions produce the Aerosmith-Ted Nugent concert, which was attended by over 5,000 — well over capacity for the Fieldhouse. The concert was an excellent one, as both artists performed to the max. The act was peaked by an 'exploding flash of light' during Aerosmith's encore, which absolutely blew the audience away, not only with visuals, but sound, too. The drummer of Aerosmith performed a drum solo, and threw his sticks out into the frantic audience, only to continue using his bare hands to play his drums! Fantastic" (Drake Times-Delphic, 11/18/1975).

November 16
Dane County Coliseum
Madison, WI
Other act(s): Ted Nugent, Rush
Reported audience: ~4,000 / 5,500 (72.73%)

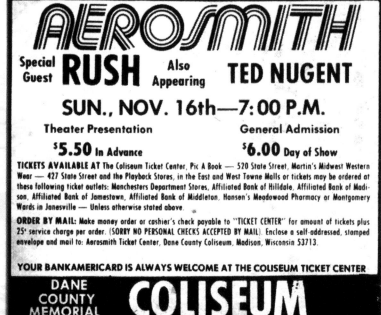

November 19
EIU Lantz Gym
Charlestown, IL
Promoter: University Board
Other act(s): Ted Nugent
Reported audience: ~5,500 / 6,000 (91.67%)
Notes:
- A week prior just 1,500 tickets had been sold, which improved slightly to around 3,300 by the day before the show. Patrons had been warned that there would be searches for drugs, alcohol, and food prior to entry to the gym. Complaints about the heavy-handed search and seizure process reverberated among the student body for several months following the show.

November 20
Athletic & Convocation Center @ Notre Dame
South Bend, IN
Promoter: Sunshine Promotions
Other act(s): Ted Nugent, Kansas
Reported audience: 8,710 / 11,800 (73.81%)
Reported gross: $48,500

November 23
War Memorial
Syracuse, NY
Promoter: Concerts East
Other act(s): James Montgomery, Black Sheep
Reported audience: (8,400 capacity)
Notes:
- Rescheduled from Oct. 29. Black Sheep was a local band which included future Foreigner vocalist Lou Gramm.

November 28
A. Wherehouse
Waltham, MA
Notes:
- Tom Scholz had rented Aerosmith's facility for his band, Boston, to perform a showcase for Epic A&R, which resulted in that band receiving a record deal with the label...

November 28
Fox Theater
Atlanta, GA
Promoter: Alex Cooley, Inc.

Other act(s): Ted Nugent
Reported audience: (4,665 capacity)
Notes:
- This booking was under a concerted effort to save the venerable venue by the nonprofit Atlanta Landmarks.

November 29 **CANCELLED
Pontiac Stadium
Pontiac, MI
Promoter: Steve Glantz Productions
Other act(s): six bands in total
Notes:
- This show (which would have been the first rock show at the venue) was postponed indefinitely in late-October due to competition with the Who concert scheduled for Dec. 6, though only 16,000 tickets had been sold in the 80,000-seat venue.

November 29
Jai-Alai Fronton
Miami, FL
Promoter: Cellar Door Concerts
Other act(s): Ted Nugent
Reported audience: (6,500 capacity)

December 2
Memorial Coliseum
New Haven, CT
Promoter: Koplik & Finkel
Other act(s): Steppenwolf
Reported audience: 10,400 **SOLD-OUT

December 3
Madison Square Garden
New York City, NY
Promoter: Howard Stein
Other act(s): Black Sabbath (HL)
Reported audience: 19,600 **SOLD-OUT
Notes:
- A party was held for the band at the St. Regis Hotel following the show, attended by Columbia executives and others including "Exorcist" actress Linda Blair. The following day, during the flight to Los Angeles, Lisa Robinson interviewed Steven Tyler for a piece that ran in the Jan. 24, 1976 issue of NME in the UK.
- From a local review: "Aerosmith — America's answer to British rock 'n roll via Boston came a rollin' to New York Dec. 3, for a stopover at Madison Square Garden... Trailed by long colorful scarfs as is his custom and dressed in striped jester clothes, Steven Tyler moves and jumps to the hypnotic pace of Joey Kramer on drums, Joe Perry on lead guitar, Brad Whitford on rhythm guitar and Tom Hamilton on bass... Aerosmith's energy is the motor of their rhythm, the power of their blues and the lower tarot card of their success... The soaring guitars take us back to the very memorable Yardbirds days when the 'Train Kept a Rollin''. This was their longest song with time

for expanded guitar solos as well as Joey Kramer's drum solo which starts off to a rattle sound similar to that of a rattle snake and continues to an off-tempo snare / bass / symbol jiveness that could have kept a train a rollin' all night long. Joey, after throwing his drum sticks to the audience continues beating the tough skin with his hands. The locomotion gets the audience clapping, suddenly, Joey whistles and the band starts playing the theme of a cartoon detective and they end... Boston has come a long way since its Tea Party and Aerosmith even farther with three gold albums. So, what if the lead singer sometimes appears like Jagger and the lead guitarist moves like Keith Richard. Aerosmith is the '70's answer to the Yardbirds with their own sound of course. There's a saying that if you see a band more than three times you really like them... Also, on the bill was Black Sabbath" (Fairleigh Dickinson University Gauntlet, 12/17/1975).

- From an industry review: "Neither act was particularly impressive. But both were solid in their performance. Aerosmith, with the vocals of Steven Tyler and lead guitar of Joe Perry standing out, did an hour of their Columbia material. Their reception was justly enthusiastic... The crowd thoroughly enjoyed the drum solos of Aerosmith's Joey Kramer and Black Sabbath's Bill Ward, neither of which were unique" (Variety, 12/10/1975).

December 5
Forum
Inglewood (Los Angeles), CA

Promoter: Fun Productions
Other act(s): Montrose, Mott
Reported audience: 18,149 **SOLD-OUT
Reported gross: $103,910
Notes:
- Sparks and Ted Nugent were initially noted as the opening acts.
- From a local review: "Persistence, youth, and attrition among the front-runners, rather than any distinctive musical style or extraordinarily exciting image, seem responsible for the continued of Aerosmith in the heart of the teenage rock audience, which has apparently transcended the threshold of boredom. That the group's supercharged, Yardbirds-derived boogie and its flashy posturing can now lure a Forum full of fans (as it did Friday night) comments less on its abilities and inspiration than it does on the treadmill condition of today's power-rock scene" (Los Angeles Times, 12/8/1975).
- From an industry review: "The last time Aerosmith played Los Angeles — not too many months ago — it opened the show for ZZ Top in a not-quite-sold-out

Forum. Dec. 5, as headliners of a particularly strong three-act show, the band played to a capacity crowd. All of which goes to indicate the still growing strength of one of the U.S.'s top-drawing bands. Steven Tyler, Joe Perry, and company are getting much the same kind of audience reaction that was once reserved for acts like the Rolling Stones (who Aerosmith, not so incidentally, shamelessly mimic). The act's set is smooth, clean, and neatly staged. The band's repertoire is drawn from its three albums, with the Stones-associated 'Walkin' the Dog' and Yardbirds' 'Train Kept A Rollin'' the only tunes not composed by group members. Tyler and company's own songs lack the kind of easy accessibility that is the hallmark of most great rock 'n' roll but try telling that to their fervid young audience" (Billboard, 12/20/1975).
- From another industry review: "At Central Park last August, their forceful sound was only partially evident, but at the Forum, a facility much more compatible, Aerosmith not only took off, but took the entire crowd with them. Steve Tyler should once and for all be recognized as his own entity, though his stage energy and antics are derived from some of the older English lead singers, there is no longer any need for comparison. Tyler, not yet jaded by the group's success, is not imitating. Aerosmith has discovered and perfected the secret to that rock 'n' roll alchemy which has provided fortunes to many greats in the past. Unlike the sweeter and more mellifluous American bands who have 'made it,' Aerosmith have mastered that erotic,

electric raunch which leads their fans to a frenetic desperation. When they stepped onstage, it was too a standing ovation" (Performance, 12/26/1975).

December 6
Winterland
San Francisco, CA
Promoter: Bill Graham Presents
Other act(s): Ted Nugent, Earthquake (opener)
Reported audience: 5,000 **SOLD-OUT
Notes:
- From a local review: "Aerosmith, already an immensely popular act on the East Coast from where the hard-rocking band hails, made its second visit to the Bay Area over the weekend. The band topped a sold-out concert Saturday at Winterland, a definite change from the band's Bay Area debut when Aerosmith opened a Winterland show for Mott the Hoople and Bachman-Turner Overdrive 20 months ago. What started out as a carbon copy Rolling Stones has now evolved beyond pure imitation into a similar, but distinct style of its own. But it is exactly the strong, deliberately drawn parallels between the Stones and Aerosmith that account for the group's impact.

Lead vocalist Steve Tyler supplied his impression of Mick Jagger, bending down to sing into the microphone or flamboyantly whirling across the stage. As if the band didn't look enough like the Stones already with Tyler and Keith Richards-look-alike-Joe Perry (Aerosmith's lead guitarist), the bass player even held his instrument upright, pointing over his shoulder, like Bill Wyman of the Stones. The loud music the band played similarly mirrored the music of the Stones: hard driving. blues-based rock, with weak melodies subordinated by crashing guitars. In addition to originals, the band has revitalized an old rhythm and blues classic — 'Big Ten-Inch Record' — in Rolling Stones style, with the antiquated double *entendres* intact" (San Francisco Chronicle, 12/8/1975).

December 7 **TEMP HOLD-DATE
Memorial Auditorium
Sacramento, CA
Notes:
- This show was noted in itineraries but appears to have not been booked.

December 9
Coliseum
Spokane, WA
Promoter: John Bauer Concert Company
Other act(s): Kansas, Ted Nugent
Reported audience: 6,010 / 8,500 (70.71%)
Reported gross: $38,312
Partial set list: Make It / Sweet Emotion / Somebody / Dream On / Toys in the Attic
Notes:
- One concert attendee waved a loaded .44-magnum at Ted Nugent during his set before being subdued by ushers and other patrons. Ted was unconcerned by the incident, though the patron was charged with intimidation with a weapon. The gun was blamed on a communication issue resulting from a slightly earlier than usual show starting time, and stampede to concertgoers once the gates opened due to the regularly scheduled police not being present. This gun-toting attendee murdered four family members, including two children, in early January.
- From a local review: "It was 'primitive culture at its finest' Tuesday night as 6,000 crazies got into a fine ol' time rock 'n' roll triple-header at the Coliseum. Aerosmith, Kansas, and Ted 'Wildman' Nugent spent three hours on stage juking, jiving, conversing with the crowd, and putting on a heck of a show. With the present trend in rock toward either kissy-sweet bubble gum or grinding acid rock guaranteed to ruin your ears, it's a pleasure to hear performers who remember something of the origins of rock. Aerosmith, led by powerful

lead singer Steven Tyler, came on the scene about three years ago behind a wave of balsa wood airplanes that some clever agent dreamed up as a publicity stunt. For a long time, no one remembered Aerosmith for anything except those planes — which were super for driving college professors crazy — until they hit the big time a year ago.

Their second album, 'Get Your Wings' did it, and they frenzied the crowd even more with a few of its cuts Tuesday. Tyler is amazing. He gyrates like a top, wrestles with his microphone stand throughout the show and dances like some sort of crazed demon. Tyler's voice sounds like a cross between Mick Jagger's rasp and Lee Michaels' whine, and when Aerosmith is going, they really do sound a lot like the tones. Tyler even exhorted the troops into singing along on one number, 'All Night Long [sic], which indeed seemed like it never was going to end. But overall, Aerosmith avoided the long unending instrumentals that drive many a reviewer to boredom. That probably is an indication of their ability. They, unlike so many groups today, can sing" (Spokesman Review, 12/10/1975).

December 11
Coliseum
Seattle, WA

Promoter: John Bauer Concert Company
Other act(s): Kansas, Ted Nugent
Reported audience: 13,902 / 15,000 (92.68%)
Reported gross: $86,105
Notes:
- From a local review: "If you were wondering where your teens were late last Thursday night, mom, and dad, they were probably among the 15,008 or so who jammed the Seattle Center Coliseum for a rock show starring Aerosmith, with Ted Nugent and Kansas sharing the bill. Aerosmith was here to collect the payoff for several low-price concerts they've done here at the Arena last July and the Aquarius Tavern about a year ago. They built up a good reputation with those shows and it paid off — tickets were $6.50 for the Coliseum gig. Aerosmith is a hard rock band in the manner of the Rolling Stones or Led Zeppelin, and it was good to see that that kind of music is popular among young people — I was afraid they only liked overly loud heavy metal groups.

It was a long time before Aerosmith took the stage — following the other two bands and long equipment changes — and the first part of the set seemed like a warmup, but the last half dozen numbers were all dynamite, showing Aerosmith has developed into an excellent rock band. Perhaps their best asset is lead singer Steve Tyler, a Mick Jagger clone who whirled around the stage in a multi-colored jump suit that had streams of cloth hanging all over the place. The band also had a pair of good guitarists in Joe Perry and Brad Whitford. Tom Hamilton played bass and Joey Kramer drums" (Seattle Daily Times, 12/15/1975).

December 12
Coliseum
Portland, OR

Promoter: John Bauer Concert Company
Other act(s): Kansas, Ted Nugent
Reported audience: 11,000 **SOLD-OUT
Reported gross: $71,396
- From a local review: "A young crowd of 11,000 swarmed over the Coliseum Friday night to pay homage to ear-crunching rock and roll music from three bands. It was almost a tossup which group the young folks cared for the most, that is until headliner Aerosmith pranced onstage. The shrieks, applause and general clamor was nearly noisier than the music, and all the physical racket was accentuated by several Roman candle fireworks which, by the way, are dangerous. However, the general mood of the crowd was a mixture of laid-back and festive. The people came to hear music but also came because if raunch-music concerts are anything at all, they are big parties...

So now we come to Aerosmith. It is a five-piece band you'd have to call third-generation rock. The players are very young, establish an empathetic rapport with their young audience, and go from there to play mighty stupendous rock and roll. The group seems to have fashioned its image of music out of English blues and American rhythm and blues, but there are times when it sounds like the early Rolling Stones, middle Led Zeppelin and any contemporary inner-city R&B group. And that's a wide range of influence. The band, at least the lead singer, is enamored of Mick Jagger or is mocking him because he has enough Jagger traits to be compared to the Rolling Stone. But he at times goes Jagger a few steps further. He has the energy that Jagger may have left behind a couple of years ago and has an excellent voice.

Aerosmith is tight rhythmically and the lead guitarist can burn the strings on up-tempo works. This is a band that can be referred to as a working band, as opposed to superstar groups who go out for two months a year. Aerosmith bas been in Portland four times and with each appearance has moved closer to the top of the bill. Friday night, Aerosmith arrived, and to prove this, the band is playing a concert at the Coliseum at 7:30 p.m. Monday, Dec. 15, same supporting bands" (Oregonian, 12/13/1975).

December 15
Coliseum
Portland, OR
Promoter: John Bauer Concert Company
Other act(s): Kansas, Ted Nugent
Reported audience: 8,186 / 11,000 (74.42%)
Reported gross: $54,455
Notes:
- From a local review: "Christmas may be a week away for most of us, but in the world of touring rock-and-roll stars it can come at any time. For the band members and traveling staff of Aerosmith, the celebration began Monday after their second Coliseum concert. The show was over 11:30 p.m. and the corks began popping shortly after. The dressing room in which the Christmas party took place looked like one of those post-World Series pictures, with lots of smiles and beverages. Aerosmith was given the party by the John Bauer concert company, which promoted the two concerts — the first one was the previous Friday and drew a sellout crowd of 11,000, while the Monday show attracted nearly 9,000 — and provided the decorated Christmas tree, a bundle of wrapped gifts, spaghetti and chicken, French champagne, ice cream cakes and plenty of goodies. Many of the gifts were toys purchased by Bauer and his wife, Ivy Liberti Bauer, at one of the many arts and craft shops they visited during the Seattle couple's four-day stay in Portland getting the two concerts on the stage. The wooden toys were purchased from a craftsman with whom Bauer attended Lewis and Clark College several years ago. Their meeting apparently was one of those, 'aren't you so-and-so?', meetings between old friends. The party wound down at about 1 a.m. when the large truck and trailer rigs outside the Coliseum began to get ready for the journey to the band's final gig of the tour, San Diego. Steve Tyler, the frantic lead singer of Aerosmith, was quite jolly during the party and was saying the two shows in Portland were great. The two concerts were the first time since 1965 that the Coliseum had successive shows by the same band" (Oregonian, 12/18/1975).

December 17
Sports Arena
San Diego, CA
Promoter:
Other act(s): Blue Oyster Cult, Ted Nugent
Reported audience: (15,000 capacity)
Notes:
- Famed photographer Fin Costello shot this show.

1975 - Toys in the Attic

1976 - Rocks

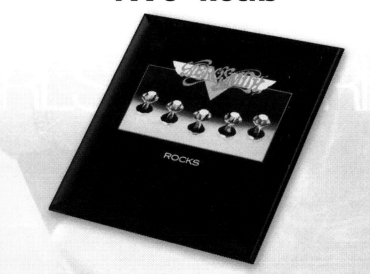

U.S. Release Details:
Columbia/CBS PC/PCA/PCT/PCQ-34165 (May 7, 1976)
Columbia/CBS PCQ/CAQ-34165 (June 25, 1976 — Quadraphonic)
Columbia/CBS CK-34165 (1987 — CD reissue)
Columbia/SME CK/CT-57363 (Sep. 7, 1993 — 20-bit SBM digital remaster)
Columbia/SME 88883760941 (Apr. 28, 2014 — 180g LP reissue)

Tracks:
A1. Back in the Saddle •
(4:40) — Steven Tyler / Joe Perry
A2. Last Child •
(3:26) — Steven Tyler / Brad Whitford
A3. Rats in the Cellar
(4:05) — Steven Tyler / Joe Perry
A4. Combination
(3:39) — Joe Perry

B1. Sick as a Dog
(4:16) — Steven Tyler / Tom Hamilton
B2. Nobody's Fault
(4:21) — Steven Tyler / Brad Whitford
B3. Get the Lead Out
(3:41) — Steven Tyler / Joe Perry
B4. Lick and a Promise
(3:05) — Steven Tyler / Joe Perry
B5. Home Tonight •
(3:15) — Steven Tyler

Album Details:
Produced & arranged by Jack Douglas and Aerosmith. Engineered by Jay Messina assisted by Rod O'Brien and Sam Ginsberg. Recorded at Wherehouse in Waltham, MA, with Record Plant Remote services, and the Record Plant, New York City, NY.

Players:
◦ Back in the Saddle - Joe Perry on six-string bass.
◦ Last Child - Paul Prestopino on banjo.
◦ Sick as a Dog - Tom Hamilton on guitar; Steven Tyler on bass; Joe Perry on bass and percussion.
◦ Home Tonight - Joey Kramer and Jack Douglas on backing vocals; Joe Perry on pedal steel.

Chart Action:
Chart Peak (USA): #3 (6/26/1976) with 53 weeks on the Billboard charts. Other countries: CAN #14; JPN #13; SWE #46.

05/29/76	06/05/76	06/12/76	06/19/76	06/26/76	07/04/76	07/10/76
25	17	7	5	**3**	3	3
07/17/76	07/24/76	07/31/76	08/07/76	08/14/76	08/21/76	08/28/76
6	10	11	9	9	8	15
09/04/76	09/11/76	09/18/76	09/25/76	10/02/76	10/09/76	10/16/76
15	15	15	17	17	18	27
10/23/76	10/30/76	11/06/76	11/13/76	11/20/76	11/27/76	12/04/76
56	55	66	110	104	95	93
12/11/76	12/18/76	12/25/76	01/01/77	01/08/77	01/15/77	01/22/77
93	89	89	89	79	68	64
01/29/77	02/05/77	02/12/77	02/19/77	02/26/77	03/05/77	03/12/77
62	66	65	65	63	72	67
03/19/77	03/26/77	04/02/77	04/09/77	04/16/77	04/23/77	04/30/77
79	121	162	159	155	155	199
05/07/77	05/14/77	05/21/77	05/28/77	06/04/77		
199	198	197	195	X		

RIAA/Sales:

In the United States, the album was certified Gold by the RIAA on May 21, 1976 and Platinum on July 9, 1976; 2X Platinum followed on October 19, 1984; 3X on December 21, 1988; and most recently 4X on February 26, 2001. Gold by the CRIA (Canada - 50,000 units) on September 1, 1976 and Platinum on November 1, 1976. During the SoundScan era, the album had sold 409,451 copies between 1991 and 2007.

Supporting Singles:

● Last Child (USA, 5/1976) - Chart Peak: #21 (8/7/1976) with 15 weeks on the Billboard charts. Other countries: CAN #26. The single, backed with "Combination, was released in the UK on July 30.

06/12/76	06/19/76	06/26/76	07/04/76	07/10/76	07/17/76	07/24/76
52	42	34	31	28	26	24
07/31/76	**08/07/76**	08/14/76	08/21/76	08/28/76	09/04/76	09/11/76
22	**21**	21	36	39	58	73
09/18/76	09/25/76					
73	X					

● Home Tonight (USA, 9/1976) - Chart Peak: #71 (10/16/1976) with 4 weeks on the Billboard charts. Other countries: CAN #82.

09/25/76	10/02/76	10/09/76	**10/16/76**	10/23/76		
86	72	73	**71**	X		

● Back in the Saddle (USA, 3/1977) - Chart Peak: #38 (5/7/1977) with 8 weeks on the Billboard charts. Other countries: CAN #26.

04/09/77	04/16/77	04/23/77	04/30/77	**05/07/77**	05/14/77	05/21/77
84	70	60	50	**38**	38	59
05/28/77	06/04/77					
73	X					

Joe Perry: "We're getting better, the songs are getting more unified and the whole band's coming up with worthwhile ideas. I'm looking forward to the next one because I know it'll be better again " (Sounds, 10/16/76) ...

Touring in support of the "Toys in the Attic" album concluded in San Diego on December 17, 1975. Aerosmith had enjoyed a strong year of popular growth and that album and tour had pushed the band's catalogue sales to over 3 million units. Additionally, each of those three studio albums had been certified Gold by the RIAA throughout the year (Platinum awards didn't exist at the time, with that certification level being created in 1976 with the first awarded in late February — though "Toys" had certainly exceeded 1,000,000 units during the year). The band had continued to pay their dues grinding through a touring schedule without the benefit of radio hits and resultant airplay, press gimmicks, or major national television appearances. It was an all-encompassing grind. More importantly, versus their progenitors, the New York Dolls, Aerosmith had diligently avoided becoming over-hyped; not that CBS had any inkling about how to market them anyway. With the band off the road, the explosive success may have felt that it had been a long time coming, but the pressure was certainly on the band to deliver a successful new album that would catapult them to the next level of rock stardom. The canon was primed to deliver a blast, but first, the band had to deliver...

In January 1976 former producer Adrian Barber filed a lawsuit against Columbia, the band members individually, Leber & Krebs, and Frank Connelly for $1.2 million. He alleged that the parties named had breached his original 1972 contract to produce the debut album on the grounds that it "gave him the option to produce further Aerosmith albums if the original achieved the success level it did reach. He attempted to exercise the option without success" (Variety, 1/28/1976). While the album had not initially been a commercial success, Barber had also not become upset being supplanted by Ray Colcord and Jack Douglas for "Get Your Wings." However, the success of his former clients trumpeted throughout the press may have been an irresistible target to attempt to leverage the fine print of a contract signed over three years previous. That the case went away with nary a further mention in the press indicates that any issue was quickly dispatched...

Following an all too short holiday break, the band convened at the Wherehouse for pre-production rehearsals with Jack Douglas. Jack recalled the genesis of the project: "The only thing we were talking about a few months before 'Rocks' was that it was going to be a real hard rock album. And we might go back to the format of the first album, which was a rock out on every tune. And again, keep it real raw. And make it as live sounding as we possible could" (Record World, 12/25/1976). Life on the road made writing and rehearsing new ideas nigh on impossible, but a handful musical ideas had taken root. Part of Douglas' role was to help marshal the band distill those raw ideas into songs, giving them form and refinement. The Wherehouse was the band's clubhouse, a refuge where they could just hang out and rehearse, but it was only a result of how the music took form that the band ended up being recorded there. Jack Douglas, ever aware to the importance of the creative environment influencing the foundation of a song, saw no reason to move the band out of the warehouse into a studio proper — at least until it was time to do overdubs and the vocals — was very aware of the creative process: "The keys the songs were written in were all dependent on the environment we were in. After a couple of weeks of rehearsal, the room started to sound really good. The very thought of moving it out of that room seemed like it would destroy everything about where we were... That record, when I put it on, sounds like truth" (Best Classic Bands, 1/31/2018). Essentially, the band were recording their album at home and there was little difference in feel between jamming, rehearsing, or recording — except during when tape would be rolling... An important part of that process would be through the jams while Tyler listened on seeking to identify a melody, lyrical phrase, or simply inspiration. When a backing track emerged from a process of revision and rearrangement, the onus would then fall to Tyler for the all-important lyrics to be added. This final stage was more often than not a painful, frustrating, and time-consuming part of the process of creation.

Over a period of six weeks in depths of the Boston winter, the basic tracks for six songs were worked out, refined, and ultimately captured to tape utilizing Record Plant's remote truck. Jack Douglas recalled, "You get a great live sound in the Wherehouse when you put a mike in the garage with cement walls. The roadies

— and they have great roadies [led by Bob "Kelly" Kelleher] — built a tent around the mobile truck, so it was 20 degrees outside, but we were warm. But being in the truck for two weeks was a little like living in a submarine, so I was a bit loony when we came out" (Circus, 6/17/1976). Loony or not, what ultimately came out of those initial sessions were the backing tracks — the bedrock that would serve as the album's foundation, and in this case those foundations were rock hard. Moreover, creating the material and capturing it in the same environment gave it a unique flavor with punchiness and rawness. Regardless, the hardest part was yet to come: There were still lyrics to be written, vocals to be recorded, and lead guitar overdubs to be captured. Lyrics would prove to be the challenge: "Aerosmith does much of the instrumental arranging before the vocal melody is even written. And when Steven's writing is coming along slowly, as it did for 'Rocks,' the sessions drag on for weeks past the delivery date, pushing back the album's release and frustrating the band's management as the opening dates of a spring tour loom nearer and nearer" (Circus, 6/17/1976).

Even as they concentrated on the creation of new material, CBS had reissued "Dream On" at the end of 1975 (it's unknown whether the pending litigation with Barber had any bearing on this release; or whether it was simply a matter of keeping the band visible at a time where they would be out of the public view — while giving a neglected gem another shot). According to Tom, "There had to be some kind of demand... Disc jockeys were calling up the record company saying, 'if you don't give us the record, we're going to play it anyway.' They were getting requests" (Phonograph Record, April 1976). It was well received: "This re-release from Aerosmith's first album is a melodic exception to the band's normal heavy metal, wreak havoc format. The hard surface is there but Tyler's plaintive vocals and some economical muscular riffing make 'Dream On' a thinker as well as a mover" (Cashbox, 12/27/1975). The song was reissued again, in November 1976 with "Sweet Emotion" as the B-side (Columbia 13-33327) as part of the "Hall of Fame" series. Promoter Fun Production's David Forest had planned to headline Aerosmith at Anaheim Stadium as early as January — suggesting activities were scheduled far in advance. It was an ambitious plan; stadium shows were usually reserved for the established veteran superstar bands with a very broad mass appeal (Zeppelin, Stones). Forest wasn't deterred, believing that the rock market was growing so big that newly established acts could also make the jump into the stadiums. With any show being a gamble for a promoter, he trusted that most singular characteristic of a successful promoter: gut instinct, though with great risk came the opportunity for a massive payoff.

On January 10, 1976, "Dream On" returned to the Hot-100 (at #81) and started a long steady climb, culminating in it hitting a high position at #6 on Apr. 10 (the single peaked at the same position on Cashbox on Mar. 27). Were that not a background distraction enough, with there being no way for the band to capitalize or promote the single at the same time as writing and recording, it would have provided a continued background drone of motivation (and pressure). There were probably several factors that played into the explosive success Aerosmith enjoyed in the second half of 1976. A strong year of touring was buttressed by the breakout of the band on the charts. The "Toys in the Attic" album had been a slow burn on the charts from the day of its release; slowly building until it reached its zenith on Sept. 13, 1975 at #11 during an impressive 82-week chart run (at the end of which it took a brief two-week break before returning for another 46 weeks through October 1977, essentially encompassing the band's golden era).

The success of the album drove sales of the back-catalogue. Sophomore effort, "Get Your Wings," returned to the Billboard Top-200 on Sept. 20, 1975 and remained active until Nov. 15, reaching as high as #74, a position that eclipsed its original chart run in 1974. It charted for the fourth time from Jan. 31 through Aug. 1976, lingering (rather than languishing) the bottom half of the Top-200. The debut album also came back on to the charts, Sept. through Nov. 1975, and again in Jan. 1976 — at a time when the band were off the road. That album ultimately climbed to #21 and stayed on the charts until Sept. 1976. The success of the reissue of the "Dream On" single initially helped continue drive the sales of all three albums; a continuation of the strategy CBS had undertaken to capitalize on whole catalogues rather than just focus on an act's current product. Until that point, the band had not had any wildly successful commercial singles, even if they had started to develop a niche on radio airplay. There would be little doubt in looking back to 1973 that "Dream On" had not been given a chance or support by the label, so regardless of its success a wrong had been righted. To celebrate the gold certification of the first three studio albums during 1975, Columbia issued a special promotional box, "Pure Gold from Rock and Roll's Golden Boys" (Columbia A3S-187). The albums were housed in a gold box and presented as a thank you for the support radio, record account and reviewer personnel in March 1976.

With the basic tracks captured, the one band member had personal matters to attend to... On Feb. 22, Brad Whitford married Lori Suzanne Philips at the North Miami garden home of her parents. Joined by the rest of the band the nuptial break was all too quickly over, with them reconvening in New York City to take up the next phase of creation at Record Plant's Studio A. As work continued on the album the lyrics became the focus. Jack recalled, "Steven moves in with me when we're working on an album. In the morning I wake him up with a cassette and a cup of coffee — 'here you go' — most of the melody lines have all been worked out and he's singing phonetically. I'll suggest a thing to him here and there; give him a kick this way and he starts to come around. He's really the main drive of the band" (Record World, 12/25/1976). Things seemed to be going according to plan and the initial run of tour dates for mid-April started to be announced in mid-March.

The first Aerosmith album to not feature a cover recording (and only one of the band's 71–79 incarnation), "Rocks" saw the members other than Tyler and/or Perry core increasing their contributions to the songwriting process. While four of the album's songs were attributed to Tyler/Perry — "Back in the Saddle," "Rats in the Cellar," "Get the Lead Out," and "Lick and a Promise" — Brad contributed two songs with Steven. Steven was adamant that the funked up "Last Child" was going to be a disco hit, and its style gave him the scope to guide Joey in a different direction for the percussion (the song had started out with Steven behind the kit infusing a more jazzy beat). Starting with a Whitford riff titled "Soul Saver," it was clear the band was full of ideas, even if they were not yet fully formed and required transformation. Given Tyler's enthusiasm, and the song's stylistic differentiation from the band's usual sound, it is hardly surprising that the song would be released as the album's first single, backed with "Combination" (Columbia 3-10359), towards the end of May. Respectably, it reached #21 on the Billboard Hot-100. Cashbox also liked the single: "Aerosmith's remarkable popularity will not be dimmed by this single. It's right in the groove: a straightforward rock tune with a slick, rhythm-oriented arrangement. From the album 'Rocks' this will rise high on the pop charts and receive tremendous FM and AM" (Cashbox, 6/12/1976). The song was fully embellished once the band reached New York with session player Paul Prestopino doubling the slide guitar with banjo.

Jack Douglas was impressed by Tom Hamilton's continued development as a songwriter and he brought in "Uncle Tom's Cabin," which became "Sick as a Dog" on the album. Tom recalled, "Jack is a very open person. He always has time for what people come up with. 'Sick' started on guitar and I wasn't sure about it but playing it for Jack I realized it had a lot of potential. We recorded it last, and I'm glad because everybody was hot then" (Circus, 6/17/1976). Jack, too, was equally complimentary towards Tom: "Tom is coming along in his writing. He's got a lot of tunes, and even though there's only one on this album, there could have been more" (Circus, 6/17/1976). For the recording Joe performed most of the bass, until leaving the control room to play a solo, and handing Steven the bass for the end. Because Tom had written the song on guitar, he'd play guitar on the recording.

Album lead-off track, "Back in the Saddle" (also a prospective album title), also served as the album's final single, backed with the second of Tyler/Whitford contributions, the apocalyptic "Nobody's Fault" (Columbia 3-10516), when released in late-March 1977. Unfortunately, the single languished on the charts only reaching #38, not a complete disaster, and it did successfully bridge the period where management had hoped the band would complete its next studio album. Musically, Joe had been inspired by Peter Green and Jack Bruce's use of a six-string bass, which he used to write the song (a Fender Bass VI). He particularly enjoyed the sound the instrument, which he described as "lead bass," gave the song. The writing of the song was straight-forward, according to Joe, "I was very high on heroin... That riff just floated right through me" (Guitar World, April 1997).

"Rats in the Cellar" started out as "Tit for Tat," and the title seemed a natural response to the previous album's title. Steven has recounted how lyrics in this song were influenced by the murder of their drug connection while recording at the Record Plant. That dealer, a peripheral music manager and hairdresser, may have been murdered (along with his young girlfriend) on Mar. 10. The swaggering "Get the Lead Out" dripped with the sleaze the band was living at the time, while "Lick and a Promise" represented the mission the band had every time they walked on to the stage: To win the audience. Joe Perry would sing his first lead vocal on an Aerosmith album, albeit as a semi-duet with Steven, on his solo contribution, "Combination." Like other songs, it was loosely based on the life the band members were living, mainly the growing involvement with drugs of various descriptions. More specifically, it was written in frustration at Steven's snail pace lyric writing.

Steven's "Home Tonight" goodnight lullaby closes the album. A seemingly natural successor to the aged "Dream On," the song was released as the album's much-hyped second single (Columbia 3-10407) in late-Aug., backed with "Pandora's Box" (the back catalogue seldom being neglected). It floundered at an unimpressive #71 on the Billboard Hot-100 during a dismal four-week run — "Rocks" may have been a Platinum album without the benefit of a top ten single (Billboard Ad, 9/3/1976), but "Home Tonight" did not end up being that single... "Hard rockers and big-sellers Aerosmith have come up with a song that has a couple of unusual shifts in it. The soft, almost ballad-like vocal holds a lot of appeal, and the harsher rock 'n' roll bridge seems to fit just right. The vocal is reminiscent of some of McCartney's hard blues numbers. The record should chart strong off of FM progressive play" (Cashbox, 9/11/1976). In late-November, in a blatant attempt to repeat the late-1975 single reissue success, "Walk This Way" was reissued with a new B-side, "Uncle Salty" (Columbia 3-10449). The exercise soon bore fruit again with the single charting for 17 weeks reaching a high of #10 on the Billboard Hot-100 on Jan. 29, 1977. It did even better on Cashbox hitting #7.

By April Jack, already involved with pre-production for Starz's debut, was recruited to help finish up Moxy's second album following last-minute "finishing touches" being put on the album, resulting in the first two weeks of shows being rescheduled. Of course, there may have been the small matter of letting "Dream On" run its course on the charts before launching the band's new material. Whatever was happening in the background, the "Rocks" project was drawing to a close. Steve wasn't completely happy with how things ended: "This last album I couldn't even stay for the final mixes. We had already cancelled two weeks of dates because of some final mastering. I insist on being there. I know what went down. Since having so much to do with the songs, I wanted at least to be able to mix the songs a little bit. I want to know where the edits are going. It shouldn't all be left up to your producer, although we have the finest producers in the world" (Sounds, 10/16/1976). Any minor gripes wouldn't matter. What resulted from the two months of grind was a powerful mix of catchy riffs and tongue-in-cheek lyrics. It was a raw slab of sleazy rock 'n' roll, Americanized Yardbirds inspired blues with punkish ferocity, but most importantly catchy, clever, and lacking in overt pretentiousness. Joe was pleased: "Well, it's better, with everyone we're getting better, the songs are getting more unified and the whole band's coming up with worthwhile ideas. I'm looking forward to the next one because I know it'll be better again. We're managing to get into a groove in the studio now and we're trying to keep it that way" (Sounds, 10/16/1976).

It was also Joe's idea to name the album "Rocks." What description could be better than what he felt was the hardest rock they'd made. He'd also suggested the title the year before for the album that became "Toys in the Attic," though this time it stuck. "Aerosmith Five" was also considered, but likely would have caused more confusion for those not considering that it described the number of band members rather than albums to that point. As had been the case with their previous album, the band returned to Ernie Cefalu's Pacific Eye and Ear for the creation of their packing. A Scott Enyart photograph of five diamonds would form the basis for the cover illustration. The inner dust-sleeve served as a more expansive canvas with a cartoon illustration of the band by old band friend Teresa Stokes on one side, and collage of photos on the other. The caricature was initially intended to serve as the band's stage backdrop for the tour, but even after having the artist paint it twice and having it made, Steve decided that he "hated" it and it wasn't used. The first version of the painting was purportedly lost in a fire and Steven requested she paint it again. The illustration would be cropped for use on the dust sleeve.

The album was released on May 14. Initially the album was not supported by a new single with "Dream On" continuing to linger on charts. That double-edged sword may have also impacted the marketing of the new album with the lead single having to be something that countered "Dream On." Entered the Billboard album charts at #25 on May 29. In the United States, the album was certified Gold by the RIAA on May 21, 1976 and Platinum on July 9, 1976; 2X Platinum followed on October 19, 1984; 3X on December 21, 1988; and (most recently) 4X on February 26, 2001. Gold was awarded by the CRIA (Canada - 50,000 units) on September 1, 1976 and Platinum on November 1, 1976. In the SoundScan era the album sold 409,451 units between 1991 and Feb. 2007. In the U.S., the album reached #3 on the Billboard Top-200 charts (6/26/1976) during a 53-week run, and the same on Cashbox (6/12/1976) for 51 weeks. The album was blocked from any chance at the top spot by "Frampton Comes Alive" and the Wing's "At the Speed of Sound." Internationally, the album reached #13 in Japan, #14 in Canada, and #46 in Sweden. Either way, the performance of the album was impressive without the benefit of a resident hit single.

For the tour, the backdrop used would be the simply black one emblazoned with large Aerosmith name in script. Other effects were kept to a minimum, deliberately, having been overdone by many another act. A single flash-pot was used as an attention grabber at the start of the show and the rest of the show was handled with lighting. Bob See's See Factor Industry lighting company pitched the idea of the descending A-frame lighting grid that was used as the show's culmination. Bob described it: "It took us six weeks from the time the go was given to build it — five weeks of engineering. But it was worth it. It's designed to withstand 60 mph winds for outdoor dates. It has a set of towers; it can be self-supporting. It's actually quite a feat of engineering. It weighs 10,000 pounds and stays up on two 12" cylinders! It's got probably more than 30 miles of wiring. Six people can have it put together, focused, and ready to go in four hours" (Circus, 10/12/1976). Other core members included Roy Bickle, who oversaw the lighting, PA crew boss Peter Alexander for Tasco, with Robert "Nite Bob" Czaykowski mixing the sound. All told, the tour entourage had grown for the "Rocks" tour. Crew Chief Henry Smith detailed, "Last time, we had 12 people on the road... There are 31 people on the road this time — six for sound, seven for lights, the group's personal people, truck drivers, stage crew" (Circus, 10/12/1976). Some of the others included Dick "The Rabbit" Hansen, whose services included teching for Joe; Nick Spigel, who'd do the same for Brad and Tom during shows, and road manager Bob Kelleher.

With original dates Apr. 13–27 rescheduled; the "Rocks" tour commenced with a sold-out show in St. Louis on Apr. 27. The set still heavily favored "Toys in the Attic" material, but that would change throughout the tour with "Lick and a Promise," "Rats in the Cellar," "Sick as a Dog," "Get the Lead Out," and "Last Child" appearing. The band also performed five stadium-sized shows throughout the initial 59-show leg — Detroit, Washington DC, Pittsburgh, Seattle, and Anaheim — to a cumulative and impressive attendance of 329,952! However, they soon tired of these massive shows. According to David Krebs, "This is the last big tour. After this one there won't be much touring... they're already big, and they just don't need to kill themselves anymore... So, next year, their touring schedule is going to be severely limited — so they can concentrate on putting out product" (Rolling Stone #220, 8/26/1976). Playing to the large crowds simply wasn't fun for the band. For Steven, it was a matter of aesthetics: "All you could see was security guys... I had trouble looking out and being able to see a kid. It's so ugly when you have to sing to security guards. F — muscle heads, who wants to sing to them" (Melody Maker, 10/16/1976). But there was also a more obvious issue with the stadium-sized shows: "The matters of sound and visibility are always a problem at outdoor shows, but they are particularly noticeable — and discouraging — when seeing a band for the first time. When the stadium shows were introduced, it was assumed that only the biggest of the veteran acts — the Stones, the Who, Zeppelin — would be able to draw enough people to fill the outdoor facilities. By the time these bands reached the stadium level, the reasoning went, their audiences would be so familiar with the groups' music and stage moves that the fans could just use their imaginations to fill in any gaps caused by the huge setting." Newer acts in a fast-expanding rock market booking shows that results in a situation where many are seeing the bands for the first time and therefore getting less out of the experience. " (Los Angeles Times, 9/14/1976). The band's schedule also changed so that they wouldn't have to perform more than two nights in a row, to help protect Steven's voice.

The "Rocks" tour saw the band's first true international jaunts. While they had expected to tour Asia in the autumn, a European run was booked instead. Steven was looking forward to the shows: "We got a progress report about England. On a lot of shows the tickets have gone on sale already and we're doing real good. We're gonna knock their tits right off their chests. I know that nobody's rockin' out over there. It's a shame" (Sounds, 10/16/1976). The tour started in England, with the band arriving in London on Oct. 9. However, the band enjoyed negligible radio play or popularity there, and like other U.S. bands making the flight across the pond, they found themselves going from 20,000-seat arenas to antiquated halls with less than 4,000 seats. If they were tired of stadiums, the European tour was a stark reminder of the other side of the spectrum. The tour concluded in Paris on Nov. 1 and the band were quickly back on U.S. soil for their next leg of dates leading to the Christmas holiday break. It was during this leg of the tour that the wear and tear of the road started to show. Following their first hometown show on Nov. 15, Steven was diagnosed with laryngitis and shows Nov. 16–24, were postponed (one date was cancelled). Touring resumed on Nov. 29 without further public drama. The band's visit to Japan took place at the end of Jan. into early Feb. with the band vacationing in Hawaii on their return. The Japanese record label marked the occasion with the release of an album, "Wild Platinum," which compiled 13 songs from the four studio albums.

Assorted review excerpts:

"Quintet has followed a formula of basic rock and has quietly sneaked up to become one of the major concert attractions and record selling acts in the country. Very basic stuff, but far better than the average heavy rock group. And, though they are not great lyrically (sounding, indeed, like a latter-day Black Sabbath at times), the energy level of the music and the skill in the instrumental work more than make up for any lyrical shortcomings. Lead singer Steven Tyler is among the best of rock's singer/screamers, the band avoids pretensions, and the result is one that is simply better than most acts of this type. One key — a marked difference between the songs. A fun music that draws the listener in — rare enough these days" (Billboard, 5/22/1976).

"Having already established themselves as one of the top rock acts of the year. Aerosmith offers an album that's chock full of rock gems. Every tune will grab the FM progressive programmers while there are several titles that will also turn up on AM stations everywhere. Among these are 'Combination' and 'Nobody's Fault,' which sound something like the Stones and Led Zeppelin respectively, proving Aerosmith to be a successfully derivative band" (Cashbox, 5/22/1976).

"Some bands — such as Bachman-Turner Overdrive and the Doobie Brothers — are either calmly enjoyed or ignored by most rock fans. But others — notably Grand Funk Railroad and Black Sabbath in recent years — have been objects of an intense love 'em or hate 'em relationship with both fans and the rock media. Aerosmith is the latest example. For those looking for 'art' or new direction in rock, Aerosmith has precious little to offer. To the hard-core, teen-age rock fan seeking power and abandon in his music, however, the band provides an abundance of high energy assault. The group's ability to deliver the latter, in fact, has enabled it to enter the rock superstar class in recent months despite little support from critics or (until the 'Dream On' single) AM airplay. The band's enormous success (its first three albums have all passed the $1 million sales mark and it headlines this summer at the 55,000-seat Anaheim Stadium) only serves to make those who shudder over the group's lack of creative vision all the more hostile. As writers and other commentators become increasingly vociferous in their attacks on Aerosmith, the group's fans, quite naturally, rally around it with growing allegiance. Being an underdog, it should be noted, has often been an advantageous position in rock.

'Rocks,' the band's fourth album, has just been released and it should add to the controversy around the quintet. After listening to the album, however, it's hard to identify fully with either side. The album (already in the Top 10 nationally) isn't substantial enough to endorse adoringly, but neither does it stir any sense of outrage. In fact, it rocks a lot more than most albums these days... 'Back in the Saddle' has all the energy, intensity, and snarl one could want from the opening track on a rock 'n' roll album. It certainly has more of the cited traits than anything on the new Rolling Stones album, to name a band whose work has often been used to point out Aerosmith's limitations and derivative nature. The truth is that — as much as lead singer Steven Tyler's pouting lips and stage manner may remind one of Mick Jagger — there is little in this song or the rest of the album to remind one of the Stones. But it is possible to see many other influences.

'Back in the Saddle,' for instance, borders so much on a Led Zeppelin-meets-Bad Company pose that you'd think Swan Records (which handles both Zeppelin and Bad Company) would be able to win an injunction for copyright infringement except that everyone in the pop music business has long stolen from everyone else anyway. Sure, it would be nice to have more imagination in the songwriting, more adventure in the arrangements, more originality in the playing and more range in Tyler's voice. But it's easy to see the band's appeal. Despite the severe limitations, Aerosmith is filling the high energy need (particularly in 'Back in the Saddle' and the explosive 'Nobody's Fault') in a time when the rock scene is all too sedate. For its audience: good of a kind. MAYBE" (Los Angeles Times, 6/5/1976).

"New England's homegrown supergroup, Aerosmith, has come of age. It's reached that point which frequently comes after several consecutive gold albums when a group thinks it can foist anything on its audience and get away with it. So, while most groups (or individual performers, for that matter) try to break new ground and spruce up their basic sound with an innovative touch here and there, the Boston based band has opted to confine itself to the well-trodden turf of simplistic heavy metal tomfoolery. Aerosmith's latest infliction is called 'ROCKS' (Columbia PC-34165). The quotation marks are appropriate, since there is considerable ambiguity as to just what the title means. If it's a noun, the answer is obvious: the jacket photo of five glimmering diamonds merely represents each of the quintet's members. A listen to the contents, though, quickly reveals that the word is more likely a verb, and a euphemism at that. There is one thing Aerosmith does NOT do here, and that's rock. Sure, they go through the motions, dishing out some fairly hard-driving contortions and borrowing blatantly from Led Zeppelin and the Stones; at least two cuts — 'Get the Lead Out' and 'Sick as a Dog' nearly take off, but somehow, they never quite generate that necessary spark. Like KISS, Grand Funk and myriads of other currently popular charlatan outfits, Aerosmith has learned it can reap the most commercial success by relying on safe, smug formulas to please the madding crowd. Plagued by lyrics which are alternately banal and obtuse, trite arrangements and sloppy mixing (Steve Tyler's vocals are often unintelligible), 'ROCKS' is hard to take all at once and best not taken at all" (Bangor Daily News, 6/12/1976).

"They had 'Toys in the Attic' in their last album and come up with 'Rats in the Cellar' for this one. Big deal. There's nothing on this release that has the tender tension of 'Dream On,' the instrumental hook of 'No More,' the momentum of 'Train Kept 'a Rollin'' or the bratty charm of 'Walk this Way" — all songs that made their earlier albums sure hits. Once Aerosmith was innovative, even when they stole their main ideas from other bands. Now they've slipped into the lazy habit of having Steve Tyler shout a few lyric lines, with the rest of the band shouting back the title as a one-line chorus. Too many of these songs sound alike. Lead guitarist Joe Perry isn't playing up to any sort of professional par. I've heard guys in local bar bands play much better. Tyler's rock ballad 'Home Tonight' is acceptable at best. The catchiest cut is 'Sick as a Dog.' That's a dubious achievement since the whole idea of the song is repulsive. At this point, Aerosmith is a drag, and that's not the way rock ought to be" (Detroit Free Press, 6/22/1976).

"Saints preserve us. The five-piece Boston band that wants stardom so very badly is achieving it. And this despite beginning in Sunapee, New Hampshire, and having a lead singer who looks and performs like a rock 'n' roll windup doll and playing home-grown material which deals mostly with adolescent sex while being more stupid than vulgar. Aerosmith's fourth album will undoubtedly sell well, moving the group further along the road from local phenom to national chartbuster. It is about as subtle as a mugging, filled with standard heavy metal guitar riffs and thinly veiled teenage titilators ('Back in the Saddle,' 'Get the Lead Out'). Despite the musical posing and calculated scruffiness, 'Rocks' will never be confused with Stones" (Boston Globe, 7/15/1976).

"Whether or not 'Rocks' is hot depends on your vantage point. If your hard-rock tastes were honed in the Sixties, as this band's obviously were, Aerosmith is a polished echo of Yardbird's guitar rock liberally spiced with the Stones' sexual swagger. If you're a teen of the Seventies, they are likely to be the flashiest hard-rock band you've ever seen. While the band has achieved phenomenal commercial success, their fourth album fails to prove that they can grow and innovated as their models did. The most winning aspect of 'Rocks' is that ace metal producer Jack Douglas and the band (listed as coproducers for the first time) have returned to the ear-boxing sound that made their second album, 'Get Your Wings,' their best. The guitar riffs and Steven Tyler's catlike voice fairly jump out of the speakers. This initially hides the fact that the best performances here — 'Lick and a Promise,' 'Sick as a Dog' and 'Rats in the Cellar' — are essentially remakes of the highlights of the relatively flat 'Toys in the Attic.' The songs have all the band's trademarks and while they can be accused of neither profundity nor originality, Aerosmith's stylized hard-rock image and sound pack a high-energy punch most other heavy metal bands lack... The material is 'Rocks'' major flaw, mostly pale remakes of their earlier hits, notably 'Dream On,' a first-album ballad that helped make the complete Aerosmith gold. Aerosmith may have their hard-rock wings, but they won't truly fly until their inventiveness catches up to their fast-maturing professionalism" (Rolling Stone #218, 7/29/1976).

"Still one of the flashiest hard rock-and-roll groups of the 70s, Aerosmith is quickly losing its fire. Its fourth LP brings little variety and does not come near matching its 'Toys in the Attic' album,' the best effort to its credit. Also, to its credit is that Aerosmith's four successive LPs are charted and selling extremely well. The group is far from entering the boredom category as some groups have, but the lack of innovation and originality is obviously noticed in this recent album. Steve Tyler's feline-vocal approach is only faintly audible in too many of the tunes, killing such well-written pieces as 'Lick and a Promise' and 'Rats in the Cellar.' His sexual Mick Jagger approach is only a cover-up for lyrics that say nothing and do nothing for a hyped-up sound. Though his delivery is polished, the groups material appears to be at best mediocre" (Spokane Daily Chronicle, 8/5/1976).

"Well, listen, the new Aerosmith album just came in the main, too. (And you thought there was no hope...) Produced in a garbage can with Japanese guitars and a 39c tape-recorder mike, there's no question that on 'Rocks,' Aerosmith mean it. That this is rock & roll. These guys aren't pretending, they're raggedy. I know for a fact that it took them as long to record this as it took KISS to record their Sgt. Pepper's grease pie ['Destroyer']. But compared with KISS, this is positively rural, this is Robert Johnson. There's nary a clean riff on this record, let alone an orchestra or a choir. Slinky is perhaps the most operative word. Listen to the riff in 'Back in the Saddle' — now you can't tell me that Joe Perry tunes his guitar. No matter what, he's a hit-it-if-you-happen-to, Chuck Berry riffer extraordinaire (Ace Frehley is more akin to The Tonight Show's Tony Mattola). On top of the rubber band guitar work you get Steve Tyler snarling definitely... While you know that the latest KISS music sounds sterile and mass-produced, at the same time you wonder how Aerosmith ever got this sprawling mess into a regularly shaped album cover. Part of the difference lies in the fact that Aerosmith don't have they knack for the hook that KISS does. KISS (along with their multitude of co-authors, whose number now includes Kim Fowley) are capable of writing a song that's catchy all the way through. Aerosmith, on the other hand, struggle, spinning off in that direction on the throb of a rhythm section which pulsates somewhat irregularly like a gelatinous monster from outer space" (Circus, 8/24/1976).

182 | Aerosmith on Tour, 1973-85

1976 - Rocks

April 13 **TEMP HOLD-DATE
Hulman Center @ I.S.U.
Terra Haute, IN

Notes:
- Appearing on early itineraries released in early February, this show was instead scheduled for May 26 and doesn't appear to have ever been put on sale. Instead, a show with Lynyrd Skynyrd was booked on this date with the Outlaws opening.

April 14 **POSTPONED
Municipal Auditorium
Kansas City, MO

Notes:
- By early April, this show was rescheduled for Apr. 28. The reason given for the batch of April postponements was "last-minute" recording required to finish up the band's new album.

April 16 **POSTPONED
Kiel Auditorium
St. Louis, MO

Notes:
- This show was rescheduled for Apr. 27.

April 17 **POSTPONED
T.H. Barton Coliseum
Little Rock, AR

Notes:
- This show was rescheduled for June 21.

April 19 **POSTPONED
Hara Arena @ U.D.
Dayton, OH

Notes:
- This show was rescheduled for May 6 on Apr. 13.

April 21 **POSTPONED
Gardens
Louisville, KY

Notes:
- This show was rescheduled for May 5. It had already sold-out at the time it was postponed on Apr. 17.

April 22 **POSTPONED
Market Square Arena
Indianapolis, IN

Notes:
- This show was rescheduled for May 3.

April 24 **POSTPONED
Roberts Stadium
Evansville, IN

Notes:

184 | Aerosmith on Tour, 1973-85

- This show was rescheduled for June 16.

April 25 **POSTPONED
Allen County Memorial Coliseum
Fort Wayne, IN
Notes:
- This show was rescheduled for May 25.

April 27 **POSTPONED
Milwaukee, WI
Notes:
- This show was rescheduled for July 8.

April 27
Kiel Auditorium
St. Louis, MO
Promoter: Contemporary Productions
Other act(s): Angel (opener)
Reported audience: 10,586 **SOLD-OUT
Reported gross: $57,250
Notes:
- The first date of the "Rocks" tour.
- From a local review: "Aerosmith played at high volume most of the set but kept it manageable so that lyrics were understandable and guitar parts were not lost in the clutter. The two guitarists in the band shared lead parts like gentlemen and even toned things down a bit when singer Steve Tyler stepped to the microphone. Tyler's style, like that of the whole band, lacked flashiness, but the fit to the music was perfect. His voice has a kind of cultivated raspiness that makes for great rock singers. He missed a note or two, probably because of difficulties in hearing himself through the sound system. Besides a lot of new material, the band did 'Dream On' and a revamped version of 'Walkin' the Dog.' That old rhythm and blues number never sounded so good" (St. Louis Post-Dispatch, 4/28/1976).

April 28
Kemper Arena
Kansas City, MO
Promoter: Contemporary Productions
Other act(s): Slade, Angel (opener)
Reported audience: 13,200 / 13,500 (97.78%)
Reported gross: $78,310
Set list: Mama Kin / Write Me / S.O.S. (Too Bad) / Lick and a Promise / Big Ten Inch Record / Sweet Emotion / Dream On / Lord of the Thighs / Last Child / Walk this Way / Sick as a Dog / Same Old Song and Dance / Train Kept A Rollin' / Get the Lead Out / Toys in the Attic
Notes:
- An AUD recording circulates from this show.

April 30
McElroy Auditorium
Waterloo, IA
Promoter: Fox Productions
Other act(s): Rush, Angel (opener)

1976 - Rocks

Reported audience: 10,000 **SOLD-OUT
Reported gross: $60,000
Partial set list(s): Walkin' the Dog / Walk this Way / Adam's Apple / Lick and a Promise / Same Old Song and Dance / Train Kept A Rollin' / Toys in the Attic
Notes:
- Reported as the first advance sell-out at the venue, even with some 5,000 fans turned away at the door. The overcrowding of the venue resulted in safety concerns about an appropriate limit on its capacity being established, with the local fire chief suggesting the official capacity of the venue was 6,977 and that concerts should be limited to 7,500. The promoter countered that shows of less than 7,800 would limit the bands that could be booked at the venue due to the financial considerations.
- From a local review: "Aerosmith played to more than 10,000 happy fans at McElroy Auditorium Friday evening... The thought of 10,000 bodies pressed inside the auditorium was a frightening one; but everything was handled smoothly. A 'rough and raunchy' (as they call themselves) rhythm and blues band, Aerosmith is a crowd pleaser; vocalist Steve Tyler's antics in a devil-red modernistic tuxedo gave the relaxed audience something to watch as well as listen to. For, it seems that the trend in rock and roll today is to give a show that will please all the senses, as this one did indeed. Murky, smoky air took care of the smell and taste, and Aerosmith took over from there. The group is pretty good — no, I should say great — simply because they produce and exciting concert; it doesn't create the urge to buy their albums, but it does make an interesting evening. A show that was fast and interesting led listeners through the group's first album, to their two current hit singles. All members of the five-man group are adequate performers, every now and then, some really exciting musical ideas would emerge... A flurry of frenzied energy, vocalist Tyler really makes this band, and his vocal variations are well planned and executed" (Waterloo Courier, 5/2/1976).
- A partial AUD recording circulates from this show.

May 1
Civic Center Arena
St. Paul, MN

Promoter: Schon Presents
Other act(s): Slade, Thin Lizzy (opener)
Reported audience: ~14,000 / 17,500 (80%)
Reported gross: $82,610
Notes:
- Apparently the band sound-checked late and were

enraged that the promoter opened the venue doors and allowed fans in before they were done. They vowed to never perform a show for him again (the newspaper article noted 1975, but that was unlikely with Wishbone Ash headlining that show, though obviously the promoter could also be confusing the headliner).
- From a local review: "Aerosmith may never become a household name like the Beatles or Rolling Stones, but the quintet has rapidly become the new rock hero to America's teen-agers... Aerosmith triumphed again Saturday night with an exciting, well-paced concert of heavy metal rock before 14,000 vociferous young people... Onstage Aerosmith, unlike its heavy metal competitors, plays with personality. Lead singer and principal songwriter Steven Tyler is the source of energy and excitement. Even if most of his words were indecipherable Saturday, he proved to be a capable heavy metal screamer. His voice was less than exceptional, but sex appeal was Tyler's chief allure. He physically resembles Carly Simon and Mick Jagger. Tyler handled himself onstage with all the charm and panache of Jagger. He danced, pranced, and leaped across the stage. The singer displayed all the classic rock star moves. Behind Tyler was a powerhouse band. Drummer Joey Kramer, bassist Tom Hamilton and guitarists Perry and Whitford were less than spectacular musicians but they did their part and let Tyler carry the show" (Minneapolis Star, 5/3/1976).

May 3
Market Square Arena

Indianapolis, IN
Promoter: Sunshine Promotions
Other act(s): Stu Daye, Montrose
Reported audience: 19,000 **OVERSOLD
Reported gross: $114,021
Partial set list: Mama Kin / Write Me / Walkin' the Dog / Big Ten Inch Record / Dream On / Same Old Song and Dance / S.O.S. (Too Bad) / Lord of the Thighs / Somebody / Adam's Apple / Walk this Way / Sweet Emotion / Train Kept A Rollin' / Toys in the Attic
Notes:
- Stu Daye was also managed by Leber-Krebs and had released his Jack Douglas produced "Free Parking" album via Columbia in March. The partial set list is not ordered in sequence of performance, just in order as noted in a review of the show in the Howe Tower (5/14/1976).
- From a local review: "Tony Orlando did it. John Denver did it. And last night the hard-rock group Aerosmith did it. Aerosmith, whose hit single 'Dream On' has become one of the all-time classics of the hard-rock set, played before a capacity crowd of 19,000 last night in Market Square Arena... Unlike the Orlando and Denver concerts, Aerosmith did not perform in the round. The concert wad 'festival seating,' which means first-come, first-serve seating" (Indianapolis News, 5/4/1976).

May 5
Louisville Gardens
Louisville, KY
Promoter: Sunshine Promotions
Other act(s): Stu Daye
Reported audience: 6,000 **SOLD-OUT
Reported gross: $39,424
Notes:
- At the time, this show marked the fastest sell-out in the venue's history.

May 6
Hara Arena
Dayton, OH
Promoter: Windy City Productions
Other act(s): Stu Daye
Reported audience: 11,905 / 13,170 (90.39%)
Reported gross: $70,970

May 8
Metropolitan Stadium
Pontiac (Detroit), MI
Promoter: Steve Glantz / Stadium Attractions
Other act(s): Foghat, Ted Nugent, The Outlaws
Reported audience: 76,900 **SOLD-OUT
Reported gross: $645,824
Notes:
- At this event there were 45 drugs-related arrests, and some 188 attendees were treated by nurses for injuries and the usual sort of concert-event-induced maladies.
- This show was professionally recorded and filmed — or perhaps more aptly the video feed from the screen was captured — and several performances were included on the 1987 "Video Scrapbook" package: "Toys in the Attic," "Sweet Emotion," "Walk this Way," "Adam's Apple," "Train Kept A Rollin'," and "S.O.S. (Too Bad)." Plans for the recording, circulated to the press in June 1976, were that the live tracks would not be used for a live album, but the best would be used in some form on a future album. A Rolling Stone magazine and photographer were on hand to capture photographs which were used in a layout for that magazine (Issue #220, 8/26/1976).

- From a local review: "Musical mayhem was rampant at Ponmet Stadium Saturday night in Pontiac when Ted Nugent, Foghat, and Aerosmith faced a throng of eighty thousand teenage rock maniacs. The show was more an event than a concert, a coldly calculated event designed to make money. The ticket prices were incredibly steep, especially since the production was mounted incompetently and exploitatively. It was virtually impossible to see the acts because of the size of the stadium. To alleviate the problem a massive video screen was suspended above the stage, which proved ineffective until the stadium got totally dark, which it never did. The acoustics were abominable: a bilevel structure built from outsize amps pumped distorted sound into a convulsive echo. No one else seemed to care however... Aerosmith, the headliners, were greeted by an insane and frenzied ovation, which was far from deserved. They are quite possibly the worst group I have ever seen, and probably the most successful of the nouveau punk-rockers. Their set consisted largely of new songs from their new album and hit singles.

The music was unimaginative, largely a background for the lead singer's wailing and unrhythmic gyrations. Judging from the audience reaction, it was obvious that the group could do no wrong, but when a group believes it as well, there is trouble in the offing. Punk-rock reaches its artistic height when the artists involved have a good sense of the ridiculous like Jagger, and Johansen (lead singer of the New York Dolls). The trouble with Aerosmith, particularly their vocalist Steven Tyler, is that they take themselves too seriously, which destroys the effectiveness of the musical style and stage performance in the genre. As a cultural event, the show was unparalleled. There was music, visuals, atmosphere, and drama that truly reflected the derangement of the teenage rock scene. As a musical event it was chaotic, and maimed at best, but even so, a testimonial to Detroit's rabid tastes in rock and roll" (Michigan Daily, 5/12/1976).
- From a mainstream review: "Only a small proportion of the 80,000 Aerosmith fans were able to see and hear the band and, in order to join this small proportion, it was necessary to suffer the extreme discomfort of being amongst those pressed close to the front of the stage. Elsewhere in the stadium it was necessary to use binoculars or imagination to watch the act. At the very back, a telescope from Jodrell Bank might have helped. A critical assessment of Aerosmith's talents as musicians is impossible under these circumstances. From where I was sitting, they sounded like a permanent drone, a rhythmic thumping punctuated by vocals squeals. It was noticeable, too, that though I was halfway up the arena, I could talk to my neighbors and be heard without raising my voice unduly, and that's rare for a hard-rock gig... One song in their repertoire is a standout these days, a new tune called 'Dream On' which has now become a recognized highlight of the act. It's a stunner and one of which they can be justly proud: a medium-paced rocker with tremendous vocals and a chorus hook of great immediacy. No other song they play, not even a rousing stab at 'Walkin' the Dog', sticks in the memory quite like 'Dream On'" (Melody Maker, 7/24/1976).

May 10
Madison Square Garden
New York City, NY
Promoter: Concerts East
Other act(s): Ted Nugent
Reported audience: 19,600 **SOLD-OUT
Notes:

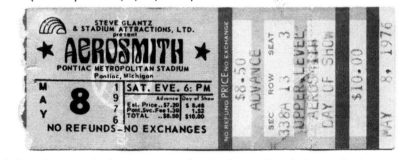

- Steven's mother and Joey's family attended the show and after party at the St. Regis Hotel. Press duties followed the next morning at the Forum club. A photo spread was included in May 1976 issue of Rock Scene.
- From an industry review: "It was an evening of 'heavy duty' rock 'n' roll, and Aerosmith and Nugent generated enough power May 10 to launch the Garden into space. Although the acts were matched in appeal, the musical results were mixed, with unknown-in-the-East Nugent delivering the quality and Aerosmith the quantity... Aerosmith's set drew a greater crowd response, but the quality of the music was considerably less. The tone of the sound and of the audience was 'very high' and 'very distorted.' Although there was a lot of energy coming from the stage, little of it was solid music. The chart single 'Dream On' was the strongest selection, but the vocal levels were all off, and 'Walk this Way,' 'Same Old Song and Dance' and 'Get Your Wings' seemed to melt into the jamming. Aerosmith may 'have its wings,' but it has to get its act more together than displayed at this particular shows" (Billboard, 5/22/1976).

- From another industry review: "Like its closest competitor, KISS, Aerosmith won its initial success the hard way: without a hit single, without much FM airplay, without a great deal of promotion, the group built up its sizeable following by touring incessantly throughout the heartlands and the east coast. Word of mouth was its meal-ticket, and the more Aerosmith returned to an area, the less audience resistance it met... Musically, Aerosmith's approach is fairly straightforward and no-nonsense. Solid power riffing by guitarist Joe Perry (who has developed into a redoubtable rhythm master) and Brad Whitford (who also slips in some stinging, tasty lead lines every now and then) propels each number as bassist Tom Hamilton and drummer Joey Kramer provide the solid bottom. Soaring over all of this, of course, are the distinctive, gritty vocals of Steven Tyler...

Aerosmith demonstrated its unflagging power. However, there was one moment that was both tender and tough; when those years of road work paid off handsomely; when the band members surely convinced themselves once and for all that they would never look back again: illuminated by a dim red spotlight, Tyler caressed and toyed with the first three verses of a song. Leaning on the mike stand, he swayed slightly to the beat of the music that rose then fell — teasingly so — in intensity. Once more the music rose. Tyler straightened up, and when his voice cut through it was powerful, urgent, magnificent — 'Sing with me / sing for the years / sing for the laughter / sing for the tears . . . dream on, dream on, dream on . . . ' Memories are made of this" (Record World, 6/5/1976).

May 12
Coliseum
Charlotte, NC
Promoter: Kaleidoscope Presents
Other act(s): Henry Gross
Reported audience: (13,000 capacity)

May 14
Coliseum
Jacksonville, FL
Promoter: Jet Set Enterprises
Other act(s): Henry Gross, Mahogany Rush
Reported audience: 9,984 / 10,000 (99.84%)
Reported gross: $64,900
Notes:
- Mahogany Rush, guitarist Frank Marino's band, had then recently signed with manager David Krebs, and released their fourth album via new label Columbia...

May 15
Bayfront Center Arena
St. Petersburg, FL
Promoter: Beach Club Concerts / Cellar Door Productions
Other act(s): Henry Gross, Mahogany Rush
Reported audience: 8,400 **SOLD-OUT
Notes:
- From a local review: "Aerosmith, while scoring well in the volume and activity departments, seemed to be too much of a rehash to impress musically. Lead singer Steven Tyler imitates superstar Mick Jagger vocally and physically, and the rest of the band follows in the Stones-Faces-J. Geils mold. But cheering thousands in the smoke-stacked arena make such criticism nonsensical. It was a party, well attended by young people out for fun. Aerosmith, playing the role of rock stars to the masses, is cashing in on the need for such attractions" (Tampa Bay Times, 5/17/1976).

May 17
Jai-Alai Fronton

Miami, FL
Promoter: Cellar Door Productions
Other act(s): Henry Gross, Mahogany Rush
Reported audience: (6,500 capacity)
Set list(s): Somebody / Sick as a Dog / Big Ten Inch Record / Lord of the Thighs / Sweet Emotion / Dream On / Walkin' the Dog / Walk this Way / Adam's Apple / Lick and a Promise / Same Old Song and Dance / Train Kept A Rollin' / Toys in the Attic
Notes:
- An AUD recording circulates from this show.

May 19
Von Braun Civic Center
Huntsville, AL
Promoter: Sound Seventy Productions
Other act(s): Henry Gross, Mahogany Rush
Reported audience: ~8,000 / 9,500 (84.21%)
Notes:
- From a local review: "Aerosmith melted 8,000 pairs of eardrums into a solid shape somewhere on the plane between absolute pleasure and total pain last night... If you were there, particularly if you were there until the end, this is merely an acknowledgement that there is another victim out here who won't be able to hear again until Friday night. If you missed the show, console yourself that another chance to experience the true meaning of the word 'sound' will come along and ask yourself if you really want to do it. Aerosmith gave the crowd everything it had, perfectly timed, and performed with a sound-studio control and depth. And no one can say that it was not loud enough. Steven Tyler is the front man for Aerosmith and the one who seems to be posturing after Mick Jagger in the photographs and on album covers. Tyler, Wednesday, was not Jagger but quite enough on his own. Changing pace from cat-like padding to leaping twirls with legs extended like a marionette in the hands of an octopus, Tyler has his own version of the moves. A powerful voice made him worth watching as long as the ear canal tissue could withstand the amplified pleasure. Tyler was the show because guitarists Brad Whitford and Joe Perry — while playing the band's four-album repertoire almost perfectly — didn't seem to know there was an audience much of the time. That was fine, because the audience didn't seem to care much what they were doing anyway" (Huntsville Times, 5/20/1976).

May 20
Municipal Auditorium
Mobile, AL
Promoter: Alex Cooley, Inc.
Other act(s): Henry Gross, Mahogany Rush
Reported audience: 13,000
Reported gross: $75,000

May 22
Omni
Atlanta, GA
Promoter: Alex Cooley, Inc.
Other act(s): Henry Gross
Reported audience: 17,000 / 17,293 (98.82%)
Reported gross: $100,000
Notes:

- Joe and Brad caught a broadcast of "The Midnight Special" following this show and enjoyed watching Chuck Berry's performance of "Johnny B. Goode." They were also interviewed by Charlie McCollum of the Washington Star for a piece that ran in that paper on May 28. Brad commented, in that piece, about the inherent dangers of performing during the summer of '76: "We did a show a couple of days ago that was incredible. They were just throwing fireworks through the whole thing. They were throwing everything on stage. One guy behind us has a roman candle, for Christ's sake. And, the last time we played the Spectrum in Philadelphia, they were building bonfires in the hall. One guy set a chair on fire and started marching around the hall with it. After a while, you keep your head up. I learned after a full whiskey bottle flew right between my head and Tom Hamilton's."

May 23
Rickwood Field
Birmingham, AL
Promoter: Alex Cooley, Inc.
Other act(s): Henry Gross, Mahogany Rush
Reported audience: (20,000 capacity)

May 25
Memorial Coliseum
Ft. Wayne, IN
Promoter: Sunshine Promotions
Other act(s): Rush, Stu Daye
Reported audience: 9,672 **SOLD-OUT
Reported gross: $57,870

May 26
Hulman Center @ I.S.U.
Terre Haute, IN
Promoter: Entam, Ltd.
Other act(s): Rush
Reported audience: (10,250 capacity)
Notes:
- Steve Marriott's All Stars were noted as the opener on some ads.

May 28
War Memorial
Rochester, NY
Promoter: Concerts East
Other act(s): Stu Daye
Reported audience: (11,000 capacity)
Notes:
- From a local review: "Last night Aerosmith performed at the Rochester War Memorial and the five-man group out of Boston proved to be an above-average rock band. But it is a group that is more a product of rock history than a maker of it. Aerosmith's music combines many of the elements that have distinguished fine rock bands in the past, but the group lacks that spark of individuality that can make the difference between a good band and a great one. Lead singer Steve Tyler has learned a lot of moves from Mick Jagger. But he hasn't added anything new to Jagger's repertoire of stage antics. Instead, Tyler comes off as a poor mimic of Jagger. He has neither the voice nor the magnetic personality of that legendary rocker. Aerosmith's sound lies somewhere between heavy metal and out and out boogie music. This is a brand of rock that has always been popular in Rochester.

Last night they came close to selling out the War Memorial, drawing the biggest crowd that hall has seen for a rock show since the second Dylan performance last December. But while heavy metal draws large crowds and sells a lot of albums, the music has a lot of built-in limitations. The basic rhythm lines and the overpowering guitars tend to make many of the songs sound alike, and this forces many heavy metal groups to rely on lighting effects and elaborate staging to make a name for themselves. It is to Aerosmith's credit that they have avoided cheap gimmicks, and a couple of their songs like 'Dream On' and 'Train Kept A Rollin" can stand comparison to anyone's heavy metal. But the group has a lot of musical maturing to do before they can be considered a first-rate rock band" (Rochester Democrat & Chronicle, 5/29/1976).

May 30
R.F.K. Stadium
Washington, DC
Promoter: Cellar Door Productions
Other act(s): Lynyrd Skynyrd, Nazareth, Ted Nugent
Reported audience: 38,600 / 50,000 (77.2%)
Reported gross: $385,000
Set list(s): Mama Kin / Write Me / S.O.S. (Too Bad) / Somebody / Lick and a Promise / Big Ten Inch Record / Lord of the Thighs / Sweet Emotion / Dream On / Walkin' the Dog / Walk this Way / Adam's Apple / Sick as a Dog / Same Old Song and Dance / Train Kept A Rollin' / Toys in the Attic
Notes:
- From a local review: "If the event was a major success in terms of security and production, it wasn't that much in the way of a rock concert. Mellowed by the combination of heat, an early starting time and heavy security, the crowd responded only politely through most of the show. A security guard, used to the more raucous Capital Centre rock fans, actually shook his head towards the end of the day and said, 'These kids are lifeless...' Aerosmith, the headline act, finally provided enough sheer energy to make the audience start acting like a hard rock crowd. As the 40,000 cheered and stomped, the band raced through a 75-minute set, at nearly unbearable sound levels. Throughout most of the afternoon, the sound had been reasonably good, but Aerosmith cranked it up to the point that quite a bit of the playing and a good portion of Steven Tyler's lead vocals were lost or badly distorted. Under the conditions, Aerosmith did rather well. The crowd seemed to react best to its all-out rockers, very basic tunes like 'Big 10 Inch' and 'Train Kept A Rollin.' The group also offered a fine version of 'Dream On,' its single hit, which drew a big response" (Washington Star, 6/1/1976).
- From an industry review: "Hard rock made a successful return to Robert F. Kennedy Stadium here May 30 as some 40,000 young people turned out for a mammoth concert headlined by Aerosmith. There were no difficulties with crowds and only a handful of arrests at the concert, the first in the stadium in two years. Hard rock had been banned from R.F.K. after a series of trouble-plagued rock and soul concerts in 1974. But the D.C. Armory Board which runs the debt-plagued stadium agreed to let Cellar Door Productions stage concerts this summer despite protests from neighbors in the area... Cool weather with a threat of rain was blamed for preventing a sellout of the 50,000-seat stadium" (Billboard, 5/22/1976). This show was a bright spot in the return of rock to the venue, with the three other pre-August shows all losing money — even with star power such as Peter Frampton, hot at the time with his "Comes Alive" album.

June 12
Three Rivers Stadium
Pittsburgh, PA
Promoter: DiCesare-Engler Productions
Other act(s): ZZ Top (HL), Point Blank

Reported audience: 47,705 / 70,000 (68.15%)
Reported gross: $425,000
Notes:
- In press reports, a stadium spokesman, noted the attendance at the event as over 54,000. Police authorities estimated as many as 70,000. Whatever the case, "More than 250 rock fans were injured — many of them cut by broken glass — while they attended a seven-hour-long concert... More than 30, after initial treatment at the stadium's first aid station, were sent on to Allegheny General, St. John's, Divine Providence, and Mercy hospitals. At least four persons were admitted, including a woman who was struck by a cherry bomb firecracker, and man who suffered fractures of the nose and pelvis, and another woman with a broken elbow. Many of the injuries occurred as the crowd pushed and shoved for several hours under a broiling sun, waiting for the gates to open at 4:25 p.m., five minutes before the start... The majority of them were treated for cuts received from broken glass when bottle-throwing erupted, and for drug overdoses and firecracker burns, a nurse said. Two unidentified security guards, assigned to keep the crowd from climbing atop the dugouts, were rushed by fans and one was struck on the head with a bottle, the other one trampled. One person suffered fractures of both ankles, another received a severe eye laceration" (Pittsburgh Press, 6/13/1976).
- Promoter Rich Engler recalled, "It was the craziest mix ever, that's for sure... It was ZZ Top, Aerosmith. They had cattle, they had rattlesnakes on stage. I liked the package, but it was weird because it was the roughneck-beer-drinkers-hell-raisers, and this American hair-type band that was a different form of rock 'n' roll. It kind of collided with the chemistry, not only of the music but the crowd. There were a lot of calamities" (Pittsburgh Post-Gazette, 6/21/2009).

June 13
Civic Center
Charleston, WV

Promoter: Entam, Ltd.
Other act(s): Starz
Reported audience: 7,699 / 8,500 (90.58%)
Reported gross: $49,616
Notes:
- At the time of this show, the debut eponymous Starz album hadn't even been released with the band having only finished its recording three weeks prior. The tough-rocking album had been produced by Jack Douglas.

- From a local review: "If someone could somehow capture and redistribute the energy expended by performers at the Aerosmith/Starz concert at the Civic Center Sunday night, the city of Charleston could run for a month. Two harder working, harder playing, bands are hard to imagine... It's easy to see why Aerosmith is a top-billed band today, though. It would be incredibly hard for another act to follow them. When their music starts it's nonstop for more than an hour... They just wouldn't stop. Aerosmith, too, plays hard rock — 'heavy metal' they call it. The music is deeply textured, building guitar upon guitar, three of them, all told and all of it on top of a deep drum backbeat. There wasn't a clunker in the bunch, assuming, of course, you go for that kind of music, and the crowd Sunday certainly did, but a few were exceedingly well-done. The boogie job done on 'Big Ten Inch Record,' for example, was excellent... 'Train Kept A Rollin',' a blues rock classic from way back, got an especially good treatment, too. A drum solo in the middle was interesting and not too long, and just when the guitar pyrotechnics near the end started to drag, the stage came alive, the band's flying 'A' logo dropped down, and it was over" (Charleston Gazette, 6/15/1976).

June 15
Municipal Auditorium
Nashville, TN

Promoter: Sound Seventy Productions
Other act(s): Starz
Reported audience: 10,137 **SOLD-OUT
Reported gross: $57,973
Note:
- Power was purportedly pulled on Starz when they started playing a second encore during their opening set...
- From a mainstream review: "The absurd is alive and kicking in rock and roll. A double dose of it reverberated in the Municipal Auditorium Tuesday night... The recorded music which introduced the band was a medley of two easily recognizable works: the theme from 'Jaws' and the 'Toccata and Fugue in D Minor' which has become famous as the organ music from 'Phantom of the Opera.' While one might be unwilling to characterize an Aerosmith concert as a horror show, they certainly take chances in their choice of background music. A physically unprepossessing group, Aerosmith managed to sell out the auditorium mainly on the basis of one song, a perfectly good one, called 'Dream On.'

It was originally released some three or four years ago and did moderately well on FM stations, but partially because of the limitations of that medium in the early '70s, soon disappeared. Re-released this year, in a time when AM stations are trying to woo some of the old FM listeners back, 'Dream On' has become a chart hit. Aerosmith's lead singer, only half the size of Starz's, wore a pink-and-black leopard print outfit with long sleeves and tails. This lizardly effect seemed to have relation to the music, which sustained the painful level. 'This band has been compared to the second coming of Christ,' said a Sound Seventy staffer. If so, Gabriel's horn may be missed in the noise" (Tennessean, 6/17/1976).

June 16
Roberts Stadium
Evansville, IN
Promoter: Sunshine Promotions
Other act(s): Rush
Reported audience: 12,615 **SOLD-OUT
Reported gross: $79,736
Notes:
- This show set a new house attendance record for the venue (also locally reported as 12,511). Stu Daye were scheduled to open but were unavailable.
- From a local review: "House records were smashed last night as 12,406 rock and rollers poured into Roberts Stadium to greet Aerosmith. The brash quintet from Boston turned in a 90-minute set that left the hot, sweaty crowd satisfied. The total attendance exceeded the previous house record for rock concerts set by KISS in its most recent Evansville appearance, by more than 1,000. The gross for the show, more than $70,000, was also a new house record. Yesterday's cool, clear weather helped account for the record attendance. Aerosmith's new album plus a top single, 'Dream On,' were additional factors. The biggest reason for the big crowd, however, is the band itself. Led by vocalist Steve Tyler, America's equivalent to Mick Jagger, the band plays a mean brand of rock and roll... The pacing of the show was fantastic. One song sped into another without losing a step, carrying the audience along in the process. Bits of fancy scenery added to the show's visual appeal. A 30-foot-wide burlap backdrop with the band's logo painted across it was unfurled, drawing a roar of approval from the crowd.

At the show's finale, the entire lighting grid, hung from the rafters of the stadium, pivoted down in front and up in the back. The structure formed a giant letter A, emphasized by blinking chase lights. The standard assortment of arc spotlights and colored lighting finished off a polished lighting display. The sound system was an earthquaker. But with the exception of 'Dream On,' the distortion completely obliterated the lyrics. Only 1 word in 10 was distinguishable. The crowd was looking for energy and excitement and Aerosmith delivered. The hit songs provided peaks as did Joey Kramer in a thunderous drum solo. The audience wanted more... Kramer responded with a bare-handed attack on his drum set which included some head-thumping on the tom-tom. As individuals, the members of Aerosmith are not knockout stars. But together, there is a special magnetism that marks them as a great stage band. It is enough to make Aerosmith the hottest American band on tour today" (Evansville Press, 6/17/1976).

June 18
Mid-South Coliseum
Memphis, TN

Promoter: Mid-South Concerts
Other act(s): Slade
Reported audience: 7,500 / 12,000 (62.5%)
Reported gross: $41,689

June 19
Mississippi Coliseum
Jackson, MS

Promoter: Mid-South Concerts
Other act(s): Slade
Reported audience: 10,030 **SOLD-OUT
Reported gross: $61,803
Notes:
- From a local review: "They came in pairs. In groups. In gangs. In virtual trances. They came in blue jeans. In evening gowns. In sweatshirts. In halters. Even in wheelchairs. Over 10,000 of them — predominantly under 21 — filled Mississippi Coliseum Saturday night, for a double bill of steamroller rock, courtesy of Aerosmith and Slade... The people at the Coliseum were hungry for rock. They roared their approval of Aerosmith's antics, from the moment Tyler took the stage and began to twirl his mike stand like a baton. The pungent odor of grass was ubiquitous as the group raced through its repertoire, from 'Dream On' (Aerosmith's biggest Top 40 hit) to 'Sick as a Dog' (from the group's latest album). The highlight came as drummer Joey Kramer tore through a spectacular solo on 'Train Kept A Rollin'' — even after he tossed away his sticks in favor of his bare hands, his drums sounded like The Panama Limited" (Jackson Clarion-Ledger, 6/21/1976).

June 21 **TEMP HOLD-DATE
T.H. Barton Coliseum
Little Rock, AR

Notes:
- Rescheduled for Aug. 16, after tickets were sold with this date printed.

June 21 **ERRONEOUS DATE
Convention Center
Pine Bluff, AR

Notes:
- Also appearing on some itineraries, this venue was still under construction and didn't open until June 28.

June 22
Expo Square Pavilion
Tulsa, OK

Promoter: Stone City Attractions
Other act(s): Fools
Reported audience: 7,950 / 8,900 (89.33%)

Reported gross: $49,000

June 24
Sam Houston Coliseum
Houston, TX
Promoter: Pantera Ten Productions
Other act(s): Stu Daye
Notes:
- Mahogany Rush were the advertised openers but did not perform.
- Part of the plot of the 1993 cult coming-of-age film, "Dazed and Confused," starring Matthew McConaughey (and Ben Affleck), involved his character, Wooderson, driving to Houston to buy tickets to this show.
- From a local review: "Festival seating in the floor area allowed an even greater number of people to jam together for a never-ending push to the front. A large black curtain beyond the ominous smoke screen generated anticipation and curiosity. Following taped chamber music, the curtain rose, but there was no great surprise unless you can count Aerosmith. Vocalist Steve Tyler was able to pantomime Mick Jagger right down to the facial expressions and microphone waltz. The music was of the heavy metal quality. Guitarist Joe Perry got in some good chops during 'Sweet Emotion' and a lengthy medley of everything from 'Batman Theme' to their hit 'Walk this Way.' A backdrop curtain later revealed the Aerosmith logo and, as if that were not enough, the original curtain unveiled a large illuminated 'A.' Excitement continued to build with rock and blues songs such as 'Big Ten Inch Record,' 'S.OS.' and 'Dream On' reinforcing their tough gang rocker image. Perhaps if the seating had been adequate and the correct performers had shown up, the good old days would not have been so old after all" (Houston Summer Cougar, 7/1/1976).

June 25
Convention Center Arena
San Antonio, TX
Promoter: Stone City Attractions
Other act(s): Stu Daye
Reported audience: 10,400 **SRO
Reported gross: $67,000

June 27
City Park Stadium
New Orleans, LA
Promoter: Beaver Productions
Other act(s): Nazareth, New Riders of The Purple Sage, KC & The Sunshine Band
Reported audience: (26,500 capacity)

Notes:
- The evening prior to this show, Joe and Steven attended the New York Dolls shows at Cord's Underground. Perry joined the band for "Pills" and Tyler on vocals and harmonica for a cover of Joe Turner's "Flip Flop and Fly." KC & the Sunshine band's Harry Wayne Casey recalled this show: "I was scared [about the Aerosmith show]. I felt like, 'God, here I'm like a teeny-bopper group" (Dubois Courier-Express, 11/24/1976)!

June 29
Moody Coliseum @ S.M.U.
Dallas, TX
Promoter: Concerts West
Other act(s): Mahogany Rush
Reported audience: (7,000 capacity)
Notes:
- From a local review: "An overflow crowd squeezed into every available hole of Moody Coliseum Tuesday night to have their senses assaulted for 80-minutes by a 5-man hard rock band, out of all places, Sunapee, NH, called Aerosmith. The question is: Why? Aerosmith is a competent band, but not an exciting one, not a special one and certainly not an abundantly talented one. In fact, they failed to live up to the anticipation created by their fourth and best album, the recently released 'Rocks,' Part of the problem may have been due to the sound system. Sitting in the outer reaches of Moody Coliseum, it was impossible to understand a word that was sung... Aerosmith showed itself to be an uninspiring rock band Tuesday night. By the fourth song, when it appeared not a word Tyler sang was going to be understood all night, the show started getting monotonous. The audience around me could not respond to what was going on down there on the stage. The applause after each number began sounding perfunctory — after all, these people paid seven bucks apiece for these tickets. This is what they came to see. They'd better applaud at some point in time to convince themselves it was money well spent.

The band seemed tired and looked like they were just going through the motions, like it was just another stop on a 50-city tour — just another day on the job. Punch the clock. Work eight hours on the assembly line. Punch the clock. Go home. What's for dinner? What's on TV? Drummer Joey Kramer stole the show right from the outset. It wasn't that he was that good during the early songs, but that he kept this constant rhythmic beat going and all of his moves seemed to have motives behind them... But even though Kramer proved himself on drums and Tyler and Perry employed a couple of not-too-novel concert tricks, the band itself emerged as a leaderless unit. No one member of the band stood out as an individual. It was impossible to relate to any of the five on a one-on-one basis" (Dallas Morning News, 7/1/1976).
- By the end of June, Amusement Business (a trade publication) reported that Aerosmith had performed for nearly 200,000 fans grossing $1.5 million.

July 2 **TEMP HOLD-DATE
Birmingham-Jefferson Civic Center
Birmingham, AL
Notes:
- Calling this a "temp" date is generous, though it did appear on various itineraries. The BJCC was nearing completion in July 1976 but wouldn't be ready in time for this show. The first concert at the facility was held by John Denver on Sept. 28... With the Rickwood Stadium show, this date would have been superfluous for the area anyway.

July 3 **TEMP-HOLD DATE
Spartan Stadium @ M.S.U.
East Lansing, MI
Promoter: Pop Entertainment
Other act(s): Peter Frampton, Jeff Beck
Reported audience: (72,000 capacity)
Notes:

- Due to issues over the promotor being required to obtain a bond to cover any damage to the stadium's turf, and the inability of the Office of Public Safety to provide adequate staffing for the event, this show had been abandoned before the contract could be signed in late May.

July 4
Groves Stadium
Winston-Salem, NC
Promoter: Entam, Ltd.
Other act(s): Black Oak Arkansas, Jeff Beck, Bob Seger
Reported audience: 14,913 / 45,000 (33.14%)
Reported gross: $157,970
Notes:
- "Replica" posters noting Nils Lofgren as the opening act for this event are junk, even though he was mentioned in advance ads along with Felix Pappalardi and Richie Blackmore's Rainbow who are equally unconfirmed as playing the date. Other early ads included bands such as J. Geils and Rick Derringer...

July 8
MECCA Arena
Milwaukee, WI
Promoter: Daydream Productions
Other act(s): Derringer, Stu Daye
Reported audience: 9,565 / 12,000 (79.71%)
Reported gross: $64,236
Set list: Mama Kin / Write Me / S.O.S. (Too Bad) / Lick and a Promise / Big Ten Inch Record / Sweet Emotion / Dream On / Lord of the Thighs / Last Child / Walk this Way / Train Kept A Rollin'
Notes:
- On the day of the show Elyssa Perry and Lori Whitford were arrested for jaywalking. According to the press, "On the way to the police station Elissa [sic] demanded that she be allowed to make one phone call — to husband Joe who was at a sound check for that evening's concert. When told that she couldn't telephone, Elissa was outraged. 'What do you mean I can't make a phone call? I watch 'Adam-12,' I know my rights!'" (Seattle Daily Times, 7/24/1976).
- The release of Derringer's debut album was still a few weeks away at the time of this show. Featuring Danny Johnson on guitar, Kenny Aaronson on bass, and Vinny Appice, the band had done a month worth of small hall dates to prepare for larger venue opening slots.
- Joe Baptista was off working as Stage Manager for the Milwaukee Summerfest Main Stage, a role he'd had for three years, but did also work the Aerosmith show (which wasn't attached to the annual festival).
- A below average AUD recording circulates from this show. It's likely missing the encores.

July 10
Comiskey Park
Chicago, IL
Promoter: Windy City Productions
Other act(s): Jeff Beck, Jan Hammer, Derringer, Stu Daye
Reported audience: 60,023 / 62,500 (96.04%)
Reported gross: $600,915
Notes:

- 28,000 tickets for this game 1 of the "World Series of Rock" had been sold by May 14. During Beck's set there were two fires (one under the press box and one in the third base upper deck), with the smoke interfering with his playing. Some 5,000 persons were evacuated, though the concert was permitted to continue (New York Times, 7/11/1976).
- From a local review: "Aerosmith has a solid following in Chicago, and the Boston rockers kept the customers satisfied. Although the sound system was excellent, visibility was not, and the band had to lean on music instead of spectacle. Happily, they had the tightness to pull it off" (Chicago Daily News, 7/12/1976).

July 11 **ERRONEOUS LISTING
Arrowhead Stadium
Kansas City, MO

Notes:
- This show appears in many lists. Ultimately, it was a ZZ Top show with the Nitty Gritty Dirt Band opening for 15,000 fans in 100-degree heat.

July 11 **CANCELLED
Cleveland Stadium
Cleveland, OH

Promoter: Belkin Productions
Other act(s): Todd Rundgren's Utopia, Jeff Beck, Derringer
Notes:
- This show was cancelled when authorities refused to allow fans on the playing field and Aerosmith refused to perform with that sort of configuration. Ted Nugent had already withdrawn from the bill. Over 13,000 tickets had been sold by June. A show in its place was booked at the Richfield Coliseum on July 28.
- Eric Singer (KISS, Alice Cooper, Black Sabbath): "I understand why people love 'Rocks,' because it sounds nasty and heavy. It's like Aerosmith at their dirtiest sounding."

July 11
Athletic & Convocation Center @ Notre Dame
South Bend, IN

Promoter: Sunshine Promotions
Other act(s): Derringer
Reported audience: 7,754 / 11,345 (68.35%)
Reported gross: $49,296
Notes:
- From a local review: "Following 30 minutes of horrid music from Derringer, activities increased. Three limousines carrying Aerosmith pulled up inside the ACC hallway. Mind you, not at the doorway but in the hall. Obviously, Aerosmith would have strained themselves if they would have to had walk the 50 yards from the outside. Steve Tyler, lead singer for Aerosmith, stepped out" (South Bend Tribune, 7/20/1976). And that is essentially as far as the journalist got describing the

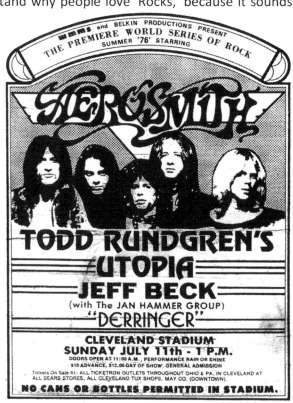

Aerosmith show, having failed to secure an interview with Steven or other members of the band. He went to suggest, "rock musicians, especially Aerosmith, are the biggest group of egomaniacs in the entertainment field. Their rapid-fire success has placed them in a position of power and like so many other rock groups they have abused it in a sense that they use the press and the public for their own gain, solely, an abuse as serious as any other public figure's disregard for those people who made him famous. The power of success has gone to Aerosmith's head."

July 15
Robertson Memorial Field House @ Bradley University
Peoria, IL
Other act(s): Ted Nugent
Reported audience: (7,800 capacity)
Partial set list: Mama Kin / Write Me / S.O.S. (Too Bad) / Lick and a Promise / Big Ten Inch Record / Sweet Emotion / Rats in the Cellar / Dream On / Lord of the Thighs
Notes:
- A partial AUD recording circulates from this show.

July 18-24
Century Plaza
Los Angeles, CA
Notes:
- The 1976 CBS Records Convention. The band received their platinum award for "Rocks," it having been certified by the RIAA on July 9. Joe purportedly commented from the stage, "Thanks. Now where's my check?".

July 23
Memorial Auditorium
Buffalo, NY
Promoter: Harvey & Corky Productions
Other act(s): Henry Gross, Derringer
Reported audience: (17,827 capacity)
Notes:

- From a local review: "Aerosmith arrives amidst peeling, deafening screams of emotion. Near the stage are cogent masses of glowering teens immersed in the idol rock that bombs all ears. The crowd stands in queue, up the aisles squeezing and crushing each other, taking consecrated cue from the 'musical' image oozing through its mind. During Aerosmith's first number, the merengue crowd peaks upon its stilting chairs to view, to be the phenomenon. Lead singer Steve Tyler dervishes wildly around stage, whirling in rapid consonance to blurts of music peppered to distortion by the ravenous multitude. His jerking, convulsive rites are repeated rimes conjuring thoughts of Mick Jagger's stage routine. Tyler uses the mike stand as a raunchy emperor's staff, repeatedly twirling it in baton-like fashion. A confident but nervously pronounced derisiveness is affected through chronic employment of this security blanket; Is it a mechanical prediction of success failing, or an overwhelming accusation of superstardom that prompts this tension? Could there be a lethargic and simple placidity beneath the Rolling Stones-accented act that is forced to hyperactivity? Tyler, in his spastic, cocky dance, covers any emotion with his mascaraed eyes; the boppers notice only the accepted, theatric persona and not the real person of Tyler and Aerosmith. In his leopard-skin leotards Tyler yells songs from 'Rocks,' seemingly admonishing himself to carry on, to finish the program without fainting from exhaustion. The stamina is adrenaline, perhaps combined with some synthetic 'ups.' Boppers admire Aerosmith's energy and praise their tunes of high school love, sneaky, sleazy, and anything at all phallic" (Spectrum, 7/30/1976). The Spectrum is the student paper of SUNY at Buffalo...

July 24
C.N.E. Stadium

Toronto, ON, Canada
Promoter: Concert Productions International
Other act(s): Henry Gross, Rory Gallagher, Derringer
Reported audience: ~25,000
Partial set list: Mama Kin / Write Me / Sweet Emotion / Dream On / Same Old Song and Dance / Train Kept A Rollin'
Notes:
- A "Summer in the City" concert series event.
- From a local review: "It was a long wait, almost an hour and a half, before Aerosmith, America's number one macho metal men from Bean Town, made the stage. There was no doubt they were most accomplished band present. They lean on stock clichés such as a Mick Jagger look-alike — acrobatic frontman Steven Tyler. He came out in a white jumpsuit with lots of multi-colored frills and waved a mike adorned with brilliant-colored scarves high in the air. Guitarists Brad Whitford and Joe Perry shared the endless number of repetitive solos, slamming them into the heads of the stunned and mesmerized audience. It all sounds a little too contrived. Take some of the Led Zeppelin sound, add the appropriate duds for the correct image, a drum solo, some exploding light, the essential leaps and by the sensuous, full-lipped Tyler and there you have it, packaged rock and roll. Their two best songs of the whole evening were 'Dream On' and 'Sick as a Dog.' But when they finished, they hardly mustered enough applause to arrant an encore. They do have drops of technique and big record sales in the United States, where they seem to be convincing the second generation of the Clearasil crowd that macho metal is a substitute for good rock 'n' roll. The ironic thing is they will probably make it in Canada too" (Toronto Globe & Mail, 7/26/1976).
- 30-minutes of AUD circulates from this show.

July 26
Onondaga County War Memorial Auditorium
Syracuse, NY
Promoter: Concerts East
Reported audience: (8,500 capacity)
Notes:
- This show was sandwiched between Elvis dates on the 25th & 27th.

July 28
Richfield Coliseum
Richfield (Cincinnati), OH
Promoter: Belkin Productions
Other act(s): Derringer, Stu Daye
Reported audience: (17,500 capacity)
Set list: Mama Kin / Write Me / S.O.S. (Too Bad) / Lick and a Promise / Big Ten Inch Record / Sweet Emotion / Dream On / Lord of the Thighs / Last Child / Sick as a Dog / Same Old Song and Dance / Train Kept A Rollin' / Toys in the Attic
Notes:

- This date was booked in place of the cancelled Cleveland Stadium show on July 11. The promoter had hoped it would be popular enough to add a second date, but it doesn't appear the 29th was booked. Prior to the show, tour manager Henry Smith and other members of the road crew were interviewed by Anastasia Pantsios for a feature that was published Circus Magazine #141 (Oct. 12).
- From a local review: "The walls of a packed Coliseum were rocking last Wednesday night. It wasn't so much the quality of the music that set them vibrating as it was the massive chunks of sound shoveled out of a P.A. system (that was turned up to its devastating full volume) ... Aside from doing a few songs from their new album, ROCKS, Aerosmith's show was virtually the same as their several past area performances. Songs like 'Dream On' and 'Train Kept A Rollin'' were done in the same manner as they've always been. Technically, the band was as tight as usual, but there was a noticeable lack of feeling in it. Lead singer Steve Tyler did his (usual) carbon copy emulation of Mick Jagger. There's nothing wrong with it because he does it well, but Tyler's performance was lifeless. Oh, he did the same movements, the same gestures (he straddled the microphone stand and rode it around like a horse or swung it around in the air at the same times in the same songs as he's always done before), but it was all very mechanical, very rehearsed, very routine. After the concert, I left with the feeling that Aerosmith has worn down its groove, and like an old record, is starting to skip in the same place every time it comes around" (Cleveland Scene, Aug. 5–11, 1976).
- A poor AUD recording circulates from this show, though the band does jam "Get the Lead Out" and "Helter Skelter."

July 29 **TEMP HOLD-DATE
Richfield Coliseum
Richfield (Cincinnati), OH

July 31
Eastwood Lake Park
Dayton, OH

Promoter: Ross Todd/Belkin Productions
Other act(s): Ted Nugent, Derringer, Rory Gallagher, Henry Gross
Reported audience: ~25,000
Notes:
- The Hydroglobe Music Festival. Four people were later indicted for a counterfeiting operation including tickets for this event and 13c "Liberty Bell" stamps.
- From a local review: "It was a mini-Woodstock for a new generation that only knows Woodstock as the name of

the baby bird in the 'Peanuts' cartoon... It was a picnic crowd, with many of the fans spreading blankets on the ground and talking above the distant din of rock and roll. T-shirts abounded, most of them with the badge of a previous concert emblazoned across the front... Promoter Ross Todd called it the most peaceful rock crowd he has seen this summer. Local police seemed to agree" (Dayton Daily News, 8/1/1976).

August 6
Civic Center
Providence, RI

Promoter: Concerts East
Other act(s): Rory Gallagher, Derringer
Reported audience: 13,228 / 14,000 (94.49%)
Reported gross: $85,716

August 9 **POSTPONED
Colt Park
Hartford, CT

Promoter: Contemporary Concerts Company
Notes:
- It was simply convenient that Tropical Storm "Belle" had forced the promoters to move this show indoors at the Springfield Civic Center, even though more than 20,000 tickets had been sold. City managers cancelled their contract with promoters Koplik & Finkel on August 15, due to the number of disturbances at previous concerts at the outdoor venue.

August 10
Civic Center
Springfield, MA

Promoter: Contemporary Concerts Company
Reported audience: ~10,500 **SOLD-OUT
Reported gross: $91,000
Notes:
- From a local review: "Aerosmith plays the kind of hard rock that makes Dad tear the tone arm off the stereo. Of course, that's a large part of this Boston quintet's charm and much of the reason why the Springfield Civic Center shook beneath the stomps of 10,500 ecstatic fans during Aerosmith's show Tuesday night... No such instrumental virtuosity was evident in Aerosmith's work Tuesday night; rather there emerged a high degree of craft in combining heavy-metal musical clichés in sometimes fresh, often effective ways. The multiple segments of 'Sweet Emotion,' joined in one artful crescendo, almost making their similarity to Led Zeppelin's 'Black Dog' irrelevant. And if 'Walk this Way,' 'Big Ten Inch,' and "Toys in the Attic' tended to sound alike, all succeeded through the precise electronic blend of Tyler's shrieks with the uninspired fuzz guitars of Joe Perry and Brad Whitford. Drummer Joey Kramer even managed to transform his musically mundane solo into an interesting piece of drumstick-throwing hoopla. Like the rest of Aerosmith's performance, Kramer's show biz came off, not because it broke new ground, but because it's often fun to see old tricks done well. Until the Zeppelin lands in Springfield, memories of Aerosmith's show will satisfy all but the most insistent appetites for hard rock" (Springfield Union, 8/12/1976).

August 11 **CANCELLED
Hartford, CT

Promoter: Contemporary Concerts Company
Notes:
- This show was cancelled as part of a compromise by the promoter with the Hartford city officials.

August 13
Spectrum
Philadelphia, PA

Promoter: Electric Factory Concerts
Other act(s): Derringer
Reported audience: 19,352 **SOLD-OUT
Reported gross: $135,507
Notes:
- From a local review: "Where was Aerosmith during the energy crisis? The five-piece band pushed enough energy into the sold-out audience at the Spectrum Friday night to light up Philadelphia for one night. The 19,000-plus people came to the Spectrum to play sardine-for-a-night... or more to the point, to attend a dance concert. There were no floor seats for the event and if one person in the front row moved, the same movement could be detected 15 rows back. Watching a band like Aerosmith is a communal effort so the crammed-in format was perfect for the concert... Friday night the group played in a wide-open stage setting giving Tyler bare expanses of floor space to move in with his patented gyrations. Aerosmith began to build its reputation as a no-holds-barred band with the release of the AM radio hit, 'Dream On.' The group's live presentation of the song seemed to have more of a biting edge to it, a sharpness which fell in line with the more hard-driving format of its present music. Visually, Aerosmith centers around Tyler. With a perpetual pout like Mick Jagger, Tyler even seems more frenzied on stage than the leader of the Rolling Stones. There is rarely a moment when Tyler is motionless on stage. His costuming is garish, but it is the type of flash

designed to take your mind off the performer's incompetence. Tyler also possesses a multi-octave vocal range. Sometimes the fullness of his vocal prowess is lost because of the heavily amplified music, but Tyler is more than an adequate singer. The band is tight and loud. Its members are practitioners of pure rock 'n roll. They possibly possess in Joe Perry and Brad Whitford the guitar duo of the future. The pair stick to tight chording and the solos are imaginative enough to skirt the riffs which have become rock 'n roll standards — overused by all of the up-and-coming groups" (Bucks County Courier, 8/15/1976).

August 14 **CANCELLED
John F. Kennedy Stadium
Philadelphia, PA

Promoter: Electric Factory Concerts
Other act(s): Foghat, Manfred Mann's Earth Band
Reported audience: (90,400 capacity)
Notes:
- The Spirit of Summer '76 festival.
- This show was cancelled on July 23 due to a conflict with a Phillies game the same afternoon which would

have put a strain on local parking and police, with the baseball team holding priority over the shared parking lots. According to press reports, "with the Phillies playing that afternoon, the city, the police department, the Phillies as well as Electric Factory officials (Larry Magid and Alan Spivak) saw it as a calamitous parking and traffic situation. In switching to Saturday night, the concert promoters found the Phillies had a night game and still had priority over the parking lots at both stadiums. Since tickets for the ball game were going extremely well, they needed all the parking space they could get. The fact that the concert would not be over until after the game did not help much. While Electric Factory was still permitted to use the stadium, it would have to be held down to approximately half of the original 105,000 capacity. With the huge expense involved in producing the rock show, Steve Apple, Electric Factory spokesman, said that almost any cutback in space would present a severe problem in staffing and services and would not allow for the full production the event called for. Moreover, Aerosmith and Foghat, co-headlining the concert, could not work out the difficulties caused by the cutback. Rather than shortcoming the fans, the groups chose to seek other venues" (Billboard, 8/7/1976). Tickets for this show could be exchanged for Spectrum tickets.

August 14
Scope
Norfolk, VA

Promoter: Entam, Ltd.
Other act(s): Derringer, Starz
Reported audience: 12,500 **SOLD-OUT
Reported gross: $87,098
Notes:
- Originally scheduled for Foreman Field on Aug. 15.

August 15 **TEMP HOLD-DATE
Foreman Field

Norfolk, VA
Promoter: Entam, Ltd.
Reported audience: (20,000 capacity)
Notes:
- Announced July 18 with "the most unbelievable guest to be announced" (Richmond Times Dispatch). By the following week, the show had been moved to the Scope.

August 17
T.H. Barton Coliseum
Little Rock, AR
Promoter: Mid-South Concerts
Other act(s): Derringer, Starz
Reported audience: (9,000 capacity)
Notes:
- Following this show, the promoter leveled charges of brutality at local police for heavy-handed treatment of concert patrons. This alleged behavior led the promoter to suggest that he'd only bring the very biggest acts to Little Rock, because they were the only acts that would guarantee that patrons would tolerate the environment to see. Mid-South rep Bob Kelly commented, "As far as police roughing up kids, they've been doing it ever since we've been having concerts there. Police behavior at Little Rock is the worst in the United States. It's the closes thing I've ever seen to Nazi Germany... I can see them [the patrons violating rules] being warned and being told to put their cigarettes out. But I can't see them being picked up by the hair and thrown out the door, which I saw 30, 40 or 50-times last night. I've never been to a show over there when I didn't see 50 kids thrown out. I do not have hits problem anywhere else. It's disgraceful the way the police are. They act autonomously" (Arkansas Gazette, 8/19/1976). The local Sheriff denied the accusations and refused to comment on a photo of a patron being escorted from the venue by his hair. He responded by ordering his deputies to stop working events so that he wouldn't be "harassed all the time."

August 18
Fairgrounds Arena
Oklahoma City, OK
Promoter: Stone City Attractions
Other act(s): Derringer, Starz
Reported audience: 10,400 / 10,500 (99.01%)
Reported gross: $67,300

August 20
Civic Auditorium
Omaha, NE
Promoter: Contemporary Productions
Other act(s): Derringer, Starz
Reported audience: 12,000 **SOLD-OUT
Reported gross: $72,043
Notes:
- Auditorium manager Charlie Mancuso was interviewed for a piece detailing artist concert riders that ran in AP syndicated press in October. Of the "elaborate" requirements noted by the likes of Peter Frampton or the Doobie Brothers, Aerosmith's was detailed as requiring that peanut butter be provided to the band. Later would come the likes of Van Halen and their "no brown M&Ms requirement" designed to ensure promoters were actually reading and meeting their more important technical aspects of the rider — those details more likely to affect the quality or safety of the performance. Of course, there were bands with demands more capricious in nature, but for many acts the rider was simply an attempt to introduce some normality and home comfort while enduring the grind of life on the road...
- From a local review: "It wasn't a night for subtlety. Aerosmith, Rick Derringer and Starz kept the music hot, heavy, and relentless at the City Auditorium Arena Friday night. Aerosmith, the main draw for the sellout

crowd of 11,300, is from Boston, but has had its greatest success in the boogie-happy Midwest. The group features two guitars, bass, drums and lead singer Steven Tyler, the main showman. Tyler, with shaggy hair, pouty lips, and some sort of long-sleeved, multihued jumpsuit, looked, pranced and at times sang like Mick Jagger. He was almost constantly in motion, flinging his streamer-festooned mike stand around him when he wasn't singing into it. When drummer Joey Kramer or lead guitarist Joe Perry were soloing, Tyler helpfully held his microphone up to the drums or the guitar speaker. Neither needed the extra amplification. When Tyler wasn't dancing around them, goading them into motion, the others in the band stood still and played elemental rock.

Aerosmith does nothing fancy musically — they just keep the beat fast and insistent. The closest thing to a slow song all night was 'Dream On,' which starts relatively calmly but builds to a screaming climax that Tyler's voice wasn't quite able to pull off. Judging by the crowd's reaction after that and every other song, nobody noticed. The only trouble the group had with the crowd was when Tyler tried a singalong on 'Train Kept a Rollin' and had to admonish: 'No, I sing 'train kept a rollin,' you sing 'all night long.'" A black curtain shielded the stage before Aerosmith appeared, although those sitting behind the stage were able to see whatever secret preparations were being made. They were repaid, however, by having their view blocked for several songs by a huge scrim (screen) with the Aerosmith logo that appeared behind the stage just after the set began" (Omaha World-Herald, 8/21/1976).

August 22
McNichols Sports Arena
Denver, CO
Promoter: Feyline, Inc.
Other act(s): Spirit, Derringer
Reported audience: 9,038 / 17,344 (52.11%)
Reported gross: $55,833

August 24 **TEMP HOLD-DATE
Salt Palace
Salt Lake City, UT
Notes:
- This show was eventually booked for Sept. 6.

August 26
Selland Arena
Fresno, CA
Promoter: Pacific Presentations
Other act(s): Derringer
Reported audience: 7,333 **SOLD-OUT
Reported gross: $47,288

August 27
Cow Palace
Daly City (San Francisco), CA
Promoter: Bill Graham Presents

Other act(s): Spirit, Derringer
Reported audience: 14,118 / 14,706 (96%)
Reported gross: $79,650
Set list(s): Rats in the Cellar / Dream On / Lord of the Thighs / Last Child / Walk this Way / Sick as a Dog / Same Old Song and Dance / Train Kept A Rollin' / Toys in the Attic
Notes:
- The day following this show the band flew to Honolulu via United flight #183.
- A partial AUD recording circulates from this show. It's missing the first four songs. The jam that night included some of "Jailhouse Rock."

August 29 **CANCELLED
Aloha Stadium
Halawa, HI

Promoter: John Bauer Concerts / KMR Productions
Reported audience: (50,000 capacity)
Notes:
- Tickets went on sale July 26, but the show was moved to the NBC on August 12, due apparently to the lack of availability of the other acts on the bill, but with the size of the venue it may have become clear sales wouldn't have been economical. The promoter had also had an issue, earlier in the year, waiting for the state to fund a covering that would protect the grass field from concert attendees. A second date at the new venue was added the following week, with the Aug. 29 show then approaching sell-out.

August 29
Neil Blaisdell Center
Honolulu, HI

Promoter: John Bauer Concerts / KMR Productions
Other act(s): Spirit, Derringer
Reported audience: 8,639 **SOLD-OUT
Notes:
- From a local review: "Nary an eardrum left the Blaisdell Center Arena last night unscathed. The packed house got what they came for — an evening of heavy metal rock by Rick Derringer and Aerosmith. It was, in short, three hours of sensory bombardment... When Aerosmith came on stage, their fans were eager and ready. Their 90-minute performance was an almost steady gush of gut-level heavy-metal rock, mixed with manic stage antics, carefully planned lighting, and an ascending and descending giant Aerosmith canvas backdrop that further heightened the emotional impact of the show... The focal point of Aerosmith was on Steve Tyler. His face has the eyes and nose of Mick Jagger and the lips of Carly Simon. Dressed in a skin-tight red and black outfit, he was in a state of perpetual motion. Never smiling or taking the microphone off its stand, he wasted no time with idle chatter. Jumping, running, screaming, pleading, spitting, he seemed to be every mother's nightmare and every high school girl's fantasy. Backing up Tyler was Joe Perry on lead guitar. Decked out in a black-leather suit and looking as if he were trying to come up with a thought, he cranked out blistering riffs that fit well with Tyler's earthy singing" (Honolulu Star Bulletin, 8/30/1976).

August 30
Neil Blaisdell Center
Honolulu, HI

Promoter: John Bauer Concerts / KMR Productions
Other act(s): Spirit, Derringer
Reported audience: 8,330 / 8,639 (96.42%)
Reported gross: $55,551
Notes:
- From a local review: "A mind-blowing force from Boston invaded the Islands recently. No, it's not another strange variety of flu, but a five-man heavy metal rock group who call themselves Aerosmith. They demonstrated their power here Sunday and Monday nights by severely infecting 16,000 at the Blaisdell

Memorial Center with a disease that used to be known as the rock 'n' roll pneumonia or the boogies-woogie flu... The loyal fans at both shows obviously got what they wanted from both performances as they showed their appreciation by screaming and yelling after the sets, for one encore after another. If you're into heavy rock and go to a show to be blasted out of your socks, Aerosmith is the group to do it. Your ears will ring for two days afterwards and you'll be in a state of shock for quite some time. Lead singer Steven Tyler also will supply enough bizarre behavior for the curious to last several months as he prances about in a leotard-like leopard skin outfit and simulates masturbation with his microphone. All in all, Aerosmith supplies what the mostly teen-age fans seem to demand, songs with a good beat you can dance to combined with outrageous behavior" (Honolulu Advertiser, 8/31/1976).

September 3
Kingdome
Seattle, WA

Promoter: John Bauer Concerts
Other act(s): Jeff Beck, Derringer, Starz
Reported audience: 51,091 / 57,000 (89.63%)
Reported gross: $422,698
Notes:
- An impressive 60 pounds of illicit drugs and paraphernalia were seized from patrons during the show... Advance itineraries for both Aerosmith and Derringer each noted a show scheduled in Portland, OR, this day, and Seattle on Sept. 4, though the Portland date was abandoned without being booked.
- From a local review: "'Welcome to the Kingdome echo chamber,' Jeff Beck snarled into the microphone after his first song Friday night. 'I can't think or a more inappropriate place for a rock concert.' Beck isn't known for being cordial and he was probably a little miffed at being second on the bill to Aerosmith ('We're here to kind of warm you up a bit for the main group, ha ha') but he was right on about the Dome that night. Despite heroic efforts by the John Bauer Concert Co. to turn the show into something special. For all but a few of the approximately 50,000 people it was another disaster... The stars of the show, Aerosmith, didn't come on until past 11:30, a half hour before the show was supposed to end. It has been reported (in Lisa Robinson's column in The Times Saturday and other places) that tile band is tired of playing huge stadia and they looked it Friday night. It was not the same highly energized, totally turned-on band that was here in the Coliseum last December.

Steve Tyler, the lead singer, kept giving signals to somebody offstage about the sound and he moved about half as much as he usually does. Joe Perry, the excellent guitarist, smoked cigarettes while he played and looked disinterested. Brad Whitford, sporting a new moustache, looked bored, too. They played their hits interspersed with songs from the new album. Tyler tried to put a little originality into some of them ('Dream on, scream on, cream on') but mostly it was the Same Old Song and Dance. The band played for a long time, until 1 a.m. But it soon became apparent that in a place the size of the Dome it's not enough to just play music. There's got to be more if you're going to focus that huge an audience's attention onto the stage. The one flash pot and the balloons from the roof at the end of Aerosmith's set weren't enough" (Seattle Times, 9/6/1976).

September 6
Salt Palace
Salt Lake City, UT

Promoter: United Concerts
Other act(s): Jeff Beck, Derringer, Starz

Reported audience: (13,075 capacity)
Notes:
- From a local review: "The music was sheer energy. Dual lead guitarists, a cross between the Stones' own Keith Richard and Jeff Beck, and Brad Whitford, who plays in much the same way as Led Zeppelin founder Jimmy Page, provided the heavy-metal sound needed to sustain the power of Tyler's raspy vocals. Tyler physically resembles Mick Jagger and Carly Simon's little sister. He sounds a bit like Alice Cooper, but softer. It is his stage presence however, that captures your attention and holds it throughout the duration of the 90-minute show. He never stops moving — dancing, prancing, singing, strutting — easily shifting from one tune to another, always in complete control. His costume Monday night consisted of a tight-fitting, multicolored jumpsuit that reminded one of a Shakespearean court jester, entertaining members of a secret Moroccan cult, high in the Atlas Mountains. He looked part Lucifer and part Cheshire Cat as he moved from one end of the stage to the other spitting out the highly sexual lyrics that heavy-rock devotees crave. Aerosmith is an extremely tight-sounding group, weaving complexity, singing and texture of sound into each piece... the boys from Boston can play powerful rock music second to none" (Salt Lake Tribune, 9/8/1976).

September 8
Stadium
Tempe, AZ
Promoter: Fun Productions
Other act(s): Jeff Beck, Derringer
Reported audience: 12,061 / 25,000 (48.24%)
Reported gross: $92,456

September 11 **POSTPONED
Balboa Stadium
San Diego, CA
Promoter: Steve Wolf & Jim Rissmiller
Other act(s): Lynyrd Skynyrd, Jeff Beck, Derringer
Reported audience: (35,000 capacity)
Notes:
- This show was booked at the Balboa Stadium due to a preliminary injunction being granted that prevented the larger San Diego Stadium being used. Managers of the smaller Sports Arena (14,000 capacity) were suing in an attempt to ban concerts from the larger venue, on the grounds that they violated terms of a contract between the city and arena. The suit was scheduled to be heard in court on Sept. 13, the day on which the show was rescheduled. Following Gary Rossington's (Skynyrd's guitarist) traffic accident, the band had to cancel touring activities.

September 12
Anaheim Stadium
Anaheim, CA
Promoter: Steve Wolf & Jim Rissmiller, Fun Productions & KLOS
Other act(s): Jeff Beck, Derringer
Reported audience: 55,633 **SOLD-OUT
Reported gross: $560,705
Notes:
- Belated birthday present for Joe, Jeff Beck jams with the group on "Train Kept A Rollin'." Unfortunately, for

reasons the band would also later note, many in the audience didn't notice the special moment: "Rock fans have long known that outdoor concerts are more social than musical events. Even with the huge closed-circuit TV screens that are sometimes employed, there is no chance to see the musicians or watch the interplay between them. I remember seeing Aerosmith last summer at Anaheim and not known until a member of the stage crew told me the next day that guitarist Jeff Beck had joined the band on stage for the encore" (Los Angeles Times, 5/10/1977).

- From a local review: "The local summer rock concert season ended Sunday at Anaheim Stadium with a sold-out Aerosmith show that not only underscored some of the limitations of massive outdoor events but told something about the new bands that are now headlining them. It doesn't seem all that long ago that many in rock were lamenting that the move by acts from small (3,000-seat) halls to the large (18,000-seat) sports arenas resulted only in poorer sound, reduced visibility and a shattering of intimacy. But it was difficult Sunday not to yearn for the 'intimacy' of the old arena days...

Aerosmith was clearly the center of attention... But the group has caused a major schism between critics and its especially young audience. For critics exposed to the Stones (and other influential bands) in the 1960s, Aerosmith suffers from a lack of originality and special vision. Rather than help define and reshape rock patterns, its music stays within the boundaries and feeds off existing designs. To its credit, however, Aerosmith replays those sounds with more sting and raw, ragged appeal than most of its rivals in the Stones-influenced area of rock. Besides, the band is less a copy of the Stones (as some have charged) than simply a group which — through such songs as 'Sick as a Dog' and 'Back in the Saddle' — revives much of the urgency, sensuality and — crucially — dramatic tension of the Stones' music. Lead singer Steve Tyler could win a Jagger look-alike contest, but his fierce, exclamatory vocal style does not lean unduly on Jagger's.

Aerosmith's musicianship is only average, but its arrangements are hard-driving, more melodic than most and nicely economical. Except for a tedious drum solo near the end, Sunday's performance — offering a generous sample of tunes from the band's four Columbia albums — was well paced and impressive. It was, in fact, good enough to make on look forward to *seeing* the band some time" (Los Angeles Times, 9/14/1976).

- From an industry review: "Sept. 12 marked the last of the marathon outdoor concerts of the season here featuring an all-out hard rock bill that easily demonstrated the impulse behind top-billed Aerosmith's rapid rise to fame. The primary focus of the set centered on lead vocalist Steve Tyler whose Jagger-ish acrobatics were simulcast on two huge screens set up on either side of the stage, making a good view of the concert available to those not able to fight the crowds at the front of the stage. Tyler worked closely with guitarist Joe Perry reemphasizing the resemblance to onstage Jagger-Richard teamwork. Comparisons, however, were only visual as Aerosmith hammered out its driving material in its own distinctive style. Drawn mainly from the 'Rocks' LP, favorites included 'Back in the Saddle,' 'Last Child,' and 'Home Tonight.' The strength of all of the band's numbers made any choice of highlights difficult, but if one could be isolated, it had to be the combination of controversial "Helter Skelter" which carried into the Tyler-Perry composition 'Get the Lead Out.' Serving as a good lead-in as well as a good contrast to Aerosmith's reckless energy, Jeff Beck meandered through his eloquent guitar passages with a subtlety that characterized his stage presence as well as his music" (Billboard, 10/2/1976).

September 13
Sports Arena
San Diego, CA

Promoter: Steve Wolf & Jim Rissmiller
Other act(s): Jeff Beck, Derringer, Starz
Reported audience: 11,559 / 14,000 (82.56%)
Reported gross: $109,810
Notes:
- This show was originally scheduled for Balboa Stadium, though rain late the week prior forced the show indoors (not to mention the likelihood that there was no point staging a show for 12,000 in a 35,000-capacity venue).

- KGB Radio's chicken mascot was knocked unconscious and arrested following a melee with security.
- From a local review: "If you like Mick Jagger, you may find Steven Tyler mildly amusing. Tyler handles the lead vocals for Aerosmith, the momentarily hot grunge-rock quintet that Monday night drew 11,000 fans to a Sports Arena concert, and his act is primarily and extended and tawdry imitation of Jagger. Bearing more than a slight resemblance to the singer and composer of the Rolling Stones, Tyler dresses like Jagger, flounces and pouts like Jagger and, lest he be accused of being too narrow in scope, throws the microphone stand around like Rod Stewart... Most of Aerosmith's fans appeared to be barely old enough to qualify for driver's licenses, with many too young even for that. These were kids who demanded horsepower more than music and Aerosmith delivered, producing an onslaught of sound: the relentless drums of Joey Kramer pounding behind the near-hysterical guitars of Joe Perry and Brad Whitford, and Tom Hamilton's bass propping up the bottom.

Kramer won ecstatic applause with a 10-minute drum solo, and the kids on the main floor stood on their seats to cream their approval when he threw his drumsticks into the crowd and attacked his drums with his fists and forehead. Tyler was the main attractions, though, clad in a red leopard-print, skintight pajama outfit, his face cast permanently in a Jagger-esque androgynous pout. He danced the same prissy-footed steps as Jagger, put his hand on the back of his hip like Jagger and wagged his finger at the front rows like Jagger. It was an astonishingly flagrant imitations, but the kids bought it as if it were the McCoy. It's been said that Aerosmith and Tyler project a raw energy that the Stones have lost over the years, and that may be true. But Jagger also projects the image of a cunning outlaw, while Tyler seems to be outlaw's little brother, the one who can never manage to get the hubcaps off the car before the cops arrive" (San Diego Union, 9/15/1976).

September 17 **TEMP HOLD-DATE
September 18 **TEMP HOLD-DATE
Nassau Coliseum
Long Island, NY
Notes:
- Tentative dates noted in Performance, these dates weren't booked.

September 18 **APPEARANCE
Hollywood Palladium
Los Angeles, CA
Notes:
- The second Don Kirshner's "Rock Awards" show. The awards were broadcast on CBS-TV and presented by Diana Ross and Alice Cooper. Aerosmith were oddly nominated for "Best New Group" award but lost to Hall & Oates. Steven and Joe attended briefly but were bored and soon split. The band members soon returned home for a break (and press duties) before the European tour. Joe planned on doing some recording work with New York Dolls' frontman David Johansen and Steven attended the Ali/Norton III fight at Yankee Stadium on Sept. 28.

October 13
Empire Theater
Liverpool, England
Promoter: Harvey Goldsmith Entertainments, Ltd.
Other act(s): Phoenix
Reported audience: (2,400 capacity)
Notes:
- Smart promotions people at CBS in London outfitted boxer John Conteh with shorts and jackets advertising the UK tour for his October 9 fight in Copenhagen against Alvaro Lopez.
- An EP was also issued for the U.K. market (CBS AS-1) with the first 1,000 tickets holders at each show being given a copy. It included "Rats in the Cellar," "Walk this Way" // "Same Old Song and Dance," and "Dream On."

- CBS signed opening act Phoenix had then been recently formed by former Argent members John Verity, Bob Henrit, and Jim Rodford, following the collapse of that band.

October 14
Apollo Theatre
Glasgow, Scotland
Promoter: Harvey Goldsmith Entertainments, Ltd.
Other act(s): Phoenix
Reported audience: (3,100 capacity)

October 16
Odeon Theatre
Birmingham, England
Promoter: Harvey Goldsmith Entertainments, Ltd.
Other act(s): Phoenix
Reported audience: (2,400 capacity)
Notes:
- Lemmy recalled: "I went to the Hammersmith Odeon show and actually thought they were quite good... But they were slagged unmercifully by the papers. One guy said Tyler looked like 'an au pair girl doing the hoovering' because he used to wear a leotard with a bustle on the backside and he used to push his mike-stand around the stage. It was cruel but very funny" ("The Fall and Rise of Aerosmith").

October 17
Odeon Theatre
Hammersmith, London, England
Promoter: Harvey Goldsmith Entertainments, Ltd.
Other act(s): Phoenix
Reported audience: (3,500 capacity)
Notes:
- From a mainstream review: "Their first London appearance at Hammersmith was rather better than expected, if almost as predictable. The physical resemblance to the Stones was uncanny: lead singer Stephen Tyler wore a fetching pink

imitation leopard skin catsuit and looked like an exaggerated caricature of Jagger (even more pretty or more ugly, depending on your taste). Guitarist Joe Perry, in a tattered leather jacket, managed to look alternatively like an exhausted Keith Richard and Ron Wood. So far, so bad, but once they started playing one could see why the Americans in the audience were getting so excited (and how well the computer had done its job). For an hour and a half, they played a non-stop, loud, attacking, and relentless mixture of rock and roll and 'heavy metal.' Musically, it was mostly extremely simple, with endlessly repeated phrases interspersed with occasional breaks for fast, unmemorable guitar solos and the mixture held together with good unmerciful drumming. But Tyler sang, as well as pranced, surprisingly well, while his band were clever and always efficient, if never inspired. If only the computer had bothered to add a little melody, Aerosmith might be on their way to matching their British counterparts" (The Guardian, 10/18/1976).
- From another mainstream review: "Finally the house lights darkened as a 'Fanfare for The Common Man' type dramatic theme blasted out of the huge PA. There was no unfolding lotus stage. I wasn't expecting to

know any of the numbers, but they kicked off aggressively with 'Helter Skelter', Stephen Tyler dressed in the poor man's Yves. St. Laurent jump suit, pouting and strutting for all he's worth. Guitarist Joe Perry has the Keith Richard imitation down perfectly, complete with menacing profile and bent knees. Perry works close to the back of the stage with Charlie Watts — whoops, Joey Kramer — pounding in his ear. During the second number Mick — sorry, I mean Steven – played harp. When Tyler and Perry come together to sing, visually they look like miniature Jagger and Richard dolls. If they sang out of tune, they'd be perfect. Tyler is a better Jagger than he is a Rod Stewart. When he'd put his hair behind his head in mock Britt Ekland style the effect was embarrassing as was his rather immature use of the mike stand, decorated with long flowing scarves. Sometimes he'd turn his back to the crowd, standing in front of Charlie's drum kit, shaking ass. While Tyler and Perry look like identical Glimmer twins, the rest of the band could smoothly fit into Status Quo. Guitarist Brad Whitford looks like a cross between Noddy Holder and Davey Johnston while bassist Tom Hamilton should be in the Sweet. Drummer Kramer favours the John Bonham school of subtle (??) drumming.

Visually, Aerosmith parody the Stones quite limply but musically they present a weird assortment of Led Zeppelin riffs and mysticism, Status Quo simplicity, and Alice Cooper aggression. Aerosmith are almost too well rehearsed. Tyler knows all the tricks from the Jack Daniels manly, rock star swig to the ability to arouse an audience. When Tyler says clap, they clapped. But it took telling the security men down front 'To fuck off' before the kids broke loose. Jagger employed the same technique at Wembley three years ago and it worked a charm. But then Jagger followed it with 'Jumpin' Jack Flash' and 'Brown Sugar'. The best Aerosmith could do was a bastardised version of 'Train Kept A Rollin' that would probably make Jeff Beck puke. They left the stage exactly 65 minutes after their arrival. Even Geoff Barton admits Aerosmith will never be the Rolling Stones. For starters, they ain't funky. Aerosmith could never play 'Hot Stuff. But they could possibly do a fair 'Whole Lotta Love'. Now the kids just loved them. Aerosmith are the first full-bodied classic British rock 'n' roll band of the seventies. And they're American. Star quality — ten. Presentation — ten. Content — four" (Sounds, 10/23/1976).
- Members of the band attended Paul McCartney & Wings' show at London's Empire Pool on Oct. 19.

October 20 **CANCELLED
Sartory Saele
Cologne, Germany
Promoter: Mama Concerts
Other act(s): Phoenix
Notes:
- A separate promotional tour EP was issued for Europe (CBS-9196) including "Dream On," "Home Tonight" // "Last Child," and "Sweet Emotion."

October 21
Erlangen Stadthalle
Erlangen, Germany
Promoter: Mama Concerts
Other act(s): Phoenix

October 23
Konserthus
Stockholm, Sweden
Promoter: EMA
Other act(s): Phoenix

October 25
New Rai
Amsterdam, Holland

Promoter: Acket & Mojo Concerts
Other act(s): Phoenix
Set list: Mama Kin / S.O.S. (Too Bad) / Lick and a Promise / Big Ten Inch Record / Sweet Emotion / Rats in the Cellar / Dream On / Lord of the Thighs / Last Child / Walk this Way / Same Old Song and Dance / Train Kept A Rollin' / Milk Cow Blues
Notes:
- A decent AUD recording circulates from this show.

October 26
Offenbach Stadthalle
Offenbach, Germany

Promoter: Mama Concerts
Other act(s): Phoenix
Set list: Mama Kin / Write Me / S.O.S. (Too Bad) / Lick and a Promise / Big Ten Inch Record / Sweet Emotion / Rats in the Cellar / Dream On / Lord of the Thighs / Last Child / Walk this Way / Sick as a Dog / Same Old Song and Dance / Train Kept A Rollin' / Toys in the Attic
Notes:
- A decent AUD recording circulates from this show.

October 28
Friedrich-Ebert-Halle
Ludwigshafen, Germany

Promoter: Mama Concerts
Other act(s): Phoenix

October 30
Volkhaus
Zurich, Switzerland

Promoter: Good News Agency
Other act(s): Phoenix
Set list: Same as Oct 26.
Notes:
- Richard Asher, president of CBS Disques International, hosted a reception for the bands during the afternoon prior to the show.
- From a local review: "Speaking of triumph still only gives a pale reflection of the flamboyant performance of Phoenix and Aerosmith on the Zurich scene. Enveloped in billows of smoke, the two groups filled space and time with an orgy of shrill sounds in a Dantesque vision of music. We asked Tom Hamilton, 'If you had a 13-year-old daughter like the one we saw tonight, would you let her attend your concert?' 'Certainly not,' he replied, 'unless she is flanked by a strong bodyguard!'" (Lausanne 24 Heures, 11/1/1976).
- A decent AUD recording circulates from this show.

November 1
Pavillon de Paris
Paris, France

Promoter: Koski/Cauchoix Productions (KCP)
Other act(s): Phoenix
Set list: Same as Oct. 26
Notes:
- A decent AUD recording circulates from this show.

November 10
Civic Arena

Pittsburgh, PA
Promoter: Pacific Presentations
Other act(s): Derringer
Reported audience: 16,470 / 17,500 (94.11%)
Set list: Mama Kin / Write Me A Letter / S.O.S. (Too Bad) / Lick and a Promise / Big Ten Inch Record / Sweet Emotion / Rats in the Cellar / Dream On / Lord of the Thighs
Notes:
- From a local review: "The teeming, rowdy crowd at the Aerosmith/Rick Derringer concert, held at the Civic Arena did not regret waiting upwards of 45-minutes in the bitter cold before being allowed to enter. The concert was all it was expected to be and more... Aerosmith played a pleasing mix of old and new material and never seemed to lag... Toward the close of the set, a giant, lit 'A' manifested itself above the group. They left to resounding cheers and cries for more. Bics were flicked in anticipation of an encore after Aerosmith left the stage. After a five-minute lapse, they reappeared on a darkened stage. Suddenly, two bright firecrackers exploded on either side of the stage and the 'A' reappeared. After several selections, they made their final exit. Tyler's vocals were superb for the duration of the concert. Clad in black and white-striped tuxedo, Tyler proved himself to be extremely versatile — a wildman on songs like 'Walk this Way' and 'Train Kept A Rollin',' tender and mellow on 'Dream On.' The band was strong and provided the perfect backing for Tyler" (Duquesne Duke, 11/24/1976).
- A decent partial AUD recording circulates from this show.

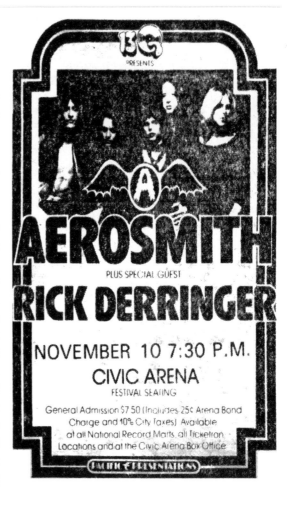

November 12
Memorial Coliseum
New Haven, CT
Reported audience: SRO
Reported gross: $81,976

November 13
Boston Garden
Boston, MA
Promoter: Don Law
Other act(s): Derringer
Reported audience: ~15,530 **SOLD-OUT

November 15
Boston Garden
Boston, MA
Promoter: Don Law
Other act(s): Derringer
Reported audience: ~15,530 **SOLD-OUT
Notes:
- Vandalism against MBTA property and equipment by concertgoers prior to the show resulted police approval being required for future rock concerts at the Garden. The promoter was also required to hire additional security for events.

- From a local review: "The 15,500 teenagers, a considerable number of them tottering alcoholically about the corridors of the Boston Garden, had come to welcome back Boston's own *enfants terribles* of rock, Aerosmith... Backstage the guys appeared drawn and tired, casualties of too many overdone hamburgers and greasy French fries. But once they got their act together onstage, Aerosmith came volcanically alive. The group detonated immediately with 'Mama Kin,' Perry's crackling solos temporarily snatching the spotlight from the lead singer who brandished the microphone as if it were a javelin. 'Dream On,' the group's first hit single, triggered a burst of recognition from the audience as Kramer fired off fusillades from his overamped drum set. 'Walk this Way,' an apparently late-blooming single from the old 'Toys in the Attic' album, found the kids singing along with Steve. A few continued to wander aimlessly about the hall, oblivious to the excitement roaring about them as one overworked usher merely shook his head in resignation. It seemed, based upon a record-setting three-night engagement that nobody liked Aerosmith — except the people" (Boston Globe, 11/16/1976).

November 16 **POSTPONED
Boston Garden
Boston, MA
Promoter: Don Law
Other act(s): Derringer
Notes:
- This sold-out show was postponed until Dec. 14 due to Steven developing laryngitis and being ordered by his physician to rest his voice completely for a week. 12 shows would be rescheduled or cancelled.

November 18 **POSTPONED
Le Forum de Montréal
Montreal, QC, Canada
Other act(s): Lynyrd Skynyrd
Notes:
- This show was postponed until Dec. 13.

November 20 **CANCELLED
Coliseum
Richmond, VA
Other act(s): REO Speedwagon
Notes:
- This show was cancelled rather than being rescheduled.

November 21 **POSTPONED
Carolina Coliseum
Columbia, SC
Promoter: Beach Club Promotions
Other act(s): REO Speedwagon
Notes:
- This show was postponed until Dec. 19.

November 23 **CANCELLED
Civic Coliseum
Knoxville, TN
Promoter: Entam, Ltd.
Other act(s): REO Speedwagon

November 24 **POSTPONED
Civic Center
Roanoke, VA
Promoter: Entam, Ltd.
Other act(s): REO Speedwagon
Notes:
- This show was postponed until Dec. 10.

November 29
Sports Arena
Toledo, OH
Other act(s): REO Speedwagon
Notes:
- The first show following the break for Steven's health. Joe Baptista filled the gap managing the stage for the Boston Globe Jazzfest & Music Fair.

December 1
Cobo Arena
Detroit, MI
Promoter: Belkin Productions
Other act(s): REO Speedwagon
Reported audience: (10,700 capacity)
Notes:

- From a local review: "It's not often a loud and long band bombs in Detroit, but try as it might, Aerosmith did just that Wednesday night. From the start, it must have hurt their collective sensibilities to not have a sell-out crowd at Cobo Hall. Worse still, those who did show up were surprisingly short of enthusiasm. In fact, lead singer Steven Tyler was reduced to virtually imploring the faithful to rush the stage about midway through the concert. The stalwarts did, but most remained in their seats. Aerosmith used its best weapon — sound, loud sound, energetic sound, writhing sound, and tumultuous sound, but it was not enough. Tyler's Mick Jagger mouth, effeminate actions, and suggestive routines with the microphone stand were wasted on all but a few dozen crushing each other against the stage barricade, as he has requested them. Lead guitarist Joe Perry's usually noteworthy windups were more like letdowns. They hauled out their old and some new material, and all met the same response — polite, contained, unsustained, but most of all, mild applause, a few half-hearted whistles, and cheers. It is unlikely Detroit audiences are mellowing, but perhaps the Aerosmith veneer is wearing a bit thin... It certainly doesn't seem much like rock and roll Detroit when the main attraction's lead singer is compelled to shout: 'Get off your ass! What the ----'s the matter with you?!' If Tyler really wants to know what the matter is, he might try looking the other way" (Windsor Star, 12/2/1976).

December 2
Cobo Arena
Detroit, MI
Promoter: Belkin Productions
Other act(s): REO Speedwagon
Reported audience: (10,700 capacity)
Set list: Mama Kin / Write Me / S.O.S. (Too Bad) / Lick and a Promise / Big Ten Inch Record / Sweet Emotion / Rats in the Cellar / Last Child / Lord of the Thighs / Walk this Way / Sick as a Dog / Same Old Song and Dance / Train Kept A Rollin' / Toys in the Attic
Notes:
- Two dates were booked, rather than a larger venue due to the band vowing never to perform at such large, enclosed facilities again.

- An AUD recording circulates from this show.

December 4
State Farm Show Arena
Harrisburg, PA
Promoter: Starview Productions
Other act(s): REO Speedwagon
Reported audience: (7,600 capacity)

December 5
Capital Centre
Largo (Landover), MD
Promoter: Cellar Door Productions
Other act(s): REO Speedwagon
Reported audience: 19,000 **SOLD-OUT

December 7
Freedom Hall
Louisville, KY
Promoter: Sunshine Promotions
Other act(s): REO Speedwagon
Reported audience: ~13,000 / 19,059 (68.21%)
Notes:
- From a local review: "The evening was one of candlelight and chaos. About 13,000 kids stuffed themselves into Freedom Hall last night to hear a few hours of rotgut rock and roll performed by two of the music business' louder elements, R.E.O. and Aerosmith. Because there were no reserved seats, the listeners wandered all over the place, some passing around booze and dope, and then passing out flat on the concrete floor, which by 9 p.m. was gooey amid wet from spilled beverages. Besides people on the floor, there were empty and broken whisky bottles, bottle caps, discarded winter wear and garbage. It was a mess. But there was music, and it was loud and pulsating. And those in the crowd who had the stamina to refrain from fainting really dug the show. Appreciation came in the form of dancing, screaming, stomping, and lighting candles in the darkness. Some decided to light a few smoke bombs in the middle of the crowd on the floor, obscuring Aerosmith for a few minutes. It was the same old Aerosmith show.

The six haven't brushed up on any of their weaknesses which are primarily their repetitiveness and lack of spontaneity. When the same riff is drummed out over and over it gets a little monotonous. But the group puts out some solid sounds, usually well-produced and energetic. The only problem is, there is not one particularly outstanding member in the group. Singer Steve Tallarico, who twirls a microphone around like a baton, is fair but no challenge to legends Like Mick Jagger, whom he seems to try to emulate. Aerosmith did some of its hits from the 'Toys in the Attic' album as well as its latest release, 'Rocks,' which is presently No. 93 on the national charts. Aerosmith is the group responsible for putting 'Dream On' in the Top 10 early this year. The song was originally released in 1973, when it steamed its way into stardom in the East" (Lexington Courier Journal, 12/8/1976).

December 9
Riverfront Coliseum
Cincinnati, OH
Promoter: Electric Factory Concerts
Other act(s): REO Speedwagon
Reported audience: 18,300 **SOLD-OUT
Reported gross: $123,057
Notes:

- From a local review: "Aerosmith — not the only band in America owning a life-size, walking-talking Mick Jagger doll (Tyler) — performed for 63 minutes for the capacity crowd. It was 63 minutes of execrable music played execrably. (The sound system wasn't much better. Words and music came out of the speakers in muddy globs of sound.) There is no craft to Aerosmith's music. Crescendos and decrescendos are alien to their musical vocabulary. They know only one dynamic level: blasting. Tyler's Jagger-isms looked pathetically humorous. He pranced, cantered, sang with his hands on his hips, brandished the microphone stand and delivered his lyrics with a defiant slap in the manner, but without the showmanship, expertise, and skill of the Rolling Stones' lead vocalist. Not only is Tyler a poseur, he is also awkward. His one dramatic leap from the drum riser started unceremoniously. As he jumped onto the riser, he slammed his forehead into the microphone suspended above Joey Kramer's drums. The guitar playing of Aerosmith's Joe Perry set rock back about 15 years. Never before has anyone with such sloppy technique and simplistic note patterns attempted to perform on the Coliseum's stage. This puts Perry in some dreadful company" (Cincinnati Enquirer, 12/11/1976).
- From another local review: "Those 'Platinum Punks' from Beantown, Aerosmith, staggered a sell-out crowd at Riverfront Coliseum here last week with heavy metal mashing and non-stop theatrics. The band proved once again why they are one of this country's premier hard-rock groups and why audiences in the region will go the extra mile to see lead singer Steven Tyler carry on with his microphone stand... Opening with the hard-rocking 'Mama Kin' from their first album, Tyler and his mates set a blazing pace that would not let up until they had heaped 90 minutes of power chording and classical British rock posturing on the mostly teen-aged mob of 18,000. The focal point of the Aerosmith group is Tyler — America's answer to Jager. The swaggering, tireless vocalist made the most of the huge stage area and, in general, made himself accessible to the adoring legions of youngsters who were crushed in the suicidal mob on the arena floor. Waving his scarf draped mike stand like a bandleader's baton, Tyler gave new life to songs like 'Lick and a Promise,' 'Big Record' and 'Sick as a Dog.'

In case the young audience needed what, they call on Madison Avenue — 'Product Reinforcement' — the Aerosmith set featured a huge backdrop with the band's logo on it. This band's formalistic approach reeks of the British influence from guitarist Joe Perry's contorted posturing to the way the band marches forward in step to present a melody line. This is as much a part of the show as the heavy musicmaking. It isn't the average vocalizing which blitzes the listener's imagination — it is the truly menacing guitar attack backed by basic drumming from the Neanderthal School by Joey Kramer... While Tyler raced and clowned throughout, the rest of the band was all business. Perry and Brad Whitford's thrilling guitar duet on 'Rats in the Cellar' didn't last long enough while Kramer's drum solo was a bit overdone. From his raised platform stage center, Kramer was a bundle of energy and set a standard for the rest of the band — nothing subtle about his drumming... It was a well-paced evening of hard rock. While the headliners barely played 90 minutes, that was enough for critic and crowd alike" (Lexington Herald, 12/13/1976).

December 10
Civic Center
Roanoke, VA
Promoter: Entam, Ltd.
Other act(s): REO Speedwagon
Reported audience: ~11,000

December 13
Le Forum de Montréal
Montreal, QC, Canada
Other act(s): Rush
Reported audience: ~12,000
Notes:
- This show marked the final time Rush opened for Aerosmith. Lynyrd Skynyrd had been scheduled to open the postponed Nov. 18 date.
- From a local review: "A double-barreled rock bottom was hit on Monday night at the Forum with the Aerosmith-Rush rock show. This was probably the loudest show at that venue this year, presenting two groups whose entire styles are based on frantically performed high-pitch volume. That the majority of the 12,000 young fans in attendance enjoyed the onslaught is a reflection of their taste... Aerosmith evidently decided it was not to be out-volumed. It blasted out a thundering sound, underpinned by relentless bass buzz (the sound of a wire spring amplified in slow motion) and moronic messy guitar. Above the din a singer named Steve Tyler — with lips larger than Mick Jagger's, and a skinnier torso (not to mention the regulation-size rock crotch) — yelled into the microphone with blurry effect. He fixed the mike stand between his legs and jumped about like a rabbit on speed. At the end of the first couple of numbers, he screeched out to the crowd: 'You're (bleeping) beautiful!' 'Nuff said" (Montreal Gazette, 12/15/1976).

December 14 **TEMP HOLD-DATE
Civic Center
Hartford, CT
Notes:
- With the rescheduling of the third Boston show, this date was not booked.

December 14
Boston Garden
Boston, MA
Promoter: Don Law
Other act(s): Derringer
Reported audience: ~15,530 **SOLD-OUT
Notes:
- Members of the audience battled with security throughout and after the show, but the local after-show violence and destruction was less than the band's previous visit had caused.

December 16
Madison Square Garden
New York City, NY
Promoter: Ron Delsener
Other act(s): Derringer
Reported audience: 19,600 **SOLD-OUT
Reported gross: $272,000 **both shows
Set list: Mama Kin / Write Me / S.O.S. (Too Bad) / Lick and a Promise / Big Ten Inch Record / Sweet Emotion / Rats in the Cellar / Dream On / Lord of the Thighs / Last Child / Walk this Way / Sick as a Dog / Same Old Song and Dance / Train Kept A Rollin' / Toys in the Attic
Notes:
- From a local review: "Thursday night, Aerosmith, riding on the success of their recent albums, five the first of two sold-out shows at Madison Square Garden. And they were good, too — which one hastens to add because success in the teen market is not always an infallible guarantee of quality. Aerosmith's forte is a steady succession of high-energy rock songs, with an unvarying guitar-bass-and-drums instrumentation, plus intermittent harmonica, and percussion. There is an occasional ballad for contrast, and the ballads work. But the essence of the act is energy. This can lead to legitimate charges of sameness. The onslaught is

steady and not very varied, and if you aren't really into it, it all begins to wash over your head. But one must remember the context in which Aerosmith is working.

In contrast to the monolithic leadenness of the heavy-metal bands and the inflated pretensions of the classical mood-rockers, it's nice to see a band that simply rocks out in a vaguely British manner... It took a while to appreciate Aerosmith's virtues Thursday because the sound was even murkier and more distorted than one is used to in large arenas. But eventually the rhythmic sharpness and executional tightness of the band began to sink in. And if Steven Tyler is still a Jagger clone, he is at least fully of spunk and he at least sings in a strong, tireless manner. It was not one of the great rock concerts, but it was amusing and, at its best, uplifting. And Aerosmith's growth over the last few years gives one hope that they can grow some more" (New York Times, 12/18/1976).

December 17
Madison Square Garden
New York City, NY
Promoter: Ron Delsener
Other act(s): Derringer
Reported audience: 19,600 **SOLD-OUT
Notes:
- Steven's parents attended both shows. Following one of the NYC shows, Rick Derringer (piano), Danny Johnson, John Belushi (vocals), Steven Tyler (drums), Brad Whitford and David Johansson (harmonica) conducted a jam session at Rick's place.
- From a local review: "Aerosmith played before an unruly capacity crowd at Madison Square Garden Friday night, and demonstrated why the group is currently America's most popular hard rock outfit. A Boston band, better known for its whizbang stage impact than for memorable material, it whipped up a potent, sonic maelstrom. Aerosmith's high-powered show is a driving blend of lightning guitar solos and cleverly sassy lyrics which cut through a rock-solid foundation of heavy blues riffs. The outfit is fronted by gruff vocalist Steven Tyler, a superbly agile leaper who soaks up the spotlight like a giant White moth. His playful antics are contrasted by the actions of guitarist Joe Perry, a raffish pirate figure in a leather vest and sloppy bandana Since its last New York appearance, Aerosmith has streamlined its set, cutting all but two ballads, and dropping Joey Kramer's drum solo, at the drummer's insistence. The band's most famous song is the drifting 'Dream On,' but its current rendition is perfunctory, in deference to churning kickers like 'Lick and a Promise,' 'Train Kept A Rollin',' and the latest single, 'Walk this Way'" (New York Daily News, 12/20/1976).

December 19
Carolina Coliseum
Columbia, SC
Promoter: Beach Club Promotions
Other act(s): REO Speedwagon
Reported audience: ~15,000
Notes:
- From a local review: "The largest crowd Carolina Coliseum has ever held turned out last night to be assaulted by more than two hours of driving heavy metal music spearheaded by a group called Aerosmith. Nearly 15,000 persons packed in to hear the five-man band, whose latest album is 'Rocks' (Columbia Records), and they were not disappointed. The group ran through most of its tunes on this LP and 'Toys in the Attic,' and although the booming sound system was not always clear, the audience obviously was familiar with Aerosmith's material. Like the lyrics of one of its songs, the band got down to the 'nitty gritty"

as a bare bones outfit with three guitars, drums, and a flashy lead singer. Aerosmith's members are not musically exciting or original, but they are competent and put on a fine show. Lead singer Steven Tyler has been compared to Mick Jagger, and he does have some of Jagger's sensual style as well as a good voice. The band also has some of the same raunchiness as the Rolling Stones or Alice Cooper but does not have the depth or fascination of these bands" (Columbia Record, 12/20/1976).

1977

January 28 **CANCELLED
Nippon Budokan
Tokyo, Japan
Promoter: Udo Artists, Inc.

January 29
Gunma Sports Center
Maebashi, Japan
Promoter: Udo Artists, Inc.
Other act(s): Bow Wow
Set list: Mama Kin / Write Me / S.O.S. (Too Bad) / Lick and a Promise / Big Ten Inch Record / Sweet Emotion / Rats in the Cellar / Dream On / Lord of the Thighs / Last Child / Walk this Way / Sick as a Dog / Same Old Song and Dance / Train Kept A Rollin' / Toys in the Attic
Notes:
- The set list performed on the Japanese leg of the tour was essentially the same that the band had been performing in December.
- An excellent AUD recording circulates from this show.

January 31
Nippon Budokan
Tokyo, Japan
Promoter: Udo Artists, Inc.
Other act(s): Bow Wow
Set list: Same as Jan. 29.
Notes:
- An excellent AUD recording circulates from this show.

February 1
Civic Assembly Hall
Nagoya, Japan
Promoter: Udo Artists, Inc.
Other act(s): Bow Wow
Set list: Same as Jan. 29.
Notes:
- A below average AUD recording circulates from this show. "Last Child" is only briefly featured on the recording before cutting out.

February 4
Kyuden Kinen Gymnasium
Fukuoka, Japan
Promoter: Udo Artists, Inc.
Other act(s): Bow Wow
Set list: Same as Jan. 29.
Notes:
- An excellent AUD recording circulates from this show.

February 6
Kyoto Kaikan
Kyoto, Japan
Promoter: Udo Artists, Inc.
Other act(s): Bow Wow
Set list: Same as Jan. 29.
Notes:
- A decent AUD recording circulates from this show. During the "Train Kept A Rollin'" jam parts of "Get the Lead Out," "Adam's Apple," and "Movin Out" are teased.

February 7
Festival Hall
Osaka, Japan
Promoter: Udo Artists, Inc.
Other act(s): Bow Wow
Set list: Mama Kin / S.O.S. (Too Bad) / Lick and a Promise / Big Ten Inch Record / Sweet Emotion / Rats in the Cellar / Dream On / Lord of the Thighs / Last Child / Walk this Way / Same Old Song and Dance / Train Kept A Rollin' / Toys in the Attic
Notes:
- "Write Me" and "Sick as a Dog" dropped from the set for the two remaining shows on the tour.
- A below average AUD recording circulates from this show.

February 9
Nippon Budokan
Tokyo, Japan
Promoter: Udo Artists, Inc.
Other act(s): Bow Wow
Set list: Mama Kin / S.O.S. (Too Bad) / Lick and a Promise / Big Ten Inch Record / Sweet Emotion / Dream On (False Start) / Rats in the Cellar / Dream On / Lord of the Thighs / Last Child / Walk this Way / Same Old Song and Dance / Train Kept A Rollin' / Toys in the Attic
Notes:
- An excellent AUD recording circulates from this show. Following the tour, the band members vacationed in Hawaii on their way back to the mainland U.S.

February 18–20 **CANCELLED
Gila River Indian Reservation
Phoenix, AZ
Promoter: Theodore Znosko / Thomas Langham / Valley of the Sun Music Association
Notes:
- Be absolutely clear, Aerosmith were never booked for what appeared to be a fraudulent music festival, the "Forty-four Hours in Concert," but they were named in promotional literature distributed by the promoter. Other bands listed included the Who, Black Oak Arkansas, Johnny Winter and Peter Frampton — none of whom had been booked either. On Jan. 14, a suit was filed against the promoter by the Arizona Consumer

Fraud Division charging that the concert was phony. A preliminary injunction against ticket sales was granted in Superior Court on Jan. 21. The promoter had allegedly printed 60,000 tickets for the event and distributed stock to ticket sellers with promise of an unusually large % of each $15 ticket sold. However, the promoter had not obtained permission from the tribe for use of their land or booked staging and lighting for the fictitious event. Aerosmith's booking agent, Hal Lazareff, denied being contacted by the promoter about any concert as did agents representing other artists linked with the purported event... Znosko was later found guilty of fraud and conspiracy and sentenced to six months in county jail and a five-years of probation.

1977 - Draw the Line

U.S. Release Details:
Columbia/CBS JC/JCA/JCT-34856 (Dec. 9, 1977)
Columbia/CBS CK-34856 (1987 — CD reissue)
Columbia/SMEi CK/CT-57364 (Sep. 7, 1993 — 20-bit SBM digital remaster)
Columbia/SME 88883760951 (Apr. 22, 2014 — 180g LP reissue)

Tracks:
A1. Draw the Line •
(3:23) — Steven Tyler / Joe Perry
A2. I Wanna Know Why
(3:09) — Steven Tyler / Joe Perry
A3. Critical Mass
(4:53) — Steven Tyler / Tom Hamilton / Jack Douglas
A4. Get It Up •
(4:02) — Steven Tyler / Joe Perry
A5. Bright Light Fright
(2:19) — Joe Perry

B1. Kings and Queens •
(4:55) — Steven Tyler / Brad Whitford / Tom Hamilton / Joey Kramer / Jack Douglas
B2. The Hand That Feeds
(4:23) — Steven Tyler / Brad Whitford / Tom Hamilton / Joey Kramer / Jack Douglas
B3. Sight for Sore Eyes
(3:56) — Steven Tyler / Joe Perry / Jack Douglas / David Johansen
B4. Milk Cow Blues
(4:14) — Kokomo Arnold

Album Details:
Produced & arranged by Jack Douglas and Aerosmith. Engineered by Jay Messina assisted by Sam Ginsberg. Recorded at The Cenacle, Armonk, NY and the Record Plant, New York City, NY.

Players:
◦ I Wanna Know Why - Stan Bronstein in saxophones; Scott Cushnie on piano.
◦ Critical Mass - Scott Cushnie on piano.
◦ Get it Up - Karen Lawrence on backing vocals.
◦ Bright Light Fright - Stan Bronstein in saxophones; Joe Perry on lead vocals.
◦ Kings and Queens - Jack Douglas on mandolin; Paul Prestopino on banjo; Steven Tyler on piano.

Chart Action:
Chart Peak (USA): #11 (1/28/1978) with 20 weeks on the Billboard charts. Other countries: N/A.

12/24/77	12/31/77	01/07/78	01/14/78	01/21/78	01/28/78	02/04/78
48	48	20	16	14	**11**	11
02/11/78	02/18/78	02/25/78	03/04/78	03/11/78	03/18/78	03/25/78
11	18	37	51	62	61	84
04/01/78	04/08/78	04/15/78	04/22/78	04/29/78	05/06/78	05/13/78
96	116	112	112	122	178	X

RIAA/Sales:
In the United States, the album was certified Gold by the RIAA on December 9, 1977 and Platinum on December 13, 1977; Its most recent certification is for 2X Platinum on August 16, 1996. Gold by the CRIA (Canada - 50,000 units) on December 1, 1977. And Platinum in Japan for sales of more than 100,000 copies. During the SoundScan era, the album had sold 120,556 copies between 1991 and 2007.

Supporting Singles:
• Draw the Line (USA, 10/6/1977) - Chart Peak: #42 (11/19/1977) with 10 weeks on the Billboard charts. Other countries: CAN #38.

10/22/77	10/29/77	11/05/77	11/12/77	**11/19/77**	11/26/77	12/03/77
79	68	57	47	** 42 **	42	42
12/10/77	12/17/77	12/24/77	12/31/77			
59	65	98	X			

• Kings and Queens (USA, 2/1978) - Chart Peak: #70 (4/1/1978) with 5 weeks on the Billboard charts. Other countries: N/A.

03/11/78	03/18/78	03/25/78	**04/01/78**	04/08/78	04/15/78
84	74	72	** 70 **	70	X

• Get It Up (USA, 4/1978) - Chart Peak: DID NOT CHART. The single mix had a sharper fade-out shortening the song by 10 seconds.

Joe Perry: "The Beatles had their white album; 'Draw the Line' was our blackout album" ("Walk this Way").

Touring for the main "Rocks" cycles ended on Dec. 19, 1976, following which the band took a short break before embarking on their Japanese tour at the end of January. While there, the band enjoyed a taste of Beatlemania with Joe and Elyssa having to get an extra hotel room in which to store all their gifts. Following the tour, the band members vacationed in Hawaii before returning to the mainland. Local press suggested that members were split, some on Maui and others, along with the road crew, in Kona and Honolulu. And then it was time for a rinse and repeat of the previous year — getting down to the work of recording a new studio album. Intended or not, the band had fallen into the tour-album-tour trap. Consequently, their lifestyles, on and off the road, also required an influx of money to fund. "Rocks" had seen the band at its most potent, with the scales of reasonableness delicately balanced between creativity and performance on one side, and tension, substance, and interpersonal abuse on the other. By early 1977, that balance was shifting, slowly, almost imperceptibly away from the creative at first; more precisely it was becoming one noted by an imbalance. A metaphorical artistic mountain had been climbed, but the band had yet to define whether there would be a plateau or descent.

What no one realized was that as the band started out to make their next album, they were standing on a precipice that would ultimately result in their decline and Joe Perry's departure. As Joe (in particular) later frequently opined, the band had gone from musicians dabbling in drugs to full-blown druggies dabbling in music. He'd later evaluate the period in which the album was created: "At that point, we were really beginning to take everything for granted... Rather than trying to move things onto the next level for us musically and maybe take some time off and put it back together, it just kind of fell apart. We were too self-indulgent. Too self-absorbed, and gain, we lost sight of what we were there for" (Billboard, 8/15/1998). "Rocks" and "Draw the Line" as albums couldn't provide a better contrast between the two states of consciousness within the band. Perhaps a better line of demarcation was the April 13 death of Father Frank Connelly, in a Norwich, CT hospital from the ravages of pancreatic cancer. A true genius, a visionary, Frank's role in the ascendancy of Aerosmith can never be understated even if he'd long been out of the band's orbit.

On the charts, the reissued "Walk this Way" remained on the Hot-100 into early March. It was followed up with the release of "Back in the Saddle," which attained top-40 status and kept the band visible on the charts into early June (when "Rocks" also dropped off the Billboard Top-200) — perfectly setting the stage for a new single from a new album... The band had enjoyed the methodology of recording "Rocks" at their Waltham rehearsal space and wanted to do similar for the new album, but with a change of scenery facilitated by using remote recording services elsewhere. Following a month's worth of preproduction at the Wherehouse, with Steven hanging at Jack's house in New Jersey while Joe worked on his own in his home basement, staff at the Record Plant located the Cenacle. Isolated on 100 acres of wooded land in Mount Kisco in Westchester County, New York, it had formerly been operated by the Congregation of Our Lady of the Cenacle. Originally bought for Broadway showman Billy Rose, the estate had become a 100-room retreat house that could "accommodate 200 people for brief periods of solitude, prayer and contemplation" (New York Times, 9/29/1974).

By 1974, the sisters had become unable to afford its upkeep, and the property had been leased by two doctors who in turn hoped to transform it into a treatment center for troubled youth (in 1979 the property would be sold to Sun Myung Moon's Unification Church). Troubled youth of a different sort were certainly those who took up residence in early 1977. Tom, Joey, Brad and Jack arrived first, and set about the task of reconfiguring the facility to be usable as a recording studio — without damaging or making any changes to the rooms used. The overall concept for the recording session was that the Cenacle would be a retreat where the band would be able to recharge and create simultaneously — separated from their worst influences and instincts in Boston or New York City. Placing the musicians in different rooms would allow the aural ambience of those rooms to be infused into the rooms: As Jack recalled, "Joey's drums were in the chapel, Steven was up on the second floor, Brad was in the living room, and Joe was in this big walk-in fireplace" ("Walk this Way"). At the Cenacle, the band came together as a group for the new project for the first time. One problem that may have been overlooked was, drugs dealers do own cars and have phones...

The problem was that the band was essentially coming into the studio from being on the road. There hadn't been much of a break in December and January, and even less following the Japan trip. "Rocks" had been born through extensive pre-production sessions at the Wherehouse as a band. There was also the question of material, or lack thereof, and Jack recalled there being discussion about possibly including covers on the album. One such song would be committed to tape, "Milk Cow Blues," and made the release. Another, Otis Rush's "All Your Love" didn't. With showing up first, Brad, Tom, and Joey worked on ideas in hopes that Joe and Steven would show up and contribute. It gave them the clearest opportunity to work on ideas, albeit as a trio, during what was almost a combined preproduction/recording session. When Joe and Steven did show up at the Cenacle, both quickly disappeared to play with new toys or indulge in a toxic chemical summer camp. Steven recalled, "I hit the wall. This was as far as I wanted to go, because I would like fall asleep for two days, just not coming downstairs to record and not caring if Joey and Brad and Tom were doing their guitar parts. Drug-wise, this is the end of it" (Billboard, 8/15/1998). The location hardly meant that drugs couldn't be delivered from the city, and friends such as David Johansen regularly visited and participated in the insanity. As illustrated by the unreleased jams — "Krawhitham," "Circle Jerk" and "Subway" — later to surface on "Pandora's Box" in 1991, Tom, Brad, and Joey clearly did try to get to work with Jack on new material. The problem was that without Steven and Joe it wasn't truly Aerosmith. With Joe, the drugs had purportedly taken control. He had ideas, new expressions he wanted to try, notably incorporating more slide guitar into songs, but was incapable of performing and focusing on the task at hand. Joe would turn up for sessions "glassy eyed" only to be thrown out when he couldn't play. He'd stowed the ideas that he'd worked on for the album in a cookie tin, like a stash of drugs. Unfortunately, he promptly misplaced the tin, so was unable to provide any collection of ideas to the rest of the band and it appeared he wasn't serious about the sessions. Or he'd be throwing up in the middle of jams... Following which, he'd disappear for days on end. Fortunately, the slide idea that became "Draw the Line" caught Steven's ear...

While the resulting album was disjointed and variable in quality in contrast to the overall strength of earlier material, perhaps one positive to come out of the situation was that shift in dynamics within the band. With the marginally less toxic trio doing more of the work there were more opportunities for them to step in and fill the void. Brad was able to contribute more guitar than usual since Joe couldn't be bothered to get out of bed at times. Regardless, his work fit the songs so there was no point replacing it. Nor was there time... It shouldn't be surprising that eventual album songs, "Critical Mass," "Kings and Queens," and "The Hand That Feeds," lacked credited input from Joe. Aerosmith's time at the Cenacle was generally unproductive, and their delays in recording resulted in the start of the Aerosmith Express tour having to be rescheduled. Their scheduling also meant that the next band who had booked the facility, KISS, had to move their recording sessions for their "Love Gun" album to the Record Plant in New York City (they had been scheduled to record May 9–27 with mixing taking place through June 11). Whatever the case, by the time the band finished up at the Cenacle, "Draw the Line" was still not completed. In the early morning of June 1, the day following the last day at the Cenacle, Joey Kramer was injured in a car accident while returning to Boston. After falling asleep while driving his Ferrari he was awoken as the car drove into the back of a truck and then collided with a guardrail. He'd receive several stitches for assorted cuts from the windscreen glass shattering, and a $19,000 ($80,000 in 2019) repair bill. Dates scheduled to start in Buffalo on June 3, followed by the year's first "World Series of Rock" stadium show in Cleveland, were postponed, or cancelled; and the tour rescheduled to start in Ft. Worth on June 21. According to Joey Kramer they performed some "God-awful shows" during this leg of the tour.

Awful or not, "Draw the Line" debuted in the band's set at this time, the first taste from the forthcoming album. It was clear that even with Joe and Steven's challenges in Armonk, the band had been able to knock the song into enough shape to be performed on the tour and freshen the set list slightly. Also present in the set was the band's cover of "Rattlesnake Shake," which raises the question of whether that was another the songs the band considered as a cover for the album (the song having been a band favorite from the beginning). Following the conclusion of the initial leg on July 9, the band headed into the Record Plant to continue trying to work on the album. If Joe had been unable to play at times in Armonk, then Steven was similarly blocked, regarding many of the album's lyrics — hardly a new situation, then or in the years to come. Ever defensive on the matter, Steven commented, "Why does it take me so long [to deliver the lyrics]? Because I'm not Patti Smith who sits down and writes poetry every time something comes to my head. I don't keep a diary or anything like that, and I have to write the words exactly to the music. You can't sit down and write all the words to an album in one week. It's got to come from somewhere, and it's hard. It doesn't come out unless you sit down and think about it and fill the fireplace, 20 times at least, with paper" (Rock Talk with Lisa Robinson via Springfield Union, 8/28/1977). He'd also suggest that life on the road was not conducive to being productive in any manner... It would be left to Jack Douglas to write the lyrics to "Critical Mass" and he would end up prodding Steven with ideas in order to get "Kings and Queens" completed. Some other songs ended up on the album as a matter of necessity. Other band members had rejected Joe's "Bright Light Fright," which he had demoed in his basement during his solo pre-production for the album and brought in fully formed. Jack, who had come to regret his decision to work with the band on the album, persuaded the others to record it, providing Joe with his first lead vocal.

For Joe, "The basic difference between this album and all our other albums is that we would make albums and then take the songs that we could play and do them on stage. This time we'll be able to play 80 per cent of the songs onstage. Also, all these songs are real rockers, real cookers. There's not a slow, draggy song on the album" (Rock Talk with Lisa Robinson via Springfield Union, 8/18/1977). One such piece was "Get it Up," which Joe had also worked up prior to the album sessions. Some of the other nearly lost cookie tin ideas included what became "Sight for Sore Eyes," a song he'd initially worked on with David Johansen. Another musical seed grew into "I Wanna Know Why." But only one idea had been fully fleshed out and the rest required work by the band to knock into shape. Work on the album continued even while the band were on the road — and in parallel, work commenced on the next project, a live album, with shows being recorded for possible inclusion. During the band's visit to Europe in August, they spent time at George Martin's AIR Studio in London, to record the solo for the song that became the lead-off single from the album. But by late-September the band were back on the road at home for another leg of the "Aerosmith Express" tour. By this time "I Wanna Know Why" and "Get it Up" had been added to the set, providing hope to stalwart fans that a new album was really coming.

Guests, no strangers to Aerosmith albums, were brought in to season the material. 1994 vocalist Karen Lawrence, who had already sung backing vocals for Jeff Beck, was brought in to sing on "Get it Up" (Brad later performed on a single track on the Douglas produced debut 1994 album released in 1978). Scott Cushnie returned to provide some boogie-woogie piano on "I Wanna Know Why" and "Critical Mass." And Stan Bronstein played saxophone and sousaphone on "I Wanna Know Why" and "Bright Light Fright" respectively. Even Jack got in on the act, adding mandolin to "Kings and Queens" with Paul Prestopino completing the treatment for the song with banjo. Unfortunately, the title track — issued far in advance of the album's release — struggled to a disappointing #42 on the Billboard Hot-100 chart and was gone after 10 weeks. And for most reviewers, it was one of the album's stronger tracks or at least a positive omen of things to come. One review noted, "This hard rock outfit's single from a forthcoming album is a high energy, driving rocker that maintains its peak energy level throughout. The charged guitar and bass riffs are delivered in a fast-paced flurry while Steve Tyler's vocals soar through the heavy instrumentation" (Billboard, 10/15/1977). On the road again, touring continued to take a toll on band members and both Joe and Steven were injured at a show in Philadelphia on Oct. 9. As the band returned to the stage for their encores, an M-80 firework lobbed from the audience exploded close by injuring Joe's hand and Steven's eye. It was hardly an unusual occurrence for bands at the time, and they certainly weren't the only musicians injured by their fans, but the injuries knocked the band off the road for a couple of weeks.

The album was finally released December 9. In the United States, it was certified Gold by the RIAA on December 9 and Platinum on December 13, 1977; Its most recent certification is for 2X Platinum on August 16, 1996. Gold by the CRIA (Canada - 50,000 units) was awarded on December 1, 1977. In the SoundScan era the album sold 120,556 units between 1991 and Feb. 2007, which was (at the time) only slightly more than "Done with Mirrors" sold in the same period. In the U.S., the album reached #11 on the Billboard Top-200 charts on Jan. 27, 1978 during a 20-week run. During 19-weeks on Cashbox the album reached #10. Internationally, the album reached #9 in Japan and #10 in Canada. The band may have been relieved to have completed the album, but they would have known that they'd dialed it in. Tom recalled, "I'll never forget when this record was done, I went to an old friend's house for a party up in New Hampshire. And everybody pretty much politely listened to it, and then I went up to my friend and I said, 'Wow, what do you think?' and he said, 'I think it sucks'" (Billboard, 8/15/1998). While the cover was stunning, with bold caricature drawn by Al Hirschfeld, many reviews interpreted the lack of logo or title as a mark of arrogance by the band — that in their minds it seemed that they had become so successful that anyone would know which band the album was from by simply looking at the art. Copies were soon modified with the application of a sticker featuring the band's logo and album title, and many international issues had those features incorporated immediately. The caricature may have been more ironic than it had seemed in concept...

Steven had had grand plans for his entrance on stage. The show would start with a holographic Tyler singing, and then the real Tyler would enter and approach the hologram, shaking hands with it, and then merge with the image. But in the end, it didn't happen, and many reviews suggested that Aerosmith 1977 was little more than a rehash of the previous year, that the band were simply resting on their laurels. Coming off the road just after the album was released spelt its doom, to a certain extent, even after the grind required to create, record, and release it. The band's visibility plummeted while they took a three-month break, so while the album may have shipped 1.5 million copies fast, it disappeared off the charts just as rapidly. Many of the reviews of the album noted one thing in common: A sameness of the album, and a perception that it broke no new ground may have only been concern to critics, but eventually fans would catch on to some new musical sound being generated by another band. "Kings and Queens" wouldn't be issued until late-February, coinciding with the band preparing to head back on the road. Backed with "Critical Mass" (Columbia 3-10699), it stiffed, only scrapped to a five-week run on Billboard's Hot-100 singles charts plateauing at #70. It was warmly received in the trades: "With a saga of Kings and Queens and guillotines, the boys from b-town romp again. Taken off the 'Draw the Line' album, the track offers a big production, driving beat and cymbal work, tight vocals, guitars and a piano-bass interlude" (Cashbox, 3/4/1978). It was quickly followed by "Get it Up," backed with "Milk Cow Blues" (Columbia 3-10727), which failed to chart at all, even with further positive reviews: "Aerosmith's power charged heavy metal sound works well here as the riveting guitars pace the rhythms. Steve Tyler's lead vocals are gutsy and bold, charged with the same high-level energy as the instrumentals" (Billboard, 4/15/1978). The single bubbled under (on Cashbox) but utterly failed to chart and the slide off the charts continued for the album. With no touring and minimal national media promotion the album was gone from Billboard's Top-200 by May 13.

In December 1977, an announcement was made that Aerosmith had signed on to participate in Robert Stigwood's $12 million treatment of the Beatles' "Sgt. Pepper's Lonely Hearts Club Band" which was expected, at least in terms of ambitiousness, to outstrip his previous adaptation of the Who's "Tommy." The band joined a cast including the Bee Gees, Peter Frampton, and Alice Cooper. The band's participation required that they cancel a string of tour dates scheduled for early January. The band members had not been inactive as touring wound down, Steven contributed backing vocals to a Jack Douglas production, Frankie Miller's "Double Trouble" album being recorded at the Record Plant in New York City. It was released in March. Richie Supa and Karen Lawrence also participated. Brad also contributed guitar on one song on Karen's band's 1994 album released later that year. While the band continued to tour from March onwards, they were now focused on their next project: A live album...

Assorted review excerpts:

"And, at the fifth fence, the prize Boston fillies tumble down. Which is a sorta fancy way of saying that for the first time on record, Aerosmith have blown it. And blown it badly... Where once there was muscle is now all flab, where once there was a tenacity is now an adamant loss of direction. Or more precisely, where once there were good hooklines, clever riffs and a real intensity of feel is now all half-baked, indolent boring riffs of little consequence and thus a dour lack of unity of purpose within the band... They're still thrashing away adeptly enough, and Jack Douglas has still got all the earmarking of a great hard rock producer but the material here is all so stiff, so uninspired... 'I Wanna Know Why' sounds like another Stones Exile-era rocker, but somehow it never rises and, like the whole album itself, you're left waiting for a punchline that never comes.

The only time Aerosmith seem at all inspired is actually on side two's epic 'Kings & Queens'. Basically, a fairly daft song with its whole 'in days of olde' slant easily worthy of the prattish posings of Freddie Mercury, 'Kings & Queens' still has its moments, principally a brilliant break where Douglas (I presume) superimposes Bernard Hermann's nerve-tensing stringed screams straight off the 'Psycho' soundtrack onto a great rush of Aerosmith amyl-nitrate rock... The main problem may ultimately reside with guitarist Joe Perry. Until now he could invariably match Steve Tyler's not unappealing lyrical bluster with good riffs and chord progressions. Here he just doesn't seem to bother — and his own solo venture, a short spew of directionless, hotcha-fast rock jive entitled 'Bright Light Fright', sounds as amateurish as any mediocre new wave band (when adequately recorded) ... At the last count it's all down to indolence, I guess. It's been a weird, rather uneventful and often downright mediocre year for Aerosmith and maybe that's all reflected in this their dour product" (New Musical Express, 12/17/1977).

"For rough, tough black-and-blue material, Aerosmith is close to the top of the heap. 'Draw the Line' won't win them new friends, but it will keep old-timers happy. Most heavyweight undertakings are chancy, and this is no exception. Much dross, strictly out-take material, fills in the gaps between some genuine blasters. 'Critical Mass' and 'Get it Up' are both bright numbers with solid rhythms while 'Draw the Line' and 'I Wanna Know Why' didn't deserve preservation. It's hard to be enthusiastic about this one, but it's impossible to write Aerosmith off" (Toronto Globe & Mail, 12/21/1977).

Aerosmith epitomizes the genre of mainstream, high-powered hard rock that cranks up its derivative '60s moves with flashy '70s production techniques. And while Aerosmith is indisputably the best of these clones (Starz, Detective, Foreigner, etc.), their albums have come to be generally lackluster affairs that are saved only by a handful of powerhouse tunes. For my money, Aerosmith hit its peak on its second album, 'Get Your Wings'; the sterling production made their Yardbirds/Stones-derived riffs jump out of the speakers and box your ears. Unfortunately, the last three albums have tread over the same territory, and the first of these ('Toys in the Attic') did it most effectively. The title single is a raving riffer that is a solid smash until the third verse, when Steven Tyler's voice starts screeching like a mating cat. The tune that follows, 'I Wanna Know Why,' is sure to be the smash of the album, as Aerosmith throws itself into a Stones grind that barely allows a moment for breath. The Stones analogy is completed on guitarist Joe Perry's 'Bright Light Fright,' which both in structure and general sound (Perry sings lead with Tyler contributing harmonies), recalls Keith Richard's 'Happy.' Would it be that it were as good. And that is precisely the problem with the rest of the album — the material doesn't command our attention, but rather starts to give a distinct feeling of déjà vu. On their fifth album, Aerosmith isn't making us think of hard rock's founding fathers as much as of their own earlier albums. If you're a fan, you already have 'Draw the Line'; if you're simply curious, consider picking up 'Get Your Wings' or 'Toys in the Attic'" (Chicago Daily News, 12/29/1977).

"'Draw the Line' is probably Aerosmith's least satisfactory album. The fact that it can still be highly recommended points out how solid a band we're dealing with. The LP offers the usual array of Aerosmith traits: slashing guitars and vocals, locomotive chord progressions, barely decipherable, punning lyrics. It's a sound as full, whooshing and searing as a Concorde's takeoff — all enhanced by another reliable, robust Jack Douglas production job. The problem is there are fewer immediately striking songs than usual. For the most part, the group seems to be merely adding to its catalogue... Each of its previous albums contains almost a half-dozen candidates for 'best of' honors. The new, nine-song package comes up with only three. There's nothing all that bad about the other six tracks — just a slight slip in quality. The three winners are the title tune, 'Get it Up' and 'Kings and Queens.' The title tune is a fast-moving, damn-the-torpedoes cooker, with a memorable guitar riff. 'Get it Up' is the gritty, sexy, shake-your-booty contribution. Highlighted by some earthy Ron Wood-style slide licks, it comes across as engagingly as any funky number the group has done. But the most outstanding song is the ambitious 'Kings and Queens.' Its Celtic folk tune-influenced verse, diverse instrumental effects, and Stephen Tyler's soaring multitracked vocals give it a driving majesty. Aerosmith is so clearly the class of the U.S. hard rock bands that even when it's in a holding pattern, like 'Draw the Line,' it far outstrips its commonplace rivals" (Los Angeles Times, 1/8/1978).

"Aerosmith is American rock's most unpopular set of would be heavyweights. Sure, they sell a lot of records, but there's something about the band quite apart from the peculiar spottiness of its performance, which keeps it outside of haute rock. Despite the Al Hirschfeld caricature on the cover of 'Draw the Line,' they seem likely to stay in their limbo — the 70's winner of the Iron Butterfly heavy metal booby prize. Aerosmith's critical unpopularity isn't hard to understand. It can be grasped by imagining rock as an absurdist high school. The literature teacher is always going to have more time for the snarling James Deans hunched in the back of the room (and the class of '78 has plenty of them) than the smirking clique of jocks next to the windows. And Aerosmith, despite the calculated androgyny of Steven Tyler, are All American jocks, not sniveling punks... None of which says anything about Aerosmith's recording problems. Here, as previously, the compositional burden falls on Joe Perry and Steven Tyler for the most part. But even with the occasional aid of other Aerosmiths, the two have yet to produce a full album of material up to their own best standards. 'Draw the Line' pretty much tells its story by the fourth track. The title song, 'I Wanna Know Why,' 'Critical Mass,' and 'Get it Up' are all rockers hard enough and bright enough (Tyler's best songs always betray his braininess) to withstand over-familiarity... " (Circus).

"Aerosmith built their reputation on riff-rock, sung through Steven Tyler's rubber lips and played in a way that reminded their barely post-adolescent audience of golden-oldie metal pioneers like the Yardbirds, Led Zeppelin and the Rolling Stones. They could get away with such essentially extended copyist technique because their songs, if derivative, were concrete, controlled and most often honed like cutting tools... 'Draw the Line' certainly boasts a panorama of those hypnotic repetitions. Unfortunately, it rarely has the accompanying melodic strength needed to make those foundation lines memorable. 'Draw the Line,' almost two years in process, contains many tunes that will be ignored on disc... 'Draw the Line' begins optimistically with the title song reverberating like high-powered chimes. Tyler's finely tuned vocals have at last broken away from sounding like either Mick Jagger or Robert Plant; he spends the bulk of the song in a comfortable, yet still punchy register. Only in its reprise does he come back screeching, and one has the option at that point of concentrating on Joe Perry's tasteful slide or enjoying a call-and-response between Perry and Hamilton. Commencing with 'Critical Mass,' the band shows a deadly wear and tear on their creativity which doesn't abate until the album's closing minutes. Solid passages leading inevitably to neat repeat lines are abandoned in favor of repeat lines alone, to the extent that even Tyler does more rhythm accompaniment than lead singing. Without necessary vocal continuity, songs like 'Get it Up' (which reeks of the Stones' current output) or 'The Hand That Feeds' never become more than bombastic chants. In fact, what sounds like an original hook on 'Draw the Line' is re-used in a mirror image for 'The Hand That Feeds,' discrediting both songs. What is frustrating about 'Draw the Line' is that many of its decidedly unoriginal numbers contain deft, captivating fragments.

Joe Perry's own 'Bright Light Fright' provides saxophonist Stan Bronstein with a raucous solo that Perry propels with sharp definition. Scott Cushnie's boogie piano pumps some life into 'I Wanna Know Why.' Even the group-composed 'Kings and Queens' spotlights a pleasing interplay of mandolin, banjo, and guitar. Yet on that tune, the only thought which stays in the listener's mind is that if it were any more a Zeppelin outtake, it would have to end with 'and she's climbing the stairway to heaven.' The members of Aerosmith did not write 'Milk Cow Blues,' a rave-up which is legendary among '60s English bands, but their arrangement of the song is the single most spectacular item on 'Draw the Line.' From the first repeated guitar note, its clarity and crispness form a sharp contrast to the rest of the album. Maybe everyone was half-asleep and going through familiar territory on most of the disc, but they certainly wake up and palpably struggle at annexing 'Milk Cow' to their own turf. Tyler's sneering vocal style owes a debt to the Kinks version of the tune, if anyone's, but the compulsion that pushes him to race against a pummeling rhythm section is sincere and totally his own. Although Aerosmith may have drawn their lines a bit much like follow-the-numbers for too much of their latest release, they're not old hat yet. The vitality expressed at the album's high points refuses to let this band be counted out" (Crawdaddy, 3/1978).

(Ted Nugent and Steven introduce AC/DC on the "Midnight Special.")

"Aerosmith have arrived for good, mates. Just check out the packaging of their new album: the front and back covers not only lack the emerging group-logo which graced their last two LPs, but also dispense with the title of the set. Instead, the denizens who haunt the record racks will be greeted with a black-and-white caricature of the group members (by Al Hirschfeld, no less), and a no-frills listing of the song titles. Only those potential buyers already acquainted with Steven Tyler's overbite (or those hip enough to turn the LP spineside-up) will know that they're holding Aerosmith's 'Draw the Line' in their cash-crossed palms; Aerosmith are playing in Led Zeppelin's if-you-have-to-tell-'em-who-you-are-you-ain't-made-it-baby! league now. Aerosmith is thus solidly anchored to ride out the shifting currents of rock taste in the late 70's, both on the album-sales charts, and in concert arenas that have always welcomed them...

'Draw the Line' advances Aerosmith a half-notch (at most) on up their great chain of being, but the accustomed pleasures of their sound are, well, quite comfortably reiterated. 'Draw the Line' frequently invokes Aerosmith's (or probably Tyler's) songwriting formula, that of seizing some cliché or figure of speech, objectifying it with a hard-rock background and a correspondingly vague plot, at last making it stand on its own as a kind of born-again bromide.... 'Draw the Line', with its echoed, pulsating fuzz hook, is a particularly tough opener. 'Get it Up's' lyrics worry over our old nemesis of secondary impotence, but the rock-hard music doesn't suffer either variety of that dysfunction. Joe Perry's 'Bright Light Fright' laments the numbing road life of rock bands for one more go-round, but his version is somehow more compelling than most other guitar-pilgrims', presumably because he moves in higher circles of superstardom... For now (and most likely for a long time to come), Aerosmith are solidly with us, and it just may be that there is something to be said for surviving the 70's together" (Creem, 3/1978).

"Since Aerosmith's name and logo don't even appear on the outer sleeve of 'Draw the Line,' someone obviously feels rather secure about the band's position in the hard-rock sweepstakes. The group is famous now — that's the message transmitted by Abe Hirschfeld's front-cover drawing. But fame and security don't always mix. 'Draw the Line' is a truly horrendous record, chaotic to the point of malfunction and with an almost impenetrably dense sound adding to the confusion. This album shows the band in a state of shock, caught for the first time in the quandary of the meaningful encore... If 'Toys in the Attic' and 'Rocks" proved that Aerosmith could pilot its own plane to the giddiest of heights, then 'Draw the Line' shows that anyone can develop a severe case of fear of flying. For those who remember times when riffs rolled hot and heavy from the Joe Perry/Brad Whitford guitar team will probably be the first to wonder what happened. For a riff-based band to come up with only one outstanding guitar hook for an entire LP is beyond belief, yet the title track features the only memorable guitar line here" (Rolling Stone #260, 3/9/1978).

1977 - Draw the Line

June 3 **POSTPONED
War Memorial Auditorium
Buffalo, NY
Promoter: Harvey & Corky Productions
Notes:
- This show was rescheduled for July 6.

June 5 **Aerosmith CANCELLED
Lakefront Stadium
Cleveland, OH
Promoter: Belkin Productions
Other act(s): Utopia, Ted Nugent, Nazareth
Reported audience: ~30,000
Notes:
- "World Series of Rock" game #1 concert announced at the end of April. Due to Joey's injuries in a car accident on June 1, Utopia were promoted to the headliner position and Southside Johnny & the Asbury Jukes with Ronnie Spector were added to the lineup.

June 16 **POSTPONED
Kemper Arena
Kansas City, MO
Promoter: Contemporary Productions / Chris Fritz
Notes:
- Rescheduled for June 28.

June 17 **POSTPONED
Civic Auditorium Arena
Omaha, NE
Promoter: Contemporary Productions
Notes:
- Rescheduled for Nov. 13.

June 19 **POSTPONED
Myriad Convention Center
Oklahoma City, OK
Promoter: Bench-Carson Attractions
Notes:
- Announced in mid-May, by early June the tour was being re-routed due to "recording commitments." The show was rescheduled for the nearby Lloyd Noble Center in Norman on Nov. 16.

June 21
Tarrant County Convention Center
Ft. Worth, TX
Promoter: Concerts West
Other act(s): Nazareth
Reported audience: 14,000 **SOLD-OUT
Notes:
- From a local review: "Heavy metal enjoyed one of its loudest hours Tuesday night as Boston rockers

The rock group Aerosmith gives two concerts: one horrible and the other barely tolerable.

Aerosmith invaded Tarrant County Convention Center in the first of two shows there. Tuesday night's concert has been a 14,000 sellout for weeks... A long break later, Aerosmith erupted into action, led, as always, by their flamboyant, Jagger-esque lead singer Steven Tyler. Besides lead vocals, Tyler plays a mean microphone stand, which was almost hidden by the long scarves that have become one of Tyler's trademarks. With the guitar trio of Joe Perry, Tom Hamilton, and Brad Whitford grinding away in front, and drummer Joey Kramer pounding true throughout, the group opened with 'Back in the Saddle,' which was appropriate. The group has been off the circuit for six months while recording a new album; and Fort Worth is only the third stop on their current trek across America. Set in a mammoth array of amplifiers, speakers, and lights, they went immediately into 'Mama Kin,' and that set the tone for the rest of the night: hard, uncompromising rock 'n' roll. Tyler was in excellent voice; and nowhere did it show better than his sensual handling of 'Lord of the Thighs.' The crowd screamed its approval on standbys like 'Dream On' and 'Walk this Way,' and the usual Bic flicking brought them back for one of their top efforts, 'Train Kept A' Rollin'.' It was enough to keep all 14,000 of their fans happy, and something another 14,000 will have to look forward to Wednesday night" (Fort Worth Star Telegram, 6/22/1977).

June 22
Tarrant County Convention Center
Ft. Worth, TX
Promoter: Concerts West
Other act(s): Nazareth
Reported audience: 14,000 **SOLD-OUT
Notes:

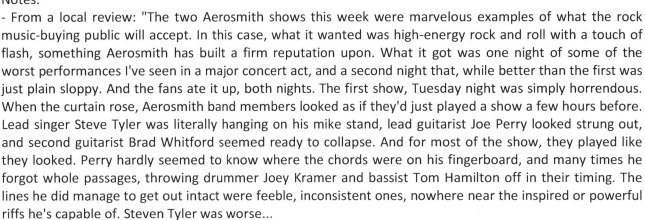

- From a local review: "The two Aerosmith shows this week were marvelous examples of what the rock music-buying public will accept. In this case, what it wanted was high-energy rock and roll with a touch of flash, something Aerosmith has built a firm reputation upon. What it got was one night of some of the worst performances I've seen in a major concert act, and a second night that, while better than the first was just plain sloppy. And the fans ate it up, both nights. The first show, Tuesday night was simply horrendous. When the curtain rose, Aerosmith band members looked as if they'd just played a show a few hours before. Lead singer Steve Tyler was literally hanging on his mike stand, lead guitarist Joe Perry looked strung out, and second guitarist Brad Whitford seemed ready to collapse. And for most of the show, they played like they looked. Perry hardly seemed to know where the chords were on his fingerboard, and many times he forgot whole passages, throwing drummer Joey Kramer and bassist Tom Hamilton off in their timing. The lines he did manage to get out intact were feeble, inconsistent ones, nowhere near the inspired or powerful riffs he's capable of. Steven Tyler was worse...

Comparatively, Wednesday's show was 100 per cent better. Almost a different set of musicians struck the opening chords of 'Back in the Saddle,' and launched into what must surely be more typical of an Aerosmith concert. But even that wasn't up to the standards the band has set for itself. Perry and Tyler were the most strikingly improved over the first night. Both moved with a confidence and professionalism so sorely missing the day before, resulting in a much tighter feel, and more coordinated, cleaner sound, and a more enthusiastic spirit. Perry's playing was much more controlled, though still sloppy during most of the set, almost as if he was trying to catch his breath from the night before. Whitford helped immensely by taking more of the lead. But by the time the band was into 'Sweet Emotion' — near the end — Perry had kicked into high gear with some dominating fluid, powerful riffs, dominating the band's guitar sound. He never completely gained control of his instrument, breezing quickly over a number of mistakes and odd notes, but the raw power he summoned from somewhere reached many thrilling peaks, especially during a new tune, 'Draw the Line.' Tyler, too, was better, though not so much as Perry. He looked rested and alert and was able to use some of his usual stage moves to a better advantage. It's just too band those moves are so hackneyed" (Dallas Morning News, 6/25/1977).

June 24
Summit
Houston, TX

Promoter: Pace Concerts
Other act(s): Nazareth
Reported audience: 19,012 **SOLD-OUT
Reported gross: $157,175
Set list: Back in the Saddle / Mama Kin / S.O.S. (Too Bad) / Big Ten Inch Record / Lord of the Thighs / Dream On / Lick and a Promise / Adam's Apple / Sweet Emotion / Sick as a Dog / Draw the Line / Walk this Way / Rattlesnake Shake / Same Old Song and Dance / Toys in the Attic / Train Kept A Rollin'
Notes:
- A pro-shot video circulates from this show. The band sometimes jammed various other songs during "Train," to varying degrees of success.

June 25 **TEMP HOLD-DATE
Taylor County Coliseum
Abilene, TX

Promoter: Stone City Attractions
Other act(s): Nazareth
Reported audience: (9,000 capacity)
Notes:
- This show was announced by the press (May 25) before the contracts had been signed and was then "postponed" on May 30 when a second (and more lucrative) date was added in Houston. That both of those Houston dates sold out with staggering grosses speaks to the pure economics behind tour routing. Mid-June trade ads for Nazareth's tour still included this date, though it had already been postponed indefinitely.

June 25
Summit
Houston, TX

Promoter: Pace Concerts
Other act(s): Nazareth
Reported audience: 19,012 **SOLD-OUT
Reported gross: $157,175
Set list: Same as June 24
Notes:
- A pro-shot video circulates from this show.

June 27
County Coliseum
El Paso, TX

Promoter: Beaver Productions
Other act(s): Nazareth
Reported audience: (10,000 capacity)
Notes:
- From a local review: "Led by the rakish lead singer Steve Tyler, the second-generation rockers stormed into the El Paso County Coliseum Monday night. The group's concert, a weak attempt at creating the same gut-level raunchiness of a Rolling Stones performance, was well received (but not greatly), by yet another large, enthusiastic local multitude. The show, though, was certainly nothing worth of excitement. Guitarists Joe Perry and Brad Whitford pelted the audience with a relentless barrage of monotonous riff after monotonous riff. Bassist Tom Hamilton was rhythmic enough, but his percussionist counterpart, Joey Kramer, showed little imagination when it came to pounding the heads. Tyler, pretentious and puckish, only served to compound the affront to one's taste and intelligence. Pretending to be Jagger rather than Tyler, the singer dashed, skirted, shuffled, and prissed about the stage in a contrived and predictable fashion. Tyler is obvious, falsely fey and does the worst Jagger shimmy I've ever seen.

All this, and more, was packaged into a keenly structured show aimed at blowing the audience away. Staged effects and an overabundance of volume proved once again that louder isn't necessarily better. The concept behind Aerosmith's show is to blast the crowd with this overly high volume, making it inevitable for the concertgoers to grab hold of the simple riffs. This technique the band used well but Tyler made a poor attempt at crowd manipulation. Throw in some hits songs in strategic places: 'Dream On' in the first quarter, 'Sweet Emotion' (with a chorus too closely styled after the Stones' 'We Love You') in the second, 'Walk This Way' in the third, and 'Toys in the Attic' at the end, add a light show patterned after Chip Monck's experiments with floodlights aimed at above-stage Mylar mirrors and the big-headed use of security guards to protect the stage and you have what is called a performance in quotation marks. In other words, the main course was cooked well in advance of the meal, but the customer was so hungry, he was gullible enough to eat the dish anyway" (El Paso Times, 6/29/1977).

June 28
Tingley Coliseum
Albuquerque, NM

Promoter: Feyline Presents
Other act(s): Nazareth
Reported audience: ~13,000 / 15,800 (82.28%)
Notes:
- From a local review: "Aerosmith and second-billed group Nazareth filed Tingley Coliseum Tuesday night to near 13,000 capacity and literally shook ear drums. It's hard to keep from comparing Aerosmith with the Rolling Stones. They have the drive and strength of a great group; every member is incredibly strong on his instrument. And then there's Tyler, prancing about in a tight leopard-skin outfit and matching coat and long tails, swinging flowing ribbons of scarf and tautly running his hands through a cat-like mane. He even has the Jagger mouth, a gorgeous creature. The only problem Tuesday was the PA system, cranked up quite a bit too loud, which is unnecessary with Aerosmith; they don't need to cover anything up. But aside from the eardrum pain, the show was extraordinary. Aerosmith opened their set with an original 'Back in the Saddle' that would have curdled cowboy Gene Autry's blood. Tyler's voice consistently approaches a scream, but is incredibly powerful and contained... Unlike most concerts, the Aerosmith song lineup was unpredictable and shot off unceasingly — clever, raunchy, but clear — the ultimate rock and roll. After they had done the hits — 'Dream On,' 'Sweet Emotion,' 'Sick as a Dog' — it seemed the one hit left would be saved for last. But after 'Walk this Way,' they remained onstage for a version of 'Rattlesnake Shake'... What could be left for an encore? 'Train Kept A Rollin',' with piercing freight engines from Joe Perry's electric guitar, and a fabulous, screeching 'Helter Skelter' that was as good as the Beatles could ever do" (Albuquerque Journal, 6/30/1977).

July 1
Kiel Auditorium
St. Louis, MO

Promoter: Contemporary Productions
Other act(s): Nazareth
Reported audience: ~10,000 / 10,586 (94.46%)
Notes:
- On this day, unbeknownst to Steve, a daughter he had fathered with Bebe Buell was born in New York City. He would only meet Liv Rundgren (who adopted his surname too) years later...
- From a local review: "When the unsung heroes of rock concerts — the ushers and the members of the security patrol — stick their fingers in their ears, chances are it's a loud concert. There were other indicators Friday night that the Aerosmith concert was going to be an ear ringer. For instance, the speaker cabinets on stage were plentiful enough to build a small house. At the end of the evening, a crowd of nearly 10,000 persons at Kiel Auditorium had every right to begin a volume vendetta against Aerosmith... Aerosmith, a band with an immense popularity that is not totally undeserved, played at a level that would fill a stadium. Obviously, the band's timing was poor because Super Jam '77 was still eight days away. Lead singer Steve Tyler wasn't as much fun to listen to as he was to watch. His moved parallel his singing style, which borders

on the sinister. It's simply part of his act to dress his microphone like a war lance. Tyler did everything but belch fire although his vocal power, at least Friday night, was not up to his wicked intentions. Still there was nothing in sweet in the way that he sang 'Sweet Emotion'" (St. Louis Post-Dispatch, 7/2/1977).

July 3
Freedom Hall
Louisville, KY

Promoter: Sunshine Promotions
Other act(s): Nazareth
Reported audience: (19,200 capacity)
Notes:
- Purportedly, the recording of "Dream On" on the "Live! Bootleg" album was sourced from this show.

July 4
Market Square Arena
Indianapolis, IN

Promoter: Sunshine Promotions
Other act(s): Nazareth
Reported audience: 19,000 **SOLD-OUT
Reported gross: $132,580
Notes:

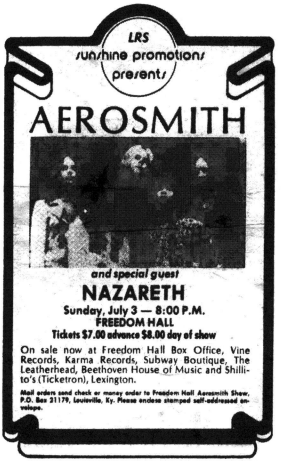

- This show was professionally recorded, and parts were used in "Live! Bootleg" the following year.
- From a local review: "The scene had all the makings of a riot. Sweat. Booze. Drugs. Smoke. And fireworks. It's crowds like last night's Aerosmith audience in Market Square Arena which could kick rock 'n' roll out of town. It was hot and nasty in the arena. The hall looked more like a battlefield than an indoor stadium. The rock 'n' roll battle raged for three hours. As one local promoter put it: 'It's stuff like this that makes me want to get out of the business. These kids don't know how much they can hurt people and this expensive equipment with the fireworks...' One could blame it all on bad timing. A hard rock group like Aerosmith, festival-seating and the Fourth of July doesn't exactly add up to a mellow show. Aerosmith is one of the world's hardest-working and most exciting groups. Its energy is bound to rub off on its followers... Aerosmith's method of delivery — both visually and audibly — is quite reminiscent to that of the early Rolling Stones. Performing hits like 'Walk this Way,' 'Toys in the Attic' and the hard rock classic, 'Dream On,' Tyler and his Massachusetts mates put on one of the wildest concerts of its kind ever in the arena, challenged only by hard rock rival KISS last year. A pentagon of mirrored Plexiglas and lights hung over the stage, giving the viewers down front a new perspective to concert-viewing. During the group's second encore someone tossed a burning sparkler on top of the overhanging mirrors and the sparkler melted a hole in the Plexiglas before it fell harmlessly on the stage. If Aerosmith does come back to Indy, one can bet it won't be on the Fourth of July. It's just too hot to handle" (Indianapolis News, 7/5/1977).

July 6
War Memorial Auditorium
Buffalo, NY

Promoter: Harvey & Corky Productions
Other act(s): Nazareth
Reported audience: 17,827 **SOLD-OUT
Reported gross: $110,000
Notes:
- Promoters Harvey and Corky were Harvey Weinstein and Corky Berger.
- Roughly four minutes of AUD filmed silent 8mm footage circulates from this show.

July 6, 7 **TEMP HOLD-DATES
Spectrum
Philadelphia, PA
Other act(s): Nazareth
Reported audience: (19,500 capacity)
Notes:
- Initially, two dates were announced in June though neither was booked, perhaps a result of earlier tour rescheduling.

July 8
Coliseum
Hampton, VA
Promoter: Entam, Ltd.
Other act(s): Widowmaker
Reported audience: 12,051 / 13,800 (87.33%)
Reported gross: $89,543
Notes:
- Nazareth was scheduled to open but was replaced on day of show.
- From a local review: "One of America's fastest growing rock groups, Aerosmith, performed to an almost sell-out crowd Friday night at the Hampton Coliseum... From the first song, 'Back in the Saddle,' the group had the audience in hysteria. The lead singer, in an outfit which resembled that of an elf, lugged his microphone around swinging its streamers wherever he went. Once the group started its performance, it never took a break. There would only be a couple of seconds between songs then the rock band would start all over again. Aerosmith played several of their most well-known songs such as 'Big Ten Inch,' 'Dream On,' Sweet Emotion,' and 'Walk this Way.' There was no need to try and put on a big theatrical performance; their music was enough to keep the crowd satisfied. The group seemed to really work at pleasing the crowd and making good music. The quality of their music was unusually fine and to put it in one word, was dynamic. Of course, as with most hard rock groups, the music was too loud. In fact, one could only really enjoy the performance if his eardrums were extremely strong. But if he could take it, [he] was in for the concert of his life. At one point of the performance, the drummer did a solo which was so sensational that the audience could not hold itself back from yelling for more. The drummer seemed to work like a madman, throwing drumsticks out to the crowd without even missing a beat. The crowd wanted music 'all night long,' and it certainly got what it wanted. After an exceptionally long performance by the hard rock group, the crowd went so crazy for more that Aerosmith returned for an encore" (Newport Daily Press, 7/13/1977).

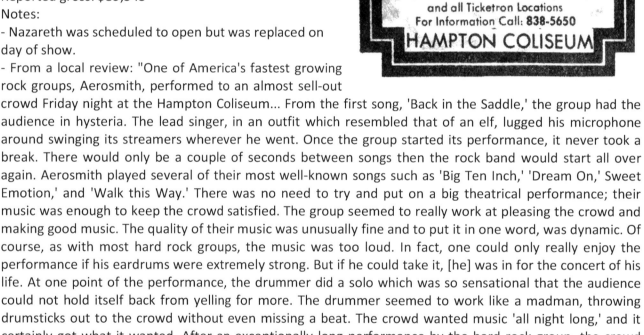

July 9
Civic Center
Baltimore, MD
Promoter: Cellar Door Concerts
Other act(s): Nazareth
Reported audience: 12,224 / 12,500 (97.79%)
Reported gross: $85,786
Set list: Back in the Saddle / Mama Kin / S.O.S. (Too Bad) / Big Ten Inch Record / Lord of the Thighs / Dream On / Last Child / Lick and a Promise / Adam's Apple / Sweet Emotion / Sick as a Dog / Draw the Line / Walk this Way / Same Old Song and

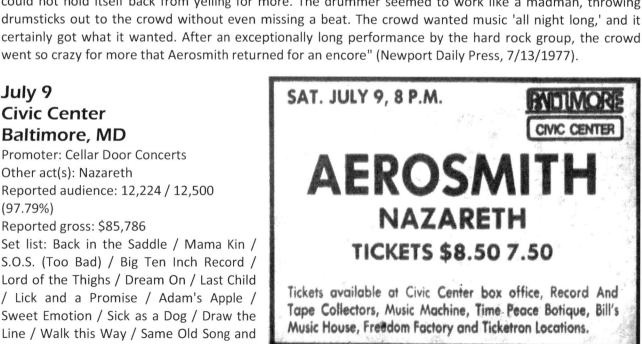

Dance / Toys in the Attic / Train Kept A Rollin'
Notes:
- From a local review: "A faulty sound system disappointed the many fans who gathered at the Civic Center Saturday night to see and hear Aerosmith. Most disappointed, however, was Joe Perry, guitarist for the heavy metal rock band, who expressed his frustration over the malfunctioning equipment through obscenities and mock violence. Perry first voiced his opinions of the equipment to the stage crew, and later to the confused audience. When, during 'Toys in the Attic,' the public address system cut off, he kicked a monitor speaker into the orchestra pit. Despite lead vocalist Steve Tyler's nightlong efforts to pacify Perry, the enraged guitarist punctuated the encore, 'Train Kept A Rollin',' with a flying kick to the amplifier. He ended the show by hurling his guitar into the air after yelling to the audience, 'This is a '57 Stratocaster. It's been in my family for a long time and this is how we do a guitar solo.' Compared to Perry, the other four members of the Boston-based band were uncharacteristically passive.

The group began the show with 'Back in the Saddle' from their latest album, 'Rocks.' Next, they performed 'Mama Kin,' their usual concert opener. They played most of their biggest hits, including 'Walk this Way,' 'Sweet Emotion,' and 'Last Child," but omitted their biggest, 'Dream On.' Aerosmith played for 75-minutes, offering 14 of their older songs and one from their soon-to-be-released album. The show was enhanced by special lighting. Colored spots were reflected off a mirrored ceiling which produced a unique glowing effect supplementing the usual stage lighting. Another unusual feature was the use of fans surrounding the stage giving the players a windswept look" (Baltimore Sun, 7/11/1977).
- Following this show, the band entered New York City's Record Plant studios to attempt some progress on the new album. They hoped to have seven songs finished by the time they departed for Europe; and planned to record an additional two following their return.
- A poor AUD recording exists from this show.

July 9, 10 **TEMP HOLD-DATES
Civic Center
Providence, RI
Notes:
- Dates were booked in October instead.

July 13, 14 **TEMP HOLD-DATES
Civic Center
Hartford, CT
Notes:
- Dates were booked in Hartford in October instead.

July 16 **TEMP HOLD-DATE
Three Rivers Stadium
Pittsburgh, PA
Promoter: DiCesare-Engler Productions
Other act(s): Lynyrd Skynyrd, Nazareth
Notes:
- This proposed show was changed to Civic Arena dates in the fall during a problematic year for concerts at the venue. The hold dates after July 4 would have concluded that initial leg of touring.

August 13
Dell
Bilzen, Belgium
Promoter: Joepie
Other act(s): The Small Faces, Ian Gillan Band, Stanley Clarke Band, Blue, Stella Marrs & Tony Scott
Reported audience: ~12,000

Partial set list: Big Ten Inch Record / Lick and a Promise / Adam's Apple / Dream On / Sweet Emotion / Sick as a Dog / Walk this Way / Same Old Song and Dance / Train Kept A Rollin' / Toys intThe Attic
Notes:
- Bilzen Jazz Festival, first date on the band's Eurofest '77 tour. They referred to the event as "Mudstock" due to the horrendous rain and resulting mud that afflicted the festival. The British NME ran a feature piece about the band at this muddy mess. David Krebs was present, awaiting the arrival of the band, and fretting over what Steven would think of the muddy mess backstage, resolving to go in search of a Wellington boots supplier.
- A partial AUD recording circulates from this show.

August 14
Eberhard-Bauer-Stadion
Esslingen, Germany
Promoter: Sunrise Concerts
Other act(s): Small Faces, Manfred Mann's Earth Band, Uriah Heep, Ted Nugent, Gregg Allman Band, Country Joe McDonald
Notes:
- The 2nd Golden Summernight Concert. While he and Aerosmith would share some European festival stages during the summer, Ted Nugent felt somewhat aggrieved at not opening for Aerosmith: "I wish the band and I could have done more with Aerosmith. I'd have liked to have played some dates with them in the East, but after a while they just wouldn't allow us to open for them anymore... I'm not taking anything away from Aerosmith, but you just don't mess with Ted" (Chicago Tribune, 7/3/1977).

August 16 **TEMP HOLD-DATE
Zurich, Switzerland

August 17
Audi Max
Hamburg, Germany
Promoter: Mama Concerts
Notes:
- A photo of the band posing outside of their airplane, taken by Ron Pownall in Hamburg on Aug. 15, would be used for tour ads throughout the remainder of the year.

August 18 **TEMP HOLD-DATE
Cannes, France

August 19
Circus Krone
Munich, Germany
Promoter: TZ Concerts

August 20
Frankfurt, Germany
Promoter: Sunrise Concerts
Other act(s): The Doobie Brothers, Small Faces, Uriah Heep, Ted Nugent, Country Joe McDonald
Reported audience: ~20,000
Notes:
- Loreley Festival, with Steven collapsing three songs into the band's set.

August 21 **TEMP HOLD-DATE

Bremen, Germany

August 23 **CANCELLED
**Gröna Lund
Stockholm, Sweden**
Promoter: EMA Telstar

August 24 **CANCELLED
Malmö, Sweden
Promoter: EMA Telstar

August 25-26 **RECORDING SESSION
**Air Studios
London, England**
Notes:
- A recording session with Jack Douglas at George Martin's studio. Joe suggests, in his autobiography, that the recording done at this studio was simply a push to put the final touches on the "Draw the Line" album, rather than recording "Come Together" which the association with Martin would seemingly suggest.

August 27
**Thames-side Arena
Reading, Berkshire, England**
Promoter: NJF/Marquee Presentations
Other act(s): Gloria Mundi, Krazy Kat, No Dice, George Hatcher Band, Ultravox, Little River Band, John Miles, Graham Parker and the Rumour, Thin Lizzy
Reported audience: ~30,000
Set list: Mama Kin / S.O.S. (Too Bad) / Big Ten Inch Record / Lord of the Thighs / Lick and a Promise / Dream On / Walkin' the Dog / Sweet Emotion / Walk this Way / Draw the Line / Same Old Song and Dance / Train Kept A Rollin / Toys in the Attic
Notes:
- Reading Rock '77 festival. Joe and Elyssa were purportedly bemused to discover that the backstage dressing rooms were little more than "gypsy caravans with wheels."
- From a local review: "At such a vast gathering, it was those with the greatest volume or the flashing lights and smoke bombs who did the best. Which must explain the appeal of American identikit rockers Aerosmith, or (top of the bill and admittedly a lot better) Thin Lizzie [sic]" (Guardian, 8/29/1977).
- A decent AUD recording circulates from this show.

244 | Aerosmith on Tour, 1973-85

September 16 **POSTPONED
Arena
Milwaukee, WI
Promoter: Stardate Productions
Notes:
- This show was rescheduled for Oct. 5.

September 19 **POSTPONED
Civic Center
Omaha, NE
Promoter: Chris Fritz / Contemporary Productions
Notes:
- This show was rescheduled for Nov. 13.

September 22 **CANCELLED
Veterans Memorial Auditorium
Des Moines, IA
Notes:
- This show was being advertised on Sept. 18, though was likely cancelled with the Oct. 4 date being advertised as the sole Iowa show for the tour.

September 28
Rupp Arena
Lexington, KY
Promoter: Entam, Ltd. / Sunshine Promotions
Other act(s): Henry Gross
Reported audience: 8,658 / 18,500 (46.8%)
Reported gross: $70,777
Notes:

- From a local review: "Thunderclap power-chording and non-stop rocking marked Rupp Arena debut last night. This morning's headache might help some of the 9,000 present recall the Boston band's hard-rocking, straight-forward set. Volume conquered all last night: Conquered feedback, conquered the applause from their fans. Aerosmith didn't even let a tune seep in — they plunged ahead with the singular purpose of bludgeoning their fans with spirited playing... Aerosmith opened their set with the ear-splitting intro to their hard-rocking standard, 'Mama Kin.' Their 80-minute set is essentially the same one they've been playing for two years (with the exception of a few songs from their upcoming LP) and it's well-paced and tight. Vocalist Steve Tyler sets up his two guitar players (Joe Perry and Brad Whitford) while drummer Joey Kramer whacks the tubs revealing basic skills. Tom Hamilton's bass bottoms out the screaming nicely.

When the guitarists are not battling it out Tyler holds most of the crowd's attention. The energetic (and macabre looking) thin man doesn't look like he can go the distance at first, but he never lets up. It helped that much of his vocals were synthesized or altered at the mixing board. Aerosmith seemed to give their fans all they asked for. There was nothing subtle about this band's music or staging. While some insist on audience participation (singing or clapping time) Aerosmith leads their fans through a set that would leave any participant gasping for air. It makes for a somewhat cold and detached performance but the end product — exhaustion — testifies to the fun and excitement of this band's brand of theater" (Lexington Herald, 9/29/1977).

September 29
Riverfront Coliseum
Cincinnati, OH

1977 - Draw the Line

Promoter: Electric Factory Concerts
Other act(s): Henry Gross
Reported audience: 13,733 / 18,000 (76.29%)
Reported gross: $101,800
Partial set list: Back in the Saddle / S.O.S. (Too Bad) / Big Ten Inch Record / I Wanna Know Why / Lord of the Thighs / Lick and a Promise / Walk this Way / Sweet Emotion / Dream On / Walkin' the Dog / Sick as a Dog / Draw the Line / Same Old Song and Dance ...
Notes:
- A partial below average AUD circulates from this show. Presumably, it's missing the encores, "Toys in the Attic" and "Train Kept A Rollin'." It does, presumably, feature the concert debut of "I Wanna Know Why."

October 2
Cobo Arena
Detroit, MI

Promoter: Belkin Productions
Other act(s): Michael Stanley Band
Reported audience: (10,700 capacity)
Partial set list: Back in the Saddle / S.O.S. (Too Bad) / Big Ten Inch Record / I Wanna Know Why / Lord of the Thighs / Lick and a Promise / Get it Up / Walk this Way / Sweet Emotion / Dream On / Walkin' the dog / Sick as a Dog
Notes:
- A partial AUD recording circulates from this show; often mislabeled "Dec. 2, 1977" (the band had performed at the venue on that date — in 1976). And, more importantly, another debut of a new song, in this case, "Get it Up." It seems likely that as many as four additional songs would have been performed during the missing part of the show.

October 4 **CANCELLED
UNI-Dome
Cedar Falls, IA

Promoter: Fox Productions
Notes:
- This show was cancelled by Sept. 22, a result of the venue being unable to fly the band's lighting rig due to its weight.

October 5
MECCA Arena
Milwaukee, WI

Promoter: Stardate Productions
Other act(s): Brownsville Station
Reported audience: 8,150 / 11,874 (68.64%)
Reported gross: $63,700
Notes:
- This show was rescheduled from Sept. 16.

October 7
Memorial Coliseum
Ft. Wayne, IN

Promoter: Sunshine Promotions
Other act(s): Brownsville Station
Reported audience: 9,672 **SOLD-OUT
Reported gross: $71,955

October 9
Spectrum
Philadelphia, PA

Promoter: Electric Factory Concerts
Other act(s): Styx
Reported audience: 19,500 **SOLD-OUT
Reported gross: $147,942
Set list: Back in the Saddle / S.O.S. (Too Bad) / Big Ten Inch Record / I Wanna Know Why / Lord of the Thighs / Lick and a Promise / Get it Up / Walk this Way / Sweet Emotion / Dream On / Walkin' the Dog / Sick as a Dog / Draw the Line / Same Old Song and Dance / Train Kept A Rollin' / Get the Lead Out
Notes:
- While returning to the stage for their encores, Steven and Joe were injured by M-80 fireworks thrown from the audience. According to press reports, "Lead guitarist Joe Perry's left hand was cut by the blast and lead singer Steven Tyler suffered a burned left cornea... The accident occurred when someone threw a firecracker on stage as the group came back for an encore... Perry and Tyler were standing less than a foot away from the firecracker when it went off... Both were treated and released from St. Agnes Hospital" (Trenton Evening Times, 10/11/1977). The promoter was unsympathetic, "Aerosmith tends to bring out that element. That's not to say that they're not nice kids or a good group. I like them, but let's face it, this stuff happens... I don't think our problems are any different from other large halls. You're dealing with immaturity here... It started with the groups using theatrics, flash-pots and so forth. Now, you get the audience mimicking the groups" (Springfield Union, 10/20/1977).
- A poor AUD recording circulates from this show.

October 10 **POSTPONED
Spectrum
Philadelphia, PA

Promoter: Electric Factory Concerts
Other act(s): Styx
Notes:
- This show was rescheduled for Dec. 19.

October 12 **POSTPONED
Coliseum
Richfield (Cleveland), OH

Promoter: Belkin Productions
Other act(s): Styx
Notes:
- This show was rescheduled for Dec. 16.

October 14 **POSTPONED
Civic Arena

Pittsburgh, PA
Promoter: Danny Kresky Enterprises
Other act(s): Styx
Notes:
- This show was rescheduled for Jan. 27.

October 15 **CANCELLED
Civic Center
Huntington, WV
Promoter: Entam, Ltd.
Other act(s): Styx
Notes:
- A show in nearby Charleston, WV was scheduled for Dec. 17.

October 16 **TEMP HOLD-DATE
October 17 **POSTPONED
Capital Centre
Largo (Landover), MD
Promoter: Cellar Door Productions
Other act(s): Styx
Notes:
- A second date, Oct. 16, was also considered but not put on sale with Santana instead performing. Regardless, due to the Spectrum incident the show was postponed until Dec. 21.

October 20 **POSTPONED
Maple Leaf Gardens
Toronto, ON, Canada
Promoter: Concert Productions International
Notes:
- Rescheduled for Dec. 10. However, on this day a Convair CV-240, that the band had considered chartering, crashed near Gillsburg, MS, killing members of Lynyrd Skynyrd and their entourage and injuring others.

October 21 **POSTPONED
Le Forum de Montréal
Montreal, QC, Canada
Promoter: Donald K. Donald
Notes:
- This show was rescheduled for Dec. 11.

October 24, 25 **POSTPONED
Memorial Coliseum
New Haven, CT
Promoter: Cross Country Concerts
Notes:
- Rescheduled for Dec. 7–8.

October 29, 30, 31
Civic Center
Providence, RI
Promoter: Phil Basile / Concerts East

Other act(s): Styx
Reported audience: (14,000 capacity)
Notes:
- The first shows following the firecracker incident.

November 2, 3
Nassau Coliseum
Uniondale, NY
Promoter: Phil Basile / Concerts East
Other act(s): Styx
Reported audience: (16,500 capacity)
Notes:
- Steven had joined Richie Supa for one of his band's shows at Trax in New York City prior to these shows, one of which Richie reportedly opened for. Interviewed backstage prior to one of the shows, Steven confirmed that the new album was finally done, but still needed to be mastered for release.

November 6
Roberts Stadium
Evansville, IN
Promoter: Sunshine Promotions
Other act(s): UFO
Reported audience: 11,199 / 13,600 (82.35%)
Reported gross: $87,798
Notes:
- From a local review: "Evansville was ready for a good concert last night and it got one from Aerosmith and UFO. Despite the increase in the ticket price from $6.50 to $7.50 and the threat of bad weather, the stadium was packed. The group has not had a top single for several months. But hard-core Aerosmith lovers turned out in full force last night. Except for a new set, the show was basically the same as every other show. They relied heavily on their most familiar pieces and that was definitely what the audience wanted. 'Walk this Way,' 'Dream On,' and 'Train Kept A Rollin'' drew the most enthusiastic audience response. 'Big Ten Inch' was another crowd pleaser with lead singer Steven Tyler playing a jazz harmonica solo. Two songs from their latest album, 'Draw the Line' and 'Get it Up' promise to next Top-40 material. Surprisingly, the group played 'Helter Skelter,' an old Beatles tune, for their encore before going into 'Toys in the Attic.' They kept the audience satisfied after an impressive show by the opening group, UFO" (Evansville Press, 11/7/1977).

November 7
U.D. Arena
Dayton, OH
Promoter: Jam Productions
Other act(s): UFO
Reported audience: (14,258 capacity)

November 10 **CANCELLED
Arena
Winnipeg, MB, Canada
Promoter: Frank Wiener

Other act(s): AC/DC, Kickin' (opener)
Reported audience: 10,000 **SOLD-OUT
Notes:
- Some 2,500 fans lineup for tickets when they went on sale on Saturday, October 8, braving near-freezing temperatures.
- From local press: "Everything was going smoothly up until early Thursday when several of the five semi-trailers transporting Aerosmith's instruments and sound and lighting equipment from Minneapolis to Winnipeg became snowbound in a freak blizzard outside Rothsay, MN, 250 miles from Winnipeg. It was obvious by late afternoon that there was little hope of pulling off the scheduled 8 p.m. performance. Promoter Frank Wiener immediately began negotiations for a make-up concert at 1 p.m. Friday. As late as midnight Thursday, chances for the new date were fairly good; Winnipeg Enterprises, which manages the arena, made it available for the Friday show. President Jim Ernst and general manager Percy Downtwon went out of their way to accommodate the show's promoters even though the show could have created conflict with the Jets-Nordiques game. Winnipeg Deputy Mayor Bill Norrie made arrangements with the North Dakota and Minnesota state police to get a wrecker to where the semi-trailers were bogged down. It appears, however, that Aerosmith simply isn't destined to appear in Winnipeg. Repeated efforts to repair one of the trucks failed to get it going in time. The alternate date also had to be scrapped" (Winnipeg Free Press, 11/16/1977).

November 12
Civic Center
St. Paul, MN

Promoter: Jam Productions / Casablanca Concerts
Other act(s): Nazareth
Reported audience: 17,500 **SOLD-OUT
Reported gross: $122,532
Notes:
- The Michael Stanley Band were noted in some ads to be opening this show.
- From a local review: "At intermission, an equipment man was checking the sound levels of the amplifiers of Aerosmith's two guitarists. He played parts of two old Rolling Stones' songs, 'Satisfaction' and 'Last Time.' It wasn't ironic. It was rather fitting, because Aerosmith has tried so hard to be in the mid-1970s what the Rolling Stones were in the mid-1960s. And the way the rambunctious, sellout crowd of 17,500 persons carried on at the St. Paul Civic Center Saturday one would suspect Aerosmith is as vital and important as the mythic Stones. However, Aerosmith didn't respond as excitedly. The musicians seemed tired and bored. Their performance was energetic but not as frenetic as usual. The quintet was clearly not in mid-tour form... To today's teen-agers, Aerosmith is the new Rolling Stones. Aerosmith even has its answer to the Stones' Mick Jagger and Keith Richard in Tyler and Perry, a pair of nasty, arrogant school dropouts. Saturday night, Tyler, who looks like a cross between Carly Simon and Jagger, was a lanky ragamuffin in a gym shirt, patched blue jeans and plenty of scarves. By contrast, Perry, who resembles the swarthy Richard, wore black leather pants and a black coat with white polka dots. Tyler and Perry were certainly arrogant enough, but neither was as nasty as usual.

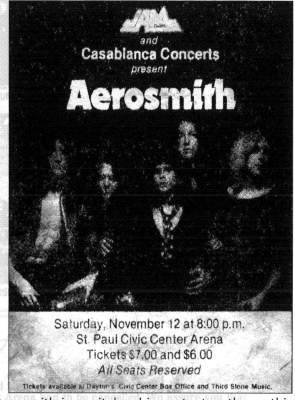

Tyler did not get wildly crazy nor did Perry play with killer instinct. Perhaps they are out of shape, merely rock-star poseurs or reaching middle-age comfort, which often afflicts rock stars after a couple of years of fleeting glory. Nevertheless, the two uninspired front men, backed by Aerosmith's reliable rhythm section, played well enough. In 75 minutes, the band whipped through a selection of hits, blues standards that influenced the group and three forgettable new songs. The revised arrangements on 'Sweet Emotion' and 'Sick as a Dog' featured strong guitar solos by Perry and Brad Whitford and showed more imagination than most highly derivative rock bands offer. However, only on the encore, 'Toys in the Attic,' did Aerosmith play with the kind of fire it had demonstrated in its three previous local appearances" (Minneapolis Star, 11/14/1977).

November 13
City Auditorium Arena
Omaha, NE

Promoter: Chris Fritz / Contemporary Productions
Other act(s): Nazareth
Reported audience: 12,000 **SOLD-OUT
Reported gross: $84,000
Notes:
- From a local review: "Sometimes it is hard to tell where 'loose' ends and 'sloppy' begins. Sunday night at the City Auditorium Arena, Aerosmith was sloppy — not all the time, and not always with damaging effect, but often enough and seriously enough to be annoying. There were many fine moments: the beginning of 'Dream On,' with echo adding a nice, spacey touch to Steven Tyler's vocals, for example. But as the song built to its climax, an uncertain sound system kept cutting out Tyler's voice and ruining the impact. Immediately preceding 'Dream On,' lead guitarist Joe Perry kicked off 'Walk this Way' with his guitar fed through a 'talk box,' the device that sends the sound through a rubber tube to the guitarist's mouth and thence to the microphone. But he started at the wrong speed, and the rest of the band floundered for a few bars before settling into a comfortable tempo. Even the lighting was uncertain. For some reason, moveable mirrors above the stage were used to reflect beams from spotlights in the wings back down to the performers. About half the time the mirrors either couldn't follow the musicians quickly enough or couldn't reach the places they were standing.

The show was by no means a disaster, though, and none of the problems was the fault of Tyler, who worked hard throughout. He pranced and pouted around the stage, swinging his microphone stand and its multicolored streamers, holding the mike out for the crowd to sing along and generally keeping things lively. The band's straight-ahead power helped cover up some of the deficiencies. At any rate, the crowd of 11,300 — the concert had been sold out since Wednesday — seemed to find things to its liking. The songs included most of the Aerosmith standards, which often are a cut above the usual hard-rock macho blast. A highlight was a version of the old, risqué blues tune 'Big 10 Inch'" (Omaha World Herald, 11/14/1977).

November 15
Assembly Center
Tulsa, OK

Promoter: Chris Fritz / Contemporary Productions
Other act(s): Wet Willie
Reported audience: 7,200 / 8,994 (80.05%)
Reported gross: $56,254

November 16
Lloyd Noble Center
Norman, OK

Promoter: Stone City Attractions
Other act(s): Wet Willie
Reported audience: 9,049 / 10,871 (83.24%)
Notes:
- From a local review: "Aerosmith is an excellent hard rock band, and in concert Wednesday night at Lloyd Noble Center in Norman, the group put on an outstanding show before 9,049 fans... But those

deserving most recognition were members of the opening group, Wet Willie" (Daily Oklahoman, 11/18/1977).

November 18
Henry Levitt Arena
Wichita, KS
Promoter: Chris Fritz / Contemporary Productions
Other act(s): Wet Willie
Reported audience: 11,000 **SOLD-OUT
Reported gross: $77,800

November 20
McNichols Arena
Denver, CO
Promoter: Feyline Presents, Inc.
Other act(s): Wet Willie
Reported audience: 15,979 / 18,000 (88.77%)
Reported gross: $121,211

November 22
Activity Center @ A.S.U.
Tempe, AZ
Promoter: in-house
Other act(s): Wet Willie
Reported audience: (14,885 capacity)

November 23
Sports Arena
San Diego, CA
Promoter: Wolf & Rissmiller Concerts
Other act(s): Wet Willie
Reported audience: 12,841 / 15,000 (85.61%)
Reported gross: $104,111
Notes:
- Days before this show co-promoter Steve Wolf was fatally shot during a burglary at his Mulholland Drive home. A 17-year-old youth was eventually arrested in Dec. 1978 for the murder. The youth later pled guilty to second-degree murder, admitting being one of four who had participated in the burglary, but denied being the murderer. He was sentenced to 7 years in prison in 1979.
- From a local review: "Wednesday's concert — which grossed an estimated $110,000 — reflected the aggressive, driving spirit of 'Rocks.' Though some of the band's material is a bit shaky, its 65-minute set was fast-paced, stylishly staged, and fervently performed. Far more substantial than the trendy, gimmicky KISS, Aerosmith shares with the new wave/punk bands an emphasis on spirit, personality, and point of view. That's why it could serve as a bridge for those rock fans who now seem somewhat confused and uncertain about groups like the Sex Pistols and Jam. Mixing sex, aggression and arrogance on stage, Steven Tyler has been repeatedly described in the press as surly, uncooperative and rude. A real punk... Aerosmith got a standing ovation when the band walked on stage Wednesday. From the opening 'Back in the Saddle,' the set bristled with energy and drive. Whether on its own material or a juiced-up remake up Rufus Thomas' 'Walking the Dog,' Tyler's vocals reflect both authority and challenge. There's no sense of musical breakthrough or new direction about the band's playing, but for those young rock fans who want to rejoice in rock's simple, celebrative dynamics it's a strong, appealing show. Even the Stones would be impressed.

More than just one of America's hottest rock bands, Aerosmith now deserves to be called one of America's best rock bands" (Los Angeles Times, 11/25/1977).

November 25
Aladdin Theater PAC
Las Vegas, NV

Promoter: Gary Naseef
Other act(s): Wet Willie
Reported audience: 7,500 **SOLD-OUT
Partial set list: Back in the Saddle / Big Ten Inch Record / I Wanna Know Why / Get it Up / Walk this Way / Sweet Emotion / Dream On / Walkin' the Dog / Draw the Line / Same Old Song and Dance / Train Kept A Rollin'
Notes:
- Parts of this show comprised the classic "5 the Hard Way" bootleg LP sourced from a decent AUD recording.

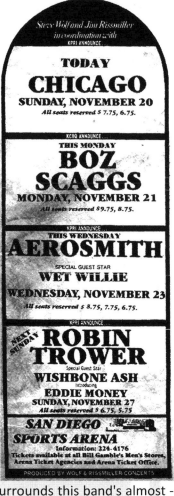

November 26
The Forum
Inglewood (Los Angeles), CA

Promoter: Wolf & Rissmiller Concerts
Other act(s): Wet Willie
Reported audience: 18,679 **SOLD-OUT
Notes:
- From an industry review: "Several critics have noted the similarity of Aerosmith's approach to their music with several bands in general and one in particular. Though there is an air of studied and well-rehearsed planning that surrounds this band's almost - formulaic sound and visual stance, Aerosmith has perfected it so well that they are one of the most entertaining rock acts around. The lion's share of praise must go to vocalist Steven Tyler whose dynamic stage antics and relentless preening is every bit as intense as the Mick Jagger of an earlier era. He doesn't just sing his material; he truly delivers it in every sense of the word. His interpretive movements and spirited dancing add much visual color to the audio bombardment that surrounds him. Much of that bombardment is led by one of rock's accomplished guitarists, Joe Perry. As front man of a talented guitar trio, Perry lays out some fast-paced melody lines that are repetitive but never overworked. The results are tunes whose melodies are unshakably hummable if the words are sometimes elusive. Aerosmith has a fine sense of pacing as well. Their most recognizable hits are scattered throughout the show achieving both a nice balance and a sense of rising momentum and increasing familiarity. Even so, one of the nicest surprises this evening was the band's version of the old Rufus Thomas tune, 'Walking the Dog.' Though many in the audience may have been too young to remember the original, Aerosmith's heavy metal 70's-style version was a sure crowd pleaser and a tasty example of their ability to do old things in a new way" (Cashbox, 12/16/1977).
- On the night of this show, Joe and Steven made a brief appearance in the crowd at the poorly attended Rocket's show at the Whiskey. Show posters with Ted Nugent and AC/DC opening for Aerosmith are inaccurate — AC/DC was on the east coast opening for UFO in Charleston, WV.

November 28
The Forum
Inglewood (Los Angeles), CA

Promoter: Wolf & Rissmiller Concerts
Other act(s): Wet Willie
Reported audience: 18,679 **SOLD-OUT
Notes:

- From a local review: "Aerosmith flew into town Thanksgiving week, performed two sold out concerts dates at the 18,000 seater arena, and proved once and for all that it's the best hard rock outfit in America The Boston super group streamlined the set to a surprisingly short 65 minutes, playing the most popular compositions off their four Columbia albums in addition to some new tunes from soon-to-be-released 'Draw the Line' disc. Aerosmith kicked the show off with the gut wrenching rocker, 'Back in the Saddle' and maintained the furious pace set by this opening number all the way through to the end of the concert But the band's 'anthem.' 'Dream On' did serve as a nice break in the electrical storm, bringing the audience to their feet as lead guitarist Joe Perry launched into the opening chords of the riveting, emotional slow tempo piece. Other concert highlights were 'Walk this Way,' 'Sweet Emotion,' 'Big Ten Inch,' 'Train Kept A Rollin' and 'Toys in the Attic.' All of these tunes were a tasty conglomeration of raw rock power, melodic lead lines, hooky choruses, punchy rhythms, snappy vocals and rather racy lyrics. Steven Tyler's spunky stage antics, distinctive lead vocals and charismatic stage presence served as the final decorations to Aerosmith's rousing brand of rock 'n' roll. Thankfully, instrumental solo outings band jams were kept to a minimum and the only disappointment in Aerosmith's set was that it was altogether too short" (Valley News, 12/6/1977).

November 30 **CANCELLED
The Forum
Inglewood (Los Angeles), CA
Promoter: Wolf & Rissmiller Concerts
Notes:
- This prospective third date was cancelled in mid-November after tickets had been put on sale.

November 30
Cow Palace
Daly City (San Francisco), CA
Promoter: Bill Graham Presents
Other act(s): Wet Willie
Reported audience: ~14,000 / 14,500 (96.55%)
Notes:

- From a local review: "It was hard to decide last night whether to laugh, cry, or scream in pain during the Aerosmith concert at the Cow Palace. A quintet from the New York area, Aerosmith has accumulated a huge following among the post-teenybopper Top-40 crowd which hasn't yet decided to enjoy music — as distinguished from noise. Fronting Aerosmith is shouter Steven Tyler, who hasn't yet decided whether he should look like Carly Simon or Mick Jagger, although in spirit (if not in voice) he is a Mick-master all the way. There are four other Aerosmith's in the ensemble, but Tyler doesn't give them much to do but play loudly. In some ways Aerosmith, which has been around and recording for five or six years, is a matured punk-rock group. They use very few chords per tune — and, come to think of it, they play very few tunes, too. Oh, they play lots of selections (another punk-rock) trait, but each is quite short, even stretching longer than five minutes. But what Aerosmith lacks in such musical refinements as melody, decipherable lyrics, harmonic ingenuity, or rhythmic inventiveness they make up for in sheer volume, power, and hard-rock pulse... Their material... has a basic common denominator — explosive, overwhelming electronic instrumental power. It's like getting caught under a waterfall of sound, trapped in an audio anxiety dream... This is pure pop-music, presented with absolutely no personality or indicated musical imagination. The massive, computerized lighting canopy was too dull most of the evening and the sound was much too loud, trending all the time toward abrasive distortion" (San Francisco Examiner, 12/1/1977).

December 1
Cow Palace
Daly City (San Francisco), CA
Promoter: Bill Graham Presents
Other act(s): Wet Willie
Reported audience: 14,500 **SOLD-OUT

December 2 **ERRONEOUS DATE
Cobo Arena
Detroit, MI
Notes:
- A mislabeled bootleg recording (from Oct. 2) is often attributed to this date but would also have been improbable in terms of routing considering the show in San Francisco the previous evening.

December 7
Memorial Coliseum
New Haven, CT
Promoter: Cross Country Concerts
Other act(s): Styx
Reported audience: 10,400 **SOLD-OUT
Reported gross: $144,972 (both nights)

December 8
Memorial Coliseum
New Haven, CT
Promoter: Cross Country Concerts
Other act(s): Styx
Reported audience: 10,400 **SOLD-OUT

December 10
Maple Leaf Gardens
Toronto, ON, Canada
Promoter: Concert Productions International
Other act(s): Derringer
Reported audience: ~17,000 / 18,815 (90.35%)
Set list: Back in the Saddle / S.O.S. (Too Bad) / Big Ten Inch Record / I Wanna Know Why / Lord of the Thighs / Lick and a Promise / Get it Up / Walk this Way / Sweet Emotion / Walkin' the Dog / Mama Kin / Draw the Line / Same Old Song and Dance / Train Kept A Rollin' / Milk Cow Blues / Toys In the Attic
Notes:
- Derringer opened the Canadian shows due to Styx having headlined their own shows in Canadian markets the previous month.
- From a local review: "A new source of emergency heat and energy may have been discovered last night at Maple Leaf Gardens. The first came from Aerosmith, the high-voltage rock band from Boston, the second from 17,000 kids who jammed and jostled all night. If that was all there had been, it wouldn't have been all that different from any number of mind-benders that go by the name of heavy-metal rock... The Aerosmith sound was so loud even some hardened rock freaks were leaving before the 75-minute show was over. 'I like it really loud,' said one, 'but this is giving me a headache.' There was yet another way the concert differed from other heavy-metal efforts. It was musical. When one waded through the din, one found a band that had matured immeasurably in the 15 months since it was last in Toronto. When lead singer Steve Tyler was starting out, he was an unabashed imitator of Mick Jagger, copying every prance and flounce. He still owes the Rolling Stones' boss a lot, but he has accomplished much on his own.

On tunes like 'Walkin' the Dog' or 'Get it Up' from the band's new album, 'Draw the Line' (Columbia), he showed a supremely intuitive rhythmic sense for the lyrics. He wasn't screaming or, if you prefer, there was much that was musical in his screaming. The rest of the band, particularly guitarist Joe Perry, gave Tyler something with which to work. Bassist Tom Hamilton and drummer Joey Kramer were discreet, if such a word can be used, allowing Perry to take off in searing solos. Joining him at moments was Brad Whitford, the other guitarist. Aerosmith, it would seem, is now at a point in its career where audiences no longer completely understand it. Crowds want to be blown away by the sound and the band gives them their wish.

At the same time, it does a lot of interesting things. Maybe someday we'll hear them the way they should be heard" (Toronto Star, 12/11/1977).

December 11 **RESCHEDULED
Le Forum de Montréal
Montreal, QC, Canada
Notes:
- This show was rescheduled for the following day during the first week of December.

December 12
Le Forum de Montréal
Montreal, QC, Canada
Promoter: Donald K. Donald
Other act(s): Derringer
Reported audience: (18,000 capacity)
Set list: Same as Dec. 10
Notes:
- From a local review: "Rock group Aerosmith has a message: Overkill. The American group has taken Rolling Stones' rhythm 'n' blues roots, stripped them of nuance, and amplified them to pounding volume. Similarly, lead singer Steve Tyler is rakish like Mick Jagger, with bigger lips and floppier hair. And with Aerosmith's penchant for rock exaggeration, Tyler has suffered injury on the battlefield. During a summer tour he was struck by an exploding firecracker, and the damage to the cornea of his eye was serious enough to postpone the tour that has just now started. Last night, Tyler looked perhaps a mite more reclusive — but within the bombast of the group's sound it was hard to tell... Surrounded by towers of speaker banks and flashing lighting, the group — Joe Perry and Brad Whitford (guitars), Tom Hamilton (bass), and Joey Kramer (drums) — goes through its paces with blitzkrieg precision. The quintet is tight and does a lot of hollering, and the kids — it was hard to spot fans over 17 years old — loved it" (Montreal Gazette, 12/13/1977).

December 13
Civic Center
Ottawa, ON, Canada
Promoter: Treble Clef / Donald K. Donald
Other act(s): Derringer
Reported audience: ~6,000 / 10,120 (59.29%)
Notes:
- From a local review: "After a shaky start they came together to give one of the best rock shows the city has had this year... Last night it was possible to catch only about one in every hundred words he sang. This lack of vocal clarity is all too common. The job can be done properly but as with many bands, Aerosmith didn't do it. Yet for all the band's minor faults, rock music is about energy and Aerosmith expended a lot of that. Their performance is aggressive and exciting — given that touch of class by the innovative guitaring of Perry and Whitford... Perry in particular

plays some superb licks and although his slide guitar work lacks a lot, he has the potential to join the league of all-time greats. He plays cleanly, fast and, for the most part, precisely. Whitford unfortunately suffers from Perry's insistence on playing (often) unnecessarily loud, but close scrutiny reveals a talent equal to that of his partner. Whitford is slower and not as flamboyant as Perry but it's all there. These two men, although physically ignoring one another on stage, are obviously listening close to each other's playing. They have a great understanding" (Ottawa Journal, 12/14/1977).

December 16
Coliseum
Richfield (Cleveland), OH

Promoter: Belkin Productions
Other act(s): Styx
Reported audience: ~20,000
Notes:
- From a local review: "Aerosmith is a totally ordinary hard rock band whose presentation has become casual to the point of sloppiness. Last night, the band let dead time elapse between numbers, made false starts, and generally kept to the back of the stage, hardly playing to the audience at all. Even when the members of the band clustered by the edge of the stage, each seemed in his own little world — they didn't seem to be playing to each other either. To pass judgement on the band's tunes (some of which are quite good) and its actual performance would be nearly impossible because the group managed to produce a sound that was close to unlistenable. There wasn't a single number in which singer Steven Tyler's voice didn't contain buzz and distortion. During the first number, the vocals were inaudible. Sometimes the bass would be too high; then it would be off. Throughout, the sound bad an unvarying buzz-saw quality that drowned out the tunes themselves. As a result of that and the band's seeming indifference, the audience's attitude also seemed rather indifferent. The greatest response came from the people close to the stage. Those in back didn't appear to be touched by what was going on. Styx, who produced a clearer sound seemed to get a response from the entire hall. At least Aerosmith managed to play a representative sample of tunes from its latest album, including 'Get it Up,' 'I Want to Know Why,' and 'Draw the Line.' These were mixed of course, with such Aerosmith concert staples as 'Walking the Dog,' 'Train Kept a Rollin',' 'Walk this Way,' and 'Big Ten Inch.' Some of these are wordy songs, but all of them would have gained much from being distinctly audible" (Plain Dealer, 12/17/1977).

December 17
Civic Center
Charleston, WV

Promoter: Entam, Ltd.
Other act(s): AC/DC
Reported audience: (8,500 capacity)
Notes:
- 48 patrons were arrested at this show as local authorities cracked down on smoking at the venue. Members of Aerosmith were fans of AC/DC, even if they were a tough act to follow. Joe told Rolling Stone magazine in 2008, "Bon had so many miles on him. You could tell when he sang... he was there, man." Steven Tyler inducted the band into the Rock and Roll Hall of Fame in 2003.

December 19
Spectrum
Philadelphia, PA

Promoter: Electric Factory Concerts

Other act(s): Styx
Reported audience: 19,500 **SOLD-OUT
Reported gross: $146,250
Set list: Same as Dec. 10
Notes:
- From a local review: "The heavy-metal rock group from Boston called Aerosmith last night completed its two-night engagement at the Spectrum — which began last Sept. 10 and was forced into a 'hold pattern' when a thrown firecracker injured the group's vocalist and lead guitarist. There was no such bombardment last night. This time the capacity crowd restricted its enthusiasm to loud shouting and a certain amount of smoking individual favorite brands. Tight security at entrances to the Spectrum did result in the confiscation of quantities of beer and wine — not to mention a tub of liquid reported to be 190-proof grain alcohol — but security personnel said no explosives had been detected. This, of course, was welcome news to Aerosmith in general and lead singer Steven Tyler and guitarist Joe Perry in particular... And so, Aerosmith completed in current Spectrum business last night, with explosives limited to the high-decibel blasting that the band has parlayed into one of the most popular rock sounds of the day, with the Mick Jagger-like swaggering of Steven Tyler and the double-guitar bashing of Joe Perry and Brad Whitford. They accounted for far more than enough fireworks for one night" (Philadelphia Inquirer, 12/20/1977).
- An AUD recording circulates from this show.

December 21
Capital Centre
Largo (Landover), MD
Promoter: Cellar Door Productions
Other act(s): Styx
Reported audience: (17,561 capacity)
Notes:
- From local press: "This week, however, the top two kid-rock bands — KISS and Aerosmith — will, at least for four nights, reverse the downward trend in the concert business. While tickets remain for KISS' shows Monday and Tuesday and Aerosmith's Wednesday and Thursday, it seems as if all the shows will sell out prior to showtime. Given some recent attendance figures at the Capital Centre — under 12,000 for Queen, 4,500 for Trower, under 10,000 for Hall & Oates — the sellouts will be more major achievements than they might seem. Unfortunately, neither Aerosmith nor KISS is enhancing the general artistic well-being of rock 'n' roll with their current contributions. In the case of KISS, this is somewhat to be expected. The failure of Aerosmith to go much beyond the more obvious manifestations of the rock 'n' roll style is much more disappointing since the group has displayed the talent to do more than simply repeat itself. Aerosmith's newest on Columbia, 'Draw the Line,' sounds like a repeat of the band's classic 'Toys in the Attic.' In retrospect, 'Toys' was an important album — most of the group's hit singles were pulled from it — but the set is at least four years old. Last year's 'Rocks,' a quality set, suggest some new directions but none of the possibilities have been followed up on 'Draw the Line'" (Evening Star, 12/18/1977).

258 | Aerosmith on Tour, 1973-85

December 22
Capital Centre
Largo (Landover), MD
Promoter: Cellar Door Productions
Other act(s): Golden Earring
Reported audience: (17,561 capacity)
Set list: Same as Dec. 10
Notes:
- Pro-shot footage circulates from this show, which would be Night Bob's last with the band for some time.

1978

January 6 **CANCELLED
Municipal Auditorium
Nashville, TN
Promoter: Sound Seventy Productions
Notes:
- This show had been cancelled by Dec. 18.

January 7 **CANCELLED
Mississippi Coliseum
Jackson, MS
Promoter: Mid-South Concerts

January 10 **CANCELLED
Omni
Atlanta, GA
Promoter: Alex Cooley, Inc.

January 17 **CANCELLED
Civic Center
Lakeland, FL
Notes:
- Several January dates were cancelled by Dec. 30 to allow for Aerosmith to film their contributions to the "Sgt. Pepper's Lonely Hearts Club Band" movie starring Peter Frampton.

January 27 **CANCELLED
Civic Arena
Pittsburgh, PA
Promoter: Danny Kresky Enterprises
Notes:
- This show had been cancelled by Jan. 1.

January 30 **QUESTIONABLE
Evansville, IN
Notes:

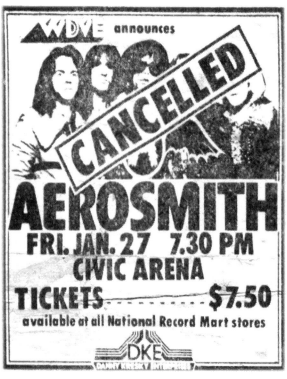

- Some regional papers noted a show scheduled in Notre Dame. Regardless, a heavy blizzard hit the area on the day of show resulting in massive disruptions to the area for the next few days, making any show highly improbable (particularly as a standalone date). Local Evansville papers make no mention of any show scheduled in town for Jan. 30.

February **CANCELLED
Madison Square Garden
New York City, NY

Notes:
- This show was reported as being cancelled in Billboard in late Feb., though it may never have been booked with touring essentially having concluded on Dec. 22.

March 5
Palace Theater
Albany, NY

Reported audience: (2,844 capacity)
Notes:
- Joining the band on their tour was vocalist and keyboard player Mark Radice, a friend of Steven's (Steven had performed on then ten-year-old Mark's debut single in 1967). Mark's father, Gene, had also produced the Chain Reaction's first recording session. After seeing him and his band performing at Trude Heller's in New York City in January, Steven begged and then bribed Mark to join Aerosmith for the tour. And Mark felt that the money could surely help him... The band conducted a week of rehearsals with him prior to hitting the road. They had felt that they had become out of touch with their audience, so they booked a series of smaller theater dates as a way to repay their diehard fans for their early support while taking a break from what had become their normal routine. Local radio stations held contests to distribute the available tickets. It was almost an inoculation against the massive shows to come...

March 6
Landmark Theater
Syracuse, NY

Reported audience: (3,000 capacity)

March 8
Leroy Theater
Pawtucket, RI

Other act(s): Streets
Reported audience: (2,700 capacity)

March 9
Palace Theater
Waterbury, CT

Promoter: Freefall Presentations
Reported audience: (2,565 capacity)

March 14
Center Coliseum
Seattle, WA

Promoter: John Bauer
Other act(s): Mahogany Rush
Reported audience: 21,289 **both nights
Reported gross: $180,957 **both nights

Notes:
- This second show was added in early March after the originally booked date sold out.
- From a local review: "Given the erratic nature of the band, Aerosmith's concert in the Coliseum last night have gone either way. In performances here the rock supergroup has been either wretched or wonderful. A Kingdome show two years ago was a disaster, and years before that the band was actually fired from a gig at the Aquarius! But on good nights, such as in the Arena in the summer of '75, the band has been nearly untouchable, comparable to the Stones and Led Zeppelin. It was like that last night, with the band putting out a total effort that never let up. Because it was the first of two shows and not sold out, the band could have held back, saving energy for the capacity crowd due tonight. Instead, it was like the old days, when the band was an opening act and had to try harder. They gave it everything they had. In many ways, Aerosmith is to the Rolling Stones what margarine is to butter: a substitute. Steven Tyler, Aerosmith's lead singer, is so close to Mick Jagger in looks and style he may as well be a clone. Last night his phrasing and tone on a couple of songs constituted plagiarism. A Yank from Boston, he even had a British accent.

And Joe Perry's guitar lines more than once borrowed from Keith Richard. But so what? If you're gonna steal, take from the best and do it with style. After all, the Stones started by ripping off Robert Johnson and Willie Dixon. What saves Aerosmith is that it also has a style of its own, a hard-edged, tough-minded, youthful style: the kind the Stones abandoned years ago. Even though Aerosmith has 'made it' and all five members are millionaires, the group last night had that raw, streetwise, angry approach they had when they were hungry. The stand and the sound systems were such that you could fully enjoy what the band was putting out. Suspended above the stage, the speakers distributed the sound evenly and didn't obscure anybody's view. The only hitch was that the sound sometimes faded. The problem to come from faulty miking on stage left. A lot of Joe Perry's guitar was lost and so was Tyler's voice whenever he wandered over there. The show was practically Aerosmith's 'greatest hits.' 'Dream On' and 'Walk this Way' showed signs of age but almost everything else was red hot... Some of the new tunes — 'Give it Up,' 'Draw the Line,' 'Milk Cow Blues' — did, too" (Seattle Daily Times, 3/15/1978).

March 15
Center Coliseum
Seattle, WA

Promoter: John Bauer
Other act(s): Mahogany Rush
Reported audience: (16,641 capacity)
Notes:
- Night two was reportedly sold-out, the first night not.

March 18
Motor Speedway
Ontario, CA

Promoter: Wolf & Rissmiller Concerts
Other act(s): Foreigner, Ted Nugent, Heart, Santana, Dave Mason, Bob Welch (w/ Stevie Nicks & Mick Fleetwood), Richie Lecea
Reported audience: 290,000 **SOLD-OUT
Reported gross: $2,500,000
Set list: Rats in the Cellar / I Wanna Know Why / Big Ten Inch Record / Walk this Way / Seasons of Wither / Sweet Emotion / Lord of the Thighs / Dream On / Chip Away the Stone / Lick and a Promise / Get the Lead Out / Get it Up / Draw the Line / No More No More / Same Old Song and Dance / Toys in the Attic / Milk Cow Blues / Train Kept A Rollin'
Notes:
- Cal Jam II was the #1 grossing musical event of 1978 though the promoters had sunk a staggering $350,000 into advertising the event. Richie Supa joined the band for "Chip Away the Stone." After Aerosmith's headlining set Mahogany Rush and Rubicon (who included Jack Blades and Brad Gillis) each played 45-minute sets following a laser light show. The promoters provided a $1-million sound system with some 150

400-watt amplifiers were driven through 1,000 JBL speakers. Loud enough even for Aerosmith to appreciate.
- From a local review: "Aerosmith was the day's standout. Working with a new keyboard player, the group delivered a marvelously paced set. Led by lead singer Steven Tyler, Aerosmith delivered with the confidence and electricity of a classic Julius Erving dunk shot. Though the day's headliner, Aerosmith performed seventh on the nine-act bill. The theory was that if Aerosmith had played last, most of the audience would have stayed until the end. The result would have been a traffic snarl as 300,000 persons hit the freeways at the same time. By putting two acts after Aerosmith... it was hoped the audience would drift out more gradually. And it worked" (Los Angeles Times, 3/20/1978).
- From a trade review: "About half of the audience left after Aerosmith's set, which turned out to have a beneficial effect on the traffic flow leaving the Speedway. If Aerosmith had gone on last, there might have been a more severe crunch of cars hitting the San Bernardino Freeway at midnight... Aerosmith and Nugent, as headliners, were offered 90-minute performance spots; but both said they'd only wanted to do 70 minutes, which is what the schedule then listed. Nugent did go about 70 minutes, but Aerosmith wound up taking the full 90 minutes" (Billboard, 4/1/1978).
- A two-hour TV late-night special from the event was broadcast on May 19 on ABC channels; hosted by Jeff Conway and Susan Sevareid. DIR's King Biscuit Flower Hour also dedicated an episode featuring Aerosmith, Santana, and Rubicon on July 30, but by that time work had been done on the recordings, and two of the three songs that appeared on the official "California Jam 2" various artists double album later in the year, "Draw the Line" and "Chip Away the Stone," are identical to their "Live! Bootleg" counterparts. Not surprisingly, those tracks, which take up much of the album's side 3, were produced by Jack Douglas. From the KBFH broadcast, only "Same Old Song and Dance" and "Big Ten Inch Record" differ from "Bootleg," so in these one may find additional tracks intended for the planned bonus EP. A full SBD of Aerosmith's set also exists.

March 23
Aragon Ballroom
Chicago, IL
Promoter: Jam Productions
Other act(s): None.
Reported audience: 5,500 **SOLD-OUT
Reported gross: $41,250
Set list: Rats in the Cellar / I Wanna Know Why / Big Ten Inch Record / Walk this Way / Sight for Sore Eyes / Seasons of Wither / Sweet Emotion / Lord of the Thighs / Dream On / Chip Away the Stone / Get the Lead Out / Get it Up / Draw the Line / No More No More / Same Old Song and Dance / Toys in the Attic / Milk Cow Blues / Train Kept A Rollin'
Notes:
- A SBD recording circulates from this show.

March 24
Veterans Memorial Auditorium
Columbus, OH
Promoter: Sunshine Promotions
Reported audience: (4,000 capacity)
Set list: Same as Mar. 23
Notes:
- A SBD recording circulates from this show. The recordings of "Sweet Emotion," "Chip Away the Stone," and "Sight for Sore Eyes" were used from this show on "Live! Bootleg."

March 26
Tower Theater
Upper Darby (Philadelphia), PA
Promoter: Electric Factory Concerts

Reported audience: (2,877 capacity)
Set list: Rats in the Cellar / I Wanna Know Why / Big Ten Inch Record / Walk this Way / Sight for Sore Eyes / Seasons of Wither / Sweet Emotion / Lord of the Thighs / Kings and Queens / Chip Away the Stone / Get the Lead Out / Get it Up / Draw the Line / Same Old Song and Dance / Toys in the Attic / Milk Cow Blues / Train Kept A' Rollin'
Notes:
- This show was broadcast on WYSP-FM. "Draw the Line" from this show was used on "Live! Bootleg."

March 27 **REHEARSALS
Music Hall
Boston, MA

Set list: Krawhitam / Kings and Queens / Sound checking Bass / I Wanna Know Why / Big Ten Inch Record (partial) / Seasons of Wither (partial) / Seasons of Wither (partial)
Notes:
- The band rehearsed at the venue working on dialing the sound in for the following two night's performances. Part of the archival recordings circulate. The "Krawhitam" jam is not the same as the version issued on "Pandora's Box."

March 28
Music Hall
Boston, MA

Promoter: H.T. Productions
Other act(s): Streets
Reported audience: ~4,000
Set list: Same as Mar. 26
Notes:

- This show was broadcast on WBCN. The opening act was managed by former Aerosmith rhythm guitarist Ray Tabano.
- From a local review: "Only ten days ago Aerosmith played before 250,000 people at the epic California Jam II outdoor rock festival in Ontario, Cal. Last night they played to a squeezed-in crowd of under 5,000 at the Music Hall, which by contrast must have seemed like a garage. Aerosmith is now purposely doing a national tour of small halls as a means of thanking their longtime fans. They last appeared in Boston in December 1976 at the Causeway Street barn, Boston Garden. The present two-night stand at the Music Hall is also a benefit for Summerthing, which expects to receive $25,000–$30,000 overall. It may be recalled that Aerosmith received its big local break from Summerthing in 1973, when the band was put on as an opening act for Sha Na Na before 40,000 fans at Suffolk Downs. Since then, Aerosmith, which used to play sidewalk lunchtime shows at Boston University in the early '70s, has risen to be one of the top concert draws in the country. However, they are now riding the rocky crest of their worst album sales in years. 'Draw the Line' is an embarrassing 96th this week on the Billboard charts — so last night's show was watched with special interest. Despite the ho-hum sales of the new album, Aerosmith dipped into it heavily. After opening with the familiar 'Rats,' where Stevie Tyler waved his gypsyish scarf with abandon, the band fired into 'I Wanna Know Why' from the new LP, and would later do 'Sight for Sore Eyes' (with the androgynous Tyler, in tight black-fringed pants, crying with an overload of echo), 'Get it Up' (with Tyler joined by Karen Lawrence, whose see-through plastic top did nothing to abate the delirium of the crowd), 'Draw the Line,' 'Kings and Queens' and, as an encore, a poor version of the oldie 'Milk Cow Blues...'

The most frustrating part of the evening, beyond Aerosmith's insistence on so much new material, which is hardly among its best, was the wall-of-noise volume maintained throughout. So loud was it that I was reminded of a stereo pushed well beyond its capacity until you have nothing but an indiscriminate blur. Tyler's vocals were swallowed up repeatedly in the noise, and what remained was mostly the guitar interchanges between Brad Whitford and Joe Perry. Perry's riffs were as convincingly raw as usual, but his slide playing was atrocious and made for an eerie assault on the ears. Tyler's strutting efforts were restricted by the smaller stage and his vocals were uncompelling except for a flat-out version of 'Toys in the Attic,' which closed the program. His work on standards like 'Chip Away' and 'Thighs' was shop-worn and little else. As the evening wore on, the most exciting mini drama pertained to the security. An armada of cops — 15 of them — tried, finally with success, to clear people out of the aisles" (Boston Globe, 3/29/1978).

March 29
Music Hall
Boston, MA
Promoter: H.T. Productions
Other act(s): Streets
Reported audience: (3,500 capacity)
Notes:
- Both Music Hall concerts were benefit shows for Summerthing. Tom Hamilton presented the check "in excess of $20,000" to the Office of Cultural Affairs on Mar. 30.
- From a local review: "The concert this week, before packed houses of 3,800 fans, dovetail with the band's current wish, in 1978, to play smaller, human-sized, venues. Still, considering the frenzy the very sight of them generated, you might've wondered if a Garden-sized crowd had been stuffed into the Music Hall. The sustained roar that greeted them Tuesday night was a wonder to hear. The band, wasting no time, charged into 'Sweet Emotion,' and inaugurated more than an hour of whiplash rock 'n' roll. Lead singer Steve Tyler was dressed to celebrate the new season. He wore (in addition to his usual Jagger-esque pout) a see-through, scoop-necked black shirt, lots of spangly bangles, and a flamboyant gypsy scarf on his head that recalled Dylan on his last tour. Steve's mike stand was bedecked with colored streamers and when he swung it around, as is his wont, it looked like a Maypole... As Matt Siegel, rabblerousing emcee and WBCN disc jockey, pointed out, there were 'probably 50-60,000 people who'd wanted to buy tickets' and BCN served the overflow by broadcasting the event live" (Boston Herald, 3/30/1978).
- According to studio cut-sheets, both "Last Child" and "Toys in the Attic" were sourced from this show for "Live! Bootleg."

April 2
Masonic Auditorium
Detroit, MI
Other act(s): Streets
Reported audience: (4,600 capacity)
Notes:
- Jack Douglas recalled that during the recording of this show a ceiling mic fell into the audience who then entertained themselves by passing it around after speaking inanities into it while the technicians scrambled to figure out which line to kill to prevent the output being broadcast. After the show ended the expensive Neumann mic was simply left on a seat.
- From a local review: "In what was termed a 'special performance' by the promoter, one of the best bands in the world, Aerosmith, sent a capacity crowd Detroit's Masonic Auditorium (yes, Masonic) into a frenzy Sunday night. It was advertised that the band wanted to play to a 'small gathering in intimate surroundings' before they embark on their U.S. tour later this month... Most of the audience was already on their feet as the five-man powerhouse came out and broke into a pulsating rendition of 'Rats in the Cellar...' During much of the period they were on stage, it was as if each member was in his own cylinder while Tyler flew around the stage, waving his mike stand around with multi-colored scarves dangling from it... It became so loud and intense at the end that I figured everyone in Ann Arbor could hear it, 'Train' provided a fitting ending to a good evening of frenzied Aerosmith music" (Michigan Daily, 4/4/1978).

April 3 **CANCELLED
Public Music Hall

Cleveland, OH
Promoter: Belkin Productions
Other act(s): I.R.S.
Reported audience: (3,000 capacity)
Notes:
- This show was scheduled to be broadcast on WMMS as part of their 10th anniversary celebrations. Unfortunately, the band cancelled citing Steven suffering from strep throat. The 1,500 pairs of tickets had been made available via lottery.

April 7
Civic Auditorium
Santa Monica, CA
Promoter: Wolf & Rissmiller Concerts
Other act(s): None.
Reported audience: 3,416 **SOLD-OUT
Partial set list: Seasons of Wither / Sweet Emotion / Lord of the Thighs / Chip Away the Stone / Get the Lead Out / Get it Up / Draw the Line / Same Old Song and Dance / Toys in the Attic / Train Kept A Rollin
Notes:
- 100,000 entries were received for the 3,000-ticket lottery available for the two shows.
- From a mainstream review: "Steven Tyler is in especially good form. Looking like a Mick Jagger kewpie doll and stomping round the stage twirling a ribboned microphone like a demented cheerleader, he screams out with a striking, sensuous voice. It's so loud you can hardly make out the songs (especially as they run into each other with barely a pause for applause) and hardly distinguish the voice from the instruments. It's a good night for the rest of the band too — high-speed, sturdy drumming from Joey Kramer, throbbing bass from Tom Hamilton, Joe Perry, and Brad Whitford play well together, and the new keyboardist is a well-chosen addition to the band. For the most part the music is tight and integrated, though at times the fuzzy sound was irritating and the lack of pacing overwhelming.

Still, needless to say, the audience of very dedicated heavy metal aficionados enjoyed every moment, applauded every note, drooled at the new tunes and went gaga at the old ones, pressed up against the stage when they weren't trying to jump it, and generally had a good time. It wasn't a long set (was that a look of relief on a few journalists' faces?), a little over an hour, and after one encore the lights came on and that was that. Songs of the show: 'Rats in the Cellar' and 'Sweet Emotion'. It was OK, but if I'd had to queue up all day for tickets with my box of Kentucky Fried, I'm afraid I'd have expected more" (Sounds, 5/18/1978).
- A poor partial AUD recording circulates from this show.

April 8
Civic Auditorium
Santa Monica, CA
Promoter: Wolf & Rissmiller Concerts
Other act(s): None.
Reported audience: 3,416 **SOLD-OUT
Reported gross: $25,620
Partial set list: Rats in the Cellar / I Wanna Know Why / Big Ten Inch Record / Walk this Way / Seasons of Wither / Sweet Emotion / Lord of the Thighs / Chip Away the Stone / Get the Lead Out / Draw the Line
Notes:
- Recorded by the Record Plant remote truck with Lee DeCarlo engineering with Jack Douglas.
- A partial SBD circulates from this show. While "Live! Bootleg" may suggest that "Chip Away the Stone" is from this show, it clearly is not.

May 2
Scope
Norfolk, VA

Promoter: Entam, Ltd.
Other act(s): Fotomaker
Reported audience: (12,500 capacity)
Notes:
- Opening act Fotomaker included former members of the Rascals, Gene Cornish, and Dino Danelli, with ex-Raspberries/Tattoo guitarist Wally Bryson (who was an Aerosmith fan), and Lex Marchesi and Frankie Vinci.

May 3
Coliseum
Charlotte, NC

Promoter: Kaleidoscope Presents
Other act(s): Mahogany Rush
Reported audience: (13,000 capacity)

May 5
Coliseum
Greensboro, NC

Promoter: Entam, Ltd.
Other act(s): Mahogany Rush
Reported audience: 12,714 / 13,500 (94.18%)
Reported gross: $93,669
Notes:
- More than 60 attendees were arrested at this show, primarily for drugs offences.
- The venue looked to book "lighter" groups, following experiences with bands such as Aerosmith. "[Coliseum Manager Jim] Oshust has to book the groups he thinks will draw the most people, and for that reason he is trying softer groups. But he is also personally pleased to see a change, having tired of the hard rock music and some of the people who work with it. 'They can't tell me that I should be impressed by five or six guys who look like runaways from Devil's Island.' he says. He also says many of those groups and their entourage are extremely demanding, unconcerned about their audiences, and generally obnoxious. A recent example was Aerosmith, which appeared this month at the Coliseum. Oshurst said the road crew got into an egg throwing episode which messed up a dressing room. He described a man who handled some of the group's financial affairs as a 'schnook' who made excessive demands and hinted the group was being cheated by the Coliseum" (Greensboro Record, 5/23/1978).

May 6
Carolina Coliseum
Columbia, SC

Promoter: Beach Club Concerts
Other act(s): Mahogany Rush
Reported audience: (13,500 capacity)

May 9
Municipal Auditorium

Nashville, TN
Promoter: Sound Seventy Productions
Other act(s): Mahogany Rush
Reported audience: 11,000 **SOLD-OUT
Notes:
- From a local review: "'Dream until your dream comes true.' These — the lyrics that first brought the Aerosmith group to fame, and once again to fame as they were recycled two years ago — were strikingly absent from last night's Municipal Auditorium performance. Nearing the end of their set, Aerosmith tempted the audience with the opening notes of 'Dream On,' promoting expectant applause, then broke — ironically — into the lyrics, 'same old story, same old song and dance.' The evening was not anyone's same old story. It was an evening of foot-stomping, mind-racing rock 'n' roll. The sold-out performance drew a young sun-blushed crowd, T-shirts advertising everything from, 'The Stones' to 'Harley-Davidson' to 'Waylon...' Lead singer Steven Tyler, clad in thickly striped pants and a black shirt, cavorted about the stage, cradling the microphone as if it were a musical instrument... Aerosmith medleyed songs one into the other until they ended with 'Toys in the Attic' and a bright flourish of searchlights. Lighting throughout was smooth and befitting each number, but nothing exotic. And, as usual at general admission shows, the floor, from the seats above, was wall-to-wall heads" (Tennessean, 5/10/1978).

May 10
Von Braun Civic Center
Huntsville, AL
Promoter: Sound Seventy Productions
Other act(s): Mahogany Rush
Reported audience: 9,000 **SOLD-OUT

May 12
Mid-South Coliseum
Memphis, TN
Promoter: Mid-South Concerts
Other act(s): Mahogany Rush
Reported audience: 11,267 / 12,000 (93.89%)
Reported gross: $82,123

May 13
Birmingham-Jefferson Civic Coliseum
Birmingham, AL
Promoter: Alex Cooley, Inc.
Other act(s): Mahogany Rush
Reported audience: 14,769 **SOLD-OUT
Reported gross: $108,185

May 15
Omni
Atlanta, GA
Promoter: Alex Cooley, Inc.
Other act(s): Mahogany Rush
Reported audience: 15,861 **SOLD-OUT
Reported gross: $123,649
Notes:
- From a local review: "It was a night for earplugs at the Omni Monday as Aerosmith, one of the most successful American hard rock bands, assaulted the aural senses of a large, young audience with its no-frills, heavy-metal rock. Aerosmith, like its loud raw cousin KISS, is known for the kind of loud, primitive music

which finds favor with so many teens these days, and the massive sound system which the group brought along was more than equal to the challenge, pulverizing eardrums in the forward part of the auditorium even when between-show tapes were being played. But while KISS resembles Aerosmith in the over-amplified simplicity of its music, that painted band at least has some noteworthy special effects and stage presence of its own. Aerosmith, by comparison, seemed positively artless. Joey Kramer's drum work was the worst heard here in a long time, consisting almost totally of a simple pounding and crashing of cymbals, while the droning playing of guitarists Joe Perry and Brad Whitford and bassist Tom Hamilton depended heavily on amplifier feedback for its power.

The main center of attention in the band's show was lead singer Steven Tyler, a Mick Jagger lookalike who continually pranced about in a stage routine obviously inspired by the leader of the Rolling Stones. Tyler dragged the mike stand, which was bedecked in colorful streamers, around the stage, occasionally carrying it over his shoulder or leaning into it and wrapping the streamers around his body. It was not exactly inspired choreography. The band, best known for the hits 'Dream On' and 'Walk this Way,' played a representative sampling of their songs, most of which unfortunately sounded very much like the repetitive, tuneless latter number. However, the audience, which was primarily of high school age, took a sort of zombie-like delight in all of this, with many of its members (including almost all those on the floor) remaining on their feet throughout, waving a clenched fist in the air. Don't worry too much, though — they'll outgrow it... Monday night's show left this reviewer yearning for some music with at least a modicum of melody" (Atlanta Constitution, 5/16/1978).

May 17
Coliseum
Macon, GA
Promoter: Alex Cooley, Inc.
Other act(s): Mahogany Rush
Reported audience: 7,837 **SOLD-OUT
Reported gross: $55,408

May 18
Civic Center
Lakeland, FL
Promoter: Beach Club Concerts
Other act(s): Mahogany Rush
Reported audience: 10,000**SOLD-OUT

May 20
Sportatorium
Hollywood, FL
Promoter: Cellar Door Productions
Other act(s): Mahogany Rush
Reported audience: (15,500 capacity)

May 21
Coliseum
Jacksonville, FL
Promoter: Jet Set Enterprises
Other act(s): Mahogany Rush
Reported audience: (10,000 capacity)

May 24
Municipal Auditorium
Mobile, GA

Promoter: Alex Cooley, Inc.
Other act(s): Point Blank
Reported audience: 13,272 **SOLD-OUT
Reported gross: $91,170
Notes:
- From a local review: "Aerosmith played the Mobile Municipal Auditorium Wednesday night and the auditorium won in a sell-out double header, the back-up band being Point Blank in lieu of Frank Marino and Mahogany Rush... Aerosmith was a 'Close Encounter' of another world apart in its intro, and mystery always holds attention. Thus, black curtains and special aura worked. The total presentation was tight, hard, moving with a pulsating, throbbing, intoxicating wave. And the audience moved with it, in perfect harmony with what was being sent forth. Guess it will always take the younger people to get off their apathies and purchase tickets to see and enjoy a live entertainment in Mobile. The auditorium books great shows but only the young seem to respond. Congrats to them both" (Mobile Register, 5/25/1978).

May 26
Riverside Centroplex
Baton Rouge, LA

Promoter: Beaver Productions
Other act(s): Point Blank or Dirty Angels
Reported audience: (15,000 capacity)
Notes:
- Dirty Angels included David Hull, future bassist for the Joe Perry Project.

June 3-4 **RECORDING SESSION
Long View Farm
North Brookfield, MA

Notes:
- "Chip Away the Stone" was cut during this session with Jack Douglas and engineer Jesse Henderson. Songwriter Richie Supa played piano. This song was also recorded for Richie's "Tall Tales" album, which had been released in July 1977. That version had included Steven on backing vocals. A live recording from the "California Jam 2" was also included on the commemorative live release from that event in June 1978. Aerosmith's studio version of the song would be released as a single, backed with the live version from "Live! Bootleg," but only reached #77 on the Billboard Hot-100 charts

June 25
Veterans Auditorium
Des Moines, IA

Promoter: Celebration Concerts
Other act(s): Cheap Trick
Reported audience: (14,234 capacity)
Notes:
- Rick Nielsen recalled, "We did a show with [Aerosmith] in Iowa in 1978, in Des Moines... There was a tornado. It was after the show. We were on the top floor of the

Holiday Inn watching it. It was wild. Steven was sitting with me, and he was enjoying it. He was going wild — kind of a precursor of things to come with that guy" (Iowa State Daily, 5/3/04).

June 27
Kiel Auditorium
St. Louis, MO

Promoter: Contemporary Productions
Other act(s): Climax Blues Band
Reported audience: 9,067 / 10,000 (90.67%)
Reported gross: $67,030
Notes:
- From a local review: "If the old saying that nice guys finish last applies to rock 'n' roll, then Aerosmith should finish somewhere near the top of the heap. After all, singer Steven Tyler didn't win adulation by smiling all the time or singing about sunshine. Darkness, nastiness, and toughness were the main themes of at least half a concert Tuesday night at Kiel Auditorium featuring Aerosmith. The other half of the show was provided by the Climax Blues Band, which was a much friendlier lot, at least on stage. That band proved to be better entertainment, too. About 10,000 persons turned out for the show. Aerosmith, a band with a new album to peddle, came on with a great deal of sinister fanfare. The sound was powerful but usually lacked definition. There was one exception — the bass drum — and the two guitarists and bass player didn't always manage to generate enough volume to rise above it. Thus, a lot of presumably hot licks got lost in the ozone. The best new material the band offered was reminiscent of the old material. That meant that the guitarists and rhythm section moved together in huge blocks of counterpoint. They were not at their best when they played standard rock, unless you care to count the oldie 'Walkin' the Dog.' Tyler's singing was sufficiently cocky, although his dancing demonstration of the walk-the-dog looked more like the funky chicken. Tyler put on his mean guy routine as expected, but also showed that he has learned some new tricks. He made use of some new harmony effects and occasionally turned his singing into percussive effects over the microphone" (St. Louis Post-Dispatch, 6/28/1978).

June 28
Kemper Arena
Kansas City, MO

Promoter: Contemporary Productions / Chris Fritz
Other act(s): Climax Blues Band
Reported audience: 11,355 / 17,614 (64.47%)
Reported gross: $85,163'
Partial set list: Draw the Line / Big Ten Inch Record / Get it Up / Back in the Saddle / Seasons of Wither / I Wanna Know Why / Critical Mass / Sweet Emotion / Same Old Song and Dance / Toys in the Attic / Milk Cow Blues / Train Kept A Rollin' (** in order as noted in local review)
Notes:
- From a local review: "With bombs bursting in air, a near-capacity crowd at Kemper Arena witnessed the most powerful rock 'n' roll show to hit Kansas City this year... Between two enormous walls sound, Aerosmith bludgeoned the audience with its brand of no-frills rock 'n' roll as it pounded out 'Big Ten Inch Record,' a song that has captured airtime in many cities (for obvious reasons). As the names of many of the

tunes imply, like 'Get It Up' and 'Lord of the Thighs," the band bases its songs on sex. Those are the songs played most frequently and the most probable reason or Aerosmith's nationwide success. Fortunately, Aerosmith stuck with these recognizable songs. All through the set, the band was so loud that clarity was lost in the onslaught of noise and conflicts between guitars, drums, and shrieking vocals. Steve Tyler, lead vocalist, has been compared to Mick Jagger. He does strut around the stage and has big lips, but that's where it stops. Tyler's from-the-gut, primal scream sent chills down the spine in 'Back in the Saddle,' a hard-hitting rocker with the catchy rhythm and bass riffs that dominate most Aerosmith songs.

Lead guitarist Joe Perry was disappointing on lead breaks in the songs 'Walkin' the Dog,' which was almost note for note with Roger Daltrey's version, and 'Same Old Song and Dance,' in which he rushed his feedback-laden playing enough to throw the band off pace. Aerosmith is potentially a good band on record, but because of what seemed to be a battle for sound dominance on stage, it lost the effect it works for in the studio. Instead of buying a ticket, next time the band comes to town, save some money, and buy its album" (Kansas City Star, 6/29/1978).
- From another local review: "Every good hard rock band should be like Aerosmith. The Golden Boys of Rock 'n Roll (there are other names for them, but that is the most common) came to Kemper Arena in Kansas City recently and performed what had to be the loudest and one of the most dynamic shows that hall has ever seen. If you were at the concert and still have your ears on, consider yourself lucky. It wasn't only the music. The concert had a carnival-like atmosphere, with firecrackers, M-80s and bottle rockets going off all around. People began lining up in the aisles in front of the stage an hour before Aerosmith came on and rushed the stage near the end of the show. The main attraction, of course, was lead singer Steven Tyler. On stage, Tyler looks and acts like Mick Jagger and the band itself has been compared to the Rolling Stones.

Tyler posed, strutted, and sashayed throughout the 1 1/2-hour set, carrying the mike and stand with him much of the time. Along with Jagger, Rod Stewart, and Peter Wolf, Tyler is one of the most physical lead singers in rock, jumping up, running from one end of the stage to the other and teasing the teenyboppers in the first row repeatedly. They — along with everyone else — loved it. The music was deafening. Lead guitarist Joe Perry and rhythm guitarist Brad Whitford combined for some thundering solos, with Tom Hamilton's bass supplying a raucous, incessant bottom. Drummer Joey Kramer, one of the best musicians in the group, nailed away at his drums, almost unheard. It was that loud. But that is what Aerosmith is all about. That is keeping in line with their reputation, and you either love them or hate them — there's no in between" (St. Joseph News Press Gazette, 7/15/1978).

July 1
Cotton Bowl
Dallas, TX

Promoter: Texxas World Music Festival, Inc
Other act(s): Ted Nugent, Heart, Eddie Money, Mahogany Rush, Van Halen, Head East, Atlanta Rhythm Section, Walter Egan
Reported audience: 83,000 **SOLD-OUT
Set list: Rats in the Cellar / I Wanna Know Why / Big Ten Inch Record / Walkin' the Dog / Walk this Way / Seasons of Wither / Sweet Emotion / Lick and a Promise / Lord of the Thighs / Get the Lead Out / Draw the Line / Same Old Song and Dance / Toys in the Attic / Milk Cow Blues / Train Kept A' Rollin'
Notes:
- The Texxas World Music Festival '78 was held June 30 through July 4, with the

Texxas Jam taking place on a single day. Other musical events included Willie Nelson's annual picnic on July 3, featuring country artists such as him, Waylon Jennings, Kris Kristofferson, and others. Aerosmith's performance was professionally filmed and later released as "Live Texxas Jam '78" in 1989, though a live album featuring three of the bands was planned at the time (excluding Ted Nugent and Aerosmith). Audio recording services were provided by Dallas' Omega Audio's remote truck which utilized a 16/25-track rig with an MCI console. Additional songs from the performance, not included on the video release, have been released on "Pandora's Box" and other releases.

July 2
Summit
Houston, TX
Promoter: Pace Concerts
Other act(s): Journey, AC/DC
Reported audience: (14,950 capacity)

July 4
Municipal Auditorium
Lubbock, TX
Promoter: Mike Clark Friends Productions, Inc.
Other act(s): AC/DC
Reported audience: 8,380 / 10,000 (83.80%)
Reported gross: $68,761

July 5
Coliseum
El Paso, TX
Other act(s): Point Blank
Reported audience: ~8,000 / 10,000 (80%)
Notes:
- From a local review: "Rock bands lacking talent often make up for the impropriety by doling out large doses of volume. That's precisely what Aerosmith did an its return appearance here Wednesday night in County Coliseum, during El Paso's first concert in nearly three months. A little more than 8,000 attended the break in the local concert drought. Fireworks blazed and few crowd members walked away from the show disappointed. The predominantly teen-aged audience seemed ignorant to the fact that Aerosmith's show was nothing more than a rehash of last year's. Aerosmith is a hard rock band with a reputation for volume and 'raunchiness.' But its main faults lie deeper. Aerosmith still depends a great deal upon the Rolling Stones for staging, image, and even music. So much so, that Aerosmith's show amounts to an imitation of what the Stones were doing six years ago. Last year, singer Steve Tyler proved less than third-rate Jagger in his pompous, ostentatious copy of that famous singer's spontaneous stage act. There is nothing new in Tyler's routine now, except an increased dependence on screeching (as opposed to singing).

Strengthening the case against Wednesday's show is that guitarist Perry now has gotten into the act. He's taken to wearing satin shirts (complete with sleeves rolled to the elbows), streaking his hair with peroxide, singing at the mike with Tyler, and playing more rhythm guitar. And if that's not emulating Keith Richards, what is? A further disappointment is that a band with the hard rock ability of Aerosmith has to depend so largely upon another established act for its material. Aerosmith is still using the Mylar mirrors (a device borrowed from the Stones' 1972 tour). They suspend them above the stage for a spotlighting technique which gave the show half of its impact. (The volume made up the rest). Aerosmith's show was mechanically packaged rock, plain and simple. The group is, in fact, the McDonald's of rock. Sure, it's easy to whip a crowd into a frenzy when you depend the pulverizing effects of a ridiculously loud sound system and upon the anticipation built by a highly hyped reputation. Even the structure of the group's show lacked imagination, spontaneity, or originality — shortcomings similar to the 1977 concert. The group reeled off a couple of less familiar tunes, sprinkled in a few hits like 'Sweet Emotion' and 'Walk this Way' at pivotal points and concluded with a volume so thunderous that it shook the floor of the hall" (El Paso Times, 7/8/1978).

July 7
McNichols Arena
Denver, CO
Promoter: Feyline Presents, Inc.
Other act(s): 1994
Reported audience: 13,693 / 18,949 (72.26)
Reported gross: $94,635

July 10
Salt Palace
Salt Lake City, UT
Promoter: United Concerts
Other act(s): AC/DC
Reported audience: 13,000 **SOLD-OUT
Notes:
- From a local review: "Ah, the smell of cheap scotch in a 7-11 baseball cup, the ironic mixture of fake satin and popcorn. Ah, the Aerosmith audience, with every hair carefully out of place, from self-destruct afros to stringy Rod Stewart imitations. Ah, Aerosmith, the little Boston band now so big it doesn't even have to put the group's name on an album cover to sell it (shades of Led Zeppelin) and which can sell out the Salt Palace, as it did Monday night, leaving disappointed latecomers wandering ticketless in the streets... For some reason, Aerosmith rushed through everything — whether to get more songs in the repertoire or to get the show over and done with faster, who knows. The result is that some of its nearly classic rock tunes (like 'Big Ten Inch Record,' 'Sweet Emotion' and 'Same Old Song and Dance') tumble and are ruined in a frantic wall of noise. Which brings up another point. The group seems unaware that what isn't played is just as important as what is played. Aerosmith employs no audial [sic] dynamics, but a constant, thunderous stream of sound, with six musicians going full-tilt full time, as the songs gasp for air.

Aerosmith was fooling visually, too. Singer Steve Tyler and lead guitarist Joe Perry, the latter-day Jagger/Richards, shared the spotlight most of the time, but Tyler's vocals rarely more than an inaudible squeak, making any and all lyrics sadly indiscernible. Perry's solos were an exercise in distortion and a waste of time. Both do beautifully on record. The real guitarist in this band is the rhythm boy, Brad Whitford. He's not as much fun to look at as Tyler or Perry, but when he was allowed a brief solo, it was not only excellent, but pulled songs like 'Walk this Way' and "Lord of the Thighs" out of the mire. Tom Hamilton on bass and Joey Kramer on drums held things together as much as possible for the nearly two and one-half hour set, which introduced the band's new single, 'Chip Away at the Stone' from an upcoming LP culled from the group's appearance at the recent California Jam... Opening act AC/DC was better than expected, in light of the fact that American audiences usually turn up their noses at English/Scottish/Australian rockers that the British kids love so much" (Daily Utah Chronicle, 7/12/1978).

July 12
Long Beach Arena
Long Beach, CA
Promoter: Wolf & Rissmiller Concerts
Other act(s): AC/DC, 1994
Reported audience: 12,677 **SOLD-OUT
Reported gross: $102,000
Notes:
- From an industry review: "During the past few years, Aerosmith has deservingly earned its reputation as one of the most invigorating, explosive hard-rock bands in live performance. When the sextet (now including Mark Radice on keyboards) last played Southern California in February, the group demonstrated

the ability to captivate audiences both at the California Jam II and at its more intimate dates at the 3,000-seat Santa Monica Civic. However, Aerosmith's concert in Long Beach was marred by numerous sound system difficulties. Throughout most of the show, the group's sound was muddled and distorted, preventing Aerosmith from building up any sense of onstage momentum. Second-billed act AC/DC's performance was not hindered by any noticeable sound problems. Nonetheless, Aerosmith gamely played its usual selection of infectious, guitar-laden rock numbers. Such tunes as 'Draw the Line,' 'Get it Up' and 'Same Old Song and Dance' received enthusiastic responses from the audience. Also, the group's innovative lighting effects helped divert the crowd's attention away from the poor sound mix" (Cash Box, 7/29/1978).

July 15
Selland Arena
Fresno, CA
Promoter: Avalon Attractions
Other act(s): AC/DC
Reported audience: 7,333 **SOLD-OUT
Reported gross: $53,473
Set list: Rats in the Cellar / I Wanna Know Why / Big Ten Inch Record / Sight for Sore Eyes / Walk this Way / Walking the Dog / Chip Away the Stone / Seasons of Wither / Sweet Emotion / Lord of the Thighs / Get the Lead Out / Get it Up / Draw the Line / Same Old Song and Dance / Train Kept A Rollin'
Notes:
- Roughly 34 minutes of video footage exists from this show. An incomplete AUD recording also circulates.

July 20
Starwood
Hollywood, CA
Promoter: in-house
Reported audience: ~1,000
**SOLD-OUT
Notes:
- The band were in town for the premiere of the "Sgt. Peppers Lonely Hearts Club Band" movie, which opened to the public on July 21.
- After midnight, the band jammed for more than 90-minutes at this Los Angeles area club as Dr. J Jones & the Interns, which they opened with "Helter Skelter." Joe recalled, "That was the first time we'd played a club for a really long time and it was more fun playing that gig than I think I've had in two years. There's lots of things you can do in one of the big places — you can use a lot more equipment, you're a lot freer to use the guitars in different ways and you have a lot more stage to fill — but I think for really getting down, clubs are the best 'cause you see the people. You get an immediate reaction if you fuck up or if you do something good. I couldn't believe how exciting it was that night at the Starwood. The place was wall-to-wall, and we just opened it up. It wasn't like it was giving away a lot of tickets to record people either. The day before the gig our manager didn't even know we were gonna play there. We booked the gig ourselves, hired the equipment, everything... We went in as Dr. J. Jones and the Interns and anybody could take a chance on that. There was a few people there that got wind of it, but the place was packed, right up against the stage.

Our crew told us that Rod Stewart couldn't get in because they said it was too full" (Creem, December 1978).
- Playing in the clubs again was important for Joe, part of a process of reconnecting with the music with all that was being lost performing in larger venues. Perhaps, in a way, it was also an attempt to press an imaginary rewind button and take the band back to a time when they had audiences to connect with where their performance, energy, and music mattered. Joe later reflected, "Two gigs. That's all we did. The Starwood as Dr. Jones and the Interns — I was Dr. Jones — and the Paradise. I always wanted to do the clubs, but we never did them. And when we finally did them, they were some of the best gigs ever. And that was where the seed was dropped. That was right after we'd played some of the biggest halls. Like, I've been through it all. I've played in front of 350,000 people. I've been in a rock movie. I've been to Europe twice. I've been to Japan. I've been through millions of dollars. I've wrecked expensive cars. I've done it all! It got to be so boring. Musically I was a fucking shell" (Sounds, 7/5/80).
- From an industry review: "Dr. Jones and The Interns — That's what the marquee at the Starwood in West Hollywood read on July 19, but when Cash Box staffer Joey Berlin dropped in for a late show, the band on stage was cranking out songs such as 'Walk this Way' and 'Draw the Line.' Yes, it was Aerosmith playing under a pseudonym, and the throngs inside and outside the club weren't fooled by the name. Hundreds milled about outside, trying to join the shoulder-to-shoulder crowd standing on chairs and tables inside. But despite the overcrowding, Aerosmith put on one of the most powerful and invigorating performances the Starwood has ever seen. In the intimacy of the small club, the group's hard-driving rock 'n' roll consumed the audience and made it a night to remember. And the evening gave the Starwood's beefed up security team practice for the anticipated appearance of the Rolling Stones with Peter Tosh two nights later" (Cash Box, 7/29/1978).

July 21
Coliseum
Portland, OR

Promoter: John Bauer Concert Company
Other act(s): AC/DC
Reported audience: 11,000 **SOLD-OUT
Reported gross: $93,364
Notes:
- From a local review: "Aerosmith drew from just the right rung of the ladder Friday night when it returned to Portland's Memorial Coliseum to play for a sellout audience of some 11,000. What the band got was a screaming, occasionally rowdy crowd that liked its music loud. The band gave loudness and more to its fans with thunderous rhythms and basic high energy guitar solos sandwiched around Steve Tyler's frenetic vocals. Although there is little variety to the total sound — tempos are mostly fast — the sound appeals to basic emotions that key an array of aggressive behavior, most of which is manifested in shouting and jumping. Aerosmith is one of those longtime rock bands that seldom gets Top-40 airtime. The band doesn't play and sing cute little pop anthems, giving its energy instead over to booming music that needs trucks full of sound amplification equipment to hammer the lyrics home. This band, nevertheless, sells records like crazy. It gets progressive rock play or manages to get heard on stations that play albums or long cuts of bands not interested in formula radio. It's also pretty close to being in the punk arena from the volume and content of its songs. The show Friday night about 90 minutes. The sound system was mushy at times, giving guitar and vocal lines muddy moments. Lights, however, were excellent. A pentagonal lighting system hovered over the band with crossbeams holding a variety of colored lights. Between the beams floated triangle shaped mirrors that bounced stage borne spots back down on the performers for a well-done effect. AC/DC opened the show with more high energy rock and a decent show to go along with it" (Oregonian, 7/22/1978).

July 23
Oakland Coliseum
Oakland, CA

Promoter: Bill Graham Presents

Other act(s): Foreigner, Pat Travers, Van Halen, AC/DC
Reported audience: 57,512 **SOLD-OUT
Reported gross: $632,632
Notes:
- The "Day on the Green #3" festival.
- From a local review: "San Francisco held out longer than any other City in the country against the Aerosmith onslaught. But last Sunday, when the band headlined a sold-out Day on the Green at the Oakland Coliseum Stadium, San Francisco finally succumbed. The hard-rocking East Coast quintet has come a long way from the band's Bay Area debut four years ago, opening a Winterland concert for Bachman-Turner Overdrive and Mott the Hoople (where are they now?), to topping a bill of heavy decibel rockers that included Foreigner, Pat Travers, Van Halen, and AC/DC before an audience of more than 55,000. Furthermore, the band is no longer the carbon copy Rolling Stones Aerosmith started out as — although the quartet still pays tribute to the sound of middle-period Stones. Opening with a thunderous version of the Beatles' 'Helter Skelter,' Aerosmith powered

through nearly 90 minutes of tough, biting rock, ringing with wonderful guitar riffs and driven by a pounding rhythm section. The band barely paused between selections, rolling through as many as six consecutive numbers with little more than one drum beat in between. Lead vocalist Steve Tyler pouted, posed, and stomped around as star rock vocalists are supposed to. His vocals tended to get lost in the sea of guitars, but he was ably supported with harmonies from other members" (San Francisco Chronicle, 7/26/1978).

July 25
Pacific Coliseum
Vancouver, BC, Canada

Promoter: John Bauer Concert Company
Other act(s): AC/DC
Reported audience: ~12,000 / 17,600 (68.18%)
Notes:
- From a local review: "Aerosmith has been hanging on in the top echelons of the heavy metal rock pile for several years now, but that's not much of a distinction anymore. After all, there's hardly any heavy metal rock pile left, and it can't feel like much of an achievement to better the remaining contenders. But there it is — and there Aerosmith was Tuesday night at The Coliseum — snapping millions of little brain synapses with its mondo-gonzo barrage of decibels and lobotomized approach to what might hesitantly be called rock 'n' roll. Hesitation because, of late, rock 'n' roll has finally started getting a good name again — and the legit, exciting contemporary stuff has little to do with what Aerosmith pounds into eardrums. It's anybody's guess why 12,000 people turned out for the event. Mine is that it was strictly that — an event. In its six years of touring and recording, Aerosmith has never played Vancouver. With any luck, it won't again. Even Nazareth, a dinosaur itself, has several distinguishable songs in its repertoire, which is more than you can say for Aerosmith.

Well, okay, you could pick out a few things, like 'Walk this Way,' 'Toys in the Attic,' and 'Sweet Emotion.' But the lung-ripping vocals of Steven Tyler and the napalm guitar of Joe Perry (with the remaining members of the band providing the necessary tonnage) is exactly the archetypal, passé buzz-saw approach the '70s contingent of brave new rockers detests so heartily. Granted, Aerosmith does put on, by definition, a power-packed show, complete with enormous sound and light systems — but these days even Tyler's Jagger-esque stage antics are unconvincing, Perry's guitar is outrageously meaningless and self-indulgent, and the rest of the group appears to be functioning in a grotesque, mindless mind lock. Somebody once called this group the middle-of-the-road of heavy metal; to be sure, they're not nearly so awful as Uriah

Heep and not nearly so good as Led Zeppelin at its best, so that's probably accurate enough. But they are leaning toward the former, and that's something that should probably be written off in the history books by now. Heavy metal of a different bent (and it is bent) was presented, for openers, by Australia's AC/DC band. Its musically redeeming qualities are also somewhat questionable, but the band has a lot of spirit and an enormous sense of humor, embodied by a lead guitarist who dresses in (and then undresses in) short-pants public school uniform and carries on an incredible repertoire of stage antics that are hopelessly ridiculous and quite amazing" (The Province, 7/26/1978).

July 26
Coliseum
Spokane, WA
Promoter: John Bauer Concert Company
Other act(s): AC/DC
Reported audience: (7,800 capacity)
Notes:
- From a local review: "Aerosmith's lead singer, Steve Tyler, thinks he's hot stuff. But judging from the reaction of last night's capacity Coliseum crowd, his popularity here has cooled considerably. Tyler was aloof on stage. 'How are you, Spokane?' he asked with no interest. Frequently he turned his back to the crowd, and many in attendance did the same. Fans milled about long the finish. Aerosmith has been to Spokane several times, and it's entertaining to hear old favorites such as 'Train Kept a Rollin',' 'Sweet Emotion' and 'Big Ten Inch.' But those are dated. What Spokane fans needed last night was something new. That they got when the warm-up band, AC/DC, appeared and lead guitarist Angus Young began his hour-long hard rock blast... Last night's entire concert was louder than most. Picking out melodies was near impossible. The whole evening like a three-hour car crash" (Spokane Daily Chronicle, 7/27/1978).
- From another local review: "As if the weatherman hadn't provided enough heat for concert goers Wednesday night, the combined efforts of rock bands Aerosmith and AC/DC added to the inferno in the Spokane Coliseum, playing for three hours at fever pitch. Neither good nor bad best describes the performance as well as LOUD, Even the ears of the heartiest hard rock fans were blistered by the thunder created by these groups. And if, by chance, there was fan or two in the overflow crowd who was not feeling the heat before the concert began, just watching the antics of Aerosmith's lead singer Steve Tyler and AC/DC's lead guitarist Angus Young was enough to send beads of perspiration falling from their brow. Although most of the 7,800 packed the Coliseum to watch and listen to Aerosmith, these same fans had to be equally impressed by the performance of AC/DC, a group hailing from Australia.

Aerosmith began its segment of the show playing 'Helter Skelter.' From that point on only a handful of the group's selections were familiar to those who follow the top 40 charts, 'Walk This Way,' 'Same Old Song and Dance' and 'Sweet Emotion' apparently sparked even the most passive concert attendees. Glaringly omitted, however, from the band's performance was the playing of 'Dream On,' its hit single which sent Aerosmith's first of five albums to platinum status. The group may have been saving 'Dream On' for a second encore. But the hot and worn-out Coliseum crowd could not muster enough enthusiasm to bring the band back a second time... Although the stage show was good and the music was loud, both group's selections seemed to melt together, just as did the throng of hot, T-shirt and tank top clad fans milling around the Coliseum floor" (Spokesman Review, 7/28/1978).

July 28
Yellowstone Metra Park

Billings, MT
Promoter: John Bauer Concert Company
Other act(s): AC/DC
Reported audience: 10,255 / 11,500 (89.17%)
Notes:
- From a local review: "Aerosmith is proof that a few American hard-rock bands can still break through the music industry's domination by British groups and rise to the top. With their music, the five-member band from Boston made the walls of Metra vibrate Friday night, drawing screams from more than 10,000 fans. The group appeared with special guest AC/DC. The arena was nearly sold out. Billed as the top band in America, Aerosmith is on tour promoting its latest album 'Draw the Line...' The crowd was mostly in the 16-to-24-year-old range... Some fans were packed like sheep for slaughter in front of the stage. Others were bouncing between corridor walls as if in a giant pinball machine...

Aerosmith kept the main-floor fans on their feet, waving and clapping their hands throughout the show, by playing some of their best hits and a few songs off the new album. But that could be as much a tribute to the Metra's hard cement floor as to the band's playing ability. The fans packed in front of the stage would have had to sit on the floor. Aerosmith opened the show with a driving rendition of the Beatles' 'Helter Skelter' and peaked with crowd-pleasing favorites like 'Sweet Emotion' and 'Train Kept A-Rollin'.' Perhaps the band's greatest talent is the ability to blend a potent mixture of soft melodies with hard rock. Another notch for their guitars is the selection of AC/DC as a warm-up band. The group from Australia, via England, has come a long way from being called a Punk Rock group playing the Marquee in London. While fans can often be restless waiting for the intro group to finish so the main event can start, AC/DC kept most of the crowd stomping" (Billings Gazette, 7/29/1978).

July 30
Exhibition Hall
Winnipeg, MB, Canada
Promoter: Advance Promotions
Other act(s): AC/DC
Reported audience: ~7,000 / 7,800 (89.74%)
Notes:
- The third attempt to bring the band to Winnipeg was finally successful!
- From a local review: "Sunday night at the Winnipeg Arena Aerosmith finally made the local scene after several abortive attempts. Judging by the audience response the jury is still out on whether it was worth the wait. About 7,000 fans responded reasonably well to the super group but only a hard-core element was wildly enthusiastic... After a lengthy intermission, lightened by the neat catching and toss-back of an errant Frisbee by an adept and friendly Winnipeg constable (the crowd gave him a rousing ovation), Aerosmith arrived. Their appearance was heralded by an attractive panoply of shifting, brilliantly colored spotlights. Their radiance was reflected effectively by the curtain of smoke which was so thick by this time that it was almost impossible to read the 'No Smoking' signs. Steven Tyler on vocals likely sings as well on stage as he does on vinyl. But who can tell? Joey Kramer's drumming is so over-amplified that for the first time in memory I couldn't hear the electric bass, let alone the singer. Tyler works very hard but his awkward and inept attempts to be cool and sexy in his handling of the floor mike constitute a parody of the rock singer in full flight.

Not too many rock groups last eight years with no personnel changes. Some don't last eight weeks. Aerosmith is the exception, and one would expect this continuity and stability to provide an assurance which would permit intelligent programming. But to follow a heavy metal group like AC/DC with an only slightly more sophisticated dose of the same smacks of disinterest, an acute lack of awareness or utter indifference to the audience's sensibilities. There wasn't a change of tempo or melodic note in the whole show. With five platinum records to their credit the fellows know what they're doing in a recording studio, and the resultant albums do offer contrasts in material and style. So why the compulsion to blow us away on every number when in concert? ... The audience seemed to display a certain ennui as the waves of sound washed over it. There was much coming and going and a demand for an encore which was less vociferous than that afforded the energetic but monotonous warm-up group. Perhaps it was just too much of a good thing. Perhaps the boredom produced by what was essentially one long, very loud riff spread over two groups and 150 minutes got to us.... Whatever the reason, Aerosmith's long-awaited show simply wasn't the spectacular event we'd anticipated and which their albums would entitle us to expect" (Winnipeg Free Press, 7/31/1978).

August 1
Rushmore Civic Plaza
Rapid City, SD

Promoter: John Bauer Concert Company
Other act(s): AC/DC
Reported audience: ~10,000
Notes:
- From a local review: "Almost 10,000 area young people attended a Tuesday concert at the Rushmore Plaza Civic Center by the rock group Aerosmith. Billed as one of the top rock groups in the country today, Aerosmith is drawing crowds of up to 80,000 at stadium concerts. The group is concluding a tour of United States cities and is getting ready for an international tour later this year. AC/DC, an Australian group, was on tour with Aerosmith and played first at the Rapid City concert. The elaborate lighting system was provided by Bee Factor of California and the sound system was the same as was used for the Heart concert, provided by Showco" (Rapid City Journal, 8/4/1978).

August 4
Alpine Valley Music Theater
East Troy, WI

Promoter: in-house
Other act(s): AC/DC

Reported audience: 11,680 / 18,500 (63.14%)
Reported gross: $109,111
Notes:
- A point of comparison, 10 days earlier Fleetwood Mac sold out three nights for 54,639 patrons.

August 5
Comiskey Park
Chicago, IL
Promoter: Jam Productions
Other act(s): Foreigner, Mahogany Rush, AC/DC, Walter Egan
Reported audience: ~40,000
Partial set list: Rats in the Cellar / I Wanna Know Why / Big Ten Inch Record / Sight for Sore Eyes / Walk this Way / Walkin' the Dog / Chip Away the Stone / All Your Love / Lick and a Promise / Sweet Emotion / Lord of the Thighs
Notes:
- Aerosmith replaced Jefferson Starship at the top of the bill in early June. That band had had issues during their European tour, featuring a legendary meltdown on stage by frontwoman Grace Slick in Germany...
- From a local review: "As outdoor venues go, Comiskey Park lent itself surprisingly well to music, being smaller than Soldier Field and — at least Saturday acoustically superior. In fact, the sound was far less terrible than might be imagined. Saturday's lineup was long on power rock and short on frills, with Aerosmith, AC/DC, and Mahogany Rush the heaviest of the lot. But though Aerosmith headlined and churned out a competent, hard-edged set, it's a good bet that a lot of the crowd had come to see Foreigner, a half-British, half-American sextet that proved itself a highly commercial comer last year with a debut album that sold 3 million copies and produced three hit singles" (Chicago Tribune, 8/7/1978).
- A excellent, albeit partial, AUD recording circulates from this show.

August 6
Giants Stadium
East Rutherford, NJ
Promoter: John Scher / Monarch Entertainment
Other act(s): Ted Nugent, Journey, Mahogany Rush
Reported audience: 51,592 / 64,000 (80.61%)
Reported gross: $608,615
Set list: Helter Skelter / Rats in the Cellar / I Wanna Know Why / Big Ten Inch Record / Sight for Sore Eyes / Walk this Way / Walkin' the Dog / Chip Away the Stone / Seasons of Wither / Lick and a Promise / Sweet Emotion / Lord of the Thighs / Get the Lead Out / Get it Up / Draw the Line / Same Old Song and Dance / Toys in the Attic / Milk Cow Blues / Train Kept A Rollin'
Notes:
- Purportedly, Aerosmith were paid $100,000 for this show. WNEW-FM had been due to broadcast the concert but ran into difficulties and only broadcast in-between the live acts.
- From a local review: "There is an old adage, that it never rains on the golf course. It also, apparently, never rains at outdoor rock concerts. Nearly 50,000 hard rock music fans jammed Giants Stadium in the Meadowlands yesterday and listened to Aerosmith, Ted Nugent, and other bands as steady afternoon showers dampened their clothes, but not their enthusiasm. Although the crowd was smaller than the mob of 64,000 that packed the sports arena for the first rock concert, the June 25 seven-hour marathon headlined by the Beachboys, promoter John Scher and Meadowlands were happy. 'The rain kept the people away. If it was a sunny day, we would have filled the place.' said Scher. 'We had over 40,000 tickets sold by Thursday. I think the weather held the crowd down.' One of Scher's aides said the day's box office gross, about $500,000, would yield a 'small profit' for the producer and the New Jersey Sports and Exposition Authority, but not much more" (New York Daily News, 8/7/1978).
- From another local review: "They came — 51,622 strong; they stayed — through well over six hours of intermittent rain; and they listened with unflagging enthusiasm — to four ear-splitting, reverberating sets of rock 'n roll. In terms of fan dedication, yesterday's concert at Giants Stadium in the Meadowlands, featuring

Aerosmith, Ted Nugent, Journey, and Frank Marino and Mahogany Rush, may well have been 'The Rock Event of the Summer,' as promoter John Scher had billed it. In terms of numbers, it was not. Beach Boys concert in June, the first rock 'n roll event staged in Giants Stadium, drew 62,000. Numbers aside, even if Scher just breaks even on this concert, as a spokesman claimed he did, a stadium full of young, less-than-mellow, hard-rock addicts, many of them packed body to body on the Astroturf-and-tarpaulin-covered playing field, enjoyed themselves under highly uncertain conditions. Those conditions had exclusively to do with the weather. Would it rain, or wouldn't it? Well, it did, and it didn't, and not until the very last minute would anyone know if the headlining group, Aerosmith, was going onstage at all.

They did. Just as someone was commenting that the group's flamboyant lead vocalist, Steve Tyler, who practically makes love to his microphone stand while performing, would light up like a fuse on the rain-slick stage, Aerosmith suddenly appeared — and played a 1 1/2-hour concluding set to a soggy, but receptive crowd. If Aerosmith had not appeared, Scher's concert literally would have gone down the drain, and he would have had to give everyone a rain check... It would be pretentious and probably inaccurate to judge Ted Nugent's and Aerosmith's performances by any conventional standards. Throughout their sets, so dense and was the sound system that even the more carefully mixed version piped into the glass-enclosed press was hardly more than a dull, roar... Aerosmith was another visual orgy Steve Tyler, the band's Jagger-esque lead vocalist — dressed in red slacks, black shirt, and white jacket — did a tight-kneed soft shoe as he jerked and contorted through the music. But it's Tyler's face that is most fascinating. It's a face that in repose must ugly, maybe frightening, but in action is beautifully expressive. Although the crowd tough — motorcycles were zipping around the parking lot, and tattoos on both sexes were almost de rigueur — it acted friendly and close to peaceful. There is almost a tradition at Aerosmith concerts for firecrackers to thrown onstage, but yesterday nothing more lethal than frisbees and beach-balls were tossed around" (Hackensack Record, 8/7/1978).
- An AUD recording circulates from this show, which marked the end of the "Aerosmith Express" era.

August 9
Paradise Club
Boston, MA
Promoter: Don Law
Other act(s): Lilith, Nightshade
Reported audience: ~1,000 **SOLD-OUT
Partial set list: Helter Skelter / Get it Up / Rattlesnake Shake
Notes:
- "Secret" show as Dr. J. Jones & the Interns recorded for "Live! Bootleg" ("Last Child" was purportedly sourced from this show). Lilith was just booked to play an earlier slot at the club that evening.
- From a local review: "It was the talk — correction, whisper — of the town, and by nightfall Wednesday what started out as a hush-hush happening turned out to be Boston's worst-kept secret. Masquerading in the hospital whites of a group billed on the marquee as Dr. J. Jones & The Interns, Aerosmith pulled off a 'sudden' concert at the Paradise. It caught most of the rock audience off guard, yet a crowd sufficiently large to fill the club apparently either had had their ears to the ground or friends in high places. Recently returned from a seven-week tour which saw the Boston-based rock stars co-headlining with Ted Nugent before 50,000 in the Meadowlands in New Jersey, the group also is broadening its audience through the success of its rendition of 'Come Together' in the motion picture version of 'Sgt. Pepper's Lonely Hearts Club Band.' On Monday night, Aerosmith's road manager contacted Don Law on the matter of staging a 'sneak show' at his club in order to complete the recording of its 'live' album. A general announcement of the concert date might have resulted in a stampede.

'We've always wanted to come into a club unannounced in Boston,' said guitarist Brad Whitford of Reading. 'Because of what we've become, we can't do it anymore on a conventional level. We'd have a riot. We also wanted to make the appearance part of our 'live' album. I think it's going to be called 'Bootleg.' We've played small facilities before and sold tickets by lotteries. We had people enter by sending letters to radio stations. When we played Santa Monica Civic Center, where they had only 3,000 seats, the radio station received over 100,000 letters.' Spot announcements broadcast over local radio stations hinted about a 'special concert by Dr. J. Jones,' but there was no explicit mention of the true identity of the performers, Whitford said. 'The date means a lot to us,' the guitarist said. 'We want to feel appreciated in our own hometown. I think we've always had a little bit of trouble with that in Boston in the past.' Inside the packed club, a festive New Year's-type atmosphere prevailed as the band arrived onstage at 11:35. It was to remain there, dealing out its peculiar brand of hard-punching rock 'n' roll, featuring Steve Tyler on vocals, for nearly two hours, and few persons were seen heading for the exits. Aerosmith was psyched for this concert in its own backyard as it stoked intense fires with 'Helter Skelter,' 'Rats," 'Ten-Inch Record,' featuring Tyler honking a boogie blues chorus on mouth harp, 'Rattle Snake,' 'Licks and Promises,' 'Get it Up,' 'Toys in the Attic' and others" (Boston Globe, 8/11/1978).

- From another local review: "Any expectations that the evening at the Paradise would be special or unusually intimate were deflated the moment Aerosmith recklessly charged into 'Helter Skelter,' never acknowledging either the audience or the occasion... Perhaps the band was concentrating on the live recording rather than the performance, but it seemed pretty pointless to play for an audience they chose to ignore... Steven Tyler never even made eye-contact with the crowd, never mind establishing rapport... Their remoteness looked more like boredom than absorption in the music. Even lead guitarist Joe Perry, whose arrogance makes up the large part of his mystique, was surprisingly cool. Perhaps the only surprise came when he mumbled an introduction to Fleetwood Mac's 'Rattlesnake Shake,' the only acknowledgement of either the crowd or Aerosmith's humble beginnings: 'This is a song we used to play here — before it was the Paradise.' One couldn't help thinking that if Aerosmith had given such lackluster demonstrations back in the days of the Boston Club, they'd still be hungry — instead of heavy metal heroes" (Boston Phoenix, 8/22/1978).

August 10 **RECORDING SESSION / REHEARSAL
A. Wherehouse
Waltham, MA

Set list: All Your Love / Come Together (Multiple Takes)
Notes:
- Assorted live run-throughs and rehearsals were recorded with roughly 40-minutes' worth circulating from the tapes. The cut of "All Your Love" is different to that released on "Pandora's Box." The band are clearly working out "Come Together" for its live inclusion on "Live! Bootleg" and as a feature piece for the new upcoming tour.

August 20 **RECORDING SESSION / REHEARSAL
A. Wherehouse
Waltham, MA

Set list: Come Together / Downtown Charlie / Come Together (Multiple Takes)
Notes:
- Assorted live run-throughs and rehearsals were recorded with roughly 27-minutes' worth circulating from the tapes. The cut of "Downtown Charlie" is different to that released on "Pandora's Box."

August 21 **RECORDING SESSION
A. Wherehouse
Waltham, MA

Notes:
- Live recording session at the rehearsal space to record "Come Together" for the live album. The studio version for the "Sgt. Pepper's" movie had been recorded at the Record Plant Studios earlier in the year. Joe recalled, "I was amazed that [producer] George Martin let me do it, because we didn't even rehearse the song 'Come Together,' and we didn't even listen to the album. All I did was remember how it used to sound when the Beatles did it, and the other guys listened to it a little bit, just to get the bass down. We just went into the studio and started playing it. And about the tenth time through, I said to George, 'Listen, what do you want?' — because I would play it halfway straight and then I'd play all these different kinds of weird things. And Martin said, 'Do whatever you want; you're doing fine.' I didn't know what the hell he had in mind... It was fun working with George Martin, but I was expecting him to come up with a lot more songs.

Apparently, however, he liked what he heard. And I have to admit, we were flattered that he dug it. We finally took the best performance, which we got on about the twelfth take" (Guitar Player, 3/1979). Joe used a B.C. Rich Mockingbird for recording of this track, a guitar that had too much presence to get used too often on stage. He had also used it for the recording on "Milk Cow Blues" (also cut live).

1978 - Live! Bootleg

U.S. Release Details:
Columbia/CBS PC2/P2A/P2T-35564 (Oct. 27, 1978)
Columbia/SME CK/CT-57365 (Sept. 7, 1993 — 20-bit SBM digital remaster)
Columbia/SME 19075896831 (Sept. 13, 2019 — 180g LP reissue)

Tracks:
A1. Back in the Saddle
(4:11) — Joe Perry / Steven Tyler
A2. Sweet Emotion
(4:43) — Steven Tyler / Tom Hamilton
A3. Lord of the Thighs
(7:13) — Steven Tyler
A4. Toys in the Attic
(3:45) — Joe Perry / Steven Tyler
B1. Last Child
(3:03) — Brad Whitford / Steven Tyler
B2. Come Together ●
(4:50) — John Lennon / Paul McCartney
B3. Walk this Way
(3:35) — Joe Perry / Steven Tyler
B4. Sick as a Dog
(4:35) — Steven Tyler / Tom Hamilton

C1. Dream On
(4:31) — Steven Tyler
C2. Chip Away the Stone ●
(4:00) — Richard Supa
C3. Sight for Sore Eyes
(3:13) — David Johansen / Jack Douglas / Joe Perry / Steven Tyler
C4. Mama Kin
(3:42) — Steven Tyler
C5. S.O.S. (Too Bad)
(2:39) — Steven Tyler
D1. I Ain't Got You
(4:00) — Calvin Carter
D2. Mother Popcorn / Draw the Line
(6:49) — Alfred Ellis / James Brown // Steven Tyler / Joe Perry
D3. Train Kept A Rollin' / Strangers In The Night
(9:49) — Howard Kay / Lois Mann / Tiny Bradshaw // Bert Kaempfert / Charles Singleton / Eddie Snyder

Album Details:
Executive producers: David Krebs & Steve Leber. Produced & arranged by Jack Douglas and Aerosmith. Engineered by Jack Douglas, Jay Messina, and Lee DeCarlo. Assisted by Sam Ginsberg, Rod O'Brien, and Julie Last. Recorded by Record Plant remote services arranged by David Hewitt (New York) and Chris Stone (Los Angeles). Mastered at Sterling Sound by George Marino. Art direction & design by John Kosh.

Players:
◦ Keyboards and backing vocals by Mark Radice.
◦ Mother Popcorn - Saxophone by David Woodford.

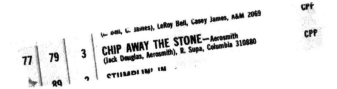

Chart Action:
Chart Peak (USA): #13 (1/13/1979) with 22 weeks on the Billboard charts. The album also hit #10 on Cashbox (12/16/1978). Other countries: CAN #27.

11/11/78	11/18/78	11/25/78	12/02/78	12/09/78	12/16/78	12/23/78
62	37	31	23	18	17	16
12/30/78	01/06/79	**01/13/79**	01/20/79	01/27/79	02/03/79	02/10/79
16	14	** 13 **	13	17	17	31
02/17/79	02/24/79	03/03/79	03/10/79	03/17/79	03/24/79	03/31/79
50	51	73	86	129	156	179
04/07/79	04/14/79					
198	X					

RIAA/Sales:

In the United States, the album was certified Gold by the RIAA on October 31, 1978 and Platinum on December 26, 1978; Gold by the CRIA (Canada - 50,000 units) on December 1, 1978. During the SoundScan era, the album had sold 403,265 copies between 1991 and 2007.

Supporting Singles:

• Come Together (USA, 7/1978) - Chart Peak: #23 (9/30/1978) with 12 weeks on the Billboard charts. Other countries: N/A.

08/05/78	08/12/78	08/19/78	08/26/78	09/02/78	09/09/78	09/16/78
81	66	50	41	38	33	29
09/23/78	**09/30/78**	10/07/78	10/14/78	10/21/78	10/28/78	
25	** 23 **	23	35	95	X	

• Chip Away the Stone (USA, 12/1978) - Chart Peak: #77 (2/3/1979) with 3 weeks on the Billboard charts. Other countries: N/A.

01/20/79	01/27/79	**02/03/79**	02/10/79			
81	79	** 77 **	X			

Of interest:

Released June 30, 1978, the "California Jam 2 (Columbia/CBS PC2/P2A/P2T -35389)" album included three Aerosmith cuts along with songs from other artists appearing at the event. Bruce Botnick served as an Executive Producer for the project. While the album has been reissued on CD (1995), and songs included on the likes of "Pandora's Box," all three cuts were also included on other releases, such as the Japan "Tour Edition" of "Just Push Play" (Sony SICP87-88) in 2002.

C1. Same Old Song and Dance
(5:09) — Steven Tyler / Joe Perry
C2. Draw the Line
(4:34) — Steven Tyler / Joe Perry
C3. Chip Away the Stone
(4:06) — Richard Supa

Joe Perry: "As far as I'm concerned, I didn't want to do a live album because there're so many perfect albums coming out, all doctored and fixed — big deal. Double live album: standard of the industry... I felt like we had to top that, do a real live album" (Creem, 12/1978).

The "Draw the Line" tour had come to a conclusion before Christmas 1977, with several shows scheduled for early 1978 being canceled to facilitate the band's filming for the "Sgt. Pepper's Lonely Hearts Club Band" movie. While Joe later suggested that the involvement with the movie was at the root of the band's demise — "Aerosmith shouldn't have tried to become actors or movie stars. We were a rock group, not movie stars. It hurt us just as it hurt Frampton" (Little Falls Journal, 10/7/1981) — the seeds had been full sown during 1977 (and before). With active support for the album having come to an end, management thought that the band was a mess and needed some downtime. David Krebs recalled, "I didn't become a manager to be a doctor... We had reached the top, but the band was dying, so we switched from a running game to a passing game... My idea was that I wanted to build a roof over their heads, to give them time to work out their problems. We came up with these giant events — Cal Jam, Texxas Jam — that would make so much money it would give them running room to deal with those problems" ("Walk this Way"). CCC started exercising another plan for its larger acts: Live albums. This format had become a bit predictable by the second half of the 1970s — they were no longer special commemoratives and had become commonplace time fillers. The format had set bands such as KISS, Bob Seger, and Peter Frampton on the road to superstardom, but they also provided break from the time, effort, and cost of recording a studio album; and for that Aerosmith time was needed. Ted Nugent, who had already firmly established himself, issued "Double Live Gonzo!" in January 1978. As was the case with Aerosmith's later live offering, his was pieced together from multiple show recordings.

The idea of using large shows as substitute for general touring backfired when the band decided that they wanted to get back to the people. The band had felt that they had become out of touch with their audience, so they booked a series of smaller theater dates to repay their diehard fans for their early support. Local radio stations held contests to distribute the available tickets. It was almost an inoculation against the massive shows to come... The idea of packaging the album similar to the unofficial merchandise the band often saw appealed to Steven in particular (multiple designs would be worked on for the packaging). As a rough 'n' tumble rock 'n' roll band they also didn't want something polished and fake sounding. They wanted it raw, but they wanted to beat the bootleggers at their own game. Joe recalled, "We started finding all these old tapes, like this one from Paul's Mall in Boston. It was right after we'd recorded the first album. All we had of it was a two-track tape off a radio broadcast. Everybody said, 'Two track! We can't put that on the album. Too much hiss, too much this and that... It's basically not gonna sound good.' And we said, 'What the fuck do you think they did ten years ago?' So, we did just a little fixing and it's gonna be on the thing. We had a sax player up there doin' a James Brown song, a lot of good shit on that tape" (Creem, 12/1978). According to Jack Douglas, "It's loaded with mistakes and we left all the mistakes on the record. But anyone who's ever to an Aerosmith concert knows their shows are loaded with mistakes. And we wanted this to a sampling of an Aerosmith concert" (Dallas Morning News, 11/4/1978). Throughout the summer of 1978 the album was simply referred to as "Bootleg," but in August it was changed to its final form: "Live! Bootleg." Joe also wasn't interested in following the formula established for live albums: "As far as I'm concerned, I didn't want to do a live album because there're so many perfect albums coming out, all doctored and fixed — big deal. Double live album: standard of the industry... I felt like we had to top that, do a real live album, like 'Live at Leeds,' 'Get Yer Ya Yas Out,' that old Kinks album [Ed. "Live at Kelvin Hall"] or 'Got Live If You Want It.' So, I was trying to think of something that would justify a live album in my head" (Creem, 12/1978).

Keyboard player Mark Radice had joined the band for the "back to the people" tour in March and only planned on staying throughout the summer. While a friend of Steven's, he wasn't a fan of the band's songs — "They all sounded the same to me" (The Record, 8/31/1978) — and he was looking forward to getting back to his own material once recording wrapped up for the album. He would, however, be persuaded to stay with Aerosmith for the live album tour. When the band wrapped up their spring tour, they and Jack Douglas got to work properly on the live album in June. A version of the album was ready for debut at the CBS Records Convention held in Los Angeles in late-July, while the band headed back out on the road.

Preview tapes at this time certainly included the wavering version of "Rattlesnake Shake," though the number of cover songs still included may have become a problem for the label. Additional recordings would be required in August, at Boston's Paradise Club and the Wherehouse, to complete the source material for the album. According to Joe, the band wanted to keep the overdubs to a minimum: "The fixing we did was just places where the guitar or the mike went out, places where we legitimately had to fix it. I've let stuff go by on this album, like guitar mistakes, and I just don't want to change it. I don't want anybody fixin' it. That was that night. There's no multi-track vocals on this to make it sound sweeter or anything like that. In a few places Steven was singing really off, so off that it would be totally offensive to hear, so we took that part of the vocal out, if we could, and put a new one in. But I think there's only one or two places where we did something like that. You hear all those live albums, and you know the band doesn't sound like that" (Creem, 12/1978). The source material, in cases like the 1973 two-tracks, also made fixing things a near impossibility.

Even while recording the live version of "Come Together" at the Wherehouse, the band's studio cut from the "Sgt. Pepper's" movie was released as a single. It became Aerosmith's final Top-20 single for nearly a decade but was noted as one of the two musical positives to come out of that disastrous movie (the other being Earth, Wind and Fire's take on "Got to Get You into My Life" which hit #9, making Columbia's demands for the singles rights for the two songs a victory when millions of copies of the RSO soundtrack were returned). Critics seemed to agree: "One of the strongest cuts on the 'Sgt. Pepper' soundtrack, Aerosmith sticks pretty much to the Beatle original. Steven Tyler's lead vocal is backed by the band's high-powered instrumentation" (Billboard, 8/12/1978). Joe recalled recording the song: "We realized our involvement with this could look cheesy, but we looked at it as another adventure. The real hook was being able to work with George Martin on our cover of 'Come Together.' We flew to New York to work at the Record Plant. Our idea was not to stray too far from the original... We'd figure he'd have a lot to say — either adding or subtracting from our interpretation. But he had no suggestions whatsoever. So, we kept playing until we formulated a good basic track" ("Rocks: My Life In and Out of Aerosmith"). Ray suggested in the "Walk This Way" book that it only took the band a couple of takes to get something George liked. The song became a centerpiece of the band's set during the Bootleg tour, the live version having also been included on "Live! Bootleg."

Columbia purportedly wasn't happy with the resulting product the band had produced for their live project and were concerned about the product's quality. Jack Douglas recalled, "Columbia didn't get it, but they were afraid to tell us they wanted a remix. They went quietly crazy but kept it in the building because they were afraid of Aerosmith and David Krebs, who was capable of giving them massive amounts of grief. Anyway, Columbia thought that Aerosmith had run its course after 'Draw the Line' bombed... they didn't believe in it" ("Walk this Way"). One way Columbia may have expressed its displeasure at the band was by torpedoing plans for an additional special EP of material. According to Jack, "After the first 700,000 albums are sold, we're going to include an EP (a 7-inch, extended play record) with the next 300,000 albums. On one side of the EP will be a 9-minute version of an old Fleetwood Mac song that we recorded in Indianapolis in 1973. We would have included it on the regular album, but it was too long, and we would have had to take at least two songs out of the album to make room for it" (Dallas Morning News, 11/4/1978). That 9-minute song likely would have been the take of "Rattlesnake Shake" recorded at Counterpart Studios on Sept. 26, 1973 (it and "Walkin' the Dog" were both issued on "Pandora's Box" in 1991). The B-side would have contained an additional three songs. There were also supposed to be three variants of John Kosh's cover art design, based on the band's distinctive period logos and alternate layouts (all based on the same basic elements). Columbia, however, did permit the inclusion of a poster.

As the band's activities wound down on the road, during the summer, Steven's certainly didn't. In late August he was became the latest Aerosmith member to wreck his car. According to press reports, "Tyler was driving down the road in New Hampshire when a deer suddenly loomed up in front of him on the highway. He swerved to avoid hitting somebody who might be Bambi's cousin and managed to total his Porsche 911 when he smashed it into a tree. Fortunately, both Steven and the deer went, uninjured, which is more than can be said for his car" (Cashbox, 8/26/1978). As a result, news rumor went to press that Aerosmith were keen sponsor a Porsche racing car... Steven was healthy enough to marry Cyrinda Foxe (born Kathleen Hetzekian, the former Mrs. David Johansen) on Sept. 1 in New Hampshire. There wouldn't have been much time for a honeymoon with rehearsals for the tour scheduled. The "Live! Bootleg" tour kicked off in Buffalo, NY on Sept. 27. Highlight in the band's set was the rendition of the recent hit single, "Come Together," but the band's next single, "Chip Away the Stone" was also featured. While there some strong attendances in some markets, fatigue was starting to show elsewhere with far lower than expected audiences. One such show resulted in the perfect confluence of circumstances to generate press. When numerous fans were arrested during a show in Fort Wayne, IN, the band dispatched their lawyer to pay bail for those still held, also criticizing purported heavy-handed tactics employed by the local police during the show. The resulting press followed the band for several months. During the shows the band were kept on their toes by the upstart Australian band AC/DC...

The tour wasn't without incidents directly affecting the band. One show, in Syracuse on Nov. 21, was rescheduled — after the opening act had already performed — Aerosmith were stranded in Boston with airplane issues. A few days later, a show at the Philadelphia Spectrum was abandoned when Steven was hit by glass from a beer bottle thrown from the crowd, before even getting to sing a word of "Sight for Sore Eyes," which the band had just started performing. Brad recalled, "Five songs into a sold-out show, someone threw a beer bottle from the balcony. It hit the stage dead center, right in front of the monitor, and exploded — sending shards of glass into Steven's face. I think some glass went right through his mouth. That's it. Backstage, Steven's holding a towel to his bloody face, and he wants to go back on! The vote was four-to-one against, and we were in the limos two minutes later. Fuck this" ("Walk This Way"). By the end of November, the tour's final four December dates were postponed or cancelled, due to Cyrinda's advanced pregnancy — daughter Mia was born on Dec. 22. The tour wrapped in Tulsa on December 10 with the band members then dispersing for an extended downtime.

The album's hype sticker promoted the inclusion of the full-color poster and the live version of "Come Together." The packaging also included specific printed inner dust sleeves for each of the albums opening a gatefold of 48 photos of the band. Details for the tracks on each LP are spartan at best. What is clear that the contents attributed to shows that circulate do not match the packaging's attributions, not that one would expect the liner notes on a bootleg to be accurate (in keeping with the theme). While it seems that tracks such as "Back in the Saddle," "Sick as a Dog," "Mama Kin" and "S.O.S. (Too Bad)" were definitively sourced from Indianapolis (Jul. 4, 1977), and "Dream On" from Louisville (Jul. 3, 1977), it's impossible to confirm without the actual recordings from those shows. In keeping with the "bootleg" ethos the facts are as irrelevant as the lack of note of the inclusion of "Draw the Line" following "Mother Popcorn." Irrefutable (probably) are songs such as "Come Together," with its enigmatic attribution as being from a "gig so secret, nobody showed up but us," and "Last Child" from the Paradise. Both "I Ain't Got You" and the edited version of "Mother Popcorn" were sourced beyond doubt from the band's March 1973 shows at Paul's Mall in Boston (originally simulcast via WBCN). The album's liner notes have an incorrect date for the show, though the band did perform at the venue again on that date, but the date of broadcast was Mar. 20, 1973.

Even the seemingly obvious "Last Child, (Boston, 8/9/1978), the "only known recording of Dr. J. Jones and the Interns," was called into question at the time of the album's release due to the purported quality of that performance. However, Jack Douglas has commented that "Live! Bootleg" was "all recorded at a club in Boston that's much smaller than this one [The Palladium in Dallas]" (Dallas Morning News, 11/4/1978). That would seem to point in the direction of the second Boston Music Hall show on Mar. 29 (as suggested by the studio sheets in the CD remaster packaging) or last gasp Paradise Club show on Aug. 9; rather than the circulating Mar. 28 show. Other songs seem to be clearly wrong: "Sight for Sore Eyes" is attributed to Columbus, "2/24/78." It's not, and the Columbus date was March 24. Bootleg indeed, at least the song titles were correct! "Sweet Emotion" and "Lord of The Thighs" are purportedly from the March Chicago show but bear little resemblance to the circulating soundboard recordings from that show, even considering various performances being overdubbed in the studio. "Toys in The Attic," attributed to Boston (3/28/1978), is clearly not — that referenced recording being an absolute train wreck lyrically in the first verse. The hypersonic speed at which the song is performed also stands out as does the "fuck off" call-out on the "Bootleg" version at 2:33. Again, the studio sheets indicate the second Music Hall show. "Walk This Way," "Train Kept A Rollin'," with its "Strangers In The Night" section are attributed to Detroit (4/2/1978) from which there is currently no SBD to directly compare. Finally, "Chip Away the Stone," supposedly from Santa Monica (4/8/1978), is clearly from the California Jam II recording from March 18, 1978. The identical guitar figure is played at the end of the song and the remnant of Steven's "alright!" comment remains. Ultimately though, none of the specifics actually matter a damn, for like any "live" recording, the album was a representation — according to the band's interesting perspective — of them in concert in 1978; with some additional subtle messaging...

Released on Oct. 27, 1978, "Live! Bootleg" was certified Gold by the RIAA on Oct. 31 and Platinum on Dec. 26, 1978. In the SoundScan era the album sold 403,265 units between 1991 and Feb. 2007. In Canada, the album was certified Gold by the CRIA on Dec. 1, 1978. The album reached #13 on the Billboard Top-200 charts on Jan. 13, 1979 during a 22-week run. During 17-weeks on Cashbox the album reached #10. The album didn't chart in international markets other than Canada, where it reached #27. The studio version of "Come Together," which had been released as single in late-July, reached #23 on the Billboard Hot-100 and #20 on Cashbox. The studio version of "Chip Away the Stone" was released in December but only reached #77 following a three-week run. Oddly, no specifically "live" single was issued from the album in the U.S...

Assorted review excerpts:

"Heavy metal works best live and no act hones a finer edge than Aerosmith, which pushed to release this 15-cut, two-record set before a bootleg version surfaced; hence, the title, bolstered by intentionally unslick artwork in the rip-off tradition. All the hits are included, recorded from 1977 through 1978; most recent, a more exciting arrangement of 'Come Together' than the single. But unusual in its appeal is a 1973 medley of 'I Ain't Got You / Mother Popcorn,' taped at Pall's Mall in Boston, in which a surprising R&B side of the fivesome emerges. Steven Tyler's vocals sparkle consistently in his dog-stuck-in-barbed-wire style" (Billboard, 11/4/1978).

"Aerosmith has always been regarded as an exceptional live outfit, and this two-record set captures the hard-rock power and sexual swagger of the group. 'Bootleg' was recorded in a variety of settings, ranging from Aerosmith's usual hockey arena gigs to its intimate club performances as Dr. J. Jones and the Interns. Steve Tyler's vocals are in top form here, as are the band's raucous guitar exchanges" (Cashbox, 11/4/1978).

"Inside the faded, ring-stained cover which opens to a centerfold of 45 color snapshots, next to the official group poster, tucked away in the neatly decorated, information-filled jackets rests Aerosmith's Christmas present to the rock world. It's their first live album, a double-record set, containing 16 songs from their five-album career on Columbia Records, and it's close to delightful. Granted, there is a desultory version of 'Dream On.' Yes, Steven Tyler's raspy tenor is occasionally reduced to a croak. OK, they are most adept at milking a guitar riff until it's watery cliché. But when has the band sounded this good? Not at their Boston Garden shows. Nor at the Paradise Theater this past August. You have to give them credit, it took a lot of work to cull the best live renditions of recorded material from all those tapes. It's a job well done.

The very good cuts ('Chip Away the Stone,' 'Come Together,' 'I Ain't Got You,' 'Mother Popcorn,' 'Mama Kin') tilt the odds in the band's favor. Too bad only one of these, 'Mama Kin,' was written by them. There is enough going-for-the-jugular rhythm and blues to make 'Live Bootleg' a big success. Their musicianship is, as they say on the liner notes, 'lusty nice and ratty.' Don't pay attention to the fact that 'Sick as a Dog' and 'Sweet Emotion' are copied from the same guitar lines, or that 'Last Child' and 'Back in the Saddle' will keep you guessing which is which. So, they can't write songs anymore. How many Rolling Stones clones has that stopped" (Boston Globe, 11/16/1978)?

"A series of greatest album hits, the Aerosmith album — unlike the band's live concert waves — sounds as if it were carefully assembled in a Harvard biology laboratory, rather than pushed through masses of amplifiers. Recorded during their recent U.S. tour, the disc's vocals are surprisingly accurate and, although there are many who would prefer to believe the opposite, the Ravaged Five (as opposed to the Fab Four) sound controversially good. 'Last Child,' from the recent Paradise show of 'Dr. J. Jones and The Interns,' was miraculously recorded as a flawless tune, much to the surprise of those in attendance that steamy August night. 'Come Together,' 'Toys in the Attic,' and 'I Ain't Got You/Mother Popcorn,' the only other tunes recorded in the Boston area, come off true to life with enough spirit for these to serve as the only recorded versions of the songs. Steve Tyler's gravelly vocals, surprisingly on key here, complement the full-blown barrage of distorted electric guitars and rhythm backings of the assorted decadents in attendance (on stage and off)" (Lowell Sun, 12/8/1978).

"Let Steve Tyler and the boys strut their stuff on your own patch, thrill to the thrum of another well-tuned hard rock machine, kiss off the final vestiges of brain detritus, stand back in awe as that East Coast derring-do nods you off into Quaalude submission. Heavy metal? Bugger my old boots, there's none heavier... The guys include all their familiar faves in the most applicable running gun order, intermeshing a couple of radiocasts from 1973 for historic credibility. Insensitive pariah that I am I cannot distinguish the overall bombast of, say, 'Back in the Saddle' from 'Walk this Way'... At this stage in the game there's little or nothing to be said that could possibly curb Aerosmith's departure for mega-universal moolah, and good luck to them for proving that there's none so dumb as Amerika's stadia regulars. Once upon a time they almost possessed some semblance of a saving grace. The resurrected five-year-old versions of 'I Ain't Got You' and 'Mother Popcorn' are cleaner sounding, nearly spontaneous average bar band blues. The sax player from their debut album, David Woodford, gets up to blow at length and Tyler waffles through a sub-J. Geils throat scat with extended aplomb. Aerosmith unleash their version of 'Come Together', the old Bee Gees chestnut which seems to these ears as vapidly unpleasant a number as it did on Stigwood's 'Abbey Road'. At least Ted Nugent is moderately amusing, but this lot take it seriously. Best of the rest: 'Dream On', the one that set the ball rolling, has effective back up piano, still the Perry-Whitford axis is desperately short of the mark. Lucky for some" (New Musical Express, 12/9/1978).

"Aerosmith's first live album looks like an under-the-counter job. The two-record set is packaged like an actual bootleg, including a crudely printed, 'stained' cover and misspellings on the dust sleeves. The credits even omit one song on Side 4 ('Draw the Line'). Beyond this clever gimmick is 65 minutes of fierce, fiery hard rock that should more than satisfy the Boston-based quintet's many followers. 'Bootleg' may even make a few more converts among those who continue to place Aerosmith on the same level as such mindless outfits as KISS. The group's powerful, often witty guitar-and-screaming-vocals blasts put most of the competition to shame. 'Bootleg' contains a representative sampling: Most of the singles — 'Dream On,' 'Walk This Way,' etc. — are rendered with a fresh vigor, and the other selections from the band's five studio albums are generally well chosen. Of more importance to the value of the LP, however, is the careful, wise choice of live versions from a wide variety of venues. These capture the manic majesty that the group is sporadically able to deliver on stage, while avoiding, with a couple of exceptions, its equally frequent sloppy renditions. The two unsatisfactory cuts are 'Back in the Saddle' and 'Sweet Emotion,' the LP's opening tracks. The band's timing and the recording balance both are off. But from there on vocalist/chief composer Steve Tyler and cohorts are in top form. 'Lord of the Thighs,' 'S.O.S.,' 'Sick as a Dog' and 'Chip Away the Stone' are especially striking examples of Aerosmith's snarling, high-strutting style" (Los Angeles Times, 12/17/1978).

"If Aerosmith has any claim to remembrance in rock history, it is through its romantic hit single, 'Dream On.' The concert version is the best-performed song on this two-record live album. The LP showcases the band in a variety of settings. Some of them, such as two cuts on side four recorded in Boston's Pall's Mall, are quite flattering. Those cuts include the blues 'I Ain't You' and James Brown's 'Mother Popcorn.' Lead singer Steven Tyler sounds good as an ersatz Brown. The high quality of performance on these two songs shows up the woeful lack of rhythmic tightness on most of the rest of the album. The song 'Last Child' also finds the group in very good form, running through a disco-funk type number. Both the Pall's Mall cuts and this one were recorded in the group's home town: Boston. It seems as though the band wanted to impress the folks at home.

Another stand out is 'Chip Away at the Stone,' the chorus of which sounds like the Rolling Stones via Ry Cooder. The rest of the song has tinges of the Band's sound. For most of the album, Tyler sounds like a bad imitation of Alice Cooper in his funkier moments. Some of the guitar-playing is genuinely exciting while the rest is purely self-indulgent. The majority of cuts are violent riffs strung beneath lyrics which glamorize mindlessness. This is particularly true on songs such as 'Back in the Saddle' and 'Lord of the Thighs.' 'Sweet Emotion' has a tantalizing melody and arrangement, but, like many of the songs, it fails to deliver because the vocals are weakly recorded" (Courier News, 2/10/1979).

(German single — Wo ist Joe?)

September 27, 1978
Memorial Auditorium
Buffalo, NY
Promoter: Harvey & Corky Presentations
Other act(s): AC/DC
Reported audience: ~11,000 / 13,500 (81.48%)
Reported gross: $80,000

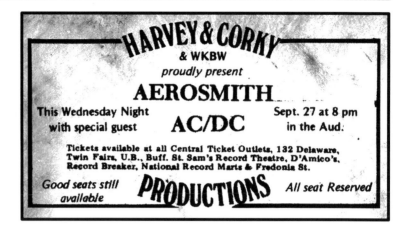

September 29
Cobo Arena
Detroit, MI
Promoter: Brass Ring Productions
Other act(s): AC/DC
Reported audience: 11,704 **SOLD-OUT
Reported gross: $101,809
Notes:
- From a local review: "There is an intriguing mystique about Aerosmith. Many still consider them one of the premier heavy metal ensembles around, but their last album, 'Draw the Line,' didn't fare as well as expected, and their popularity seems potentially on the wane. At the band's concert at Cobo Arena in Detroit Friday night, a real question hung in the air: can they still crank it out with the best of them? As far I'm concerned, the answer is an unqualified 'yes.' Following AC/DC, which attempted to fire the crowd up with some loud and monotonous punk rock, Aerosmith walked on stage and the packed house went berserk. The stage set-up was similar to Boston's from a previous concert, except that mirrors were mounted directly above the stage, I suppose to create a special effect when beamed on by the spotlights. It didn't work. But while Aerosmith doesn't claim to have an illustrious stage show, they performed brilliantly without the benefit of gimmickry. Their pure physical presence is intimidating enough. As usual, a spotlight remained on the flamboyant Steve Tyler, as he flew around the stage clad in a black and white striped tightsuit. The rest of the band remained rather placid, with the exception of lead guitarist Joe Perry, who occasionally sauntered downstage to deliver an ear-piercing solo.

The band's forte was their exceptional jamming, and they did a lot of it. 'Back in the Saddle,' 'Train Kept a Rollin',' 'No More, No More,' and 'Lick and a Promise' were all first-class renditions, although 'Sweet Emotion' suffered, the only bright spot being when Perry's talk-box took over. Two of the highlights, 'Seasons of Wither' and 'Chip Away the Stone,' were ironically the only tame moments in an otherwise frenzied performance. During 'Same Old Song and Dance' and 'Draw the Line,' most of the main floor ushers were useless in containing the onslaught of fans trying to get near their heartthrobs. Aerosmith is about to release their first live album — entitled 'Live Bootleg' — after five solid studio efforts. The future direction of their popularity will surely be indicated by the album's sales. But if Friday evening at Cobo Hall was any clue, then their live LP may just put them right up to the top. Clearly, they haven't lost it all" (Michigan Daily, 10/1/1978).

September 30
Athletic & Convocation Center @ Notre Dame
South Bend, IN
Promoter: Sunshine Promotions
Other act(s): AC/DC
Reported audience: 6,994 / 11,800 (59.27%)
Reported gross: $56,020
Notes:
- From a local review: "On Saturday night, an unsuspecting crowd of 7,000 people witnessed the transformation of the Notre Dame ACC from a concert hall into the rock 'n' roll pits. The siege, which was cleverly disguised as an Aerosmith concert, began with the first chord played by the warm-up group,

AC/DC... As the curtain rose, the PA system simultaneously erupted with a force that could have straightened the hair of any Afro in the crowd. And once again, the talents of the group became lost in an onslaught of distortion... In the case of Aerosmith, their volume level was twice what was needed for the ACC. Most of the audience stood motionless through the entire performance. This, unlike the usual party-like atmosphere at a show of this nature, served as an indication that the crowd was either awestruck by the presence of Aerosmith, or that they were just stunned... It would seem unlikely for one to sit through an entire three-hour concert without coming away with at least a few redeeming moments of enjoyment. Unfortunately, though, it happened with the Aerosmith show. Along with the sound problem, the act itself was lacking in professionalism. At times, the Aerosmith material sounded completely unrehearsed. On two occasions the group literally stopped and restarted their songs in order to catch up with each other... Sometimes it seems that a group that has made it to the top becomes so caught up in their stardom, they forget what merits it took to become a star. Obviously, Aerosmith needs their memories jarred" (South Bend Tribune, 10/4/1978).

October 2
Sports Arena
Toledo, OH

Promoter: Belkin Productions
Other act(s): AC/DC
Reported audience: (8,000 capacity)

October 3
Memorial Coliseum
Fort Wayne, IN

Promoter: Sunshine Promotions
Other act(s): Exile
Reported audience: 4,788 / 9,500 (50.4%)
Notes:
- AC/DC were the opening act noted on tickets.
- The band posted $500 bail for 13 fans who'd been arrested during their concert, after Steven had promised to do so during the concert when he stopped a song to protest the "gestapo" tactics arrests by local police. In total, some 62 patrons were arrested during the show for various offences. The following day they paid an additional $3,500 to cover the fines incurred by some 25 of those charged with misdemeanors.
- Steven later recalled, "We paid in Ft. Wayne because the cops were too rowdy. They were coming down like such gestapo scumbags. Most of the places we play the police are cool, but Ft. Wayne already had a reputation for being super-restrictive. A lot of bands had cancelled out shows before we even played, and a one-third house was not considered bad. The kids knew what they were in for when they bought the tickets. The police wouldn't even let our road manager light up a cigarette, and he's 48... We went there to try and change things, but I don't think we did, so we have to be careful. Besides, the towns really pissed about the bad publicity, and next time we might be set up for something bad" (Circus, April 1979).

October 5
Riverfront Coliseum
Cincinnati, OH

Promoter: Riverfront Concerts
Other act(s): Starcastle
Reported audience: 15,700 / 16,000 (98.13%)
Notes:
- AC/DC were noted as the opening act on advance advertisements for the show. Starcastle was a progressive rock band signed to CBS. The band's singer, Terry Luttrel, had been replaced by Kevin Cronin in REO Speedwagon. He left the band after the dates with Aerosmith.
- From a local review: "It is a wanton Thursday night at Riverfront Coliseum — a kingdom of adolescent delight where the hard-driving sounds of Aerosmith's rock overshadow the harrowing teenage fears of

acne, flunking out, and hooking a good catch for the next major concert. It is 9:30 p.m. The swarms of screaming teens begin flicking their Bics, stomping their feet on the Coliseum floor — now inundated with erect bodies — and demanding the group that promises to produce ear-splitting sounds and lyrics that stroke their pubescent fantasies... The band pumps out the fierce, firing number as lead singer Steve Tyler bolts across the stage in a shiny pair of tight white pants, a shirt the same color and a black-and-white-striped sweater. He swings around a long thin mike draped with five-foot streamers the colors of his attire. He dances with it, caresses it, sings into it, and sends it flying into the crowd, retrieving it before the star-hungry souls physically devour the thing. The Jagger mannerisms are down pat. It's hard to believe the 27-year-old Tyler and the rest of Aerosmith nearly starved in Boston while trying to make it big back in 1970...

The music of Aerosmith continues nonstop for 90 minutes, producing the compulsive, rhythmic drive. And the sound system is turned up to an almost deafening decibel. The crowd screams, punching fists in the air doing everything to express the wild new adrenaline flow implied in the music. The flashing lights. The smoke. The assembly of close to 16,000 people. The crowd is pleased... Heavy-metal guitarist, Brad Whitford — a former student at the prestigious Berkeley School of Music — spins around stage belting out those rough, scintillating tunes on his shrieking, often droning, guitar. The time flies for the red-hot rockers. Soon, the clock strikes 11. The group finishes its encore with 'Train Keep a Rollin'' (from the 'Get your Wings' album). The lights go up. The audience is displeased. It has not heard 'Dream On,' the success that stayed at the top of the charts for what seemed to be forever. It has not heard 'Walkin' the Dog,' a Cincinnati favorite. A few fans mutter on the way out. Some turn and ask each other, "Why didn't they play the tunes?' Anticlimax out the door as Aerosmith leaves its Cincinnati fans a wee-bit disappointed" (Cincinnati Enquirer, 10/7/1978).
- On his day off, the following day, Steven attended the Boyzz / 1994 benefit show for the Little City Foundation at the Riviera Theater in Chicago, where the band were basing themselves out of for the Mid-West leg of the tour. Admission was a donation of two cans of food. A photo of Steven backstage with singer Dirty Dan Buck appeared in various trade publications.

October 7
Market Square Arena
Indianapolis, IN
Promoter: Sunshine Promotions
Other act(s): Exile
Reported audience: 19,000 **SOLD-OUT
Reported gross: $135,570
- Aerosmith's five trucks and two busses blocked Median Street forcing police to have them move. Local music critic Zach Dunkin was disappointed that Billy Joel, who performed at the arena on Oct. 9, only drew 8,000 while

"a noise-belching group like Aerosmith can fill the arena with 19,000 like it did for the third straight time last Saturday night" (Indianapolis News, 10/10/1978).

October 8
Wings Stadium
Kalamazoo, MI
Promoter: Aiken Management
Other act(s): Exile
Reported audience: (8,038 capacity)

October 11
Convention Center Arena
Pine Bluff, AR
Promoter: Chris Fritz & Co. / Contemporary Productions
Other act(s): Exile
Reported audience: 8,055 / 9,000 (89.5%)
Reported gross: $58,328

October 12
Myriad Arena
Oklahoma City, OK
Promoter: Chris Fritz & Co. / Contemporary Productions
Other act(s): Exile
Reported audience: 10,210 / 14,885 (68.59%)
Reported gross: $73,629
Notes:
- From a local review: "An estimated 10,000 rock fans turned out Thursday night at the Myriad for rock and roll — and they got it, courtesy of Aerosmith and Exile. Exile, with a No. 1 hit, 'Kiss You All Over,' on the record charts, led off with clean rockin' music... As the black curtain rose to reveal lead singer Steven Tyler, dressed in white, prancing to the front of the stage with his streamer-draped microphone, the crowd erupted into non-stop screaming which almost drowned out the music — almost. It was hard to differentiate between Aerosmith's first song, 'Toys in The Attic,' and the last, or the ones in-between because of the screaming minions and the eight-foot wall of speakers, apparently at full blast. 'Come Together,' the Beatles hit Aerosmith performed in the movie, 'Sgt, Pepper's Lonely Hearts Club Band,' stood out during the concert as it did in the flick, primarily as a tribute to Lennon-McCartney.

It seemed half the crowd, mostly teen-agers who didn't know Paul McCartney was in another band before Wings, made their way to the stage as soon as the first chords were struck. Bodies were four-deep between the front-row seats, quickly abandoned by their rightful owners, and the wire mesh surrounding stage... The eight-year-old Boston band put on a show no doubt, as Tyler leaned seductively close to those around the stage and later lewdly placed the microphone stand between the legs of guitarist Joe Perry during a rock solo. The raucous crowd loved it, dancing and clapping as drummer Joey Kramer tossed his sticks into the audience, causing more than a few scuffles on the arena floor" (Daily Oklahoman, 10/14/1978).

October 14
Civic Center
St. Paul, MN
Promoter: Casablanca Concerts / Jam Productions
Other act(s): Exile
Reported audience: 17,646 **SOLD-OUT
Reported gross: $132,950
Notes:

- From a local review: "Who says heavy metal is dead? If Aerosmith, the quintessence of screaming, thumping hard rock, can still sell out the St. Paul Civic Center Arena — 17,500 tickets sold by noon Saturday — heavy metal is, if not here to stay, at least very healthy at the moment... One can't help noting every time Aerosmith comes through town how the opening act does, whether at some point the positions will reverse and it will be Aerosmith that is outshone by the newcomer. Not so, this time anyway — Exile, the opener at the civic center Saturday night, kept the crowd entertained, but apparently stole no fire from Aerosmith. Except for sound quality, this was an impressive 85-minute set from Aerosmith and its live-wire lead singer, Stephen Tyler. Expectedly, the emphasis is on flashy theatrics and a kind of manic energy...

The material is simple: simple riffs and ostinato patterns in the bass, though there's an occasional nod to an old rhythm-and-blues tune, like Bullmoose Jackson's risqué number from the early '50s, 'Big Ten Inch Record.' Tyler provides most of the visual excitement, bounding about the stage in frenzied fashion, though much of his time Saturday night was spent throwing things offstage that had been thrown onstage — hats, T-shirts, paper cups, etc. — from the fans crowding the barricade at the front of the stage. The show built to a fine finale, but the sound was a mess from the beginning. Close to the stage, it was all garbled. Further back, it was better, but Tyler's vocals were being mixed, not higher, but evenly with the instruments, so there was no aural sense of background-foreground. Apparently, that's what they wanted" (Minneapolis Star Tribune, 10/16/1978).

October 15
Dane County Coliseum
Madison, WI
Promoter: Landmark Productions
Other act(s): Exile
Reported audience: 10,000 **SOLD-OUT
Reported gross: $75,000

October 18
Civic Center
Huntington, WV
Promoter: Entam, Ltd.
Other act(s): Exile
Reported audience: 7,382 / 7,500 (98.43%)
Reported gross: $58,645

October 19
Civic Center
Roanoke, VA
Promoter: Entam, Ltd.
Other act(s): Exile
Reported audience: 9,793 / 11,000 (89.03%)
Reported gross: $76,797

October 21 **POSTPONED
Freedom Hall
Louisville, KY
Promoter: Sunshine Promotions
Other act(s): Golden Earring
Notes:
- This show was rescheduled for Dec. 19.

October 22
Coliseum
Richfield (Cleveland), OH
Promoter: Belkin Productions
Other act(s): Golden Earring
Reported audience: ~17,000 / 17,500 (97.14%)
Notes:
- From a local review: "About 17,000 people shelled out as much as $8.50 apiece for tickets to Sunday's Aerosmith extravaganza at the Coliseum. But more than a few weren't convinced the jarring rock and roll act was really going to show. Afterall, an assortment of unexpected problems — including car crash and firecracker wounds had forced the band to cancel its last three area appearances.

And a lot of frustrated Aerosmith fans were still leery. But shortly before 9 p. m., any suspicions of another no-show were obliterated. Because when the big, black stage drapes parted at the north end of the arena, cool-aqua blue and warm-red spotlights illuminated Steve Tyler and his five-man rock and roll machine. They were already in motion and racing into a frenzied delivery of 'Toys' as the crush of customers became one gigantic salvo of pandimonious approval...

Aerosmith's music — though it's the same hard-core rock and roll as the Stones' — has a heavy metal texture to it that runs through most of the band's melodies and gives a distinctive sameness. It's that sameness that has zoomed Aerosmith to top of the rock pile. Fans know exactly what to expect and apparently can't get enough of a good thing. Aerosmith's driving, high velocity sounds penetrate the mind and body like a needle-tipped battering ram... 'Ten Inch,' 'Walk this Way' and the band's duplication of the Beatles' 'Come Together' were also highlights of the 90-minute Aerosmith onslaught. One of the few problems with the show was an inability to clearly hear Tyler's vocals... When Aerosmith left the stage, nonstop cheers and a sea of flickering matches brought them back for 10 more minutes of supersonic syncopation. And then they were gone" (Akron Beacon Journal, 10/23/1978).

November 2
Civic Arena
Pittsburgh, PA
Promoter: Danny Kresky Enterprises
Other act(s): Golden Earring
Reported audience: (15,000 capacity)
Notes:
- The Doobie Brothers were the announced opening act in some papers when the show was announced in late-September.

November 3
U.D. Arena

Dayton, OH
Promoter: Jam Productions
Other act(s): Golden Earring
Reported audience: 10,159 / 12,962 (78.38%)
Reported gross: $70,784

November 5
Roberts Stadium
Evansville, IN
Promoter: Sunshine Promotions
Other act(s): Golden Earring
Reported audience: 7,897 / 12,000 (65.81%)
Notes:

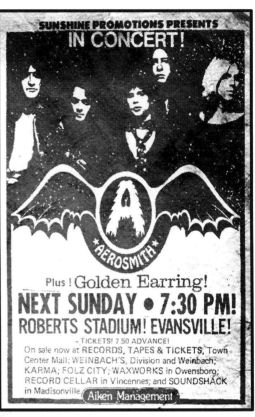

- From a local review: "Aerosmith came into Evansville last night with a stage reminiscent of 'Close Encounters of the Third Kind' and gave 7,897 listeners an encounter with rock of the hardest kind. The rock came in the form of a 90-minute set that was non-stop except for an encore... The band played songs ranging from 'Sweet Emotion' and 'Big Ten Inch' off their album 'Toys in the Attic' to John Lennon's 'Come Together,' which they performed in the recently released movie "Sgt. Pepper's Lonely Hearts Club Band.' The band opened with 'Toys in the Attic' from the album of the same name, while black curtains hanging from the top of the five-sided stage rose. Lead singer Steve Tyler belted out the song at a frantic pace that continued throughout the evening. Guitarist Joe Perry, who had two patches of blond hair on his otherwise dark brown head, roamed around the front of the stage while the other musicians — Tom Hamilton on bass, Brad Whitford on guitar, and Joey Kramer on drums stayed relatively stationary. It was Tyler who attracted the most attention. He used his microphone stand more as a prop than to sing with. He knelt at the foot of the stage and jabbed it at the first few rows while making them sing the chorus to 'Walk this Way.' At other times he twirled the stand around his head, put it between his legs, shoved it under Kramer's drums and used the white and purple ribbons attached to it to drag it around the stage... The crowd reacted to most of the songs with foot stomps and hand claps. At the end, they applauded, whistled, held up matches, and flicked lighters for about three minutes to get an encore" (Evansville Press, 11/6/1978).

November 6
Civic Coliseum
Knoxville, TN
Promoter: Entam, Ltd.
Other act(s): Golden Earring
Reported audience: (7,200 capacity)

November 8
Richmond Coliseum
Richmond, VA
Promoter: Cellar Door Concerts
Other act(s): Golden Earring
Reported audience: ~6,000 / 10,000 (60%)
Notes:
- From a local review: "Aerosmith on stage has nothing to do with Aerosmith on record, even though the bulk of the show comes from their most recent album release, 'Live Bootleg,' a collection of on-location tracks recorded at various concert stops over the past five years. It still isn't the same. There is just too much energy onstage to ever be compressed between the grooves of an album. Aerosmith obviously knows that, and so does the audience. From the time Tyler pranced on stage and began tossing his microphone

about to the finale of the encore when the prancing finally did him in and he fell flat on his back (without injury), the key word for the performance was energy. Working their way through the whole range of their recent recording repertoire, they relied heavily on the strong guitar work that has always been their strong point, and on power drumming. You could seldom hear Tyler's vocals, but nobody seemed to mind. The rest was shaking the walls with its energy, and that was the key. The overall feeling was aided by the creative use of an overhead bank of multicolored lights used in many different ways in addition to the usual half-dozen spots, and a curtain that the entire stage area made for a dramatic entrance. It would be hard to pick out a highlight in the program, but their new version of 'Come Together' drew one of the most enthusiastic crowd reactions, even though it was only one of many obvious favorites in the Aerosmith line" (Richmond Times Dispatch, 11/9/1978).

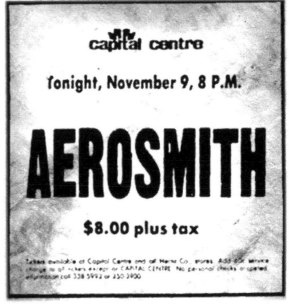

November 9
Capital Center
Landover (Largo), MD

Promoter: Cellar Door Concerts
Other act(s): Golden Earring
Reported audience: (17,561 capacity)
Notes:
- From a local review: "Three years ago; they were hyped as the 'best' band in America. With the newness gone, Aerosmith came into Capital Centre Thursday night to try to prove they were worthy of the acclaim. The typical hard rock organization did little more than show they were indeed a rehash of their many predecessors' styles... The chords were very loud Thursday night, accented by thunderous drums and bass. This pounding shook the superstructure of the Capital Centre. The crowd reacted enthusiastically to the high volume of the music and the individual performance of the strutting and screaming Tyler, rather than individual musicianship. And somehow the repetitive line droning on for the hour-and-a-half show was accepted by the young and gullible crowd as unique. Tyler's normal singing voice, which could be described as a rhyming shout, managed to project over the loud group. As per the manner of his style, the lyrics remained unintelligible through his snarl. But he seemed to have trouble letting loose with the occasional primal scream — it didn't carry over the band. This is what happens to a human voice when it's strained like that every night of a road trip. He did manage to display some affinity for the blues in a harmonica introduction he played to 'Big Ten Inch,' but the pounding boogie beat still remained a far cry from the real thing" (Evening Star, 11/11/1978).

November 12
Nassau Veterans Coliseum
Uniondale, NY

Promoter: Mark Puma / Freefall Presentations, Ltd.
Other act(s): Golden Earring
Reported audience: (17,000 capacity)
Set list: Toys in the Attic / S.O.S. (Too Bad) / Mama Kin / I Wanna Know Why / Big Ten Inch Record / Sight for Sore Eyes / Lick and a Promise / Come Together / Back in the Saddle / Sweet Emotion /

Lord of the Thighs / Seasons of Wither / Get the Lead Out / Chip Away the Stone / Walk this Way / Draw the Line / Same Old Song and Dance / Rats in the Cellar / Milk Cow Blues / Train Kept A Rollin'
Notes:
- From a local review: "The crowd was at its feet, cheering, clapping, calling for more, as Aerosmith blasted through 90 minutes of hard rock Sunday at Nassau Coliseum. Their fans weren't reveling in the show's musical content — there were very few new inroads presented — rather they were standing, gaping at a performance overwhelming with energy. Aerosmith has been called the 'hardest rock band' America has ever produced. These musicians are loud, arrogant, [and] hostile, as if they embodied a caged animal roaring its frustration at a world it doesn't comprehend. Their fans, mostly teenagers, are attracted by the boldness of their disdain. Aerosmith's statement isn't articulated in their songs, but rather through fervent energy which amplifies their pent-up hostilities. Traditionally, this type of brash defiance stirs up the young. So be it, there are a lot worse groups than Aerosmith. Musically, they are limited, but proficient in what they play. All their songs are anchored by a heavy bass, a pumping beat, spiraling guitar solos, and the manic vocals of Steve Tyler. Only the pace seems to change around the same guitar chord progressions. The current darlings of hard rock bask in songs such as 'Sick as a Dog,' 'Sight for Sore Eyes,' 'Lord of the Thighs,' and 'S.O.S.' — tunes which are super-saturated with energy but whose lyrics are indecipherable. Oddly enough, the song performed at Nassau Coliseum which showed Aerosmith to be a formidable band was the Beatles' 'Come Together.' In essence, Aerosmith showed they had enough artistry to perform mainstream rock but chose to reach for effect and hyperbole instead" (New York Daily News, 11/19/1978).
- An AUD recording circulates from this show, the first complete recording currently known from the tour; though sadly not with particularly good sound quality.

November 15
Civic Center
Springfield, MA
Promoter: Cross Country Concerts
Other act(s): Golden Earring
Reported audience: 8,822 **SOLD-OUT
Reported gross: $72,647
Set list: Toys in the Attic / S.O.S. (Too Bad) / Mama Kin / I Wanna Know Why / Big Ten Inch Record / Sight for Sore Eyes / Lick and a Promise / Come Together / Back in the Saddle / Sweet Emotion / Lord of the Thighs / Seasons of Wither / Get the Lead Out / Chip Away the Stone / Walk this Way / Draw the Line / Same Old Song and Dance / Rats in the Cellar / Bright Light Fright / Train Kept A Rollin'
Notes:
- A decent AUD recording circulates from this show. Amusingly, during his intro to "Sweet Emotion," Steven playfully suggests various songs for the audience to request, including "Major Barbara."

November 16
Civic Center
Providence, RI
Promoter: Mark Puma / Freefall Presentations, Ltd.
Other act(s): Golden Earring
Reported audience: (14,000 capacity)
Set list: Same as Nov. 15.

November 18
Veterans Memorial Coliseum
New Haven, CT
Promoter: Cross Country Concerts
Other act(s): Flint
Reported audience: 9,973 **SOLD-OUT
Reported gross: $80,750

November 19
Cumberland County Civic Center
Portland, ME
Promoter: Mark Puma Presents
Other act(s): Golden Earring
Reported audience: (9,000 capacity)
Notes:
- Both Steven and Joe appreciated the convenience of commuting to shows via Lear Jet. As Joe told music journalist Lisa Robinson for her "Rock Talk" syndicated feature: "We fly in and out of each city in a private Lear Jet, and aren't staying in any hotels. The other night we had a concert in Portland, ME. We left Boston at 6:30 in the evening, had a 15-minute plane ride, and after the gig we came back home. It's more like going to rehearsal every night" (Durham Sun, 12/2/1978).

November 21 **Aerosmith CANCELLED
Onondaga County War Memorial
Syracuse, NY
Promoter: Cedric Kushner
Other act(s): Golden Earring
Reported audience: ~8,000 / 8,400 (95.24%)
Notes:
- After Golden Earring performed their set (stretching it as long as they could to give the headliner time to arrive) there was an hour delay before the promoter took to the stage to announce that Aerosmith would not be appearing. Apparently, the band's plane had experienced an engine fire and had had to make an emergency landing in Boston. After a further delay he returned to the stage explaining that the band was unable to repair their plane or find alternative transport to the venue but would cancel their Rochester show and perform a make-up date in Syracuse instead.

November 22 **TEMP HOLD-DATE
Civic Center
Providence, RI
Notes:
- This date had been announced in early October, but within weeks was moved to Nov. 16.

November 24
Madison Square Garden
New York City, NY
Promoter: Ron Delsener
Other act(s): Golden Earring
Reported audience: (20,000 capacity)
Set list: Toys in the Attic / S.O.S. (Too Bad) / Mama Kin / I Wanna Know Why / Big Ten Inch Record / Sight for Sore Eyes / Lick and a Promise / Come Together / Back in the Saddle / Sweet Emotion / Lord of the Thighs / Seasons of Wither / Get the Lead Out / Chip Away the Stone / Mother Popcorn / Walk this Way / Draw the Line / Same Old Song and Dance / Rats in the Cellar / Bright Light Fright / Train Kept A Rollin'
Notes:
- The night of this show, for a taped appearance of the "Midnight Special," Steven Tyler and Ted Nugent introduced AC/DC for their performance of "Sin City." Ted, who was hosting, also played "Cat Scratch Fever" and other songs with his band. Other musical guests during the episode included Golden Earring, Cheap Trick, and Thin Lizzy. A clip of "Come Together" from the "Sgt. Pepper" movie was also broadcast.
- An AUD recording circulates from this show.

November 25
Spectrum

Philadelphia, PA
Promoter: Electric Factory Concerts
Other act(s): Golden Earring
Reported audience: 19,500 **SOLD-OUT
Reported gross: $158,280
Set list: Toys in the Attic / S.O.S. (Too Bad) / Mama Kin / I Wanna Know Why / Big Ten Inch Record / Sight for Sore Eyes...
Notes:
- From a local review: "An empty bottle shattered on the stage of the Spectrum during a performance by the rock group Aerosmith last night, injuring the band's lead singer and causing the concert to be cut short. The bottle, hurled by a spectator from the upper levels, smashed at the east end of the stage, and a piece of flying glass cut the face of singer Steve Tyler, who was injured last year in a similar incident. Mitchell Bass, an assistant public relations manager at the Spectrum, said the band, which plays hard driving rock, was about 40 minutes into its set when the bottle crashed to the boards just before 10 p.m. The band 'just walked off the stage,' Bass said. Tyler was treated in his dressing room by a Spectrum doctor, Bass said. Because of the injury and the 'emotional upset' the incident caused, Tyler said he was unable to continue the concert, Bass said. About 15 minutes after the band left the stage, officials announced that the concert would be ended, sending an estimated 19,500 fans home early. They left without incident, Bass said. Promoters have not yet decided whether to offer refunds, he said. Bass said that the crowd became hushed when Tyler was hurt and reacted without anger when the concert was called off. 'It was as if they understood (why the concert had to be cut short),' Bass said" (Philadelphia Inquirer, 11/26/1978).
- An AUD recording circulates from this show.

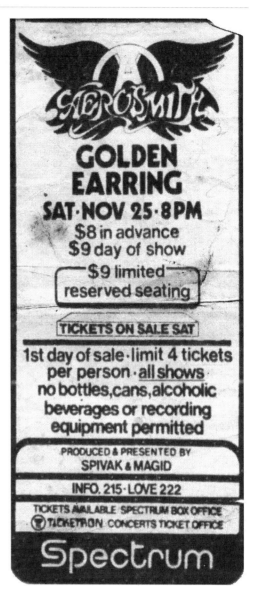

November 27
Boston Garden
Boston, MA
Promoter: Don Law
Other act(s): Golden Earring
Reported audience: 14,200 **SOLD-OUT
Reported gross: $130,219
Notes:
- From a local review: "Tyler showed no ill effects from Saturday's injury — and in fact sounded better than I have ever heard him in Boston — but there was almost another ugly incident. A youth in one of the front rows lit a firecracker and was making ready to heave it toward the stage, when a special cadre of security guards (Aerosmith carries its own security force, and it was joined by a few of Don Law's Red Shirts) pounced on him and eliminated the threat. It all seems ironic when you realize that Aerosmith probably cares more about its own fans than virtually any other rock group... The problem is that Aerosmith still attracts as rowdy a crowd as you'll see at a rock concert, and last night was no exception. There was craziness everywhere, and, after a while, there was a sense of suspended time as one felt as if he were walking through a demilitarized zone. Those of you who have heard about an Aerosmith — in which there are more leather jackets per concert square foot than at a motorcycle club — probably need no clarification. Yet Aerosmith, contrary to expectation (the band's Summerthing gig at the Music Hall and its sneak concert at the Paradise last summer were both less than memorable), performed quite decently. The sound level was not as deafening as in the past, and Tyler's vocals this time cut through and were not buried in the sledgehammer heavy metal of Joe Perry's and Brad Whitford's guitars.

Tyler led his hometown charges out for a set keyed around the band's new 'Live Bootleg' album. Amid whirling spotlights, Tyler blistered through 'Toys in the Attic,' then commented that 'we ain't gonna let anything bother us tonight.' He meant it, for he never turned back. Aided by Perry's authoritative riffs and Joey Kramer's jungle rhythms on drums, Tyler belted through 'Mama Kin,' 'S.O.S.,' 'I Don't Know Why [sic],' 'Sight for Sore Eyes' and 'Lick and a Promise' before doing the Beatles' 'Come Together,' which was the one redeeming feature to the 'Sgt. Pepper's' movie fiasco. A series from 'Bootleg' followed, including the James Brown-influenced 'Back in the Saddle,' as Tyler's tonsils proved to be in lusty working order. Now if he can just calm down some of his fans, he and the band won't have to be among the walking wounded. As raunchy as Aerosmith can sometimes get, it doesn't deserve missiles from its own crowd" (Boston Globe, 11/28/1978).

- From another local review: "Aerosmith, Boston's answer to the Rolling Stones, returned to the land of their birth Monday night and were given a hero's welcome by the fans convened for the occasion. The show starred lead singer Steve Tyler and guitarist Joe Perry, the self-described Lords of the Thighs, who camped it up in their customary style, their reward being the customary adulation. Though his scream was in robust shape, Tyler looked even frailer and more sensitive than usual, and wore well the signs of dissolution that the rock star's lot.

As for Perry, the zealousness with which his bushy hair guarded his face was so intense as to give rise to curious speculation. One theory held that the guitarist wasn't even under there at all, but in Aruba recuperating from the ravages of the tour while a sympathetic session stood in for him. Aerosmith's music was the same pale Rolling Stones-Yardbirds rip-off they've always traded upon. Even though the band with what appeared to be genuine enthusiasm, there's not much you can say about what they play, except that some songs are catchier than others" (Boston Herald, 11/29/1978).

November 28 **TEMP HOLD-DATE
Boston Garden
Boston, MA
Notes:
- Initially noted as the band's Boston date for the tour but was not booked.

November 28 **CANCELLED
War Memorial
Rochester, NY
Promoter: Cedric Kushner
Notes:
- This show was cancelled on Nov. 21, to facilitate the make-up date for the aborted Syracuse concert.

November 28
Onondaga County War Memorial
Syracuse, NY
Promoter: Cedric Kushner
Other act(s): Boyzz

Reported audience: (8,400 capacity)
Notes:
- The rescheduled show from Nov. 21. The Boyzz were an Illinois band signed with Epic.
- From a local review: "Aerosmith launched its high energy assault on the ears of many area rock fans Tuesday night at the Onondaga County War Memorial in Syracuse. Whether the band would appear or not was a question right up until show time, but as the curtain rose, and the band began blazing through the initial strains of their fast-paced title song of their third Columbia album (of six) 'Toys in the Attic,' the faint cloud of speculation that had shrouded the auditorium gave way to a more familiar cloud of smoke that usually lingers in the rafters at concerts such as this one... Aerosmith followed their opening number with some earlier favorites ('Mama Kin.' 'S.O.S.') and proceeded through an hour and a half set of a variety of material sampled more or less equally from all studio albums except the first. The band strayed from their 'Live-Bootleg!' album in order as well as in form (though predictably not in content.) This was welcomed by a crowd who, after all they'd been through, did not want to hear something that they could've stayed at home and played on their turntables... Aerosmith ended their action-packed set, leaving the audience chanting for more, and returned to do one encore (with 'Train Kept a Rollin') that kept the crowd at its frenzied peak. As they left for the second time, the lights in the auditorium went up, and the fans, finally having received their long-awaited dose of rock n' roll, after a rather unexpected delay, queried themselves on whether what they saw was worth the wait. Judging from the next time Aerosmith can be expected in the area, they'd better hope so" (Oswegonian, 11/30/1978).

December 2
Tarrant County Convention Center
Fort Worth, TX

Promoter: Pace Concerts / Friends Productions
Other act(s): Liberation
Reported audience: 13,878 **SOLD-OUT
Reported gross: $116,196
Notes:

- Originally scheduled for Dec. 16. Local press suggested that Liberation, a local power-trio, may have been a last-minute addition to the bill.
- From a local review: "If it's Monday and my ears are ringing, that can mean only one thing: Aerosmith's been here. Just like last year, the Boston rockers sold out the 14,000-seat Tarrant County Convention Center Saturday night, spearheading what amounted to three nonstop hours of floor-to-ceiling rock and roll... Aerosmith's show was little changed from their last one, probably because they haven't had time to make any changes. They still work under what must be the ultimate in mirrored ceilings — five giant moveable mirrors anchored in a pentagon of lights. And the star of the show is still irrepressible Steven Tyler, whirling, dancing, jumping, and taunting with his microphone stand, streamers, and all. The band was onstage for an hour and 45 minutes, playing 20 songs and two encores at a volume that approached Ted Nugent" (Star Telegram, 12/4/1978).

December 3
Convention Center Arena
San Antonio, TX

Promoter: Stone City Attractions
Other act(s): Dirty Angels
Reported audience: (16,000 capacity)
Notes:
- Originally scheduled for Dec. 17. The band stuck around in Texas to conduct an in-store appearance at the Lemmon Avenue Sound Warehouse in Dallas attended by 300-400 fans on Dec. 5. Peter Mensch (Leber-Krebs representative): "We haven't made any kind of personal appearance like this in over a year. But we played before 78,000 persons July 4th at the Cotton Bowl, we sold out Fort Worth last weekend and we obviously like our fans here. We try to spend a lot of time here" (Dallas Morning News, 12/6/1978).

December 6
Mississippi Coliseum
Jackson, MS
Promoter: Mid-South Concerts
Other act(s): Dirty Angels
Reported audience: 7,284 / 7,500 (97.12%)
Reported gross: $51,795
Notes:
- One of the songs in the Dirty Angels' set was the Beatles "I'm Down," later covered by Aerosmith (1987). The band also performed Jimi Hendrix's "Red House" (which became a Joe Perry Project standard and was also performed on Aerosmith's "Back in the Saddle" and other tours), and "Buzz Buzz" (recorded by the Project in 1981)

December 7
Mississippi Coast Coliseum
Biloxi, MS
Promoter: Sound Seventy Productions
Other act(s): Dirty Angels
Reported audience: 9,197 **SOLD-OUT
Reported gross: $63,927

December 9
Hirsch Memorial Coliseum
Shreveport, LA
Promoter: Beaver Productions
Other act(s): Dirty Angels
Reported audience: 10,150 **SOLD-OUT
Notes:
- From a local review: "Puke rock — not a misspelling — invaded Shreveport last night. That isn't a pleasant word to use, but it adequately describes Aerosmith's 'music' before a sold-out crowd at Hirsch Coliseum last night. Granted, rock 'n roll was never meant to be pleasant. But rock, no matter how anti-establishment or outrageous, always trod on the melodic side of the thin line between order and chaos. Aerosmith was as musical last night as the barbarians were Roman. In short, this concert was the loudest this reviewer has heard. The five members of Aerosmith took a good crowd — one that had been warmed up by a decent band, just starting out in music — and burned it to a crisp (almost literally) with unintelligible lyrics, shrieking guitars, muddied bass notes, and occasionally shouted four-letter words. The words that were understandable, unfortunately, were the four-letter ones, and their ugly impact was heightened by the presence of a large number of teens and preteens in the audience...

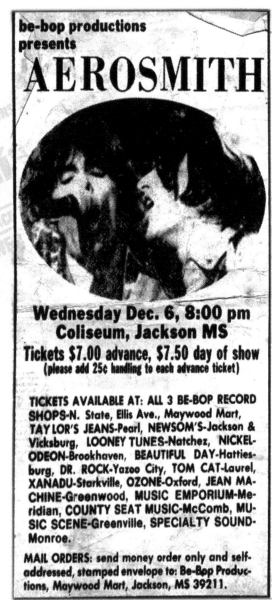

The band members seemed to glory in the sheer decibel power their mountain amplifiers and speakers provided. Drummer Joey Kramer provided most of what passed for rhythm during the band's set. Though his playing occasionally deteriorated into a hypnotizing 'tom-tom' rain dance beat, he doggedly pounded the skins even during the occasional moments when the group's roar subsided, and the band members seemed at a loss of noise. Bassist Tom Hamilton should have stayed at home. This isn't a cut at his playing. Rather, it is a comment on the effectiveness of any bass player attempting to work in Hirsch's echo chamber. Guitarist Joe Perry was interesting during the first few songs, but he soon proved the rock 'n roll adage that anyone can sound good if amplified enough to break eardrums. Lead vocalist Steve Tyler sang loud and scratchy toward the end of the set and is the only singer I have heard who can inject a dirty word into the song 'Happy Trails.' Perhaps the most memorable moments of the concert occurred when

Aerosmith's hydraulically operated, mirrored, and tasteful light show went into operation. It quickly proved the superiority of the sense of sight over that of hearing" (Shreveport Times, 12/10/1978).

December 10
Fairgrounds Pavilion
Tulsa, OK
Promoter: Contemporary Productions
Other act(s): Dirty Angels
Reported audience: 9,134 **SOLD-OUT
Reported gross: $71,405
Notes:
- The final show of the "Live! Bootleg" tour. Band members were soon at work at the Wherehouse, starting the process of working up musical ideas for a new album. One of the earliest titles to be mentioned was "Bone to Bone," and Joe also teased that they were messing around with Aerosmith's "version of what we think disco should be" (Daily Tribune, 2/22/1979) .... The period between this show, and their next (in March), would be one of their longest layoffs from the road during their history.

December 12 **POSTPONED
Britt Brown Auditorium @ Kansas Coliseum
Valley Center (Wichita), KS
Promoter: Chris Fritz & Co. / Contemporary Productions
Reported audience: (12,200 capacity)
Notes:
- This show was rescheduled for Apr. 5, 1979.

December 13 ** POSTPONED
Civic Auditorium
Omaha, NE
Promoter: Chris Fritz & Co. / Contemporary Productions
Notes:
- Cancelled in advance, on Nov. 21, due to Steven's wife's (Cyrinda) pregnancy. The couple's daughter, Mia, was born on Dec. 22. This show was eventually rescheduled for Apr. 3, 1979.

December 14 **CANCELLED
Freedom Hall
Louisville, KY
Promoter: Sunshine Promotions
Other act(s): Exile
Notes:

- Originally scheduled for Dec. 19 with Golden Earring opening. Unfortunately, it was cancelled on the day of show due to Steven reportedly suffering from laryngitis.

December 16 **RESCHEDULED
Tarrant County Convention Center
Fort Worth, TX
Promoter: Pace Concerts / Friends Productions
Notes:
- In mid-November, this show was rescheduled for Dec. 2.

December 19 **RESCHEDULED
Freedom Hall
Louisville, KY
Promoter: Sunshine Promotions
Notes:
- Rescheduled for Dec. 14.

1979

March 27 **TWO SETS
Main Act Concert Club
Lynn, MA
Promoter: in-house
Reported audience: (1,200 capacity)
Set list: Make It / Big Ten Inch Record / I Wanna Know Why / Walkin' the Dog / Seasons of Wither / Bone to Bone / Mama Kin / I Ain't Got You / Mother Popcorn // S.O.S. (Too Bad) / Somebody / Walk this Way / Get the Lead Out / Chiquita / Come Together / Lick and a Promise / Same Old Song and Dance / Toys in the Attic
Notes:
- A not too secret show at the former Harbour House venue. The band performed this show using their "Dr. J. Jones & The Interns" pseudonym.
- A below-average AUD recording circulates from this show, though it's great to hear the band's performance from their first show following a long layoff. Tom introduces the first new song: "Excuse me, we've been working on a new album... We've got this song that we think you're really gonna dig. If anyone wants to dance — If anyone's got room to dance, please do so on the next song! Now, you're gonna hear this on our next album, you're gonna hear it a little different, but we're gonna play it for you the way it is." Steven intros "Chiquita:" "Alright motherfuckers! We're gonna give you a little biddy taste of a song we've been doing for our next album. All you people with the tape-recorders on, we're gonna get ya, 'cause I'm gonna be cussing at you the whole time." The second set has improved sonic quality.

April 3
City Auditorium Arena
Omaha, NE
Promoter: Chris Fritz & Co. / Contemporary Productions
Other act(s): Trillion
Reported audience: 8,542 / 12,000 (71.18%)
Notes:
- From a local review: "Has Aerosmith mellowed? Or matured? Or become more sure of itself? Or gone stale? Tuesday night's concert at the City Auditorium Arena raised those questions for at least one in the crowd of 8,542 — probably more, judging by the number of people heading for the exits immediately after the obligatory first, and only, encore. The problem, if you can call it that, was the band played more skillfully than during its first two Omaha concerts. Last time, in fact, Aerosmith was downright sloppy, and lead

singer Steven Tyler and lead guitarist Joe Perry openly battled on stage. Tuesday night, though, the band was tight and the playing polished. Trouble is, Aerosmith is a high energy band, and when it harnesses the energy in the interest of good musicianship, the spark seems to fade a bit. In other words, Aerosmith is a 'people's band,' not a critic's band...

The group may have made things harder for itself by not playing as many of the hits as usual. It did perform 'Walk this Way,' 'Come Together,' and 'Train Kept a Rollin',' the old Yardbirds number that is Aerosmith's trademark concert closer, but 'Dream On' was skipped. Possibly the group finally realized that Tyler's voice seldom can reach the song's high notes after a long night of singing. Also, 'Dream On' is a slow number, and every song performed Tuesday night was up-tempo. Aerosmith stressed its blues roots, with Tyler playing occasional harmonica on such blues oldies as 'Big 10-Inch Record.' Tyler certainly did his best to keep things fired up, waving his streamer-decorated microphone stand and running through his full neo-Mick Jagger repertoire of prancing and grimaces. Then again, maybe that act is wearing a bit thin, too" (Omaha World-Herald, 4/4/1979).

April 5
Britt Brown Auditorium @ Kansas Coliseum
Valley Center (Wichita), KS
Promoter: Chris Fritz & Co. / Contemporary Productions
Reported audience: (12,200 capacity)

April 8
Memorial Coliseum
Los Angeles, CA
Promoter: Wilf & Rissmiller Concerts
Other act(s): Brownsville, Cheech & Chong, Van Halen, UFO, Eddie Money, Toto, April Wine, Boomtown Rats, Head East
Reported audience: 61,000 / 180,000 (33.89%)
Set list: Train Kept A Rollin' / S.O.S. (Too Bad) / Mama Kin / I Wanna Know Why / Big Ten Inch Record / Bone to Bone / Lick and a Promise / Come Together / Back in the Saddle / Lord of the Thighs / Seasons of Wither / Get the Lead Out / Chiquita / Walk this Way / Draw the Line / Same Old Song and Dance / Toys in the Attic / Milk Cow Blues / Bright Light Fright
Notes:
- The "Califfornia World Music Festival," which like the "Florrida" festival featured a deliberate misspelling (for attention and copyright purposes). Mother's Finest were on the bill but were a no show. Head East had been scheduled to perform on the Saturday but were bumped to Sunday's show. Mahogany Rush were scheduled to perform after the closing fireworks/laser show that followed Aerosmith's co-headlining (honors shared with VH) set but were cancelled with the audience exiting rapidly. This show was announced, and tickets went on sale, in January, but attendance only totaled 106,000 for the weekend with the promoter taking a $220,000 loss.
- From a local review: "Because co-headliners Aerosmith and Van Halen both deal in a numbing, high-energy attack, it was easy to think of their back-to-back appearances Sunday as a private battle of the bands. Would the Pasadena-based newcomer Van Halen be able to upstage East Coast veteran Aerosmith and thereby claim the American hard-rock title? The bands offered an interesting contrast. Both have flashy, crowd-stirring lead singers, but Aerosmith's strength is in the quality of its material, while Van Halen's main weapon on the stage is the guitar excellence of Eddie Van Halen. The one advantage Van Halen had going into the show was freshness. Aerosmith has been around here a lot with the same songs.

Even with that handicap, Aerosmith worked hard and overcame what looked initially like sure defeat. By coming on first, Van Halen drained the audience. Nothing during Aerosmith's set drew as much response as Van Halen's, but there was little the audience could offer except its presence. The fact that Aerosmith kept most of the audience in the Coliseum was a moral victory. So, the decision was clouded. Van Halen won — if you measure crowd response. But you've got to put an asterisk by the win. If Aerosmith had gone on first, the result could have been reversed. In either case, no one had to follow Aerosmith. With much of the exhausted audience already streaming out of the Coliseum, the festival staff decided at 11:30 p.m. to simply cancel the final act. It's not fair to ask anyone to play to an empty field" (Los Angeles Times, 4/10/1979).

- From a trade review: "During the past year in Southern California, Aerosmith has played to 250,000 at the Cal Jam at Ontario Speedway, to 15,000 at the Long Beach Arena and to 1,000 at its special Starwood concert. The band has proven it can win over crowds at any size gig, and before the huge audience at the Coliseum, Aerosmith demonstrated its resourcefulness again, giving the crowd a solid dose of its swaggering, raucous rock 'n' roll. Steven Tyler and gang, with standards like 'Walk this Way' and 'Draw the Line,' brought the crowd up on its feet on several occasions, despite the fact that most of the fans at the Coliseum were weary and exhausted by the end of the show, slowly filing out of the Coliseum one last time" (Cashbox, 4/21/1979).

- An AUD recording circulates from this show.

April 14
Tangerine Bowl
Orlando, FL

Promoter: Beach Club Concerts / Cellar Door Productions
Other act(s): Ted Nugent, Cheap Trick, Mahogany Rush, Brownsville, Blackfoot, Hoochie
Reported audience: 61,075
Notes:

- The "Florrida World Music Festival," with Aerosmith and Ted Nugent as the co-headliners, was the brainchild of Leber-Krebs (the deliberate misspelling of 'Florida' was a ploy to attract attention).

- From a local review: "An archeologist on a dig sifts through old bones and rubble in search of a new discovery. He may suffer in the hot sun and harsh conditions of a hostile environment, but when he finds something special, something unique, it all becomes worthwhile. The Florrida World Music Festival was not unlike an archeologist's quest for treasures. Approximately 55,000 people jammed into the Orlando Tangerine bowl Saturday, despite the hot sun and hostile environment, to hear an all-star line-up of hard rock bands featuring Ted Nugent, Aerosmith, and Cheap Trick. Stadium concerts are notorious for conditions that should be outlawed by the Geneva Convention. The sun took a heavy toll on the crowd and casualties lay strewn beneath the stands. It took hours to fight through the crowd for something to eat or drink and an overwhelming stench of vomit and sweating bodies permeated the lower regions of the stadium. And the crowd seemed to love it... Aerosmith delivered little more than it promised, a repeat of old Aerosmith shows. Tyler and guitarist Joe Perry are a foppish imitation of the Rolling Stones' Jagger-Richard combination, but without even the semblance of spontaneity. The other Aerosmith members saunter across the stage like models looking for predesignated spots to stand and pose..." (Tampa Tribune, 4/16/1979).

May 8 **CANCELLED
Offenbach Stadthalle
Frankfurt, Germany

Promoter: Mama Concerts
Other act(s): Golden Earring

May 9 **RESCHEDULED
Friedrich-Ebert-Halle
Ludwigshafen, Germany

Notes:
- After being announced, this date was rescheduled for May 15.

May 11 **RESCHEDULED
Messehalle

Stuttgart-Sindelfingen, Germany

May 12 **CANCELLED
**Circus Krone
Munich, Germany**
Notes:
- This show was on the initial German itinerary which included May 8-11 dates first announced in early-January.

May 12 **CANCELLED
**Messehalle
Stuttgart-Sindelfingen, Germany**
Promoter: Mama Concerts
Other act(s): Golden Earring
Notes:
- The initial itinerary for run of German dates was modified in early March with dates being rescheduled or cancelled.

May 14 **CANCELLED
**Hemmerleinhalle
Neunkirchen am Brand, Germany**
Promoter: Mama Concerts
Other act(s): Golden Earring

May 15 **CANCELLED
**Friedrich-Ebert-Halle
Ludwigshafen, Germany**
Promoter: Mama Concerts
Other act(s): Golden Earring
Notes:
- All German dates were cancelled at the end of March.

June 27 **HEARTBREAKERS
**Mudd Club
New York City, NY**
Notes:
- Joe attended this Johnny Thunders show and joined the band for encores including "Bright Lights, Big City," "Just Because I'm White," and "I Can Tell."

June 30 **TWO SHOWS
**Stage 1
Clarence, NY**
Promoter: Harvey & Corky Presentations
Other act(s): None.
Reported audience: 400 **SOLD-OUT
Notes:
- A pair of "shake off the dust and cobwebs" club gigs to prepare for the run of July dates.
- From a local review: "Last Saturday night was hardly an ordinary one for many area rock fans patronizing Harvey & Corky's Stage 1. A different kind of anticipation, and even mystery, surrounded the place with the

news that some Boston group, Dr. J. Jones and the Interns, was to perform that evening. Or at least that was the belief running the musical grapevine, and the skeptics. However, many of us were quickly convinced by the attendants, posted at all entrances, barring entry to even the lot without a ticket. The "sold out" sign on the door along with the scalpers (asking almost $20 for $4.50 tickets) was the final proof. Later, $13 poorer, my suspicions were confirmed: the fictitious Dr. J. Jones and his Interns weren't coming — Aerosmith was. Inside, after an hour and a half of pushing, shoving, and near brawls for standing room, Aerosmith entered to thunderous cheers.

The band put on a show (not unlike their bigger concerts) and never seemed to ease off with the lack of a stadium-sized crowd. Lead singer Steve Tyler (clad in tight red satin) shook hands with the fans up front and proceeded to be as verbally and visually obscene as his reputation has it. Tyler's vocals were as raspy and tough as everyone expected. Guitarists Joe Perry and Brad Whitford were in good form despite lacking some of their recorded luster. The band played at least three songs off their soon-to-be-released album; and though they were well received, they didn't evoke the response quite like the favorites ('My Big Ten Inch,' 'Walk This Way,' their Sgt. Pepper hit, 'Come Together,' and especially 'Sweet Emotion') did. The 'oldies' were the highlight of their two 45-minute sets" (The Spectrum, 7/6/1979).

July 2
C.N.E. Stadium
Toronto, ON, Canada
Promoter: Concert Productions International
Other act(s): Ted Nugent, Nazareth, Johnny Winter, Ramones, Goddo, Moxy
Reported audience: ~50,000 / 70,000 (71.43%)
Set list: Train Kept A Rollin' / S.O.S. (Too Bad) / Mama Kin / Big Ten Inch Record / Reefer Head Woman / Lick and a Promise / Think About It / Seasons of Wither / Bone to Bone / Lord of the Thighs / Sweet Emotion / Get the Lead Out / Walk this Way / Draw the Line / Same Old Song and Dance / Rats in the Cellar / Milk Cow Blues / Toys in the Attic
Notes:
- The "Canadian World Music Festival 1979."
- From a local review: "Aerosmith headlined the festival. They deserved that status. Those Ottawans who witnessed this band's performance a year ago last December at the Civic Centre would not recognize last night's explosive set as belonging to the same musicians. In Ottawa, they slopped out low-energy noise. Last night they ripped out excruciatingly high-powered rock. Steve Tyler, vocalist, and visual focal point of Aerosmith, was a non-stop energy source of snakeskin and silk scarfs. The band was loose enough to bring out its flavor but at the same time so kinetic that one felt the tower of amplifiers and speakers might cringe under the pressure. Aerosmith's appeal is their ragged stage delivery and reckless musicianship. They give an image common enough for their audience to identify with, and in so doing provide a good fantasy for listeners to 'dream on'. Aside from old favorites the band played three songs from a forthcoming unnamed album which included a bluesy number called 'Reefer Headed Woman,' which points to their new musical direction. The Canadian World Music Festival will be the biggest concert in the area this summer, which is just as well. It would be a tough act to follow" (Ottawa Journal, 7/3/1979).
- From another local review: "The evening hours of the munificent Canadian World Music Festival (an event which surely had certain Fathers of Confederation turning over in their graves) are the hours specifically set aside for Star Time, but it was one of the curiosities of the event that two of the three headliners were acts which could well be considered to be in popular decline. Of Nazareth, Aerosmith, and Ted Nugent, only the latter is still enjoying healthy and rising album sales, and one wonders what per cent of the 50,000-plus audience would have been in attendance had not Nugent, the Head Gonzo of pain-rock, not been on the bill... There was little the headliners, Aerosmith, could have done to top Nugent. The fact that they even tried was a point in their favor. Aerosmith's late set was like a denouement. Not only was their sound system muddied and static-filled in comparison to Nugent's, but their attempt to build slowly was a mistake after Nugent's pyrotechnics. Their music was powerful but controlled, and the trickle of fans leaving at the beginning of their set became a steady stream as the set progressed late into the night. Had they preceded

Nugent, or even Nazareth for that matter, they would have come off much better. All told, the Canadian World Music Festival ran a nerve-shattering 12 hours. Those who endured every mega-decibel minute will, like Dan McCafferty, have something to tell their kids. They were there, and survived" (Toronto Globe & Mail, 7/3/1979).

July 7
Grant Field @ Georgia Tech
Atlanta, GA

Promoter: Alex Cooley, Inc.
Other act(s): Atlanta Rhythm Section, Cars, Mother's Finest, Dixie Dregs, Whiteface
Reported audience: ~40,000 / 62,500 (64%)
Notes:
- The "Champagne Jam '79" Festival. Attendance was substantially down from the 57,000 who attended in 1978. There was no mention of Aerosmith's performance in the Atlanta Constitution's review of the show, other than the band's last-minute demand for an additional stuffed 10lb turkey... A local music critic suggested "a good portion of the crowd didn't even stay for the group's entire set" (Atlanta Constitution, 7/14/1979).

July 21
Oakland Stadium
Oakland, CA

Promoter: Bill Graham Presents
Other act(s): Ted Nugent, AC/DC, Mahogany Rush, St. Paradise
Reported audience: 57,561 / 60,000 (95.94%)
Reported gross: $720,733
Set list: Back in the Saddle / Train Kept A Rollin' / Mama Kin / Big Ten Inch Record / Reefer Head Woman / Lick and a Promise / Think About It / Seasons of Wither / Bone to Bone / Lord of the Thighs / Sweet Emotion / Get the Lead Out / Walk this Way / Draw the Line / Same Old Song and Dance / Come Together / Toys in the Attic
Notes:
- The 1979 edition of "Day on the Green," with the band appearing for the second year running.
- Somewhat ironically, St. Paradise featured lead singer/guitarist Derek St. Holmes and was his first post-Ted Nugent project. The band's album wasn't successful, and he and Brad Whitford would work together on an equally unsuccessful album in 1981.
- Pro-shot VID footage circulates from this show.

July 28
Municipal Stadium
Cleveland, OH

Promoter: Belkin Productions
Other act(s): Ted Nugent (HL), Journey, Thin Lizzy, AC/DC, Scorpions
Reported audience: 65,807 / 72,000 (91.4%)
Reported gross: $834,690
Notes:
- This event caused massive headaches for the promoters and local authorities, due to related trouble the resulted in "violence outside the stadium, the shooting death of one person, and a number of robberies and

beatings" (Dayton Daily News, 8/13/1979). These issues threw into confusion plans for additional events, with the promoter flip-flopping between venues to downsize the scale amidst local political and safety concerns. Ultimately, additional events were ultimately cancelled. The show would provide German band, the Scorpions, with their U.S. debut.
- The night prior to the show members of the band were interviewed by Denny Sanders at WMMS' studio. During this hot and humid "World Series of Rock Game #1" festival show, 33 fans were injured and 31 arrested. There was also a post-show spat backstage between band member's wives, and as a result this was Joe Perry's final show with the band. For a while...
- From a local review: "That was the score yesterday at the Fourth World Series of Rock concert at the Stadium. A total of 65,800 came to see six acts that started about 11 a.m... Aerosmith, led by skinny hyperactive singer Steve Tyler, scored with songs such as 'Bone to Bone,' but the audience was waiting for its 'Come Together,' the Beatles song they had sung in the movie, Sgt. Pepper's Lonely Heart's Club Band. The audience brought them back for an encore. Aerosmith put out as much energy as they did at their last Coliseum appearance, but their sound did not come through as clearly as it did then. This was a series with no base loaded, home-run players like Led Zeppelin or the Rolling Stones. Those bands are not touring now. But it was a hard-hitting, successful series anyway" (Plain Dealer, 7/29/1979).

1978 - Live! Bootleg

1979 - Right in the Nuts

U.S. Release Details:
Columbia/CBS FC/FCA/FCT-36050 (Nov. 16, 1979)
Columbia/CBS CK-36050 (1989 — CD Issue)
Columbia/SME CK/CT-557366 (Sep. 7, 1993 — 20-bit SBM digital remaster)
Columbia/SME 88883760961 (Apr. 25, 2014 — 180g LP reissue)

Tracks:
A1. No Surprize
(4:25) — Steven Tyler / Joe Perry
A2. Chiquita
(4:24) — Steven Tyler / Joe Perry
A3. Remember (Walking in the Sand) •
(4:04) — Shadow Morton
A4. Cheese Cake
(4:15) — Steven Tyler / Joe Perry

B1. Three Mile Smile
(3:42) — Steven Tyler / Joe Perry
B2. Reefer Head Woman
(4:01) — Joe Bennett / Jazz Gillum / Lester Melrose
B3. Bone to Bone (Coney Island White Fish Boy)
(2:59) — Steven Tyler / Joe Perry
B4. Think About It
(3:34) — Keith Relf / Jimmy Page / Jim McCarty
B5. Mia
(4:14) — Steven Tyler

Album Details:
Produced by Gary Lyons and Aerosmith. Engineered by Gary Lyons. Additional engineering by Rod O'Brien and Peter Thea. Recorded at Mediasound and Record Plant studios.

Players:
◦ No Surprize - Richard Supa on additional guitars.
◦ Chiquita - Louis del Gatto, Lou Marini, George Young and Barry Rodgers on brass; Neil Thompson on additional guitars.
◦ Remember (Walking in the Sand) - Mary Weiss on background vocals.
◦ Three Mile Smile - Jimmy Crespo on additional lead guitars.

Chart Action:
Chart Peak (USA, 1/1980): #14 (1/19/1980) with 19 weeks on the Billboard charts. Other countries: CAN #8; JPN #39.

12/01/79	12/08/79	12/15/79	12/22/79	12/29/79	01/05/80	01/12/80
115	46	21	19	19	16	16
01/19/80	01/26/80	02/02/80	02/09/80	02/16/80	02/23/80	03/01/80
14	14	20	26	25	31	31
03/08/80	03/15/80	03/22/80	03/29/80	04/05/80	04/12/79	
76	96	108	137	181	X	

RIAA/Sales:
In the United States, the album was certified Gold by the RIAA on March 13, 1980 and Platinum on October 28, 1994; Gold by the CRIA (Canada - 50,000 units) on December 1, 1979. During the SoundScan era, the album had sold 82,370 copies between 1991 and 2007.

Supporting Singles:
• Remember (Walking in the Sand) (USA, 12/1979) - Chart Peak: #67 (2/9/1980) with 6 weeks on the Billboard charts. The single managed five weeks on Cashbox peaking at #91 (1/26/1980). Other countries: CAN, #29.

01/12/80	01/19/80	01/26/80	02/02/80	02/09/80	02/16/80	02/23/80
84	73	71	69	**67**	99	X

Performed Live:
"Bone to Bone" and "Chiquita" had debuted with Joe in April 1979. Covers included on the album, such as "Think About It" and "Reefer Head Woman" had previously been performed while Joe was still a member of the band during the first half of 1979; in the case of the former at their very first show in November 1970, and the latter during 1971. Regardless, these songs also appeared in the set while Joe was still in the band in 1979 while the band struggled to record an album. By the time Jimmy joined the band, "No Surprise" and "Remember (Walking in the Sand)" were included in the set.

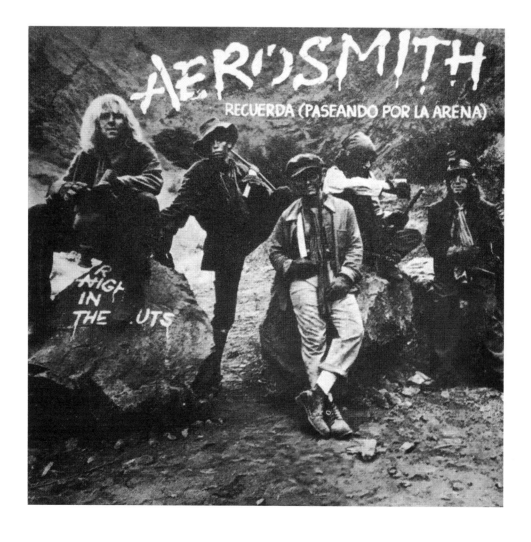

Steven Tyler: "Heroin. Shooting coke. Eating opium and it was just... I love that album — Night in the Ruts. It's like a fuckin' solar eclipse" ("Walk This Way").

"Bootleg Live!" segued into the "Night in the Ruts" era as neatly as the transition between "Rocks" and "Draw the Line." Well, perhaps not, but the underlying plan remained the same: Take some time off from the inevitable grind of touring and start working on ideas for a new album. The problem was, more so than in 1977, the band's toxic dependencies had finally caught up with them and were no longer stalking in the shadows. The band were fatigued, battle-scarred from internal and external fights, and paranoia, with the bonds that had once made them so formidable having been severed, cut by cut, until only the thinnest of strands remained. During 1978, "Come Together" had done well for the band, but its non-album follow-up "Chip Away the Stone" had failed to live up to expectations. "Draw the Line" was considered a flop, having failed to build on the success of "Rocks" or deliver any hits. That is of course regardless of the challenging proposition of following two albums such as "Toys in the Attic" and "Rock," or even approaching the plateau both had attained. Aerosmith were no longer the new guys, and a plethora of other bands were working hard to gain the attention of the record-buying and show-attending youth of America. The band was off the road by Dec. 18, and while Steven was busy with his Daddy duties, the rest of the band got soon to work at their Boston Wherehouse, rehearsing five days a week preparing material for a new studio album.

If the band were ready for an extended period off the road, there certainly wouldn't be an extended break from work. Preproduction for Jack Douglas was expected to take a while. From these sessions some 30-minutes of the band woodshedding out "Three Mile Smile" circulate, illustrating the process of just attempting to get the musical arrangements down. Steven is clearly heard as the band's director trying to get the others to capture and execute the sounds he hears in his head. Musical ideas could often be a grind, developing a promising riff or passage into a fully arranged musical track was a time consuming and frustrating process. And then there would be the inevitable wait for Steven's lyrics, which often came last, dragged out of him kicking and screaming like unruly children. In the interim, between the completion of the live album and starting work on the new album, Jack Douglas had also changed, both in his personal life and he faced challenges similar to those faced by the band. One thing that had not changed was the pressure on the band. Daisann McLane opined, "The pressure is still on Aerosmith. They are not original, nor are they instrumental virtuosos; they play basic, loud rock & roll... Their albums have a raucous edge that keeps them off of tight AOR playlists. In a way, Aerosmith is a dinosaur among bands, the last of a generation of rock & rollers being edged out by more streamlined competition... What keeps Aerosmith alive is their ability to related to their loyal, largely male adolescent audience" (Rolling Stone #285, 2/22/1979). Problem was, under the continuous barrage of toxic elements, the band were finding it harder to relate with one another, let alone teenagers...

One of the earliest new song titles mentioned in public was "Bone to Bone," which at that point was still the instrumental Joe originally envisaged. He also teased that the band were fooling around with some disco sounds, or at least "our version of what we think disco should be" (Wisconsin Rapids Daily Tribune, 2/22/1979). It wouldn't have been a particularly shocking diversion into the genre (other rock bands such as KISS and Angel dabbled with the genre during the year) but following the lackluster critical response to the previous album it may have been deigned too risky. But in terms of completed tracks, some of the first to hit the can were the hard rocking "Chiquita" (amusingly Steven was spotted sporting a Chiquita banana sticker on his wrist in 1977), the bluesy revisit of "Reefer Head Woman," and a fierce cover of "Remember (Walking in the Sand)." For the latter of these, original Shangri-Las' vocalist Mary Weiss joined the band in the studio on backing vocals for the transformation of the George "Shadow" Morton written 1964 hit. It was a song that Steven had always wanted to record, dating back to the Chain Reaction opening for the girls in the 60s; a reminder of a far simpler time to what Aerosmith had become, emmeshed within the corporate machine. "Reefer Head Woman" was an amalgamation of two interpretations of a standard 12-bar blues composition. One was Jazz Gillum & His Jazz Boys 1938 take on the song had been one of the first recordings to include an electric guitar accompaniment (by George Barnes) and established the melody later used on a 1945 version by the Buster Bennett Trio produced by Lester Melrose. The Aerosmith version followed the latter lyrical form since Gillum's original was more a lament: "She musta have smoked that reefer and it's bound to carry her down." Tom Hamilton described the song as being a tune about "a guy with a dope-smoking girlfriend who's upset because he has to drink twice as much to get half as high" (Rolling Stone #298, 8/23/1979). More notably, within the context of Aerosmith album production progress, Steven had only to write the lyrics for one song with the other two being covers. Other material was still in the process of transformation. A jam from the Wherehouse pre-productions sessions, "Let It Slide," was adapted and became "Cheese Cake."

By the end of March, the band had been recording in New York City, and the slow pace left them considering releasing an EP prior to a full album. But in the middle of rehearsals, the band had to head out on the road again. They had dates in Wichita and Omaha to make up for postponements the previous December, and pre-scheduled festivals in Los Angeles and Orlando. The band prepared for the short road jaunt with a warm-up gig at the Main Act in Lynn on March 27, with local fans getting first performances of "Chiquita" (clearly a work in progress) and "Bone to Bone." Interestingly, the opening act on the mid-west make-up dates was Trillion, a band that had released their Fergie Frederiksen fronted Gary Lyons produced debut via Epic in 1978. While the tour may have been disruptive to recording, unlike during the recording of "Draw the Line," shorter tour outings would be scheduled. And the tours were primarily for large stadium events planned many months in advance rather than short regional legs. The first of these large shows, the Callifornia [sic] World Music Festival had been announced in January. It was followed in March with the addition of a Florrida [sic] version, both taking place in April. Technically, one might consider these dates part of the "Night in the Ruts" tour, though the press considered the band to still be supporting "Live! Bootleg." During the April dates, the band debuted both "Bone to Bone" and "Chiquita," two of the harder-rocking tracks. Performing new material was a challenge, according to Joe: "I would try to get Aerosmith to play some of the new stuff; I thought it would work for the fans. But there was a fear of doing anything new unless it'd been on a record, and it was frustrating. Aerosmith sold itself short in that respect. We were ripping off the audience" (Circus, 5/27/1980). Yet the band did perform new material that was clearly a work in progress lyrically. "Bone to Bone" hadn't taken on it's more familiar album arrangement but was a full-frontal assault that certainly illustrated that the band's direction was closer to the sonics of "Rocks" than "Draw the Line." According to Tom, "We're going for a more focused sound on the instruments, more separation, less adding tracks upon tracks" (Sounds, 7/7/1979), though he introduced the song in Lynn as a "danceable" song.

With the album progressing at snail's pace a planned European tour scheduled for May was also cancelled. Producer Jack Douglas was also out, and a new producer brought in; it would be the first time in five years Douglas wasn't behind the board for the band. Douglas was soon back at work, utilizing the Record Plant's then new 3M digital recording and mastering system for the debut album by Rick Dufay. The album would be one of the first all-digital rock productions. Joe wasn't happy, suggesting that he'd been outvoted by the other band members on retaining Jack's services (Circus, 5/27/1980). His replacement on the Aerosmith project, Gary Lyons, had initially been a musician who slowly became more interested in the technical side of the studio. Initially, he'd been hired to finish the build out of Command Studios in London, a process where he learned about how a studio was cabled. He became particularly known for the sound on his recording of drums and worked with the likes of Humble Pie, and by 1979 had engineered and co-produced the first Foreigner album. For Steven, it wasn't just his drum sound, but the freshness of working with someone new. He admitted that "things were on the fritz between us and Douglas" (Rolling Stone #298, 8/23/1979) and that Gary was a breath of fresh air: "He's excellent and he does it real fast — like he's playing an instrument he's practiced on all his life. He's that old English type — fuck-it-put-it-there" (Sounds, 7/7/1979). The band also wanted a more spontaneous and less produced sounding album.

Things were on the fritz elsewhere. It wasn't long until rumors of malcontent started to swirl around the band, with the suggestion that Joe was considering leaving the band. Without doubt he had become frustrated by the marathon of frustration the process of making Aerosmith albums had become. He was holding back material from the band and started to consider doing a solo project to get the surplus of material out, rather than go through the tortuous process of transforming the material into Aerosmith suitable songs. This was not a new thought that grew out of the rut, but something he had considered around the "Draw the Line" album. However, in 1977 it was the band album that prevented Joe from working on solo material. Initially, it was stressed that Joe had no intention of leaving the band, with him telling Lisa Robinson: "Ron Wood has done something similar in that he did his own album and stayed in the

Stones, but he's a different kind of guitar soloist and songwriter than I am... I feel strongly about Aerosmith because I put nine years of my life into it. I want to keep doing it as much as I can. It's my first love. It's a club that I've been in for a long time, and I don't want to quit it" (Green Bay Press-Gazette, 7/13/1979). If one takes Joe at his word, he wasn't feeling restricted by Aerosmith and had all the space he needed within the band to breathe artistically. The solo album he envisaged, which he'd once stated would be called "Guitar Wars" would be produced by Jack Douglas and contain 1/3 instrumentals with the rest split between him on lead vocals and someone else. He was also interested in possibly covering a Jimi Hendrix song.

At the end of June, the band took another break from the studio for an additional brace of festival dates. Following a warm-up at Harvey & Corky's Stage 1 in Clarence, NY the band headlined the "Canaddian [sic] World Music Festival" in Toronto, Canada, followed by the "Champagne Jam '79" Festival in Atlanta, GA. Additional "new" covers returned to the set, "Reefer Head Woman" and "Think About It." The former had been performed by the band in 1971. The latter of these was another cover familiar to the band — they had performed it at their first ever show in Nov. 1970, making it part of their core musical DNA. While the solo on the Yardbird's original had later been recycled by Page for "Dazed and Confused," Perry had more scope to inject his frustration into crafting a unique and ferocious sonic attack for the song. The month concluded with two final stadium shows, July 21 in Oakland, CA, and July 28 in Cleveland, OH. The latter of these shows was a jarringly ragged performance by the band. Steven was purportedly substance affected, and Joe appeared supremely disinterested in proceedings. Following what were by all accounts were stunning performances by Ted Nugent, Journey, AC/DC, and the U.S. debut of the Scorpions, the band's decline was laid bare for all to see. One DJ, who'd been present at the previous evening's band interview at WMMS, recalled Steven on top of a table on all fours, snorting a line as long as the table... Backstage, before the fated performance, interpersonal relationships had declined to the point of becoming a forecast of "festering, with a high chance of volatility." Joe had already distanced himself from the band, who continued to struggle along in the studio. He'd completed his final session for them a month earlier, a brief jam titled "Shit House Shuffle," and had moved on to working on demos for his solo project. Even the generally stolid Tom Hamilton was driven mad to the point of distraction by the continued lack of progress on the material. That tensions were running high within the band would be stating the case too mildly.

There had been a shift in the dynamics within the band. It was clear Joe was frustrated by the pace of the creativity of a new Aerosmith album, and had material in pocket that he wanted to develop outside of those confines. As he later described it, "I was wasting my time with Aerosmith, getting frustrated and miserable" (Trouser Press, 2/1980). But this desire was being leveraged against the band with the presentation of an $80,000 debt to the band, a solo album seemed an ideal way to clear the debt and assuage the artistic itch in a low-risk manner. Conversely, what may have been a play designed to keep Joe in the band may have backfired in an unintended manner. An offer of solo deal could easily be read to a drug-affected mind of being able to break away, seemingly with the backing of management. What started prior to the Cleveland show was just another bickering interaction between Elyssa and another band member's wife. It was hardly a fiery catalyst igniting some biblical conflagration, the glass of milk was a metaphorical final wet slap of indignity. According to Steven, "He was just a pain in the butt. He was paying more attention to his wife and other people than to music" (Los Angeles Times, 8/2/1983). The stage had already been set, tension and distance always present, and literally anything could have caused the scene that erupted following the band's performance. The usual accusations were brandied around, countered with "Maybe I should leave" and "Get the fuck outta here!" If ever there had been need of an adult in the room, a referee with an offer of a long vacation and a period of detox, then that might have been the moment best suited for an intervention. Perhaps Brad sums it up best: "Being in Aerosmith was like walking into a dogfight and both dogs bite you" ("Walk this Way"). Problem was that the dogs were also biting themselves... Regardless, Joe Perry was out of the band and returned to Boston where he soon got on the phone with Ralph Morman, a singer he'd met a few weeks earlier backstage at a gig...

When did Joe Perry quit Aerosmith? The exact date is probably contained on some dense legalese document, but it doesn't matter when the result was the same. That a planned European tour in August had been cancelled makes it clear that Joe had walked away, even if the members kept up appearances of normality in the music press — that Joe was working on a solo album. Joe made it clear: "I had the

Aerosmith itinerary in one hand and my demo tapes in the other and it was a question of playing the same songs again and again in the same songs and again in the same big arenas" (Circus, 3/4/1980). So, the same old song and dance had become old hat. Whenever the case, by October 1979 the band's next run of dates was being announced to the press, with Joe's departure was often mentioned as a side note citing the usual played-out "amicable split" and "new musical direction" excuses. The long festering situation was anything but amicable, but for the remaining band members there was a long lingering studio album to finish. The rest of the band returned to New York City to continue trying to work on the album at Media Sound. The lack of Joe Perry didn't keep the band from claiming victory in the battle of the rut. Stalwart band friend Richard Supa was brought in to complete the guitars on the autobiographical Perry/Tyler tome, "No Surprize." Within its context, charting the history of the band in the beginning, even with its fist-pumping up-tempo tone it's impossible to separate it from the melancholy of the band's situation at the time and the frustrations within the business that had become life. "Chiquita" was given the treatment that had served classic songs such as "Same Old Song and Dance" and "Big Ten Inch Record." Neil V. Thompson, who had worked with the band for several years before signing on fulltime as their guitar tech in 1978, more than capably performed on Steven's "Mia" (along with Richard), the lullaby written for his daughter. "Chip Away the Stone," the underperforming single had been intended to be included on the album but was likely left off simply for that reason in addition to having been produced by Jack Douglas and already having been included in live form on "Bootleg Live" and the "California Jam II" albums and failing on the singles charts.

By September, rumors of Joe's departure, imminent or actual, were already circulating in the press. On the 8th, Joe appeared at the Paradise in Boston and jammed with David Johansen's band during their show encores including "Personality Crisis" and probably "Babylon." For Aerosmith, as work on the album neared completion, the process of finding a replacement for Joe had commenced. Michael Schenker was purportedly the first to audition. After leaving UFO, he had briefly rejoined the Scorpions, but had walked out on them during the "Lovedrive" tour in April 1979. He had been advised by his manager, Peter Mensch, to audition for the band and flew to New York to rehearse with Aerosmith. The German riff-meister didn't relate with the band members on any level, if one takes comments by the band in "Walk this Way" at face value: Steven: "It was Raymond all over again. Personified. 'Hello, I'm taking over. Before I join your band, I vant [sic] it clear, I'm taking over right now. Here — my jacket — take and hang up'." But it was clear that the black leather clad Teuton with an English language challenge was too much. If there was any perception that he seemed to think that Aerosmith were looking to join his band rather than vice-versa, then it would seem likely that it was simply the result of a culture clash or communication issues. Michael, while troubled, was also gifted and had been a member of several big-name bands previously, in addition to having been invited to join a formative Motörhead. Tom recalled, "He was this boy genius that couldn't speak English too well. He had these classical-sounding guitar riffs, echo-reverb stuff, very European-sounding leads played on classical scales instead of blues scales. Gary Lyons insulted him, and I think he ended up walking out" ("Walk This Way"). And therein lies the rub.

Musically and visually, Michael would have clashed with America's band. But if Michael was in bad shape, then the same was certainly true of the members of Aerosmith, particularly Steven. Michael has recounted being penned up in his hotel room for days on end waiting for Aerosmith to be ready to rehearse with him. When they finally were, no one (including himself) was in the best shape to make things work out on a musical. Michael has suggested that Steven headed off to hospital and he briefly worked out with Joey and Tom, who had expressed an interest in working with him on his new project. However, Steven was soon back in the picture, so Michael worked in Boston with Billy Sheehan and Denny Carmassi on demos for what became the first MSG album. Somewhat ironically for Aerosmith, Michael's former band would be the opening act scheduled for the first dates on the "Night in the Ruts" tour...

The band also jammed with Danny Johnson (Derringer) at S.I.R. Studios in New York City for a week and both Tom and Brad liked him — Brad had already recorded demos with him and other members of his then band (Axis) at Cherokee Studios for a prospective solo project in late-1978. Steven, on the other hand, had issues with Danny's then short hair. Danny recalled, "I was straight, which made Steven Tyler nervous. Initially, I thought, 'this is cool!' But they were spiraling out of control. It was a dysfunctional situation... Tyler ultimately picked Jimmy Crespo since he had long hair and Steven thought he looked like Joe Perry. Plus, Crespo was a New Yorker. I think it was for the best. At that time in my life, I didn't need a vampire lifestyle" (Guitar World, 11/18/2019). A member of the Los Angeles band Valentino was also rumored to have been considered for the position and Salem Witchcraft's Arlen Viecelli is purported to have auditioned. Another possible replacement was Punky Meadows, who recalled, "David [Krebs] later offered me $500,000 a year to take over Joe Perry's place in Aerosmith. He's a great guy, and I was sorry to refuse him but I'm too dedicated to Angel" (Miami Hurricane, 4/25/1980). He'd also previously turned down Krebs on an offer to join the New York Dolls preferring to focus on the formation of his own band in 1975...

Jimmy Crespo had the benefit of being a mutual friend of Richie Supa. Crespo had been in an ideal position in 1979. His previous band, Flame, had come to an end and he and the band's singer, Marge Raymond, were shopping demos and looking for management. They approached David Krebs with a demo, but later David suggested that Jimmy audition of Aerosmith. He had enough of a session background and was more than technically proficient to fit into any situation. As noted by Danny Johnson, he also had Steven's stamp of approval for fitting certain image prerequisites and could certainly play in the requisite style. Before the audition Jimmy was introduced to Steven at Privates in New York to see if he passed muster visually and on a personal level. Steven later recalled, "I replaced Joe with Jimmy Crespo because he looked just like Joe, and played really good, too. Nice long hair, skinny fucking guy, I thought, 'Hey, bingo! What do I need fucking Joe Perry for?" ("Does the Noise in My Head Bother You?"). There wasn't much of an involved process for Jimmy, and he only did a couple of auditions with the second one providing a positive vibe from his point of view. Steven was looking for a foil, with someone who looked right but could provide the roll previously filled by Joe. As such there wasn't much interest in changing the underlying dynamic of the band.

Jimmy, though, had second thoughts about joining Aerosmith. He was doing well for himself working sessions for various projects in New York, but ultimately decided that he would regret it if he didn't take up the opportunity, even after discovering how dysfunctional the band had become with their addictions. Crespo came in at a very late stage of the album's production but was able to contribute a solo to "Three Mile Smile;" much to the chagrin of Brad Whitford whose own solo was rejected by Tyler in favor of Jimmy's. Still, it started his integration into the band... Even out of the band, Joe had some gripes about the album: "I'm not happy with the way the album sounds, 'cause I wasn't there for the mix. I don't claim any responsibility for the sound. But I know the basic tracks. I know the potential was there... I was just starting some new things on the Aerosmith album and for some reason it's not mixed up quite as loud. At least they didn't take them off! They were mixing after I quit the band, so I expected them to erase all my playing" (Trouser Press, 2/1980). Steven disputed that suggestion in the same feature, "I don't think he's particularly mixed down, either. If he had something to say, it's there." Perry's later evaluation of the album was more measured: "We were still fucked up, but the record sounds more cohesive than 'Draw the Line'" (Guitar World, 4/1997).

If Jimmy had been unaware of how dysfunctional Aerosmith had become, it soon became apparent. After making his debut with the band during a club gig within the friendly confines of the Main Act, the Aerosmith traveling circus hit the road for the tour supporting the album in early December 1979. Joining the band for the tour was Richard Supa on keyboard. After a successful show in upstate New York, the tour's second date was scheduled for Portland, ME. Early during the show Steven keeled over, hit the stage, and didn't get up. Jimmy told Eddie Trunk in 2012: "I thought it was part of the act. Like James Brown would fall down and come back up... He fell down, so I just kept playing... I look over and Brad is kicking him, not hard, just kicking him to see if he's alright." At that point Jimmy realized that the job he had signed on for was going to be more of a challenge than he'd envisaged. As noted in the Portland Press-Herald, "[Steven] made a phone call later from backstage and received no medication from the paramedics on duty" calling into question the reality of the situation. The band limped back to Boston so that Steven could see his doctor, though he suggests in his autobiography that he was simply falling-down drunk that night and no fainting was involved — it being a tender mercy to euthanize the show as a matter of self-interest. The press reported obediently that Steven was the victim of viral exhaustion. He recalled, "Happened twice in my career that I was so soused and so dizzy that I became a fall-down drunk. Well, rather than fall-down drunk in front of the audience and act like a pathetic idiot for an hour while they through apples at me, I said, 'Fuck this!'... I knew they'd never stop the show just because I was drunk, so I lay down and didn't move, as if I'd fainted. And to make it look convincing I twitched my foot spastically... I really did it good, and Joe Baptista dragged me offstage" (Steven Tyler, "Does the Noise in my Head Bother You"). However, a string of dates were postponed, suggesting it must have been a pretty good hangover or sales were poor enough to justify a delay...

(Photograph © BC Kagan 1979, 2021 — Used with permission)

The tour was scheduled to resume on Dec. 16 in Charlotte, NC, but that date was then postponed at the last moment with the promoter reporting that Steven had been hospitalized, this time with hypertension as the culprit. Prior to Christmas, the band did successfully complete three shows, plus two more afterwards, but further postponements left the tour on hiatus until January 10. From that point the band were able to string together a consistent run of dates through February 3, following which the remainder of the tour was ignominiously axed. Steven later suggested the cancellations were a simple matter of quality control: "I was exhausted then. We had a Lear jet at the time, and you can imagine what a Lear jet does to your sense of time when you travel. You get out of bed and you're someplace else... We said the heck with it. Why should be burn ourselves out and do any lousy shows? Of course, the press jumped on it and said, 'Golly, he's been taking drugs again'" (Boston Globe, 11/11/1982). It was ironic that tour PR was proclaiming that Aerosmith was "back with a vengeance," something that was probably only partially true when listening to the album.

In March, the band were expected to book a 45-date arena tour May through July booked through ICM (Billboard, 3/22/1980). Whatever the case, the band instead switched gears and booked dates that comprised the "Mystery Club Tour." The decision to downscale was multifold but partially fueled by the economic downturn that derailed several larger tours by bands at the time. Prior to the club run, Jimmy Crespo played dates as part of Helen Schneider band — he also did session work for her "Crazy Lady" album (which included Marge Raymond) on backing vocals. Marge's band Kicks would open some dates on the club jaunt, with her occasionally joining Aerosmith on stage for backing vocals. From April 20 the band performed limited club dates thorough June with the dates in West Hartford being recorded for a King Biscuit Flower Hour radio broadcast. Any hopes for supporting the "Night in the Ruts" album ended when Steven was involved in a mini-bike accident while in Sunapee on August 18 — though it was reported in the local press that he had been riding a moped. A 21-year-old passenger, Kathleen Bickford, was "treated for cuts and bruises" (AP), but Steven was hospitalized at the New London Hospital following the crash. Steven recounted, in "Walk this Way," that he had been drunk and had picked Kathleen up to babysit Mia. His injuries were more severe, having nearly torn off the heel on his foot, having been riding with inadequate protection. He would be hospitalized for an extended period. Steven later expanded on the accident: "I went flying and hit a tree upside down. I had a concussion and I almost died... I was pumped full of pain killers and injections. I was in bed eight months and had a cast up to my knee" (Boston Globe, 11/11/1982). In terms of the actual injury, Steven's foot had slipped as he tried to down-shift, nearly ripping the heel off his foot. The injury was serious and the rehabilitation and healing process a lengthy one.

(Photograph © BC Kagan 1979, 2021 — Used with permission)

The band would perform just twice more in 1980, once for a single song at an election party for their management, and the final time for a muted first decade celebration broadcast in Boston. At home, the band had been eclipsed by the likes of the resurgent J. Geils Band and emergent Cars, who'd go so far as to purchasing Intermedia Studios, and renaming it Syncro Sound. As 1980 drew to a close, Columbia issued "Aerosmith's Greatest Hits" in November, succinctly distilling the band's first decade down to just ten tracks in various forms. As Joey Kramer put it, "The best that we could do was to issue 'Greatest Hits' to fill the gap. We had nothing else to offer. We were done" ("Hit Hard").

Finally released on Nov. 15, 1979, "Night in the Ruts" was certified Gold by the RIAA on March 13, 1980 and Platinum on Oct. 28, 1994. It was certified Gold by the CRIA in Canada, for sales of 50,000 units, on Dec. 1, 1979. In the SoundScan era the album sold 82,370 units between 1991 and Feb. 2007. In the U.S., the album reached #14 (1/19/1980) with 19 weeks on the Billboard charts. The album charted for the same duration on Cashbox and reached #16 (1/12/1980). "Remember (Walking in the Sand)" had originally been a #5 hit on the Billboard Hot-100 charts in 1964 for the Shangri-Las, and while it wasn't a hit for the band — only scraping to #67 on Billboard singles chart — it did garner positive reviews as a stand out track from the album: "This Shangri-Las hit is given a hot metallic treatment by singer Steve Tyler, lead guitarist Joe Perry and the boys on the first single from the "Night In The Ruts" LP. Crackling with razor sharp guitar work and Tyler's slicing vocals, this is an AOR killer" (Cashbox, 12/22/1979). The positive review didn't help the single on the Cashbox charts with it languishing for five weeks in the 90s. It was likely an ill-conceived choice for the sole single off the album, a version by Louise Goffin having already charted in the Billboard Hot-100 at #43 in October 1979. No further singles were issued with the band's touring collapsing, though both "Three Mile Smile" and " No Surprise" received extensive airplay. The latter was one of two Aleks Rosenberg and John Fraker produced videos — they'd only established their partnership earlier that year but had done several clips for Columbia artists such as Janis Ian and the Laughing Dogs — the other being "Chiquita." The album's cover had been shot by Jim Shea at Griffith Park in Los Angeles, CA, a movie lot where Star Trek and Buck Rodgers were filmed. Featuring the band in 1920s costumes, the art had already been promotionally used for the "Chip Away the Stone" single in 1978, though the session did provide a unified session from which to source the album's packaging.

Assorted review excerpts:

"Aerosmith has been chipping away at the stone for a long time now and this album erases any doubt that the band was losing its sledgehammer-like edge. 'Night in the Ruts' is as blissfully loud and raunchy as any album in the past. New cuts like 'Chiquita' and the earth moving 'Cheese Cake' will guarantee that the stadiums will be full once again when these heavy metal kings decide to tour. A bluesy, ballsy package of 'sweet emotion" for AOR" (Cashbox, 11/24/1979).

"If hard driving raunch 'n' roll is your cup of tea, then this latest Aerosmith offering is for you. Relying once again on screaming guitar lines and unrelenting boogie beats, producer Gary Lyons pulls it together with a flair" (Record World, 11/24/1979).

"The first song on Aerosmith's seventy album is called 'No Surprize,' and that about sums up 'Night in the Ruts.' After some tentative attempts to expand its basic jock-rock sound with mandolins, banjos, and an occasional female backup vocal on its last studio record, 'Draw the Line,' Aerosmith returns to what it does best: playing America's crass, punkier version of the Rolling Stones... But the fact that the finest moments on 'Night in the Ruts' sound like inspired outtakes from 'Rocks' and 'Toys in the Attic' suggests that Aerosmith may be stuck in a hard-rock rut of its own. 'Cheese Cake,' 'Bone to Bone (Coney Island White Fish boy)' and 'No Suprize' are typical chain-saw rockers, Tyler howling like a wolf in heat while the guitars ricochet around him. 'Think About It,' an obscure Yardbirds B-side, is also rendered with a reverential bluster that doesn't cut the original, yet at least credits roots where credit is due.

So far, so-so, but the deviations from this norm are disastrous, if not in concept then in execution. Aerosmith's attempt to redo the old Shangri-Las weeper, 'Remember (Walking in the Sand),' is a regrettable example of stylistic indecision, sitting uncomfortably between the band's hard-rock attack and the song's original pseudo-Spectorian grandeur, with no small blame due Gary Lyons for his rather bland production. The one ballad here, Tyler's 'Mia,' is cloned from Aerosmith's 1975 hit, 'Dream On,' but all possible tension between the group's electricity and the acoustic guitar and piano is negated by a surprisingly lifeless performance that's as unsettling as it is unnecessary" (Rolling Stone #310, 2/7/1980).

"So here it is, the last Aerosmith album featuring the original line-up. Now that Joe Perry has left, this album will no doubt stand as the point of comparison for upcoming Aerosmith efforts. And what is there here to compare with? Well, it starts off rocking enough with 'No Surprize,' which is aptly titled since it is pure Aerosmith — hard rockin', slightly unintelligible, and nothing at all new. For a while Aerosmith were the biggest U.S. band of them all, even in the league of the biggest of British rockers like Queen and Led Zep. But whether this album will keep them in that slot remains to be seen. There is a great deal about this LP in sound in contents that is old hat. In fact, it's hard to believe that the band spent as much time and dinero as they're reported to have done in making this epic. They might well have done better by recording it all in a week. The thing that bothers us most about this album is that it seems to be hard to hear what's going on. Yes, there are big drums music and big guitars and a big voice, but the general effect on our hi-fi at least is mush. High level intense mush, but nothing we can walk away humming. More Tylenol music than anything new, exciting, or exciting and new. Is this how it all ends? All that big time ending in nothing more than a repeat, some sort of electronic indigestion? Well, yes, in a way" (Rock Scene, 5/1980).

August 1979 **Aerosmith CANCELLED
Knebworth House Grounds
Stevenage, Hertfordshire, England
Promoter: Frederick Bannister
Notes:
- Aerosmith had been invited to perform during the Aug. 4–11 event, which Led Zeppelin headlined two nights at, but withdrew due to the delays surrounding the recording of their studio album. This show would have formed part of a larger European tour.

November 2
Main Act Concert Club
Lynn, MA
Reported audience: (1,200 capacity)
Notes:
- Aerosmith's first show with new guitarist Jimmy Crespo, with the "Night in the Ruts" tour scheduled to start in Binghamton, NY the following month.

November 8 **CANCELLED
Coliseum
Charlotte, NC
Notes:
- This show had been cancelled by Sep. 21.

November 18 **CANCELLED
Tarrant County Convention Center
Ft. Worth, TX
Notes:
- Among a batch of dates announced in mid-October, this show had been cancelled by the second week of November, due to illnesses and other reasons. There were likely other dates from this initial touring itinerary, and a show at the International Amphitheater in Chicago on Oct. 3 had been announced in July.

November 28 **CANCELLED
Civic Center
Providence, RI
Promoter: Freefall Productions

December 5
Veterans Memorial Arena
Binghamton, NY
Promoter: Cedric Kushner / Magic City Productions
Other act(s): Scorpions
Reported audience: 7,200 **SOLD-OUT
Notes:
- First show of the "Night in the Ruts" tour which followed three day of final production rehearsals at the venue.
- From a local review: "Aerosmith, one of America's most popular hard-rock bands, opened its three-month national tour with a blast last night at the Broome County Veterans Memorial Arena. The arena was filled to capacity. The concert's 7,200 tickets — all general admission — had been sold out four weeks before the concert. A purple haze accompanied Aerosmith as the band opened its 90-minute set, and a well-designed stage show followed through the course of the evening. The group did a fine job performing a number of its past hits but managed to come off with a few misses. Aerosmith had spent the last three days setting up the

tour's premier show. The most effective number of the night was Aerosmith's 1975 top-ten hit, 'Dream On,' followed close behind by the encore, their well-arranged rendition of the Beatles song 'Come Together,' which the group performed in the film version of Sgt. Pepper's Lonely Hearts Club Band. Naturally, Aerosmith played quite a few songs from the latest album, 'Night in the Ruts.' Although cuts from this disc weren't all bad, it seemed that the audience preferred the band's earlier music. 'Reefer Head Woman' was a particularly weak number.

Crowd control at the arena seemed well-organized, with a standard contingent of 18 to 20 security men on duty. Earlier this week 11 people were killed at a rock concert in Cincinnati when the crowd rushed for the doors. Broome's arena is designed so concertgoers must walk up a long ramp, and police limit the number of people allowed onto the ramp at any given time. All the rock fans questioned at last night's concert said they doubted that dangerous crowding could occur while people were entering the Arena... Joe Perry, the group's original lead guitarist and music writer, recently left Aerosmith to form his own group. This is Aerosmith's first tour without Perry. He has been replaced by Jimmy Crespo; the former lead guitarist of a group called Flame. Last night Crespo's skill proved a sufficient substitute for Perry's, and listeners did not seem to notice much change in the quality of the music. The vitality of lead Singer Steven Tyler created a high energy level on stage, which Aerosmith managed to maintain all through the show... All in all, however, rock fans were thrilled by last night's concert, and showed it with the wild enthusiasm that Binghamton's young audiences are known for" (Binghamton Press and Sun-Bulletin, 12/6/1979).

December 6
Cumberland County Civic Center
Portland, ME

Other act(s): Scorpions
Reported audience: ~8,600 / 9,000 (95.56%)
Notes:
- If the previous night's show bespoke a successful start to the tour, the band's luck didn't hold for long. This show was abandoned when Steven passed out on stage during the fifth song, "Reefer Head Woman." According to tour manager, Henry Smith, Steven "had not been feeling well and was unable to keep food down" (Boston Globe, 12/7/1979) when he collapsed. Carried off stage by roadies, the show was abandoned, though it was soon rescheduled for Jan. 20.

December 8 **POSTPONED
Coliseum
Hampton, VA

Promoter: Entam, Ltd.
Other act(s): Mother's Finest, Scorpions
Reported audience: (13,800 capacity)
Notes:
- This show was postponed on Dec. 8, the result of Steven's collapse in Maine, and later rescheduled for Feb. 9. The date also would have been the first of the tour with R&B-Rock fusion Mother's Finest opening.

December 9 **POSTPONED
Civic Arena
Pittsburgh, PA

Promoter: Danny Kresky Enterprises
Other act(s): Mother's Finest, Scorpions
Reported audience: (15,000 capacity)
Notes:
- This show was postponed on Dec. 8, the result of Steven's collapse in Maine. It was rescheduled for Jan. 24.

December 12 **CANCELLED
Civic Coliseum
Knoxville, TN
Promoter: Entam, Ltd.
Other act(s): Mother's Finest, Scorpions
Reported audience: (7,200 capacity)

December 13 **POSTPONED
Augusta-Richmond Civic Center
Augusta, GA
Promoter: Beach Club Productions
Other act(s): Mother's Finest
Reported audience: (9,167 capacity)
Notes:
- Approximately 6,000 tickets had been sold for what would have been the first concert at the venue. The show was rescheduled for Feb. 14.

December 15 **POSTPONED
Coliseum
Greensboro, NC
Promoter: Entam, Ltd.
Other act(s): Mother's Finest, Scorpions
Reported audience: (13,500 capacity)
Notes:
- Nearly 6,000 tickets had been sold for this show, which was rescheduled for Feb. 8.
- While the Scorpions still appeared on many show advertisements, for this and shows listed afterwards, they had returned to Germany to continue work on their next album ("Animal Magnetism") and would not have performed.

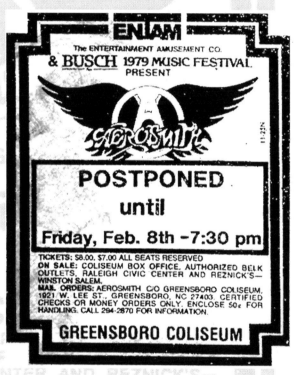

December 16 **POSTPONED
Coliseum
Charlotte, NC
Promoter: Kaleidoscope Concerts
Other act(s): Mother's Finest, .38 Special
Reported audience: (13,000 capacity)
Notes:
- This show was postponed until Jan. 27 with the promoter reporting that Steven had been hospitalized for hypertension. Original tickets were honored at the new date.

December 18
Omni
Atlanta, GA
Promoter: Alex Cooley, Inc.
Other act(s): Mother's Finest, The Miles Brothers
Reported audience: 15,000 **SOLD-OUT
Notes:
- The Miles Brothers Band was a local act (they became Miles Per Gallon / MPG) who regularly gigged with Mother's Finest.

- From a local review: "The house might have been full and the audience most receptive, but the members of Aerosmith probably don't think too much of Atlanta hospitality after their Tuesday night at the Omni. I mean, how polite is it to have a bunch of locals come onstage before the headliners and steal the show completely, as Atlanta-based Mother's Finest did to Aerosmith? ... Aerosmith seemed to be coasting on its audience's built-in good will. That audience, composed of numerous drunk and drugged teen-agers, responded loudly but almost mechanically to the same old heavy-metal riffs and lead singer Steven Tyler's well-worn (and second rate) imitation of Mick Jagger. The band played a cross section of its songs, with heavy emphasis on its new LP, 'Night in the Ruts.' If you like Aerosmith, you would have liked the show. Considering Aerosmith's past drawing power, it may be a sign of slippage on the group's part that promoters felt they had to add two other bands" (Atlanta Constitution, 12/19/1979).

December 19
Birmingham-Jefferson Civic Coliseum
Birmingham, AL

Promoter: Watermark Productions
Other act(s): Mother's Finest
Reported audience: (15,000 capacity)
Notes:
- Steven reportedly didn't perform "Dream On" at this show.

December 20 **CANCELLED
Fairgrounds Coliseum
Columbus, OH

Promoter: Sunshine Promotions
Notes:
- This show was cancelled by the Ohio Exposition Commission on Dec. 13, "In the interest of controlling the crowd and for safety's sake" (Dayton Journal Herald, 12/14/1979). Their view was that the general admission show posed a risk to patrons and there was no provision to convert the show to reserved seating. The promoter sued the administrators of the facility for cancelling the show, in light of the Who concert crush, first attempting to claim $50,000 in losses and then attempting to recover their costs for advertising and printing associated with the show. The show would have used general admission seating...

December 21 **CANCELLED
Riverfront Coliseum
Cincinnati, OH

Promoter: Electric Factory Concerts
Other act(s): Mother's Finest, Scorpions
Reported audience: (17,000 capacity)
Notes:
- Initially postponed by the promoter in the immediate aftermath of the Who concert tragedy.
- In the aftermath of the Who concert stampede, where 11 fans lost their lives, this show was cancelled while the future of the venue was being considered by authorities. The behavior of fans at general admission shows, where free-for-alls would often occur when a venue's doors opened and fans scrambled for the best possible standing position in front of the stage, was called into question and many venues started switching to reserved seating. For the promoters, the arrangement had often been one of

convenience: One price structure, no seating to be arranged, and greater capacity. Unfortunately, by the late-70s concert crushes had seen the general admission areas often become warzones with security beating back patrons from knocking down barriers or pressing forward, not to mention throwing bottles, fireworks, and other objects.

December 22 **TEMP HOLD-DATE
Louisville Gardens
Louisville, KY

Notes:
- In the initial run of dates announced in November, Dec. 5–30, this show appears to have been the only one not to have been booked.

December 22
International Amphitheater
Chicago, IL

Promoter: Celebration/Flipside Concerts
Other act(s): .38 Special, Mother's Finest
Reported audience: 9,450 / 11,513 (82.08%)
Reported gross: $98,280

December 23 **TEMP HOLD-DATE
Mid-South Coliseum
Memphis, TN

Reported audience: (12,500 capacity)
Notes:
- Variety's itinerary for the band published on Dec. 19, included this date as the final show prior to the holiday break.

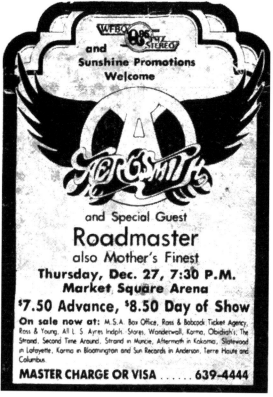

December 26
International Amphitheater
Chicago, IL

Promoter: Celebration/Flipside Concerts
Other act(s): .38 Special, Mother's Finest
Reported audience: 9,367 / 11,513 (81.36%)
Reported gross: $97,416

December 27
Market Square Arena
Indianapolis, IN

Promoter: Sunshine Promotions
Other act(s): Mother's Finest, Roadmaster
Reported audience: ~18,200 / 19,000 (95.79%)
Notes:
- 56 patrons were arrested during this show. For the second year running, readers of the Indianapolis News voted this show the worst concert of 1979... The show was, at the time, the final event hosted without reserved seating.
- From a local review: "Tyler and company roared into town for the fourth time in four years last night and for the fourth time more than 18,000 filled the hall. Which brings us to the most important question: Why? The answers surely will come via mail in the next week or so. Unlike respectable bands such as Kansas and Foreigner, who took Led Zeppelin's idea of the late '60s and polished it in the '70s, Aerosmith has failed to grow beyond its 1976 level. Tyler is still a poor imitation of the original white prancer, Mick Jagger, and

Aerosmith never has been able to surpass the talents of Zep, a group that has managed to keep up with the times. Last night's show had all the pitfalls of a hard rock concert — a stacked P.A. at the corners of the stage, overwhelming instrumentals, muddy vocals, and a shoddy stage presentation. Only decent opening sets from Mother's Finest and Roadmaster saved this show from a one-star rating, which is given to anyone who shows up on stage. Although the most ardent Aerosmith fan will probably disagree (because he and she were probably screaming so loud they could hear no one else), last night's crowd just wasn't into the show like an audience can be for high-energy concerts of this sort.

Perhaps the best example of this came when Tyler assumed the crowd was singing the chorus to 'Walk This Way.' Just as he does at all the shows when he gets to the chorus, Tyler turned the microphone to the audience to let it sing while he remained silent. The result? Silence. The crowd wasn't singing along, but it finally caught on and finished out its part. The song, one of the group's best recorded efforts, turned into one of the show's worst with Tyler and the band on two slightly varying tempos. Tyler's slower vocals finally caught up with the instrumentals. Tyler became so disgusted with the fellows at the sound board that he stopped in the middle of 'Same Old Song and Dance' and told the audience to pass the word back to the sound board to 'turn the (expletive deleted) drums up'"
(Indianapolis News, 12/28/1979).

December 29 **POSTPONED
Municipal Auditorium
Nashville, TN
Promoter: Sound 70 Presentations
Other act(s): Mother's Finest
Reported audience: (11,000 capacity)
Notes:
- This show was rescheduled for Jan. 30 in mid-December.

December 30 **POSTPONED
Mid-South Coliseum
Memphis, TN
Promoter: Mid-South Concerts
Other act(s): Mother's Finest
Reported audience: (12,000 capacity)
Notes:
- This show was rescheduled for Jan. 29.

1980

January 10, 1980
Le Forum de Montréal
Montreal, QC, Canada
Promoter: Donald K. Donald
Other act(s): Teaze
Reported audience: ~9,000 / 18,000 (50%)
Notes:
- From a local review: "With the dawn of the 80s, Aerosmith is on the comeback trail, touring in support of 'Night in the Ruts,' their first album in two years. The heavy metal revival hit the Forum last night and whether out of nostalgia or new-found appreciation for a dormant style — the concert bowl (about 9,000) was packed to the rafters... And Aerosmith was more than up to the task of satisfying the crowd's craving for roof-shaking boogie. Once Teaze had polished off a 45-minute warm-up set — devoted mainly to the screeched praises of Montreal, its food, and its women — Aerosmith got down to the serious business of

reestablishing their reputation as live killers. The show began, appropriately, with 'Back in the Saddle Again,' a rousing rocker that lead singer Steve Tyler belted out in the style that has endeared him to a generation of high school girls. Prancing around the stage, straddling the mike stand, pouting, and sneering in the best Mick Jagger tradition, Tyler is the consummate rock star, and the four-man group provides thunderous support for his high-energy performance.

Tyler describes Aerosmith's current style as 'the raw-guts, grab-everything sound — the sound of blood pumping through our veins.' While it may read like Mickey Spillane is writing in his material, Tyler's is an apt description of the roaring sound that set blood to pumping at a feverish pace among the Forum faithful. Aerosmith's set was a nicely-balanced combination of material off the new album and certified group classics like 'Walk this Way' and 'Dream On' — both of which drew immediate, standing-O recognition. With the addition of lead guitarist Jimmy Crespo, who replaced Joe Perry just after 'Ruts' was released, Aerosmith has strengthened its sound" (Montreal Gazette, 1/11/1980).

January 11
Maple Leaf Gardens
Toronto, ON, Canada

Other act(s): Mother's Finest
Reported audience: (18,815 capacity)
Notes:
- From a local review: "When Aerosmith played in Toronto last summer, they closed that mega-noise heavy metal music festival at Exhibition Stadium. It was generally agreed by critics and fans alike that Aerosmith's performance was something of an anti-climax after Ted Nugent's 90-minute sonic barrage. All of which makes the fact that Aerosmith was able to fill Maple Leaf Gardens Friday night, for what was basically just another go-round of last summer's show, all the more surprising. One suspects that it was more the dearth of major rock events over the last two months which filled the hall, than any real desire on the part of 20,000 of the city's noise junkies to see this outfit again. Aerosmith have made a pretty lucrative career out of posing as a poor man's Rolling Stones. The fact that lead vocalist Steve Tyler bears more than a minor resemblance to Mick Jagger has been parlayed, over the years, into an out and out mimicry of The Stones in virtually every aspect of the band's performance. Tyler even goes so far as to drape himself and the microphone in long scarves, a prop that is as identifiable with Jagger as the pouting lips and hippy-hippy shake.

There are myriad reasons why Aerosmith will probably be forgotten two days after the group disbands. The main one is the oppressive sameness of their material. After opening with a thundering (but then, they were all thundering) version of their 'Back In The Saddle Again,' the band slugged through about a half dozen more similar sounding heavy metal dirges before coming back down to melody with 'Walk This Way.' It is No Surprize that the only songs with which the band has had any real success, 'Dream On' and their reworking of the Shangri-Las' old hit 'Walking in The Sand,' are numbers which shy away from their basic formula. In all fairness, however, the young audience ate it all up from the outset. Aerosmith provided the sort of raw and energetic rock work-out that the crowd had come for, and they in turn responded in the accepted manner — screaming until hoarse, singeing their little fingers with disposable lighters — and all the rest of the responses which make attending over-loud rock concerts so much fun" (Toronto Globe & Mail, 1/12/1980).

January 13
Nassau Coliseum

Uniondale, NY
Promoter: Mark Puma
Other act(s): Mother's Finest
Reported audience: ~15,000 / 16,500 (90.91%)
Set list: Back in the Saddle / Mama Kin / I Wanna Know Why / Big Ten Inch Record / Three Mile Smile / Reefer Head Woman / Bone to Bone / Walk this Way / Dream On / Rats in the Cellar / No Surprize / Remember (Walking in the Sand) / Lord of the Thighs / Same Old Song and Dance / Milk Cow Blues / Toys in the Attic / Come Together / Train Kept a Rollin
Notes:
- The night following this show Tom and Steven recorded their radio appearance on the Robert Klein hour. Other guests on the episode included Beatles producer George Martin and Desmond Child & Rouge.
- From a mainstream review: "Aerosmith fans turned out Jan. 13, 19,000 strong pledging allegiance to the banner behind their notoriously hard-rocking favorite. Smart scheduling placed the band's only metropolitan area appearance in suburbia, homeland of its loyal teen following. Fans got what they paid to hear — sound and fury in a near non-stop adrenalin rush. The classic 'Dream On' served as a breather, but the majority of the 14 songs exploded with Joey Kramer's drum muscle and the guitar work of Brad Whitford and Jimmy Crespo. Crespo is the new member of the group and did not waste time commanding the spotlight. Rocketing confidently through Aerosmith hits, he won favor with his aggressive use of straight and slide stylings, and electronic shadings that filled the hall. The band's weak point was in its visual impression, of which it made little. Steve Tyler's razor-edged vocals are appropriate for the music, but his skip-kick, mike-twirling mannerisms hardly varied and wore thin early on. The band also uses no props, except for two alternating backdrops in need of an overhaul. Mandatory in the 90-minute set were barnstorming versions of 'Walk this Way' and signature piece 'Train Kept A-Rolling,' while radioactive rocker 'Three Mile Smile' introduced the band's new Columbia album to the crowd. Only cover versions of 'Remember (Walking in the Sand)' and 'Come Together' were exercises in slow motion flatulence, but fans didn't seem to mind" (Billboard, 2/2/1980).
- From an industry review: "Aerosmith's brand of lavish kilowatt rock is made for the masses, and the group could do no wrong for an enthusiastic but orderly crowd of over 15,000, mostly teenage admirers. Following the departure of founding member Joe Perry to pursue a solo career, Aerosmith is making its first tour with new lead guitarist Jimmy Crespo, formerly of Flame. The fans' acceptance of Crespo was immediate and unanimous, but the lion's share of their adulation was reserved for the androgynous heroics of lead vocalist Steve Tyler. Sporting a flowing red shaman's robe over a striped yellow and black jester's suit, Tyler was the focal point throughout the show — a study in nasty insouciance. The band opened with 'I Wanna Know Why,' then got the crowd jumping with 'Big Ten Inch Record.' Crespo took his first solo on the exotic B.C. Rich flying cutaway guitar he used throughout most of the evening, giving the crowd a taste of things to come with an intense burst of workmanlike overdrive.

Rhythm guitarist Brad Whitford transmitted a barrage of thick chord textures with his Les Paul as the two guitarists kept throwing smoke through 'Coney Island Whitefish Boy.' Crespo was on time with the rolling signature lick on 'Walk this Way,' displaying the glamorous physicality essential to the Aerosmith format. The arena went ecstatic for 'Dream On' backed by shimmering drum dynamics from Joey Kramer. Tyler then led the boys into the propulsive, crowd-pleasing twelve-bar 'Rats in the Cellar,' before bringing on guest guitarist Richard Supa for a rousing 'Chip Away.' Milking his raspy falsetto and a variety of vamping, mike-twirling poses, Tyler stirred up a frenzy on 'No Surprize' and 'Same Old Song and Dance,' while 'Lord of the Thighs' featured hot soloing by Whitford and crying slide work from Crespo on a vintage Stratocaster" (Cashbox, 2/9/1980).
- An AUD recording circulates from this show.

January 15
Richfield Coliseum
Richfield (Cleveland), OH
Promoter: Belkin Productions
Other act(s): Mother's Finest, Rockets
Reported audience: (17,500 capacity)

Notes:
- From a local review: "Three hard-rock acts stormed into the Coliseum Tuesday night, decibels flying, for the first major rock 'n' roll concert of 1980... Aerosmith's performers were, as usual, battling their own worst problem: themselves. This time they didn't quite defeat themselves totally... In its show Tuesday, the band didn't butcher its best works with apathy, nor did its members completely turn their backs on the audience. But it didn't play with the sparkle and panache that a good hard-rock band needs to drive such basic music home. Lead vocalist Steve Tyler, rock's best-known Mick Jagger lookalike, still shuffles around stiffly in outfits resembling hand painted long underwear, looking vague and listless. He always appears to be halfheartedly looking for the key to the audience's hearts. On the other hand, the other members of the group — drummer Joey Kramer, bassist Tom Hamilton and guitarists Brad Whitford and Jimmy Crespo (the latter replacing Joe Perry who recently departed) — seem far more into playing, and playing as a living unit, than they have previously. They are more active, projecting their solos into the audience instead of standing off to the side looking bored, as they've been known to do.

Musically, the group is over-indulging in solo breaks. Nearly every number comes to resemble those long bluesy-rock jams of 1969, where each member plays a long solo in each and every song. I suppose it's great if you're stoned, and if the individual members of the band are all effective players, but this music should have a driving edge. Instead, the long solos, together with the floppy disinterested antics of Tyler, give the music a strangely flat feel. The audience seemed to be reacting less to peaks in the music than to artificial stimuli (such as Tyler moving toward their side of the stage). Aerosmith has always been a band of good ideas which it has had either no energy or no inclination to spin out into a dynamic full-length show. It is a band of fits and starts rather than a totality. This year at least it was mildly entertaining" (Plain Dealer, 1/17/1980).

January 17
Memorial Auditorium
Buffalo, NY
Promoter: Harvey & Corkey Productions
Other act(s): Mother's Finest, Talas
Reported audience: (17,827 capacity)
Reported gross: $80,000
Set list: Back in the Saddle / Mama Kin / I Wanna Know Why / Big Ten Inch Record / Three Mile Smile / Reefer Head Woman / Walk this Way / Dream On / Rats in the Cellar / No Surprize / Remember (Walking in the Sand) / Lord of the Thighs / Same Old Song and Dance / Milk Cow Blues / Toys in the Attic / Come Together / Train Kept A Rollin'
Notes:
- An AUD recording circulates from this show. Presumably, it's missing the final two songs from the set.

January 18
Coliseum
Springfield, MA
Promoter: Cross County Concerts
Other act(s): Mother's Finest
Reported audience: 9,200 **SOLD-OUT

Reported gross: $74,775
Notes:
- From a local review: "The big question prior to Friday's Aerosmith concert at the Civic Center was: What effect would new guitarist Jimmy Crespo have on the band and its performance? After Smith's latest album, 'Night in the Ruts' was recorded, founding member Joe Perry started his own band, the Joe Perry Project, Crespo, ex-Flame lead guitarist, filled in as a full-fledged member of the band. Many felt Perry was the driving force behind Aerosmith, and that the relatively unknown Crespo couldn't possibly measure up. But judging from the band's show, Crespo should have no problem fitting in, musically or with the fans. Jimmy's lead guitar on the Aerosmith standards was above par, but he really won over the sold-out crowd of 9,500 when the band let him take off on his own during an extended version of 'Lord of the Thighs.' All doubts about him were dashed as he flew into a solo, complete with guitar-wrenching special effects. Crespo also knew when to take the back seat, letting second guitarist Brad Whitford take the spotlight several times...

Also on stage was keyboardist Richard Supa, who joined the band for their three-month cross country tour. Supa also played guitar on several songs. One of the biggest raps against Aerosmith is the poor quality of its live show. While Tyler may be one of the most exiting performers around, many believe they fail to capture the sound of their studio albums by playing much too loud and ruining whatever subtlety their songs may have. These beliefs were backed up by the 1978 double 'Live Bootleg' package: an album that sold well but had questionable recording quality. The 1980 edition of Aerosmith seems to have changed for the better. Ninety percent of the songs played Friday were faithful to the studio cuts, especially 'Mama Kin,' 'Toys in the Attic,' 'Same Old Song and Dance' and their first real hit, 'Dream On.' Tyler's harp-playing talents were showcased on 'Big Ten Inch' and 'Woman of the World,' and extended his cloth-draped microphone into the crowd during parts of 'Wake this Way.' Songs from the new album included 'No Surprize,' the bluesy 'Reefer Headed Woman' and a killer version of the hit single 'Walking in the Sand'" (Springfield Union, 1/22/1980).

January 20
Cumberland County Civic Center
Portland, ME
Other act(s): Mother's Finest
Reported audience: (9,000 capacity)
Notes:
- The make-up date for the aborted Dec. 16 concert.

January 22
Onondaga County War Memorial
Syracuse, NY
Promoter: Mark Puma / Cedric Kushner
Other act(s): Mother's Finest
Reported audience: ~6,000 / 8,400 (71.43%)
Notes:
- From a local review: "Rock 'n' rollers Aerosmith, who played to just under 6,000 wildly cheering fans Tuesday night at the War Memorial, are a well-intentioned and very hard-working band with a glaring weakness — uneven material. Even with new lead guitarist Jimmy Crespo, who replaced Joe Perry when he left for a solo career, Aerosmith seems destined to remain the poor man's Led Zeppelin unless Steven Tyler and company can more consistently come up with engaging numbers like 1975's 'Dream On' and 1976's 'Walk this Way.' Aerosmith's strengths lie in a driving rhythm section, Tyler's often-arresting vocals and a seemingly endless supply of energy. The band sounds at its best when doing straight-ahead blues. But too frequently the band settles for an all-too-simple groove that gets plain boring. It would be nice to hear the band do more slow numbers and songs with more dramatic tempo changes. That almost certainly would gain the players the recognition they have unjustly been denied by those who have written Aerosmith off as simply an undistinguished heavy-metal group capable of little more than pulsating volume. Much to their credit, Aerosmith has been touring almost constantly since the band formed in New Hampshire in summer 1970. As a result, Tyler and the players work as if they can anticipate each other's moves and thoughts and

it makes for exciting showmanship. But without topnotch material, flash, instrumental proficiency, and energy can only go so far" (Syracuse Post Standard, 1/23/1980).

January 23 **CANCELLED
Boston Garden
Boston, MA

Notes:
- Announced on Jan. 18, the show was pulled from the schedule the following day, apparently an error of the band's PR company, Rogers & Cowan. However, there was initially an intention to book a date at the venue later in the tour.

January 24
Civic Arena
Pittsburgh, PA

Promoter: Danny Kresky Enterprises
Other act(s): Mother's Finest
Reported audience: (15,000 capacity)
Set list: Back in the Saddle / Mama Kin / I Wanna Know Why / Big Ten Inch Record / Three Mile Smile / Reefer Head Woman / Bone to Bone / Walk this Way / Dream On / No Surprize / Remember (Walking in the Sand) / Lord of the Thighs / Same Old Song and Dance / Milk Cow Blues / Toys in the Attic / Come Together / Train Kept A Rollin'
Notes:
- An AUD recording circulates from this show.

January 25
Capital Centre
Landover (Largo), MD

Promoter: Cellar Door Productions
Other act(s): Mother's Finest, .38 Special
Reported audience: (17,561 capacity)
Set list: Back in the Saddle / Mama Kin / I Wanna Know Why / Big Ten Inch Record / Three Mile Smile / Reefer Head Woman / Bone to Bone / Walk this Way / Dream On / Rats in the Cellar / Get the Lead Out / Remember (Walking in the Sand) / Lord of the Thighs / Same Old Song and Dance / Milk Cow Blues / Toys in the Attic / Come Together / Train Kept A Rollin'
Notes:
- On this evening, the previously taped appearance of Steven and Tom on the Robert Klein Hour aired. 24 patrons were arrested during the show as police cracked down on drug offences.
- From a local review: "It was hard rock with a box-your-ear wallop for fans who turned out to hear Aerosmith at last night's Capital Centre concert. In the first leg of a world-wide tour, Aerosmith played with unrelenting vengeance while lead singer Steven Tyler sang with the shrieking brutality of a sadist — and the thought was inescapable that maybe most of the audience who'd come to hear them were masochists. As he screamed himself hoarse Tyler created a rather bizarre vision on stage. His red Japanese kimono worn over a striped, yellow-black-and-red bodysuit, and his frizzy hair, lent a fiendish air to his vocals. Except for the blues number 'Reefer Headed Woman' and The Beatles' 'Come Together' the sound emanating from stage was undistinguished. Their music embodied the worst of rock 'n' roll excesses deafening decibels, imitative chording, and unimaginative rhythms. Aerosmith insists on oral overload — the result of which was more often noise than music last night" (Evening Star, 1/26/1980).
- From another local review: "As long there is a thing called rock 'n' roll there will be groups like Aerosmith bent on pushing the fundamental rhythms of the music to the limit. Sometimes that approach demands

more stamina than imagination — not just from the musicians but from the audience as well. Nonetheless, last night at the Capital Centre Aerosmith managed to focus on the primitive power of rock without falling prey to its excesses. With the departure of lead guitarist Joe Perry, Aerosmith now relies more than ever on vocalist Steven Tyler to keep things moving. On a visual level Tyler does that as well as anyone. Dressed in a Jagger-esque body suit and a loose-fitting robe, he pranced around the stage twirling his microphone stand as if it were a baton and taunting the crowd with his spastic gestures. Although he was in good voice throughout, Tyler was most effective on older material like the manic 'Toys in the Attic' and the softer 'Dream On.' The one exception — the Shangri-La's' 'Remember Walking in the Sand' — was a vast improvement over the group's recent recording" (Washington Post, 1/26/1980).

- Pro-shot video footage and an SBD circulate of nearly the full show.

January 27
Coliseum
Charlotte, NC

Promoter: Kaleidoscope Concerts
Other act(s): Mother's Finest, .38 Special
Reported audience: (13,000 capacity)
Partial set list: Back in the Saddle / Big Ten Inch Record / Bone to Bone / Walk this Way / Rats in the Cellar / Lord of the Thighs / Same Old Song and Dance / Milk Cow Blues / Toys in the Attic / Train Kept A Rollin'
Notes:
- Three teens returning home from the show were killed in an automobile accident with two other passengers being left seriously injured.
- From a local review: "For once, the featured act didn't steal the hearts and minds of the audience. Aerosmith had neither the material nor the talent... The whole concert was an anachronism. I was reminded of the early '70s, the height of the commercial popularity of rock music, when there were so many acts touring together that you could guarantee one loser out of every two or three performances. Tonight, the booby prize was Aerosmith's" (Charlotte Observer, 1/28/1980).
- A chopped up AUD partial recording circulates from this show, but it offers the first taste of Jimmy Crespo and the band in flight.

January 29
Mid-South Coliseum
Memphis, TN

Promoter: Mid-South Concerts
Other act(s): Mother's Finest
Reported audience: 7,894 / 12,000 (65.78%)
Reported gross: $61,133

January 30
Municipal Auditorium
Nashville, TN

Promoter: Sound 70 Presentations
Other act(s): Mother's Finest, .38 Special

Reported audience: (7,000 capacity)
Notes:
- From a local review: "The worst weather of this winter couldn't keep thousands of young fans away from an evening of hard rock music — headlined by Aerosmith — Wednesday night in Municipal Auditorium. By show time, the only seats left were those to the side and rear of the stage where the view was partially blocked by banks of speakers. As usual, 1,000 or so stood on the auditorium floor... While the set was being changed for Aerosmith, many in the audience moved from their seats down to the floor. Their excitement grew as black curtains were drawn around the stage and shrieking electronic sounds were heard. The curtains were pulled back with the crash of Aerosmith's first chord. And there they were — five guys (plus a keyboard player for the tour) standing there, playing very loudly. The volume level was quite a bit higher than that of the two opening acts, and it made Aerosmith seem (according to crowd response) a much more powerful band — when they were at that point only louder.

The group's four musicians performed without very much of the standard rock posing, so the focus of attention was usually on lead singer Steven Tyler. Dressed in geometrically patterned black and red tights, a loose-fitting shirt and a frizzed hairdo, Tyler screamed and jumped around and had his own affair with his mike stand. (Tyler's had black and red ribbons hanging from it for a stand-o'-nine-tails effect.) In calmer moments ('calm' is relative; there is nothing calm about this group), Tyler showed that he does have a good, strong, unaffected voice and that he is perfectly able to hit any note right on pitch throughout his wide range. The band, too, showed some abilities that weren't immediately evident. Their harmony singing was clear and tight, and (though the volume covered this up) they showed a good feel for dynamics. Those are qualities that distinguish Aerosmith from bands who might play just as loud and just as hard. That's why their records sell. And that's why, to Wednesday night's audience, the bad weather and the two-hour-plus wait for Aerosmith were only minor inconveniences" (Tennessean, 2/1/1980).

February 2
Sportatorium
Hollywood, FL

Promoter: Cellar Door Productions
Other act(s): Mother's Finest
Reported audience: ~12,000 / 17,400 (68.97%)
Notes:
- From a local review: "Now, a few words about a joke called Aerosmith. This is as worthless a bunch of dinosaurs as ever roamed a concert stage. Aerosmith is an absolutely awful band with nothing to offer but volume. The really pitiful part is that their fans swallow this narcissistic tripe. You have to feel sorry for a generation of fans that don't know when they're being duped by a gaggle of no-talents. Having observed this farce long enough, I walked out after four songs. As for Mother's Finest, they've succeeded in becoming a top-flight opening act for superstar shows but haven't developed enough appeal to win stardom in their own right. I'm glad they want to rock, but they needn't follow such tasteless examples as Aerosmith when Sly Stone's individualism seems so much more appropriate. The group may enjoy the exposure they get at superstar gigs but playing to 12,000 Aerosmith fans is about as artistically important as entertaining a pile of bricks" (Fort Lauderdale News, 2/8/1980).

February 3
Civic Center
Lakeland, FL

Promoter: Cellar Door Productions
Other act(s): Mother's Finest
Reported audience: (10,000 capacity)
Notes:
- This show ended up being the final date at the attempted second leg of the tour.
- From a mainstream review: "Sometimes a band can go through crucial personnel changes and make a hit of it or at least hold its own. A lot of times, though, the band is mortally wounded; unable to capture the

magic and power of its firmer lineup, the group fades into obscurity with saddening attempts to recapture a lost audience. So, what is to become of Aerosmith? After witnessing the bad boys from New Hampshire play their first Bay area gig without the aid of guitarist Joe Perry, Aerosmith seems to be destined to fade from headlining status. Crowd response was thunderous at Lakeland Civic Center Sunday night when the black curtains surrounding the stage rose slowly to reveal screamer Steve Tyler hunched over and leaning on his scarf-draped microphone stand for support. Hair falling down in his face, Tyler screeched the opening lyrics for Aerosmith's thud-rocking single, 'Back in the Saddle.' If anything, Tyler, and crew were insecure in the saddle, and during the show the band rode unsurely. Although aided by lead-guitarist Jim Crespo (ex of Flame), Tyler seemed tired, and repeated efforts by him to crank up the onstage activity seemed to exhaust him. The prevailing rumor being circulated Sunday night was that the gypsy-like Tyler was suffering from a cold and, to his credit, his voice sounded in usual form except he did appear to shy away from the high notes.

Shimmying, strutting, and marching across stage, Tyler tried his best to help the audience forget that the ever-smiling Crespo was not the usually snarling Perry. Crespo is a competent guitarist — although no virtuosity was ever required for an Aerosmith tune — but he looked bewildered when Tyler would crook his finger and asked Crespo to join him at the microphone for the band's standard Jagger-Richard rip-off. It just didn't work without Perry. While the rest of the group enjoys a relative anonymity, the figureheads of Aerosmith were the departed Perry (reportedly working-on his own band) and the sometimes-tiresome Tyler. So now, with one-half of the legend gone, Aerosmith has taken on a new personality. Most of the spunk and decadence the group supposedly stood for have evaporated, leaving residual boredom and repetitiveness. The show was a live version of Aerosmith's greatest hits performed half-heartedly. 'Dream On,' the Led Zeppelin-like single that first brought Aerosmith to fame, was watered down to a slower version, minus the hard-driving ending. Making 'Dream On' a ballad relieves the repetition, but without the power, the song loses its punch. If the band is in trouble, the final blow is still far off; the capacity crowd in the center loved the band as if it still had Perry snarling around his power chords. But Aerosmith's future — if it is to have one — must be in developing a new and powerful personality without relying on the charisma and sex appeal of Steve Tyler" (Tampa Tribune, 2/5/83).

February 6 **CANCELLED
Riverside Centroplex
Baton Rouge, LA
Promoter: Beaver Productions
Other act(s): Mother's Finest
Notes:
- Due to Steven Tyler's illness, patrons were only given 4 hours' notice of the cancellation of this show. The remaining dates of the tour were cancelled the following day. At the time, a piece on the band was appearing on the AP newswire under the ironic headline, "Aerosmith is still happening" ...

February 8 **CANCELLED
Coliseum
Greensboro, NC
Promoter: Entam, Ltd.
Other act(s): Mother's Finest
Reported audience: (13,500 capacity)
Notes:

- 6,000 tickets had been sold by the time this show was cancelled on Feb. 7, though Phil Lashinsky, the promoter, heard of the band's cancellation through the local press first — the band's agents had reportedly told him on Feb. 6 that the show would go ahead despite the issues that lead to the initial postponement in Baton Rouge.

February 9 **CANCELLED
Coliseum
Hampton, VA
Promoter: Entam, Ltd.
Other act(s): Mother's Finest
Reported audience: (14,000 capacity)

February 14 **CANCELLED
Augusta-Richmond Civic Center
Augusta, GA
Promoter: Beach Club Promotions
Other act(s): Mother's Finest
Reported audience: (9,000 capacity)
Notes:
- This show was also cancelled on Feb. 7 with ticket holders being offered refunds or exchanges for the Nantucket/Molly Hatchet/.38 Special show on Feb. 28.

February 18 **CANCELLED
Memorial Coliseum
Corpus Christi, TX

February 28 **CANCELLED
MECCA Arena
Milwaukee, WI
Notes:
- There would have been additional dates scheduled that were affected by the tour cancellation.

April 20 **TWO SETS
Speaks Island Park
Island Park, NY
Promoter: Mark Puma Presents
Set list: Back in the Saddle / Mama Kin / I Wanna Know Why / Big Ten Inch Record / Dream On / Three Mile Smile / Reefer Head Woman / Bone to Bone // Rats in the Cellar / Remember (Walking in the Sand) / Walk this Way / Lord of the Thighs / Same Old Song and Dance / Milk Cow Blues / Toys in the Attic / Train Kept A Rollin'
Notes:
- While the dates of this "Mystery Club Tour" were announced in advance the venues were kept secret until the last moment. The night prior to this show Steven attended the T.J. Martell Leukemia Research Foundation dinner at the Waldorf-Astoria's Grand Ballroom. The 1,500 in attendance were present to honor Clive Davis, then president of Arista Records, who was receiving the 1980 Humanitarian Award and raise money for the charity.
- "Profiles in Rock," a 30-minute rockumentary segment produced by Watermark, aired on radio stations, Apr. 12-13. Shows were written and produced by Bert Kleinman.
- An AUD recording circulates from this show.

April 22
Club Detroit
Port Chester, NY
Promoter: Mark Puma Presents
Set list: Back in the Saddle / Mama Kin / I Wanna Know Why / Big Ten Inch Record / Dream On / Three Mile Smile / Reefer Head Woman / Rats in the Cellar / Remember (Walking in the Sand) / Lick and a Promise / Walk this Way / Lord of the Thighs / Same Old Song and Dance / Milk Cow Blues / Toys in the Attic
Notes:
- Sometimes confused as being in Boston, the club was located on Boston Post Road.
- G.D Praetorius has described this tour as the toughest he worked with the band: "In the clubs you weren't dealing with professionals, to put it mildly, and the bad situation that you had to make the best of was only a matter of degree, from a three-flight-of stairs load in coked-up club owner accusing Tyler of stealing their mirror to goombahs not wanting to pay the band if not beat the shit out of them" (Classic Rock Revisited).
- An AUD recording circulates from this show.

April 27
Fountain Casino
Aberdeen, NJ
Promoter: Mark Puma Presents
Other act(s): James Montgomery
Reported audience: 2,308 / 3,000 (76.93%)
Reported gross: $20,772

April 28
Soap Factory
Palisades Park, NJ
Promoter: Mark Puma Presents

May 2
St. Louis, MO

May 3
Kansas City, MO

May 6
Denver, CO

May 8
Long Beach, CA

May 9
San Diego, CA

May 13 **TEMP HOLD-DATE
Cow Palace
Daly City (San Francisco), CA

May 16 **TEMP HOLD-DATE
Seattle, WA

May 17 **TEMP HOLD-DATE
Portland, OR
Notes:
- Dates for May 2–17 were listed in the May 13 issue of Circus Magazine.

June 3
Emerald City
Cherry Hill, NJ
Notes:
- Not so subtly promoted in the local press, apart from ads offering tickets: "On Tuesday, however, Aerosmith will be performing in the area — at a club where attendees 'must be 19 or over' according to information passed on WMMR. The radio station is promoting the event as 'The Aerosmith Mystery Concert,' and sooner or later will get around to naming the exact location. I figure it's got to be a South Jersey club where liquor is served, and rock names are regularly featured. Somewhere over the rainbow" (Philadelphia Daily News, 5/30/1980).

June 7
Mr. C's Rock Palace
Lowell, MA

June 8
Uncle Sam's
Nantasket, MA
Promoter: Frank Petrella
Reported audience: 1,300 **SOLD-OUT
Notes:
- From a local review: "This time, the mystery wasn't who but where. Two years ago, Aerosmith 'sneaked' into the Paradise under the pseudonym of Dr. J. Jones and the Interns. Last weekend they went back to the local club circuit — two months before embarking upon a national stadia tour — under their own name. The catch was that the venues were kept secret until the tickets went on sale. This proved to be little problem — and maybe even an enticement — for the 1,300 or so people who packed Uncle Sam's Sunday night. Circus-like stadium shows don't allow for much intimacy. Clubs, however, provide the opportunity to communicate at close range. It's a challenge to get involved with the audience, but Aerosmith sidestepped it by reverting to larger-than-life star strutting and tired gambits such as which-side-can-clap- louder battles. Despite the potential for interaction, Aerosmith remained on a hard-rock pedestal, figuring their aura would overwhelm. But rock 'n' roll is not about hero worship — it's establishing an electric rapport, it's breaking down barriers, it's making the moment all that matters.

Even though Aerosmith are preparing to record their eighth album, they didn't work in any new material. It was the same old song and dance Sunday night. Aerosmith dished out the steamroller rock and tried to flatten the faithful with decibel overkill. A bottom-heavy mix frequently overcame Steven Tyler's cat-screech vocals, making the band's ponderous rhythmic lockstep the prime musical feature. Attempts to boogie ('Big 10-Inch Record') got bogged down and the hard blues ('Reefer Headed Woman') were leaden and uninvolving. The lead guitarist is a key figure in any hard-rock outfit — it's Ted Nugent's technical prowess that liberates his bone-crunching music. Aerosmith is, of course, in a transitional period as they work in ex-Flame ax man Jimmy Crespo (replacing former co-leader Joe Perry who left last fall). Crespo did not play a prominent or convincing part Sunday. As front man, Tyler did his best to involve him, but Crespo's lead lines were often buried in the thumping rhythm; the solos, when he took them ('Train Kept A Rollin''), mostly led to a dead end" (Boston Globe, 6/11/1980).

June 11, 12
Stage West
West Hartford, CT
Other act(s): Kicks
Set list: Back in the Saddle / Big Ten Inch Record / Three Mile Smile / Reefer Head Woman / Dream On / Lick and a Promise / Walk this Way / Milk Cow Blues / Rats in the Cellar / Toys in the Attic / Train Kept A Rollin'
Notes:
- The second night's show was recorded by Criteria Recording Studios' mobile unit for King Biscuit Flower Hour by engineer Steve Klein with Felix Pappalardi producing. The edited version of the show was broadcast on June 29. Somewhat embarrassingly, a swear word by Steven was left unedited at 2:08 of "Dream On," forcing DIR Broadcasting to include a notice with distribution copies of the show, warning radio stations.

July 13 **CANCELLED
Victoria, BC, Canada
Promoter: David Krenbrink
Other act(S): Streetheart, Doug & The Slugs, Roxlyde, Paachena
Notes:
- This planned 10-hour festival was cancelled when local authorities objected to the event, having not been consulted by the promoter prior to its announcement. The band was essentially on hiatus at the time, and any hopes for additional activities during 1980 would come to a screeching halt the following month. Steven's moped accident was more serious than suggested by Columbia Records, who noted that his injuries were minor, though he remained hospitalized at the New London Hospital a week after the August 18th accident. Press reports indicated that Steven had hit a tree while riding a mini-bike with 21-year-old passenger Kathleen Bickford, who also suffered minor injuries.

November 3
Privates
Manhattan, NY
Promoter: Contemporary Communications Corp.
Other act(s): Humble Pie, Don McLean, Richie Havens, Felix Cavaliere, Elliott Murphy, Shirts
Reported audience: (800 capacity)
Set list: Come Together
- This club was owned by Aerosmith's management, Leber-Krebs... They had started booking live acts in the upstairs ballroom with Humble Pie on Oct. 9–10. Aerosmith had been expected to make a surprise guest appearance under their "Dr. Jones & The Interns" guise. A week following this performance the band's first U.S. compilation, "Greatest Hits," was released.
- "America Live" was a nonpartisan "get out and vote" show with Steven still wearing his foot-cast. Aerosmith closed the 90-minute show broadcast on AOR radio stations. Each act on the bill performed a single song. The broadcast was intended to later be released as an album.

December 3
Boston-Boston
Boston, MA
Promoter: Patrick Lyons
Reported audience: (1,200 capacity)
Set list: Rats in the Cellar / Walkin' the Dog / Lord of the Thighs / Three Mile Smile / Reefer Head Woman / Mother Popcorn / Think About It / Seasons of Wither / I Wanna Know Why / Big Ten Inch Record / Walk this Way / Lick and a Promise / Milk Cow Blues / Come Together / Train Kept A Rollin'
Notes:

344 | Aerosmith on Tour, 1973-85

- This performance was broadcast as Starfleet Radio Network celebration of Aerosmith's first decade, broadcast locally on WCOZ at 11pm. As a result, an SBD circulates from the show. This venue later became the House of Blues, and Aerosmith opened their Mama Kin Music Hall nearby at #36.
- Some archives note a Dec. 1 show at the Metro, however, Boston's Metro, at this same address (15 Lansdowne St.), didn't open until Feb. 1981...

(Photograph © BC Kagan 1979, 2021 — Used with permission)

1979 - Right in the Nuts

1980 - Aerosmith's Greatest Hits

U.S. Release Details:
CBS/Columbia FC/FCT/FCA-36865 (Nov. 11, 1980)
CBS/Columbia CK-36865 (1986, CD Issue)
Columbia/SME CK/CT-57367 (Sep. 7, 1993 — 20-bit SBM digital remaster)
Columbia/SME 19075846981 (2014, 140g LP reissue)
Columbia/SME 19075977671 (2019, Wal-Mart white vinyl LP reissue)

Tracks:
A1. Dream On
(4:28) — Steven Tyler
A2. Same Old Song and Dance (Edit)
(3:04) — Steven Tyler / Joe Perry
A3. Sweet Emotion (Edit)
(3:15) — Steven Tyler / Tom Hamilton
A4. Walk this Way (Edit)
(3:33) — Steven Tyler / Joe Perry
A5. Last Child
(3:28) — Steven Tyler, Brad Whitford

B1. Back in the Saddle
(4:41) — Steven Tyler / Joe Perry
B2. Draw the Line
(3:24) — Steven Tyler / Joe Perry
B3. Kings and Queens (Edit)
(3:48) — Steven Tyler / Brad Whitford / Tom Hamilton / Joey Kramer / Jack Douglas
B4. Come Together
(3:47) — John Lennon / Paul McCartney
B5. Remember (Walking in the Sand)
(4:05) — George "Shadow" Morton

Album Details:
Songs produced by their respective original producers. This compilation package includes several non-album single edits. According to Steven, "It was supposed to have been 'A DECADE of Greatest Hits,' ... After all, most bands which put out a 'Greatest Hits' album are either folding, or about to. Which is far from true with us. I tried to explain that, and got nothing but bullshit" (Rock Scene, 5/1980). Track A2 is from the 1974 single edit. Shortens the opening and intro section with the vocal starting. More noticeably, the second verse lyric is changed from the original "Gotcha with the cocaine, found with your gun," to "You shady lookin' loser, you played with my gun. Finally, the outro section is shortened, and a harder fade-out applied. The brutal single edit of track A3 chops nearly 1:30 from the original track length. It removes the whole of the talk-box intro and starts on the refrain of the chorus. The break section, prior to the second chorus, is shortened from 8 to 4 measures. The ending simply starts to fade from the chorus following the second verse, over repetitions of the chorus, cutting the drum crescendo and guitar/talk-box jam of the original that continues to fade-out on the album version.

Track A4 is also a slight edit from the original album version, somewhat pointlessly removing the second repetition of the chorus at the first instance — saving roughly 8 seconds. Finally, track B3 is also the single edit of the song with wholesale slaughter of the intro with the first 20 seconds simply being cut. The first symphonic break is shortened leading into the second verse. The piano/bass interlude is also cut from 4 to 2 measures, the solo shortened, and the fade-out started earlier. Joe Perry: "I remember walking through the supermarket at 2 in the morning in Boston and someone walking up to me with the (Aerosmith) greatest-hits record. I didn't even know it was coming out. I was too angry. This was the band I'd put together with Tom Hamilton, and these guys were off doing this (stuff)" (Orange County Register, 7/29/1993).

From a trade review: "One of the top-heavy metal bands of the 1970s, Aerosmith was capable of some great moments. All those moments are here... The Aerosmith catalog is full of material for a set such as this, but these tracks represent the cream of the crop of hits... and not so big hits... The result is the perfect distillation of the band's goal of being a hard rocking but melodic outfit" (Billboard, 11/1/1980).

From another trade review: "Rumor has it that the '70s were a dull and uninspiring time musically. Common beliefs have it that not until the Sex Pistols opened that idiosyncratic Pandora's box called 'new wave' did the current scene really begin to soar. Bollocks! Aerosmith was, and still is, one of America's premier heavy rock outfits, and this 1 greatest hits package more than amply proves it" (Cashbox, 11/1/1980).

Chart Action:
Chart Peak (USA): #53 (12/20/1980) with 16 weeks on the Billboard charts. The album returned to chart in for two additional runs in 1987 & 1988 for an added 24 weeks. The album also reached #55 on Cashbox (1/17/1981) during a 14-week run. Other countries: N/A.

11/29/80	12/06/80	12/13/80	12/20/80	12/27/80	01/03/81	01/10/81
85	70	61	** 53 **	53	53	63
01/17/81	01/24/81	01/31/81	02/07/81	02/14/81	02/21/81	02/28/81
73	73	73	84	110	145	157
03/07/81	03/14/81	03/21/81				
178	193	X				

Second charting:

03/07/87	03/14/87	03/21/87	03/28/87	04/04/87	04/11/87	04/18/87
161	159	154	161	156	161	163
04/25/87	05/02/87	05/09/87	05/16/87	05/23/87	05/30/87	06/06/87
171	187	185	176	168	171	182
08/01/87	08/08/87	08/15/87				
198	197	X				

Third charting:

03/12/88	03/19/88	03/26/88	04/02/88	04/09/88	04/16/88	04/24/88
169	169	173	181	179	187	176
04/30/88	05/07/88					
182	X					

RIAA/Sales:
Certified Gold by the RIAA on Mar. 3, 1981 and Platinum on Jan. 27, 1986. 2x Platinum followed on Nov. 24, 1986, 4x on Nov. 21, 1988, 5x on Apr. 29, 1991, 6x on Mar. 10, 1992, 8x on Oct. 21, 1994, 9x on Aug. 1, 1996, 10x on Feb. 26, 2001, and 11x on Dec. 13, 2007. During the SoundScan era, the album had sold 4,955,290 copies between 1991 and 2007. The album was also certified Gold in Japan by the RIAJ for sales of 100,000 copies. And concurrently certified Gold and Platinum in Canada by the CRIA on Feb. 27, 1997.

Supporting Singles:
- There were no singles issued in support of this compilation. However, Columbia promotionally issued Aerosmith's "The First Decade" box set, which included the band's then catalog of eight albums, in Jan. 1981.

1980 - Let the Music Do the Talking

U.S. Release Details:
CBS/Columbia JC/JCT/JCA-36388 (Mar. 10, 1980)
Columbia/CBS PC/PCT-36388 (July 1983 — Reissue)
Columbia/CBS CK-36388 (Dec. 1989 — CD reissue)

Tracks:
A1. Let the Music Do the Talking •
(4:42) — Joe Perry
A2. Conflict of Interest
(4:43) — Joe Perry
A3. Discount Dogs
(3:42) — Joe Perry / Ralph Morman
A4. Shooting Star
(3:39) — Joe Perry
A5. Break Song
(2:06) — Joe Perry / David Hull / Ronnie Stewart

B1. Rockin' Train
(6:02) — Joe Perry / Ralph Morman
B2. The Mist Is Rising
(6:30) — Joe Perry
B3. Ready on the Firing Line
(3:54) — Joe Perry
B4. Life at a Glance
(2:41) — Joe Perry

Album Details:
Produced by Jack Douglas and Joe Perry. Engineered by Lee DeCarlo assisted by Chris Tergesen. Mix engineers: Lee DeCarlo and Jack Douglas, assisted by Julie Last. Pre-production at the Wherehouse, Waltham, MA. Bed tracks and overdubs recorded in Studio A6 at the Hit Factory, New York City, NY. Mixed in Studio A at the Record Plant, New York City, NY. Mastered by Greg Calbi at Sterling Sound, New York City, NY.

Players:
◦ Joe Perry — Rhythm and lead guitars; lead vocals on A2, A4, B2, and B4; backing vocals; bass synthesizer on A1; percussion.
◦ Ralph Morman — Lead vocals.
◦ David Hull — Bass guitar; bass synthesizer on B3; backing vocals.
◦ Ronnie Stewart — Drums & percussion.
◦ Jack Douglas — Percussion.
◦ Rocky Donahue — Percussion.

Chart Action:
Chart Peak (USA): #47 (5/24/1980) during 13 weeks on the Billboard Top-200. The album also reached #50 (5/10/1980) during 13 weeks on Cashbox.

04/12/80	04/19/80	04/26/80	05/03/80	05/10/80	05/17/80	05/24/80
157	108	74	59	52	51	** 47 **
05/31/80	06/07/80	06/14/80	06/21/80	06/28/80	07/05/80	07/12/80
47	70	68	73	175	183	X

RIAA/Sales:
"Let the Music do the Talking" has never received a RIAA certification, but the album had purportedly sold more than 200,000 copies during its first two months on sale (Billboard, 5/24/1980).

Supporting Singles:
• Let the Music Do the Talking (USA, 3/25/1980) - Chart Peak: DID NOT CHART. However, the single did "bubble under" for one week at 110 on the Billboard Hot-100. A 3:21 edit (Columbia 1-11250) was issued, and the single included the non-album B-side Project version of "Bone to Bone" (a somewhat substandard transfer of this was also included on the Australian "Best of The Joe Perry Project" compilation in 1999). The full song was also issued on a promotional 12" with the LP version backed with "Discount Dogs" (Columbia AS-741).

1980 - Let the Music Do the Talking

> *"I haven't really made it yet. I haven't peaked yet. My playing's obviously gotten a lot more sophisticated and expressive in the last five, seven years, but I still have to prove to myself to myself through this this project I'm doing now"* (Boston Herald, 10/29/1979).

Throughout 1979 Joe Perry had regularly mentioned in interviews that he was planning a solo project, but at that time had no plans for departing Aerosmith. Instead, he would juggle the two projects simultaneously. Ultimately, though, realities lead Joe to depart Aerosmith. The challenges in the studio, and his desire to solely step into the limelight was tempered with a feeling of being held back by the tortuous recording process, particularly with Steven's role in the process. He noted, "While all this had been going on, I had been working with these other guys on this solo album on the side, and there was resentment there. They'd say, 'Why don't you go down and help Steve with that', and I'd say, 'I already did my part, I already wrote the tunes, it's down on the fucking tape, you know, what more do you want from me?' So, it came down to I called up Tom Hamilton and said, 'It's off, I just don't think I'm going to be able to go on the road with you this time, I'm going to stick with my own solo thing, and I can't put up with it anymore.' That was the last official word I said to the group." Their reaction? "I don't know. I never got a phone call from any of them. I got a telegram from Steven congratulating me on my 'new vinyl,' quote. That's it" (Sounds, 7/5/1980). But the relationship with Steven was far from the sole factor. He recalled, "If I had left just because of the personal difficulties between me and Steven [Tyler, lead singer of Aerosmith], I'd have left the band a long, long time ago" (Rolling Stone, 3/6/1980). Instead, it was more about the lumbering machine Aerosmith had become and his increasing conflicts with management. After a decade of work, Joe felt the dynamics within the band had become too rigid: "In the band, everybody had his little role to play. I left basically because I wanted to write lyrics and sing lead vocals and that wasn't part of my role... I wanted to be able to step out without feeling like I was stepping on someone's toes — or being made to feel that way" (Hartford Courant, 3/7/1980). But he also expressed contradictory views, illustrating an inner turmoil. He also reflected at the time that quitting the band was "nothing bad about Aerosmith. Within the confines of the band, I had my place, and I could breathe... but it just left me wanting more as far as knowing what I could do" (Kingsport Times, 5/9/1980).

Joe had decided to call his solo project, the "Joe Perry Project," long before he left Aerosmith, though he wasn't entirely sure how it was going to differ from his sound within Aerosmith. He soon settled on describing it as "high-powered R&B, sort of funk-rock." Initially, he envisaged the project would be 1/3 instrumental, 1/3 with him singing, and the other 1/3 with another singer; so, the resulting product wasn't too far off that original vision. With his work completed for "Night in the Ruts," Joe had commenced work on his solo album. He recalled, "I wrote all the music for the first Project album right after we wrote the Aerosmith album... Before I left Aerosmith, I already had the first Project put together, because I was getting pretty bored" (Boston Rock #44). That boredom was interrupted by the stop-go routine of studio/home/tour, depending on what the band were booked to do. Joe explained the impact: "When we were on the road we wouldn't work right through. We'd work three or four days a week and then do nothing for another three, and I'd be stuck in some hotel or motel somewhere and I like to keep active. Those days on the road when we weren't playing were rough on me. And, when you lay off like that you lose your momentum" (Pottsville Republican, 2/2/1980).

The situation had become distracting and frustrating, particularly in conjunction with the internal band issues. Joe felt held back: "I had all this material and I kept saying, 'Let's get this ['Night in the Ruts'] done. Then I started playing with studio people and started coming up with all of these great musicians. I wanted to put a band together to go out on the road like Keith Richards (of the Rolling Stones) did with the New Barbarians" (Indianapolis News, 2/1/1983). The final straw ended up being the carrot management and label had been dangling over his head: the solo album. Married with the other factors, such as the band's financial position or Joe owing management money for room service. What initially seemed a distraction from Joe's weak attempt to have the band's accounts audited, became leverage. From the initial suggestion as a way to pay off his debts, and massage the creative streak outside of the band, it was soon being used against him. Joe recalled, "I was set up. It felt like that. It was: 'Do a solo record, but don't break the band up.' Leber-Krebs are going, 'Yeah, let him do the solo record, let him fail, and then we'll get him back'" ("Walk this Way").

For Joe, it was like being caught between a rock and a hard place: "There was no way I could have made my own album while I was with Aerosmith, and that's what I've want to do for a long, long time. You see, we weren't a terribly well-organized group, our schedules were always so crazy there was no way to work out time in advance to undertake making an album" (Pottsville Republican, 2/2/1980). The band couldn't even get their own albums completed with interruptions for touring, chemical dysfunction, and interpersonal strife. Then Joe felt that he wouldn't be allowed to do a solo album while still a member of Aerosmith. He had a decision to make: "I had to decide which way I was going to go... I wanted to do more writing and singing and playing, but Aerosmith had a way of doing things, and it was hard to change the system around... It was me that changed, it wasn't them. I didn't want to leave the band, but I couldn't do the solo thing and remain in Aerosmith" (Cashbox, 8/30/1980). Freed from the perceptions of any artistic limitations and the duress of band drama, Joe embarked on his solo career with a stolid fury, even before the body of his prior life with Aerosmith was cold. For a very short time, Joe was without a band, or record contract. All he had was Elyssa and his music. Coupled with the band drama of his final years with Aerosmith, Joe was adamant that his new project was going to be the opposite. As he put it, "I was tired of all the bullshit. I just wanted to get in a van and go play rock and roll. I was willing to play clubs — any clubs. If there were a hundred people, as opposed to a hundred thousand, fine. If there were forty, fine... No complications, no weird management, no drama. Just music" ("Rocks: My Life in and Out of Aerosmith").

The band had come together in an almost pre-ordained manner. Joe had known vocalist Ralph Morman from his tenure with Bux, a renamed version of Daddy Warbux. With a lineup that included future Angel members Punky Meadows (guitars) and bassist Mickey Jones (bass), the band had been signed by then Aerosmith manager Frank Connolly. They recorded a Jack Douglas produced album for Capitol Records in 1973, but it wasn't released with the band splitting up (one of the band's songs, "White Lightning," was resuscitated for Angel's 1977 "On Earth as it is in Heaven" album; and Bux's album had finally been released in 1976 at a time Ralph, and guitarist James Newlon, had reconstituted a new lineup of the band and were working on a second album). By 1979, Ralph was working in construction in Florida and came backstage at as show and asked Joe if he knew anyone needing a vocalist. He recalled, "About three weeks later Joe called and said, 'I found a band for you.' I asked, 'What kind of stuff do they do?' He said, 'Kind of Aerosmith stuff.' I asked, 'Do I know any of them?' He said, 'Me!' and explained there had been a huge fight and he had quit Aerosmith. I said, 'Have you lost your mind?'" (Ashland Daily Independent, 3/27/2011). Joe had also known bassist David Hull from the early Boston days. He recalled, "I'd loved his bass playing for years, ever since I saw him playing with Buddy Miles. Last summer, he was between bands, between managers, so... bang!" (Creem, 8/1980). David's funk credentials would have been appealing, having played on four Buddy Miles' albums, and recording an album with White Chocolate in 1973 before that band transformed into the more mainstream Dirty Angles. And that band had previously opened for Aerosmith. Following several unsuccessful drummer auditions, Joe asked around about the best local drummer and found powerfully technical Ronnie Stewart working as a salesman at a Wurlitzer store. The blend of a soulful vocalist from the Paul Rodgers school married to a solid and inventive backing group, infused by a plethora of influences, allowed Joe to incorporate more of his new musical ideas into the material. This freshened the sonic palette and allowed the exploration of some directions that Joe felt he'd been prevented from doing while in Aerosmith. However, he initially suggested that the members keep their day jobs in case things didn't work out...

The band started rehearsing at the communal Wherehouse, pulling Joe's ideas together at a rapid pace. Joe recalled, "I still like to play rock 'n' roll, and that's what I'm doing... And I wasn't getting enough of it near the end of my stay with Aerosmith... I'm proud of everything I did with Aerosmith, but it was time for me to move on. I was working on my solo album ('Let the Music Do the Talking') at the same time as I was working on 'A Night in the Ruts,' and it was turning out that the Aerosmith sessions were totally conflicting with my rehearsals for the Project, and I was getting so much satisfaction from the Project that I had to make a decision one way or the other, because if I split my time I really wouldn't have been able to give my best to either" (Nyack Journal News, 10/11/1981). He was trying to fuse a love of the energy of punk with his love of funk and R&B, to create a hybrid that he felt didn't yet have a label. Initially, the challenges of putting a band together were one matter, persuading Columbia to roll the dice with him another. Joe recalled, "The Project did about ten gigs before I signed an album deal with Columbia. The label wasn't that eager because

Aerosmith had been bringing albums in way late. But I went down and convinced them I was a walking, talking viability instead of the burn-out they thought I was" ("Walk this Way"). Toward the end of the year, he been signed by Columbia to a reported eight album deal. With Aerosmith planning on hitting the road in late-November, Joe initially planned to record his album at the Wherehouse utilizing a 24-track remote truck reminiscent to various sessions with his former band.

The album was deliberately raw. Following the initial rehearsals, the band's initial gigs were regional shows, mostly under the radar, to tighten both themselves as a band and the material, before going into the studio with producer Jack Douglas. The decision to use Jack wasn't solely a result of Joe's comfort level working with him. He'd been unceremoniously dumped from the "Night in the Ruts" sessions, and Joe's efforts to bring him back had been met with failure at the time. There was a desire for a bit of revenge, going back to the producer who had given Aerosmith their sonic wings and delivering a completed album in record time. On hearing the demos Joe had been working on, once he'd finished recording an album for a new Polydor artist, Rick DuFay, his schedule was free, and he jumped at the opportunity. Shaking up his sonic signature also meant that Joe moved away from his trusted arsenal of Les Pauls and Strats. Joe "put this mongrel left-handed Telecaster together, with Barcus Berry pickups, which I haven't been able to find another set of. It's a guitar that shouldn't really sound as good as it does" (Guitar World, 3/31/2010). What it helped deliver was more than an apparent dose of rawness. Joe has suggested: "[The] album was definitely a spurt of energy that was let loose after being fenced up in Aerosmith. Jack Douglas [long-time producer for Aerosmith who was fired during the 'Night in the Ruts' sessions] and I just clicked. I'd pre-produced, arranged everything. We went into the studio and played the songs live. There was no bullshit, no magic... the album's like a soundtrack for the live shows" (Creem, August 1980). Ronnie disagreed: "The way we did the first album wasn't live. We did it in the studio, and when we heard it, we all said, 'that's not us'" (Boston Rock #17). Whatever the specifics, the results literally spoke for themselves, and Joe was (at least at the time) pleased with the album's "good, rough sound" (Hartford Courant, 3/7/1980).

Joe had set himself a challenge with the solo album, which wasn't just about him leaving a safe cocoon: "Aerosmith was a way of life for 10 years. It was family. But I knew I had to leave. No one was listening to me. I was stereotyped as the second singing lead... Everyone I knew in New York opposed me. But I decided I'd make it if I had to go back to playing Boston clubs again" (Plain Dealer, 4/24/1980). An additional factor that frustrated him was his limited lead vocal opportunities, and he took some vocal coaching classes to work on his singing for the album. He recalled, "The guys (at Aerosmith) didn't think I was good enough to sing, but I do the lead on several of the numbers and its okay" (Pottsville Republican, 2/2/1980). If it was a matter of ego for him to sing more of his songs, it was certainly a matter of ego about being the creative force in his own band. Joe made this abundantly clear: "It's a real ego thing for me to know that I wrote all the music on 'Let the Music Do the Talking' (his new album). I don't owe that to anybody. I don't owe anything to anybody anymore" (Green Bay Press-Gazette, 5/2/1980). However, while Joe may have written the bulk of the album, there was still scope for input from his new band. He and Ralph collaborated on the funky "Rockin' Train" and "Discount Dogs." The instrumental "Break Song" was shared with David Hull and Ronnie Stewart and was present in the band's set performed at the Wherehouse for Boston Herald music critic Bill Adler on October 24. An additionally collaborator may have done so unknowingly, with the Project recording an instrumental version of " Bone to Bone" — it retained its shared credit with Steven Tyler and was only used as a B-side for the sole single issued in support of the album. The rest of the songs were generally autobiographical Perry compositions, though naturally some arrangement suggestions and other modifications would be expected from the other band members.

"Let the Music Do the Talking" literally spoke for itself, being the whole ethos that summarized the events and era that led to its birth. When released as the album's sole single it was duly noted: "The bass-drum intro of this title cut from the ex-Aerosmith guitarist's first solo album has all the subtlety of an approaching freight train. Nor does it let up. Perry's muddy slide guitar and a saw-toothed vocalist recall early Stewart & the Faces to memory. Speaker-rattling energy for pop-AOR playlists" (Record World, 4/12/1980). As also the lead-off track for the album, the album's title track, the song had to be an unrelenting declaration of musical intent. Joe: "We're a little more into R&B than Aerosmith. There are similarities in rhythm... But there's more energy, track for track. I haven't gotten such a rush from making a record since we did 'Rocks'" (LA Times, 5/18/1980). "Conflict of Interest" was based on Joe's perception about his relationship with

Aerosmith's management. He recalled, "It's about people in the music business, the not caring, the not wanting to commit themselves to me [when I left the band]. I got help from newer people, but the veterans took real convincing... They figured I was just an irresponsible drugged-out rock star. They didn't know me from Steven... They didn't want that all over again" (Circus, 5/27/1980). More than that the song clearly illustrated the distrust that Joe had developed with Leber & Krebs, who continued to nominally represent him, even though he was essentially being managed by attorney Bob Casper. Joe would later admit that his relationship with the business side of the band was partially of his own doing: "I was living the classic rock 'n' roller's life during the last couple of years with Aerosmith. I was burning the candle at both ends, into drugs and not paying attention to what was going on around me" (Montreal Gazette, 10/14/1983). That events served to fuel a new direction is entirely a different matter.

Other material also spoke of Joe's frame of mind in late-1979. "Shooting Star" was born out of that initial period in-between bands, having immediately left Aerosmith with nothing lined up for the future. Joe recalled, "I wrote it during that hard time, so it's a lot more telling than I wanted it to be" (Circus, 5/27/1980). "The Mist is Rising" provided another opportunity for Joe to take the lead vocal on the song that would be closest described as the album's ballad, even with its brooding dark and down-tempo pace. Joe would usually introduce it by noting that while it was a ballad, "it's not 'Dream On', believe me." "Ready on the Firing Line" would be one of Joe's efforts turned over to Ralph to sing but was noted by reviewers as one of the album's standout tracks. If one takes Joe's contemporaneous comments at face value, then "Life at a Glance" was literally written on Nov. 15, 1979, the night prior to the band's debut at the Rat. By that time, the band had only been together a month, but the material was coming together quickly. When they played their Boston debut the following month five songs from his former band were present to buttress the set. To be fair, "Reefer Head Woman" and "Think About It" were both technically covers while representing his final work with Aerosmith (and in the case of the latter, his very first work with Aerosmith, with the song having been performed at that band's first show a decade earlier). The set also included four other covers, but the bulk of the new album was represented with only "Conflict of Interest," "Rockin' Train," and the "Break Song" excluded. During a late-night WBCN broadcast and interview following the show, demos of "The Mist is Rising" and "Discount Dogs" were broadcast for listeners to get an early taste of the band's direction.

With recording completed, Joe hit the road with his band in February 1980. An initial two month run, paired with Capitol Records act William Oz, saw them playing the east coast club scene. It was precisely the place Joe wanted to be, and nearly as far away from the stadium shows as one could get. He noted that it tied in with his approach to the music: I've gotten back to basic music, basic rock 'n' roll. And a club tour is the way I always wanted to do it. Everybody gets their money's worth. I could have gone on a big arena tour, but I'm not looking to play the rock 'n' roll game anymore and get the most exposure in front of the most numbers. Right now, I feel like a local boy playin' rock 'n' roll in a local club with guys who are real hot, eager to play and gettin' off on it" (Creem, August 1980). It was similar to the early days of Aerosmith: "Aerosmith broke out of Detroit and Cleveland and we did it with the live gigs and that's how I plan to set the Joe Perry Project up. I'm not putting the band together to go out and try to make a lot of money and just scam it. I'm really into the music and the sound I'm getting, and the best place for that is the theaters and the clubs" (Kingsport Times, 5/9/1980). He'd had offers to tour on a more traditional national scale. He recalled, "We've been approached to play guest slots opening for some really big acts on the stadium circuit, but I don't' want to do that anymore. If I was in this for the money, I wouldn't have left Aerosmith" (Rolling Stone, 3/6/1980). The project were beneficiaries of several radio broadcasts during the year, dialing in powerful performances for local radio stations. For the first half of the year, Joe stuck to his initial plan, essentially that of a "band in a van" playing often and staying out on the road. He wanted to work, and it had been one of the smoldering embers that had led to the solo project: "It grinds me down only when I can't play every night. It's when we play four nights a week that it gets to be a drag. What are you supposed to do on the off-nights? Sit around Rapid City and stare at the walls? If you're gonna be on the road, you might as well be on the road for real" (Boston Herald, 10/29/1979). However, not all of the band was made for the rock 'n' roll pirate's life.

Ralph purportedly became unreliable on the road. Understandably, it was an odd situation for the vocalist, who would sing the first few songs and then leave the stage while Joe sang or played instrumentals, before returning to the stage in time for band introductions and final songs. And while alcohol may have been his bane, Joe was at least still a functional druggie. He was also the boss and now had to make the hard decisions for the best of the band himself. According to Joe, "I fired Ralph Morman and replaced him with J. Mala [the singer for the New York club band Revolver] for the rest of the tour. He lasted three gigs" ("Walk this Way"). By 1980 Mala had been fronting New York band Revolver, who had a track, "Mama Said," included on the WNBC Radio 66 "Hometown Album II" album in February. But he wasn't just a club singer pulled from those environs to work with the band and had an impressive resume dating back to early days of Aerosmith's interactions with the New York Dolls in the city in 1972. At that time, Mala had been a member of an incarnation of the Magic Tramps, having replaced vocalist Eric Emerson. As such, he'd been a part of the Warholian scene that gave birth to the New York glitter movement and had even seen the embryonic KISS at their Coventry gigs. Earlier still, he'd been a member of Koala who released a garage punk album in 1969 for Capitol (another member of that band ended up in the Brats). Ralph, out of the band, hit the road singing in a new formation of Savoy Brown (he'd record "Rock 'N' Roll Warriors" with the band in 1981.). Joe would decline to go into detail about Ralph at the time, simply commenting, "I don't want to say anything bad about him, but it just got to the point where he wasn't all there" (Circus, 8/31/1981). With Mala in the band (for certainly more than three shows), the Project were paired with bigger name acts, such as Heart, Journey, the Rossington-Collins Band, but even with the greater exposure the record had quickly plateaued following its release. CBS also declined to issue further singles, following the release of the title track, leaving the promotion of the album dead in the water.

Touring petered out towards the end of the year. Joe had been working on ideas for the next album throughout the year and wanted to record an album every 18 months. Even mid-1980, he had a plan: "The next album comes out this year and it will be a lot more R&B oriented, because I wrote two albums basically within eight months. It was a breaking-away period, and the next album will break away even further. I mean it's going to rock but it's going to be more to the point. It's called 'Soldier of Fortune' and it's going to be a smoker!" (Sounds, 7/5/1980). However, by early 1981 he needed another new vocalist...

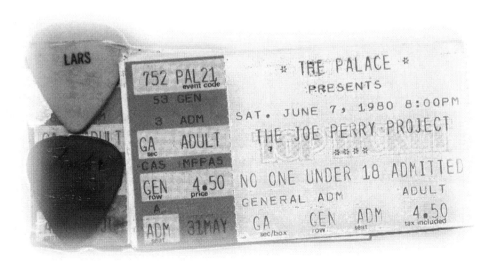

Assorted review excerpts:

"Perry, one of the driving forces behind hard rocking Aerosmith, steps out on his own with a hard-hitting debut. Material isn't all that different from some of the Aerosmith catalog though much of Perry's playing is more clear in the mix here. Still, it is the same type of high-energy blues rock Perry helped to create with Aerosmith. Vocalist Ralph Morman and Perry have a gutsy Foreigner type of appeal. Many rock fans have been waiting for this one" (Billboard, 3/22/1980).

"Until very recently Perry was the lead guitarist of Aerosmith and this debut solo LP continues in that same solid rock vein. The energy here is blasting and Jack Douglas adds the appropriate thick production" (Record World, 3/22/1980).

"Despite the difficulty in finding anyone over 18 who'll admit to liking it, heavy-metal rock has continued to survive since its inception a score of years ago when Link Wray's 'Rumble' blew Frankie Avalon and Fabian off the radio. Though Aerosmith is hardly in a class with the genre's consummate past and present groups (The James Gang, Deep Purple, Led Zeppelin), the group has managed to represent the best (addictive power riffs, voluminous guitar antics) and worst (tedious songs filled with say-nothing lyrics) characteristics of heavy-metal. And on his first album since leaving Aerosmith, lead guitarist Joe Perry has managed to equal the best and worst music of his former band. 'Let the Music Do the Talking' is predominantly a showcase for Perry, whose heavy chording and hot solos dominate the album, no more so than on the thunderous title track where Perry makes even his own guitar hero, Jeff Beck, sound like the laid-back Mark Knopfler of Dire Straits. The hard and fast pace is maintained throughout the album, especially on the relatively funky 'Rockin' Train' and the manic 'Life at a Glance.' But, as is the case with most heavy-metal albums, there are moments of tedium and self-indulgence. 'The Mist is Rising' (only adequately sung by Perry) is ponderous and irritating, and the instrumental "Break Song" should have remained in the can. A few Aerosmith devotees may miss Steven Tyler's vocals in combination with Perry's guitar (lead singer Ralph Morman has a strong but nondistinctive voice), but not enough to keep them or any heavy- metal magnets from being attracted to the Joe Perry Project's clamorous debut" (Boston Globe, 3/27/1980).

"Is it just the plethora of bad punk-new wave-power pop albums we've been hearing lately, or is this the last grand gasp of heavy metal? Whatever, Aerosmith's former guitarist has come up with a set that is vulgar, crude, tasteless, indulgent and (just often enough) really exciting, in the way a riveter can be. He lacks Ted Nugent's sense of humor, but that doesn't mean that it's not a kind

of in-joke anyhow" (Rolling Stone magazine's David Marsh for newspaper syndication, 4/1980).

"Steve Tyler's shrieks may have been the fire of the hard-rocking Aerosmith, but it was Joe Perry's searing guitar that gave the band its spark. Perry left Aerosmith earlier this year to get away from the arenas and stadiums the platinum band had found itself playing for in the last few years. While his departure was certainly Aerosmith's loss, I think the move may have hurt Perry as well. The instrumental roar still lives with the Joe Perry Project. The guitarist may have switched bands, but he certainly hasn't changed styles. Ear-ripping chords and ricochet solos are supplied in even greater abundance on 'Let the Music Do the Talking.' But the vocal tracks just don't do the record justice. Singer Ralph Morman is possessed of a competently raspy rock 'n' roll voice that bleats over the mayhem with suitable authority. But he's nothing special. And when Perry himself tries to play lead singer with his listless drone of a voice it's plain pitiful. Perry should try a Jamaican trick and release a dub (instrumental) version of the album. Frankly, I'd rather do my own screaming to this disc" (San Bernardino County Sun, 4/27/1980).

"Perry, who left Aerosmith late last year, has come up with one of the best hard rock albums of the past few years. Some tracks resemble his former band's work too much, but the album mostly evokes guitarist-writer Perry's idol, Jeff Beck, to good gain. Cuts such as the six-minute 'Rockin' Train' and the trimmer instrumental 'Break Song' particularly seem to draw their appealing R&B-rock style from Beck's 'Rough and Ready' period. Perry's Project is a smooth, strong vehicle for his ably conceived songs — with Ralph Morman's vocals, ranging from Rod Stewart-ish to rasps to more individual approaches, a standout contribution. But the central strength is Perry's inventive playing and arrangements, which have resulted in a work far more satisfying than Aerosmith's last LP" (Los Angeles Times, 5/11/1980).

"If Steven Tyler is Aerosmith's big mouth, then hawk-nosed guitarist Joe Perry was the band's main muscle. Now, on Perry's first LP since leaving the group last year, he flexes that muscle like champ. 'Let the Music Do the Talking' overflows with molten riffs and the kind of smoking guitar solos that made 'Get Your Wings' and 'Toys in the Attic' such head-banger delights. The Joe Perry Project delivers all of the rock & roll moxic that Aerosmith couldn't manage on their last album with him, the prophetically titled 'Night in the Ruts.' At only 2:06, the instrumental 'Break Song' is 'Let the Music Do the Talking's pivotal raver, a microcosmic demonstration of the chops that Perry deploys throughout the record. Against bassist David Hull and drummer Ronnie Stewart's manic rhythms, Perry trots out his entire bag of tricks — feedback, fuzz-tone harmonics, vibrato wails, hammer-on-anvil power chords — but with a practiced musicianly class that further fuels the guitar-star cool with which he slams on his strings. The LP's eight other blitzkriegs crackle with similar electricity. Jack Douglas, Perry's co-producer, and former Aerosmith mentor has done a good job.

'Shooting Star' and the title track bristle with double-time heavy-metal tension, while 'Life at a Glance' kicks to a punkier beat. 'Rockin' Train' and 'Discount Dogs' are effectively funked-up James Brown-style numbers. The only weak link in this chain of churning jock-rock is lead singer Ralph Morman, who can howl with the best of the hard-rock hounds but whose voice lacks the cutting edge that would distinguish him from the rest of the pack. Joe Perry takes a few unspectacular turns at the vocal mike, too, but any singer might feel intimidated by the locomotive pace and guitar-army sound of this album. Any singer except maybe one. If Steven Tyler were here, 'Let the Music Do the Talking' would probably be the finest record Aerosmith never made" (Rolling Stone, 5/29/1980).

"Perry is the heavy metal guitarist who has had the foresight to desert the good ship Aerosmith before it ultimately sinks under the weight of its own redundance. On his first solo album, he has aimed straight for the heart of the massive Ted Nugent audience — the predominantly high school-aged males who still believe in long hair, naked guitar riffs, and massive volume overdoses. That Perry is dead on target is illustrated by this album's almost immediate rise into the top 40, despite being too heavy for consistent radio (AM or FM) airplay. The album is ploddingly formulaic — Ralph Norman's vocals are gruff but unadventurous, and the rhythm section here is brutally repetitive, although effective just the same. The star of the show is undoubtedly Perry, with his slick power chording and flashy fret work" (Toronto Globe & Mail, 6/7/1980).

"There aren't very many guitar heroes (in the traditional arena sense) left in America, but if there's one that has come out of the seventies to typify and wave the banner for that vanishing breed, it's Joe Perry. Playing a variety of custom axes, deft of technique and possessed by a rocker's pure lunge for power, Joe is a Powder Keg of amplitude just waiting to be set off. His album reflects the genre, with good hook-laden songs that none-the-less are just vehicles for his guitar pyramidizations. The title cut is the smoker here, and cranked up on ten, it should sizzle nicely live. Kudos as well to Jack Douglas as producer, who knows how to milk every last decibel of wattage for maximum effect" (Rock Scene, 11/1980).

"Aerosmith guitarist Joe Perry formed his project and released his first solo album, 'Let the Music Do the Talkin.' Although album sales were surprisingly disappointing, the music was fantastic — especially such as powerful rockers as the title cut, 'Discount Dogs,' Break Song,' and 'Rockin' Train.' 'Let the Music' had everything the last couple of 'Smith albums were lacking, and, incidentally, blew away the music being made by the revamped Aerosmith. Perry's smoldering, blues-based guitar style was in fine form, the rhythm section was unbeatable, and the production merged heavy metal bite with a groovy funk warmth. Unfortunately, this hard work magic only worked for one more album" (CD Review, June 1990).

1980 - Let the Music Do the Talking

October 24, 1979
The Wherehouse
Waltham, MA

Notes:
- Two weeks after officially departing Aerosmith, Joe debuted the Joe Perry Project for an audience of one: Boston Herald Pop Music Critic Bill Adler, following an interview. Since he was still 1/5 owner of the Wherehouse, and Aerosmith were finishing up the "Night in the Ruts" album, the parties agreed that Joe could use the facility to audition musicians and rehearse.
- Without a lead vocalist, Ralph Morman, Joe, Ronnie Stewart (drums) and David Hull (bass) powered through the band's set. The resulting piece on the occasion ran in the Oct. 29 issue of the Herald: "Minus the fanfare, the flashing lights, and the glandular-fed fever that animates 15,000 rock fans packed into a hockey arena, Joe Perry kicked his new band into an absolutely crushing heavy-metal groove. His guitar was slung low, his shoulders were hunched, and through his hair (of course) was in his eyes, he played intensely right into his cohorts faces, taking them through the tune step-by-step. Loathe to compare his music to anyone else's, Joe has nonetheless ventured earlier that his ideal of the Joe Perry Project would sound like 'Duane Eddy meets Led Zeppelin.' In fact, there was a definite rockabilly twang at the edge of his guitar's wild Hendrix-based screams as he closed out the tune now known only as 'The Break Song'." Other songs from the album were performed along with covers including "Red House" and "Heartbreak Hotel," which would remain staples for the next 5 years.

November 16
Student Union Rathskeller @ B.U.
Boston, MA

Promoter: UGBC Social Committee
Other act(s): Shane Champagne
Partial set list: Same Old Song and Dance / Get the Lead Out / Pills / Discount Dogs / Reefer Head Woman / Ready on the Firing Line / Bone to Bone / Walk this Way / Shooting Star / The Mist is Rising / Talk Talk / Heartbreak Hotel / Life at a Glance / Let the Music Do the Talking
Notes:
- The public debut of the Joe Perry Project, appropriately back in the confines of Boston University paralleling the dues Aerosmith had paid nearly a decade earlier. Steven Tyler and Brad Whitford stopped by before the show, to wish Joe well. Steven didn't stay for the performance (not wanting to wait through the opener), but Brad did. By this time, the Paradise Club show had been booked as a single 8:30 p.m. performance. Perry was satisfied with that first show: "It went pretty well for our first gig. I think we'll be even better with a little more time together... It feels like a natural situation. Tonight, everything seemed to click, like in the rehearsals. Spontaneously, quickly. We felt at home playing together. We were a little nervous at first, but once we got out there, things went fine" (Boston Heights, 12/3/1979).
- From a local review: "All the knives were drawn, the swords raised, and the executioner's axes sharpened. Overhead, vultures circled ominously, ready to strike. The night had finally arrived. Joe Perry, the former lead guitarist for Aerosmith, was about to put his balls on the chopping block for keeps, with the debut of his new band, The Joe Perry Project at the BC Rathskeller... Plugging in his Stratocaster, Joe led the rest of the band (David Hull, bass; Ron Stewart, drums; Ralph Mormon, vocals) into 'Same Old Song and Dance,' with his guitar pouring out the familiar lead. Smart move number one. The song was familiar enough to get the crowd going, yet the version rendered here was more straight-ahead, led by one guitar, and a vocalist distinctly non-Tyleresque. The result, as on the second song 'Get the Lead Out,' was a rawer, funkier sound than the Aero-versions. Mormon's voice and style especially kept these songs from Aero-dom, as he strutted and wailed in a boisterous style, I can only compare to Rod Stewart at his finest with The Faces, and the original Jeff Beck Group. In addition to Mormon's raspy voice, Joe's wailing power riffs and nifty solos seemed to give the Project a very early Beckish sound... I'd have never known that this band has only played together for three weeks, or that this was their first gig ever, and neither would anyone else, from the performance. Joe Perry, away from Aerosmith, is now able to play guitar more naturally, without the limits of a band to confine what he can do onstage. This ain't no Aero-clone. Perry's new material has more

variety in its style, ranging from punkish N.Y. Dolls-type material to Cream power to Yardbirdish, Beckish, funky bluesy rock to even plain electric blues, all the while distinct in itself" (Boston Heights, 12/3/1979).

- From a mainstream review: "Finally, the p.a. blasted out the 'William Tell Overture,' and the Joe Perry Project came out to meet the world. Kids stood on cafeteria tables and cheered. The band ran through a ragged but enthusiastic set of Aerosmith songs... a couple of covers... and some new Perry compositions. Besides Perry on guitar, the band comprised Ronnie Stewart on drums, former Dirty Angel David Hull on bass, and singer Ralph Morman. Perry, however, sang enough leads to qualify as a front man — and his heavy, explosive guitar generated the set's excitement. Even those who avoid this sort of music in an arena would conceded that to have heard all this guitar power, all these sounds, wailing out of one guitar in a cramped school cafeteria was a gas" (Trouser Press, 2/1980).

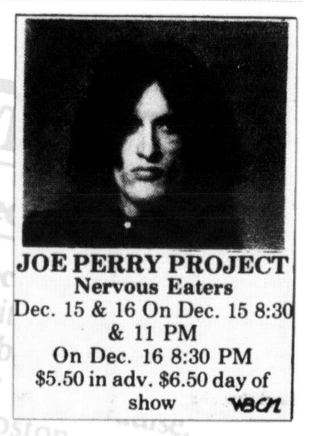

December 15 **TWO SHOWS
Paradise Club
Boston, MA

Other act(s): Nervous Eaters
Set list: Same Old Song and Dance / Get the Lead Out / Pills / Discount Dogs / Reefer Head Woman / Ready on the Firing Line / Bone to Bone / Heartbreak Hotel / Shooting Star / The Mist is Rising / Talk Talk / Red House / Walk this Way / Think About It / Life at a Glance / Let the Music Do the Talking
Notes:
- From a local review: "The stirring strains of the 'William Tell Overture' were still bouncing off the walls when Joe Perry, rock's newest Lone Ranger, drew up onto the stage at the Paradise in a cloud of dust last week. The gunslinging guitarist, recently departed from his long-standing gig with Aerosmith in search of individual fame and fortune, was debuting his new Joe Perry Project. 'Hi. How ya doin'?' Joe said with typical low-key diffidence. 'Nice of y'all to show up.' With that he kicked the Project into a version of 'Same Old Song and Dance,' a classic Aerosmith favorite. As it turned out, the tune was prophetic of the shape of things to come. Not only is the JPP pretty strictly in the wind-it-up, grind-it-out, heavy-metal tradition of Aerosmith, convivial, leather-lunged lead-singer Ralph Mormon is doubtlessly capable of matching Aerosmith's Steve Tyler rasp for rasp.

What's different about the JPP is Perry's increased dosage of limelight time. What's at least slightly humorous is the fact that even the most sharply focused spotlight failed to penetrate the guitarist's dark bangs, and the matter of whether or not Joe was ever even issued the standard set of eyes remains a mystery. What's not news is that the guy can play the hell out of his guitar and did so to the noisy delight of two packed houses. Joe's lead vocals were a little monotonous, but no one seemed to mind. The JPP encored with a crusher called 'Let the Music Do the Talking,' a tune which could serve as Joe's motto, and it was evident that most folks agreed the music was speaking pretty eloquently right into their faces" (Boston Herald American, 12/20/1980).
- From another local review: "After spending the past month playing scattered dates at various New England colleges, the Joe Perry Project had its 'official' Boston corning-out over the weekend at the Paradise Theater. Somewhat surprisingly — especially in the light of rumors that Perry's Project would lean toward a more funky, rhythm and blues-based sound — the tack taken was not really dissimilar from Aerosmith's straight ahead, blast furnace hard rock, tempered with an occasional heavy blues-rock digression. The two primary differences evidenced in the 17-song set which included five Aerosmith songs — were: (1) as the sole guitarist, Perry was responsible for playing both lead and rhythm parts, and (2) as the undisputed leader, he had total control over the material. However, in staking this second claim he cut a cloud over the

set's intent — was this the effort of a band led by Joe Perry or a Joe Perry showcase? The answer likely lies somewhere between the two. the central part of the show things slid, rather indulgently, toward the latter shading the evening in musical schizophrenia.

The set opened With Ralph Morman handling the lead vocals on two Aerosmith standards, 'Same Old Song and Dance' and 'Get the Lead Out' — an admittedly difficult task considering the identification Aerosmith singer Steven Tyler has with the songs. Perry followed by singing lead on a New York Dolls-inspired arrangement of Bo Diddley's 'Pills' and, later, Morman and Perry generated a hot musical rapport (as Morman's bluesy harp playing intertwined with Perry's stinging licks) on 'Reefer Headed Woman.' However, after one more tune Morman left the stage for seven straight songs, appearing, ironically enough, just in time for Perry to introduce 'the boys in the band.'

Although Perry did not seem uncomfortable in the spotlight, he did not project any kind of special charisma. His singing, while earnest, showed little range — this may be partially attributable to the DC-10 volume the band played at which often overwhelmed whoever was singing — and the songs never really caught fire. One hesitates to harken back to the over-used Aerosmith/Rolling Stones comparison — with Perry playing the Keith Richard foil to Steve Tyler's Jagger — but it seemed that Perry missed that driving force, that extra push, while he was fronting what had become essentially a power trio. To some extent Morman fills the role when he's on stage. Morman's gravelly voice — not to mention his hairstyle and stage mannerisms — is reminiscent of Rod Stewart. Although Morman doesn't possess Stewart's versatility, his singing and Perry's guitar playing give the Project a sound which, at its best, reminds one of the old Jeff Beck Group. Perry though, unlike Beck, is not a particularly inventive guitarist. His fast, hard-rock licks serve the purpose, but they rarely take the songs up to a higher level; the result then, despite the energy and volume, is just mildly satisfying" (Boston Globe, 12/19/1979).
- An AUD recording circulates from the first show.

December 16
Paradise Club
Boston, MA
Other act(s): Nervous Eaters

1980

February 29 **TWO SHOWS
The Place
Manchester, NH
Other act(s): Kid Morocco

March 1
Mr. C's Rock Palace
Lowell, MA
Other act(s): William Oz, Barker Gang
Notes:
- Opening act for this initial tour run, William Oz, were signed to Capitol Records and had released their debut in January.

March 6, 7
Toad's Place
New Haven, CT
Other act(s): William Oz

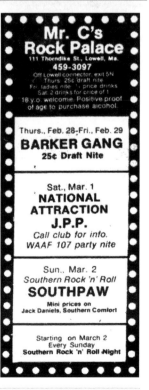

March 8
Shaboo
Willimantic, CT

March 13
Alexander's
Browns Mills, NJ
Other act(s): William Oz

March 14, 15
Fast Lane
Asbury Park, NJ
Other act(s): William Oz

March 16
Lupo's
Providence, RI

March 19
Triangle Theater
Rochester, NY

March 20
Uncle Sam's
Cheektowaga, NY
Promoter: Harvey & Corky Present
Other act(s): William Oz
Reported audience: (1,000 capacity)

March 23
The Factory
Staten Island, NY

March 28, 29
My Father's Place
Roslyn, NY
Other act(s): William Oz
Set list: Same Old Song and Dance / Get the Lead Out / Pills / Discount Dogs / Reefer Head Woman / Ready on the Firing Line / Bone to Bone / Heartbreak Hotel / Shooting Star / The Mist is Rising / Talk Talk / Bright Light Fright / Break Song / Walk this Way / Rockin' Train / Life at a Glance / Let the Music Do the Talking
Notes:
- The second date from this engagement was broadcast on WLIR-FM. The set followed the same general form for other headlining dates, including the New York Dolls' version of Bo Diddley's "Pills," Elvis' "Heartbreak Hotel," and the Music Machine's 1966 garage rock "Talk Talk" (not to be confused with "Talk Talkin'" from Joe's 2005 solo album).

April 5
Estadio Hiram Bithorn

San Juan, Puerto Rico
Promoter: First Class Rock Concerts
Other act(s): Blackjack
Reported audience: (20,000 capacity)
Notes:
- Blackjack included singer Michael Bolton and future KISS guitarist Bruce Kulick.

April 10
Penalty Box
Pennsauken, NJ
Promoter: Electric Factory Concerts
Reported audience: (3,500 capacity)
Set list: Same Old Song and Dance / Get the Lead Out / Pills / Discount Dogs / Reefer Head Woman / Ready on the Firing Line / Bone to Bone / Heartbreak Hotel / Shooting Star / The Mist is Rising / Talk Talk / Bright Light Fright / Walk this Way / Rockin' Train / Life at a Glance / Let the Music Do the Talking / Red House
Notes:
- An FM broadcast was recorded at this show.

April 11
Orpheum Theater
Boston, MA
Other act(s): The Stompers
Reported audience: (2,700 capacity)

April 13 **TWO SHOWS
The Bayou
Georgetown, Washington DC
Promoter: Cellar Door Presents
Reported audience: (~500 capacity)
Set list: Same Old Song and Dance / Get the Lead Out / Pills / Discount Dogs / Reefer Head Woman / Ready on the Firing Line / Bone to Bone / Heartbreak Hotel / Shooting Star / The Mist is Rising / Bright Light Fright / Rockin' Train / Life at a Glance / Let the Music Do the Talking
Notes:
- The Project were scheduled to perform sets at 8 and 11p.m.
- From a local review: "Joe Perry was once lead guitarist for Aerosmith, and nothing short of a lobotomy could make you forget that fact at the Bayou last night when his new band — the Joe Perry Project — made its first Washington appearance. Among the reminders were his fans; cheering, chanting droves of them jammed the club early for the first show and formed a line that stretched more than a block down K Street for the second. Then there was his prerecorded theme song: the 'William Tell Overture,' which heralded his appearance and not-so-subtly pointed to his new 'Lone Ranger' status in rock. And finally, there was his music. Next to Aerosmith, Perry's Project on a visual plane at least, is a model of rock decorum. Yet musically, the similarities outweigh the differences. Even allowing for some technical problems and Perry's inadequate singing (lead singer Ralph Mormon is a far more convincing vocalist in a raspy Rod Stewart vein), the band could have been easily cloned from one of Aerosmith's power chords" (Washington Post, 4/14/1980).

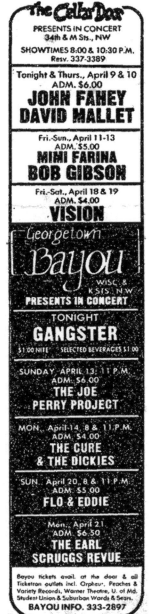

- An AUD recording circulates from the late show.

April 15
Mancini's Lounge
McKees Rocks, PA
Other act(s): Le Slick

April 16 **TWO SHOWS
Bogart's
Cincinnati, OH
Promoter: Electric Factory Concerts
Notes:
- The band performed 8 and 11p.m. sets.

April 18
Agora
Columbus, OH
Promoter: Paradise Island Productions
Other act(s): Ron Goedert Band
Notes:
- Smokin' were originally noted as the opener.

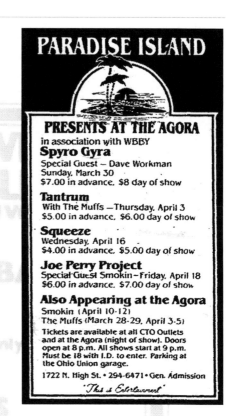

April 19
Park West
Chicago, IL
Promoter: Jam Productions
Other act(s): Ron Goedert Band
Set list: Same Old Song and Dance / Get the Lead Out / Pills / Discount Dogs / Reefer Head Woman / Ready on the Firing Line / Bone to Bone / Heartbreak Hotel / Shooting Star / The Mist is Rising / Talk Talk / Rockin' Train / Life at a Glance / Let the Music Do the Talking
Notes:
- An FM broadcast was recorded at this show.

April 22 **TWO SHOWS
Agora Ballroom
Cleveland, OH
Promoter: in-house
Other act(s): Ron Goedert Band
Set list: Same Old Song and Dance / Get the Lead Out / Pills / Discount Dogs / Reefer Head Woman / Ready on the Firing Line / Bone to Bone / Heartbreak Hotel / Shooting Star / The Mist is Rising / Talk Talk / Bright Light Fright / Break Song / Rockin' Train / Life at a Glance / Let the Music Do the Talking
Notes:
- Joe performed 7 and 10p.m. shows. He was interviewed by the Plain Dealer following the shows.
- From a local review: "Joe Perry showed Tuesday night at the Cleveland Agora why Aerosmith is hurting without him. The wiry, dark-maned lead guitarist for his new group, The Joe Perry Project, turned in an electric rock and roll performance. The three-piece band, which included Perry on lead, a bassist, a drummer, and a lead singer, played several Aerosmith songs as well as material from The Joe Perry Project's recently released first album, 'Let the Music Do the Talking...' Perry and his band played 12 songs in the one-hour set, including the single 'Let the Music Do the Talking,' as an encore. They performed five songs from Aerosmith. Perry altered certain portions of the Aerosmith selections, changing the tempo, or adding

longer solo guitar parts for himself. The lack of variation in music, it was reported, was the crux of Perry's disagreement with Tyler and led to the subsequent separation. Perry appeared to struggle with concentration while playing yet played to perfection, the way he had with Aerosmith. He maintained a determined facial expression throughout the show.

The Joe Perry Project began with two Aerosmith songs, 'Same Old Song and Dance' and 'Get the Lead Out.' The other three Aerosmith songs in the concert were 'Reefer Head Woman,' 'Bone to Bone (Coney Island Whitefish Boy)' and 'Bright Light Fright.' 'Reefer' and 'Bone' were good examples of Perry's rebelliousness toward his former group. 'Reefer,' which uses a rhythm and blues tempo, was played even more deliberately. 'Bone' was a Perry instrumental, differing from Aerosmith's version with lyrics. While Perry strayed from the Aerosmith style at times, his former group couldn't be forgotten. Some of the equipment to the rear of the stage displayed Aerosmith decals. Aside from songs from his Aerosmith days and songs off his new band's first album, Perry played and sang Elvis Presley's classic, 'Heartbreak Hotel'" (Elyria Chronicle Telegram, 4/23/1980).
- An AUD recording circulates from this show.

April 23 **TWO SHOWS
Music Theater
Royal Oak, MI
Promoter: Brass Ring Productions
Other act(s): Ron Goedert Band
Reported audience: 2,500 / 3,400 (73.53%, both shows)
Reported gross: $22,500
Set list: Same Old Song and Dance / Get the Lead Out / Pills / Discount Dogs / Reefer Head Woman / Ready on the Firing Line / Bone to Bone / Heartbreak Hotel / Shooting Star / The Mist is Rising / Talk Talk / Bright Light Fright / Break Song / Walk this Way / Rockin' Train / Life at a Glance / Let the Music Do the Talking
Notes:
- Show broadcast live on WRIF-101. The bootleg is often misdated Apr. 25.

April 24
Bus Stop Night Club
East Lansing, MI
Promoter: in-house
Other act(s): Angel City
Notes:

- From a local review: "Thursday's show proved that it takes more than just a hot-shot guitarist to make for a good band or an interesting show. Much of the Joe Perry Project's live material came from its recently released album 'Let the Music Do the Talking,' which showcases Perry as a songwriter and vocalist as well as a guitarist. In addition, some old Aerosmith favorites like 'Same Old Song and Dance' and 'Walk This Way' drew an enthusiastic response from the very partisan crowd, while the group's versions of such old faves as 'Heartbreak Hotel,' 'Talk Talk,' and the Bo Diddley New York Dolls tune 'Pills' were surprising to hear. Unfortunately, none of this material came off very well on stage. Oh, sure, Perry was as flashy as his fans could have hoped for, but without some strong song structures to improvise around he tended to overplay, and most of his new material is weak in this respect. Only 'Life at a Glance' and the title song from the new album have really memorable changes to them, and even these were plowed through in such a way as to make them nearly indistinguishable from every other tune. The Aerosmith covers, meanwhile, suffered by not having the dual guitars they were written for, and lead vocalist Morman is no Steve Tyler. In fact, Morman is easily the band's weak link, so it was almost a relief whenever Perry would sing or — better yet

— do an instrumental. If Perry wants to make something of his new band, his first move should be to replace this hack with a hot vocalist and stick to guitar playing himself" (Michigan State News, 4/28/1980).

April 25
Great Northern Music Hall
Grand Rapids, MI
Set list: Same Old Song and Dance / Get the Lead Out / Pills / Discount Dogs / Reefer Head Woman / Ready on the Firing Line / Bone to Bone / Heartbreak Hotel / Shooting Star / The Mist is Rising / Talk Talk / Bright Light Fright / Conflict of Interest / Break Song / Rockin' Train / Life at a Glance / Let the Music Do the Talking
Notes:
- A AUD recording circulates from this show.

April 26
The Palms
Racine, WI
Set list: Same Old Song and Dance / Get the Lead Out / Pills / Discount Dogs / Reefer Head Woman / Ready on the Firing Line / Bone to Bone / Heartbreak Hotel / Shooting Star / The Mist is Rising / Talk Talk / Break Song / Bright Light Fright / Rockin' Train / Life at a Glance / Let the Music Do the Talking
Notes:
- A decent AUD recording circulates from this show.

April 28
Sam's
Minneapolis, MN

May 1 **POSTPONED
Omaha Auditorium
Lincoln, NE
Promoter: Schon Productions
Notes:
- The postponement of this date was later noted as being the result of the promoter wanting more time for Perry to build an audience...

May 2 **CANCELLED
Uptown Theater
Kansas City, MO
Promoter: The Concert Group
Notes:
- Tickets for this show were honored at the June 4 date.

May 3
Music Hall
Selina, KS

May 5
Rainbow Theater
Colorado Springs, CO

May 8 **TEMP HOLD-DATE
Commodore Ballroom
Vancouver, BC, Canada

May 8 **TWO SHOWS
Euphoria
Portland, OR
Promoter: Double Tee Productions
Notes:
- The Project was scheduled to play shows at 7 and 10p.m.

May 9
The Place
Seattle, WA

May 10 **TEMP HOLD-DATE
Brothers Music Hall
Birmingham, AL

May 13, 14
Oasis Ballroom
Sacramento, CA
Notes:
-From a local review: "For all intents and purposes, the Joe Perry Project concert in Sacramento Tuesday night was a one-man show. At the Oasis Ballroom, Joe Perry gave a masterful lesson on how to be a successful rock guitar hero in the process of numbing everyone's hearing and proving that even a wealthy escapee from a group such as Aerosmith can rock with honest enthusiasm. Tearing through 16 songs, including five Aerosmith covers, in an hour and 20 minutes, Perry pulled out all the stops in his guitar work. Perry and his band played crunching heavy metal rave-up endings. Perry played slide guitar. Perry played blues, after a fashion. Perry played using a wah-wah pedal. Perry played blues and wah-wah at the same time. Essentially, Perry played the kind of rock designed to get kids up and out of their seats in the back rows of hockey arenas, and in a place the size of the Oasis ballroom, the effect bordered on overkill, but was a lot of fun anyway. By the time the Joe Perry Project's set was half over, it had become evident that Perry is one of the premier commercial heavy metal guitarists around, easily outclassing such people as Eddie Van Halen and many others. Despite his stature though, it was refreshing to see that Perry abstained from the egotistical strutting and posing typical of most heavy metal heavies. Instead, Perry, hair hanging in his face and wearing an old T-shirt, seemed eager to just play his music. He was humorously self-deprecating about his role in the band, introducing himself as playing 'occasional lead guitar.' Perry also seemed pleased to announce that a second show had been added the next day for under eighteen-year-olds, normally excluded from the Oasis.

Perry's band was equally enthusiastic, but not nearly as distinguished as their leader. Bassist David Hull and drummer Ronnie Stewart gave Perry a firm foundation to work from but didn't contribute much beyond that. Lead vocalist Ralph Morman seemed even more dispensable, working the stage with a manner derivative of Rod Stewart, and singing with an unexceptional voice. In fact, during five songs in mid-show,

Morman left the stage entirely, and Perry took over on vocals... Just about the only detraction from Perry's show was the volume. Playing at a level that makes walls in the back vibrate, sterilizes insects, stuns small animals, and turns human ears into vestigial attachments, the band's loudness obliterated whatever subtleties were imbued in the music. Fifteen feet in front of the stage all the instruments could be heard fairly clearly, but anywhere else in the club the resonance was bad enough to make most vocals unintelligible and smear the bass and drums into an undistinguishable mess. Given the all-important role Perry plays in his new band, the circumstances of his split with Aerosmith, and the way he drowned out the rest of his group in concert, it would be easy to say that Joe Perry is merely interested in self-indulgence, not having to share the spotlight with anyone. Seeing the frank enjoyment with which Perry played Tuesday night though, I'm willing to give him the benefit of the doubt, as was the rest of the audience" (California Aggie, 5/17/1980).

May 15
Keystone
Berkeley, CA
Promoter: in-house
Other act(s): Earth Quake
Notes:
- Joe was interviewed backstage by Dave Zimmer for a feature that ran in Creem magazine in August.

May 16
The Stone
San Francisco, CA
Promoter: in-house
Other act(s): Snail, The Scooters (opener)

May 17
Keystone
Palo Alto, CA
Promoter: in-house
Other act(s): Snail, The Scooters (opener)

May 20
Star Palace @ Warnors Theater
Fresno, CA
Other act(s): The Scooters (opener)

May 22
Club House
Santa Ana, CA
Notes:
- An AUD recording circulates from this show.

May 23
Civic Auditorium
Santa Monica, CA
Promoter: Avalon Attractions
Other act(s): Carmine Appice's Rockers
Reported audience: 2,612 / 3,500 (74.63%)

Reported gross: $22,855
Notes:
- Joe was interviewed backstage by Sylvie Simmons for a feature that ran in Sounds (UK, 7/5/1980).
- From a local review: "Friday night at Santa Monica Civic, the Joe Perry Project showed that it is three bands in one — an Aerosmith spinoff carrying on that group's sound, a re-creation of the late-'60s Jeff Beck Band, and a new outfit forging a hard rock pretty much its own. Overall, this mix was satisfactory, but overemphasized its leader's nostalgic leanings. Perry, the guitarist who left Aerosmith a few months ago, formed this quartet around his flavorful if seldom top rate playing. An encouraging debut album resulted, and the band is just as enjoyable onstage. It would have been more praiseworthy, though, had its chief left some of his idolizing behind. Not only does Perry often approximate Beck's style, but he's hired a singer (Ralph Morman) who generally copies the raspy vocals of Rod Stewart — who sang with Beck early in his career.

Though agreeable enough, this tactic became a bit ludicrous Friday when 'Reefer-Headed Woman' (from Aerosmith's last LP) came out sounding very much like the Beck-Stewart 'Blues De Luxe.' Two more Aerosmith numbers, 'Walk This Way' and 'Same Old Song,' were understandable bows to the many Aerosmith fans attending (the hall fell only a couple hundred short of a sellout). But ideally, they'll be dropped to make room for more original material. The latter made up the set's highlights: 'Rockin' Train,' 'Life at a Glance' and the stirring encore 'Let the Music Do the Talking,' some of which Perry sang himself with considerable effectiveness. If he expands on the groundwork he's laid with these songs, and if Morman can find more to do than copy Stewart and constantly hold the mike stand at a 50-degree angle, the Project might become a great rock band rather than a merely good one" (Los Angeles Times, 5/26/1980).

May 24
Raincross Square
Riverside, CA

Promoter: Climax Productions / Laguna Seaberg
Other act(s): The Scooters, The Look
Notes:
- Ted Nugent, who was performing nearby at the Swing Auditorium, hoped to jam with Joe at a nightclub following their respective gigs. Ralph later recalled that they jammed Savoy Brown's "Needle and Spoon" with him.

May 26
Civic Center
Yuma, AZ

Promoter: Climax Productions
Other act(s): The Scooters, Spider Kelly (opener)
Reported audience: 880

May 27 **TWO SHOWS
Roxy Theatre
San Diego, CA

Promoter: Fahn & Silva Presents
Other act(s): The Scooters
Reported audience: 1,037 / 1,258 (82.43%)
Reported gross: $7,545
Notes:
- The Project performed shows at 7:30 and 10p.m in the 629-seat venue.
- From a local review: "When one particular member of a rock band emerges as the star, there's usually a good reason. Generally, the reason is that that person's combination of skills and personality — charisma if

you will — automatically attracts public attention. Most often, of course, the star is the lead singer, who in the course of performing focus not on an instrument but exclusively on the audience and keeps in closest touch with it. So, when an instrumentalist strikes on his own, he undertakes the adventure at great risk. Joe Perry, until last October the lead guitarist for Aerosmith, has taken that chance. Judging from the first of two shows last night at the Roxy Theater by Perry and his new group, the Joe Perry Project, he shouldn't have bothered. Perry's performance was reminiscent of the New Barbarians tour undertake a year or two back by guitarists Ron Wood and Keith Richard of the Rolling Stones and a retinue of sidemen. Bit highly respected musicians, neither Wood nor Richard had the force of personality needed to glue a show together and keep it in focus. The menacing power of Mick Jagger was greatly missed, and it was easy to see why he, and not Wood or Richard, is the star of the Stones. Likewise, it was plain at the Roxy why lead singer Steve Tyler, and not Joe Perry, became the star of Aerosmith. His androgynous pout, his fey campy gestures and his slinky costumes may only be juvenile imitations of the Jagger shtick, but they are what the crowd watches.

Perry provided the slam-bang-crash guitar licks for Aerosmith, and he continues in the same vein with his new group. But his own stage personality is stiff and awkward, obviously, ill at ease as the target of the spotlight. He has none of Tyler's cuteness, and there is little reason to watch him, even when he plays the guitar while holding it behind his head. Ralph Morman now serves adequately as part-time lead vocalist, with David Hull on Bass and Ronnie Stewart on drums, but Perry sings himself quite a bit. Most of the time his vocalizing was passable, but in 'Heartbreak Hotel' it was hopeless. The Project's style, like that of Aerosmith, is basic, straight-ahead rock 'n' roll, but now with the emphasis on endless guitar solos. Without the distraction of Tyler's posturing, however, Perry's guitar work is cruelly exposed in all its repetitive emptiness. All were at their best in the oldie, 'It's All Over Now,' which was offered in agreeably bluesy fashion, and in 'Rockin' Train,' one of the several tunes taken from Perry's first solo album, heavy featured Morman's vocal impersonation of James Brown" (San Diego Union, 5/28/1980).

May 28 **TWO SHOWS CANCELLED
Dooley's
Tucson, AZ

Promoter: Evening Star Productions
Notes:
- These shows were cancelled due to Joe not feeling well and poor ticket sales, though the promoter felt that the show would have had decent walk-up attendance.

May 29
Dooley's
Tempe, AZ

Promoter: Evening Star Productions
Notes:
- From a local review: "One thing about heavy metal music: You know what you're going to get long before it comes — a sound as relentless and powerful as a locomotive on full throttle. Along with the power come risks — musical and technical. For one thing, distortion and a lack of balance can smother all other aspects of the music. A venue such as Dooley's, which has all the acoustic merit of a box canyon, is particularly susceptible. Not only on musical grounds but also, it seems, on technical. Joe Perry's band blew out one of the club's two speaker banks Thursday. Perry left Aerosmith last year amid the usual talk of developing potential but also with encouraging promises of a strong rhythm-and-blues influence in his ensuing work. Naturally, he also was expected to continue in a heavy rock 'n' roll tradition.

On that level, the Joe Perry Project satisfied expectations Thursday. The group was a little weak in the vocal section. Neither Perry nor lead vocalist Ralph Morman has a distinctive voice. But the rhythm section — drummer Ronnie Stewart and bassist David Hull — was strong, and some of the tightest numbers were as a trio with Perry's lead guitar. With Perry at his most sensitive and Stewart and Hall laying a good solid beat, I couldn't help making distant comparisons with Cream. But the strength of Cream was that it never lost sight of that beat, whereas, once Project speeded up, the group disappeared in a thick fog of distortion and blanket sound. What was most disappointing was that the promised R&B influence never amounted to much more than window dressing. It was doubly frustrating because Perry and company clearly had the ability to go beyond heavy metal to the subtler tempo of R&B. Stewart and Hull showed that when they were given free rein to develop the rhythm during the number that blew the speakers" (Arizona Republic, 5/31/1980).

May 30
Ballroom @ U.N.M
Albuquerque, NM
Promoter: ASUNM Popular Entertainment Committee

June 2
Stages
St. Louis, MO

June 3
Bushes
Omaha, NE

June 4
Pogo's
Kansas City, MO
Promoter: The Concert Group

June 6
The Opry
Austin, TX
Promoter: Pace Concerts
Other act(s): Laurie & The Sighs
Reported audience: (1,700 capacity)

June 7 **TWO SHOWS
The Palace
Houston, TX
Promoter: in-house / Pace Concerts
Other act(s): Laurie & The Sighs
Reported audience: 1,370
Reported gross: $6,922
Notes:
- The project performed sets at 8 and 11p.m.

June 8
Agora
Dallas, TX
Other act(s): Laurie & The Sighs
Notes:
- Some ads noted the Project appearing at the Bijou.
- From a local review: "The kindest thing one can say about a performance by rock guitarist Joe Perry is that it is bearable longer than a concert by Perry's former

associates, Aerosmith. Perry also seems to have a keener sense of the direction of his music than the more scattered Aerosmith, and according to a comment he dropped during his show Sunday night at the Agora, that is precisely the reason he suddenly left that band last year to form the Joe Perry Project. As an introduction to the song 'Bright White Fright,' Perry said, 'Here is a song I wrote when I was with Aerosmith, but they wouldn't let me play it.' But there are two things Perry doesn't have. The first is a talent for playing the blues guitar. He tried it twice Sunday night, and his blues technique involves adding a little more reverberation to his rock sound. The second is a talent for vocals.

Although Perry has enlisted a lead vocalist for the Project, a singer named Ralph Morman who sounds like a Rod Stewart who hasn't mastered voice control, Perry's Project too often performed as a trio (with Ron Stewart on drums and David Hull on bass), and on these occasions Perry sang lead. His rendition of 'Heartbreak Hotel,' for instance, made a mockery of Elvis Presley's original, and I don't think that was Perry's intention. In fact, Hull, who sang lead on one chorus of 'It's All Over Now,' sounded better than Perry. Although the first 10 or so rows closest to the stage seemed to be excited by Perry's performance, the feeling wasn't contagious. Those situated farther back in the club sat on their hands throughout the evening. A measure of the Perry group's accessibility is that it even made the Bobby Womack classic 'It's All Over Now' sound terribly dull" (Dallas Morning News, 6/10/1980).

June 10
Skip Willey's
San Antonio, TX

June 11
Columbia Studios
New York City, NY
Other act(s): Bram Tchaikovsky
Reported audience: ~150
Set list: Life at A Glance / Rockin' Train / Shooting Star / Heartbreak Hotel / The Mist is Rising / Ready on the Firing Line / Break Song / Let the Music Do the Talking
Notes:
- Recorded for a live radio program, "Afternoon Live." The show was an experimental broadcast by D.I.R. Broadcasting to engage younger listeners during a more favorable time slot. According to DIR's Peter Kauff, the company felt the show "circumvents the competition most live broadcasts get from other evening activities, such as actual concerts and primetime TV, and he also points out that the feature, scheduled for 3–4:30PM, will come 'at a time when the kids are coming home from school; it's drive-time, the heaviest listening period in radio'" (Record World, 6/14/1980). Fortunately for fans, the Project engaged in numerous radio broadcasts during their lifespan.

June 13 **TWO SHOWS
Poet's Inn
Memphis, TN
Other act(s): Laurie & The Sighs
Notes:
- The Project were booked to perform 8 and 11p.m. shows.

June 14
This New Place
New Orleans, LA
Other act(s): Laurie & The Sighs

June 15
Slick's Music Hall

St. Martinville, LA
Promoter: in-house
Other act(s): Laurie & The Sighs

June 17
Brothers Music Hall
Birmingham, AL
Other act(s): Laurie & The Sighs

June 18
The Agora Ballroom
Atlanta, GA
Other act(s): Laurie & The Sighs

June 20
Palladium
New York City, NY
Other act(s): .38 Special
Notes:
- From a local review: "Joe Perry spent much of the 70's playing in stadiums and arenas as lead guitarist for Aerosmith. One suspects his years on this circuit kept him well insulated from the economic realities of the rock world's lower echelons. In any event, he's deluding himself if he thinks he's going to achieve overwhelming success as a solo artist with shows like the one he gave at the Palladium on Friday night. Mr. Perry seems to want to project a wasted-but-tough stage presence, something like Johnny Thunders. But he's too cute and clean cut, and his playing lacks the discipline and rhythmic drive that characterizes Mr. Thunder's and other guitarists of the Keith Richards school even when they're more wasted than tough.

His band, especially the Rod Stewart sound-alike on lead vocals, is ordinary; his own singing is pleasant enough but severely limited. There's no reason why Mr. Perry can't succeed as a solo artist; he has some good ideas, and his playing doesn't lack drama. But he's going to have to rethink his plan of attack — the competition is a lot stronger than he seems to think it is. The .38 Special, an energetic but fairly ordinary Southern guitar band, preceded Mr. Perry's group and connected with the audience much more easily. Despite a certain lack of imagination, .38 Special has a firm grasp of rock-and-roll basics and is unself-conscious about using them. One hopes Mr. Perry was listening" (New York Times, 1/23/1980).

June 23 **CANCELLED
Capital Centre
Largo (Landover), MD
Promoter: Cellar Door Productions
Other act(s): Laurie & The Sighs
Notes:
- This was initially a tentative booking date for the "Summerfun" series of concerts that ran June 21–28, though tickets were certainly printed.

June 25
Poplar Creek Music Theater
Hoffman Estates, IL
Promoter: Nederlander Organization
Other act(s): Sammy Hagar (HL)
Reported audience: ~2,500 / 20,000 (12.5%)
Notes:
- Sammy was supporting his "Danger Zone" album on his first major headlining tour in the U.S.

June 26
Pine Knob Music Theater
Clarkston (Detroit), MI
Promoter: In-house
Other act(s): Sammy Hagar (HL)
Notes:
- After the tour Morman was fired and temporarily replaced with J. Mala. Ralph quickly hooked up with Kim Simmonds and was singing for Savoy Brown by mid-August. According to Joe, "I fired Ralph Morman and replaced him with J. Mala [the singer for the New York club band Revolver] for the rest of the tour. He lasted three gigs" ("Walk this Way"). Clearly, he lasted more than that, but it's not clear if he was in place for the band's next scheduled show (with Sammy Hagar) ...

July 9
Open Air Amphitheater @ S.D.S.U.
San Diego, CA
Other act(s): Sammy Hagar (HL)

July 13
Toledo Speedway
Toledo, OH
Promoter: Belkin Productions / Chicago
Other act(s): Heart (HL), J. Geils, Blackfoot, Triumph
Reported audience: 32,424
Reported gross: $410,932
Notes:
- Heart were touring in support of their "Bébé le Strange" album which marked a down-shift in their commercial appeal.
- From a local review: "The Joe Perry Project, featuring Joe Perry of the Aerosmith group, opened, and proved that Perry should definitely get back with Aerosmith as soon as possible" (South Bend Tribune, 7/20/1980).

July 14
Civic Arena
Pittsburgh, PA
Other act(s): Heart (HL)
Notes:
- From a local review: "Heart's opening act, the Joe Perry Project, was a less happy affair. If this band has something of value to offer its public, it successfully hides it behind brutal overamplification. Sheer volume can traumatize and audience, but it cannot, in itself, move it. Loudspeaker feedback, in likewise, is not an expressive device; it simply blinds (or deafens) us momentarily to what is essentially a paucity of musical substance" (Pittsburgh Post-Gazette, 7/15/1980).
- From another local review: "Last night's warm-up group was the Joe Perry Project, headed by the ex-Aerosmith guitarist; their album peaked at No. 47 in late May and now is off the charts completely... Perry and his trio offered exactly what you'd expect from an Aerosmith member (so how come he left Aerosmith — artistic differences? Not hardly.) — loud, hard rock, loud enough to make singer Ralph Morman largely excess baggage. The few times Perry sang, it was obvious why Steven Tyler was and is Aerosmith's lead

vocalist. 'Life at a Glance' was the way to start a set; 'Discount Dogs,' the all-instrumental 'Bone to Bone,' 'The Mist Is Rising,' 'Rockin' Train' and the touch more melodic 'Let the Music Do the Talking' were pretty good ways to continue it. Drummer Ron Stewart had a good solo on 'Break Tune' and Perry fired off some mean guitar licks the whole time, but Perry's lackluster vocals on 'Heartbreak Hotel' won't cost Elvis Presley's ghost any sleep" (Pittsburgh Press, 7/15/1980).

July 15
Cambria County War Memorial
Johnstown, PA
Promoter: DiCesare-Engler
Other act(s): Heart (HL)
Reported audience: 4,197 / 6,000 (69.95%)
Reported gross: $33,440
Notes:
- From a local review: "The excellent performance of Heart contrasted sharply with the warm-up act, 'The Joe Perry Project.' Hard, loud and little else, the effort by Aerosmith's former guitarist only drew audience response with Elvis' 'Heartbreak Hotel,' Aerosmith's 'Walk this Way,' which Perry wrote and at their introduction, when they entered to a recording of 'William Tell Overture'" (Daily American, 7/19/1980).

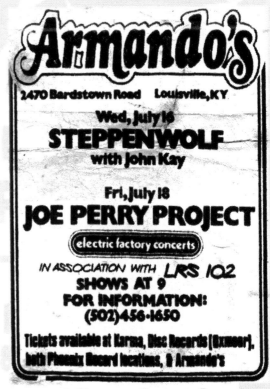

July 18
Armando's
Louisville, KY
Promoter: Electric Factory Concerts

July 19
Market Square Arena
Indianapolis, IN
Promoter: Sunshine Promotions
Other act(s): Heart (HL)
Reported audience: 7,093 / 18,000 (39.41%)
Reported gross: $61,332

July 20 **POSTPONED
Riverfront Coliseum
Cincinnati, OH
Promoter: Electric Factory Concerts
Other act(s): Heart (HL)
Notes:
- This show was postponed until July 30, and the Project were replaced by The Silencers for that date.

July 22
Five Seasons Center
Cedar Rapids, IA
Promoter: The Amusement Conspiracy
Other act(s): Heart (HL)
Reported audience: 6,987 / 9,000 (76.63%)
Reported gross: $62,253
Notes:
- From a local review: "The only drawback to the evening was the opening act, Joe Perry Project — which was just that, a project. The group should go back to the neighborhood garage and work on its original

material, which lacks creativity and finesse and has too much noise. Perry, who recently left as lead guitarist for Aerosmith to form his own band, was loud, incongruous, and difficult to understand. But the crowd voice approval of the songs, and a couple of Aerosmith fans sitting next to me were surprised Perry 'was so good.' They were going to buy his latest album as soon as they could locate it" (Cedar Rapids Gazette, 7/23/1980).

July 23
Rosenblatt Stadium
Omaha, NE
Promoter: Schon Productions
Other act(s): Heart (HL), Blackfoot, Head East
Reported audience: 14,514 / 25,000 (58.1%)
Reported gross: $164,614
Notes:
- From a local review: "The Joe Perry Project, which opened the show, won't be worth watching — or rather, listening to — until it gets somebody who can sing. Perry himself, who used to be Aerosmith's guitarist, can't, as he demonstrated on 'Heartbreak Hotel.' Neither can lead vocalist Joey Mala, as he demonstrated on most of the rest of the songs" (Omaha World-Herald, 7/24/1980).

July 25
MECCA Arena
Milwaukee, WI
Promoter: Stardate Productions
Other act(s): Heart (HL)
Reported audience: (12,000 capacity)
Set list: Life at a Glance / Same Old Song and Dance / Pills / Discount Dogs / Ready on the Firing Line / Bone to Bone / Heartbreak Hotel / Shooting Star / The Mist Is Rising / Rockin' Train / Break Song / Let the Music Do the Talking
Notes:
- A review in the Milwaukee Sentinel doesn't mention the Project but did note that the concert was barely half sold.
- A SBD recording circulates from this show.

July 26
Met Center
Bloomington, MN
Promoter: Schon Productions
Other act(s): Heart (HL)
Reported audience: 11,199 / 16,000 (69.99%)
Reported gross: $99,372
Set list: Life at a Glance / Same Old Song and Dance / Pills / Discount Dogs / Ready on the Firing Line / Bone to Bone / Heartbreak Hotel / Shooting Star / The Mist Is Rising / Break Song / Rockin' Train / Let the Music Do the Talking
Notes:
- An AUD recording circulates from this show.

July 27
Rockford Speedway
Loves Park, IL
Promoter: Kelso Jam Productions, Inc.
Other act(s): Heart (HL), Judas Priest, Scorpions

Notes:
- The Rockford Jam.

July 29
Dane County Memorial Coliseum
Madison, WI
Promoter: Stardate Productions
Other act(s): Heart (HL)
Reported audience: (10,000 capacity)
Notes:

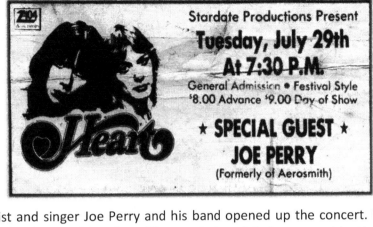

- From a local review: "Ex-Aerosmith guitarist and singer Joe Perry and his band opened up the concert. I certainly hope his old group is not mourning his loss, as his guitar riffs sounded as dated as a presidential candidate's rhetoric. Many in the crowd, bored with the opening act, milled around the Coliseum floor, chitchatting, swilling, and spilling beer and setting off firecrackers" (Wisconsin State Journal, 7/30/1980).

August 8 **TWO SHOWS
Magic 'til Midnight @ Six Flags
Jackson, NJ
Promoter: Six Flags
Notes:
- Entertainment series at Six Flags Great Adventure theme park with shows at 8 and 10p.m.

August 14
Memorial Auditorium
Buffalo, NY
Promoter: Harvey & Corky Presentations
Other act(s): Journey (HL)
Reported audience: (17,827 capacity)
Notes:
- The project opened for Journey, who were supporting their "Departure" album.

August 15
War Memorial Auditorium
Rochester, NY
Promoter: Monarch Entertainment Bureau
Other act(s): Journey (HL)
Reported audience: 8,784 / 20,721 (42.39%)
Reported gross: $76,031

August 16
Fountain Casino
Aberdeen, NJ
Promoter: in-house
Notes:
- Journey played Nassau Coliseum this night, with the Project opting for a solo show.

August 17
Civic Center
Providence, RI

Promoter: Mark Puma Presents
Other act(s): Journey (HL)
Reported audience: (13,000 capacity)

August 20 **PROJECT CANCELLED
Spectrum
Philadelphia, PA

Promoter: Beaver Productions
Other act(s): Journey (HL)
Reported audience: (19,500 capacity)
Notes:
- The Project were replaced by Sterling at this show.

August 21
Stabler Arena @ Lehigh University
Bethlehem, PA

Promoter: Makoul Productions
Other act(s): Journey (HL)
Reported audience: (6,000 capacity)
Notes:
- From a local review: "From the moment Journey took the stage you knew it was going to be a night to remember. Of course, it did help that the opening act, The Joe Perry Project, fell below the mediocre classification. Though Perry is a highly touted musician since he was lead guitarist with Aerosmith, the band could be overshadowed by some of the area's local bands. Journey was just the opposite of the Perry Band as the five members of Journey exemplified professionalism at its best" (Wilkes-Barre Citizens' Voice, 8/29/1980).

August 22
Coliseum
New Haven, CT

Promoter: Cross Country Concerts
Other act(s): Journey (HL)
Reported audience: (10,500 capacity)

August 23
Capital Centre
Largo (Landover), MD

Promoter: Cellar Door Productions
Other act(s): Journey (HL)
Reported audience: (19,000 capacity)
Notes:
- A pro-shot video of Journey's set circulates from the in-house cameras...

August 24
Civic Center
Springfield, MA

Promoter: Cross Country Concerts
Other act(s): Rossington-Collins Band (HL)
Reported audience: 5,778 / 10,347 (55.84%)
Reported gross: $49,286

October 11
Show Place
Dover, NJ

October 17 **TEMP DATE-HOLD
E.M. Loews Theater
Greenfield, MA

October 25 **POSTPONED
Mr. C's Rock Palace
Lowell, MA
Promoter: Rockfever Productions
Notes:
- Show rescheduled for Nov. 1.

October 25
Stage West
Hartford, CT

October 27
Paradise Theater
Boston, MA
Other act(s): The Mirrors
Notes:
- A "Duane Glasscock for President" WBCN fundraising benefit.

November 1
Mr. C's Rock Palace
Lowell, MA
Promoter: Rockfever Productions
Other act(s): The Barker Gang

November 6
Cleveland, OH
Notes:
- When the Statler Office Tower, which housed the studios of Cleveland's WMMS-FM, caught fire, DJ Denny Sanders quickly threw on a Joe Perry Project concert before evacuating, so that the station wouldn't

immediately go off the air. His timing was near perfect, as workers were cleared by authorities to enter the building just before the show concluded.

November 8
Municipal Auditorium
Barre, VT

Promoter: Sundance Talent Productions
Notes:
- A local promoter recalled issues at this show: "Milne was on his way to a radio interview with Perry in Montpelier when the concert hall doors opened and 1,200 fans who were supposed to buy tickets at the door rushed in without paying. He lost all of his savings in one night, he said" (BT Digger, 10/27/2014).

December 31 **PROJECT CANCELLED
Market Square Arena
Indianapolis, IN

Promoter: Sunshine Promotions
Other acts: REO Speedwagon (HL)
Reported audience: 18,000 **SOLD-OUT
Reported gross: $142,232
Notes:
- While they had been scheduled to open this show, which ended up being a monster, it was instead opened by Prisoner.

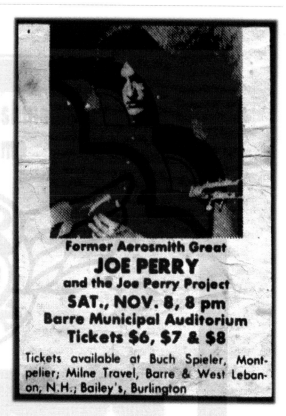

1981

January 6, 1981
Auditorium
Utica, NY

Promoter: John Scherr
Other act(s): Allman Brothers Band (HL)
Reported audience: ~3,500 / 6,000 (58.33%)
Notes:
- From a local review: "The Joe Perry Project, the warm-up band, played a set of uninspired rock, apparently not having learned that loudness does not substitute for ability" (Utica Daily Press, 1/7/1981).

January 9
Headliners North
Nashua, NH

January 10
Hole in the Wall
Rochelle Park, NJ

January 11
El Greco

Bricktown, NJ

January 15
Stabler Arena @ Lehigh University, Bethlehem, PA

Promoter: Monarch Entertainment Bureau
Other act(s): Allman Brothers Band (HL)
Reported audience: 3,700 / 6,000 (61.67%)
Reported gross: $33,300
Notes:
- Joe's son, Adrian, was born 10 days after this show, by which time Joe had placed an ad in the Boston Phoenix and Village Voice seeking a new vocalist...

(Boston Phoenix, 1/13/1981)

1980 - Let the Music Do the Talking

1981 - I've Got the Rock 'n' Rolls Again

U.S. Release Details:
Columbia/CBS FC/FCA/FCT-37364 (June 19, 1981)
Columbia/CBS PC/PCT-37364 (July 1983 — Reissue)
Columbia/CBS CK-37364 (Sept. 1990 — CD issue)

Tracks:
A1. East Coast, West Coast
(3:06) — Charlie Farren
A2. No Substitute for Arrogance
(3:25) — Joe Perry / Charlie Farren
A3. I've Got the Rock 'N' Rolls Again
(4:34) — Joe Perry / Charlie Farren
A4. Buzz Buzz •
(3:41) — David Hull / Andrew Resnick / Charlie Karp
A5. Soldier of Fortune
(3:05) — Joe Perry

B1. TV Police
(4:11) — Joe Perry / Charlie Farren
B2. Listen to the Rock
(3:20) — Charlie Farren
B3. Dirty Little Things
(3:42) — David Hull
B4. Play the Game
(5:20) — Joe Perry / Charlie Farren
B5. South Station Blues
(4:10) — Joe Perry

Album Details:
Produced by Bruce Botnick. Recorded at the Boston Opera House, Boston, MA and Wherehouse, Waltham, MA, by Rik Pekkonen with Record Plant mobile facilities; Engineered by Jack Crymes and James Sandweiss assisted by David Bianco and Jim Scott. Mixed at Oceanway Studios, Los Angeles, CA by Rik Pekkonen assisted by Mark Ettel. Mastered at A&M Studios, Los Angeles, CA, by Bernie Grundman.

Players:
◦ Joe Perry — Lead guitar; vocals.
◦ Charlie Farren — Rhythm guitar; vocals.
◦ David Hull — Bass; vocals.
◦ Ronnie Stewart — Drums & percussion.

Chart Action:
Chart Peak (USA): #100 (8/8/1981) during 10 weeks on the Billboard Top-200 album charts. The album also reached #79 on Cashbox (8/8/1981). Other countries: N.A.

07/04/81	07/11/81	07/18/81	07/25/81	08/01/81	**08/08/81**	08/15/81
174	146	136	115	105	** 100 **	112
08/22/81	08/29/81	09/05/81	09/12/81			
137	146	193	X			

RIAA/Sales:
This album has never received any sales certification.

Supporting Singles:
● "Buzz Buzz" (Columbia 18-02497) was released as a single, backed with "East Coast, West Coast." The 2:40 edit failed to chart on the Billboard Hot-100. However, "Listen to the Rock" did appear in the non-mainstream Billboard "Top Tracks" chart reaching #48 during three weeks.

"I called the album 'I've Got the Rock 'n' Rolls Again' because I did. Like the first Project record, this one was made without strife or procrastination. I was hoping that my promptness might convince Columbia not only that I was still taking my band seriously, but that my band was here to stay..." (Perry, Joe - "Rocks: My Life In and Out of Aerosmith").

Early 1981 was a life changing period for Joe Perry. The Mk.II version of the Projects played a final run of shows at the start of January, mixing club dates with a couple of opening slots for the Allman Brothers Band. More important to the guitarist personally, was the birth of his son, Adrian, on January 25. With his debt load causing personal consternation, and the results of an only moderately successful band at the time, the pressures were mounting on the Admiral he quickly realized that it was time to get back to work. The first album had been a positive start to his solo career, but the challenges the band had faced meant that they had not quite attained what Joe had hoped. During the year Leber-Krebs had dropped from the scene fully, and Joe had switched from his reliance on lawyer Bob Casper to more musically suited management in the form of Don Law, who he hoped would be better placed to serve his needs. The band's vocalist, J. Mala, had moved on — he soon became the production manager for Rage Records prior to advancing further on the business side of the industry. Seeking a replacement, Joe placed an ad for a "singer and rhythm guitar player" in New York's seminal Village Voice and his local Boston Phoenix. Joe received over 100 responses, and there commenced the challenge of sifting through the tapes to find suitable candidates to call, and then perhaps audition. He recalled, "I got everything from women to guys who play Vegas... I got guys who couldn't play guitar to save their lives; I got guys who couldn't sing, and I got a lot of talented people. But out of all those tapes. Charlie was the one" (Nyack Journal News, 10/11/1981).

Charlie Farren had become a solid part of the Boston music scene at the time. He submitted an application that included two of his original songs, "Listen to the Rock" and "East Coast, West Coast," to illustrate his musical strengths. By that time, he'd been working the region for most of the previous decade, having started his professional career with the band Live Lobster; after playing with a series of cover bands after finishing high school. The band was developing a solid reputation in the clubs of the Northeast and was soon playing the club grind, often five sets a night, five nights a week. Charlie recalled, "although we mostly played cover songs, we didn't play the hits, rather focusing on artists like Savoy Brown, Led Zeppelin and Jeff Beck, with a few hits sprinkled in to keep us employable" (Goldmine, 9/5/2014). It would be with this band where Charlie developed his vocal chops by covering a plethora of other vocalist's material night after night. However, he wanted to focus on writing and performing original material, so he and Berklee trained guitarist Ken Kalayjian left to form Balloon. Charlie recalled, "we started developing an all-original repertoire and began to really catch on. Loud and heavy! We started to try to establish ourselves as a one or two set act, and began filling places like The Club, The Rat, Jasper's in Somerville, and eventually started headlining and filling The Channel" (Malden Wicked Local, 10/2/2008). Demos recorded at home on a 4-track machine received airplay on local radio stations, WAAF, WBCN and WCOZ, regularly dominating their hit lists and Atlantic Records' Ahmet Ertegun took note of the band's songwriter.

Charlie recalled the audition process, "I sent in some pictures and I sent in those two songs. I heard back from their manager Don Law. He said, 'Come in, and let's meet. Let's see if it leads to the next step.' So, I met him, and I met Joe. I went down to the Orpheum Theatre for the audition. It's a big 2,700 seat theater in Boston. I walked in and there were probably 15 to 20 guys sitting there, sitting in their seats with their guitars, waiting for their turn. Everybody played in front of everybody else. I remember looking around and thinking 'I got this. No way I'm not going to get this gig.' It immediately clicked right away" (MusicGuy247, 2/8/2019). Perry liked him, he sang well and was a solid enough rhythm guitarist that would allow Joe a more familiar musical structure within the band. The two quickly got to work in Joe's basement knocking some of Joe's rough ideas into shape. Joe already had "Station Song," "First One's for Free," "TV Police," the planned title track "Soldier of Fortune," and "I Got the Rock & Rolls Again" in various forms of completion. Charlie noted, "He had a mansion with a really nice studio in the basement and we'd go down there. I was really surprised at his work ethic. He played, and played, and played... rolled tape... listen back. I'd write all the time, but I'd sit down for maybe an hour. Then I'd put it down and come back to it. Joe would go for four or five hours... just grinding it out" (MusicGuy247, 2/8/2019). The strong songwriting of Farren was clearly seen as a benefit to Joe's riffing strengths and the band was soon finalizing arrangements during their rehearsals at the Wherehouse. To keep his head above water financially, Joe had to move fast. Charlie: "Joe wanted something completely different than either Aerosmith or the first JPP record... [He] was also very open to co-writing, which I thought to be generous. We co-wrote four songs on that record, and we also did two of mine, two of David's, and two of Joe's. That was a great band, and it would have developed into a really powerful unit" (Malden Wicked Local, 10/2/2008).

In early March, the band performed a limited series of regional engagements billed as the new Joe Perry Project. It was simply an opportunity "to get their feet on the ground, work out the new songs in front of live audiences, and generally loosen-up" (PR). The band made their local debut at Boston's Paradise Theater on March 10 and it was during those sets that songs such as "No Substitute for Arrogance" and "Soldier of Fortune" received their first public performances. It's also somewhat incredible to consider that just weeks after joining Charlie the band, the band had commenced recording an album. It was hardly surprising that the Opera House was utilized. Not only was it suitable for capturing the essence of rock and roll the band were creating, but there were also cost savings benefits. It also provided a unique atmosphere. Joe recalled, "every day there'd be something going on... like pimps beating up their whores right in front of the sound truck. It was pretty heavy" (Circus, 8/31/1981). Located near the Combat Zone, the city's adult entertainment district, it wasn't too far removed from the societal seediness that had influenced "Get Your Wings" and "Rocks." Joe also noted, "the theater was like a gorgeous woman gone to seed. You could see and feel traces of her former glory, but the paint was peeling, and the floors were cracked. I liked all that decay. The rooms were huge marble affairs ... the acoustics were naturally sublime" (Perry, Joe - "Rocks: My Life In and Out of Aerosmith"). However, the appeal of the environs he described could easily be read as a metaphor for his own current state. However, it should be noted that the Boston Opera House had ended its life as a movie theater in 1980 and been refurbished for the Opera Company of Boston (which had a disappointing 1980 season, but 300 dates booked for 1981) though other nearby theaters were still run-down.

While there had been some initial conversations about a second record, producer Jack Douglas was unavailable. He had been working with John Lennon and Yoko Ono at the time and was reeling from Lennon's murder in December 1980 (the recordings that would be posthumously released as "Milk and Honey" in 1984). An alternative was required... Bruce Botnick is probably best known for his work with the Doors. However, by mid-1980 he was a Columbia staff producer working with popular acts such as Kenny Loggins and generating top-20 hits such as "Don't Fight It" and "Heart to Heart" which followed Kenny's "Caddyshack" theme "I'm Alright." Whatever the case, Joe's appreciation of his work on the Doors' "L.A. Woman" was more than enough to vouch for Bruce's credibility — for that release he had directed the band away from the embellished sound of then recent efforts and dialed in a perfectly stated stripped-down sound. Joe was known for regularly getting amped up for a show by listening to the Sex Pistols' "Never Mind the Bollocks..." album, and to a certain extent, elements of that genre and album show through with the sound and attitude on "Rock 'n' Rolls Again." When approached about working with Joe, Bruce (who had wanted to work with Aerosmith and had served as Executive Producer on the "California Jam 2" album in 1978) suggested that he and Joe get together so that he could first get a feel for where Joe wanted to head with the project. Joe sent Bruce some demos for review, and then played additional songs for him when the two got together in Boston. Initially, there was no overriding plan for the album to bear any sonic relation to anything else, Bruce was most interested in the material that Joe had, rather than thinking about how the final product might sound. There was a decent amount of material to choose from, though some songs were incomplete ideas and were finished during the sessions.

Recording was quick, utilizing the Record Plant's remote truck at the Boston Opera House to capture a band playing live on the studio. The Opera House had been Bruce's idea, with him feeling that the material would be best translated into a recording by having the band on a stage performing it. Charlie recalled, "They parked in the alley behind the Opera House. We set up on the stage and did it live... no audience. A lot of these were first takes" (MusicGuy247, 2/8/2019). There would be overdubs, including some recorded at the Wherehouse, but there was a deliberate attempt to capture the band and not have an overthought-out sound and production and with Botnick's history and having come off Loggins' "Alive" album he was dialed in for that methodology (as an experienced Columbia staff producer he was ready to hit the ground for any project). For Charlie, though, it was a somewhat unexpected experience. He later noted, "I was surprised by

Joe's approach. Aerosmith's calling card, besides the big guitar riffs, is great grooves and clever, punchy, precisely played arrangements. So, I was expecting that. Joe had those big riffs alright, but he was much more in the moment, much more raw and edgy. He wanted to make a punk-rock record, more Clash or Sex Pistols" (Malden Wicked Local, 10/2/2008). The process of woodshedding some of the idea pieces into songs during recording added an essence of rawness to the song, something that would usually have been smoothed over during a lengthy pre-production period. Even the lobby would be used for recording, with its construction providing a solid reverb.

The material released on the album can be split into three categories: Joe's, band member contributions, and collaborations. While Joe only received two songs credited specifically to himself, it wasn't due to him being devoid of ideas or lazy. Several of his initial ideas were fully worked into songs with Charlie, once he joined the band. Those two solo compositions, "Soldier of Fortune" and "South Station Blues," were generally already fully formed. The latter of these had been based on a riff born at the tail-end of his Aerosmith career as "Shit House Shuffle." Both were later included on Aerosmith's "Pandora's Box" to illustrate the point, and the 1981 album version was also included on the Various Artists compilation "Guitar Wars" (Columbia FC/FCT-36842) released in late-1982. "Soldier of Fortune" bore the title Joe had hoped to use as the album's title and had regularly mentioned in the press the previous year. He and Charlie would use four of the songs they wrote together. Charlie recalled, "The four I wrote with Joe were mostly just kind of strumming and listening in the studio. He was very generous with his time and allowed me to throw in my two cents" (MusicGuy247, 2/8/2019). These included "No Substitute for Arrogance," eventual title-track "I've Got the Rock 'n' Rolls Again," "TV Police," and "Play the Game." The first of these, a very Steven Tyler-esqe turn of phrase, was even considered for use as the album's title due to all the band members feeling so strongly about it as a song during pre-production rehearsals. The song-writing process was very collaborative, and Charlie recalled, "Joe and I have very different writing styles. When I write, I think of the melody first. Joe, on the other hand, rips out these great guitar riffs first and builds on that. It all seems to work out. So, he gives me these licks, and I think of what to sing. It's a very different approach — mine is more melodic — but it's all working out well. I'm excited about a new song called 'Third World War.' He's come up with the guitar parts, and I got a melody on it. So far it's working out nicely" (Boston Rock #17). The new input, buttressed by a supportive rhythm player, allowed Joe to expand into new areas of expression.

Both of the songs included Charlie's application demo were recorded by the Project. "Listen to the Rock," a song that he had originally recorded on his own had served as a vehicle for him to learn various recording techniques though. According to Charlie, the song had been recorded "around 1977 on a Teac 3440 1/4" 4-track machine in my bedroom of my parent's house, with Bobby Sutton's drums in my attic" (reverbnation). It proved popular on Boston's powerhouse radio stations even though it didn't sound like a band performance. It also proved popular with Joe, and the preexisting local popularity may have been tempting to co-opt. However, the opportunity to rerecord the song was also an opportunity for it to be recorded properly. Another Balloon recycle was "East Coast, West Coast," which had also been popular on WBCN the previous year, though lyrical changes were made. Bassist David Hull also contributed to the songwriting providing "Dirty Little Things." "Buzz Buzz," a second song, which he had written with Andrew Resnick and Charlie Karp, had been recorded by his previous band, the Dirty Angels. It had originally been released on their self-titled album (A&M SP/CS-4716) in 1978. Perhaps surprisingly, the song became the album's first (and only) single, backed with "East Coast, West Coast" (Columbia 18-02497), though it failed to chart. Other former Balloon songs were also considered for the sessions, including "Political Vertigo" and "I'm No Loner," and Charlie noted that the band had essentially recorded enough material for two albums because of the whole band effort on material. That Balloon's "Political Vertigo" was due to be released on WCOZ's "Best of the Boston Beat, Volume II," may ultimately have precluded its use. Charlie commented, soon after the band's Boston debut, "I'm singing more than I originally expected to, and I'm doing a lot of writing. Everybody in the band is too, it really is a band effort. In a way, it's all something I didn't anticipate" (Boston Rock #17).

Other leftovers from these sessions purportedly include a version of "Heartbreak Hotel," which had regularly featured in the Project's live sets, and Joe's "First One's for Free" (copywritten in May 1981 along with other material from the album) though neither they or extra Balloon tracks were necessarily recorded during the short, focused Opera House sessions. In fact, Botnick has recalled that the sessions were extremely focused, with only a specific list of songs being recorded for the album from the initial catalogue of ideas that he reviewed with Joe. He suggests that if there were any extras, then they would have had to have been really good to carry any weight for consideration for inclusion and that no covers were recorded (other than the songs being recycled from earlier band member projects). There was, after all, only so much that could be put on an album in the days where vinyl had a sweet spot for the duration of each side and quality of pressing and sound. Tape and studio time costs money, and the Opera House had been booked on a flat-rate in-between the stage productions scheduled there.

The sessions went fast, with bed tracks being captured at the Opera House in roughly a week. For Charlie, the speed was more a result of the effort that had gone into pre-production Ronnie felt, "There are bands spending a lot of time going over stuff in the studio and it just doesn't sound live or free. We wanted more excitement. Like, you know, what they got on the old Led Zeppelin stuff. It's still just at the experimental stage, it's just what we're about now" (Boston Rocks #17). Ultimately, there wasn't much for Botnick to do to "capture a spontaneous, live feeling on the sessions" (PR). The band were prepared and were blasting through the material, while Botnick focused on capturing the best performances from the musicians. Charlie recalled, "We were writing lyrics on paper taped to the floor and just were ripping through and keeping first takes. I thought it was fun, and we ended up with a pretty cranked-sounding record. So, Joe wanted something completely different than either Aerosmith or the first JPP record" (Malden Wicked Local, 10/2/2008). The band's preparation and professionalism made fast possible, though Bruce was also working on rough mixes of the songs while still in the remote truck! Another notable factor may have been that Joe was singing less on the album. It may simply have been a case of the previous year getting it out of his system, and him wanting to focus more on his playing. His voice was what it was, and certainly suited some of the material he wrote, but the show had certainly been impacted in the first half of 1980 with extended sections as a trio. At least when Joe sang, Charlie could continue with his rhythm playing.

In advance of the album's release, the band hit the road in May with a short run of East Coast club shows, plus a single opening slot for Ozzy which Don Law was promoting at Springfield's Civic Center. A tour with the Rossington-Collins Band was postponed when that band needed more time in the studio (an album scheduled for August release was delayed until October), leading to the Project having to scramble for work to plug the gap. If there was a drop-off in label effort promotionally, new cuts were still included on CBS loss-leader type albums such as "Guitar Wars" ("South Station Blues") and "Speaker Death! (Heavy Metal Head-Bangers)" ("No Substitute for Arrogance") along with additional label radio promo sampler albums. Basic no-frills performance videos were shot for "I've Got the Rock 'N' Rolls Again" and "East Coast, West Coast," but until August 1981 there were few places to broadcast them. Whatever the label situation, the album was certainly distributed in fewer markets than its predecessor. The band did appear on Rockline on Aug. 17, on an episode shared with Def Leppard and The Ramones. Ronnie had hoped that the band would visit Japan, with the first album having sold about ten or fifteen thousand copies" (Boston Rock #17) there, but that excursion wasn't possible without substantial backing. The band eventually lined up separate opening runs with ZZ Top and Nazareth, but by the end of the year they were back in the regional clubs with an album that had died a quick death on the charts.

With the financial noose tightening around Joe's neck, and the knock-on effect of cutting costs with the band, departures from the ranks were inevitable. Sensing that Aerosmith was not just a part of Joe's past, Charlie and David's departed the Project, though their leaving didn't immediately translate into musical success. Charlie went to work at Boston Music Company but soon formed The Enemy with David, and members of Charlie's old band, Balloon (Ken Kalayjian and drummer Bob Sutton). They'd heat up WBCN during the summer of 1982 with the anthemic "America Rocks" independent single. Joe, on the other hand, had found that Don Law wouldn't bail him out, but had at least met someone who thought he could do something for him...

Assorted review excerpts:

"Second LP by the former Aerosmith guitarist keeps alive the head banging kind of intense rock that Perry has been playing since Aerosmith. Perry's lead guitar blazes its way through 10 rough and tumble tracks that hard rock fans (and radio) should embrace almost instantly. For some reason, no matter how indistinguishable these licks are, there is a huge demand for ferocious heavy metal" (Billboard, 6/27/1981).

"The incendiary guitarist for Aerosmith ventured off into his own solo career last year and got a thumbs up from AOR programmers. His second time at bat is another barroom brawl of a rock album. Perry plays a gruff and bloozy form of rock that's closer to Keith Richards than it is to heavy metal honchos like Angus Young or Eddie Van Halen, and it should please mainstream rollers to no end" (Cashbox, 7/4/1981).

"Joe Perry probably caught the 'small is beautiful' ethic when Aerosmith was playing the Paradise under the pseudonym of 'Dr. Jay and the Interns.' When Perry left the band in late 1979, he set out to squander his Beckian postures in smaller halls — places which became anomalies for Aerosmith. It shouldn't be an oddity, then, that this new album was recorded using the Boston Opera House as the studio. Whether it's a token or grand gesture, Joe Perry can lay down classy licks anywhere. The title cut is a sneaky variation of 'Milk Cow Blues Boogie,' but Perry works it over nicely — strutting it as if he were playing in a garage band. Perry doesn't hide his influences but relishes them by lending a charged enthusiasm. 'South Station Blues' is an Alvin Lee foot-stomper. 'Soldier of Fortune,' a wry number with a thug-like harmony, unleashes a run of guitar pyrotechnics. When affairs cool down with the starry-eyed 'Play the Game,' Perry magnetizes with a sharp guitar. What holds this album back is its terse economy, although there's no doubt rhythm guitarist Charlie Farren, bassist David Hull, and percussionist Ronnie Stewart round out a solid quartet that rocks beneath the ribs" (Boston Globe, 7/9/1981).

"Joe Perry's second album shows some promise but has a lack of direction. But this is not as big a putdown as you might think, because it was not Perry's intention to make a sleek, slick, rock and roll record. Thus, the name 'project.' Perry's brilliant, and violent, guitar work was the heart of the old Aerosmith band, but wisely he decided to quit taking a back seat to hammy Steve Tyler. Perry is an imaginative and powerful guitarist, with a distinctive style that has been heard for more than a decade. But Perry wants to pursue a new sound, a new direction, for 'heavy metal' and this album was recorded live in an empty Boston auditorium to forge that sound... Many of the songs are 'first takes,' and you can hear the musicians 'feeling' their way through the songs with drummer Ronnie Stewart and bassist David Hull forming a bedrock rhythm section... 'Rock and Rolls' is more interesting than it is proficient, but it is nice to see someone at least trying to find a new frontier for heavy metal. Now that Brad Whitcomb [sic] has also left Aerosmith, don't be surprised if he and Perry reunite on the next 'Project' album. A lineup of guitarists Whitcomb, Perry, and Farren could have awesome potential" (Jackson Clarion-Ledger, 7/19/1981).

"The second solo effort by ex-Aerosmith guitarist Perry is built around a 'live performance' sound, achieved through a week's worth of recording at the Boston Opera House. Although there was a little studio polishing afterward, the overall result is an album of hard, unvarnished rock 'n' roll. With the addition of rhythm guitarist Charlie Farren, Perry is freed from excessive guitar chores. An added bonus: Farren can sing! 'South Station Blues' and 'Play the Game' in particular display the quality of the man's throat. The former is rock 'n' blues potent enough to drop Dead heads, the latter a jazz-blues fusion with a very controlled Perry displaying Robin Trower/Jeff Beck finesse. Elsewhere on this LP, there are echoes of Blue Oyster Cult, the Ramones, and Led Zeppelin. The least appealing cuts, 'East Coast, West Coast' and 'No Substitute for Arrogance,' reek of Perry's prehistoric Aerosmith train of thought. This disc is good; the next one should be a classic" (Allentown Morning Call, 7/25/1981).

"This is everything Joe Perry's first solo album wasn't. Basically, it rocks and rolls, and in some instances, Perry displays a guitar aggressiveness which outdoes his contributions with Aerosmith. There are several songs here, like 'East Coast, West Coast,' 'No Substitute for Arrogance,' and 'TV Police,' which are guaranteed to ravage your stereo. Clean, solid rock with power to spare. Welcome back, Joe" (San Pedro News-Pilot, 7/31/1981).

"For one album, Perry's post-Aerosmith act was amusing as a heavier metal than thou kind of in-joke. Second time around, unfortunately, we're left with a fairly witless hot guitarist and his pedestrian band singing mediocre tunes. Personal to Joe: 'No Substitute for Arrogance' doesn't mean that there's not complement to it" (Dave Marsh, Rolling Stone Magazine review for national syndication).

"So, Joe Perry didn't rejoin Aerosmith, as recently rumoured in this here organ. However, he did give Ralph Morman the big E. Not to worry Ralph, now you can re-form Bux with your china plate Punky Meadows. The Bux LP is well worth having, but the way, called 'We Come to Play' (Capitol ST-11459). And as a must for Angel fans, there is a new version of 'White Lightning.' 'I've Got the Rock 'N' Rolls Again' was recorded in a Boston opera house of all places, and probably explains why this album sounds so ruff 'n' shoddy. Even Sounds own Deaf Barton gave the Project's newie the thumbs down. However, yours truly has always " (Sounds, 8/15/1981).

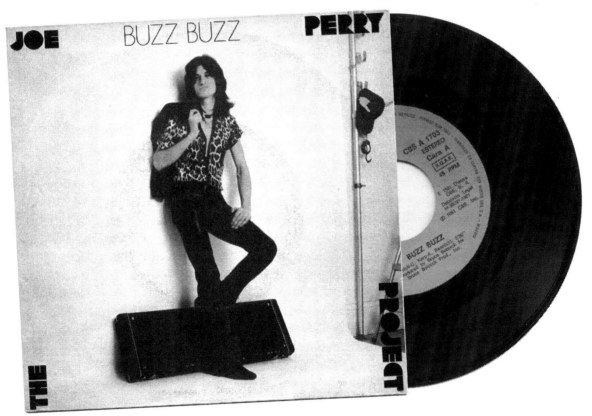

(Spanish 7" picture sleeve)

1981 - I've Got the Rock 'n' Rolls Again

February 5, 1981 **CANCELLED
Paradise Theater
Boston, MA

Notes
- This show, which would have been a WBCN benefit concert for Citizens for Handgun Control. By that time, Joe was busy auditioning guitarists...

February 28 **Cheap Trick
Garden
Boston, MA

Reported audience:
Partial set list: Day Tripper / The Last Time / Cold Turkey
Notes:
- Joe jammed with Cheap Trick for their encores. Steven also joined for the last two, marking the first time in over a year that the two had shared a stage. Joe recalled, "It was the first time we'd actually seen each other in over a year and right in the middle of the Cheap Trick show he came up on stage. I had no idea he was going to be there; it was kind of a déjà vu... I talk to Steve maybe about once every two months. Sometimes we'll go out and have dinner or something like that, but very rarely do we talk about music. In fact, I can say that we just about don't" (White Plains Journal, 10/11/1981).

March 6
Shaboo
Willimantic, CT

March 10
Paradise Theater
Boston, MA

Other act(s): Guy Williams Band
Reported audience: (900 capacity)
Partial set list: Toys in the Attic / No Substitute for Arrogance / Soldier of Fortune / Same Old Song and Dance / Train Kept A Rollin'
Notes:
- The band was billed as The New Joe Perry Project... Having only had Charlie in the band for three weeks, it was a good opportunity to break in the band and test new material on a live audience.

Spring **RECORDING SESSIONS
Opera House
Boston, MA

Notes:
- Recording of the "I've Got the Rock 'N' Rolls Again" album, which had been using the working title, "Soldier of Fortune," in press mentions during late-1980.

May 1
Showcase South
Pawtucket, RI

Other act(s): The A's, Minglewood

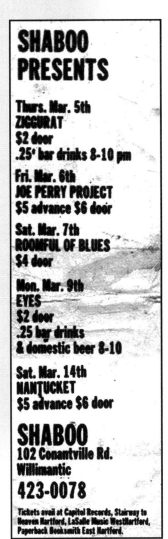

May 4
Civic Center
Springfield, MA
Promoter: Don Law Company
Other act(s): Ozzy Osbourne (HL), Motorhead
Reported audience: 4,058 / 5,000 (81.16%)
Notes:
- From a local review: "Next up was the Joe Perry Project. Since he left Aerosmith two years ago, Perry has decided to maintain a low profile by putting together a band of virtual unknowns and playing smaller rock showcase clubs, rarely appearing in large concert halls. Perry got the crowd's attention in a big way by tearing through a rousing version of the old Aerosmith song, 'Toys in the Attic.' The cord's response, however, indicated that it would have preferred the older Aerosmith material to Perry's new songs. Even an engaging rock song, 'East Coast, West Coast,' from his coming LP, lost out to Aerosmith fare such as 'Same Old Song and Dance.' The improvement in the Joe Perry Project is new lead vocalist Charlie Farren, whose strong, sure tenor gave the band the vocal assurance it has always lacked. The highlight of Perry's set was letting bassist David Hull come out front to since 'Buzz Buzz,' a song he once performed with his former band, the sadly underrated Dirty Angels. It was a refreshing respite from most of the pompous droning during the evening. Even though Perry was able to stimulate the crowd a bit, the wild enthusiasm was saved for headliners Ozzy Osbourne... Three hours of so much noise. Except for the brief interim by Joe Perry, all of this heavy metal seemed like so much scrap iron" (Springfield Daily News, 5/5/1981).

May 8
Hole in the Wall
Rochelle Park, NJ

May 9
El Greco
Bricktown, NJ
Other act(s): T.T. Quick, Papa

May 16
Mr. C's Rock Palace
Lowell, MA
Promoter: Rockfever Productions

May 23
Painter's Mill Star Theater
Owings Mills, MD

May 24
Bayou

Georgetown, Washington DC
Other act(s): Nightman

May 25
Stone Balloon
Newark, NJ
Other act(s): The Pedestrians

May 29
Show Place
Dover, NJ

June 13 **PROJECT CANCELLED
William & Mary Hall
Williamsburg, VA
Promoter: Cellar Door Concerts
Other act(s): April Wine (HL), Frankie & the Knockouts (opener)

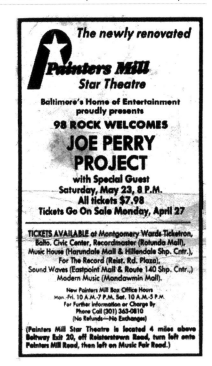

June 29 **NOT BOOKED
Metro
Boston, MA
Promoter: WBCN
Notes:
- WBCN rejected offers by the Project and New England to be special surprise guests at the Rock 'N' Roll Rumble, "claiming they wouldn't fit the progressive musical mood" (Boston Globe, 7/1/1981). However, Farren's former band, Balloon, did perform on June 22, their demos having been popular on local radio stations such as WCOZ and WBCN, leading to Farren's recruitment by Perry. Amusingly, Farren would be back at the 1982 event with his new band, The Enemy.

July 2, 3
Met Center
Minneapolis, MN
Promoter: Schon Productions
Other act(s): Rush (HL)
Reported audience: 23,691 **both nights
Reported gross: $249,390 **both nights

July 4, 5
Alpine Valley Music Theater
East Troy, WI
Promoter: in-house
Other act(s): Rush (HL)
Reported audience: 40,000 **SOLD-OUT
Reported gross: $394,900 **both nights

July 8
Wendler Arena
Saginaw, MI

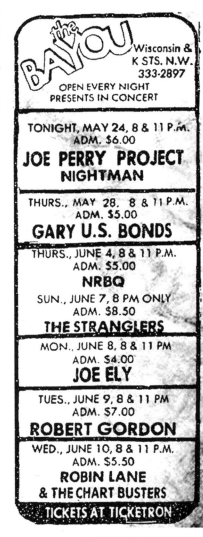

Other act(s): Alice Cooper (HL), Spyder (opener)
Notes:
- Initial tour dates supporting the album, through July 28, were noted in the June 27 issue of Billboard. None of the initially scheduled dates, opening for the Rossington-Collins Band, took place due to that band's tour being postponed. In some ways that proved a blessing for the band. Joe recalled, "We played Detroit with Alice Cooper, and we played at the Chicago Summerfest, with Cheap Trick, which is something we wouldn't have done if we'd been on the Rossington-Collins tour" (Nyack Journal News, 10/11/1981).

July 10, 11
Joe Louis Arena
Detroit, MI
Promoter: Brass Ring Productions
Other act(s): Alice Cooper (HL), Spyder (opener)
Reported audience: 26,490 **SOLD-OUT
Reported gross: $274,888 **both nights

July 12
Civic Center
Lansing, MI
Promoter: Brass Ring Productions
Other act(s): Alice Cooper (HL), Spyder (opener)
Reported audience: 4,981 **SOLD-OUT
Reported gross: $47,320
Notes:
- During the afternoon, Joe jammed with local band Lady Grace for one song during their show at Riverfront Park.
- From a local review: "The civic sauna had been heated up earlier mostly by the efforts of the Joe Perry Project. The old Aerosmith guitarist had a new band that rocked with a familiar heavy metal style which gave some old sounding stuff new freshness. Most of it anyway. A version of 'Heartbreak Motel' featured Perry as lead vocalist. The best part about that one number was that it was short. The 45-minute Perry set mostly had the thin fellow with the hair in his eyes playing flashy leads on about a dozen different guitars. The project did include three other musicians that were also front-man material" (Lansing State Journal, 7/13/1981).

July 16 **POSTPONED
Garden State Arts Center
Holmdel, NJ
Promoter: in-house
Other act(s): Rossington-Collins Band (HL)
Notes:
- This show was rescheduled for Aug. 2, and then Sept. 11.

July 17 **POSTPONED
Music Mountain
Woodbridge, NY
Promoter: Frank J. Russo
Other act(s): Rossington-Collins Band (HL)

July 18 **POSTPONED
Kingston Armory
Wilkes-Barre, PA
Promoter: Electric Factory Concerts
Other act(s): Rossington-Collins Band (HL)
Notes:
- This show was rescheduled for Sept. 17, though was then cancelled. Perry was not scheduled as the opening act for the Sept. show.

July 21 **POSTPONED
Merriweather Post Pavilion
Columbia, MD
Promoter: Nederlander Organization
Other act(s): Rossington-Collins Band (HL)
Notes:
- This show was postponed and rescheduled for Aug. 13, then Sept. 12.

July 22 **POSTPONED
Civic Center
Springfield, MA
Promoter: Don Law Presents
Other act(s): Rossington-Collins Band (HL)

July 24 **POSTPONED
Mid-Hudson Civic Center
Poughkeepsie, NY
Promoter: Harvey & Corky / Austen-Fagen Productions
Other act(s): Rossington-Collins Band (HL)

July 25 **CANCELLED
Cape Cod Coliseum
South Yarmouth, MA
Promoter: Don Law Presents
Other act(s): Rossington-Collins Band (HL)

July 26 **CANCELLED
Jai-Alai
Bridgeport, CT
Other act(s): Rossington-Collins Band (HL)

July 26
Fairgrounds
Allentown, PA

Promoter: Makoul Productions
Other act(s): Judas Priest (HL), Iron Maiden (opener)
Reported audience: ~5,100
Set list: Toys in the Attic / Discount Dogs / No Substitute for Arrogance / Buzz Buzz / Same Old Song and Dance / East Coast, West Coast / I've Got the Rock 'n' Rolls Again
Notes:
- From a local review: "A small fight broke out between the first and second sets but was quickly broken up. The Joe Perry Project played before Judas Priest. Former Aerosmith guitarist Perry has assembled a polished sound, with help from fine drummer, Ronnie Stewart. The opening act, Iron Maiden, illustrated the theory that even loud can be boring" (Allentown Morning Call, 7/27/1981).
- An AUD recording circulates from this show.

July 28 **CANCELLED
Performing Arts Center
Saratoga, NY
Promoter: in-house
Other act(s): Rossington-Collins Band (HL)

July 29 **POSTPONED
Pier
New York City, NY
Other act(s): Rossington-Collins Band (HL)
- Dr. Pepper Music Festival. Rescheduled for Aug. 18.

July 30 **POSTPONED
Convention Hall
Asbury Park, NJ
Other act(s): Rossington-Collins Band (HL)

July 31
Coliseum
New Haven, CT
Promoter: Cross Country Concerts
Other act(s): Foghat (HL), New England (opener)
Reported audience: 3,100 / 10,400 (29.81%)
Reported gross: $28,887

August 1 **CANCELLED
Wicomico Youth & Civic Center
Salisbury, MD
Other act(s): Rossington-Collins Band (HL), Cold Chisel
Notes:
- This show was cancelled due to the band still being in the studio recording what would become their final album, "This is the Way."

August 2 **POSTPONED
Garden State Arts Center
Holmdel, NJ
Promoter: in-house
Other act(s): Rossington-Collins Band (HL)
Notes:

- This show was rescheduled for Sept. 11, by which time the Project were unavailable.

August 4 **RESCHEDULED
Ohio Center
Columbus, OH
Other act(s): Rossington-Collins Band (HL)
Reported audience: (7,000 reserved capacity)

August 5
Navy Pier
Chicago, IL
Promoter: Chicago Fest
Other act(s): The ODd, The Kings, Loose Lips, Garrison
Notes:
- Chicago Fest '81 "Rock Around the Dock."

August 7 **POSTPONED
Hara Arena
Dayton, OH
Promoter: Sunshine Promotions
Other act(s): Rossington Collins Band (HL), Cold Chisel (opener)

August 7, 8 **JOE PERRY CANCELLED
Convention Center Arena
Dallas, TX
Promoter: Pace Concerts
Other act(s): The Kinks (HL)
Notes:
- Following this show, Perry's band was bumped from the opening slot by the promoter, and replaced with local act Lightning, due to backstage problems between his and the headliner's road crew. Promoter Lou Messina noted, "There was trouble backstage and I just told them (Perry) to stay home" (Fort Worth Star-Telegram, 8/10/1981).

August 11 **POSTPONED
Gardens
Louisville, KY
Promoter: Sunshine Promotions
Other act(s): Rossington Collins Band (HL), Cold Chisel (opener)

August 13 **POSTPONED
Merriweather Post Pavilion
Columbia, MD
Promoter: Nedelander Organization
Other act(s): Rossington-Collins Band (HL)
Notes:
- This show was postponed and rescheduled for August 13.

August 14
Nassau Coliseum
Uniondale, NY
Promoter: Delsener, Ruffino & Vaughn
Other act(s): Ozzy Osbourne (HL), Def Leppard (opener)
Reported audience: 13,640 **SOLD-OUT
Reported gross: $145,423
Notes:
- Charlie Farren recalled, "One night, on a three-band bill, we opened for Ozzy... But Def Leppard opened for us — imagine that! I also remember meeting Randy Rhoads — who was a pretty innovative guy at the time — and having this little sound check moment with him backstage. It was all really cool" (Goldmine, 9/5/2014).

August 18 **POSTPONED
Pier
New York City, NY
Other act(s): Rossington-Collins Band (HL)

August 21
T.H. Barton Coliseum
Little Rock, AR
Promoter: Beaver Productions
Other act(s): ZZ Top (HL)
Reported audience: (9,000 capacity)
Notes:
- ZZ Top were on their "El Loco-motion Tour."

August 22
Myriad
Oklahoma City, OK
Promoter: Beaver Productions
Other act(s): ZZ Top (HL)
Reported audience: (15,000 capacity)
Notes:
- From a local review: "The proper mood was set by the Joe Perry Project, who opened the evening with a substantial dose of incendiary heavy metal music. Perry, former lead guitarist with Aerosmith, was resplendent in black leather and in fine form on such rockers as 'No Substitute for Arrogance' and the hyper-drive rockabilly of 'Buzz Buzz.' The big talent in Perry's new assemblage is rhythm guitarist Charlie Farren, who looks like a young Keith Richard and sings like nobody's business, especially on the group's reworking of Aerosmith's 'Same Old Song and Dance,' a screaming rendition which puts that other band's singer, Steve Tyler, to shame" (Daily Oklahoman, 8/24/1981).

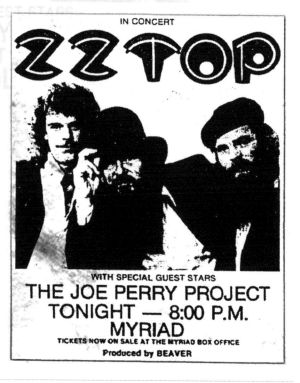

August 23
Hirsch Memorial Coliseum

Shreveport, LA

Promoter: Beaver Productions
Other act(s): ZZ Top (HL)
Reported audience: ~9,200 / 10,150 (90.64%)
Notes:
- From a local review: "Now the Joe Perry Project is an interesting band, and Perry has a fine reputation as a guitarist and songwriter with the band Aerosmith dating back to the early '70s. But his music is to that of ZZ Top as Perrier waters is to a fine, vintage wine. Some may want each liquid, but not at the same time. So, it was Saturday. Perry and his three fellow players belted out nine heavy rock 'n' roll tunes that were fast, flashy, and too darned businesslike for a crowd that seemed eager to hear the active-but-still-somewhat-laid-back musical connivance of 'that little ol' band from Texas'" (Shreveport Times, 8/24/1981).
- From another local review: "Opening last night's show was The Joe Perry Project. Joe Perry is best known for his guitar work with Aerosmith and, judging from last night's performance, we think his is likely to stay that way. Perry left Aerosmith in October of 1979 and in 1980 The Project released its album, 'Let the Music Do the Talking.' The group played the title tune from that release last night, and it proved to be one of the better numbers in an otherwise mediocre set. The rest of the set was drawn from the group's new album, 'I've Got the Rock 'N Rolls Again.' Vocalist Charlie Farren shouts lyrics like a heavy-metal Tarzan; the back-up vocals from David Hull and Perry are no help. The only thing you can't fret about is the Perry guitar work. He still delivers the straight Aerosmith sound that made him a name" (Shreveport Journal, 8/24/1981).

August 25 **CANCELLED
Ohio Center
Columbus, OH

Other act(s): Rossington-Collins Band (HL)
Notes:
- Ultimately, due to studio delays and health issues, Rossington-Collins cancelled a string of dates that the Project would have opened for.

August 27
Civic Center
Springfield, MA

Promoter: Don Law, Inc.
Other act(s): ZZ Top (HL)
Reported audience: 8,448 / 10,347 (81.65%)
Notes:
- From a local review: "The Joe Perry Project's fifty-minute set was considerably weak because of the lack of really distinctive, original material, but was bolstered by Aerosmith's familiar 'Toys in the Attic' and 'Same Old Song and Dance.' A few songs from Perry's two albums, including the 'Let the Music Do the Talking' and 'I've Got the Rock and Rolls Again' title tracks, stood out, but aside from some fine leads by Perry, the majority of the others were very ordinary" (Springfield Union, 8/29/1981).

August 29
Merriweather Post Pavilion
Columbia, MD
Promoter: Nederlander Organization
Other act(s): Kansas (HL)
Notes:
- From a local review: "Somehow the Joe Perry Project ended up on the same bill as Kansas Saturday night at Merriweather Post Pavilion. A strange combination this. Perry comes across as your typical rock 'n' roll Hun. Wearing leather pants and with a couple of guitars strapped across his bare chest, the guitarist did everything in his power to blast the amphitheater off the ground, but to no avail. The response to his unrelenting volume and theatrics were polite at best; and when Perry, in one final attempt to get a rise out of the crowd, trashed the guitar and amplifier, the show short-circuited along with a good deal of equipment on the stage" (Washington Post, 8/31/1981).

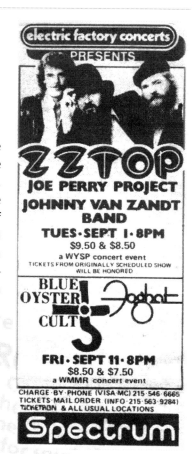

August 31
Cumberland County Civic Center
Portland, ME
Promoter: Ruffino & Vaughan
Other act(s): ZZ Top (HL)
Reported audience: 6,400 / 9,000 (71.11%)
Reported gross: $60,024

September 1
Spectrum
Philadelphia, PA
Promoter: Electric Factory Concerts
Other act(s): ZZ Top (HL), Johnny Van Zant Band
Reported audience: 9,309 / 19,500 (47.74%)
Reported gross: $85,629

September 7
Shoreline Arena @ Playland
Rye, NY
Reported audience: (1,600 capacity)

September 9
Riverfront Coliseum
Cincinnati, OH
Promoter: Electric Factory Concerts
Other act(s): ZZ Top (HL)
Reported audience: (17,000 capacity)

September 11
Civic Center
Glens Falls, NY
Other act(s): ZZ Top (HL)
Reported audience: (8,400 capacity)
Notes:

- From a local review: "Last Friday night the fans in attendance at the Glens Falls Civic center were treated to an outstanding array of talent in The Joe Perry Project and the ever-popular ZZ Top. Joe Perry and his band opened the show with an old Aerosmith tune, 'Toys in the Attic.' They increased their assault on the crowd with songs from their new LP, 'I've Got the Rock 'n' Rolls Again,' which included 'East Coast, West Coast,' 'No Substitute for Arrogance,' 'Buzz Buzz' and the title cut which drew a healthy response from the crowd. The set ended in what is considered Perry's theme song, 'Let the Music Do the Talking,' and it did. There was nothing wrong with the music, I only wish The Joe Perry Project could have showed a little more enthusiasm and a lot more energy and I'm sure they would have had a bigger impact on the crowd" (Greenwich Journal, 9/17/1981).

September 12 **CANCELLED
Merriweather Post Pavilion
Columbia, MD
Promoter: Nederlander Organization
Other act(s): Rossington-Collins Band (HL)

September 12 **PROJECT CANCELLED
Coliseum
Jacksonville, FL
Other act(s): Blackfoot (HL), Johnny Van Zant Band

September 12
New Jersey State Fairgrounds
Hamilton, NJ
Promoter: Monarch Entertainment Bureau
Other act(s): The A's, Castle Brown Band
Notes:
- This was a free show as part of the State Fair followed by a firework display. It was initially billed as a show with ZZ Top headlining with New Riders of the Purple Sage with the Project opening.

September 19
Field House Gym @ Plattsburgh State
Plattsburgh, NY
Promoter: PSUC Student Association Concert Committee
Other act(s): Southside Johnny and the Asbury Jukes (HL)
Reported audience: ~2,100 / 3,500 (60%)
Notes:
- A local review only noted that the reviewer thought the Project were sloppy.

September 26
Orpheum Theater
Boston, MA
Promoter: Don Law., Inc.
Other act(s): New England (opener)
Reported audience: (2,800 capacity)

October 15
Wings Stadium

Kalamazoo, MI
Other act(s): Nazareth (HL), Vic Vergat (opener)
Reported audience: (8,038 capacity)
Notes:
- Vic Vergat was a Swiss guitarist whose backing band for the tour included Bobby Blotzer and Juan Croucier, later members of RATT.

October 16
Wendler Arena
Saginaw, MI
Promoter: Brass Ring Productions
Other act(s): Nazareth (HL)
Reported audience: 3,753 / 7,169 (52.35%)
Reported gross: $35,651
Notes:
- Nazareth guitarist Billy Rankin: "The first few gigs I spent boring Mr. Perry with teary-eyed tales of how my old band Phase used to open with 'Back in the Saddle' to enthusiastic U.S. Marines at Dunoon Naval Base; and he was always polite in nodding his approval, or so I thought. Fact is, Joe, for the most part, didn't understand my accent or, as I realized eventually, couldn't give a fuck. Depending on the time of day, he was either capable of remembering my name (which always blew me away) or he was merely incapable of recalling how I'd bored him before. Don't get me wrong, Joe Perry was, and no doubt still is, one of the sweetest guys on the planet, but sometimes he was on another planet from the rest of us. Every night of the tour, you'd find me beside the onstage monitor guy enjoying Joe's unique guitar playing despite not being familiar with any of the Joe Perry Project's material. He was cool. He looked cool. He played some Aerosmith too.

One night, during a rendition of 'Same Old Song and Dance,' he leaned back into his Marshall stack for the solo and my monitor guy buddy sensed something was amiss. 'Fuck, he's lost it! Backup!' I joined four other stagehands to prop up Joe's speakers from behind while a fifth roadie hauled him upright. Joe won't remember this, but I do. In fact, his on/off best friend, Steven Tyler will have me to thank a year later during another episode but won't recall it either. That's the thing about meeting your heroes. They'll never disappoint, so long as they don't expect you to think they give a fuck" (Billyrankin.com).

October 17
Sports Arena
Toledo, OH
Promoter: Belkin Productions
Other act(s): Nazareth (HL), Vic Vergat (opener)
Reported audience: (7,500 capacity)

October 18
Civic Center Coliseum
Charleston, WV
Promoter: Entam, Ltd.
Other act(s): Nazareth (HL), Vic Vergat (opener)

October 21
Hara Arena
Dayton, OH
Promoter: Sunshine Promotions
Other act(s): Nazareth (HL), Vic Vergat (opener)
Reported audience: 3,717 / 8,000 (46.46%)

Reported gross: $30,773

October 22
County Fieldhouse
Erie, PA
Promoter: Belkin Productions
Other act(s): Nazareth (HL), Vic Vergat (opener)
Reported audience: (5,250 capacity)

October 23
Maple Leaf Gardens
Toronto, ON, Canada
Other act(s): Nazareth (HL), Vic Vergat (opener)
Reported audience: (19,000 capacity)
Notes:
- From a local review: "An indication of just how good Nazareth is can be obtained by comparing it to the Joe Perry Project, the evening's middle-billed act. Perry, a former lead guitarist for the Boston-based heavy metal outfit Aerosmith, gets by predominantly on unimaginative riffing taken at ear-bleeding volume. The redundancy of numbers such as 'Let The music Do the Talkin'' and 'Same Old Song and Dance' made Nazareth's carefully planned set look all the more appealing" (Toronto Globe & Mail, 10/24/1981).

October 24
Civic Arena
Pittsburgh, PA
Promoter: Danny Kresky Enterprises
Other act(s): Nazareth (HL), Vic Vergat (opener)
Reported audience: (17,500 capacity)

October 26
Mid-Hudson Civic Center
Poughkeepsie, NY
Promoter: Harvey & Corky / Austen-Fagen Productions
Other act(s): Nazareth (HL), Vic Vergat (opener)
Reported audience: (3,000 capacity)

October 27
Tower Theater
Upper Darby, PA
Promoter: Electric Factory Concerts
Other act(s): Nazareth (HL), Vic Vergat (opener)
Reported audience: (2,877 capacity)

October 29
Memorial Coliseum
Fort Wayne, IN
Promoter: Sunshine Promotions

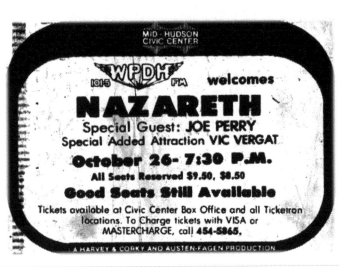

Other act(s): Nazareth (HL), Molly Hatchet
Reported audience: (10,000 capacity)

October 30
Louisville Gardens
Louisville, KY
Promoter: Sunshine Promotions
Other act(s): Nazareth (HL), Vic Vergat (opener)
Reported audience: (6,800 capacity)

October 31
Joe Louis Arena
Detroit, MI
Promoter: Brass Ring Productions
Other act(s): Nazareth (HL)
Reported audience: 7,703 / 15,924 (48.37%)
Reported gross: $83,921

November 1
Public Hall
Cleveland, OH
Other act(s): Nazareth (HL)

November 2
Second Chance
Ann Arbor, MI

November 4 **CANCELLED
Civic Center
Springfield, MA
Other act(s): Nazareth (HL), Vic Vergat (opener)
Notes:
- This show was cancelled due to poor ticket sales.

November 5
Stabler Arena @ Lehigh University
Bethlehem, PA
Promoter: Electric Factory Concerts
Other act(s): Nazareth (HL)
Reported audience: (6,000 capacity)

November 6
Cumberland County Civic Center
Portland, ME
Promoter: Don Law Company
Other act(s): Nazareth (HL)
Reported audience: 6,777 / 9,500 (71.34%)
Reported gross: $58,118

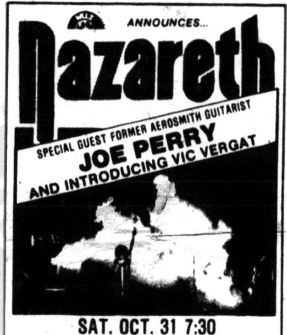

November 7
Uncle Sam's
Nantasket Beach (Hull), MA
Notes:
- During a brief break for Joe, Nazareth appeared at the Orpheum in Boston on Nov. 7, with Vic Vergat and New England.

November 11
Palmer Auditorium
Davenport, IA
Other act(s): Nazareth (HL), Vic Vergat (opener)

November 12
MetroCentre
Rockford, IL
Other act(s): Nazareth (HL), Vic Vergat (opener)
Reported audience: (10,000 capacity)

November 13
Uptown Theater
Chicago, IL
Other act(s): Nazareth (HL), Vic Vergat (opener)
Reported audience: (4,351 capacity)
Notes:
- At the time, it was rumored that Joe would be producing a local band, the Chicago Connection.

November 15
Met Center
Minneapolis, MN
Promoter: Schon Productions
Other act(s): Nazareth (HL), Vic Vergat (opener)

November 16
Arena
Winnipeg, MB, Canada
Other act(s): Nazareth (HL), Vic Vergat (opener)
Notes:
- With his run completed at this show, Joe's slot on the tour was taken over by Australian Billy Thorpe.

November 18 **TEMP HOLD-DATE
The Cove
Duluth, MN

November 19
S.M.U. Main Auditorium
Dartmouth, MA
Promoter: Lightwaves Productions
Other act(s): Berlin Airlift

December 7
El Mocambo
Toronto, ON, Canada

December 11
Capital Theater
Concord, NH
Promoter: in-house / La Muzika
Other act(s): .44 Magnum
Reported audience: (1,200 capacity)

December 27
Civic Center
Augusta, ME
Promoter: Frank J. Russo
Other act(s): Blue Oyster Cult (HL)
Reported audience: 3,228 / 6,000 (53.8%)
Reported gross: $27,910

December 29
Cape Cod Coliseum
South Yarmouth, MA
Promoter: Don Law, Inc.
Other act(s): Blue Oyster Cult (HL)
Reported audience: 3,800 / 7,200 (52.78%)
Reported gross: $40,814

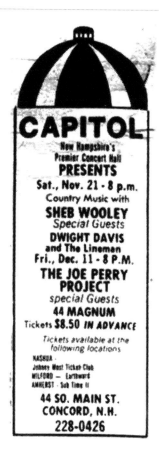

1982

January 15, 1982
Showcase South
Pawcatuck, CT

January 22
Fountain Casino
Aberdeen, NJ
Promoter: in-house

January 29
Toad's Place
New Haven, CT

January 30
Toad's Place
Waterbury, CT

February 20 **CANCELLED

The Chance
Poughkeepsie, NY

Notes:
- This show had been cancelled by Feb. 12, by which time the band were preparing to audition new bassists and lead singers following the departure of Charlie Farren and David Hull.

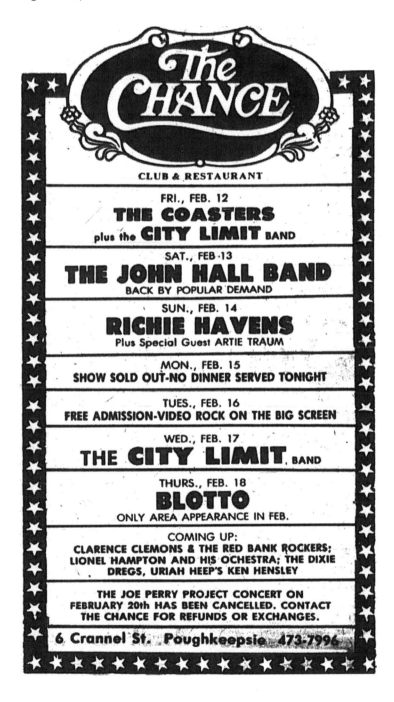

1981 - I've Got the Rock 'n' Rolls Again

1981 - Sharpshooter

U.S. Release Details:
CBS/Columbia NFC/NCT-37365 (July 31, 1981)
Columbia/CBS CT/CK-66986 (1994 — Reissue)
Columbia/CBS CK-66986 (2001 — CD reissue)
Pasco Melvin, LLC PM-10001 (2015 — CD reissue)

Tracks:
A1. I Need Love
(3:18) — Derek St. Holmes
A2. Whiskey Woman
(3:51) — Derek St. Holmes
A3. Hold On
(2:59) — Derek St. Holmes / Brad Whitford
A4. Sharpshooter
(5:29) — Derek St. Holmes / Brad Whitford
A5. Every Morning
(4:49) — Derek St. Holmes

B1. Action
(3:45) — Derek St. Holmes
B2. Shy Away •
(4:12) — Derek St. Holmes
B3. Does It Really Matter?
(4:25) — Derek St. Holmes
B4. Spanish Boy
(4:09) — Derek St. Holmes / Brad Whitford
B5. Mystery Girl
(3:19) — Derek St. Holmes / Brad Whitford

Album Details:
Produced by Tom Allom. Engineered by George Pappas assisted by Chuck Fedonezak. Mastered by Stew Romain at CBS Recording Studios, New York City, NY. Recorded at Axis Sound Studio in Atlanta, GA.

Players:
- Derek St. Holmes — Vocals & guitars
- Brad Whitford — Guitars
- Dave Hewitt — Bass
- Steve Pace — Drums

Chart Action:
Chart Peak (USA): Bubbled under at #208 on the Billboard Top-200 (10/3/1981). The album also reached #167 on Cashbox (9/26/1981) during a four-week appearance. Other countries: N.A.

09/05/81	09/12/81	09/19/81	09/26/81	10/03/81		
178	173	169	** 167 **	X		

RIAA/Sales:
Exact sales figures for this album are unknown.

Supporting Singles:

• "Shy Away," backed with "Mystery Girl" (Columbia 18-02555, 10/1981), as a 3:49 edit (which neutered Brad's solo), was released as a single but did not chart.

"Starting all over with a new band's a little scary. But playing clubs and opening act gigs is very exciting. It kind of brings what rock 'n' roll is all about back into focus" (Asbury Park Press, 9/6/1981).

Joe Perry mentioned in press interviews in early July 1981 that he had then recently spoken with Brad who'd told him that he'd left Aerosmith and was committed to a new band — working with Derek St. Holmes on their album. Standing in the shadows of "others" was a common theme in early interviews from both Whitford/St. Holmes (WSH) band principals. For Brad, it was that Joe would usually perform the solos during concerts even though Brad contributed quality work on the studio cuts. And by the time of "Night in the Ruts," Brad got no solos, even though Joe had departed the band after his contributions were complete. Jimmy Crespo had joined and provided the last-minute solos for "Three Mile Smile" while others also made contributions. According to Brad, "I didn't even get to do a solo on (the most recent Aerosmith album) 'Night in the Ruts...' Ridiculous stuff like that kept happening, so eventually I told them, 'I'm gonna walk — see ya later'" (Detroit Free Press, 10/23/1981). That album had also taken far too long to complete, and the process was so tortured, that in 1981 Aerosmith were faced with a similar situation when trying to create their first post-Perry album. Once Steven had recovered from his injuries, and they started thinking about recording a follow-up, it became a process mired in near futility, even though musical ideas were being generated. Even then Brad remained committed to Aerosmith. He recalled, "My original plan was to manage (playing in) two bands at once — Aerosmith and Whitford/St. Holmes. But after I finished recording with Derek, I went back into the studio with Aerosmith and things had gotten worse. So, I quit" (Detroit Free Press, 10/23/1981). Like Joe, Brad had initially considered that he would be able to foster a side project in addition to remaining in Aerosmith. But the tale of two studio experiences made the case for him, and Aerosmith had clearly stagnated to the point where new options were more appealing that trying to salvage his formative band.

As Brad told Metal Express Radio, "It was a really rough time for the band at that moment. Joe had left and there was nothing musical happening. I was working with Derek and before I'd left, I'd already completed the first Whitford St. Holmes album and we did that album in a couple of weeks all recorded and finished. I went back to Aerosmith and we couldn't even get a song. I was there right at the start of that record and we tried working on it, but we really had no success. It was very hard to get anything done and I was very frustrated. I had to walk away from it" (12/31/2016). Steven, though, was particularly unforgiving towards Brad at the time, suggesting, "he had no patience when I was in the hospital" (Los Angeles Times, 7/31/1983), and that his marital issues and need for money pushed him to commit everything to the new project. Having married Karen Lesser in 1980, by early 1981 she was expecting their first child and the financial pressures mounted, forcing efforts to look for new opportunities.

Derek St. Holmes had experienced a situation very similar to that which Brad experienced within Aerosmith. He had written with Ted, but forever was secondary to the star — something which he had no rancor against, but he needed more from the music on a personal level. As he made clear, Ted "is incredible. He taught me more than anybody could have taught me. But after a while I started slacking off and that's when we both decided it wasn't going to work out. I told him, 'I'm not happy and there's no way in hell you can give me as much freedom as I want. It's time for me to be a star.' I was tired of standing in his shadow" (Indianapolis News, 10/20/1981). Feeling that their talent was over-looked, their contributions under-valued, but were simply ready to move on to something of their own, even if it mean they had to choose between being "poor and happy or rich and unhappy" (Indianapolis News, 10/20/1981). Forming a new band project was something that Derek had already tried with his St. Paradise project in 1979. That band had included Nugent bassist Rob Grange and drummer Denny Carmassi (Montrose), but their Mike Flicker produced self-titled album for Warner Bros. stiffed. More importantly, perhaps, Derek remained with Leber-Krebs.

As a band project, with the two having initially reconnected in the summer of 1980 and discussing the possibilities of working together, one of the first things that both Whitford and St. Holmes discovered was that music could be fun again when they were in control. The synergy was quickly apparent and the two knocked out six songs. As Brad put it, "We jammed some tunes he'd written, and everything was magic from the word go" (Indianapolis News, 10/20/1981). The band was completed with bass player Dave Hewitt, who had moved to Atlanta from the U.K. the previous year (he had previously played with the group Babe Ruth), and drummer Steve Pace, both of whom had been working with Derek. Initially considering the idea of working as a trio, Derek had invited Brad to come down and jam. He recalled, "Everything just seemed to fall right into place. We decided to all make a commitment to the group and started working on material, which, I might add, almost came too easy. We had something like six songs finished in a matter of days. We never realized that we were so creative" (Asbury Park Press, 9/6/1981). Derek would be solely responsible for the lyrics on the album.

The album was released during the last week of July but did nothing on the Billboard charts (bubbling under on the Billboard Top-200 at #210 on Sept. 26 and #208 on Oct. 3), though it did chart on Cashbox, debuting at #178 on Sept. 5. The album was supported by a non-charting single, "Shy Away" (Columbia 18-02555), backed with "Mystery Girl" issued in September. "Whiskey Woman," along with the Project's "No Substitute for Arrogance," were included on the CBS sampler, "Speaker Death! (Heavy Metal Head-Bangers)" issued promotionally as a label catalog sampler during the year. The same Whitford/St. Holmes song plus "Every Morning," were also featured on the CBS loss-leader compilation "Exposed II: A Cheap Peek at Today's Provocative New Rock" the following year. A decade later "Sharpshooter" represented the less-Aero-era on Aerosmith's "Pandora's Box" in 1991. Mixed reviews also led to a degree of consumer confusion who expected the band to be she same as the member's former bands. Dave Hewitt commented, "A lot of people expect us to be heavy metal, but we're not heavy metal — we're just showing off the fact that Derek can sing" (Johnson City Press, 9/5/1981).

Like Joe Perry, Brad Whitford initially appreciated the regression in performing in clubs rather than stadiums, and the challenges the new band presented: "When you're in a very successful group like Aerosmith, and all you really get to do is play huge ballparks and arenas, you tend to lose touch with the people. That may be the most important part of the music to me — to know how the people feel, and what they think about what you're doing. With this band that special energy has been turned back on again" (Asbury Park Press, 9/6/1981). The band hit the road throughout the south, since they hadn't played live together in public, and their booking agency (Starmount Agency) was based out of Atlanta (as was Derek). By the time they reached New England in mid-August they were ready to record a show for the King Biscuit Flower Hour, which would be broadcast the following month on a show shared with Ozzy Osbourne. Starmount also paired them with another client, Mother's Finest, who had opened for Aerosmith the previous year, for a larger venue tour slot through the south.

The following month WSH was attached as the opening act for the Blue Oyster Cult / Foghat tour. Theoretically, it was a decent tour package for the new band, even if some dark humor might be present with either principal opening for the Cult again... Foghat were touring in support of their "Girls to Chat & Boys to Bounce" album which reached #92 on the Billboard charts with "Live Now, Pay Later" bubbling under on the Hot-100, but performing well on the Mainstream Rock chart (#15). Headliners, Blue Oyster Cult, were doing markedly better with their "Fire of Unknown Origin" album hitting #24 on Billboard bolstered by the strength of their top-40 single, "Burnin' for You." The band had then recently undergone their first line-up change since 1970 with the departure of founding drummer Albert Bouchard. Touring with the package continued throughout the middle of November. It's not clear at what point Hewitt and Pace left the band. Regardless, they were replaced by bassist Chase Chitty (Magic Cat) and drummer LaRue Riccio roughly halfway through the touring cycle. Hewitt went on to work with a version Humble Pie that Steve Marriot was attempting to launch, but nothing came of the recordings, and he ended up as the original bassist in the Georgia Satellites. Steve Pace joined Krokus for their 1983 "Headhunter" album. A final run of dates was completed with Billy Squier at the end of November with WSH concluding activities with a solo show at the Country Club in Reseda, CA on Nov. 24. Once the tour was completed the band essentially petered out.

Derek returned to Ted Nugent's band for the preproduction for the "Nugent" album which started in Dec. 1981, with the album being recorded in Hollywood between Feb. and Apr. 1982. Derek recalled, "When we got to the end of our touring schedule, Brad was asked to return to Aerosmith and Ted wanted me back. We felt we had to do those things" (Classic Rock, 6/7/2016). Ted was enthused for a while, gushing, "I'm telling you; this is the cat's ass. I've got the best rock 'n' roll band in the world here... Carmine is the best drummer in the world. And Derek St. Holmes sang with me on all my best records. I hired him because Derek pioneered all the best vocal styles you hear in rock 'n' roll today. And Dave Kiswinney, my bass player, is responsible for all that jackhammer bass playing on my 'Wango Tango' stuff. Between the four of us, the bottom line is we're in danger here. I think we ought to hire our asses out on the weekends for anti-terrorist missions" (Santa Fe New Mexican, 7/22/1982). Unfortunately, even that firepower failed to stop the decline in Ted's fortunes, and Derek was soon out of the band again, next teaming up with one-time Aerosmith trialist Michael Schenker. Chase landed with Pat Travers.

More important to the context of Aerosmith, by early 1982 Brad had reunited musically with Joe Perry with the pair rehearsing new members for the Project. He had simply found himself unable to return to Aerosmith. Instead, Brad was part of the band for the auditions of new bassists, with Danny Hargrove being selected, and new vocalist, "Cowboy" Mach Bell. The band immediately transitioned into recording demos and then hit the road with Brad remaining with them into early May. At that time, he received an offer to work with TV personality, and then "Solid Gold" show host, Rex Smith, for a project produced by Ron Nevison. At the time, however, Brad had no idea what was going on with the project after recording his parts. He later recalled, "I don't even know what happened to that one. I don't even know if the record company knows what happened to it, but it was fun to do" (Detroit Free Press, 1/10/1985). The resulting album, "Camouflage," was eventually released in March 1983, with Brad receiving a co-writing credit for the jazz-tinged song, "Get It Right." By that time, his finances were in dire straits. Brad recalled, "No money, no income, all my savings going to alimony and mortgages. Karen's parents had to loan us money to buy a crib when Zach was born [in Sept. 1982])" ("Walk this Way"). He'd return sporadically to the Project for shows in late-1982 following the birth of his son but spent much of 1982 out of public view. Interestingly, even as late as February 1982, a prospective second WSH album was being mentioned in trade press, as pointless as it likely would have been following the less than lackluster commercial response to the debut. Fortunately, WSH fans would receive a follow-up album decades later...

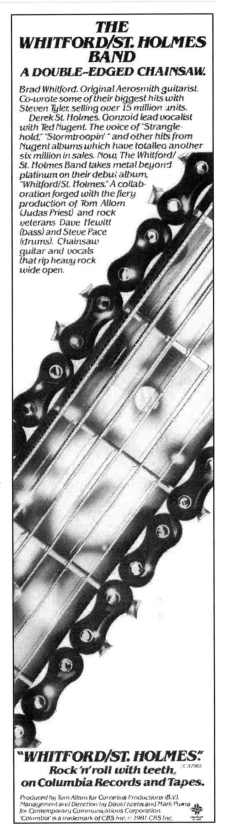

1981 - Sharpshooter

Assorted review excerpts:

"Brad Whitford, when he played guitar in Aerosmith, penned such songs as 'Last Child' and 'Kings and Queens.' Derek St. Holmes sang with Ted Nugent on his LPs from 1974 to 1978; writing 'Hey Baby' on the Ted Nugent LP. He also appeared on the 'Double Live Gonzo' album. The two met in 1976 during the tour that included Ted Nugent, Aerosmith, Lynyrd Skynyrd and Nazareth. The troupe played in RFK Stadium in Washington on May 30. 1976. Whitford and St. Holmes became friends and talked of forming a group. It has become a reality and the LP reminds me of Aerosmith and Ted Nugent in the younger days when they could really cook and this LP does that; from 'I Need Love,' the opening cut, to 'Mystery Woman,' the closing one. In between there's some blistering rock that should establish the Whitford-St. Holmes band as superstars. Dave Hewitt plays bass and Steve Pace is the drummer" (Cumberland Sunday Times, 8/2/1981).

"As Aerosmith's racy rhythm guitarist, Brad Whitford was overshadowed by Joe Perry's blistering licks. Similarly, vocalist Derek St. Holmes ceaselessly yielded the spotlight to the raucous guitar antics of his boss Ted Nugent. On this album, lifted out of their usual scenarios, Whitford and St. Holmes are tamer yet craftier than their colleagues. Whitford discloses a hidden talent on lead guitar with the emphasis on tight material with just the right amount of licks, riffs and gimmickry to make the album glisten with a genuine rock heart. 'Mystery Girl' is frenetic enough to be a dance tune. The irresistible 'Does It Really Matter' and the ever-catchy 'Shy Away' showcase pretty harmonizing. The social commentary of 'Hold On' rocks with a reggae lining. But Whitford and St. Holmes are also determined to belt out sonic attacks. 'Sharpshooter' is a magnum opus of guitar and heavy wailing that ought to make first-rate heavy metal bands blush. As part of their mega-buck ensembles, Whitford and St. Holmes are subjected to stinging criticisms for pandering to empty-headed rock. Their stylish radiance here should spare these two such dismissals" (Boston Globe, 8/13/1981).

"Brad Whitford, former Aerosmith guitarist, and Derek St. Holmes, a lead vocalist with Ted Nugent, team up on some good, strong rock and roll, reminiscent of both groups. The heavy metal edge is blessedly softened, thanks to some nice harmonizing by the two pros. Still, it is the more hard-rocking songs that make this album a potential hit. Dave Hewitt on bass and Steve Pace on drums keep the beat pounding for two solid sides" (Billboard, 8/15/1981).

"Derek St. Holmes (former Ted Nugent lead vocalist) creates pinched vocal urgency, while Brad Whitford (original Aerosmith lead guitarist) lets loose with mega-watt axe havoc on this rocker from the duo's new self-titled LP. Explosive stuff for AOR and young rockers" (Record World, 10/10/1981).

"The big guitar sound of Whitford/St. Holmes is a textbook example of current mainstream hard rock, with high, strutting vocals leading the ballsy beat. High speed axe licks and muscular drumming provide the flash trimmings around the crack hook. Ace AOR and rock-oriented pop fare" (Cashbox, 10/17/1981. Review for "Shy Away.").

1981 - Sharpshooter

August 5, 1981
Whippin' Post
Augusta, GA

Other act(s): Slyder
Notes:
- From a local review: "Whitford-St. Holmes brand of standard, competent hard rock never really won over the audience, which was attracted more by the former bands of the two lead performers than anything else. Playing live together for only the third time, Whitford-St. Holmes' performance was respectable if unexceptional, but was not up to the level of the all-out efforts of Slyder" (Augusta Chronicle, 8/9/1981).

August 6
Agora Ballroom
Atlanta, GA

Reported audience: (800 capacity)
Notes:
- Brad wasn't a real fan of being back in the clubs and doing the grind: "It was a real drag, but it had to be done to break in the act. When we recorded our album, we hadn't done any touring" (Detroit Free Press, 10/23/1981). That's not to say he didn't find the prospect exciting. After years of being on the massive stage Aerosmith had grown to enjoy, he had pressed the rewind button on his career and was once again one the ground floor with two directions to go. This venue was the renamed Electric Ballroom...

August 14
Mr. C's Rock Palace
Lowell, MA

Promoter: in-house
Other act(s): Kid Gloves

August 15
Stage West
West Hartford, CT

August 16
Paradise
Boston, MA

Other act(s): Guy Williams Band
Notes:
- Four songs from this show ("I Need Love," "Shy Away," "Every Morning," and "Sharpshooter") were broadcast on King Biscuit Flower Hour on Sept. 13.
- From a local review: "Guitarist Brad Whitford and singer Derek St. Holmes have spent too much time in hockey barns and civic centers. From the indications given before a sparse crowd at the Paradise Sunday night, it appears they'd like nothing more than to be right back in those barns and civic centers. St. Holmes, Ted Nugent's lead singer and rhythm guitarist from 1974 to 1978, and Whitford, ex-Aerosmith guitarist, have formed Whitford / St. Holmes (they're joined by bassist Dave Hewitt and drummer Steve Pace) and released their debut album on Columbia. Despite the role each played in their respective, and extremely popular, groups, Whitford and St. Holmes are now at the starting-over-but-with-a-reputation stage — similar to the position Joe Perry, another ex-Aerosmith guitarist, was in last year. Fans can expect hard rock, but without a string of hits following them Whitford / St. Holmes must develop a following. As such, they're presently at the club level. Unfortunately, they wear their eagerness to be back in the arenas right on their sleeves. And arenas are, of course, the best places to make money and the worst places to communicate. 'How's everybody feeling

tonight!?' St. Holmes screamed at the outset, shouting over the few bodies. 'You've been great, thank you, goodnight!' St. Holmes screamed at the end, shouting over the same few bodies.

In between, he assumed the all-too-usual arena technique of over-projecting and singing over — not to — the audience. Sunday's show seemed like a scrimmage, an exercise to work out the kinks before meeting the big tests surely on down the line. In fact, St. Holmes' goodnight cry came at the end of a no-encore set. It was if they'd done what they set out to do and couldn't play too hard at this stage of the season. Whitford / St. Holmes play competent, at times ('Sharpshooter') burning, high energy hard rock that is probably a shade more pop oriented than Aerosmith or Nugent. But it's standard crankshaft fare — rock for show. Song titles include 'I Need Love,' 'Whiskey Woman' and 'Mystery Girl' (get the idea?) and, oh, 'Does It Really Matter?' to which the answer is, no, not really. Whitford / St. Holmes don't have a bad attitude; they don't really have any attitude. When songs succeed, they're reasonably well-executed escapist blasters; when they fail, they're plodding, unimaginative escapist blasters. Whitford introduces 'Spanish Boy' as being about El Salvador (politics!?), but St. Holmes' treats the song as just another love-and-action strutter. And yes, give 'em a few years as the warmup act for a major hard rock band on an arena tour and Whitford and St. Holmes could be stars again" (Boston Globe, 8/18/1981).

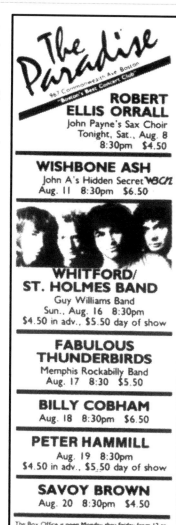

August 20
Mississippi Coliseum
Jackson, MS
Other act(s): Mother's Finest (HL), Point Blank, Sassy Jones (opener)
Reported audience: (10,000 capacity)
Notes:
- Having had Mother's Finest opening for Aerosmith on the "Night in the Ruts" tour, both they and Whitford-St. Holmes were signed with the Starmount Agency. Mother's Finest were touring their heaviest album, "Iron Age."

August 21
Tennessee Theater
Nashville, TN
Promoter: Sound Seventy Productions
Other act(s): Mother's Finest (HL)
Reported audience: (2,028 capacity)

August 22
Freedom Hall
Johnson City, TN
Promoter: Entam, Ltd.
Other act(s): Mother's Finest (HL), The Producers (opener)
Reported audience: (7,500 capacity)

August 23
Township Auditorium
Columbia, SC
Other act(s): Mother's Finest (HL), The Producers (opener)
Reported audience: (3,400 capacity)

Notes:
- From a local review: "Once the house lights finally went down, a roar erupted from the crowd... A couple of guys walked onto the stage, strapping on guitars, and right away I recognized Brad Whitford, ex-Aerosmith, and Derek St. Holmes, ex-Ted Nugent. We were hot and ready, they were hot and ready, and they were smiling... Whitford and St. Holmes both smiled as they cut loose with their first song, a cut from their debut release. The sheer raw power the band displayed surprised us, but the crowd had clearly come to see Mother's Finest. They were reluctant to get on their feet with any feeling and it looked like the first two rows would be the only ones gettin' down all night. Wrong again. Not that I'm trying to say very little about Whitford-St. Holmes, but they only got to do about a 30- or 40-minute set. This is par for the course for an opening band, especially a new band. But they were excellent, and it was good for the soul to see Brad Whitford, who had been hidden behind Joe Perry in Aerosmith, step out with his Stratocaster with one pick-up on it and literally burn the strings off it. It was just as good to see St. Holmes, who had been downtrodden by Ted Nugent, a noted guitar overkill artist, playin' so hard that he broke two strings on his guitar within five minutes from the beginning of the show. But St. Holmes never missed a note while he was singing the song, and was taking the guitar off, motioning for the roadie to bring him his Hamer, jumping back at the mike for the next notes, stepping back again to take off the Strat, putting on the Hamer and lunging at the mike once again, with perfect timing, to finish the notes and launch into a short burner himself with that Hamer. When they went off, we wanted more. But the house lights came up..." (Orangeburg Times & Democrat, 8/30/1981).

August 27 **TWO SHOWS
Bogart's
Cincinnati, OH
Promoter: in-house
Notes:
- The band were scheduled to perform two sets, at 8 and 11p.m.

August 30
Cardi's
Houston, TX
Set list: I Need Love / Shy Away / Whiskey Woman / Does it Really Matter? / Spanish Boy / Every Morning / Action / Sharpshooter
Notes:
- This show circulates from a supposed FM broadcast but sounds more like an AUD, but the band does perform nearly the full album.

September 6
Rock Saloon
San Antonio, TX

September 7
Barton Coliseum
T.H. Little Rock, AR
Promoter: Beaver Productions
Other act(s): Blue Oyster Cult (HL), Foghat
Reported audience: (9,000 capacity)
Notes:
- It's not clear whether WSH had joined the tour at this point.

September 8
Assembly Center
Tulsa, OK
Promoter: Contemporary Productions
Other act(s): Blue Oyster Cult (HL), Foghat
Reported audience: (9,000 capacity)
Notes:
- It's not clear whether WSH had joined the tour at this point.

September 11
Spectrum
Philadelphia, PA
Promoter: Electric Factory Concerts
Other act(s): Blue Oyster Cult (HL), Foghat
Reported audience: (19,500 capacity)
Notes:
- This was the seventh show of Blue Oyster Cult's tour, but it's currently not known if WSH opened any of the earlier dates, even though the tour started regionally close to the last confirmed show of August in Houston.

September 12
Civic Center
Providence, RI
Promoter: Frank J. Russo
Other act(s): Blue Oyster Cult (HL), Foghat
Reported audience: (14,000 capacity)

September 13
Civic Center
Springfield, MA
Promoter: Frank J. Russo
Other act(s): Blue Oyster Cult (HL), Foghat
Reported audience: (9,200 capacity)

September 15
Memorial Auditorium
Buffalo, NY
Promoter: Festival East Concerts
Other act(s): Blue Oyster Cult (HL), Foghat
Reported audience: (17,827 capacity)

September 17
Civic Arena
Pittsburgh, PA
Promoter: DiCesare-Engler Productions
Other act(s): Blue Oyster Cult (HL), Foghat
Reported audience: 10,177 / 17,000 (59.87%)
Reported gross: $95,449
Notes:
- A weekend press piece noted that Shooting Star opened the show, while Billboard's Boxscore noted Whitford-St. Holmes. The review in the Pittsburgh Post-Gazette (Sept. 18) notes two opening acts, but only discussed Foghat's set specifically.

September 19
Boston Garden
Boston, MA
Promoter: Don Law Co.
Other act(s): Blue Oyster Cult (HL), Foghat
Reported audience: 13,800 /15,000 (92%)
Reported Gross: $155,018

September 20
Coliseum
New Haven, CT
Promoter: Cross Country Concerts
Other act(s): Blue Oyster Cult (HL), Foghat
Reported audience: 9,069 / 10,000 (90.69%)
Reported gross: $90,035
Notes:
- Following this show "Shooting Star" and other acts took over the opening slot for a few shows.

September 27
Wicomico Youth & Civic Center
Salisbury, MD
Promoter: Cellar Door Presents
Other act(s): Blue Oyster Cult (HL), Foghat
Reported audience: (5,130 capacity)

September 29
Civic Center
Roanoke, VA
Promoter: Cellar Door Concerts
Other act(s): Blue Oyster Cult (HL), Foghat
Reported audience: (11,000 capacity)

September 30
Coliseum
Hampton, VA
Other act(s): Blue Oyster Cult (HL), Foghat
Reported audience: (13,800 capacity)

October 1 **CANCELLED
Carolina Coliseum
Columbia, SC
Other act(s): Blue Oyster Cult (HL), Foghat
Notes:
- This show was cancelled, though it's unknown whether WSH was scheduled to open.

October 2
Coliseum
Charlotte, NC
Promoter: Kaleidoscope Presents
Other act(s): Blue Oyster Cult (HL), Foghat

Reported audience: 8,667 / 10,000 (86.67%)
Reported gross: $74,193
Notes:
- From a local review: "Opening act Whitford/St. Holmes brought together two journeymen rock musicians who displayed talent and promise. Derek St. Holmes, formerly vocalist with Ted Nugent, has a good rock shouter's voice. Guitarist Brad Whitford, formerly second-string guitarist (to Joe Perry) in Aerosmith, played with controlled abandon. On 'Sharpshooter,' the final number of a brief opening set, St. Holmes sang melodically and energetically when he could be heard over the din. But on the whole, the band didn't have much new to say" (Charlotte Observer, 10/3/1981).

October 3
Municipal Auditorium
Nashville, TN
Promoter: Sound Seventy Productions
Other act(s): Blue Oyster Cult (HL), Foghat
Reported audience: 9,900 **SOLD-OUT
Reported gross: $80,690

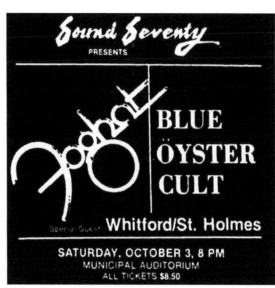

October 4
Riverside Centroplex
Baton Rouge, LA
Promoter: Beaver Productions
Other act(s): Blue Oyster Cult (HL), Foghat
Reported audience: (15,000 capacity)

October 6
Omni
Atlanta, GA
Promoter: Alex Cooley, Inc.
Other act(s): Blue Oyster Cult (HL), Foghat
Reported audience: (16,000 capacity)

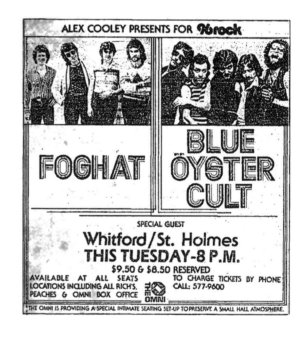

October 8
St. Lucie County Civic Center
Ft. Pierce, FL
Promoter: Fantasma Productions
Other act(s): Blue Oyster Cult (HL), Foghat
Reported audience: 3,917 / 5,000 (78.34%)
Reported gross: $35,253

October 9
Sportatorium
Hollywood, FL
Promoter: Fantasma Productions
Other act(s): Blue Oyster Cult (HL), Foghat
Reported audience: 7,001 / 7,500 (93.35%)
Reported gross: $59,508

October 10
Civic Center
Lakeland, FL

Other act(s): Blue Oyster Cult (HL), Foghat
Reported audience: (10,000 capacity)

October 11
Lee County Arena
Ft. Myers, FL
Promoter: Fantasma Productions
Other act(s): Blue Oyster Cult (HL), Foghat
Reported audience: 6,603 / 9,000 (73.37%)
Reported gross: $56,125

October 13 ???
Mississippi Coast Coliseum
Biloxi, MS
Promoter: Superstar Productions
Other act(s): Blue Oyster Cult (HL), Foghat
Reported audience: (9,200 capacity)

October 15
Roberts Stadium
Evansville, IN
Promoter: Sunshine Promotions
Other act(s): Blue Oyster Cult (HL), Foghat
Reported audience: 4,560 / 10,000 (45.60%)
Reported gross: $40,174
Notes:
- Whitford/St. Holmes are mentioned in trade box office reports, though may have performed too early to be mentioned in the local show reviews (Evansville Courier & Press and Evansville Press, 10/16/1981).

October 16
International Amphitheater
Chicago, IL
Promoter: Jam Productions
Other act(s): Blue Oyster Cult (HL), Foghat
Reported audience: (11,513 capacity)

October 17
MetroCentre
Rockford, IL
Promoter: Jam Productions
Other act(s): Blue Oyster Cult (HL), Foghat
Reported audience: (10,000 capacity)

October 18
Horton Fieldhouse @ I.S.U.
Normal, IL
Other act(s): Blue Oyster Cult (HL), Foghat
Notes:
- Unconfirmed, though other shows didn't note the third act on the bill.

October 21
Sports Arena
Toledo, OH
Promoter: Sports Arena, Inc.
Other act(s): Blue Oyster Cult (HL), Foghat
Reported audience: (7,500 capacity)

October 22
Civic Center
Saginaw, MI
Other act(s): Blue Oyster Cult (HL), Foghat
Reported audience: 6,190 / 7,169 (86.34%)
Reported gross: $58,805

October 23
Joe Louis Arena,
Detroit, MI
Promoter: Brass Ring Productions
Other act(s): Blue Oyster Cult (HL), Foghat
Reported audience: 9,513 / 15,924 (59.74%)
Reported gross: $103,375

October 24
Market Square Arena
Indianapolis, IN
Promoter: Sunshine Promotion
Other act(s): Blue Oyster Cult (HL), Foghat
Reported audience: 12,500 / 13,263 (94.25%)
Reported gross: $114,517
Notes:
- From a local review: "The Whitford-St. Holmes Band also made its Indy debut Saturday night although fans familiar with Aerosmith and Ted Nugent might have recognized Brad Whitford as a former guitarist for Aerosmith and Derick St. Holmes as a former guitarist and vocalist for Ted Nugent. The group's half-hour set featured music from the band's self-titled album. Despite the audience's unfamiliarity with the tunes, the group earned a respectable response for a respectable set, highlighted by moving presentation of 'Spanish Boy'" (Indianapolis News, 10/26/1981).

October 25
Louisville Gardens
Louisville, KY
Promoter: Sunshine Promotions
Other act(s): Blue Oyster Cult (HL), Foghat
Reported audience: 5,622 / 6,800 (82.68%)
Reported gross: $49,186
Notes:

- From a local review: "The Whitford-St. Holmes Band opened last night's show. Their set was brief and had the crowd attentive, if not enthusiastic" (Louisville Courier-Journal, 10/26/1981).

October 27
Coliseum
Richfield (Cleveland), OH
Promoter: Belkin Productions
Other act(s): Blue Oyster Cult (HL), Foghat
Reported audience: 10,373 / 17,500 (59.27%)

October 29
Metropolitan Center
Bloomington, MN
Promoter: Rose Presents
Other act(s): Blue Oyster Cult (HL), Foghat
Reported audience: 12,660 **SOLD-OUT
Reported gross: $118,395

October 30
Five Season Center
Cedar Rapids, IA
Other act(s): Blue Oyster Cult (HL), Foghat
Reported audience: 7,528 / 10,000 (75.28%)
Notes:
- From a local review: "Opening the show with a 30-minute set was the Whitford St. Holmes Band, which did an adequate job in getting the crowd wound up for the two headliners" (Cedar Rapids Gazette, 10/31/1981).

October 31
Kemper Arena
Kansas City, MO
Promoter: Contemporary Productions / New West Presentations
Other act(s): Blue Oyster Cult (HL), Foghat
Reported audience: 12,500 **SOLD-OUT
Reported gross: $122,310
Notes:
- From a local review: "The promoters did a disservice to the audience by announcing the opening act, Whitford/St. Holmes, only a day before the concert. Though the band bears the name of former Aerosmith guitarist Brad Whitford and singer Derek St. Holmes, who formerly sang and wrote with Ted Nugent, the other two members are veterans of other, not quite so rock bands. Bassist Dave Hewitt formerly played with Babe Ruth, and drummer Steve Pace used to beat the skins for Hydra. Although that set also was short, it may have been the most powerful of the evening. It was missed by most of those attending the concert, however, because it started at 7:30p.m. and the concert was scheduled to begin at 8p.m." (Kansas City Times, 11/2/1981).

November 1
Checkerdome

St. Louis, MO
Promoter: Contemporary Productions
Other act(s): Blue Oyster Cult (HL), Foghat
Reported audience: 9,750 **SOLD-OUT
Reported gross: $98,541
Notes:
- From a local review: "The leaders of the Whitford-St. Holmes band are veterans of Aerosmith and Ted Nugent bands, respectively. Musically the quartet is tight, and it fit right into the music of the evening. Of the half dozen or so songs that were performed one called 'Sharpshooter' had the most potential, lyrically, and melodically" (St. Louis Post-Dispatch, 11/2/1981).

November 2
Hammons Student Center
Springfield, MO
Promoter: Contemporary Productions
Other act(s): Blue Oyster Cult (HL)
Reported audience: 3,853 / 5,000 (77.06%)
Reported gross: $32,750

November 3
Kansas Coliseum
Wichita, KS
Promoter: Contemporary Productions
Other act(s): Blue Oyster Cult (HL), Foghat
Reported audience: 9,000 **SOLD-OUT
Reported gross: $85,111

November 4
Pershing Auditorium
Lincoln, NE
Promoter: Contemporary Productions
Other act(s): Blue Oyster Cult (HL), Foghat
Reported audience: 7,129 / 7,500 (95.05%)
Reported gross: $65,304
Notes:
- From a local review: "It was simply your average, maybe above average, heavy metal concert in which three bands are each progressively less boring. In one corner, you had the tag team of Derek St. Holmes — a marriage made in a promoter's heaven, a former Aerosmith, and a former Ted Nugent, but they were quickly dismissed as featherweights" (Lincoln Star, 11/5/1981).
- From another local review: "The first band was alright, Derek St. Holmes. Somebody said one of the guys used to be in Aerosmith and that another guy was in Ted Nugent. Everybody wanted to see Foghat and Blue Oyster Cult, though, so we didn't clap too much" (Lincoln Journal Star, 11/5/1981).

November 5
Dane Country Coliseum
Madison, WI
Promoter: Stardate Productions
Other act(s): Blue Oyster Cult (HL), Foghat
Reported audience: 6,953 / 10,100 (68.84%)
Reported gross: $61,077
Notes:

- From a local review: "The 4 1/2-hour program opened with a 30-minute sound check attempting to pass as an opening set by the Whitford-St. Holmes band. Brad Whitford was the rhythm half of the Aerosmith guitar duo. Derek St. Holmes was the vocalist and support axeman on the first four Ted Nugent albums. So, what have they done lately? Got themselves and drummer and bass player and formed a band. Now all they need is some material that will stick in the old memory banks longer than it takes to wander off to the concession stand for popcorn. Until then, the paying public should be spared" (Wisconsin State Journal, 11/6/1981).

November 6
Lake View Arena
Marquette, MI

Promoter: Stardate Productions
Other act(s): Blue Oyster Cult (HL)
Reported audience: 4,610 / 5,400 (85.37%)
Reported gross: $27,910
Notes:
- The final show opening for Blue Oyster Cult.

November 19
Fox Theater
San Diego, CA

Other act(s): Billy Squier (HL)
Reported audience: ~2,400
Notes:
- From a local review: "The show opened with Whitford-St. Holmes, a not-too-subtle group headed up by guitarist Brad Whitford, once of Aerosmith, and vocalist-guitarist Derek St. Holmes, who was until 1978 in the employ of Ted Nugent. Excessive volume could only help this quartet. They needed as much noise as they could get to divert attention from the emptiness of their material. The 40-minute set featured an extended solo by drummer Steve Pace, whose two best tricks were stolen from Art Blakey and Buddy Rich. Blakey, 62, and Rich, 64, will until they die perform them better than Pace can ever dream of" (San Diego Union, 11/20/1981).

November 20, 21
Civic Center
Santa Monica, CA

Promoter: Avalon Attractions
Other act(s): Billy Squier (HL)
Reported audience: (3,500 capacity)
Reported gross: $59,998.25 **both nights
Notes:
- From a local review: "Whitford/St. Holmes, featuring former Aerosmith guitarist Brad Whitford and ex-Ted Nugent vocalist Derek St. Holmes, opened the concert with a journeyman display of corporate rock at its most faceless. They have talent; they simply don't have a clue what to do with it" (Los Angeles Times, 11/23/1981).

November 22
Warfield Theater
San Francisco, CA

Promoter: Bill Graham Presents
Other act(s): Billy Squier (HL)

424 | Aerosmith on Tour, 1973-85

November 24 **CANCELLED
Keystone
Palo Alto, CA
Promoter: in-house

November 24
Country Club,
Reseda, CA
Promoter: Wolf & Rissmiller Concerts
Other act(s): Tim Bogert

November 25 **CANCELLED
Keystone
Berkeley, CA
Promoter: in-house

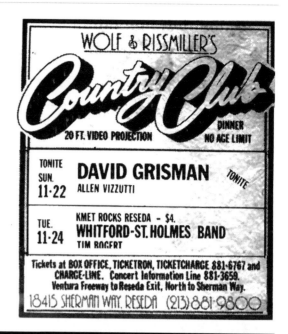

1986

May 1986
Thirsty Whale
River Grove, IL
Reported audience: 1,000 **SOLD-OUT
Notes:
- Brad and Derek got together for a one-off club show (Billboard, 6/21/1986). A proper "Reunion" would follow decades later ...

1981 - Sharpshooter

1982 - Rock in a Hard Place

U.S. Release Details:
Columbia/CBS FC/FCA/FCT 38061 (Aug. 27, 1982)
Columbia/CBS CK-38061 (1989 — CD Issue)
Columbia/SMEi CK/CT-57368 (Sep. 7, 1993 — 20-bit SBM digital remaster)
Columbia/SME 88883761441 (2014 — 180g LP reissue)

Tracks:

A1. Jailbait
(4:38) — Steven Tyler / Jimmy Crespo

A2. Lightning Strikes •
(4:26) — Richard Supa

A3. Bitch's Brew •
(4:14) — Steven Tyler / Jimmy Crespo

A4. Bolivian Ragamuffin
(3:32) — Steven Tyler / Jimmy Crespo

A5. Cry Me a River
(4:06) — Arthur Hamilton

B1. Prelude to Joanie
(1:21) — Steven Tyler

B2. Joanie's Butterfly
(5:35) — Steven Tyler / Jimmy Crespo / Jack Douglas

B3. Rock in a Hard Place (Cheshire Cat)
(4:46) — Steven Tyler / Jimmy Crespo / Jack Douglas

B4. Jig is Up
(3:10) — Steven Tyler / Jimmy Crespo

B5. Push Comes to Shove
(4:28) — Steven Tyler

Album Details:
Produced by Jack Douglas, Steven Tyler, and Tony Bongiovi. Engineered by Godfrey Diamond, Tony Bongiovi, and Jack Douglas; assisted by Josh Abbey, John Agnello, Bruce Hensal, Malcolm Pollack, Gary Rindfuss, Jim Sessody, Zoe Yanakis. Overdubs recorded on Key Biscayne by Criteria on Wheels and engineered Godrfey Diamond, Joe Foglia and Bob Kosiba. While Rick Dufay is credited, and pictured on the album's packaging, he did not perform on any of the studio recordings.

Players:
◦ Lightning Strikes - Brad Whitford on rhythm guitar.
◦ Joanie's Butterfly - Reinhard Straub on violin; John Lievano on acoustic guitar.
◦ Rock in a Hard Place (Cheshire Cat) - John Turi on saxophone.
◦ Push Comes to Shove - Paul Harris on piano.
◦ Jack Douglas contributes percussion throughout.

Chart Action:
Chart Peak (USA): #32 (10/16/1982) with 18 weeks on the Billboard charts. The album fared worse on Cashbox only reaching #42 (11/13/1982) during a 17-week run. Other countries: CAN #24.

09/25/82	10/02/82	10/09/82	**10/16/82**	10/23/82	10/30/82	11/06/82
53	39	35	** 32 **	32	32	32
11/13/82	11/20/82	11/27/82	12/04/82	12/11/82	12/18/82	12/25/82
44	55	76	76	103	163	167
01/01/83	01/08/83	01/15/83	01/22/83	01/29/83		
167	167	199	199	X		

RIAA/Sales:
In the United States, the album was certified Gold by the RIAA on Nov. 10, 1989. It has never been recertified. In the SoundScan era the album sold 101,014 units between 1991 and Feb. 2007.

Supporting Singles:
• While "Lightning Strikes" was issued to video music channels such as MTV, it was not accompanied (in the U.S.) with a physical single release. However, the song did feature on Billboard's Album Top Tracks chart reaching #21 during a nine-week run.

10/09/82	10/16/82	**10/23/82**	10/30/82	11/07/82	11/13/82	11/20/82
51	26	** 21 **	24	28	40	35
11/27/82	12/04/82	12/11/82				
52	49	X				

• A promotional 12" was issued in 1983 with "Bitch's Brew," for which a Jonas McCord produced and directed 3-Dimensional live performance video (that remains unreleased).

Performed Live:
Five songs from the album debuted at the first show of the supporting tour: "Bolivian Ragamuffin," "Jig is Up," "Jailbait," Rock in a Hard Place (Cheshire Cat)," and "Lightning Strikes." While that number quickly dropped, "Bitch's Brew" and "Cry Me a River" were added to the set in December (albeit briefly).

Steven: "We've been away too long. We miss all the bad reviews" (Boston Globe, 11/11/1982).

A follow-up studio album to "Night in the Ruts" would be a long time coming. During the years that followed the initial recording sessions for that album, both of the band's guitarists had departed, the vocalist had been laid up recovering from physical injuries for an extended period, and the band essentially ground to a halt. Perhaps it was an ideal situation for Aerosmith to have become incapable of releasing new material — 1981 certainly wasn't particularly kind to another 70s behemoths who had similarly suffered internal dysfunction. With Steven's injury, Aerosmith had been limited to just one full show during the latter half of 1980, a limp celebration of the band's first decade broadcast live on the Starfleet Radio Network. While rumors abounded, suggesting Steven would be going solo (Leber & Krebs were looking for film opportunities for him to broaden his career), Columbia took advantage of the break to release a spartan celebration of the band's first decade in the form of "Aerosmith's Greatest Hits." It was clear that much of the Blue Army had gone elsewhere, with that album scraping to RIAA Gold certification on March 3, 1981. For the album that ultimately became the band's marquee catalog seller, it took a further half decade for the title's sales to truly ignite. Wrapping up the band's muted first decade celebration was the promotional "First Decade" box set issued to programmers in Jan. 1981, simply containing promotional versions of the first eight Columbia albums.

Fortunately, by the end of 1980, Aerosmith was starting to think about the next studio album. Former Mountain bassist Felix Pappalardi was mentioned in the trade press as being connected with the band as a prospective producer. He had already worked with them, helping to engineer their June 1980 King Biscuit Flower Hour broadcast from West Hartford. The musical core of the band had continued rehearsing and trying to write new songs, which they would send up to Steven to review while he recuperated. It was less than an ideal situation, though Steven seemed to think that things were working out with Jimmy Crespo: He told Lisa Robinson, "I've been writing. Doing the same thing I did with Joe, only with Jimmy which is a lot faster. Jimmy doesn't have a lot of extracurricular activities... [Joe] had a lot of interests in other departments: The Joe Perry Project... that's what caused the whole breakup... It just started not to work... I couldn't write with him anymore. He wanted to write himself and wanted to be his own superstar. I guess that's what's all behind it, he wanted to be his own frontman... He was into so many side trips" (10/1982). Even at this point, there was a still palpable bitterness towards Joe, who Steve accused of not even visiting him while he was recovering from his crash injuries.

It was a less than satisfactory situation for the band members. Brad had worked on a side project with Derek St. Holmes, but by July 1981 had decided that Aerosmith was a lost cause, particularly at a time when both musicians were tired of standing in the shadows in their respective bands. During August Whitford/St. Holmes hit the road in support of their album. Following the tour, Aerosmith called for Brad to return to the studio for the continued album sessions and soon afterwards Ted called on Derek. The dissolution of the band, and its failure in becoming and ongoing entity, was simply a matter of the two going separate ways by necessity. They'd re-experienced the ground-floor touring as an unestablished opening act in contrast to what they'd enjoyed previously with their respective headlining bands. That Brad ultimately decided that he couldn't continue with Aerosmith simply led to new opportunities to explore. He recorded with actor-musician Rex Smith, brother of Starz's Michael Lee Smith, and reunited with Joe Perry making occasional appearances with the Project, in addition to participating in the group's initial demo sessions. Steven doesn't appear to have been much bothered by Brad's departure, instead continuing to fixate on Perry: "Joe won't be missed except in the hearts of the diehard fans. He thought he has a lot more to do with the band than he really did. The very fact his (solo) albums are not doing so good show the kids where he could do the most good — in a band framework. He knows where he should be — or it's a shame that he doesn't" (AP, 9/24/1982). Regardless, with both of his guitarists gone, all of the pressure was on him to produce an "Aerosmith" album.

While Aerosmith had reconvened in New York City in September 1981 to try and work on a new album with producer Tony Bongiovi, Steven remained lost within the clutches of his personal issues. With Brad having released his "Whitford-St. Holmes" and permanently departing the group, the other members of the band were twiddling their fingers waiting for Steven, the pressure was mounting, and it didn't take much longer for more threatening cracks to appear. Joey, wanting to stay busy — while Aerosmith appeared to be going down the drain — put together a side project he named Renegade. With Tom and Jimmy, he added the powerful vocalist from Jimmy's old band Flame, Marge Raymond, and keyboard player Bobby Mayo. Marge and Jimmy had signed with Leber-Krebs following the demise of Flame. When Crespo was coopted by Aerosmith, Marge had formed a band, Kicks, opening several Aerosmith shows during 1980. Kicks, who included Tommy Derossi, Jimmy Iommi, and PJ Mumola, had also been working on material with producer Felix Pappalardi and recorded a 10-song demo. Steven had even able to provide backing vocals for one song, "Raceway Rock" (the group's set opener). It was a return of the favor for Marge having joined Aerosmith on stage for background vocals on songs such as "Come Together," "Lick and a Promise," and "Train Kept A Rollin'." Marge was a vocal powerhouse, almost a female version of Steven Tyler and then some, whose style could compete with the likes of Pat Benatar or Laura Branigan and raise the bar a notch or six. The band started rehearsing at S.I.R. studios and quickly developed a batch of prospective material.

Renegade progressed far enough to perform a single showcase for record labels at S.I.R. Studios. The also had recorded rough demos of seven songs, including a re-recording of "One More Night" (a song from the abandoned third Flame album). Other songs included "Do It Again," "All Night Long," "Badlands," "Angry Times," "Ride On," and "Cinderella Dreamer," all written by Crespo. With a record deal in the offing, the band began basic tracking/pre-production for an album. According to Joey, David Krebs deliberately used the leverage of this record deal for getting the Aerosmith album completed. It provided a direct threat to the Aerosmith's singer. Once he heard that the remaining members of his band were working on a separate album project, Steven found the requisite motivation to get back to work — at least with enough impetus to stagger forward. And that (essentially) was the end of Renegade, until a couple of the recordings ("Do it Again" and "One More Night") surfaced decades later leaving fans to ponder the question, "what if?" Where Joe and Brad had failed, would a powerhouse female vocalist fronted band with highly accessible rock material have had any better success?

Whether Renegade was the motivational medicine Steven needed to get things back on track, or the leverage Leber-Krebs needed to get Jimmy, Tom, and Joey recommitted to finishing the Aerosmith album, it's unknown which was the greater factor in kicking Aerosmith forward. Whatever the case, towards the end of 1981 activities in the studio got more serious for Aerosmith as a band. Steven once again had a goal, telling Lisa Robinson, "[Aerosmith] is going to make its niche again like it did before. We were definitely a species of our own, this thoroughbred in here... Where's it gonna fit? It's just gonna go out and kick ass. There's not many out there doing it now a la Aerosmith. They're doing their own style; I know what our music is about... [Aerosmith] is such a raunchy good-time rock 'n' roll band... I don't think there's anybody out there who can say an Aerosmith song all sound the same... Format rock." While the band had recorded many of the album's basic tracks with Tony Bongiovi at the Power Station Studios, it was clear things weren't working out with him as producer and further changes were required.

The band weren't completely missing from the public eye during the period. Their visibility benefitted from the then emergence of cable channels specializing in broadcasting music features. In late-1981, USA's "Night Flight" program broadcast "Boston Rocks," a special including interview segments with Joe Perry, Brad Whitford, and video excerpts from the "Chiquita" and "No Surprize" videos. It was ironic that a feature about the band included only two former members of the band. By late 1981 Jack was firmly back in the trenches with the band. He was ultimately credited for contributions on two of the album's tracks ("Joanie's Butterfly" and the album's title track). Not only was there a comfort level with Jack, as he had done during the "Draw the Line" sessions, he could fill specific lyrical gaps during an emergency. According to Steven, "Tony Bongiovi did the bulk of the recording of the songs and then we decided to get Jack in. It's not that we weren't happy with what Tony was doing, but we felt it would be real good to have Jack involved again. We've been through a lot of different producers in the past but we kind of missed that feeling we'd always got with Jack. And I felt that he could capture some of those elements on this LP. He's got a great concept of what Aerosmith is about" (Kerrang #29). Tony's engineering was great for quickly capturing the basic sound for the bed tracks, and he had captured the basic element of the band providing them the foundation from which to build on. But it wasn't enough, and perhaps doubts were entering Steven's mind as co-producer of the album. He later admitted that things hadn't gone as well as hoped with Tony during the four-months they worked together: "We didn't get along. We didn't like the way things were going" (Los Angeles Times, 8/2/1983).

Some of that perceived friction may have been due to Tony's more arcane style — he was neither musician nor studio-techno-wizard; he was more interested in the crafting of records by bringing the best various elements together. Joey Kramer has recalled how dysfunctional and wasteful the sessions were, and that that may have played a larger role in Tony's departure: "Tony Bongiovi, who owned the place, was pulling what little hair he had left on his head. Tony was the consummate professional, and he just couldn't deal with the nonsense that was going on among us. After a while he gave up, and they brought Jack Douglas in, because he was just as much into the drugs as we were" (Kramer, Joey — "Hit Hard"). Additional producers were considered before the band returned to the comfort zone provided by Jack; though the material worked on with Tony wasn't abandoned. Steven, though, was happier and more comfortable with Jack returning to the fold: "Well, he's one of the all-time greatest. You look at his track record, all the Aerosmith records he's done in the past. We've been through three different producers since we did leave him a couple of years back and we wanted to get back to something old with a new flavor, which was Jimmy Crespo being in the band. Jack Douglas was just missed. It was a bit of that sound, the old sound, that we hadn't been getting co-working with other producers, so we found it necessary to call the young lad up" (Creem, 1/1983).

Steven certainly leaned on Jimmy Crespo to step into the roll that had been vacated by Joe Perry and he seemed happy with the developing relationship: "Jimmy (Crespo) took over where Joe left off, and writing songs is fun again (the two collaborated on six of the 10 cuts on the current album, 'Rock in a Hard Place')" (Pittsburgh Press, 11/24/1982). But the dynamic of working with Jimmy was likely part of the events that ultimately led to the departure of Brad. Tom recalled, "When Joe left, it wasn't a case of, 'OK, you guys, I'm leaving. See ya later.' Things within the band had gotten a little tense and it seemed best for him to leave. We all miss Joe personally, but at the time it seemed best for him to do his thing... When Brad left, he was restless. He didn't want to go for the long haul. He had songs and he had been talking about doing a solo album. I was ticked off at first because it happened so suddenly and in the middle of everything, but I can't be bitter... We're committed to staying together as a band, and that took a lot of energy. We wanted to make sure whatever we did was very Aerosmith" (Moline Dispatch, 12/5/1982). Brad had been considering solo work at least as early as late-1978. Jimmy was up to the task and took a leading role on the material written for the album. Steven recalled, "First of all, it was him (Crespo) and only him. We'd go and put down the band, as the band was then, so there wasn't much room for leakage. It was nice and clean and/or dirty one time, the first time that he put it down and then anything we wanted to add over it we put on afterwards which we didn't do much of. Jimmy consequently played lead and rhythm on the album. Coming from the same guy he left room for himself. It all does fall into place a lot more" (Creem, 1/1983). Another beneficiary of the changing band dynamics was Tom Hamilton. Brad's departure left greater scope for Tom to be noticed and his visibility in interviews increased.

Jimmy's fresh roll and very specific methods were the opposite of how Joe and Brad had worked during their decade together — little in that relationship needed to be communication. Brad recalled, "Jimmy was a trained musician, a stickler for getting precise. I found it hard to work with that attitude. Joe and I, we didn't have to say two words to each other about the guitar parts. It was a big part of the guitar magic that had sustained Aerosmith for ten years" ("Walk This Way"). For "Rock in a Hard Place," Jimmy, with a few minor exceptions, would provide all the guitar work himself. There was no one for him to play off, or against, no underlying guitar tensions, competition, or collaboration. That's not to say that Brad's replacement, Rick Dufay, wouldn't play an important role. For Jack, Dufay was also critical to completing the album: "There was a tremendously different atmosphere all the way around. You didn't have Joe and Brad. You had Rick Dufay who was a real ball of fire. That kinda made it fun. I think we were all in a drug daze at that time. Drugs were not fun at that particular time... Let's just say that Rick really held things together at that point, you know, for the band. I mean, Tom and Joey were just rooting that we would get the thing done. Steven was at a loss for lyrics. It took them a long time to make that record. And Rick, because of his humor and energy, was able to drive us all. Drove us crazy, mostly. But that helped a lot. Kept us awake" (RoughEdge.com). There were mixed explanations for the amount of time the album took to produce, and in the end the album purportedly cost well over $1 million. According to Steven, "We were actually in and out of the studios for pretty much the bulk of a year. And the main reason it took so long was because we were in the midst of a writing frenzy. There were so many songs coming out all at once that we decided to hang on in the studio and at least get them down on tape for the next album. So consequently, we ended up with two LP's worth of material" (Kerrang #29).

Dufay may have been something of an accidental band member, certainly initial press reports noting his involvement simply suggested that he was "helping out" on a few tracks. He certainly wasn't a fan of the band (he did like the sound of "Rocks," which is why Jack ended up as producer of "Tender Loving Abuse"), wasn't particularly impressed by them, and even had to be coerced into auditioning. Those may form part of the reason that he was perfect for the band. Jimmy was serious, Tom and Brad had seldom been particularly active on stage, and Rick had a laissez-faire performance attitude that didn't accept any rule book. He was into having fun and was a musical renegade. Coming into the sessions at such a late stage, Jimmy had already performed the majority of guitars for the album and the songs were fully composed and arranged. If he added anything to the recordings, then there were only bits and pieces. He and Steven certainly did work on musical ideas together, including a song titled "Written in Stone" that would be released by Rick years later. With the band having worked on and off for a year, Rick was in place by the time they were finishing overdubs in Florida. The band used both Criteria Studios and the studio's remote unit to record at a location on Key Biscayne. If there was an MVP for the album, then that person would be Jimmy Crespo. With Brad out of the picture he was left carrying the full weight of providing all the guitars on the album, a task that had previously been split between two vastly different personalities and styles. Rick, too, became a babysitter to get Steven cleaned up enough to complete the album.

Some of the earliest song titles mentioned (to the press in August 1981) in relation to the project included "Jailbait," "Bitch's Brew," and "Dr. Nickadick's Magic Wishing Pills." "Jailbait" would become the album's lead off track and with "Bitch's Brew" sonically illustrated the contributions Jimmy was bringing to the band and his importance to this period of the band's career (so much so that it would be the sole representative off the album included on "Gems" in 1988). Not only was he writing material through which the essence of Aerosmith still flowed, but he understood Aerosmith as a musical powerhouse. If he couldn't replicate the guitar magic previously created by Brad and Joe, he did at least respect the band and the band's musical legacy. While he couldn't get Steven straight, that was one area where Dufay became the ideal partner. While Steven later admitted defeat on the lyrical front, he resorted to covering Julie London's "Cry Me A River" (originally written for Ella Fitzgerald). At least he had a creative story to justify its inclusion: "I think we've just about done 'em all, haven't given it much thought. 'Cry Me A River' I heard in Beaumont, Texas or somewhere. It was an overnight stand, I had this old honkytonk station on, and they happened to play the oldie by Julie London, and I thought to myself it would be terrific to try bring it back" (Creem, 1/1983). It was something that certainly hadn't hurt the band on the previous album...

Tom was adamant that the new lineup wasn't going to change the band: "They're not gonna get a down-the-road, derivative band — it'll be Aerosmith. I know there's a lot of so-called heavy metal bands out here, but I know we're gonna go out there and show them that style with some class" (Moline Dispatch, 12/5/1982). For all the dysfunction and drama involved in its creation, "Rock in a Hard Place" was chock full of experimentation and embellishment. Douglas incorporated a brass section to buttress the album's title track; strings were added to season "Joanie's Butterfly" with a vocoder being deployed for the song's prelude. There were layers and textures that harkened back to the basic ingredients of the band's classic era. Steven recalled the creation of that song: "It was taken from a riff that Jimmy came up with sitting around a hotel room... then I had a dream one night. I wrote down my dream, in fact it's on the inner sleeve of the album. The dream was so fucking vivid... from that the song came out. It definitely has an Indian/Ethiopian flavor to it... It's a threefold song anyway. It starts off, we use vocoder. That's what they used in Germany when Hitler would send secret messages. He would have a voice over a band playing, a voice that sounds like a trumpet and somebody got ahold of it in France or wherever and put it to use. That's where it's nice and melodic and ballad-y but then it goes into the second part which cuts it right in half. Most of our ballads have been like that anyway. The front will be nice and sweet, then it will break into... I kinda love it, it's the second step for us" (Creem, 1/1983). "Lightning Strikes" was a song brought into the band from stalwart contributor Richard Supa. When first demoed in 1980, it was fully titled "When the Lightning Strikes" (interestingly, he wrote "Once Is Enough" soon afterward). The Aerosmith version included Brad Whitford's final contributions during his original tenure.

Album closer "Push Comes to Shove" would be the only song credited solely to Steven. He recalled, "I wrote that song on piano years ago, it used to sound like a Burt Bacharach thing... I was real loose down in Florida, we were recording at Criteria Studios and I sat down at the piano and I had my machine running, Godfrey

Diamond, who was our engineer on this project, sat down with me and we stayed up for 54 hours solid and put that song down. I played piano on it, I played the drums, I did all the vocals, I did the background vocals, and it was such a trip" (Creem, 1/1983). But, as good as any of the material may have felt to the band it wouldn't be enough, competing against a plethora of bands that had filled the gap during their absence. A video for "Lightning Strikes" went into rotation on MTV the week of November 15. Directed by Arnold Levine, the combo video saw the band's soundstage performance intercut with 50's styled "West Side Story" greaser rumble footage acted out by the band members.

AEROSMITH: BACK WITH A SPLASH!
"We still p—— all over the opposition" sez Steven Tyler

(Kerrang #27 headline)

Released on Aug. 27, 1982, "Rock in a Hard Place" was certified Gold by the RIAA on Nov. 10, 1989. It has never been recertified. During the SoundScan era the album sold 101,000 units between 1991 and Feb. 2007. In the U.S., the album reached #32 on the Billboard Top-200 charts on Oct. 16, 1982, during an 18-week run. During 17-weeks on Cashbox the album reached #42. The album didn't chart in international markets other than Canada, where it reached #24. No single was commercially released for "Lightning Strikes," and the song only charted on Billboard's Album Top Tracks chart, reaching #21 during a 9-week run. It was off the chart by early December. For touring preparations, following such a lengthy layoff (plus personnel changes), the band spent nearly two months rehearsing at the Capitol Theater in Concord, NH. The extensive rehearsals were buttressed with efforts to improve Steven's health for the rigors of the road. There was certainly a lot of work to be done. A harsh review of Steven's guest appearance with Cheap Trick on August 27, may have played a part. Joining the band at the Ritz in New York City, a critic noted: "Steve Tyler of Aerosmith joined Cheap Trick for the first of two encores, sharing vocal duties with Robin Zander on several numbers, including 'Day Tripper.' The Beatles tune brought out Rick Nielsen's best effort, played on a triangle guitar illustrated with the likenesses of the original fab four. The whole group seemed pleased as punch to share the stage with Tyler, a fellow protege of producer Jack Douglas. Unfortunately, Tyler on stage revealed only a faint glimmer of the great talent that sparks Aerosmith" (Billboard, 9/11/1982).

During the rehearsals it was as important to fully incorporate the new musicians into the lineup while knocking the rust off the band, individually and collectively. The rehearsals were beneficial. The new lineup built the requisite tightness critical for successfully taking the show on the road and avoiding a repetition of the 1979 tour implosion. Starting what was essentially a brand-new thing was a new experience where the new members, particularly Rick, brought in a fresh energy that forced the others to step up their own performances. Dufay was an injection of caffeine to a band that was often static on stage. He kept Steven on his toes, with his unrestrained rock-'n'-roll-and-don't-give-a-fuck attitude which forced Steven to respond, sometimes chasing him around the stage. If his antics enraged Steven, it also made him focus and get involved in the performance on stage. It certainly annoyed the ever-stolid Jimmy, who was left alone to dial in the quality guitar performance required by his position as Joe Perry's replacement.

The new members did more to change the band both visually and sonically. Tom recalled, "In the old days the band used to be extremely loud. But 80 per cent of that [sound] was coming out of Joe's amp, which meant the monitors had to be constantly pushed to the brink of feedback, which took the raunch too far. It's different now. The band works together more as a team. Everybody listens to each other more and everybody works off the rest of the band as a whole. We've got a much better stage mix and it transmits out front, too" (Indianapolis News, 12/4/1982). Jimmy concentrated on the music and while some saw him visually as an analogue for the departed Perry it certainly wasn't the case with his precise and more restrained performances. Rick was left to be the Wildman, who quickly learned that it was best to leave Jimmy to his craft on stage. Jimmy shouldered the weight of the "Where's Joe" garbage, having been with the band longer, and due to his looks and style. Not that he would have been able to hear any audience negativity from the stage. Rick has commented that Jimmy took the criticisms personally, whereas he just didn't give a shit.

Steven, perhaps, was finally happy at last, able to hear himself through the PA. Whatever the case, he was ready to get back on the road, commenting, "There's a lack of real good kickin' rock 'n' roll out there. Nobody has filled the gap. Kids are dying to see the band" (AP, 9/24/1982). Whether the band could reclaim their crown was a completely different matter. In their period of absence, they had been replaced with the emergence of numerous new, young, and exciting bands who had shifted rock 'n' roll to a different level.

A 31-date tour through the end of December was booked, with the band then planning to go back into the studio to work on new 3-D videos for several songs. Purportedly, the beer brewer Schlitz approached the band with an offer of tour sponsorship, only to be countered by Steven suggesting, "Aerosmith would pay Schlitz one half cent a bottle to print 'Aerosmith presents Schlitz' on every one of its labels. The brewery stopped calling" (Cashbox, 1/8/1983). A new stage show was being created, featuring an eight-foot 3-D head that would sing along with the band on "Lightning Strikes." Following a "thank you" show for the residents of Concord — who had tolerated the band's presence in their town — the tour kicked off at Stabler Arena in Bethlehem, PA on November 7. The band debuted an impressive five songs from the album that night — "Bolivian Ragamuffin," "Jig is Up," "Jailbait," "Rock in a Hard Place (Cheshire Cat)," and "Lightning Strikes" — though they would quickly start the process of culling songs and reduce that number to two. Steven was enthusiastic in the press commenting that the first nine shows had sold-out, a somewhat unexpected occurrence during the economic challenges of the time. Enthusiastic he might as well have been, the tour was not without drama. Steven collapsed towards the end of the band's second hometown show on Nov. 16, though unlike the previous tour the event didn't cause the cancellation of any dates. While many songs from the album came and went, and catalog songs were brought in to rebalance the set, during the tour both "Cry Me A River" and "Bitch's Brew" also made appearances.

It was clear from that first run of dates that there were still plenty of customers who wanted to see Aerosmith, and while reviews were mixed major disasters were avoided. On the strength of a near SRO first leg, the DMA Agency booked Aerosmith for a second run throughout the anticipated unusually quiet Jan./Feb. period, seeing the lack of competition as an opportunity to maximize their draw. Whereas a similar risky strategy backfired for KISS and their booking agency, ICM, Aerosmith were able to benefit from some surprisingly strong attendances that were not reflective of the band's album's performance on the charts or airplay. Following a break for the winter holidays, the band returned to the road on Dec. 26 and toured through a raucous homecoming at the Cape Cod Coliseum on March 5. Several shows were recorded by the Record Plant "black" remote truck #2 for a prospective live album, and mixed-down masters from the show multi-tracks were produced. Show attendances were patchy during second leg, with the economic situation undoubtedly having some effect. This leg also saw the set shortened to just 13 songs, with the majority comprised of classic catalog songs (only "Lightning Strikes" survived from the new album).

Following two Florida music festival shows in April, playing second to Journey, the band took on a brief third leg of touring at the end of May. While "Bitch's Brew" had been issued promotionally, and the band's hyped 3-D video premiering in early May, the band were dead on the charts. The smaller venues and attendances reflected the diminishing returns being earned on the road. Many fans had likely simply come out to see the band their elder siblings had listened to or caught up with an old friend after an absence of a few years. A final tour leg starting July 26 was cut short after several substance afflicted performances and Steven's arrest in Arizona. After a promising start, reality had caught up with the band, and the wheels on the bus had fallen off... As had been the case in 1980, the band attempted to downscale in December with a club date run, though initial dates had to be postponed when Joey fell ill with pneumonia. He was temporarily replaced by Bobby Rondinelli (ex-Rainbow) for several dates into early 1984. Another final short run of live dates took place in February, with Kramer returned to the band, with them playing clubs and smaller halls. By that time Aerosmith had seemingly run out of steam, and other plans were being worked on in the background. The Dufay/Crespo version of the band played their final show on Feb. 17 in Providence, RI.

Assorted review excerpts:

"What's this — Aerosmith doing 'Cry Me A River' and 'Bitch's Brew'? Fear not, headbangers, Steve Tyler screams rather than cries that old ballad, and the latter is a typically raunchy hard rock original, not the Miles Davis classic. In fact, despite a brand-new guitar front line in Jimmy Crespo and Rick Dufay, this Boston quintet returns with the style and format of its biggest selling '70s albums intact, and with AOR on its hard rock rampage, these new performances could return the band to prominence" (Billboard 9/11/1982)

"To be quite frank, I've always been a die-hard Aerosmith fanatic. From the day I first procured a copy of the classic 'Dream On' it was instant addiction. Over the years the boys from Boston have delivered a string of high-grade rock 'n' roll albums: 'Toys in the Attic', 'Get Your Wings', 'Rocks'... the list goes on. During the seventies, the band became huge in their native America and always seemed to have a steady cult following in Britain. Aerosmith were very much a force to be reckoned with. However, when their last studio LP 'A Night in the Ruts' surfaced back in '79 it was announced that guitarist Joe Perry had left the band. The news came as a bitter disappointment since Perry and vocalist Steven Tyler had been the spearhead of Aerosmith's attack and many cited the axeman's departure as the start of the group's demise.

And to be frank, it's been a pretty tough ride for Tyler's gang over the past couple of years. Jimmy Crespo was enlisted as Perry's replacement and the band subsequently went back on the road but gradually Aerosmith were to gig less and less. Some blamed their inactivity on Steven Tyler's health whatever the reason things became very quiet on the Aerosmith front. It therefore came as a great relief to hear that the band has started work on a new LP earlier this year. And finally, it's arrived in the form of 'Rock in a Hard Place'. I'm happy to report that the wait has definitely been worthwhile and after continual spins over the past few days I'm convinced that the record will stand as one this year's output from Priest, Van Halen and the Scorpions. It's possibly the band's best LP to date and proves beyond all doubt that Aerosmith was always very much Tyler's baby. From the vicious opening track 'Jailbait' the band never let up — the intensity is maintained throughout. I'm not going to give you a track-by-track run down of the material, my advice is pure and simple: if you like hard 'n' dirty, mean 'n' moody rock 'n' roll played at its best then get a hold of 'Rock in a Hard Place'... FAST!" (Kerrang #25).

"This is Aerosmith's first release without founding member Joe Perry, the guitarist who already has released two serviceable solo LPs... Nothing really new here, but is that so surprising?" (Allentown Morning Call, 10/2/1982).

"Tyler and his muscle rock will have to kick their way back into our hearts. 'Rock in a Hard Place' sounds the call to arms. It's time to tighten the hinges on that hardest place of all, the fickle consumer heart" (Saskatoon Star-Phoenix, 10/16/1982).

"At times Aerosmith played as if they invented hard rock but things have changed with this, their ninth album. Although there's been personnel changes, the band is mired in a formulaic rut... If you're an Aerosmith diehard, this may be a worthy addition for sentimental reasons. But for freshness try something else" (Boston Globe, 10/21/1982).

"Tyler and company were forced to choose between the old sound with new faces or a complete change in approach. They went for the former, and on first hearing, it almost seems to work. Perry lookalike Jimmy Crespo is no slouch at turning out hard-edged guitar hooks that make up in drive what they lack in swing, and both 'Jailbait' and 'Lightning Strikes' throb with the sort of nasty glee that's always been an Aerosmith trademark. But despite an occasional burst of primal energy, much of the LP rocks by rote. In all fairness, it's a good formula, and even the weakest examples here hold up well enough under repeated listening. Not so the ballads, though: Steve Tyler is unable to energize the slow numbers, and they drag interminably, undercutting the album's pacing in their wake. Maybe next time Aerosmith will stick to the rock; for now, however, they're really stuck in a hard place" (Rolling Stone #381, 10/28/1982).

The new album "shows that the new people have the same taste. The group is as good (or bad) as it has always been... The record is filled with original locomotive rock, with lots of quick licks and Tyler tricks... Tyler's yells are as strong as ever. His raunchy wails sometimes fit the music and sometimes don't" (Lansing State Journal, 11/20/1982).

Oct–Nov 1982
Capitol Theater
Concord, NH

Notes:
- The band conducted several weeks of rehearsals a theater in preparation for the tour. According to Tom, "We knew every song had to be really tight and everything had to go just right, so when it came time to go on stage all we had to think about was going up there and having a good time... Jimmy's over there on stage left and puts on a great show. He really screams, but with a lot of finesse. And Rick is on the other side with me. He's real flamboyant and plays everything really nice and tight and keeps it cooking. It's a great mix of personalities with great musicianship and showmanship" (Indianapolis News, 12/4/1982). The time invested meant that the band had the opportunity to gel as a unit. He expanded, "Being together all these years, we knew what the chemistry was we needed, the personalities that worked. We've been taking apart all the old stuff for the first time in years, taking the songs part by part and putting some oomph in them. We went and did a video rendition of 'Lightning Strikes,' and after that we realized the new band had just done its first gig. The chemistry was great" (Moline Dispatch, 12/5/1982).

October 31
Capitol Theater
Concord, NH

Reported audience: (1,200 capacity)
Notes:
- Since the band had been rehearsing in the run-down theater for a while, they performed a special "Halloween Night" show for the locals who had tolerated their noise and disruption. This show marked Rick Dufay's first public performance with the band.

November 7
Stabler Arena @ Lehigh University
Bethlehem, PA

Promoter: Makoul Productions
Other act(s): Pat Travers, Rose Tattoo
Reported audience: 6,164 / 6,300 (97.84%)
Reported gross: $61,640
Set list: Back in the Saddle / Big Ten Inch Record / Three Mile Smile / Reefer Head Woman / Lord of the Thighs / Bolivian Ragamuffin / Lick and a Promise / Jig is Up / Jailbait / Mama Kin / Sweet Emotion / Dream On / Rock in a Hard Place (Cheshire Cat) / Lightning Strikes / Walk this Way / Same Old Song and Dance / Milk Cow Blues / Toys in the Attic / Train Kept A Rollin'
Notes:
- Joining the band on the tour was keyboard player, and backing vocalist, Bob Mayo, who had played with Peter Frampton and had just come off 14-months on the road with Foreigner. By that time, he had also recorded with Joey, Jimmy, and Tom for the Renegade project. Impressively, five songs from the "Rock in a Hard Place" album were performed at this show. During their final technical rehearsals for the tour at the venue, TV crews visited the band for an interview with Tom and Steven.
- Pat Travers was placed on the tour by Doug Thaler, who was working for Leber-Krebs in various capacities. By the end of the year, he had teamed up with Doc McGhee after seeing a young band, Mötley Crüe, in Los Angeles...
- From a local review: "Aerosmith in concert always has been a motley mixture of color, noise, glam, and merry prurient sleaze. At Lehigh University's Stabler Arena last night, the veteran Boston-based band performed before 6,400 fans, who welcomed their heroes with a jubilant frenzy no doubt brought about in large measure by the band's three-year absence from rock 'n' roll wonderland. Certainly, there were no

surprises. The riffs were in the right place. The strobe lights flashed on time. And vocalist Steven Tyler knew precisely when to act like Mick Jagger. Trouble was, the band sounded hopelessly dated. Protracted soloing and sluggish tempos no longer are the cornerstones of contemporary hard rock. Today's hip noisemakers pack their licks into tighter, brighter arrangements, while at the same time pay homage to their rock-blues roots. Of course, this has been documented many times before. Let's just say Aerosmith has some homework to catch up on. Especially guitarists Rick Dufay and Jimmy Crespo, the latter replacing Joe Perry who had the good sense to leave the band three years ago.

The undynamic duo did put some spunk into a wild version of 'Jailbait,' overlaying the song's herky-jerky rhythm with searing, spiraling leads. But too often, notably on 'Lord of the Thighs,' they merely indulged on their fretboards, prompting at least one concertgoer to search out the soft drink stand. In all fairness, though, the crowd responded enthusiastically to all-time Aerosmith faves 'Sweet Emotion' and 'Dream On' plus 'Mama Kin,' a surprise selection culled from the band's debut LP. Musical considerations aside, the Aerosmith persona also needs a quick overhaul, coming as it does from the mid-'70s broom closet: leather, headbands, rings and sequined scarves. Tyler's microphone was decked out with colored streamers, f'rcryingoutloud! Talk about time warps. So, considering all this lunacy, one could have thanked Pat Travers for lending some respectability to last night's double-bill show" (Allentown Morning Call, 11/8/1982).
- An AUD recording circulates from this show.

November 9
Coliseum
New Haven, CT

Promoter: Cross Country Concerts
Other act(s): Pat Travers, Rose Tattoo
Reported audience: 8,892 **SOLD-OUT
Reported gross: $96,913
Set list: Same as Nov. 7
Notes:
- An AUD recording circulates from this show.

November 11
The Centrum
Worcester, MA

Promoter: Don Law Company
Other act(s): Pat Travers, Rose Tattoo
Reported audience: 10,820 **SOLD-OUT
Reported gross: $216,694 **both nights
Set list: Same as Nov. 7
Notes:

- This show sold-out in minutes, shocking some. Tyler retorted, "We've been away too long. We miss all the bad reviews... This band was always so big, especially in its home area that how can anyone be surprised we wouldn't sell out? I was more shocked by people who thought we wouldn't" (Boston Globe, 11/11/1982).
- From a local review: "As brash as ever, Aerosmith has boasted of returning with a bang after a two-year absence from the big arenas. They've sounded almost too cocky — especially in view of their sludgy, scattershot days of old — but they backed up their boast with a convincing thunderclap of a snow Thursday. Rather than lapse into murky metallic sound, inaudible lyrics, and clumsy musicianship, which were pitfalls in the past, they shed their old skin and played unexpectedly clear, barn burning rock 'n' roll. There was plenty of grinding pelvic rock — an old Aerosmith trademark — but this time the rock was much sharper, more lively and more rhythmic. It was dance music, not Quaalude Muzak. The reasons for the vast improvement were several — fresh personnel (new guitarists Jimmy Crespo and Rick Dufay are flashy but electrifying); time spent in rehearsal (two months rather than the few days of prior tours); and a solid recommitment from charter members Tom Hamilton on bass, Joey Kramer on drums and, most emphatically, Steven Tyler on lead vocals.

Looking his androgynous self in a purple Edwardian dandy suit with flowing tails, Tyler, fully recovered from a motorcycle accident, whipped the band into one peak after another.

Thanks to a superb sound system that boomed the music but did not distort it, Tyler was audible on every song, whether belting his witchy tales of hedonism, scratching out a blues phrase or throwing in soulful hysteria on the back-to-back 'Sweet Emotion' and 'Dream On,' two of the band's best-known hits which came midway through and prepped the capacity 13,500 crowd for a savage stretch drive. But Tyler was hardly the night's only focus. Crespo's rapid-fire slide guitar riffs were galvanizing (he's a much cleaner player than former axeman Joe Perry), as was Dufay's crunching rhythm guitar and not infrequent lead licks of his own. Dufay was also a great crowd-pleaser, stalking the stage with a wireless guitar, spinning around, and often challenging the other musicians in face-to-face duals. Songs were chosen from every phase of the band's 12-year career. Oldies were raved up considerably (from the appropriate opener 'Back in the Saddle' to an all-out 'Walk this Way,' while new ones leapt out of the speakers with more intensity than the new album 'Rock in a Hard Place' would indicate. Regardless of how skeptics view the band's machismo (there were no feminists in the crowd, that's for sure), Aerosmith put on the finest high-energy' display since AC/DC. Hard rock lovers are urged to scoot out to Worcester for a repeat show Tuesday" (Boston Globe, 11/13/1982).
- A poor AUD recording circulates from this show.

November 13
War Memorial
Rochester, NY
Promoter: John Scher
Other act(s): Pat Travers, Rose Tattoo
Reported audience: (10,200 capacity)

November 16
The Centrum
Worcester, MA
Promoter: Don Law Company
Other act(s): Pat Travers, Rose Tattoo
Reported audience: 10,820 **SOLD-OUT
Set list: Back in the Saddle / Big Ten Inch Record / Mama Kin / Three Mile Smile / Reefer Head Woman / Lord of the Thighs / Rock in a Hard Place / Bolivian Ragamuffin / Lick and a Promise / Jig is Up / Jailbait / Sweet Emotion / Dream On / Lightning Strikes / Walk this Way / Toys in the Attic (abandoned)
Notes:
- This second date was added after the first sold-out rapidly. While local fans may have been supportive of the return of Aerosmith, local critics were, well, critical: "Although there's been personnel changes, the band is mired in a formulaic rut... Tyler seems to have lost rock sensibility and fantasy... Worse, Jack Douglas' use of extra musicians is superfluous... If you're an Aerosmith diehard, this may well be a worthy addition for sentimental reasons. But for freshness try something else" (Boston Globe, 10/21/1982).
- Steven collapsed towards the end of this show, blamed on food poisoning, as the band started "Toys in the Attic." The show ended without explanation.
- An AUD recording circulates from this show.

November 17
Civic Center
Providence, RI
Promoter: Frank J. Russo
Other act(s): Pat Travers, Rose Tattoo
Reported audience: ~10,000 / 14,000 (71.43%)
Notes:
- Several fans were mugged outside the venue following the show resulting in one bringing a $2 million suit against the band, promoter, venue, and city. Two other fans were assaulted with baseball bats and their

tickets stolen. From local press: "Most people who go to rock concerts bring tickets and money, and a lot bring liquor and marijuana. But some are beginning to bring baseball bats. That's how some fans came to the Aerosmith concert at the Civic Center last night, and the results were broken teeth, bloody noses and at least one young man hospitalized with serious head injuries... In all, 13 persons were arrested on charges that included assault, possession of narcotics, delivery of narcotics, obstructing police officers, malicious mischief, and disorderly conduct. A 17-year-old Cranston girl, who was ejected from the Civic Center, screamed angrily on the steps near the soldiers' memorial and kicked over a 50-gallon trash container filled with beer cans and bottles. The trash spilled into the street. Then she did the same to a second trash container. Two Providence police officers grabbed her wrists and quietly asked her several times to stop yelling and pick up the litter. She continued to yell and struggle and then, according to police, kicked one of the officers in the groin. She was immediately handcuffed and charged with assault. Police later released her in the custody of her parents, pending a Family Court hearing. Some concertgoers threw rocks. Ptlm. Ralph Garofano was hit twice. He shrugged off the first rock, which grazed his head about 9:20. But the second, which hit him in the cheek, sent him to St. Joseph Hospital for treatment. The same rock thrower also hit Ptlm. Dennis C. Lambert, according to police. A 16-year-old Fall River youth was arrested and charged with two counts of assault with a deadly weapon. He was released to his parents, pending action in Family Court" (Providence Journal, 11/18/1982).

November 18
Civic Center
Hartford, CT

Other act(s): Rose Tattoo
Reported audience: (16,300 capacity)
Set list: Same as Nov. 7.
Notes:
- Pat Travers was performing solo at the Agora in West Hartford.
- An AUD recording circulates from this show.

November 19
Cumberland County Civic Center
Portland, ME

Promoter: Freefall Presents
Other act(s): Rose Tattoo
Reported audience: (9,500 capacity)
Set list: Back in the Saddle / Big Ten Inch Record / Mama Kin / Three Mile Smile / Reefer Head Woman / Rock in a Hard Place (Cheshire Cat) / Lord of the Thighs / Bolivian Ragamuffin / Lick and a Promise / Jig is Up / Jailbait / Sweet Emotion / Dream On / Lightning Strikes / Walk this Way / Same Old Song and Dance / Milk Cow Blues / Toys in the Attic / Train Kept A Rollin'
Notes:
- An AUD recording circulates from this show.

November 21
Wendler Arena
Saginaw, MI

Promoter: Brass Ring Productions
Other act(s): Pat Travers, Rose Tattoo
Reported audience: (7,647 capacity)
Notes:
- Pat Travers and Rose Tattoo performed unconnected shows in Madison, WI on Nov. 22, and Burlington, IA (with Ohm) on Nov. 23, something they'd do throughout the tour.

November 24
Rosemont Horizon

Chicago, IL
Promoter: Jam Productions
Other act(s): Pat Travers, Rose Tattoo, Saga
Reported audience: (14,000 capacity)
Set list: Back in the Saddle / Big Ten Inch Record / Mama Kin / Three Mile Smile / Reefer Head Woman / Rock in a Hard Place (Cheshire Cat) / Lord of the Thighs / Lick and a Promise / Jig is Up / Jailbait / Sweet Emotion / Dream On / Lightning Strikes / Walk this Way / Same Old Song and Dance / Milk Cow Blues / Toys in the Attic / Train Kept a Rollin'
Notes:
- Both AUD and SBD recordings circulate from this show.

November 26
Civic Arena
Pittsburgh, PA
Promoter: Danny Kresky Enterprises
Other act(s): Pat Travers, Rose Tattoo
Reported audience: (17,500 capacity)
Notes:
- By the time the tour reached Pittsburgh, Steven was pleased with how things were going: "The kids are showing up in droves. It's butt-kicking, boogie-woogie rock 'n' roll. They love it. When the tour started, people were saying the economy is bad, but the concerts have all gone clean (sold out). Up here in New England (where the quintet is based) there were people telling us, 'Take thee heed, young man,' but we've gone out there with 10 amplifiers and a good sound system and done it like we used to. People are going crazy. It's a lot of old fans and a lot of young kids. There are older people — people my age (34) — boogying out there with their girlfriends. I'm loving it more than any other tour" (Pittsburgh Press, 11/24/1982).
- From a local review: "The natives were pretty restless, but they finally got Aerosmith at the Civic Arena last night in some of the hardest rock music of its kind. The three-ring marathon concert began at 7:30 with Rose Tattoo and continued with Pat Travers and his band as a second warmup... 'Festival seating' — that maniacal invention that gave us the Who concert disaster in Cincinnati — was employed for the arena's floor space, and boy is it a hazard. People were being squished against the stage down front, but, surprisingly, no paramedics were required. Police, on the other hand, were required to help break up some spirited fistfights that helped pass the time at intermission. After the endless interval, Aerosmith finally materialized for a relentless set of the 'butt-kickin', boogie-woogie rock 'n' roll' that is the group's trademark. Vocalist Steven Tyler is Aerosmith's leading light. His rasping voice and bouncing antics make him — not unintentionally — the band's functional equivalent of Mick Jagger, whose decadent delivery he emulates and embellishes. He was powerfully backed by bassist Tom Hamilton, drummer Joey Kramer, and guitarists Rick Dufay and Jimmy Crespo.

The androgynous Tyler, in black leather-fringed duds and one dangling earing, stomped the stage authoritatively, which is saying something considering that he ripped off a heel in a 1979 motorcycle accident, and it took him a long time to recover. There's a heavy-duty relationship at work between Aerosmith and the fans. Tyler whips 'em into a frenzy by playing touchy-feely with the zanies down front, and then the stagehands and bodyguards beat them back into line. Sort of a sadomasochistic Pavlovian conditioned response. Tyler the showman rubs backs with the guitarists and also does a lot of bizarre things with his stand-up microphone. If he doesn't exactly make love to it, it's at least the heaviest petting you've seen in a long time. But then he's known for eccentric behavior... If I write one more time about the excruciating decibel levels these days, they're going to send me my AARP membership early. But honestly — it's Pain City. Even Tyler had to hold left index finger in left ear on some songs, presumably to avoid (more) damage. Aside from pain, it is difficult even to concentrate on what is essentially a very good, very disciplined band that makes exciting music. Forget lyrics entirely, unless you know them in advance" (Pittsburgh Post-Gazette, 11/27/1982).

November 27
Joe Louis Arena
Detroit, MI
Promoter: Brass Ring Productions
Other act(s): Pat Travers, Rose Tattoo
Reported audience: 15,924 **SOLD-OUT
Reported gross: $189,367

November 29
Jenison Fieldhouse @ M.S.U.
East Lansing, MI
Promoter: Brass Ring Productions
Other act(s): Pat Travers, Rose Tattoo
Reported audience: 5,746 / 7,000 (82.09%)
Reported gross: $63,206
Notes:
- From a local review: "The wide-mouthed vocalist looked like he'd have no trouble swallowing a harmonica sideways. In between some on-stage spitting, he made screams that would make a horror flick soundtrack sound peaceful. How could anyone not like Steven Tyler? He led Aerosmith through a concert Monday night on the Michigan State campus. The more than 6,000 fans in Jenison Field House seemed to love anything Tyler tried. The performance showed why the band is often billed as Steven Tyler and Aerosmith. When he yelled or played mouth harp, Tyler was the center of attention. Wearing a long coat with tails that sometimes looked like a dress from the back didn't make him any less noticeable. It was also hard to ignore Tyler's spitting, or the fat sounds the skinny guy made with a harmonica. And only a cement zeppelin couldn't be moved by his voice. Jimmy Crespo did manage to steal the spotlight at times with his lead guitar. He masterfully wrestled his 6-string machine through some familiar tracks off of old Aerosmith LPs" (Lansing State Journal, 11/30/1982).

December 1
Hara Arena
Dayton, OH
Promoter: Jam Productions
Other act(s): Pat Travers, Rose Tattoo
Reported audience: (13,170 capacity)

December 3
Coliseum
Knoxville, TN
Promoter: Future Entertainment / Belkin Productions
Other act(s): Pat Travers, Rose Tattoo
Reported audience: (10,000 capacity)

December 4
Market Square Arena

Indianapolis, IN
Promoter: Sunshine Promotions
Other act(s): Pat Travers, Rose Tattoo
Reported audience: 9,842 / 10,200 (96.49%)
Reported gross: $84,237
Set list: Back in the Saddle / Big Ten Inch Record / Mama Kin / Three Mile Smile / Reefer Head Woman / Rock in a Hard Place (Cheshire Cat) / Lord of the Thighs / Lick and a Promise / Jig is Up / Sweet Emotion / Dream On / Lightning Strikes / Walk this Way / Milk Cow Blues / Toys in the Attic / Train Kept A Rollin'
Notes:
- From a local review: "Judging the response of the nearly 9,500 fans assembled in Market Square Arena Saturday night, the triple-bill concert with Aerosmith, Pat Travers, and Rose Tattoo was quite a success. From a concert that lasted nearly four hours, the crowd certainly got its rock 'n' roll money's worth. The only thing that would have improved the show — aside from toning down the volume — would have been a reshuffling of the line-up... Opening with, appropriately enough, 'Back in the Saddle Again,' Aerosmith did satisfy the house with its powerhouse rock and flashy stage show. Led by Steve Tyler's vocals and his intriguing stage presence, the band rocked through most of its biggest hits, and then some, for about 75 minutes.

Tyler, when it comes down to it, is Aerosmith. Without his blues influenced vocals and crazed prancing onstage, Aerosmith would probably sound like most other good heavy metal bands. Indeed, when Aerosmith was playing something other than one of its 'classics,' the songs all sounded pretty much the same. But the band did play an impressive assortment of its better-known tunes including 'Sweet Emotion,' 'Dream On,' 'Walk this Way' and 'Toys in the Attic,' the latter of which was used to close the show. Despite a long and loud ovation, Aerosmith returned for just a brief one-song encore" (Indianapolis Star, 12/6/1982).
- An AUD recording circulates from this show.

December 6
Memorial Auditorium
Buffalo, NY
Promoter: Harvey & Corky Inc.
Other act(s): Pat Travers, Rose Tattoo
Reported audience: (17,827 capacity)

December 8
Coliseum
Richfield (Cincinnati), OH
Promoter: Belkin Productions
Other act(s): Nazareth, Rose Tattoo
Reported audience: ~12,500 / 17,500 (71.43%)
Partial set list: Back in the Saddle / Reefer Head Woman / Bitch's Brew / Cry Me a River / Rock in a Hard Place (Cheshire Cat) / Come Together / Sweet Emotion / Dream On / Walk this Way / Toys in the Attic (** Not in order; songs noted in reviews)
Notes:

- From a local review: "It's hard telling what Steve Tyler was hopped-up about Wednesday. But whatever it was, it seemed to put him in a nasty mood and make him spit and swear a lot more than usual. It also detracted considerably from what otherwise might have been a mighty showing for him and his band, Aerosmith, after more than a two-year absence from the Coliseum in Richfield. Despite the skinny singer's preoccupation with just about everything from crowd and security to the sound system and assorted refreshments surrounding Joey Kramer's drum kit, the band still managed to put a powerful — albeit erratic — 90 minutes the thundering sounds that lifted them to rock superstardom in '70s. The addition of guitarists Rick Dufay and Jimmy Crespo in place of Brad Whitford and co-founder Joe Perry doesn't seem to have noticeably diminished the band's effectiveness. Though both occasionally appeared uncertain on stage, their licks were raw-edged and full of fire and meshed well with Kramer's crisp drumming and Tom Hamilton's ever-solid bass work. The problem was that every time the band built a head of steam, Tyler would shut it down... Only a of tunes into set, he was signaling to the sound man, then repeatedly storming off stage to have words with him and eventually yelling right into the microphone at him. Later, he focused on the 11,000 in the audience, swearing at them for not showing more emotion ('Don't you know how to express yourselves?') and issuing instructions for to ignore security personnel. All the while, he was spewing gobs of saliva and streams of some kind of beverage all over the stage... The band is still at least capable of picking up where it left off in the late '70s. But something will have to be done about Tyler" (Akron Beacon Journal, 12/9/1982).
- From another local review: "Aerosmith was back in the saddle at the Coliseum last night with a rejuvenated band — two new members and an added keyboard player. Good thing. Lead singer Steven Tyler, pale looking in a black outfit with fringed panels, wasn't his usual exuberant self. He seemed to be fighting a headache, once leaning his forehead up against an amplifier as the lights faded. He scowled, rather than smiled, and sang with his eyes closed most of the time, rarely making eye contact with the audience. About halfway through, just before 'Sweet Emotion,' he suddenly stopped and sat down at the front of the stage and swore at the crowd for its reactions. The people in back were 'getting off' more than the ones up front, he said. 'I'm not asking for a riot, but do you know how to express yourselves?' he asked. 'F--- it, we're only here once a year.' Then he cussed out the men in yellow shirts (Hall Security) and told the crowd not to pay attention to them.

Tyler did make a valiant effort, even if his 'Cry Me a River' wasn't as poignant as on the latest 'Rock in a Hard Place' LP. The sound was a little murky on this and Tyler punctuated it by spitting on the floor. 'Reefer Head Woman' was a knockout. Joey Kramer outdid himself on the drums and Tyler pulled out his mouth organ. Bassist Tom Hamilton had said the band was more of a unit now, not just Tyler and lead guitarist Joe Perry up front. True. Rick Dufay, the new rhythm guitarist, was the showpiece of the musicians, jumping down in front of the stage, dancing around, and keeping up visual fireworks. New lead guitarist Jimmy Crespo, replacing Perry, didn't move much, but did fine work on his guitar. The band was tight, though at times it was hard to tell because it was so loud, and the mix seemed muddy. The band's 'Dream On' was given a good play, but its old 'Walk this Way,' with a more staccato rhythm, topped that. Those who have not seen Tyler before might have been impressed, but we Aerosmith watchers know he can do better. As we left the backstage area, a reporter said that Tyler had complained of a strep throat that afternoon" (Plain Dealer, 12/10/1982).

December 9
Maple Leaf Gardens
Toronto, ON, Canada
Promoter: Concert Productions International (CPI)
Other act(s): Nazareth, Rose Tattoo
Reported audience: ~15,000 / 19,000 (78.95%)
Set list: Back in the Saddle / Mama Kin / Big Ten Inch Record / Three Mile Smile / Reefer Head Woman / Rock in a Hard Place (Cheshire Cat) / Lord of the Thighs / Bitch's Brew / Lick and a Promise / Jig is Up / Sweet Emotion / Dream On / Lightning Strikes / Walk this Way / Milk Cow Blues / Toys in the Attic / Train Kept a Rollin'
Notes:
- Robert Lawson (Author, "Razama-Snaz!: The Listener's Guide To Nazareth"): "Scotland's Nazareth had dominated much of the 70's hard rock landscape with stellar albums such as 'Razamanaz' (1973}, 'Loud n

Proud' (1973), 'Hair of the Dog' (1975), 'Expect No Mercy' (1977) and 'No Mean City' (1979). But after the departure of guitarist Zal Cleminson, whose presence had done so much to invigorate the band, and a pretty solid double live album 'Snaz,' fortunes were changing. By 1982 Nazareth were supporting their most recent album 2XS featuring the single 'Love Hurts' written by new member axe-slinger Billy Rankin. The album was a slightly slicker affair then previous releases and unfortunately didn't make much of an impact on the charts (#122 in the U.S.). Subsequent albums would continue this trend (the band eventually reclaimed their status of releasing quality albums by the early 90's). Although still a potent live act the band no longer would headline arenas in North American. Nazareth joined the new Mk 4 incarnation of Aerosmith on the 'Rock in a Hard Place' tour for a series of dates as that group slowly imploded." Nazareth had headlined the same venue the previous year.

- From a local review: "Last night at Maple Leaf Gardens, a trio of rock acts which included two has-beens and one never-was managed to draw a nearly full house on what had to be the coldest night of the season. The fact that the total record sales of Aerosmith, Nazareth and Rose Tattoo (has-been, has-been, never-was, respectively) over the last two years probably wouldn't add up to one gold record over-all doesn't seem to matter to the heavy metal fans. Like Toronto's wrestling and hockey crowds, they don't really seem to care what the draw is, as long as they get their regular fix. How else to explain it? ... It [Nazareth] was a hard act for Aerosmith to follow, but it succeeded largely on the strength of strong audience support. I've never understood Aerosmith's success or staying power. Somehow this Boston-based band has managed to combine the strident Jagger-esque vocals of Steven Tyler with a crunching but unappealing twin guitar attack and stay in business for more than a decade. Thursday night, Aerosmith, too, presented a show that was basically just another rerun. There was Tyler, ever fey in swirling scarves, wailing out 'Back in the Saddle Again' to an audience of Bic-flicking kids, most of whom hadn't even graduated kindergarten when Tyler perfected this act. In this battle of tired old warhorses, give the nod to Nazareth, with Aerosmith closing fast at the finish. Rose Tattoo barely got out of the gate" (Toronto Globe & Mail, 12/10/1982).

- An AUD recording circulates from this show.

December 11
Civic Center
Huntington, WV

Promoter: Future Entertainment / Belkin Productions
Other act(s): Pat Travers, Rose Tattoo
Reported audience: (9,000 capacity)
Notes:
- A new stage debuted at this show, in time for the following day's video shoot. One feature was a "six-foot, three-dimensional head that will sing along with the band on one song" (Newport Daily News, 12/17/1982).

December 12 **VIDEO SHOOT
Civic Center
Huntington, WV

Notes:
- Material was filmed via the Optimax process (the same method used to create "Jaws III") for use as part of a full-length 3-D home video release. The video was produced and directed by Jonas McCord, who commented, "Lots of groups can only tour 20 or so cities. Now 3-D video will be able to tour for them. It's watching Steven Tyler walk out into the audience, kicking right through the screen" (R&R, 12/17/1982). The audience was filled with local contest winners.
- Plans, the following year, were to screen the 8-minute video which purportedly featured "Bolivian Ragamuffin," "Bitch's Brew," and "Sweet Emotion" at one lucky venue towards the end of the tour before sending the tape off to MTV. Miramax Films, at one point picked up the distribution rights for a "Rock 'N' Roll 3D" feature film which was intended to star Aerosmith and Devo, and other groups, for satellite, cable, and syndicated TV broadcast ultimately leading to a home video release. To date only a very short video clip from "Sweet Emotion" has surfaced, though the live performance recording was used on "Classics Live" in 1986.

December 13
Battelle Hall @ Ohio Center
Columbus, OH

Promoter: Sunshine Promotions
Other act(s): Pat Travers, Rose Tattoo
Reported audience: (6,864 capacity)
Notes:
- From a local review: "Steven Tyler wants Mick Jagger's job. And if he keeps performing like he did Monday night at the Ohio Center; he just might get it. The nearly sold-out show was a 4 1/2-hour exercise in multinational styles of rock 'n' roll, from Rose Tattoo and the Pat Travers Band to the salacious Steven Tyler and Aerosmith. Tyler doesn't need to try hard to emulate Jagger. Both have the same build, the same pouty lips, and inexhaustible amounts of vocal and physical energy onstage. But the groups are different, and — like the Stones — Aerosmith has cemented its style into a one-of-a-kind act... Excitement inside the center peaked when huge black curtains were lowered to cover both the stage and Aerosmith's entrance. Fans rose to their feet, chairs or someone else's shoulders as the band began its set with 'Back in the Saddle.' As he would be for the next 1 1/2 hours, Tyler was the star of the show, strutting, twirling the microphone stand, and making suggestive moves with 'I-don't-care-if-you-like-me' flippancy. The audience couldn't get enough of him. Despite the recent defection of lead guitarist Joe Perry, Aerosmith's dual guitar attack was in textbook form. With Tyler alternately dancing, running, and slinking across the stage, the group powered its way through a stack of what are now Aerosmith classics... Steven Tyler and Aerosmith may not be able to write the classics like they used to, but after Monday night's show it is obvious that they sure can perform them" (Columbus Dispatch, 12/14/1982).

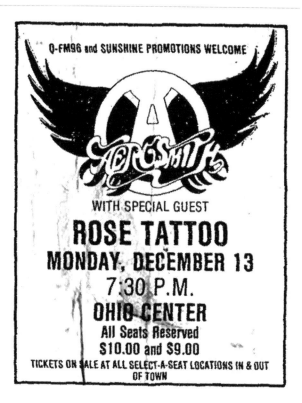

December 15
The Omni
Atlanta, GA

Promoter: Concert Promotions, Inc. / Southern Promotions
Other act(s): Pat Travers, Rose Tattoo
Reported audience: (16,000 capacity)
Notes:
- Nazareth was also added to the bill at one point but did not perform. Local radio station WKLS ran a contest with the winner becoming the band's "Roadie for the Day" and watching the show from the side of the stage.
- From a local review: "If pressed to find something unique about Aerosmith's performance Wednesday night at the Omni, I'd have to admit it was the first rock show I've ever seen where the lead singer reminded me of Morticia Addams on the old 'Addams Family' TV series. Dressed in a black outfit featuring a low-cut top with long streamers hanging off the sleeves and back, and sporting a Carolyn Jones-ish hairdo and earrings, Steven Tyler, Aerosmith's androgynous, screeching vocalist, looked just this side of ludicrous. But in just about every other way, Aerosmith's show was the same as the last time they came through town a couple of years ago: loud and

boring. And Tyler's third-rate Mick Jagger clone act hasn't improved any, either. Actually, there was one major difference between Wednesday's concert and the Boston band's last visit to Omni — the size of the crowd, which had the arena's half-house seating arrangement barely more than half full despite the stacking of the bill with two other groups appealing to the hard audience: Rose Tattoo and Pat Travers. Still, the faithful who showed up — a young crowd prone to raising fists and tossing firecrackers — gave Tyler and company an enthusiastic response as Aerosmith played such older as 'Back in the Saddle Again,' 'Big 10 Inch Record,' 'Mama Kin' and 'Lord of Your Thighs' as well as songs from its new 'Rock in a Hard Place' album. Aerosmith's set often bogged down with extended, cacophonous solos that went nowhere" (Atlanta Constitution, 12/16/1982).

December 17
Coliseum
Greensboro, NC

Promoter: Beach Club Concerts
Other act(s): Pat Travers, Rose Tattoo
Reported audience: (13,500 capacity)
Notes:
- From a local review: "Aerosmith's performance Friday night at the Greensboro Coliseum proved how blah a rock concert can be and still draw enthusiastic applause. The show was undisguisable from any other hard rock concert, and Aerosmith was no better or worse than the two groups that preceded it, Rose Tattoo and Pat Travers. If you closed your eyes, you'd have only even odds of guessing which was performing. Aerosmith, around since 1970, is making a much-heralded comeback to the stage after a three-year absence prompted when lead singer Steven Tyler was injured in a motorcycle accident. They are riding the crest of their ninth consecutive gold album, 'Rock in a Hard Place.' But gold albums or not, they did little to earn the standing ovations they received from an easy-to-please audience. From the opening song, 'Back in the Saddle Again,' it was clear that this would be another electronic facsimile of quality rock 'n' roll, a band that uses the same old mass audience appeal — plug it in and let it whine.

Tyler wore black tails and tatters, and twittered back and forth across the stage, tossing the stand-up microphone around like a broom dance partner. If that was supposed to be an energetic star performance, it had little starch. Those who can't do it like Mick Jagger shouldn't try. It may or may not be to the group's credit that they had no fancy light shows or gimmicks such as smoke, snakes, or rocket ships. And with practically no talking by Tyler, the show had to stand on its music. It turned out to be misplaced confidence. Melodies, which Tyler has described as 'very sexual to me' were drowned in runaway decibels. There was little imagination in the music, which translated into a lot of seemingly interminable guitar jamming that went nowhere. Almost every song was filled to the brim with screeching guitars. Even the ever-standing, whistling, match-lighting audience got bored with a couple of them, though it is unlikely anyone would admit it.

It's not as if Aerosmith members — Tyler; Tom Hamilton, bass guitarist; Jim Crespo, lead guitarist; Joey Kramer, drummer, and Rick Dufay, guitarist — are poor musicians. They've produced some solid rock 'n' roll hits such as 'Sweet Emotion,' and 'Walk this Way,' both part of their show. And Tyler is no slouch on a harmonica. But, instead of stopping the ceaseless beat and treating the audience, he only teased with a few bars before a couple of songs. It may be simply their adherence to what appears to be a rock-concert-code, i.e., crank it up until their eardrums are on the floor. Quite often, such groups' albums sound considerably better without such distortion. Each song melted electronically into the other. 'Bitch's Brew,' 'Lightning Strikes' from their new album, 'Toys in the Attic,' the title song from a 1975 album produced little variation in performance. Aerosmith promoters say the group is America's number one, home-grown hard-rock group, and that they draw large crowds. The first claim is debatable, and the second was unsupported, at least in Greensboro, by lots of empty Coliseum seats" (Greensboro Daily News, 12/18/1982).

December 18 **CANCELLED
Civic Center
Lakeland, FL
Notes:
- This venue saw its booking of show particularly affected by the recession and had been cancelled by Nov. 26. The date was replaced by a show in Hampton, though Pat Travers and Rose Tattoo instead performed several dates in Florida in the run up to the holiday break (Tampa [cancelled], Miami and Cocoa Beach).

December 18
Coliseum
Hampton, VA
Promoter: Future Entertainment / Belkin Productions
Other act(s): Johnny Van Zandt Band, Fortnox
Reported audience: (13,800 capacity)
Notes:
- Rose Tattoo was the advertised special guest but did not open.
- From a local review: "The near-sellout audience at the Aerosmith concert at Hampton Coliseum Saturday night screamed and applauded for a show that was little different than some of the mind-numbing rock extravaganzas of nearly 10 years ago. Although the niche in rock that Aerosmith maintains has received a lot of criticism, this kind of music will probably last as long as young people love screaming guitars, pounding drums and thunderous bass playing at such a high-decibel level that lyrics are usually inaudible. That's not to say Aerosmith doesn't do its job well. Although by now heavy metal has run into a dead end, rehashing clichéd guitar riffs, and rendering obligatory, long drum solos, these guys have as good a set of rock 'n' roll chops as some players who've achieved more notoriety. For instance, Joey Kramer, whose drumkit was surprisingly small for a player in his field, was a nearly flawless percussionist. Tom Hamilton handled his bass well too. But the show's highlights were the flamboyant performances of singer/songwriter Steven Tyler and guitarist Rick Dufay.

Tyler, whose pooched-out lips make him resemble Mick Jagger, played his role as the wild and raucous rock 'n' roll front man to the hilt, even pulling a girl onto the stage from the audience during the encore and embracing her passionately. Dufay was the band's image of the bad boy rocker, sometimes staggering across the stage and, at one point, actually turning an apparently accidental fall into a backward roll while still playing his guitar. Before changing guitars during one song, he actually threw the one he was playing over his head, letting it crash to the floor as the audience applauded approval. Basically, the set ran a gamut of material from the group's recordings, including 'Walk this Way,' 'Sweet Emotion,' and 'Lightning Strikes.' Unfortunately, the sound mix had some of the same blurred quality that too often is part of heavy metal performances, rendering songs such as the boogie rocker 'Big Ten Inch Record' much weaker than the recorded version on the 'Toys in the Attic' album" (Newport News Daily Press, 12/21/1982).

December 26
Reunion Arena
Dallas, TX
Promoter: Pace Concerts
Other act(s): Rose Tattoo
Reported audience: (14,939 capacity)
Notes:

- Initially, only Rose Tattoo rejoined the tour with Pat Travers embarking on a short solo run through early Jan.

December 27
The Summit
Houston, TX
Promoter: Pace Concerts
Other act(s): Rose Tattoo
Reported audience: (14,950 capacity)

December 29
Lloyd Noble Center
Norman, OK
Promoter: Contemporary Productions / Stone City Attractions
Other act(s): Rose Tattoo
Reported audience: ~8,000 / 11,000 (72.73%)
Notes:
- From a local review: "It was the last electric waltz of '82 for the city area, and Aerosmith rocked out the old and rolled in the new in prodigious style Wednesday night at Lloyd Noble Center... But when the lights went down again, and the darkness was accompanied by the slashing violin strains from the shower-murder scene in Alfred Hitchcock's 'Psycho' (a remarkably perfect synthesizer re-creation), the crowd began to stir once again. The moment Aerosmith finally bounded on-stage; enthusiasm exploded anew. Lead singer Steven Tyler still looked his lean and fit self in tight-fitting basic black as he plunged into the throbbing opener, 'Back in the Saddle.' It's been five years since the band's last Oklahoma City appearance and three years since its last national tour. But drastic personnel changes and uncertain times have failed to dampen Aerosmith's energy or heavy-metal dash.

New guitarists Jimmy Crespo (formerly of Flame) and Rick Dufay reeled through letter-perfect renditions of the old Joe Perry-Brad Whitford duets on boilers such as 'Mama Kin,' 'My Big 10-Inch (Record)' and 'Lord of the Thighs.' Their imposing sound was clean and technically well-mixed, allowing their much-improved vocal harmonies to shine through, and temporary road member Bob Mayo added extra texture on electronic keyboards. Newer rockers like 'Rock in a Hard Place' and 'Jig is Up' were less interesting than their old standbys ('Sweet Emotion' and their classic anthem of troubled youth, 'Dream On'), but their showmanship and instrumental skills were as impressive as ever. While Aerosmith was never known for innovation, its stage prowess has seldom failed to stir the ardor of 8,000-plus sweating, bouncing fans and Thursday's performance was a prime example" (Daily Oklahoman, 12/31/1982).

December 30
Convention Center Arena
San Antonio, TX
Promoter: Stone City Attractions
Other act(s): Rose Tattoo
Reported audience: (16,000 capacity)

Set list: Back in the Saddle / Mama Kin / Big Ten Inch Record / Three Mile Smile / Reefer Head Woman / Rock in a Hard Place (Cheshire Cat) / Lord of the Thighs / Lick and a Promise / Sweet Emotion / Dream On / Lightning Strikes / Walk this Way / Milk Cow Blues / Toys in the Attic / Train Kept a Rollin'
Notes:
- Last show with Rose Tattoo, who moved on to open a few dates with ZZ Top and Tommy Tutone, before ending their U.S. tour. According to Angry Anderson, "We were falling apart. In fact, the band was in danger of splitting up there and then, which would have been terrible. So, we curtailed the tour and came back home to break up... There were quite a few people who suggested we get rid of Pete Wells, 'Digger' Dallas and Rob Riley (the trio who've now departed), get in some American guys and plough on through America. But we never even considered this as an option. We preferred to get back to Australia to find some home-grown talent" (Kerrang #55).
- A SBD circulates from this show.

1983

January 4, 1983
Neal Blaisdell Center Arena
Honolulu, HI
Promoter: New West Productions / John Bauer Concert Company
Reported audience: (9,000 capacity)
Set list: Same as Dec. 30, 1982
Notes:
- A SBD circulates from this show, which features an insane 14-minute version of "Milk Cow Blues," along with some epic Steven stage rants.

January 6
Long Beach Arena
Long Beach, CA
Promoter: Avalon Attractions / Beach Club
Other act(s): Pat Travers
Reported audience: 13,000 **SOLD-OUT
Reported gross: $149,692
Set list: Same as Dec. 30, 1982
Notes:
- From a local review: "The big question surrounding red-hot Aerosmith in the mid-'70s was whether this Boston-based band was too much like the Rolling Stones. Most critics felt they were. But the band's staunch fans, including this one, argued that Aerosmith was more than just a copy. To us, the hard-rock outfit had its own fresh, driving sound. The Stones connection seemed mostly superficial: Singer Steve Tyler resembled Mick Jagger, and both groups worked the same blues-based rock territory. But Aerosmith's sold-out concert Thursday night at the Long Beach Arena suggested the other critics may have been right. This was an Aerosmith that has slipped into middle or even old age, as rock bands go, and this 'big return' show after an absence of almost five years in Los Angeles did remind me of one of the Stones' many comebacks. Just as on those Stones second (or third or fourth) comings, the enthusiastic fans greeted Aerosmith on Thursday with a roaring chorus of applause and yells, lit matches in salute, waved banners, and threw several scarves at the ever-be-scarved Tyler's feet. And even more than the Stones, Aerosmith is now concentrating on evoking its peak days rather than exploring anything new. Like Jagger & Co., these guys are very good at it.

Opening with the aptly titled 'Back in the Saddle,' they concentrated on their better-known oldies during the 90-minute show. Even the few selections from the group's new LP sounded like excellent pastiches of the past biggies, capsule summaries similar to what the Stones did with songs like 'Start Me Up.' To keep the

Stones comparison going, Aerosmith is also missing a founder-guitarist. And there was surely some grumbling Thursday that the group's music isn't as dynamic without Joe Perry. If Aerosmith's intention, however, was to put on a typical Aerosmith show and nothing more, they succeeded. Tyler wore his scarves and struck the same old but still effective rock-star poses. His strong voice has faded a bit, but he still moves well through witty lyrics in a way that suggests he's racing to squeeze in as many words as possible between the booming riffs. But there's a danger in sticking too closely to the past. Even the Stones sound flat on some nights. You just can't get the same stimulation hearing the same songs done in the same way again and again. At some point, a band has got to come up with new ideas. Besides interesting new material, the Stones live get away with avoiding cobwebs through Jagger's charisma and warmth. Unfortunately, Tyler seemed distant most of the night. You wonder if his heart is really in it anymore. The fans seemed satisfied, but this may have been a last hurrah unless the group offers something more than replays next time" (Los Angeles Times, 1/8/1983).
Notes:
- A reasonable AUD recording circulates from this show. Unfortunately, it cuts during Toys, so the presumed final song is not present.

January 7
Coliseum Arena
Oakland, CA

Promoter: Bill Graham Presents
Other act(s): Pat Travers
Reported audience: 14,472 **SOLD-OUT
Reported gross: $170,481
Set list: Same as Dec. 30
Notes:
- An AUD recording circulates from this show.

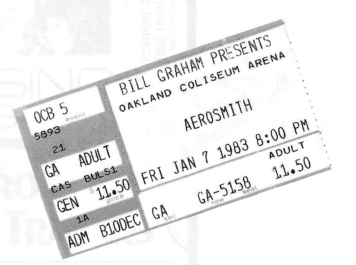

January 9
Salt Palace
Salt Lake City, UT

Other act(s): Pat Travers
Reported audience: (13,075 capacity)

January 11
McNichols Arena
Denver, CO

Promoter: Feyline Presents
Other act(s): Pat Travers
Reported audience: 14,712 / 18,000 (81.73%)
Reported gross: $132,408
Set list: Same as Dec. 30
Notes:
- An AUD recording circulates from this show, which may be partial (it's missing "Sweet Emotion") since "Lick and a Promise" cuts.

January 13
Tingley Coliseum
Albuquerque, NM

Promoter: Feyline Presents
Other act(s): Pat Travers
Reported audience: 8,612 / 10,000 (86.12%)
Reported gross: $84,290
Set list: Same as Dec. 30

Notes:
- From a local review: "There was a long wait before Aerosmith took the stage. This is the band's first tour in more than three years and the crowd milled about the Coliseum apprehensively. When the band finally took the stage, it began playing behind a black curtain that rose to reveal the musicians under blazing blue spotlights. The opening song, 'Back in the Saddle Again,' a hard-driving screamer that had the audience on its feet cheering the return of one of America's most popular hard-rock bands, set the tone for the show. The focal point of Aerosmith is lead singer Steven Tyler. Dressed in a silver-black outfit with numerous scarfs and streamers, he strutted about the stage with an odd blend of Mick Jagger and Jams Joplin antics. Often Tyler would turn his back to the audience, facing instead the drummer or bass player. The rest of the band was less animated and concentrated on producing the wall of heavy metal sound. For sheer loudness, Aerosmith is to be rivaled by only Judas Priest, AC/DC, and Grand Funk Railroad.

The choice of material was varied, some songs from the most recent LP, 'A Rock and a Hard Place,' and others from the best-selling 'Toys in the Attic.' Early on the group played an intriguing mix of 'Oh Well,' — the Fleetwood Mac rocker — and 'Big 10 Inch.' On this number (and a couple of others) Tyler played mouth harp, either to demonstrate that he was more than a vocalist or to merely embellish the songs with a bluesy sound. Lead guitar player Joe Perry left the band a couple of years ago, but newcomer Jimmy Crespo adequately filled his shoes. Playing a black Stratocaster, he deftly handled the blues runs, although most of his leads were of the heavy-handed, distorted variety. The biggest cheers came during his solo on 'Sweet Emotion.' Neither Aerosmith nor Pat Travers will win any awards for breaking new musical ground, but they did give the young crowd a large dose of loud, heavy metal" (Albuquerque Journal, 1/15/1983).
- An AUD recording circulates from this show.

January 14
County Coliseum
El Paso, TX
Promoter: Stone City Attractions / Pace Concerts
Other act(s): Pat Travers
Reported audience: 8,050 **SOLD-OUT
Reported gross: $79,845

January 16
Convention Center Rotunda
Las Vegas, NV
Promoter: Michael Schivo Presents
Other act(s): Pat Travers
Reported audience: (6,500 capacity)

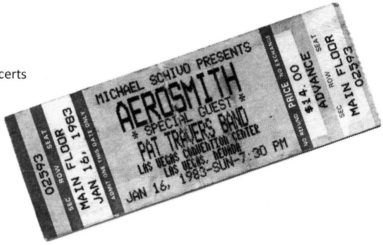

January 18
Memorial Coliseum
Portland, OR
Promoter: John Bauer Concert Company
Other act(s): Pat Travers
Reported audience: (11,000 capacity)

January 20
Center Coliseum
Seattle, WA
Promoter: John Bauer Concert Company
Other act(s): Pat Travers
Reported audience: (16,641 capacity)
Notes:

- From a local review: "Aerosmith sounded better than ever last night in the Coliseum, and it's no wonder. The band has been off the road for four years while lead singer Steven Tyler recuperated from injuries suffered in a motorcycle accident, and Aerosmith now has roared back with renewed energy and dedication. The newly restructured group did all the gutsy, hard rocking tunes that made it famous, but played them as if they were new. Tyler's voice sounded a little older and raspier during the opening lines of 'Dream On,' but was back in top form for the screaming climax. Probably because they haven't done them for years, Tyler and the band worked hard to put across Aerosmith classics such as 'Walk this Way,' 'Dream On,' 'Train Kept A-Rollin',' 'Sweet Emotion,' and 'Toys in the Attic.' They played only a few tunes from the new 'Rock in a Hard Place' album, sticking to tried-and-true material.

Arriving on stage to the soundtrack of 'Psycho,' the whirling, dancing Tyler looked like his old self in a black outfit with material trailing from the arms. As usual, his mike stand was decorated with long strands of colored ribbons. The new guitarists — Jimmy Crespo and Rick Dufay, who replaced Joe Perry and Brad Whitford — added new twists to the old songs with high-energy solos... As usual with Aerosmith shows, the sound and lights were first-rate without being gimmicky. The band resisted the temptation to shine bright lights on the audience — the latest rock-concert gimmick — until the end. The only complaint was that the 75-minute set was too short. In past years, Aerosmith has played twice that long" (Seattle Times, 1/21/1983).

January 21
Pacific Coliseum Concert Bowl
Vancouver, BC, Canada

Promoter: Perryscope Concerts
Other act(s): Pat Travers
Reported audience: 10,925 / 12,199 (89.56%)
Reported gross: C$139,445
Notes:
- In November 1982, a show at the Corral in Calgary was also being considered for Jan. 1983.
- From a local review: "Fans of hard-rock are called headbangers. As the name implies, headbangers like the sheer blistering volume of hard-rock in their ears and the gut-level kick it gives to their bodies. About 10,000 headbangers liked what they saw and heard at the Coliseum Friday night: Aerosmith and Pat Travers. But for me, the concert didn't end soon enough. It was dull, lifeless, and devoid of original expression. But then, that's hard rock for you... Sure, Aerosmith may be one of the leading practitioners of hard rock. But the band lacks style, flair, originality. After all, so many other bands do what Aerosmith does and they do it so much better. For flash and showmanship, I'll take the bizarre antics of Ozzy Osbourne any day. For sheer heavy rock guitar mastery, I'll choose Van Halen's namesake Eddie Van Halen. What Aerosmith amounts to is a band with limited ideas — sort of a poor-man's Led Zeppelin. Or rather, a Led Zeppelin for today's teenagers who were too young to enjoy the real thing (the average age Friday was about 16) ... It appears that the members of Aerosmith — veterans Tyler, Tom Hamilton on bass, and Joey Kramer on drums, and newly added guitarists Jim Crespo (lead) and Rick Dufay — still believe in the old hard-rock maxim, the louder the better" (Vancouver Sun, 1/22/1983).

January 26
Civic Center
Bismarck, ND

Promoter: John Bauer Concert Company
Other act(s): Pat Travers
Reported audience: ~3,500 / 8,200 (42.68%)
Notes:
- From a local review: "For the second time in less than a month the Bismarck Civic Center brought in a big-name rock group, and for the second time, as a movie producer once said, the public stayed away in droves. Not that Wednesday night's Aerosmith concert attendance was sparse. Approximately 3,500 were there, estimated Harlo Thon, assistant manager of the Civic Center, which edged it ahead of December's KISS concert. Like many of its concerts, the Civic Center was not financially involved in staging the event, Thon

said; the risk, and almost certain loss, on Wednesday's concert was absorbed by the promoters. Ticket prices of $10 may have deterred some rock fans, but Thon said he thought the necessity of bringing in Aerosmith on a weeknight may have hurt the most. Many in the crowd were from Jamestown, Dickinson and a host of small towns between and beyond, and Thon said fans from the states and provinces surrounding North Dakota came to the concert, but not as many out-of-towners showed up as producers usually count on in staging a major concert.

The small crowd for Aerosmith, and KISS before it, are the exception rather than the rule, Thon said. In the last year, circumstances led the Civic Center to stage an unprecedented string of major concerts, including rock, country, and pop performers, and almost all were successful, Thon said. The 15-20-minute intermission that is normal between a warm-up performer in this case rock singer Pat Travers — and the main attraction stretched to over an hour Wednesday night. The delay was reportedly due to Aerosmith's lead singer, Steve Tyler's, star temperament. After playing to at least one, concert of over 300,000 fans, Tyler was reluctant to have his group stage a full-scale concert for little more than 1 percent of that in Bismarck. And throughout the hour-long set, Tyler scolded the audience for its inhibition. Ironically, Aerosmith played few of its best-known songs, though it has been placing singles on the chart since 1975. Though those were precisely the numbers that brought the most enthusiastic response from the audience, Aerosmith mostly performed songs off its new LP, 'Rock in a Hard Place,' which its present tour is designed to promote" (Bismarck Tribune, 1/27/1983).

January 28
Met Center
Minneapolis, MN
Promoter: Jam Productions
Other act(s): Pat Travers
Reported audience: 14,823 / 16,777 (88.35%)
Reported gross: $154,211
Set list: Same as Dec. 30
Notes:
- An AUD recording circulates from this show.

January 29
MECCA Auditorium
Milwaukee, WI
Other act(s): Pat Travers
Reported audience: (12,000 capacity)

January 31
MetroCentre
Rockford, IL
Other act(s): Pat Travers
Reported audience: (10,000 capacity)

February 1
Civic Auditorium Arena
Omaha, NE
Promoter: Contemporary Productions
Other act(s): Pat Travers
Reported audience: 5,428 / 6,000 (90.47%)
Reported gross: $54,516
Notes:

- From a local review: "Afternoon classes may have been canceled, but Tuesday's snowstorm didn't dissuade 5,421 fans from attending the evening Aerosmith concert at City Auditorium Arena. Only 500 ticket holders were no-shows because of the weather, Auditorium Manager Terry Forsberg said. An undaunted 700 bought tickets at the door... Their old hits — from 'Dream On' to 'Sweet Emotion' to 'Walk this Way' — were enough to coax the old fans back (although most of the crowd seemed too young to have seen any earlier Aerosmith shows). The band was without original guitarists Joe Perry or Brad Whitford. Replacements Jimmy Crespo and Rick Dufay didn't really pack their power on the oldies but held their own during the band's newer material. Lead singer. Steve Tyler was the main attraction, in black headgear, long lace coat (which looked more like a dress), a microphone stand draped with streamers and the usual antics. He's long been snubbed as a Mick Jagger imitator but he's in good company. His jumping around, spitting, theatrical facial expressions and an almost perverse preoccupation with bubble gum kept things on stage visually interesting almost all night.

Frankly, I was expecting a third-rate concert from a washed-up band. But the refreshing thing about Aerosmith is that after all these years, they're just as sloppy as they ever were. That is, they occasionally miss a beat or let their solos go way out of hand. But fans dulled by over planned concerts, where everything works like clockwork, got a chance to see a real rock band in action. Aerosmith fiddles around with the songs, changes plans, and allows things to go awry. The band still has the spontaneity that its successors in corporate rock have long since smoothed over. Aerosmith is actually fun to watch. Heck, they even brought back opening guitarist Pat Travers for the final song 'Toys in the Attic' and it honestly looked as if they hadn't planned it all out first... Aerosmith's encore was a cover of the Burnette Brothers' classic 'Train Kept A Rollin'.' I usually hate their heavy handling of it but even that sounded OK Tuesday. Maybe it was a pretty good show. Or maybe it was just nice not to be cooped up indoors on a snowy day" (Omaha World-Herald, 2/2/1983).

February 3
Checkerdome
St. Louis, MO

Promoter: Contemporary Productions
Other act(s): Pat Travers
Reported audience: 10,117 **SOLD-OUT
Reported gross: $103,555
Notes:
- From a local review: "Between one classic and another Thursday night came nearly three hours of hard, blues-based rock served up at the Checkerdome by Aerosmith and Pat Travers' Black Pearl. The bands originally made their names in the '70s when that brand of music was in its prime... Back in the saddle after their three-year hiatus from recording and performing was headliner Aerosmith. Both of Aerosmith's guitarists, Joe Perry, and Brad Whitford, left during the hiatus and were replaced. New guitarists Jimmy Crespo and Rick Dufay showed in this performance just how much the band has lost with the departure of, in particular, Perry's distinctive style. Lead vocalist Steve Tyler's charm and presence is as distinctive was ever. In his rags and tatters, his lipstick and mascara, he is a distillation of the worst aspects of Mick Jagger, Keith Richard, and Alice Cooper. His onstage banter and general demeanor are equally vulgar, tasteless, and irresistible to his fans.

Interestingly, the absence of an inventive melodic foil for Tyler has brought the band's rhythm section out front. While not the best drummer in the business, Joey Kramer creates catchy percussive figures for the band's melodies and — as opposed to most heavy rock — interacts with bassist Tom Hamilton to form a rhythmic carpet as deep as funk. After their mid-'70s standards, 'Sweet Emotion' and 'Dream On,' and new numbers such as 'Lightning Strikes,' the band ended with the blues and rock classic 'Train Kept A-Rollin' in a version reminiscent of no one so much as Savoy Brown — clearly an early mentor of Aerosmith's undeniably successful old sound" (St. Louis Post Dispatch, 2/4/1983).

February 5
Kemper Arena
Kansas City, MO

Promoter: New West Presentations / Contemporary Productions
Other act(s): Pat Travers
Reported audience: 10,345 **SOLD-OUT
Reported gross: $104,204

February 6
Five Seasons Center
Cedar Rapids, IA

Promoter: Jam Productions
Other act(s): Pat Travers
Reported audience: ~7,000 / 10,000 (70%)
Notes:
- From a local review: "One of Aerosmith's fans got carried away at the group's concert last night at the Five Seasons Center literally. During their 'old chestnut,' 'Sweet Emotion,' the blonde-haired lass beckoned to lead singer Steven Tyler from the massive crowd crammed in against the Five Seasons Center stage. Tyler pulled her onstage after the words 'Here I am' were heard, and the unidentified young woman managed to sing a chorus with Tyler before she was whisked offstage by a 'roadie.' Ten minutes later, she was back in the crowd, beckoning again from someone's shoulders. This was about halfway into their set, and it kicked off the excitement that followed a rather plain first half. Perhaps it's because Aerosmith saved their more recognizable hits for last. And one wonders whether their new material will ever be as recognizable as, say, 'Dream On,' or 'Walk this Way,' on which the crowd of 7,000 took over for the chorus Sunday night. By then, both crowd and band were having a good time.

Newer Aerosmith material is faster paced than their plodding, heavy sound of yore. Fortunately, lead singer Tyler restrains himself from letting his voice sink into a shriek, as so many lead singers these days seem to do. A band has to progress, but Aerosmith treads a path taken by others, losing a bit of originality as they do. Feed that new sound through a system that distorted Tyler, and you have an audience waiting for excitement to happen. So, if Aerosmith is telling reporters around the country that their lyrics are 'explicit,' as reported in Friday's Gazette, it's hard to tell. Tyler's voice just became lost amid the work of lead guitar Jim Crespo, bassist Tom Hamilton, guitarist Rick Dufay, and drummer Joey Kramer. But that isn't to say any of the five weren't trying last night. They performed" (Cedar Rapids Gazette, 2/7/1983).

February 8
Wings Stadium
Kalamazoo, MI

Promoter: Danny Kresky Enterprises
Other act(s): Pat Travers
Reported audience: (8,038 capacity)

February 9
Civic Center
Wheeling, WV

Promoter: Future Entertainment / Belkin Productions
Other act(s): Pat Travers
Reported audience: (10,000 capacity)

February 11
Civic Center
Springfield, MA

Promoter: Cross Country Concerts
Other act(s): Pat Travers
Reported audience: 9,718 **SOLD-OUT
Reported gross: $93,321
Set list: Same as Dec. 30
Notes:
- Aerosmith's set started an hour late after Steven was delayed arriving at the venue due to atrocious weather conditions. As a result of the late finish and weather several hundred fans ended up stranded at the venue overnight.
- An AUD recording circulates from this show.

February 13
Brendan Byrne Arena
Meadowlands, NJ

Promoter: John Scher
Other act(s): Pat Travers
Reported audience: 16,773 **SOLD-OUT
Reported gross: $181,750
Set list: Back in the Saddle / Big Ten Inch Record / Mama Kin / Three Mile Smile / Reefer Head Woman / Rock in a Hard Place (Cheshire Cat) / Lord of the Thighs / Lick and a Promise / Sweet Emotion / Dream On / Lightning Strikes / Walk this Way / Milk Cow Blues / Toys in the Attic / Train Kept A Rollin'
Notes:
- Dan Hedges from Circus was with the band to write a feature that appeared in the May 31 issue.
- From a local review: "Aerosmith, one of the most popular rock bands of the 1970's, played its first engagement in the New York City metropolitan area in several years Sunday in the Brendan Byrne Arena, in East Rutherford, N.J. The band's absence from the concert scene, the result of a motorcycle injury suffered by its lead singer, Steven Tyler, had not appreciably diminished its largely teen-aged audience. If after 10 years and recording and extensive touring, Aerosmith's fans remain largely male and teen-aged, the band's music also remains resolutely pseudo-savage. Flouncing about in purple tails, Mr. Tyler offered his usual gawky parody of Mick Jagger, and his anguished over-wrought yelps recalled Led Zeppelin's Robert Plant. But Aerosmith has neither the rhythmic of the Rolling Stones nor the dynamic control of Led Zeppelin. The music at Sunday's concert was a rhythmically overbearing sludge dominated by the drummer Joey Kramer's militaristic preening. Only twice, in the group's signature ballad 'Dream On,' and in the pre-rap rock song 'Walk this Way,' did Aerosmith begin to sound like a cohesive musical unit" (New York Times, 2/17/1983). How strange that "Walk this Way" should be described as "pre-rap..."
- From a trade review: "Aerosmith has long been known as one of the hardest-rocking American bands on the concert scene. Yet in recent years, the band has been largely inactive due to a multiplicity of factors, not the least of which was the state of lead singer Steve Tyler's health. Touring now as a sextet, Aerosmith drew nearly 16,000 fans on one of the worst nights of the year. Forty-eight hours before showtime, the East Coast was paralyzed by the blizzard of '83. It seemed everything but rock 'n' roll stood still. Weather conditions or not, the Feb. 13 concert came off without a hitch. Aerosmith immediately established a rapport with the audience as Tyler cavorted from one end of the stage to the other. Newcomers Jimmy Crespo and Rick Dufay, both guitarists, have joined forces with founders Tyler, Joey Kramer, and Tom Hamilton. Super-session man Bob (Foreigner) Mayo played keyboards and synthesizer throughout the show. Opening with 'Back in the Saddle Again,' Aerosmith said little to the audience, but worked hard and well as a musical unit. Crespo, Joe Perry's replacement in the band, was impressive, unleashing long and biting solos between Tyler's vocals. Other songs performed early on included 'Big 10-Inch,' 'Reefer Head Woman' and 'Cheshire Cat.' But it was clear the band had not yet reached its musical stride. After 'Lord of the Thighs,' the tall, lanky Tyler ambled to the front of the stage and announced, 'Now we're gonna shift into second gear!' And so, they did, as Aerosmith ran off a blistering string of hits including 'Sweet Emotion,' 'Dream On,' 'Lightning Strikes,' 'Walk

this Way,' 'Milk Cow Blues,' and 'Toys in the Attic.' With that, the band scrambled off, but returned for an encore of the Yardbirds classic, 'The Train Kept A-Rollin'" (Billboard, 2/26/1983).
- From another trade review: "The Boston-based quintet staged a lavish show with Tyler, un-mindful of his mishap, prancing around the stage in purple tails, and doing blatant imitations of Mick dagger's antics and Robert Plant's trademark high tenor shouting. The rest of the group was clad as loudly and as severely as their music would dictate. The majority of the show was devoted to high volume noise that seemed to lack cohesion. Even their self-proclaimed sole 'political' song, 'Three Mile Smile' communicated no message except possibly for the volume of a nuclear explosion. The best moment of their show came when they did 'Dream On,' their somewhat slower-paced 1975 hit. A light keyboard flourish added to its intro set the contrast for the tune's more haunting nature" (Cashbox, 2/26/1983).
- An AUD recording circulates from this show, which has "Big Ten Inch Record" and "Mama Kin" flipped in performance order as the only difference from the standard Dec. 30 set list.

February 14
Spectrum
Philadelphia, PA
Promoter: Electric Factory Concerts
Other act(s): Pat Travers
Reported audience: 13,721 / 14,063 (97.57%)
Reported gross: $123,442
Set list: Same as Feb. 13
Notes:
- From a local review: "Aerosmith's latest album, 'Rock in a Hard Place' (Columbia), has barely made a dent on the national record charts. Perry left the band a couple of years ago to start a superior band, the Joe Perry Project, and was replaced by Jimmy Crespo, whose agile soloing is as nondescript as Perry's was distinctive. Yet despite these signs of slippage, Aerosmith sold out last night's Spectrum show — the arena was packed, with fans braving the snow to cheer lustily even when their heroes didn't find the stage until nearly an hour and a half after the opening act, the Pat Travers Band, had finished. Indeed, Aerosmith is so popular in Philadelphia that another Spectrum date has been scheduled for Feb. 28, a rare occurrence in the midst of the current music-industry depression. This suggests that Aerosmith has become what is known in the pop-music industry as a regional act — a strong draw in some cities, a liability in others. This is definitely a step down from aspiring to be the American Rolling Stones, but it keeps one in electric guitars, I suppose.

Last night, Aerosmith concentrated on their best-known songs, tunes dating back almost a decade now; material from 'Rock in a Hard Place' was inserted here and there in discreet interludes. This is certainly the only band around that begins its show by playing Bernard Herrmann's music from the movie 'Psycho,' but that's not all that makes Aerosmith notable. Tyler's Jagger mannerisms have become stylized and fluid: Dressed in tights and a flowing tunic, Tyler trailed the microphone stand behind him like a manic-depressive Hamlet — leaping and giddy one moment, somber and glowering the next. Aerosmith's music may be ordinary stuff these days, but Tyler is fun to watch" (Philadelphia Inquirer, 2/15/1983).
- A poor AUD recording circulates from this show

February 16
Civic Center
Baltimore, MD
Promoter: Talent Coordinators of America
Other act(s): Pat Travers
Reported audience: 8,268 / 12,000 (68.9%)
Reported gross: $82,645

February 18
Rupp Arena
Lexington, KY

Promoter: Sunshine Promotions / Future Entertainment
Other act(s): Pat Travers
Reported audience: 7,533 / 9,244 (81.49%)
Reported gross: $72,436
Notes:
- From a local review: "Lexington's hard rock buffs got something old and something new last night when metal wrights Aerosmith made an increasingly rare tour stop at Rupp Arena. The seminal heavy metal group, which inspired newer hard rock bands like Van Halen and AC/DC and was once one of the biggest selling rock acts in the world, has gone through some changes since its last tour ... Part of the excitement at last night's show, for the over 8,000 fans who showed up, was the speculation over whether band leader/songwriter Steve Tyler and the two new guitarists, Jimmy Crespo, and Rick Dufay, could haul the mail the way the old band did. The new band started out, appropriately enough, with 'Back in the Saddle,' a near-hit from the old band, and continued with lesser-known material and blues cover versions for the better pan of the night.

The idea, apparently, was to prove they could rock out without resorting to an every-third-song's-a-hit pace. Tyler was in great voice, and the new players are technically equipped to handle the job. In addition, it seemed like the group had tightened up its stage act. The ghosts of concerts past crept in as the night wore on, however, and when it came time to put together a string of well-known songs, it seemed to be too little and too late. Although a good part of the crowd was relieved enough to finally start enjoying the night, the band had somehow lost its punch, and a surprisingly large number of fans were leaving just when the fun was supposed to start" (Lexington Herald-Leader, 2/19/1983).

February 19
Freedom Hall
Johnson City, TN

Promoter: Future Entertainment / Belkin Productions
Other act(s): Pat Travers
Reported audience: (19,000 capacity)
Notes:

- From a local review: "Direct, loud, and obnoxious. Those are adjectives with that musical form we so lovingly call rock 'n' roll. They also are adjectives synonymous with the members of Aerosmith, the bad boys of the Boston rock scene. A decade after rising to the national limelight, the sextet proved its durability in a Freedom Hall concert last night. While J. Geils may be the shirt-sleeved Carl Yastrzemski, the group Boston the technocratic MIT grad, and the Cars the aristocratic Kennedy family, Aerosmith is the true power-broker — the Tip O'Neill, if you prefer — of that city's musical heritage. From the opening salvos of 'Back in the Saddle' through such anthems as 'Walk this Way,' 'Sweet Emotion' and 'Dream On,' singer Steven Tyler strutted his way into the hearts, if not other organs, of the appreciative, but-not-quite-capacity audience. Interspersing newer, more-drawn-out compositions with the band's scorecard of past successes, Aerosmith showed it can be: Direct, as in such lyrics as 'I'm in heat, I'm in love, but I just couldn't tell her so.' loud, as in the five-minute solo the main set and in the feedback-laden guitar displays. Obnoxious, as in the Mick Jagger-esque poses Tyler strikes and the Keith Richards-ian stances the guitarists assume. Despite such factors — or perhaps because of them — Aerosmith puts on a thoroughly enjoyable show, more energetic than one would expect from a group after 10 years near the top" (Kingsport Times News, 2/20/1983).

February 21
Civic Center
Glens Falls, NY

Promoter: Freefall Enterprises
Other act(s): Anvil
Reported audience: (8,400 capacity)
Set list: Same as Dec. 30
Notes:
- The Civic Center's take from the show was $7,418. At the time, this show attracted the largest number of patrons to ever attend a rock show at the venue. Up to 200 patrons were also ejected from the show...
- From a local review: "Aerosmith is a rock group. It plays loudly. It uses in an evening sufficient wattage to illuminate the Town of Fort Ann for ten minutes. Aerosmith played at the Civic Center Monday night. I attended to celebrate an anniversary. Thirty-two years ago, that night, I first heard and reviewed Elvis Presley. I wanted to experience, before my ultimate lapse into senility, what had happened to rock in the interim: not much, yet a multitude of things... After a too-long intermission, in which canned rock undifferentiated from actual performance blasted away, Aerosmith did its stint. The group's lead, Steve Tyler, ought to have been a revival minister: if a man can make the stoned seem alive, no sinner could withstand his message... With Tyler and company, the show's the thing. They trucked in enough lighting to reproduce First Day. Everything's worked out. So many beats, so many paces, a series of hue changes (garish, but striking). A random walk across the stage by the lead guitarist finds him in a keyed light.

Tyler, fetchingly costumed in a cerise or heliotrope caftan, an aniline green jerkin and pantyhose (it seemed), with knee-high boots, is two thirds of the act. He wails a Leadbelly-style harmonica, sings, rides a microphone stand like a hobbyhorse, whacks at the drums alongside the drummer. It's all lunatic, but slick. Even if at times I thought I was caught in a unique Circle of the Inferno, it was a helluva lot of fun. It's a pity the kids weren't sensate enough to enjoy it. Even their howls of approval were sedate. At any rate, as we fogies say, there used to be a Golden Age which, in fact, never was. There was as much tinsel and—brass back when Elvis and I were young. But it was a good deal less harmful to eardrums" (Glens Falls Post Star, 2/23/1983).
- An AUD recording circulates from this show, though it's missing the presumed final song of the night.

February 22
Broome County Arena
Binghamton, NY

Promoter: Freefall Enterprises
Other act(s): Anvil
Reported audience: ~5,500 / 7,200 (76.39%)
Set list: Back in the Saddle / Mama Kin / Big Ten Inch Record / Three Mile Smile / Lord of the Thighs / Lick and a Promise / Sweet Emotion / Dream On / Lightning Strikes / Walk this Way / Milk Cow Blues / Toys in the Attic / Train Kept A Rollin'

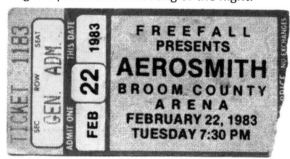

Notes:
- From a local review: "The black velvet curtains parted, the lights came up on stage, and Aerosmith lead singer Steven Tyler dug into his first line of the band's opening song, 'Back in the Saddle,' with a special vengeance. 'I'm BACK,' he screeched. 'I'm Back in the Saddle again.' Back indeed. After hearing the band's masterful performance before 5,500 at the Broome County Veterans Memorial Arena last night, you've got to believe that Aerosmith isn't just back, but Aerosmith is back and better than ever. With all that's happened to the members of the group in the three years since they last visited Binghamton, many thought the group had been put out to pasture. After the critical and commercial flop of its 1979 release 'Night in the Ruts' Aerosmith proceeded to lose both of its guitarists — first Joe Perry, then Brad Whitford. To add injury to insult, singer Steven Tyler then suffered a motorcycle accident that seriously injured his heel. The time spent

in a cast must have given him a chance to have his vocal cords restrung, because never in Aerosmith's 10-year career has Tyler sung with more confidence and control.

Dressed in silver Spandex pants with yellow leg warmers, a lavender waistcoat, and a black peasant blouse, he belted out numbers like 'Lick and a Promise,' 'Lord of the Thighs' and 'Sweet Emotion' with surprising strength. Why Steven Tyler even hit those treacherously high notes in 'Dream On' that used to have him squeaking like an unoiled door hinge. Steven Tyler proved he can still do the Mick Jagger jiggle-alike better than anyone, scurrying across the stage and teasing the people in the front rows with his microphone. Newcomers Rick Dufay — the guitarist who replaced Brad Whitford — exhibited quite a knack for showmanship himself. Dufay soaked up the spotlight with a boyish charm, at one point he even carried Tyler around the stage on his shoulders. Seeing how Tyler's prancing brought comparisons to Mick Jagger and former guitarist Joe Perry's lurking presence brought comparisons to Rolling Stones' guitarist Keith Richards, it's just a matter of time before Dufay's playfulness is compared to the Stones' other guitarist, Ron Wood. The addition of both Dufay and guitarist Joe Crespo seems to have pumped new blood into Aerosmith's sound. With the band's blues-based boogie combining heavy metal power with Tyler's crafty song writing, one can only hope they soon return to Binghamton. Those same warm feelings turn cold toward the opening act, Anvil" (Binghamton Press & Sun Bulletin, 2/23/1983).
- An AUD recording circulates from this show, though the band cut two songs from their set. With the final performance, the night before, of "Rock in a Hard Place (Cheshire Cat)," "Lightning Strikes" becomes the sole remaining "Rock in a Hard Place" song in the set list.

February 24
War Memorial Auditorium
Syracuse, NY
Promoter: Freefall Presentations / Syracuse University Concert Board
Other act(s): Anvil
Reported audience: (8,200 capacity)
Set list: Same as Feb. 22
Notes:
- From a local review: "Unlike the heavy-metal bands who are primarily concerned with form and rhythm, and the new music practitioners who are interested in synthesizing a new sound and approach to pop music, Aerosmith's music is firmly grounded in the blues roots that spawned much of the '60s and 70s hard rock. Surprisingly, though, the audience that attended last night's show was fairly young, and certainly wasn't the group that bought all the records that brought Aerosmith their initial success... Little in the concert lineup was of recent vintage. Instead, the old warhorses were given preferential treatment. 'Sweet Emotion,' 'Dream On,' 'Walk this Way,' 'Toys in the Attic,' and 'Ten Inch Record' were the linchpins of the set, with only a few newer tunes interspersed during the hour-long performance. While the group's playing wasn't exactly inspired, it was enjoyable, especially during the middle of the set when the band stretched out a bit and let both their age and roots show through. For some in the audience, though, it seemed as if the highpoint of the show was during the obligatory drum solo when the drummer proved how capable (?) he was by playing his kit with his forehead. Steven Tyler, the group's vocalist, seems to have toned down the Jagger-inspired mannerisms that used to be a bone of contention with his critics in the past. That he superficially looks like Jagger and has a fondness for dressing in jumpsuits and with flowing scarves ala Jagger wasn't much help either. His movements onstage and between song patter last night gave the audience a strong focal point for its attention, and his voice seems to have lost little of its strength over the years. There may not have been a huge audience applauding Aerosmith's music last night, but those who were there obviously felt the band had provided a worthwhile evening's entertainment" (Syracuse Post Standard, 2/25/1983).
- An AUD recording circulates from this show.

February 25
Le Forum de Montréal
Montreal, QC, Canada
Promoter: Donald K. Donald

Other act(s): Anvil, Bryan Adams
Reported audience: (18,000 capacity)
Set list: Same as Feb. 22
Notes:
- Bryan Adams (on opening for Aerosmith): "Let's just say they were a little more intense than our regular audience. We were the boys in the trenches out there. Ready for assault. It was war. But you do it because you want to walk away with a victory, make a few more friends" (Montreal Gazette, 2/28/1983).
- An AUD recording circulates from this show.

February 28
Spectrum
Philadelphia, PA
Promoter: Electric Factory Concerts
Other act(s): Anvil
Reported audience: 9,886 / 14,587 (67.77%)
Reported gross: $90,335
Set list: Same as Feb. 22
Notes:
- An AUD recording circulates from this show.

March 1
Nassau Coliseum
Uniondale, NY
Promoter: John Scher
Other act(s): Zebra
Reported audience: (16,500 capacity)
Set list: Same as Feb. 22
Notes:
- Partial audience filmed VID circulates from this show.

March 4
Civic Center
Augusta, ME
Promoter: Ruffino-Vaughan Productions
Reported audience: (7,000 capacity)
Set list: Same as Feb. 22
Notes:
- This show, and others around the time, was professionally recorded by the Record Plant remote truck by engineer Jay Messina, purportedly for a live album that was abandoned.

March 5
Cape Cod Coliseum
South Yarmouth, MA
Other act(s): Enemy, Gary Shane & Detour
Reported audience: ~6,500 / 7,200 (90.28%)
Set list: Same as Feb. 22
Notes:

- From a local review: "What better way a group of salty hard rockers to end a comeback than with raucous party starting two songs into their tour's final concert? So, it was Saturday the Cape Cod Coliseum, as Aerosmith worked a crowd of 6,500 into a frenzy with a rowdy, musically freewheeling show often bordering on pandemonium. It began with a frantic version of 'Back in the Saddle.' Lead vocalist Steven Tyler — dressed in simple shirt and jeans instead of his usual flowing Edwardian garb — acted out the lyrics by riding his microphone stand while rhythm guitarist Rich Dufay took full advantage of his cordless guitar, executing dizzy spins and mad dashes across the stage. But the real mania started during 'Lord of the Thighs' when Tyler challenged a bottle-thrower to come on stage and take over the vocals. The dumbfounded culprit answered the challenge but froze at the mike and was quickly whisked off by a burly roadie. Meanwhile, Dufay was engaged in a wrestling match on stage with another roadie. His further antics included: tearing bassist Tom Hamilton's shirt and taking over the bass while Hamilton changed; tussling good-naturedly with Tyler; and hurling full drinks into the audience during the encore.

The actual music flew by with equally chaotic intensity, though there were a few sags. Tyler sounded as if he were being strangled when he reached for the high notes in 'Dream On,' and the band botched the transitions to 'Sweet Emotion.' But the overall performance featured instrumental flights zooming far above the bland, craft-conscious music of inferior hard rock bands. Lead guitarist Jimmy Crespo obliterated any lingering memories of his predecessor, Joe Perry, with solos that sounded like music from another planet. The riveting power riffs of Dufay and Hamilton were almost as galvanizing as those of AC/DC's rhythm guitarist Malcolm Young and bassist Cliff Williams. And drummer Joey Kramer's solo spot — a convenient excuse to visit the rest room at most concerts — erupted into a tribal ritual. Tyler joined in on timbales and cowbell. Taking a page from Led Zeppelin's late drummer John Bonham, Kramer ended the solo by playing with his bare hands. Arena hard rock rarely functions as anything more than passive entertainment for the masses. But Aerosmith proved that the times uncontrollable power of rock 'n' roll emanates from the spirit, not from the amplifiers" (Boston Globe, 3/7/1983).
- A SBD recording circulates, featuring an edit of the show which was professionally recorded by the Record Plant remote truck. The full "Milk Cow Blues" was 34 minutes in duration (likely combining multiple recordings).

April 23
Tangerine Bowl
Tampa, FL

Promoter: Beach Club Concerts / Beaver Productions / Cellar Door Concerts
Other act(s): Journey (HL), Sammy Hagar, Bryan Adams
Reported audience: 50,022 / 60,000 (83.37%)
Reported gross: $792,139
Notes:
- Poor weather conditions resulted an estimated 40,000 actually attending the event.
- From a local review: "The rain was hard, the mud was thick, and plastic garbage bags were selling for $1 apiece Saturday at the Rock Super Bowl XVII. Nearly 50,000 die-hard partyers and roll 'n' roll fans filled the Tangerine Bowl to hear the straight-ahead heavy metal of four of America's premier rock acts. The crowd huddled in the rain some of the fans armored against the water in their overpriced plastic bags — heaved mud balls and crumpled soda cups at each other between sets. They generally did their best to have a good time under the circumstances... The crowd was wet, but much happier after the [Sammy Hagar] set — happy, in fact, that it got a nice little mud and garbage-throwing fight going while waiting for Aerosmith to take the stage — which the band did an hour behind schedule.

As dusk fell, the schizophrenic violins of the soundtrack to the movie Psycho pierced the air as Aerosmith roared onto the stage for a jolting set of their Boston-bred rock 'n' roll. Although the sound was far muddier than it had been earlier in the day, vocalist Steve Tyler snarled his way through the distortion in a shimmering version of 'Back in the Saddle.' Brandishing the microphone stand as if it were a pikestaff, long purple coattails fluttering about his knees, Tyler's fine rock tenor soared through the band's best material. The chunky, pole-ax guitar chords of the band fueled nice and nasty renditions of 'Sweet Emotion,' 'Dream On' and the grinding blues-rock classic that made the band one of the country's best-known heavy metal acts, 'Train Kept A-Rollin'" (Tampa Bay Times, 4/24/1983).

April 24
City Park & Baseball Stadium
Miami, FL

Promoter: Beaver Productions / Cellar Door Concerts
Other act(s): Journey (HL), Sammy Hagar, Bryan Adams
Reported audience: 30,000 / 32,000 (93.75%)
Reported gross: $464,954
Notes:
- From a local review: "The show's lively pace and fairly melodic and fresh sound fizzled when Aerosmith took the stage. They played, too loud, droned on too long and unwittingly proved that their best days and best songs, such as 'Dream On' and 'Sweet Emotion,' are 10 years old. Sandwiched between Hagar and Journey, Aerosmith seemed like a dinosaur fighting for breath. Still, you could not prove that by the band's fans who turned out in force and love hearing it — whatever *it* was — loud... Aerosmith lead singer Steven Tyler, resembling a gypsy king dressed in blues, mauves, and purples was side stage watching Sammy Hagar and talking to a couple of young string bikini-clad ladies. When one of the women asked who he was, he replied, 'Keith Richards.' She appeared to believe him" (Fort Lauderdale News, 4/29/1983).

May 3 **VIDEO PREMIERE
Studio 54
Manhattan, New York City, NY

Notes:
- The Aerosmith 3-D video premiered at this event. Attendees were provided with special 3-D glasses with which to view the video. Producer and Meat Loaf guitarist Bob Kulick and other industry figures were in attendance.

May 22
City Island
Harrisburg, PA

Promoter: Makoul Productions
Other act(s): Kix
Reported audience: (12,000 capacity)

May 24
Cambria War Memorial Auditorium
Johnstown, PA

Promoter: Belkin Productions
Other act(s): Kix
Reported audience: (6,000 capacity)
Notes:
- From a local review: "The furniture was moving, and the windows were cracking in Johnstown homes Tuesday night It wasn't a flood — it was an earthquake. Aerosmith and Kix, two of America's hardest hard rock bands, assaulted a full Cambria War Memorial Auditorium with their styles of ground-shaking rock, and the tremors haven't died down yet... From the opening 'Back in the Saddle' to the closing 'Long Train Running' [sic], Aerosmith blew the fuse of every rock fanatic in the place. Part of their electricity was in their pace — Aerosmith never gave the audience a second to recuperate. The sound and lighting complimented the effect for a strong performance with songs like 'Mama Kin,' 'My Big Ten

Inch Record,' 'Sweet Emotion,' 'When the Lightning Strikes,' 'Walk this Way' and 'Toys in the Attic.' Coupled with new tunes like 'Jailbait' and the classic 'Dream On,' and Aerosmith's show left a fast impression. The three Aerosmith guitarists — Jim Crespo, Rick Dufay, and Tom Hamilton — kept the speed of the show quick. Experience must have taught them how to use guitar jamming in their performances, because there was just enough jamming to leave the audience between anticipation and boredom. Drummer Joey Kramer was less reserved. He played the drums with headless abandon. If the audience wasn't loud enough, he threw his sticks into the crowd and finished the piece with his bare hands. Aerosmith should make sure he's chained down during the next performance.

Aerosmith's show center is sparked by Steve Tyler. He is the original rock gypsy, complete with flowing scarves and erotic dance. His lyrics are delivered with a defiance to sexual humility. Tyler succeeds in his show because of experience — he always knows how much taunting the audience can take so he can taunt them just a little more. Most of Aerosmith's electricity, however, was administered in vain. The Johnstown audience was not ready for this performance. It was the first hard rock show in the area for a while, so promoters probably thought the audience would be hungry for an act of this caliber. They weren't hungry — they were already starved to death, and. unlike surgery, shocks delivered from a rock performance can't bring the dead back to life" (Altoona Mirror, 5/26/1983).

May 25
Capital Centre
Landover (Largo), MD
Promoter: Cellar Door Presents
Other act(s): Kix
Reported audience: ~6,000 / 17,561 (34.17%)
Notes:
- From a local review: "Perhaps nothing illustrates the sagging fortunes of a rock band more graphically than the sight of a huge arena that's less than half full at showtime. That was the scene at the Capital Centre last night, where Aerosmith, one of the kingpins of mid-'70s hard rock, performed for about 6,000 people. But say what you will about these musicians: As unoriginal, unimaginative, and increasingly unfashionable as they are — and they are all of these things — they still set out to rock an audience, no matter what its size. The band opened with 'Back in the Saddle Again,' which found vocalist Steve Tyler straddling the microphone and riding it like a hobby horse across the stage. Even though Tyler continues to wear Mick Jagger hand-me-downs, and many of his stage antics are similarly affected, his harsh, high-pitched voice still is powerful enough to carry the band's most guitar-laden anthems. Except for the blues number 'Reefer-Headed Woman' and a particularly strong version of 'Dream On,' Tyler wisely avoided the band's ballads in favor of more raucous material. On most of these tunes, guitarist Jimmy Crespo and drummer Joey Kramer provided him with all the momentum necessary" (Washington Post, 5/26/1983).

May 27
Cincinnati Gardens
Cincinnati, OH
Promoter: Electric Factory Concerts
Other act(s): Johnny Van Zandt
Reported audience: (20,410 capacity)
Set list: Back in the Saddle / Big Ten Inch Record / Mama Kin / Three Mile Smile / Reefer Head Woman / Lord of the Thighs / Lick and a Promise / Sweet Emotion / Dream On / Lightning Strikes / Walk this Way / Milk Cow Blues / Toys in the Attic / Train Kept A Rollin'
Notes:
- An AUD recording circulates from this show.

May 28
Alpine Valley Music Center
East Troy, WI
Promoter: in-house
Other act(s): Head East, Johnny Van Zandt
Reported audience: (20,000 capacity)
Set list: Same as May 27
Notes:
- An AUD recording circulates from this show.

May 30
Pine Knob Music Theater
Clarkston (Detroit), MI
Promoter: in-house
Other act(s): Johnny Van Zandt
Set list: Same as May 27
Notes:
- An AUD recording circulates from this show.

July 23
Pier 84
New York City, NY
Other act(s): Clarence Clemons, Stevie Ray Vaughan & Double Trouble
Set list: Toys in the Attic / Train Kept A Rollin' / Milk Cow Blues / All Your Love
Notes:
- The "Tennis / Rock '83" event was a benefit for the Special Olympics. The band was introduced by tennis stars John McEnroe and Vitas Gerulaitis and jammed with blues legend Buddy Guy on the final two songs.
- From a local review: "While they may make more money than most rock stars, guitar-toting tennis pros still cannot lure hordes of teen-agers to a concert, even a benefit for a worthy cause. As hosts of an evening of 'tennis rock' at Pier 84 on Saturday, John McEnroe, and Vitas Gerulaitis drew one of the lightest turnouts of the season in an event whose proceeds will benefit the Special Olympics. The concert opened strongly with the ubiquitous Texas guitarist Stevie Ray Vaughan leading his trio Double Trouble through a workmanlike set of blues and boogie-woogie. Mr. Vaughan was shortly joined by his fellow blues guitarist Buddy Guy, who sang 'Stormy Monday.' It was followed by the first of several impromptu jam sessions, which grew increasingly shapeless as the evening wore on.

While Eddie Van Halen didn't appear in person, one of his guitars did and was donated as a door prize. Finally, Mr. McEnroe and Mr. Gerulaitis straggled onto the stage along with an 'all-star' band that included Bruce Brody from Patti Smith's group, Billy Squier's drummer Bobby Choumard, the guitarist Alex Lifeson of the rock trio Rush and the bassist Kenny Passerelli for a desultory blues jam that focused on Buddy Guy. While the two tennis pros, both of them on guitar, spent most of the set awaiting serve, they managed to keep time as well as to land a few scattered musical chop shots.

Bruce Springsteen's saxophonist Clarence Clemons and his band followed with a sluggish set of 60's soul standards. By the time Aerosmith, the final act on the bill, arrived, the group had time for only three numbers. Understandably irate, Aerosmith's lead singer Steven Tyler halfheartedly suggested that the crowd stage a riot. Wielding the mike stand as a hobby horse, a baton and a bludgeon, Mr. Tyler yelped and whined and strutted in a doomed effort to work the crowd into a lather. But as the evening limped to a close with a final all-star jam, the mood was as cool and serene as the night air" (New York Times, 7/25/1983).

July 26
Red Rocks Amphitheater

Morrison (Denver), CO
Other act(s): Dio
Notes:
- This was only the second public live show that Dio had performed, having played their first a few days earlier at the Concert Barn in Antioch, CA with Rough Cutt opening. The band's debut album, "Holy Diver" had been released in May. Wendy Dio later suggested, "They (the old agency) put him [Dio] out as a special guest for Aerosmith... I found Ronnie was outselling Aerosmith four-to-one in merchandise, so obviously the kids were coming to see him" (Tampa Tribune, 6/6/1986).

July 28
Colorado State Fairgrounds
Pueblo, CO
Promoter: Feyline Presents
Other act(s): Dio
Reported audience: (10,000 capacity)
Notes:
- Prior to the show Jimmy and Tom were interviewed at the KILO radio station.

July 30
Compton Terrace
Tempe, AZ
Promoter: Feyline Presents
Other act(s): Dio
Reported audience: 7,832 / 16,000 (48.95%)
Reported gross: $84,928
Set list: Back in the Saddle / Big Ten Inch Record / Mama Kin / Three Mile Smile / Reefer Head Woman / Lord of the Thighs / No More No More / Lick and a Promise / Sick as a Dog / Sweet Emotion / Same Old Song and Dance / Walk this Way / Milk Cow Blues / Toys in the Attic / Train Kept A Rollin'
Notes:
- While in town for this show, Steven appeared in court in Kingman to plead not guilty to charges of possession of cocaine and dangerous drugs (Serax). He had been arrested on June 23, while band members were vacationing in Lake Havasu City, AZ. At the time Tyler was ordered to attend a trial starting Sept. 20. Steven was sentenced on Jan. 23, 1984 to three years' probation and fined $5,000 in a deal that saw the more serious charges of possession of cocaine and paraphernalia dropped when he pled guilty to possession of Serax. The conviction was cleared from his record in 1998, when it was determined that the offence should have been designated a misdemeanor following his successful completion of probation.
- From a local review: "What the fans received for their money seemed to satisfy them. But the show really didn't say much for the development of Aerosmith. Whatever they were doing during those three years, it wasn't contribution to the possibilities of rock 'n' roll. Aerosmith's brand of hard rock is very explicit and direct by nature. Tyler yells out lyrics characteristically sexual; bassist Tom Hamilton and drummer Joey Kramer provide a crunching beat; and guitarists Jim Crespo (the replacement for group founder Joe Perry) and Rick Dufay cooperate on some twin lead work" (Arizona Republic, 8/2/1983).
- This show was voted the 2nd worst show of 1983: "The show dragged. With several rising stars in the hard-rock/heavy-metal firmament, Aerosmith seems passé and mundane" (Arizona Republic, 1/1/1984).
- An AUD recording circulates from this show.

July 31
Community Center Arena
Tucson, AZ
Other act(s): Dio
Reported audience: ~4,700 / 9,713 (48.39%)
Notes:

- From a local review: "Playing hot and wild, fast, and juicy, Aerosmith is back on the road and is just as outrageous as ever. If they made a movie about this band, they'd have to call it 'Rock 'n' Roll Comes to Porky's...' Fans of Aerosmith got their money's worth last night, from the band's opening fanfare of screeching horror movie noises through drummer Joey Kramer's showboating solo and on to a massive rush for the stage — at lead singer Steve Tyler's suggestion — just before the encore. There were some 6,000 people in the Tucson Community Center Arena for this concert, which opened with the heavy metal band Dio, and at least three-fourths of them had moved down closer to the front by the time Aerosmith had finished its 86-minute performance. The frenetic Tyler was forever running back and forth across the stage or jumping up on the drummer's platform. Using a microphone stand with long red and black streamers attached, Tyler was swinging the stand in huge arcs overhead; or else pulling it up between his legs; or holding it as if it were a rifle with a bayonet attached, and charging toward lead guitarist Jimmy Crespo... With rhythm guitarist Rick Dufay and bassist Tom Hamilton joining in, the band played several lengthy guitar jams that included tons of trite Southern rock stylings. They were played with so much good humor, though, who could be offended?

These guys have never been out to impress anyone with their musical hipness. They know what, the little girls understand, and they want to play it. The songs rolled by practically non-stop, played so convincingly and at such high-volume levels that someone in the crowd got stirred up enough to throw a bottle of booze at the band. Not long after that, an Arena chair was tossed onstage, too. Tyler took it all in stride. Later he even announced from the stage that it had seemed like a slow night. Toward the show's end, he urged people in back to come down front and urged the people down front to come up on stage. By the time Tyler sat behind an electric piano to perform his drawn-out version of 'Dream On' — the closest Aerosmith came all evening to playing a ballad — the screams were absolutely quivering. The song list included hits from the band's half-dozen platinum albums as well as the present one. The collection of songs has a remarkable homogeneity. There is no evidence of any modern music influences, no awareness of time passing at all — which, some would say, proves Aerosmith is timeless. On the other hand, Aerosmith never has sounded contemporary, either" (Tucson Citizen, 8/1/1983).
- From another local review: "Aerosmith's music is not for the weak of heart. Or ears, for that manner. Aerosmith plays hard, trashy, nasty music. Aerosmith plays music about living hard and loving women. Aerosmith plays some fearsome rock 'n' roll. Their opening number at the Tucson Community Center Arena last night warned the crowd of 4,700 that they were 'Back in the Saddle,' which meant they were going to cause a veritable stampede of sound. Get close to the speakers and you just might get tromped on — or at least get a sizable and persistent ringing in your ears for a few days... But basically, Aerosmith put on a high-charged show. Thankfully, they chose some of their better, more rock-oriented tunes instead of the slam-bam hard rock ones, with 'Dream On' slowing the pace and 'Same Old Song and Dance' slithering along sultrily. Drummer Joey Kramer and bassist Tom Hamilton had a good feel for sensual and propulsive rhythms" (Arizona Daily Star, 8/1/1983).

August 2 **CANCELLED
Selland Arena
Fresno, CA
Promoter: Avalon Attractions

August 2
CAL Expo Amphitheater
Sacramento, CA
Promoter: Bill Graham Presents
Other act(s): Dio
Reported audience: 4,075 / 10,000 (40.75%)
Reported gross: $56,251
Set list: Back in the Saddle / Big Ten Inch Record / Mama Kin / Three Mile Smile / Reefer Head Woman / Lord of the Thighs / No More No More / Lick and a Promise / Sick as a Dog / Sweet Emotion / Dream On / Same Old Song and Dance / Walk this Way / Milk Cow Blues / Toys in the Attic / Train Kept A Rollin'
Notes:

- From a local review: "Steven Tyler, loudmouthed lead singer for the rock band Aerosmith, likes attention. Lots of it. And he's not exactly shy about getting it. Take, for example, his performance at Cal Expo Amphitheater Tuesday night. He strutted, he spit, he bared his bottom. He cussed, he gyrated, he clutched his crotch. Et cetera. Yes, indeed, Tyler lived up to his well-earned rabble-rouser reputation and then some. The band's reputation, however, is clearly at stake. In many important ways, it let the audience down. It's not that Aerosmith's five members are untalented. As rock musicians go, they can hold their own — even without the help of former and much-missed guitarist Joe Perry. But the show they put on Tuesday was sloppy, uneven and, most unforgivable of all, reeked of bad attitude.

True, the band has seen troubled times of late... so, in a sense, Aerosmith is now trying to make a comeback. If Tuesday's concert was any indication, though, their prospects of doing so don't look particularly promising. The show — which drew a good-sized crowd of young, restless teens — focused on tunes from Aerosmith's earlier, more affluent years. Sadly, some very fine songs were given some very shabby treatments... The crowd's response was erratic, depending on the particulars, but it never came close to the pandemonium commonly generated and concerts of this sort. It did, however, give with glee when Tyler demanded that they turn over some pot. 'All I want's a joint, man,' he announced, only to be showered with a pair of shades, a bra, cigarette lighters and other miscellany (including, naturally, the desperately desired dope)" (Sacramento Bee, 8/4/1983).
- An AUD recording circulates from this show.

August 3
County Fairgrounds
Ventura, CA

Promoter: Avalon Attractions / Bill Graham Presents
Other act(s): Dio
Reported audience: ~7,000 / 12,000 (58.33%)
Set list: Back in the Saddle / Big Ten Inch Record / Mama Kin / Three Mile Smile / Reefer Head Woman / Lord of the Thighs / No More No More / Sweet Emotion / Walk this Way / Milk Cow Blues / Toys in The Attic
Notes:
- Contrary to popular opinion, based on trade publications in which it was suggested that Steven had collapsed, the lead singer was clearly wasted during this show, though Dio's set reportedly went down so well that some fans were still chanting his name when Aerosmith was performing. As a result, several songs were cut from the set and the band performed for less than an hour. "Aerosmith — a band that still owes Ventura a concert — suffered a meltdown after just five songs, leaving amid a chorus of boos" (Los Angeles Times, 3/2/2001). Ronnie James Dio, in the same LA Times article, recalled, "I remember that show. We had done just 10 days with them when they completely melted down. I love Aerosmith and I'm glad they got it back together, but Steven Tyler was blotto that night. He attacked the bass player, then passed out. They broke up for quite a while after that one. That's the only time I ever saw them like that."
- An AUD recording circulates from this show.

August 5
Pacific Coast Amphitheater
Costa Mesa, CA

Promoter: Nederlander and Associates
Other act(s): Dio
Reported audience: (18,765 capacity)
Set list: Same as Aug. 2
Notes:
- Aerosmith were featured in that night's broadcast of cable channel music show, "Night Flight."
- An AUD recording circulates from this show which is missing the presumed last song of the set.

August 6
Sports Arena

San Diego, CA
Promoter: Avalon Attractions / Mark Berman Concerts
Other act(s): Dio
Reported audience: 5,678 / 14,217 (39.94%)
Reported gross: $68,617
Set list: Same as Aug. 2 (probably)
Notes:
- Krokus and Zebra were advertised as the opening acts in some ads.
- From a local review: "Although otherwise an altogether undistinguished affair, Aerosmith's concert at the Sports Arena Saturday night did pose one intriguing question, namely: Should mandatory retirement be required for all over-the-hill rock stars? As extreme as such a proposition might sound, it would protect unwitting fans from having to witness the kind of sad debacle which transpired here Saturday evening, an event which saw a once-potent musical ensemble stumble through their paces with all the grace of a troupe of clubfooted ballerinas. Indeed, the Boston-based quintet performed so listlessly and with such complete disregard for its audience that one had to wonder why they even bothered to appear. Once among the premiere hard rock bands in this country, Aerosmith has been plagued by a series of misfortunes, not the least of which is that their monolithic brand of pile-driving music now serves merely as some sort of cultural artifact, being devoid of either vision or purpose.

This was best illustrated by their performance here, which relied almost exclusively on previous hits, some as much as six or seven years old. Certainly, a band like this needn't discard its past altogether, but the fact that the group itself chose to feature such a preponderance of older songs sorely illustrates a dearth of compelling new tunes. (The presence of only 4,000 fans in the 12,000 seat Sports Arena also provides evidence that this act has fallen by the wayside.) Singer Steven Tyler and his cohorts were able to set off some sparks, most notably during 'Big Ten Inch Record' and 'Sweet Emotion,' but the majority oi their set was so ragged and perfunctory as to verge on the inept. True, both of the band's guitarists demonstrated remarkably powerful arms when flinging cups of beer at the crowd and Tyler took a dramatic leap from the drum riser, an endeavor which saw him fall flat on his face. As entertaining as these antics may have been, though, they hardly compensated for a lack of memorable music, and if Aerosmith continues to degenerate at this pace, their next San Diego appearance may well be at the Wild Animal Park as the opening act for Three Dog Night" (San Diego Union, 8/8/1983).
- A choppy AUD recording circulates from this show, so it's presumed that the set was the same as at other shows around the time.

August 8 **CANCELLED
Sparks Convention Center
Reno, NV
Promoter: Bill Graham Presents
Other act(s): Dio
Reported audience: (7,000 capacity)
Notes:
- As reported in the trade press: "Steven Tyler of Aerosmith collapsed recently from exhaustion during Aerosmith's concert at the Ventura, Calif. Fairgrounds, forcing the cancellation of the final three dates of the band's West Coast mini-tour" (Billboard, 8/20/1983).

August 11 **CANCELLED
Stampede Corral
Calgary, AB, Canada
Promoter: Perryscope Concert Productions
Other act(s): Dio
Reported audience: (7,500 capacity)

August 12 **CANCELLED
Northlands Coliseum
Edmonton, AB, Canada
Promoter: Perryscope Concert Productions
Other act(s): Dio
Reported audience: (12,300 capacity)

September 3–5 **TEMP-HOLD DATE
Bam Webster Farm
Columbia, TN
Promoter: Electric Cowboy Festival, Inc.
Notes:
- Aerosmith were one of several acts still reportedly being negotiated with for the festival in early August.

December 22 **POSTPONED
Calderone Concert Hall
Hempstead, NY
Notes:
- These dates, for what was dubbed the "Toys in the Attic Christmas Tour," would have been warm-ups for the Centrum New Year's show after the band's long lay-off. The band requested fans bring gifts for redistribution to those in need by local charities.

December 23 **POSTPONED
Fountain Casino
Aberdeen, NJ
Notes:
- This show was rescheduled on the day of show for Jan. 6, due to Joey Kramer reportedly being ill with pneumonia

December 26 **POSTPONED
Civic Center
Glens Falls, NY
Notes:
- This show was rescheduled on Dec. 23 for Jan. 3. Local press reported that a temporary drummer had been found but wouldn't be ready in time for the show.

December 28 **POSTPONED
The Ritz
New York City, NY
Notes:
- This show was rescheduled for Feb. 9.

December 29
Cumberland County Civic Center
Portland, ME
Promoter: Freefall Productions
Other act(s): Cathedral
Reported audience: (9,000 capacity)
Notes:

- Michael Gandia (Cathedral drummer): "The band was managed by Paul O'Neil for Leber and Krebs who also managed Aerosmith. At rehearsal one night I was reading a music paper that had an ad for Aerosmith playing all over the area. Turning to Paul, I flippantly said to him, 'Hey! Why aren't we opening up for them?' He laughed and left — calling us back at home the next day saying we were put on the tour for some shows! Paul did it all for us. Steven Tyler gave us great recommendations on radio, and we did great — they loved us."

December 31
The Centrum
Worcester, MA
Promoter: Don Law Company
Other act(s): Orion the Hunter, Cathedral
Reported audience: (11,000 capacity)
Set list: Back in the Saddle / Big Ten Inch Record / Mama Kin / Three Mile Smile / Reefer Head Woman / Lord of the Thighs / Lick and a Promise / Sweet Emotion / Dream On / Lightning Strikes / Walk this Way / Auld Lang Syne / Come Together / Milk Cow Blues / Toys in the Attic
Notes:
- Former Rainbow drummer Bobby Rondinelli filled in for Joey at this show and other shows through early January. The band initially planned on filming and recording this WAAF New Year's Eve Party show for a live album for

Japanese fans (which would likely have become impossible due to Joey's illness), and Steven had invited Joe and Brad to join the band for the event as special performing guests (Boston Herald, 12/26/1983). Brad joined the band for "Come Together."
- An AUD recording circulates from this show.

1984

January 3, 1984
Civic Center
Glens Falls, NY
Reported audience: ~7,000 / 8,400 (83.33%)
Notes:
- The only item of note mentioned in the brief report on the show was that only one concert-related arrest took place!

January 6
Fountain Casino
Aberdeen, NJ
Reported audience: (3,000 capacity)
Set list: Back in the Saddle / Big Ten Inch Record / Mama Kin / Three Mile Smile / Reefer Head Woman / Lord of the Thighs / Lick and a Promise / Sweet Emotion / Dream On / Lightning Strikes / Walk this Way / Milk Cow Blues / Toys in the Attic / Train Kept A Rollin'
Notes:
- An AUD recording circulates from this show. This was the same set as performed during the May 1983 tour.

February 8
Agora
West Hartford, CT

Reported audience: (1,500 capacity)
Set list: Back in the Saddle / Big Ten Inch Record / Mama Kin / Three Mile Smile / Reefer Head Woman / Lord of the Thighs / No More No More / Lick and a Promise / Sweet Emotion / Dream On / Train Kept A Rollin'
Notes:
- Joey Kramer is back with the band following his short health-induced hiatus.
- An AUD recording circulates from this show.

February 9
The Ritz
New York City, NY

Other act(s): Anvil
Reported audience: (1,500 capacity)
Partial set list: Lightning Strikes
Notes:
- An AUD recording from this show exists, but only a single song circulates, likely the last performance of that song by the RIAHP line-up.

February 11
Calderone Music Hall
Hempstead, NY

Other act(s): Anvil
Reported audience: (2,500 capacity)
Set list: Back in the Saddle / Big Ten Inch Record / Mama Kin / Three Mile Smile / Reefer Head Woman / Lord of the Thighs / No More No More / Lick and a Promise / Sweet Emotion / Dream On / Sick as a Dog / Walk this Way / Milk Cow Blues / Toys in the Attic / Train Kept A Rollin'
Notes:
- David Krebs had signed Anvil to a management deal in 1983. According to Steve Kudlow, "David had little or no knowledge of metal music. He managed Aerosmith and thought we were a great opener, but beyond that he couldn't find us a deal without including our first three albums in a deal. The company Attic refused to license or release those recordings in the USA. This made it impossible for David to go forward with us. He pulled us out of the contract with Attic and left us to die" (Metal Shock Finland, 2012).
- An AUD recording circulates from this show.

February 14
Orpheum Theater
Boston, MA

Promoter: Don Law Company
Other act(s): Anvil
Reported audience: 2,860 **SOLD-OUT
Set list: Sane as Feb. 11
Notes:
- Joe Perry was invited to the show but declined. However, he did attend the after-show hangout at the Parker Hotel. Two days later he'd tell the members of the Project that he would be returning to Aerosmith.
- From a local review: "Valentine's Day is meant to be an intimate time for lovers. What it isn't meant to be — at least not in the story books — is a noisy night in the trenches with Boston's brash and

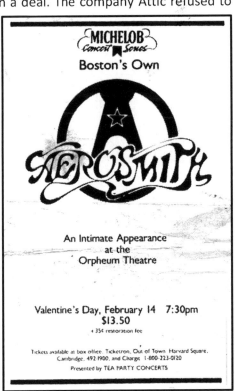

nasty Aerosmith. Rather than peaceful intimacy, there was the adrenaline rush of jet-engine decibels and guitar blasts that could be heard in Chelsea. Romantic pretensions were quickly squashed, for this was mainly a boys' night out with only hangovers waiting for later on. All kidding aside, however, it was another convincing display of brute powerhouse rock by Aerosmith, the Boston veterans who have been shell shocking fans for the past decade. Aired live on WBCN via the Kopper Broadcasting sound truck, the concert marked a special homecoming for Aerosmith, who for the past year have played at the Worcester Centrum and the Cape Cod Coliseum but not in Boston, where they haven't played since sneak gig at the Paradise Theater more than three years ago...

It was fitting, then, that singer Steve Tyler should come on stage and change the opening verse of 'Back in the Saddle again' to 'Back in Boston again.' As the capacity crowd pent up a blood-curdling roar, he climbed on top of the mike stand and rode it like horse raising the hysteria level to a plateau from which it rarely dropped the rest of the night... Following a stylized but potent set from the Canadian band Anvil, they stuck with tried-and-true favorites, playing a show very similar to their New Year's Eve bash at the Centrum. High points were oldies like the searing 'Sweet Emotion,' the momentum-building 'Dream On,' the crunching 'Toys in the Attic,' the suggestive 'Lick and a Promise,' the walloping 'Sick as a Dog' and the provocative 'Reefer Head Woman,' a torrid blues in which Tyler, wearing frilly horror-movie black clothes, edged his voice into an eerie shriek. But unlike some of their recent New England shows, this one saw a minimum of horsing around. There were no wrestling matches with roadies or throwing of drinks into the crowd, which happened at their unruly Cape Cod gig last summer.

The concentration this time was firmly on music, not mayhem. Lead guitarist Jimmy Crespo, when he wasn't flicking his flowing scarf away from his strings, played with more authority than ever, especially on rave-up transitions. Rhythm axman Rick Dufay was more subdued than usual but still a pillar of strength. Bassist Hamilton, whose blond hair flapped in the breeze from a fan blowing at stage side, kept a stable lid on the music, while muscular drummer Joey Kramer again took a bare-handed solo a la Led Zeppelin's John Bonham. It wasn't the kind of valentine that sells greeting cards, but it helped restore Aerosmith's credibility as a band that can still shake the rafters at will" (Boston Globe, 2/15/1984).
- A result of the show being aired on WBCN, an SBD circulates from this show. Recordings of "Train Kept A Rollin'," "Mama Kin," "Three Mile Smile," "Reefer Head Woman," and "Lord of the Thighs," purportedly with additional over-dubs, were officially released on "Classics Live!" in 1986.

February 16
Mid-Hudson Civic Center
Poughkeepsie, NY
Promoter: Harvey & Corky / Donald K. Donald
Other act(s): Anvil
Reported audience: 3,002 **SOLD-OUT
Reported gross: $39,082
Set list: Same as Feb. 11
Notes:
- A partial AUD recording circulates from this show.

February 17
Civic Center
Providence, RI
Other act(s): Jon Butcher Axis
Set list: Same as Feb. 11
Notes:
- The final show with Rick Dufay and Jimmy Crespo.
- A partial AUD recording circulates from this show. It's missing most of "Sick as a Dog," "Walk this Way," "Milk Cow Blues," and "Toys in the Attic," due to an unfortunate tape jam.

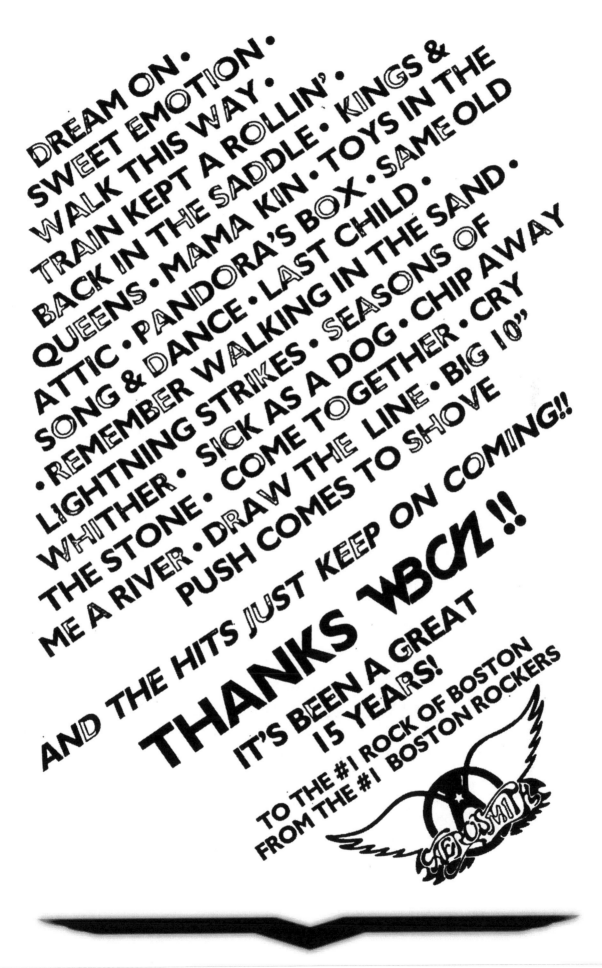

1982 - Rock in a Hard Place

1983 - Always a Rocker

U.S. Release Details:
MCA/MCAC-5446 (Sept. 15, 1983)
MCAD-11028 (Apr. 1994 — CD reissue)

Tracks:
A1. Once a Rocker, Always a Rocker
(2:56) — Joe Perry / Mach Bell
A2. Black Velvet Pants
(3:20) — Joe Perry
A3. Women in Chains
(4:01) - Ronnie Brooks / Harold Tipton / Tom Deluca
A4. 4 Guns West
(3:27) — Joe Perry / Mach Bell
A5. Crossfire
(5:36) — Joe Perry / Mach Bell

B1. Adrianna
(3:20) — Joe Perry / Mach Bell
B2. King of the Kings
(3:50) — Joe Perry / Mach Bell
B3. Bang a Gong
(3:56) — Marc Bolan
B4. Walk with Me Sally
(3:16) — Joe Perry / Mach Bell
B5. Never Wanna Stop
(4:23) — Joe Perry / Mach Bell

Album Details:
Produced by Joe Perry. Associate producers: Harry King and Michael Golub. Engineered by Michael Golub. Recorded, mixed, and sequenced at Blue Jay Recording Studios, Carlisle, MA. Mastered at Sterling Sound Studios, New York City, NY. Horns arranged by Joe Perry, Harry King, and Michael Golub.

Players:
- Joe Perry — Rhythm and lead electric and acoustic guitars.
- Cowboy Mach Bell — Lead vocals; percussion; pagan inspiration.
- Danny Hargrove — Bass guitar; backing vocals.
- Joe Pet — Drums & percussion; backing vocals.
- Harry King — Piano.
- Jim Biggins — Saxophone.
- Ric Cunningham — Saxophone.

Chart Action:
Chart Peak (USA): DID NOT CHART.

RIAA/Sales:
"Once a Rocker, Always a Rocker" has never received a RIAA certification. It purportedly initially sold 40,000 copies, but that number would have grown over the years due to reissues and increased availability of product in consumer channels. Regardless, contemporaneously, the performance was less than its

predecessors even with the shenanigans MCA pulled on the band during its recording and minimal promotion afterward.

Supporting Singles:
• No single was issued in support of the album. However, a video was distributed for "Black Velvet Pants" which went into rotation on MTV in late-October.

"Imagine a cat like a tiger or panther that grew up in the wild suddenly being caged for an arbitrary number of years and then let out to the wild. That's how I feel. So, lock up your wives and lock up your girlfriends. I'm back" (Boston Herald, 9/22/1983).

By late-1981 Joe Perry was beset with problems. Perhaps forefront in his mind was the effect the deaths of rockers such as John Bonham and Bon Scott; and the death of John Belushi. Joe recalled, "That was the turning point for me. It made it easy to turn around and say, 'What's going on here?' That's when I began to climb out of the hole" (Boston Herald, 9/22/1983). The hole, however, was deep, and his ascent was one fraught with perils. Joe Perry was also in a period of reappraisal following the end of the problematic "I've Got the Rock 'N' Rolls Again" touring and album cycle. As was expected, the album had been buried by the label and had not been successful outside of a core of diehard fans — and even some of them had difficulty finding it in stores. Touring had also been challenging with the band ending up on the bills of acts with less and less stature; and the Rossington-Collins tour fiasco had thrown the period immediately surrounding the album's release into disarray. Joe's personal problems were also magnified by his precarious financial position. Most of the issues affecting the band revolved around money and management. Simply put, the band wasn't generating enough money to cover all the demands on the revenue stream. The band had become unsustainable and Joe's debt level was increasing and the IRS was badgering him. Don Law may have seen the writing on the wall and was unwilling to bail Joe out. Joe's road manager Doc McGrath was pushing him to ditch Law on the grounds "Don Law isn't doing shit for you" ("Walk this Way"), though there was only so much that could be done considering the amount of financial baggage attached to the project. As a result, Joe was introduced to Tim Collins, then better known as a booking agent and somewhat inexperienced minor local player than manager extraordinaire he would become. For any shortcomings, Tim had one thing: He believed in Joe Perry and was willing to take on a massive financial risk in the short term in hopes of a payout down the road. And he had a semblance of a plan and enough belief in Joe to take on a dangerous gamble. That was certainly more than Joe had at the time, and he was willing to try anything...

On that somewhat tenuous thread Joe committed his immediate future to Collins/Barrasso, Inc. in January 1982. Elyssa and Charlie were not fans of Tim, but he'd ultimately persuaded Joe that he had nothing to lose by giving him a chance, and there weren't any other prospects knocking on Joe's door. Joe recalled, "I didn't see what choice I had. I called Don Law and told him that Collins was taking over. I told Elyssa the same thing. No one could argue with me, because no one else was willing to put his money on the line. Collins was, and that was all I needed to know" ("Rocks, My Life In and Out of Aerosmith"). Joe's friend, Mark Parenteau recalled, "We were hanging out a lot at that time... Joe got a divorce from his wife, found himself out on the streets of Boston by himself, and I think that sort of jolted him into reality... It was a low period for Joe, but it was actually strength-giving. Being out on his own got him a lot more clearheaded in the long run" (Spin, July 1986). And with Tim, the long, slow process of getting Joe sorted out commenced. Tim also had other percolating in the back of his mind...

One of the immediate changes was Tim's plan to tour the Project heavily. He also wanted them to incorporate more Aerosmith songs into the set, something that didn't sit well with Charlie Farren, who was ready to take a break and focus on writing a second album with Joe. He recalled that the process had tentatively started: "It wasn't really a studio; it was a room with gear in it. We got Ronnie's drum kit down there. We'd get together and the road manager would bring Joe. We never really got Joe on the demos for the second record... Tim came into my studio and said, 'OK this is the plan... We're gonna go on the road. We're gonna go to South America and tour down there and we have to do twice as many Aerosmith tunes.' I thought, 'Wait a minute???' That didn't sound like a good plan to me. I love Aerosmith and I love those songs, but it really isn't my kind of voice. My plan... was let's get off the road and write another record. Joe was not touring well at that point. Joe owed me a lot of money. They just decided to go in another direction. They said, 'Listen, this is what we're doing. You're out and come and get the money.' We had a month or so of batting that around. We ended up settling. There was [sic] no hard feelings" (MusicGuy247, 2/8/2019). It wasn't a matter of any falling out, just a diverging of paths, but it would have been a frustrating situation for Charlie considering the amount of material amassed over the previous year. However, Hull and Farren likely saw the writing on the wall regarding the band's prospects when the name "Aerosmith" was mentioned; and generating revenue on the road rather than spending it in the studio.

Charlie and David opted out and formed "The Enemy" with other former members of Balloon and the style of that band's music makes it evident that there were other musical direction issues involved in the decision. The band released the first of two independent singles, "America Rocks," later that year, eventually even opening for Aerosmith. In 1986 Hull changed his surname to "Heit" and the pair formed Farrenheit. They'd have a modest hit with "Fool in Love" from their eponymous album.

Money was the key and at the core of the big plans. Tim knew that he'd pissed off Don Law, and the two would battle over the managerial situation, while the Project needed to be prepared to start building what Collins referred to as a "war chest." There was only so much backing Collins could pour into the Project to pay debts and bills, fight Law, and get the band into the studio. More concerningly, the band's public visibility had dropped with fewer and fewer mentions and even less features appearing where rock fans could read them. Joe was starting to disappear from the public conscious. With David Hull having been with the band since 1979, and Charlie having pedigree and drive, there were financial implications for the running of the band. Cutting of salaries also played into the economics of the band's situation. Cheaper players were needed to execute Collins' plan of keeping the band on the road. By February 1982, a slightly more significant factor had come into play: Brad Whitford had reunited with Joe. At a time of upheaval, the reunion brought a certain amount of musical normalcy, with Joe being far from his finest condition. News reaching the music pressed set off interesting conjecture about that prospective reunion while Aerosmith worked on mixing a new LP. Whitford was be an active participant in the auditioning of new members of the Project at the Cambridge Music Complex. And it was immediately clear that the pair's musical symbiosis had survived their period of professional estrangement. First recruited was ex-Rage bassist Danny Hargrove, who quickly locked in with Ronnie Stewart providing a solid backbeat from which Brad and Joe could riff. The following day, February 26, 1982, Mag-4 (and former Thundertrain) vocalist Mach Bell auditioned.

Mark, known by his nickname Mach, was cut from the same cloth as Joe. From the next town over from Joe, they shared a similar outlook, not just musically. Thundertrain had been styled on the raunch of "Exile on Main Street" era Rolling Stones fused with the volume of Blue Cheer; so, he had a similar perspective to that which infused Aerosmith. His band had been booked by Tim over the years, and their 1977 debut, "Teenage Suicide," had been produced by Earthquake Morton, a member of Duke & The Drivers who recommended Mark for the gig. Another member of that band, Doc McGrath was Perry's road manager at the time. Somewhat interestingly, considering Collins' plan for the band, Mark had only been asked to learn one Aerosmith song for his audition, along with six Project songs. An impromptu "Going Down" from the Jeff Beck Group closed the session. Whether other vocalists considered is unknown, but he was asked back as the band immediately transitioned into rehearsing and adding new songs to the repertoire. With the loss of two members, Joe wanted something different for the new lineup, apart from something cheaper. He noted, "For the first two albums I picked guys just for their talent, but we'd get out on the road and there'd be personality conflicts. This time I wasn't looking just for talent, but also for compatible people so we could grow together and be more of a gang" (Ottawa Citizen, 12/10/1982).

By early March, Mach still wasn't officially a member of the band. He'd kept learning the new material, as requested, and kept returning to rehearsals as scheduled, but no position within the band had been offered or accepted. Mach would advance his case by adlibbing lyrics to one the new riffs Brad and Joe were prone to jam during rehearsals; and one quickly gave birth to the track that later became the title track of the third Project album. Even that contribution didn't lead to an immediate solidification of his position, but it changed the dynamic of the rehearsals from just working on existing songs to creating new music. And that brief spark served more than just a transition for the embryonic unit, it broke the ice between Joe and Mach, resulting in Joe handing over his notebook of song ideas which Mach quickly started mining for unused nuggets. What he discovered was a mine of material that was just screaming for attention, and some would be quickly drafted as the band found its creative feet. It was just as well when Collins announced the band's schedule: Three more weeks of rehearsals followed by the recording of a demo which would be shopped to prospective labels once the band hit the road. It wasn't particularly an ambitious plan, but with even Joe's state of health Mach was more concerned by the initial plan to record an album using several guest vocalists in addition to himself. If he felt pressure, it was channeled into learning to sing the catalog of songs previously sung by a broad range of vocalists: Tyler, Morman, Farren, Tench, Presley, McCartney... It was enough to infect a lesser vocalist with musical schizophrenia!

Between March 24–26, the Project recorded their demo at Blue Jay Studio in Carlisle, MA. At the time it was relatively new and very modern, having opened in 1979. It had been utilized by the likes of George Thorogood & The Destroyers, The Enemy, and Jonathan Edwards. Five songs were recorded during this initial session: "Going Down" (a Freddie King cover written by Don Nix), "First One's for Free," "Black Velvet Pants," "When Worlds Collide," and "No Time for Women." Four recordings from these sessions circulate for collectors with "When Worlds Collide," "No Time for Women," and "Black Velvet Pants" also being available in differing quality from a different mix (they feature some sonic/instrument differences). An additional song from the period, titled "Wait for the Night," was noted in "Walk this Way" as being written by Brad and Joe, but it may have become known under a different title or was discarded. Certainly, "First One's for Free" appears to be the only song to have not escaped the vault to wide dispersion to date, though it was performed live by the band. Whatever the case, even with Mach not caring for the title the Admiral gave to the song he thought was titled "Once A Rocker," the demo session was a resounding success (as evidenced by the resulting work).

The band hit the road on March 27, for a series of club dates that followed a warm-up in front of a sold-out audience at the Capitol Theater in Concord, NH. That debut show for the lineup also saw the debut of three news songs: "No Time for Women," "Black Velvet Pants," "When Worlds Collide," plus the cover of "Going Down." Brad stayed with the band until May 7, following which he left for opportunities on the West Coast recording with TV star Rex Smith. With Joe struggling with his addictions, the Project only managed to keep things together for a few days following Brad's departure before the tour was derailed. At a show in Jacksonville, NC, performing near USMC Base Camp Lejeune, Joe suffered a seizure during the beginning of the set, resulting in the abandonment of the show and tour. It made the situation abundantly clear for Collins. Detox or die, Joe had to get clean. So, with the help of Joe's mother, Tim persuaded Joe dry out, at least for a time, which he did during June. It wasn't a cure, but it was the start of a process that took years to get control of on a day-by-day basis. According to Joe, "I realized I was caught in a dead-end situation. I'd lost my friends and I'd lost my control. So, I put the brakes on my lifestyle and my foot on the accelerator to regain control of my future. [But] Hey, I'm not an angel" (Montreal Gazette, 10/14/1983).

Aero folklore has been rewritten to suggest that Steven Tyler collapsed during a show at the Centrum, forcing its cancellation due to Joe and his reunion hijinks prior to the show. No doubt, there's more than a grain of truth to the heroin-fueled fiasco, but Steven did make it some 70-minutes into the show on Nov. 16, 1982. That the "toxic twins" broke bread with quality illicit substances is not disputed either, nor ultimately was the fact that it affected one of Aerosmith's sold-out hometown shows on the "Rock in a Hard Place" tour. The optics were horrible, and Tom and Joey were rightfully enraged. If Joe had stayed clean up to that point, it certainly hadn't stuck enough for him to resist old temptations. Yet, it was an important step on the road to the eventual reunion. Collins would have had more than an inkling, that a reunion was a prospect somewhere down the road, if a multitude of factors worked out. And with Aerosmith still selling out 14,000-seat venues, not with the regularity they'd once done, that road would be a long one to travel. His focus remained firmly planted on keeping Perry as viable as possible as an artist. And more importantly, keeping him alive. The seed of reunion had always been planted, but it would take time to germinate. But at this time, Joe's tone seemed to indicate the inevitable: "There is the possibility I may team up with Aerosmith again. We've talked about it, but the way my career is, now is not the time for it — not for a year or two" (Ottawa Citizen, 12/10/1982). If the aftermath of the Worcester fiasco, the Project returned to Blue Jay Studio for a second demo session between November 22–24. During this session new versions of three songs originally recorded in March were re-recorded by a road-tested four-piece lineup. New material that had been written in the interim was also added: "Walk with Me Sally," "They'll Never Take Me Alive," and "When Do I Sleep?" All told, the band nearly had enough new material for the album with "Heartbreak Hotel" and "Going Down" having remained in the set.

Songs such as "Adrianna" (originally "When Do I Sleep?") were born on the road, specifically during one of the band's rare international forays — in that particular case, a pair of shows in Venezuela in July 1982. A new album was teased throughout the second half of 1982, with the working title "Persona Non Grata," perhaps inspired by Collins' perception of the efforts to get Joe a new record deal. As had been the case for the first demo at the beginning of the year, some songs, such as "They'll Never Take Me Alive," was a recent creation born out of jams during band rehearsals. With covers still forming an important part of the set it's hardly surprising that the older style of music would become fused during the creative process, with the stylistically different "Walk with Me Sally" being birthed during the year. The Project continued performing wherever and whenever they could into early 1983. The demo of "Once a Rocker, Always a Rocker" went into regular rotation on local Boston radio stations such as WCOZ and WBCN while Collins continued to search for the illusive record deal. The period of stability, and perhaps stagnation, was interrupted when drummer Ronnie Stewart gave notice in late-February 1983. Ronnie was the last member standing of the original band from 1979 and had been through thick and thin with Joe, though the band quickly moved to replace him with Berlin Airlift drummer Joe Pet. Ronnie remained with the band while they rehearsed with Pet, who made his debut with the band in Monterey, CA on March 17.

The West Coast tour was seen as the last chance for the band with them hitting the road with a focus and fury, masking the usual touring shenanigans in hopes of staying out of jail long enough to sign a record deal. While not wholly successful, the initial list of prospective labels was whittled down, and Collins signed a deal with MCA Records in mid-April. The downside to signing with MCA wasn't immediately apparent. The label was actively working to realign their industry profile while shuffling senior executives to different roles to deal with a more bullish approach to signing artists, with a particular focus on major established ones. The label had, by then, lost marquee acts such as the Who and Elton John and had seen a substantial decline in their revenues. In early May, Front Line Management chairman Irving Azoff assumed the presidency of the label. His immediate vision included closer ties between MCA and its more successful sister company, Universal Pictures, which he saw as a conduit to boosting the visibility of acts on the label. Ultimately, he sought a transformation of the company into a "music delivery business... which means everything from records to cable to music publishing to merchandising to home video" (Billboard, 5/7/1983). As part of the shakeup Azoff assumed near total control above the various divisions, but he was clear that his vision was ruled from that of a practical businessman's perspective. The Project, without the visibility or stature of established current acts (an early signing under the new administration was Joan Jett being prissed from Boardwalk where she'd enjoyed her first real solo success).

On June 1, the project entered White Dog Studios in Newton, MA, to conduct pre-production for the album sessions. Rough ideas would be recorded with Phil Adler engineering, assisted by Harry King. However, even as the band wrapped up pre-production, word came through that the band had fallen victim to Azoff's axe and were being dropped. It was a kick in the guts. Joe recalled, "halfway through the record, MCA tried to drop me. They had a new president [Irving Azoff] and he just didn't want to know. In the end, they figured it would be cheaper to finish the record — and bury it — than to buy out my contract. I didn't really give a shit. I just wanted another record so that I could tour" ("Walk this Way"). However, if the label's aim was to bury the record, it doesn't explain their willingness to provide a small budget for the "Black Velvet Pants" music video. It was trite and vapid, yet immediately catchy and certainly one of the most commercial songs on the album. Thus, with a video for the increasingly important MTV it would serve the purpose as the album's single, albeit in visual format only (no physical singles were issued). That song had essentially written itself at the beginning of Mach's tenure with the band. Joe had already written lyrics in his notebook, and once Mach had possession of it, he was able to complete the idea and give it the form required to become fully realized.

The MCA issue left Tim Collins scrambling, but the band were instructed to continue with their plans and move to the now familiar confines of Blue Jay Studio to record the album. He'd figure something out... Local concert promoter Michael Striar, with whom Collins had partnered in Jan. 1983 for TFI records in hopes of placing Jonathan Edwards' album with major label distribution, again came to the rescue purportedly backing the Project for the recording costs. According to a later lawsuit report, "Striar further claims he laid out $70,000 for a Joe Perry Project recording which MCA Records agreed to release. MCA was to pay $75,000 plus points so Striar could recoup all his money. Striar contends that Collins paid him $25,000, less a 25% commission through Collins/Barrasso" (Billboard, 2/8/1986). Michael received a "very special thanks" in the liner notes for backing his faith with cold hard cash. With funding in place Joe produced the album with Michael Golub, and Harry King assisting.

Covers had always played a part in the Project's live set. Hendrix's "Red House" provided one of Perry's vocal slots and had been a consistent inclusion since 1979. Other songs came and went, such as "Pills" or

"Talk Talk," but during early touring with the Mach lineup, "The Wanderer" was dug up and tried out. Elvis' "Heartbreak Hotel" was a favorite and had been considered as a single. As the band approached the recording of the album other songs filled spots in the live set: "Manic Depression," "Something Else," and "Bang A Gong." It would be the latter of these that was recorded for the album. It had received positive responses from the young audiences, who were oblivious to the fact that it had been a hit for T. Rex over a decade earlier. Sadly, for Joe, another cover of the song was a #9 hit for The Power Station in 1985... Eddie Cochran's "Something Else," also made it into the studio, only to be left on the cutting room floor... Of the other material on the album, "Women in Chains" was regularly noted as a standout track due to its feminist-leaning lyrics. It had been written by Ronnie Brooks, Harold Tipton, and Tom DeLuca. Brooks and Tipton had been members of the Nashville 50s revival band, the Sh-Booms, and by 1983 were noted jingle/songwriters for the Pi-Gem & Chess music stable, in addition to being in an eclectic rock band named the Piggy's. That band had demoed their recording of the song at Quadraphonic Studios in March 1983. Joe recalled, "I thought it was cool to do a pro-woman song after all the heavy metal misogyny that was around" ("Walk this Way"), plus stylistically different to the rocking material already written for the album and it was different enough to perhaps get the album noticed.

Recording of the album took place between June 6–23 and 25–28 followed by a break to perform in Canada. Mixing started on June 29 and the album was completed on July 5 and delivered to MCA. And the band returned to the road. The Bob Tingle directed video for "Black Velvet Pants" was filmed at the Strand Theater in Dorchester, MA, and surrounding areas, between July 26–28, based on a concept story-boarded by Mach. Additional filming was captured in early August and the completed video went into rotation on MTV in October. By this time, the filming of the video had already changed Joe Perry's life. When casting the model to play the central female character, Joe's world collided with the gorgeous Billie Montgomery and the pair soon commenced a relationship (they married Maui in Sept. 1985). The band continued to perform throughout the summer of 1983 wherever Collins could scrounge gigs, but it was apparent (perhaps only in hindsight) that the Project was stagnating. The venues were generally the same smaller clubs that Joe had been performing in since departing Aerosmith. At some, the appearance of a new album provided a bump to both attendances and the local airplay surrounding their visits, but not consistently. Opening slots for large viable acts were becoming less and less frequent and so the band continued doing what they'd been doing, albeit with more of that lineup's material in the set. Once the album was released on Sept. 15, 1983, it plummeted from sight. There was no national tour lined up to expand on Perry's visibility and promotional efforts were minimalistic (other than the video). For MCA, there was no reason to spend any further money on an act Azoff had wanted dumped months earlier, and once it had met its minimum contracted obligations to was clear to move on. For the Project, little would be telegraphed by the label and they stuck to the road to promote the album as best they could, playing and making in-store appearances wherever possible.

During the period, the number of Aerosmith songs in the set decreased with the bulk being featured from the new album, plus the beloved "Red House." Steven Tyler and Rick Dufay attended the band's performance at the Bottom Line in New York City on Oct. 24. Broadcast on WNEW-FM, for such a large market, the show was important for the Project. During the November 1983 Californian tour several things occurred that likely changed Joe's direction. Collins recalled, "By October [1983], we knew that 'Once a Rocker' had bombed and that Joe's solo career was going down the tubes... Joe hit bottom in Los Angeles, while he was playing some gigs at the Country Club is Reseda... He'd played there before and done well; now he couldn't even sell out one gig... After the show, we went back to this apartment I'd rented while I was dealing with MCA. Joe didn't look happy... And he opens up: the pain, the separation from his family, the fighting, the drugs. He just broke down. I'd never seen that before from Joe" ("Walk this Way"). Whether the Reseda show referenced was in Nov. 1983, or the following visit in March 1984 is almost moot considering the actual timeline of events. If the pressure of leading a band alone was getting to Joe, he was still able to keep it together in public and kept moving forward, at least for the time being. But the cracks, that had always been present, were becoming chasms. Joe added, "There were still demons at my door. The thrill of the Project was starting to wear thin. Collins was still able to hustle up gigs, but the failure of the MCA album to make a dent in the marketplace was a blow. I was still drowning in debt" ("Rocks: My Life in And Out of Aerosmith").

Debt was a powerful motivating force, as was his new relationship that contrasted the brutal divorce-process he remained mired in. Elyssa was a continuous reminder of the dysfunction he'd been a part of and the damage they had caused to those around them. Billie was an oasis of supportive non-toxic love. It was clear that Joe needed additional revenue. Joe recalled, "I figured I'd try doing a little journeyman work — write with this one, work with that one, play on this one's album. In fact, I started to work with Alice Cooper" (Creem, June 1986). Joe first met with Alice in Nov. 1983, and the two got together during the following January. Alice recalled, "I get out of rehab [in 1983], and [Aerosmith guitarist] Joe Perry got out of rehab at the same time. I was going to write two songs for this movie I was going to be in and thought, 'I'll call Joe, and we'll do this together.' My manager set up this house in upper New York. Joe's assistant went up there. My assistant went up there. We checked into this big old house in the middle of farm country — this big gothic-looking thing. I'm putting my clothes away. I leave the room and come back, and the closet door is closed. The drawer I was packing is closed. Hmm, I don't remember closing that. This house was so full of whatever that on the second night we're there, we're sitting there eating dinner, and it sounds like somebody is moving furniture in the basement. It's making so much noise. It's not even trying to be subtle. I say to Joe, 'We're the only ones here, right?' I'm not going down into the basement to find out what's down there. I say, 'This house — every time I put my coat down, I come back, and it's gone.' Joe says, 'The same exact thing is happening to me too. I thought I was just going through a recovery thing — being forgetful.' I say, 'No, this place is insane.' So, we ran out of the place" (Cleveland Scene, 10/24/2007).

The resulting Claudio Fragasso directed movie, "Monster Dog," was released in Dec. 1984. It did feature two Alice Cooper songs, "Identity Crisis" and "See Me in The Mirror," performed for his character, Vincent Raven. However, Joe was not involved in the writing of those songs, so as is often the case the memory is possibly a confluence of several activities and actual events. Regardless the two certainly got together for a writing session at a mansion in Taconic Shores near Copake, NY. Joe has also suggested that he had six songs ready with Alice, but Alice's movie was scheduled to begin filming in Torrelodones, Spain during the spring. While rumors abounded that Joe and Alice would work together, the Project had plenty of dates lined up through the same period. Joe also continued to look for additional side jobs. Joe provided the screaming guitar on the title track on The Lines' "Dirty Water" in January 1984. Mark Parenteau, one of WBCN's DJ, was a strong supporter and had helped the band out by them getting airplay. He was friends with Joe and had helped him with support when he was down and out, during the rougher parts of the Project years. He had also been associated with Paul Carchidi, business manager of The Lines who also owned Sideman Recording Studios. Joe's financial challenges and Tim Collin's desire to find him additional work made a paid-for-work situation appealing, regardless of any overall visibility of the project.

With the Project's winter layoff lasting most of the month, activities in the background were ongoing, and to a certain extent the rest of the Project was blissfully unaware of those activities as road duty resumed on January 27. Perry had even had the band learn a new song to add to the set: Chuck Berry's "Sweet Little Rock and Roller." But something in the background was changing, as Joe at least confronted his demons and started to analyze his situation and future. Whatever the case, as his band mates prepared for the tour, Joe was really still in the same situation he'd been in, in early 1982 when the current incarnation of the band even after circling the nation in vans and clocking up over 200 gigs. He'd even had some fun, somewhat unkindly recalling later, "The last Project was more a get-along-with-the-guys than the talent" (Creem, June 1986).

Assorted review excerpts:

"His newfound optimism is the guiding force behind the new 'Once a Rocker' album, the first record Perry's produced himself. The album showcases his improving two-year-old band of Perry, singer Cowboy Mach Bell, drummer Joe Pet and bassist Danny Hargrove. It even departs from hard-rock macho to include a sensitive feminist song, 'Women in Chains,' about women office workers being enslaved by male bosses. The album is still loud and aggressive enough to capture old fans, but it reveals that Perry has a lot more depth than often given credit for" (Boston Globe, 9/22/1983).

"For sheer unpretentious catchiness, this is nearly as good as Perry's previous album, "Let the Music Do the Talkin'.' Perry's guitar playing is his usual job of blunt concision, and the lyrics are even more blunt — crude, in fact. But that's what hard rock is about, most of the time, isn't it? Let's put it this way: I could really do without 'Women in Chains' and 'Black Velvet Pants,' and you can probably guess why. But the rest of this is fun" (Philadelphia Inquirer, 10/14/1983).

"After a decent first solo album and a dismal follow-up, former Aerosmith axe man Perry's third LP may seem like a risky buy. But for those who revel in no-frills rock and who remember when they played with toys in the attic, it should be a safe investment, because the songs on 'Rocker' will never go out of style. The best tracks are '4 Guns West,' 'Adrianna' and 'Crossfire,' in which Perry does his thing: Intro with a grabbing guitar hook and layers of snappy guitars and drums on top. Be careful not to punch out any walls or windows when you listen. Perry really shows good taste by covering the late Marc Bolan's 'Bang A Gong;' his is a much rougher version than the one Bolan did with T. Rex. And Perry should be praised for doing such a fine job instilling with classic rock 'n' roll 'Walk with Me Sally,' a frenetic, Jerry Lee Lewis-inspired shouter, complete with the barrelhouse piano, and 'Never Wanna Stop,' with the unmistakable jungle-rhythm-charged Bo Diddley guitar beat. You're entitled to look smug on the album cover, Joe" (Allentown Morning Call, 10/15/1983).

"Unfortunately for all but the least discriminating listeners, the title of this album is true. While rehashing stale guitar licks and singing like a bullfrog with swollen glands, Perry finds it necessary to remind himself he's a rocker by propagating one of the most disturbing trends in heavy rock — singing about yourself. On 'Black Velvet Pants,' 'Crossfire,' the title track and several others, Perry sings unconvincingly and narcissistically about the rock lifestyle. The results are loud, loud, loud, and dull, dull, dull. Perry's remake of Marc Bolan's 'Bang a Gong' only makes matters worse. T. Rex's original version was a classy teaser, but Perry proceeds to remove every semblance of talent from the song. The former Aerosmith guitarist has certainly not learned much musically since leaving the group, and his voice could easily be considered a felony. On 'Women in Chains,' the one redeeming song on the album, Perry explores the various ways that women are exploited in today's society. It is too bad, however, that Perry has to be the outlet for this song, for it is doubtful that the message will reach many understanding ears. On this album, the Joe Perry Project is a lot like the Iranian hostage rescue project — ill-advised and doomed to failure" (Columbus Dispatch, 10/16/1983).

"With the third release from the Joe Perry Project, 'Once a Rocker, Always a Rocker,' Perry produces some of the finest music of his 10-year recording career. 'Once a Rocker' is filled with a variety of rock styles, from the honky-tonk boogie of 'Black Velvet Pants' to the Chuck Berry-influenced 'Walk with Me Sally.' The common denominator throughout the album is Perry's unmistakable guitar, which emits a rawness missing from much of the slick productions of today's heavy metal chart toppers. The album's finest moments come when Perry, who produced the album, integrates the blues saxophones of guest performers Jim Biggins and Ric Cunningham with the stripped-down sound of the Project. In 'Crossfire,' Perry and company seem to battle with the horn section, culminating in an all-out war midway through that continues as the song fades away. 'Black Velvet Pants' and 'Adrianna' feature a more blended use of the horns and Project rhythm section of bassist Danny Hargrove and drummer Joe Pet. Pulling both of the songs together are Perry and vocalist Cowboy Mach Bell. Perry has found in Bell a singer who effectively compliments the style of the 33-year-old guitarist. Bell's whiskey-flavored voice projects a streetwise toughness that Perry's previous vocalists, Ralph Morman and Charlie Farren, both lacked. Bell doesn't match former Perry sidekick Steve Tyler in reckless abandon but has a distinctive growl of his own" (Indiana-Purdue Communicator, 10/20/1983).

"On his third album and MCA debut, former Aerosmith guitarist Perry reveals 'the funkier side of his personality,' which translates here to a no-frills hard rock set performed with passion and panache" (Billboard, 10/22/1983).

"Noisy, simple, with about the same texture as a wad of gum stuck under a Cobo Arena seat after a Ted Nugent show, Joe Perry's rock is good, dumb fun. The former Aerosmith guitarist has a lot more authentic claim to rock and roll's basics than plenty of the self-conscious new-wave revivalists. 'Walk with Me Sally' punches the same guts as Little Richard's old piano-pumping; 'Bang a Gong' oils the same innuendo as the late T. Rex; 'Women in Chains' proclaims men's guilt like poster paint daubed on a wall. Perry strikes the standard guitar-hero poses, all haughty sneers and bare chest, but at least half the songs crash and bang with the kind of fundamental energy that even the heavy-metal crews often submerge" (Windsor Star, 10/29/1983).

"Perry, the former lead guitarist with Aerosmith, is just a headbanger, too. But he's no good at it. His rendition of T Rex's 'Bang a Gong' is especially ham-fisted, and 'Women in Chains' and 'Black Leather Pants' ("I love the way they look] I love the way they feel]") are especially dumb" (Providence Journal, 10/30/1983).

"Joe Perry's an adequate heavy-metal guitarist who manages to project his own sense of enjoyment, but his lead vocalist, a dyed-blond screecher named Cowboy Mach Bell, ought to be exiled to wherever they've got Jim Dandy Mangrum. And he can take these songs with him" (Times-Picayune, 11/4/1983).

"Former Aerosmith guitarist Joe Perry, burns his musical signature into this debut for MCA (his third album release) and that includes Gibson and Ovation acoustic guitars, Gibson six string bass, various Stratocasters, and what he describes as his 'red string Rich Bitch,' lap steel slide, and a prototype Bill Lawrence electric, which he calls 'the balls,' and a Leslie Guitar, six string bass solo on the 'King of Kings' track. The vocals are handled by Cowboy Mach Bell, who cowrites several of the tracks with Perry — key tracks being 'Adrianna' and 'King of the Kings.' The remaining members of the quartet are drummer Joe Pet and Danny Hargrove on guitars. Also key is the Marc Bolan penning of 'Bang A Gong.' Perry emphasizes 'there are no synthesizers on this album.' The sax inserts are provided by Jim Biggins and Ric Cunningham" (RPM, 11/12/1983).

"Former Aerosmith leader Joe Perry gives hard rock new life with his MCA comeback album 'Once a Rocker Always a Rocker.' Perry approaches the wired vitality of Aerosmith on the best tracks, which happen to be the first and last — the title cut, 'Walk with Me Sally' and 'Never Wanna Stop.' 'Once a Rocker' kicks off the record with hard boogie; the last two are Bo Diddley-meets-Led Zeppelin powerhouses. 'Women in Chains' may be a first — a heavy metal feminist song. (Joe Perry a liberated man? Ironically, it follows 'Black Velvet Pants.') But Perry, too, turns in a turkey — a Quaaluded cover of T. Rex's 'Bang a Gong.' Perry also makes clear his feelings toward New Music on the back cover, whose credits note, 'There are no synthesizers on this album.' Maybe he'll invite Duran Duran to step outside — all of them" (Huntsville Times, 11/25/1983).

<A面>①オールウェイズ・ア・ロッカー②ブラック・ベルベット・パンツ③ウイメン・イン・チェインズ④フォー・ガンズ・ウエスト⑤クロス・ファイアー<B面>①エイドリアナ②キング・オブ・ザ・キングス③バング・ア・ゴング④ウォーク・ウィズ・ミー・サリー⑤ネバー・ウォナ・ストップ

★いつまでも熱く／ジョー・ペリー・プロジェクト

MCA
VIM-6317
¥2,500(11/21)
★★★☆

ロックのかっこいい部分を，音楽面にもヴィジュアル面にもしっかり出せる人という意味では，この人は数少ないそうしたベテラン・ミュージシャンのひとりだ。とにかくA①の出だしのかっこいいこと，胸がすーっとするし，思わず熱いものがこみあげてくる。とはいえ，聴き進むと少しずつヘヴィな気分になり，そのプロ根性ゆえに，今の若いバンドが持っている体あたり的なエネルギーにやや欠けるのは惜しい。しかし，キッスといい，ジョー・ペリーといい，栄光の中年は不滅なのだ／ (水上)

(Music Life, Japan, Dec. 1983)

"The Project's third outing has been long overdue, but now I've finally managed to lay me mits on Joe's newie I wish I hadn't bothered. 'OAR' simply isn't a patch on the two albums he recorded for Columbia. Oh, didn't I tell you? The Project are now on the ever-improving MCA and, not only that, but there's a new line-up as well: Cowboy Mach Bell (vocals), Joe Pet (skins), and Danny Hargrove (bass). I tried to get into this album, but even after the fifth spin I'm still left with an empty hollow feeling. It's as if the master (Perry) is taking the piss. Sure, the title cut is up to his usual standard and 'Black Velvet Pants' has touches of the Stones about it, but that's hardly surprising is it? 'King of the Kings', meanwhile, which could quite easily be an Aerosmith outtake, is the only toon where frontman Cowboy Mach Bell tries and fails to clone Steven Tyler — elsewhere he seems to be more at home with a Rod Stewart type of voice, but that just doesn't go with Joe's music. The real low point here, however, has got to be the cover version of the Marc Bolan klassic 'Bang A Gong' which fails miserably. Come on now Joe, you can do better than this! Third time unlucky" (Kerrang #56).

"The Joe Perry Project approaches heavy metal [to Mötley Crüe's formulaic approach] from the opposite direction by trying to inject as much originality into its sound as possible. Perry, whose guitar playing pretty well defined Aerosmith's style during his tenure with that group, left to pursue his own idea, and 'Once a Rocker' is ample prove that he made a wise choice. Few guitarists imbue hard rock with the kind of personality Perry brings to all his guitar playing. He owes a structural debt to the Stones' Keith Richards but deserves to be called a great player for adapting that influence into his own style and expanding it into other directions as well. The spectacular Leslie cabinet effect achieved with the guitar sound on 'King of the Kings' is an innovative heavy-metal approach that unites musical ideas from Muddy Waters, Jimi Hendrix, and Led Zeppelin. The Perry Project's 'Once a Rocker' is one of the best hard-rock albums of the year" (Circus, 1/31/1984).

March 24–26, 1982 **RECORDING SESSIONS
Blue Jay Studio
Carlisle, MA

Set list: Going Down (cover) / First One's for Free / Black Velvet Pants / When Worlds Collide / No Time for Women
Notes:
- With a lineup that included new guys Cowboy Mach Bell and Danny Hargrove, drummer Ronnie Stewart, and Brad Whitford, the band moved straight out of auditions and recruitment into rehearsals and were quickly writing new material. Four of the five new songs would be performed at the line-up's first show.

March 27
Capitol Theater
Concord, NH

Promoter: Michael Striar
Other act(s): The Dream
Reported audience: 1,200 **SOLD-OUT
Set list: Toys in the Attic / Life at a Glance / Discount Dogs / No Substitute for Arrogance / Back in the Saddle / The Mist is Rising / Heartbreak Hotel / No Time for Women / Black Velvet Pants / Going Down / When Worlds Collide / Rockin' Train / Soldier of Fortune / East Coast, West Coast / I've Got the Rock 'n' Rolls Again / Let the Music Do the Talking / Train Kept A Rollin'
Notes:
- The first Project show featuring Cowboy Mach Bell, Ronnie Stewart, Danny Hargrove. And Brad Whitford.
- The opening act included lead singer Gary Cherone and drummer Paul Geary (both later of Extreme).

March 31
J.B. Scott's
Albany, NY

April 1
Fountain Casino
Aberdeen, NJ

Other act(s): Good Rats

April 2
Left Bank
Mt. Vernon, NY

April 3
The Circus
Bergenfield, NJ

April 9
Uncle Sam's
Nantasket Beach (Hull), MA

Set list: Toys in the Attic / No Substitute for Arrogance / Heartbreak Hotel / No Time for Women / Going Down / Buzz Buzz / Black Velvet Pants / I've Got the Rock 'n' Rolls Again / East Coast, West Coast / Let the Music Do the Talking
Notes:
- A SBD was recorded at this show for National Network Radio's "Captured Live" broadcast in early May.

April 10
E.M. Loew's Theater
Worcester, MA

April 15
The Chance
Poughkeepsie, NY
Set list: Toys in the Attic / Life at a Glance / Discount Dogs / No Substitute for Arrogance / First One's for Free / Back in the Saddle / Heartbreak Hotel / Once a Rocker, Always a Rocker / Black Velvet Pants / Going Down / Buzz Buzz / Rockin' Train / East Coast, West Coast / I've Got the Rock 'n' Rolls Again / Let the Music Do the Talking
Notes:
- An AUD recording circulates from this show.

April 16
Showcase South
Pawcatuck, CT

April 17
New Hampshire College
Manchester, NH
Other act(s): Private Lightning

April 23
North Stage Theater
Glen Cove, NY

April 30
Farrell Hall @ S.U.N.Y. Delhi
Delhi, NY
Promoter: College Union / College Players
Other act(s): Paul Strowe

May 1
Roger Williams College
Bristol, RI
Notes:
- This performance took place in a tent for the college's annual spring festival.

May 7
Club Casino Ballroom
Hampton Beach, NH
Other act(s): Johnny A.
Notes:
- The last show with Brad Whitford as a regular member of the band. Brad received an offer to work with the multi-talented Rex Smith (actor/singer) on an CBS album project and headed to the West Coast. Rex had enjoyed a top-40 hit, a duet with Rachel Sweet, the previous year.
- Johnny A had been a member of Streets, managed by Raymond Tabano...

May 13
Coast to Coast
Catonsville, MD
Other act(s): Sidewinder

May 14
Wax Museum Nightclub
Washington DC

May 15
Back of the Rack
Ocean City, MD

May 16
Much More Club
Richmond, VA

May 17
Chateau Madrid
Jacksonville, NC
Notes:
- Joe made it a few songs into the set before collapsing mid-guitar solo, resulting in the show (and the rest of the run) being cancelled, patrons refunded, and Joe flown home. The band remained inactive for over a month while Joe sought treatment.

May 19 **CANCELLED
Agora
Cleveland, OH

May 20 **CANCELLED
Cardi's
Houston, TX
Other act(s): Charlie Midnight
Notes:
- In terms of tour routing, this show and the accompanying stub make no sense, so the date was likely rescheduled. An attendee noted that bluesman Robert Willie opened.

May 26 **CANCELLED
Harpo's
Detroit, MI

May 27 **CANCELLED
Agora Ballroom
Columbus, OH

June 5 **CANCELLED
Haywires
Chicago, IL

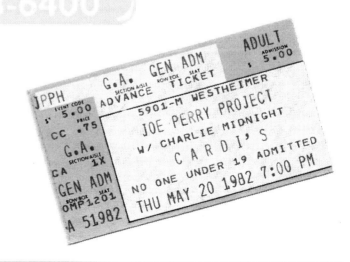

July 3 **CANCELLED
Lakeshore
Milwaukee, WI
Other act(s): Your House, Whiz Kid, Zeke
Notes:
- The band would have been performing on the "Rock Stage" at the Summerfest, with local bands playing prior.

July 4
State Fairgrounds
Topsham, ME
Promoter: J&M, Inc.
Other act(s): Joan Jett (HL), Stray Cats, Katahdin (opener)
Notes:
- This was the Project's first show back in action after Joe's collapse and stint in rehab. The show nearly didn't take place, and an injunction against the event was only rejected by a Sagadahoc County Superior Court judge on July 2.

July 8
The Channel
Boston, MA
Promoter: in-house
Other act(s): Johnny Barnes & The Back Bay Beat, August

July 9
Rocky Point Amusement Park
Warwick, RI
Other act(s): Cracked Actor
Set list: Toys in the Attic / Life at a Glance / Discount Dogs / No Substitute for Arrogance / Once a Rocker, Always a Rocker / Walk this Way / The Wanderer / Black Velvet Pants / East Coast, West Coast / Walk with Me Sally / Rockin' Train / I've Got the Rock 'n' Rolls Again / Buzz Buzz / Let the Music Do the Talking / Train Kept A Rollin'
Notes:
- An AUD recording circulates from this show.

July 10
Ichabod's
Madison, CT

July 15
The Chance
Poughkeepsie, NY

July 16
North Stage Theater
Glen Cove, NY

Set list: Toys in the Attic / Life at a Glance / Discount Dogs / No Substitute for Arrogance / Once a Rocker, Always a Rocker / Walk this Way / The Wanderer / Black Velvet Pants / East Coast, West Coast / Walk with Me Sally / Rockin' Train / I've Got the Rock 'n' Rolls Again / Let the Music Do the Talking
Notes:
- An excellent video bootleg circulates from this show.

July 17
J.B. Scott's
Albany, NY
Notes:
- This show was followed by several days off to prepare for the Venezuela trip.

July 20, 21
Poliedro
Caracas, Venezuela
Promoter: Adrishows
Other act(s): Wrabit, ArkAngel, La Misma Gente
Notes:
- One of the things Joe liked about his independence from Aerosmith was the ability to "get up and go" when he wanted and not needing a band vote to make decisions. This show offer came in just weeks before the show took place, though Collins had always planned to take the band far afield.

July 23
Memorial Auditorium
Lowell, MA
Promoter: Tom Kalil Presents
Other act(s): Rick Derringer, unknown opening act

July 24
Courtcliffe Park
Carlisle, ON, Canada
Other act(s): Mountain (featuring Leslie West), Teenage Head, Rough Trade, and more...
Notes:
- Massive festival topping off a brief 3 countries in 3 days touring activities.

July 30
Uncle Sam's
Nantasket Beach (Hull), MA
Promoter: Frank P. Petrella
Other act(s): The Dangerous Birds
Notes:
- On this evening, a taped interview with Joe was broadcast on Providence Channel 12's "Off the Record" monthly TV program.

August 8
The Compass
Cape Cod, MA

August 11
Harpo's
Detroit, MI

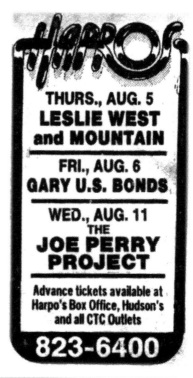

August 13
St. Patrick's Pavilion
South Bend, IN
Promoter: Peter Kernan
Other act(s): Marshall Tucker Band (HL), Straight Flush (opener)
Reported audience: ~4,000
Notes:
- From a local review: "Joe Perry Project preceded the Marshall Tucker Band and displayed some improvement since an appearance two years ago at the Toledo Jam. The group played several tunes from its new release, 'Persona Non Grata,' including the hard driving 'Always a Rocker.' Joe Perry Project also performed it fast tempo hit 'East Coast, West Coast' and 'Black Velvet Pants" (South Bend Tribune, 8/16/1982).

August 14
Agora Ballroom
Columbus, OH
Promoter: Paradise Island Productions
Notes:
- From a local review: The Joe Perry Project is a vehicle for Perry to display the thundering style of music he helped create when he was a member of Aerosmith. The first song the group played at the Agora Saturday night was the Aerosmith classic, 'Toys in the Attic.' Perry proved quickly that there was no need to lament his former band. He can still produce the same roaring steamroller sound of his Aerosmith days. There is little need to mention the members of the Project at all. They performed their perfunctory roles, but the concert was all Perry's. Perry has changed band members throughout his brief solo career, but he has never changed the sound or style of his playing. Every song, except two slower blues tunes, was in the pounding manner of Aerosmith. Perry displayed his full, slashing form, creating sound that it would have taken three lesser players to make. The audience cheered every heavy-metal nuance the group showed. The Project has released two albums to date, and a third called 'Persona Non Grata,' is due out shortly. The band played a mix from all three of them. The songs included 'Discount Dogs,' 'Always a Rocker,' 'Rockin' Train,' and 'Buzz Buzz.' These all had the similar flavor of Perry's past work. It didn't matter that the vocals were unintelligible because Perry never let up on guitar" (Columbus Dispatch, 8/16/1982).

August 15
Sheridan Center
Taylor, MI

August 19
Bacchanal
San Diego, CA
Notes:
- First date of a West Coast excursion, the band flew into San Diego on day of show.

August 21, 22
The Country Club

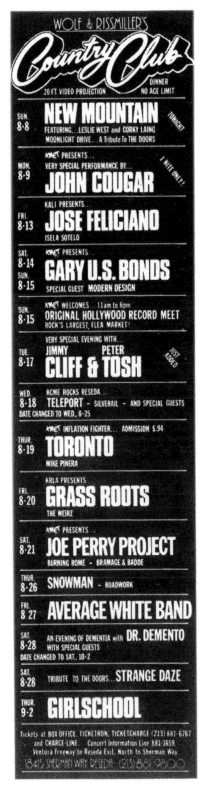

Reseda, CA
Other act(s): Burning Rome, Bramage & Badde

August 24
Golden Bear
Huntington Beach, CA
Other act(s): Tim Bogert
Set list: Toys in the Attic / Life at a Glance / Discount Dogs / No Substitute for Arrogance / Once a Rocker Always a Rocker / Walk this Way / Heartbreak Hotel / First One's for Free / Black Velvet Pants / East Coast, West Coast / Rockin' Train / I've Got the Rock 'n' Rolls Again / Let the Music Do the Talking / Walk with Me Sally
Notes:
- An AUD recording circulates from this show.

August 26
Keystone
Berkeley, CA
Promoter: in-house
Other act(s): Violation, Bleu Food

August 27
The Stone
San Francisco, CA
Promoter: in-house
Other act(s): Head On

August 28
Keystone
Palo Alto, CA
Promoter: in-house
Other act(s): Hyts, RedVette
Set list: Toys in the Attic / Life at a Glance / Discount Dogs / No Substitute for Arrogance / Once a Rocker Always a Rocker / Walk this Way / Heartbreak Hotel / Red House / Black Velvet Pants / East Coast, West Coast / Rockin' Train / I've Got the Rock 'n' Rolls Again / Let the Music Do the Talking / Walk with Me Sally
Notes:
- An AUD recording circulates from this show.

September 1
Pan American Center
Las Cruces, NM
Promoter: ASNMSU
Notes:
- This was a free concert for students. The band had been advertised (in early August) as appearing on a bill with the Randy Hansen Group, Mötley Crüe, Riot and Saxon at Concord Pavilion in CA, but played this headlining show instead.

September 3
Will Rogers Auditorium
Fort Worth, TX

Promoter: Concerts International Associates
Other act(s): Lightning, Easter Island
Notes:
- From a local review: "On Friday night he performed before a small audience at Will Rogers Auditorium, and he'll play another show at the Agora in Dallas Monday night. Perry's Will Rogers performance was a 15-tune, 70-minute affair that featured plenty of Aerosmith-style hard rock but also spotlighted the guitarist's love of the blues. Perry and his Project opened with 'Toys from the Attic [sic],' one of many tunes he cowrote with Steven Tyler during a 10-year career with Aerosmith. Perry also dipped into his old group's song bag for 'Walk this Way.' However, most of the night's selections ('Rockin' Train,' 'Discount Dogs' and 'No Substitute for Arrogance' among others) came from the Project's two album releases ('Let the Music Do the Talking' from 1980 and 'I've Got the Rock 'n' Rolls Again' from '81). Also previewed were a handful of numbers from an as-yet unreleased third LP that is due around Christmas. The hard-rocking quartet also performed Elvis Presley's 'Heartbreak Hotel' and Freddie King's 'Goin' Down'" (Fort Worth Star Telegram, 9/6/1982).

September 6 **TEMP HOLD-DATE
Milwaukee, WI
Other act(s): Krokus, The Romantics, Badfinger, Zzynx, Grey-Star
Notes:
- This date was a planned Muscular Dystrophy benefit concert.

September 6
Agora Ballroom
Dallas, TX

September 7 **TEMP HOLD-DATE
Club Foot
Austin, TX

September 7, 8
Cardi's
Houston, TX
Other act(s): Robert Willie
Notes:
- Rescheduled from May 20.

September 11
Pleasant Valley Speedway
Wichita Falls, TX
Promoter: Rock-It Productions
Other act(s): Point Blank (HL), Steppenwolf, Blackhorse, Turnabout, Mitchell Toalson, Sage, Creed

September 14
Richie's
Kenner, LA

September 16
Slick's Music Hall
Martinville, LA

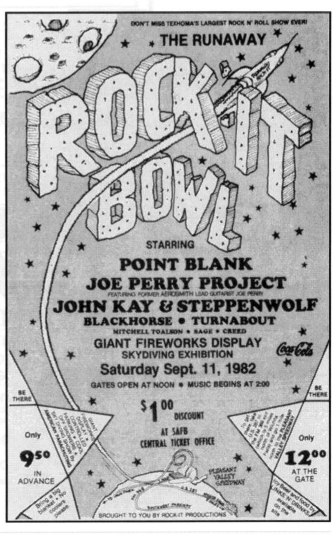

Other act(s): Nazareth (HL), Toronto (opener)
Notes:
- Frank Marino was original scheduled in the middle slot at this show.
- From a local review: "After a quick set change, the lights went down as the notes of the 'William Tell Overture' came up. The Joe Perry Project, however, immediately switched tracks, playing their unrefined brand of rock and roll for almost an hour. During that time, they drew a hearty reaction from the audience for their version of 'Walk this Way' and songs from 'East Coast, West Coast.' Most ears were tuned in when the lead singer announced the song 'Black Velvet Pants,' adding to the lyrics, 'I love the way they move and the way they feel, especially when you unzip them.' It seems very little is sacred when it comes to rock and roll" (Lafayette Advertiser, 9/17/1982).

September 17
The Spectrum
Thibodeaux, LA

September 18
Rumors
Atlanta, GA
Other act(s): Savoy Brown, Kick City (opener)
Notes:
- At the time of these shows with Savoy Brown, former Project vocalist Ralph Morman had departed, and guitarist Kim Simmonds was handling the vocals with the band a power-trio. Ralph had been working with guitarist Rusty Anderson and producer Paul Ratajczak.

September 19 **PROJECT CANCELLED
Bavarian Festhaus
Daytona Beach, FL
Notes:
- The Project cancelled (or were cancelled from this slot) and Savoy Brown headlined with APA opening.

September 21
Stage East
Stuart FL
Other act(s): Savoy Brown

September 23
Agora Ballroom
Hallandale, FL

September 24
Astro Skating Center
Tarpon Springs, FL

October 8
E.M. Loew's Theater
Worcester, MA
Set list: Toys in the Attic / Life at a Glance / Discount Dogs / Buzz Buzz / No Substitute for Arrogance / Once a Rocker Always a Rocker / When Worlds Collide / Soldier of Fortune / The Mist is Rising / Heartbreak Hotel

/ Black Velvet Pants / East Coast, West Coast / Rockin' Train / I've Got the Rock 'n' Rolls Again / Let the Music Do the Talking / Walk with Me Sally
Notes:
- An AUD recording circulates from this show.

October 13 **QUESTIONABLE
The Ritz
New York City, NY
Notes:
- This show was advertised in the New York Times.

October 16
Stanley Showcase
Pittsburgh, PA
Promoter: DeCesare-Engler Productions

October 17
After Dark
Lockport, NY
Other act(s): Talas

October 19
Purple Moose
Hamburg, NY

October 22
Circus Circus
Bergenfield, NJ

October 23
Mr. C's Rock Palace
Lowell, MA
Other act(s): Azroc
Set list: Life at a Glance / Discount Dogs / Buzz Buzz / No Substitute for Arrogance / Once a Rocker Always a Rocker / When Worlds Collide / Soldier of Fortune / The Mist is Rising / Heartbreak Hotel / Manic Depression / Going Down / Black Velvet Pants / Rockin' Train / Red House / East Coast, West Coast / I've Got the Rock 'n' Rolls Again / Let the Music Do the Talking / Walk with Me Sally / Train Kept A Rollin'
Notes:
- An AUD recording circulates from this show.

October 29
My Father's Place
Roslyn, NY
Set list: Life at a Glance / Discount Dogs / Buzz Buzz / No Substitute for Arrogance / Once a Rocker Always a Rocker / When Worlds Collide / Soldier of Fortune / The Mist is Rising / Heartbreak Hotel / Manic Depression / Going Down / Black Velvet Pants / Red House / Rockin' Train / East Coast, West Coast / I've Got the Rock 'n'

Rolls Again / Let the Music Do the Talking / Walk with Me Sally
Notes:
- An AUD recording circulates from this show.

**October 30
The Chance
Poughkeepsie, NY**
Other act(s): Richie Scarlet Band

**October 31
Coleman's
Rome, NY**

**November 6
Northeastern University
Boston, MA**

**November 12
Harpo's
Detroit, MI**

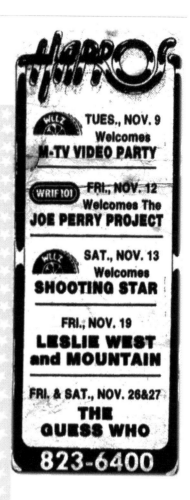

**November 14
Pointe East
Lynwood, IL**

**November 22–24 **RECORDING SESSIONS
Blue Jay Studio
Carlisle, MA**
Set list: Once a Rocker, Always a Rocker / Walk with Me Sally / Black Velvet Pants / They'll Never Take Me Alive / Worlds Collide / When Do I Sleep?
Notes:
- Following the better part of a year touring with a stable lineup the project records a six-song demo of the now road-tested material and some new songs. Three of the cuts had been recorded in February with Brad Whitford. Mixing takes place Nov. 29. This demo circulates.

**November 25
Cumberland County Civic Center
Portland, ME**
Other act(s): Nazareth (HL)
Notes:
- Nazareth would open for Aerosmith during their "Rock in a Hard Place" tour the following month.

**December 4
Sam's
Wallaceburg, ON, Canada**

**December 6
Fryfogels
London ON, Canada**

December 7
El Mocambo
Toronto, ON, Canada

December 8
Orient Express
Toronto, ON, Canada

December 10
Barrymore's Music Hall
Ottawa, ON, Canada
Notes:
- Initially scheduled for Nov. 9.

December 15
Station Inn
Wilkes-Barre, PA

December 17
S.C.C. Athletic Center
North Branch, NJ
Promoter: SCC Activities Program Council
Other act(s): Prophet

December 18
Sandbar
Baltimore, MD

1983

January 28, 1983
Agora Ballroom
Cleveland, OH
Other act(s): The Godz
Notes:
- The first Project show of 1983, following a winter layoff and brief rehearsal session at the Wherehouse.

January 29
Agora Ballroom
Columbus, OH

January 31
Bogart's
Cincinnati, OH
Promoter: Casablanca / Belkin Productions
Other act(s): Zummo

February 1
Vogue Theater
Indianapolis, IN

February 2
Stage West
Davenport, IA

February 3
Expo Center @ Kankakee County Fairgrounds
Kankakee, IL

February 4
Haymaker's
Wheeling, IL

February 5
Harpo's
Detroit, MI

February 9
Hulla Baloo Music Club
Rensselaer, NY

February 10
Community College
Nassau, NY
Promoter: Nassau Concerts

February 11
The Chance
Poughkeepsie, NY
Other act(s): Black Lace
Notes:
- A heavy winter storm dumped 8-10" of snow on Poughkeepsie in the evening.

February 12
The Circus
Bergenfield, NJ
Other act(s): Innocent Victim

February 20
Paramount Theater
Staten Island, NY

March 3
The Chance
Poughkeepsie, NY

Notes:
- Tickets for the Feb. 11 show were honored at this show.

March 4
Capitol Theater
Concord, NH
Promoter: in-house
Other act(s): The Dream

March 5
J. Bee's Rock 3
Middletown, NY

March 6
Player's
Norwalk, CT

March 10
Mohawk Club
Shirley, MA

March 11
Memorial Middle School
Laconia, NH

March 12 **TWO SHOWS
Channel
Boston, MA
Other act(s): Mike Viola's Alliance (early), Gary Shane & The Detours, Athens (late)
Early set list: Train Kept A Rollin' / Life At A Glance / Discount Dogs / Buzz Buzz / Black Velvet Pants / When Worlds Collide / No Substitute for Arrogance / Break Song / Red House / Heartbreak Hotel / The Mist is Rising / South Station Blues / Once a Rocker, Always a Rocker / East Coast, West Coast / I've Got the Rock 'n' Rolls Again / Let the Music Do the Talking / Walk with Me Sally
Late set list: Train Kept A Rollin' / Life At A Glance / Discount Dogs / Buzz Buzz / Black Velvet Pants / When Worlds Collide / No Substitute for Arrogance / Break Song / Red House / Rockin' Train / Once a Rocker, Always a Rocker / East Coast, West Coast / I've Got the Rock 'n' Rolls Again / Let the Music Do the Talking / Walk with Me Sally
Notes:
- The Project were booked to play 3 and 9:30p.m. shows. The latter was drummer Ronnie Stewart's final performance with the band.
- AUD recordings circulate from both these shows.

March 17
The Club
Monterey, CA
Promoter: Offshore Productions
Other act(s): Nasty Habit
Notes:

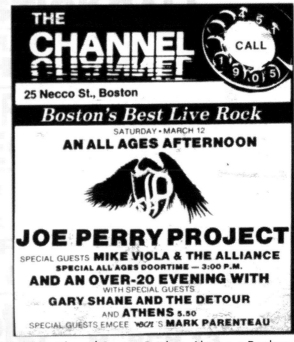

- Drummer Joe Pet's live debut with the band.

March 18
Keystone
Berkeley, CA
Other act(s): US, Sabotage

March 19
Keystone
Palo Alto, CA
Other act(s): Traveler, HotRok

March 20
The Stone
San Francisco, CA
Other act(s): Michael Spears, Steele

March 23
Crazy Horse Saloon
Merced, CA
Other act(s): Aurora

March 24
The Palace
Hollywood, CA

March 25
Golden Bear
Huntington Beach, CA

Set list: Train Kept A Rollin' / Life at a Glance / Once a Rocker, Always a Rocker / When Worlds Collide / Buzz Buzz / Break Song / Red House / Heartbreak Hotel / No Substitute for Arrogance / Discount Dogs / Black Velvet Pants / I've Got the Rock 'n' Rolls Again / Let the Music Do the Talking / Walk with Me Sally
Notes:
- An AUD recording circulates from this show.

March 26 **TWO SHOWS
Red Coat Inn
San Diego, CA
Notes:
- The band were scheduled to perform 7:30 and 10:30p.m. sets.

March 30 ** TEMP HOLD-DATE
Agora Ballroom
Dallas, TX

March 30
Rocker's
Houston, TX

March 31
Nick's Upstairs
Dallas, TX

April 1
Daddy's
San Antonio, TX

April 2
Yellow Rose
Corpus Christi, TX

April 5
Cardi's
Beaumont, TX

April 6
Oasis
Killeen, TX

April 8
Coliseum
San Angelo, TX
Promoter: Elite Concert Production
Other act(s): Huey Lewis & the News (HL)
Reported audience: (6,000 capacity)

April 12
Rumours
Decatur, GA
Other act(s): Black Swan

April 14
The Rockin' Crown
Bradenton, FL
Promoter: in-house

April 15
Crown Lounge
New Port Richey, FL

April 16
The Rockin' Crown
Pinellas Park, FL
Promoter: in-house

April 29
Dean Jr. College

Franklin, MA

April 30
Gym @ Roger Williams College
Bristol, RI
Other act(s): Gary U.S. Bonds (HL), Dish (opener)
Notes:
- A return visit for the college's annual spring festival, though unlike the previous year the shows had been moved from a temporary tent into a newly completed gym. Reportedly, the acoustics were horrendous.

May 5
Boston McGee's
Wallingford, CT

May 7
Uncle Sam's
Nantasket Beach (Hull), MA
Set list: Train Kept A Rollin' / Life at a Glance / East Coast, West Coast / Black Velvet Pants / Once a Rocker, Always a Rocker / When Worlds Collide / Something Else / Break Song / Red House / No Substitute for Arrogance / Rockin' Train / You Got to Move / I've Got the Rock 'n' Rolls Again / Walk with Me Sally
Notes:
- An AUD recording circulates from this show.

May 14
Sherwood Beach
Spencer, MA
Promoter: Jim Cappuccio Presents
Other act(s): Stompers, Tornado Alley
Set list: Train Kept A Rollin' / Life at a Glance / East Coast, West Coast / Black Velvet Pants / Once a Rocker, Always a Rocker / Something Else / When Worlds Collide / Red House / Break Song / No Substitute for Arrogance / Rockin' Train / You Got to Move / I've Got the Rock 'n' Rolls Again / Let the Music Do the Talking / Walk with Me Sally
Notes:
- A May Day festival. The following day was booked as a rain date.
- An AUD recording circulates from this show.

May 21
Scotch 'n Sounds
Brockton, MA
Other act(s): John A's Hidden Secret
Set list: Train Kept A Rollin' / Life at a Glance / Black Velvet Pants / When Worlds Collide / Something Else / Once a Rocker, Always a Rocker / Break Song / Red House / No Substitute for Arrogance / Bang A Gong / Rockin' Train / You Got to Move / I've Got the Rock 'n' Rolls Again / Let the Music Do the Talking / Walk with Me Sally
Notes:
- An AUD recording circulates from this show.

May 27
Hampton Beach Casino Ballroom
Hampton Beach, NH
Other act(s): The Lines, The Reflectors

May 28
Salem Theater
Salem, MA

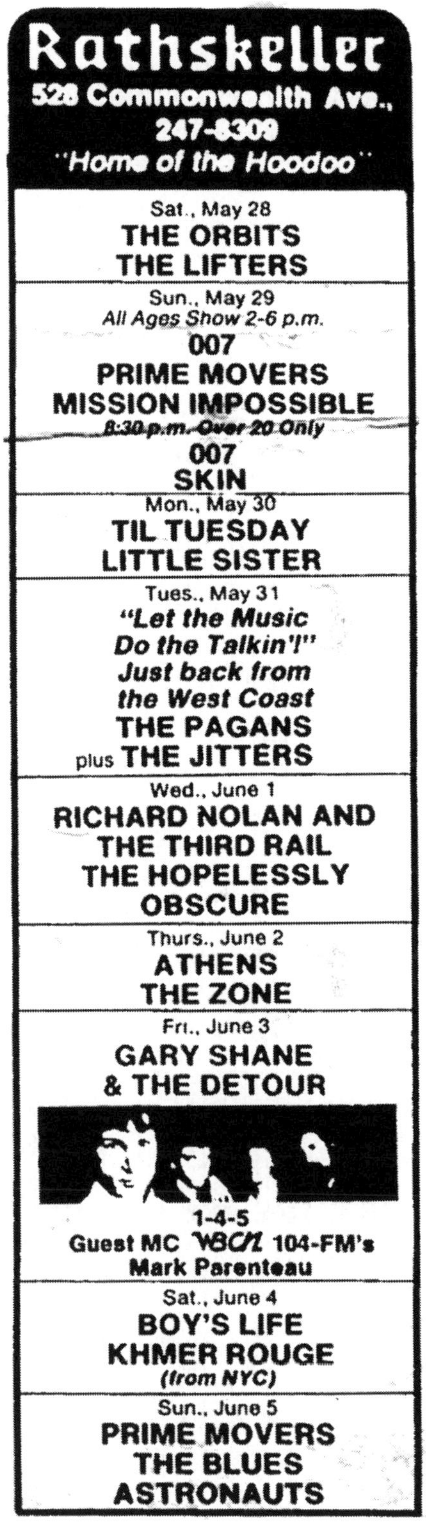

May 29
Bridgeton, ME
Other act(s): Stompers, NRBQ, Pousette-Dart Band
Notes:
- An afternoon appearance at this outdoor event.

May 29 **EVENING
Cape Channel
Mashpee, MA
Other act(s): Minus One
Notes:
- This was a 9p.m. show.

May 31
Rathskeller
Boston, MA
Other act(s): The Jitters
Notes:
- Not so secret show billed as "The Pagans...." Perhaps the "Let the Music Do the Talkin'!" hype was too obvious for this show at The Rat. The following day the band started pre-production for the album.

June 1–5 **RECORDING SESSIONS
White Dog Studios
Newton, MA
Notes:
- Preproduction sessions for the "Once A Rocker" album. Numerous ideas, jams, and covers would be recorded... Recordings of "Into the Night" and Eddie Cochran's "Something Else" circulate from these sessions.

June 6–23 **RECORDING SESSIONS
Blue Jay Studio
Carlisle, MA
Notes:
- The recording of the "Once a Rocker, Always a Rocker" album, with Joe Perry producing. Two outtakes from these sessions include "First One's for Free," an alternate vocal version of "Adrianna," and "Something Else."

June 24
La Salle Paroissiale

Saint-Charles-de-Bellechasse, QC, Canada
Other act(S): Frank Marino (HL), Coney Hatch (opener)
Notes:
- This show took place during a brief break in recording, which continued the following day.

**June 30
Fairgrounds
Kingston, NH**
Promoter: Mark-O-Hildonen
Other act(s): The Fools

**July 22
Regal Theater
Franklin, NH**

**July 26–29 **VIDEO SHOOT
The Strand
Dorchester, MA**
Notes:
- Over three days crowd scenes and close-ups were filmed for the "Black Velvet Pants" video in front of an audience of 200. Other location shots were filmed around the area.

**August 14
New England Dragway
Epping, NH**
Promoter: Mark-O-Hildonen / Rockfever
Other act(s): Cheap Trick (HL), Krokus, Blackfoot, Lipstick (opener)
Reported audience: ~15–20,000

**August 18
Skyway Club
Scotia, NY**

**August 19
Penny Arcade
Rochester, NY**

**August 21
Westboro Speedway
Westboro, MA**
Other act(s): Outlaws (HL), Gregg Allman Band, Stompers (opener)
Set list: Train Kept A Rollin' / Black Velvet Pants / Something Else / Once a Rocker, Always a Rocker / No Substitute for Arrogance / Crossfire / Red House / I've Got the Rock 'n' Rolls Again / Let the Music Do the Talking / Walk with Me Sally
Notes:
- Rockfest '83. An AUD recording circulates from this show.

August 27
J. Bee's Rock 3
Middletown, NY

Set list: Train Kept A Rollin' / Black Velvet Pants / No Substitute for Arrogance / Something Else / Bang A Gong / Once a Rocker, Always a Rocker / Woman In Chains / Crossfire / Break Song / Red House / King of the Kings / Adrianna / Rockin' Train / You Got The Move / I've Got the Rock 'n' Rolls Again

Notes:
- An AUD recording circulates from this show. The day following, drummer Joe Pet sat in at a concert-recital, as special guest, at John Horrigan's School of Modern Drumming at North Quincy High.

September 16 **CANCELLED
Show Ring
Brewer, ME

Notes:
- This show was cancelled due to poor ticket sales. Newport's Illusion II appeared in their place.

September 17
Oasis
Methuen, MA

September 23
Capitol Theater
Concord, NH

Other act(s): The Dream

September 24 **TWO SHOWS
The Channel
Boston, MA

Other act(s): The Dream

Set list: Train Kept a Rollin' / Something Else / 4 Guns West / Bang a Gong / Crossfire / Break Song / Red House / Women in Chains / Black Velvet Pants / Rockin' Train / Once a Rocker, Always a Rocker / Never Wanna Stop / Let the Music Do the Talking / Walk with Me Sally

Notes:
- The first show, at 3p.m., was all-ages with the second at 9:30 for the over-20s. This date served as the official kick-off for the tour supporting the new album, which had been released on Sept. 15. On that day, the band had celebrated by attending an album signing party at Strawberries in Cambridge, MA.
- An AUD recording circulates from this show.

September 25
Toad's Place
New Haven, CT

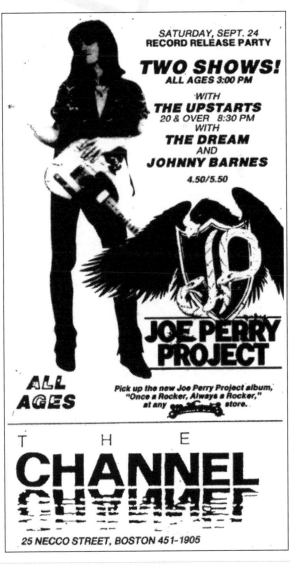

September 27
Lupo's Heartbreak Hotel
Providence, RI

September 28
The Chance
Poughkeepsie, NY

September 29
Rusty Nail Inn
Sunderland, MA
Other act(s): Fat, The Lines

September 30
L'Amour
Brooklyn NY
Promoter: in-house
Other act(s): Cities
Set list: Train Kept a Rollin' / Something Else / 4 Guns West / Bang a Gong / Crossfire / Red House / Women in Chains / Black Velvet Pants / Once a Rocker, Always a Rocker / Never Wanna Stop / Let the Music Do the Talking / Walk with Me Sally
Notes:
- An AUD recording circulates from this show, which may have a couple of songs chopped.

October 1
Sandbar
Ocean City, MD

October 2
Pocono Downs Raceway
Wilkes-Barre, PA
Other act(s): Joan Jett (HL), Foghat, Cheap Trick, The Elvis Brothers (opener)
Reported audience: ~7,000 / 12,000 (58.33%)
Notes:
- The Project performed second on the bill at Pocono Jam '83.
- From a local review: "The Joe Perry Project, the next act onstage, was unable to wake the crowd. Perry, the ex-lead guitarist for the super-group Aerosmith, formed his own combo in 1979, combining his blaring guitar leads with the screaming vocals of singer Mach Bell. In a word, the band's versions of Eddie Cochran's 'Something Else' and T. Rex's 'Bang a Gong' were loud. In another word, dull. The Joe Perry Project added little to the jam in the way of music and nothing to make the day exciting" (Wilkes-Barre Times Leader, 10/3/1983).

October 3
The Bayou
Washington DC
Notes:
- From a local review: "The Joe Perry Project hit the Bayou's stage Monday with all the blustering force of a tropical squall. Perry, guitar roaring, led a trim quartet through riotous sets of new originals, road-tested crowd pleasers and

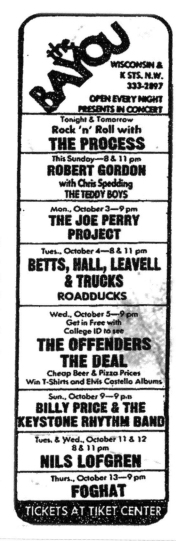

some surprising oldies. The band opened with a cocky 'Train Kept A Rollin,' the rockabilly chestnut that became the trademark of his one-time comrades, Aerosmith, in homage to the Yardbirds. Tough, no-nonsense readings of Eddie Cochrane's 'Something Else' and T. Rex's 'Bang A Gong' followed shortly, showing off Perry's twitchy, gutter-visionary brand of rhythm guitar playing. Perry's material tended toward standard boogie and blues fare and crude rock 'n' roll performed with a maximum of fuss and minimum of finesse. A solid but unimaginative rhythm section provided a sparse backdrop for flashy, facile lead pyrotechnics. As the evening wore on, the solos grew longer and the individual tunes less and less distinctive" (Washington Post, 10/5/1983).

October 4
Ripley Music Hall
Philadelphia, PA

Set list: Train Kept a Rollin' / Something Else / 4 Guns West / Bang a Gong / Crossfire / Break Song / Red House / Women in Chains / Black Velvet Pants / Rockin' Train / Once a Rocker, Always a Rocker / Never Wanna Stop / Let the Music Do the Talking / Walk with Me Sally
Notes:
- An AUD recording circulates from this show.

October 6 **LUNCHTIME SHOW
2001 Club
Buffalo, NY

Set list: Train Kept A Rollin' / Something Else / 4 Guns West / Bang a Gong / Black Velvet Pants / Crossfire / Break Song / Red House / Women in Chains / Once a Rocker, Always a Rocker
Notes:
- This show was broadcast on local FM radio for a free "Lunch Break" concert.

October 6 **EVENING SHOW
After Dark
Lockport, NY

Notes:
- After playing a lunchtime set, the band played a club gig in the evening.

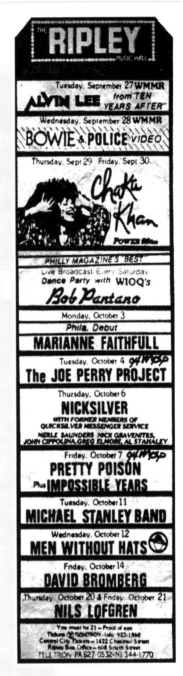

October 7
Harpo's
Detroit, MI

October 8
Fryfogels
London, ON, Canada

October 10
El Mocambo
Toronto, ON, Canada
Notes:

- From a local review: "There are several reasons why guitarist Joe Perry's appearance at the El Mocambo might have been just another lost night in the rock and roll Twilight Zone. First, he was once lead guitarist for Boston's Aerosmith, an inconsistent and unimaginative, heavy-metal product of the mid-seventies. Second, his much-publicized split with the band led to a solo career that has been slow to develop. What's more, reason number two is probably rooted in reason number three — Perry's equally well-publicized heroin addiction, which he now claims to have licked. So, with all those three strikes against him, it's nice (and somewhat surprising) to note that Perry's performance late Monday night was both electrifying and exciting enough to conclude that he is one veteran on his way back.

The Joe Perry Project is still the banner Perry uses for himself and his working band, although the current project is entirely different from the one that backed him on his last album and tour. Its major interest is singer Mach Bell, a leather-clad and leather-voiced screamer in the Bon Scott mold, someone more than willing to grab the centerstage spotlight that Perry is still reluctant to take. Most of the performance centered, naturally enough, on the music from Perry's latest album, 'Once a Rocker, Always a Rocker.' By and large, the numbers combine typical, time-worn heavy-metal structures with lengthy instrumental breaks that allow Perry to show off his derivative but flashy style. Songs such as '4 Guns West' and 'Crossfire' sound like what might happen if Jeff Beck were invited to join AC/DC. Of more interest were some unexpected moments. For example, the venerable 'Train Kept A Rollin'' was a concert standard for Aerosmith and, as a punchy opening number, it helped set the tone for the rest of Perry's set.

Also, a rendition of 'Bang-a-Gong,' the old T-Rex hit, was an amusing interlude. But the best moments of the evening for Perry's real surprise: 'Red House,' the Jimi Hendrix standard. Here the guitarist shone. But stepping outside the heavy-metal formula into a blues-rock vein, Perry showed himself to be a far more capable and interesting player than he has demonstrated in the past. Mumbled attempts at vocals, however, indicated why he has always contented himself working along bigger voices (and egos). A full house of appreciated, wild-eyed, beer-sodden, ultra-loud, fist-in-the-air fans indicated that Perry still has a hard-core audience — although it's a lot easier to fill the El Mocambo that they hockey arenas of his past. Even so, if he can continue to generate this kind of excitement, it's a cinch that this crowd serve as the foundation for a new and much larger following for Joe Perry" (Toronto Globe & Mail, 10/12/1983).

October 12
Nag's Head
Markham, ON, Canada

October 13
Orient Express
Burlington, ON, Canada

October 14
Barrymore's Music Hall
Ottawa, ON, Canada
Promoter: in-house
Other act(s): Killer Dwarfs

October 16
Le Spectrum de Montreal
Montreal, QC, Canada

Other act(s): Lee Aaron
Reported audience: (1,200 capacity)
Set list: Train Kept a Rollin' / Something Else / 4 Guns West / Bang a Gong / Crossfire / Break Song / Red House / Women in Chains / Black Velvet Pants / Rockin' Train / Once a Rocker, Always a Rocker / Never Wanna Stop / Let the Music Do the Talking / Walk with Me Sally
Notes:
- An AUD recording circulates from this show.

October 17
Café Campus
Quebec City, QC, Canada
Other act(s): Shade

October 20
Fitchburg Theater
Fitchburg, MA
Promoter: Bill Hanney Presents
Other act(s): Black Diamond
Set list: Train Kept a Rollin' / Something Else / 4 Guns West / Bang a Gong / Crossfire / Break Song / Women in Chains / Black Velvet Pants / Once a Rocker, Always a Rocker / Never Wanna Stop / Let the Music Do the Talking / Walk with Me Sally
Notes:
- A SBD circulates from this show due to the show being broadcast on WAAF-FM.

October 21
Acton-Boxborough Regional High School
Acton, MA
Notes:
- Photos from the show were included in the school's 1984 yearbook. From that yearbook page: "Joe Perry told me during supper that he would play that set for Dave [Ed: A student who had passed away during the school year] and that Dave would hear it. It thought he was talking about some spiritual communication. I didn't realize he meant he was going to play it loud enough for David to actually hear it."

October 22
Scotch 'n Sounds
Brockton, MA
Other act(s): The Mike Viola Alliance

October 24
Bottom Line
New York City, NY
Other act(s): Sighs Five
Set list: Train Kept A Rollin' / Something Else / 4 Guns West / Bang a Gong / Crossfire / Red House / Women in Chains / Black Velvet Pants / Once a Rocker, Always a Rocker / Never Wanna Stop / Let the Music Do the Talking / Walk with Me Sally
Notes:
- Live broadcast on WNEW-FM, this show was attended by Steven Tyler and Rick Dufay.
- From a trade review: "'We're the loudest band to play this gig,' yelled

the Joe Perry Project's flamboyant vocalist/screamer Cowboy Mach Bell halfway through the group's hour-plus set Oct. 24. No argument there, and while the excessive volume apparently delighted most of the crowd, it often turned some talented performances into a mud puddle of noise. Perry pierced the din often enough to maintain his reputation as a great guitarist and stuck in enough Aerosmith riffs to keep fans of his former group happy. 'Caught in the Crossfire' was one of the precious few tunes that featured saxophonist Bobby Sterns and keyboardist Harry King, who added a sophisticated blues touch. Other blues favorites such as 'Take A Walk with Me Sally' augmented the hard rock set, which drew heavily from the group's current MCA LP 'Once a Rocker, Always a Rocker'" (Billboard, 11/19/1983).

October 26
Agora,
Cleveland, OH
Promoter: in-house / WMMS
Notes:
- This 1p.m. show was broadcast live on Matt the Cat's WMMS-FM "Coffeebreak Concert."

October 27
Haymaker's
Wheeling, IL

October 28 **TWO SHOWS
Colony Theater
Chicago, IL
Promoter: AV&W Music Video Enterprises
Other act(s): The B'zz
Partial set list: Bang a Gong / Crossfire / Break Song / Red House / Women in Chains / Black Velvet Pants / Rockin' Train / Never Wanna Stop / Let the Music Do the Talking/Draw the Line / Walk with Me Sally
Notes:
- An incomplete AUD recording circulates from this show.

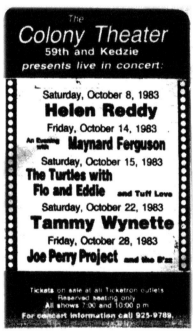

October 30
Cabooze
Minneapolis, MN
Set list: Train Kept A Rollin' / Something Else / 4 Guns West / Bang a Gong / Crossfire / Break Song / Red House / Women in Chains / Black Velvet Pants / Rockin' Train / Once a Rocker, Always a Rocker / Never Wanna Stop / Let the Music Do the Talking / Walk with Me Sally
Notes:
- An AUD recording circulates from this show.

November 4
Keystone
Berkley, CA
Other act(s): Head On, The Hyts
Notes:
- Dates Nov. 4-20 were advertised in a fan club flyer.

November 5
The Stone
San Francisco, CA

Other act(s): The Hyts, Atom

November 6
Grand Ballroom
Reno, NV
Promoter: Michael Schivo Presents

November 7 **POSTPONED
Keystone
Palo Alto, CA
Other act(s): Lemans, The Hyts
Notes:
- This show was rescheduled for Nov. 9.

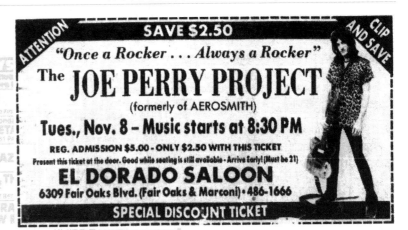

November 8
El Dorado
Carmichael, CA
Other act(s): The Boyz, Swedish Films
Notes:
- From a local review: "It was a far better 'version' of Aerosmith that played the El Dorado Saloon Wednesday night than the group which showed up at the Cal Expo during the summer... Perry has now surrounded himself with talented musicians in a group that bears many similarities to Aerosmith, from the opening song Wednesday, 'Train Keeps a Rollin' [sic],' to the eye makeup and gyrations of singer Mach Bell. However, Bell is energetic without being overbearing like Aerosmith's Tyler, and overall, the band definitely has Perry's identity. While Perry butchered one bluesy Jimi Hendrix relic Wednesday, he is an adequate guitarist, and the sound was excellent. Better yet were his drummer and bassist. Joe Pet is one of the finer hyper rock drummers around and Danny Hargrove laid down such a solid bass backbone that, arguably, it was Perry who was the musical lightweight in this group" (Sacramento Union, 9/?/1983).

November 9
Keystone
Palo Alto, CA

November 10 **TEMP HOLD-DATE
Eureka, CA
Notes:
- This show, and dates on Nov. 12 & 14, were included on the tour itinerary included with fall fan club mailings.

November 11
Catalyst
Santa Cruz, CA
Other act(s): Hyts, T.K.O.

November 12 **TEMP HOLD-DATE
Visalia, CA

November 14 **TEMP HOLD-DATE
The Graduate
Santa Cruz, CA

November 16
Belly Up Tavern
Solana Beach, CA
Promoter: in-house
Other act(s): Dreamer
Notes:
- Following this show, venue booker Dave Hodges suggested that he would never book another hard rock band like Joe's (Times-Advocate, 1/5/1984) ...

November 17
Golden Bear
Huntington Beach, CA

November 18
Country Club
Reseda, CA
Promoter: Wolf & Rissmiller
Other act(s): Lazer
Set list: Train Kept A Rollin' / Something Else / 4 Guns West / Bang A Gong / Crossfire / Break Song / Red House / Women in Chains / Black Velvet Pants / Rockin' Train / Once a Rocker, Always a Rocker / Never Wanna Stop / Let the Music Do the Talking / Walk with Me Sally
Notes:
- An AUD recording circulates from this show.

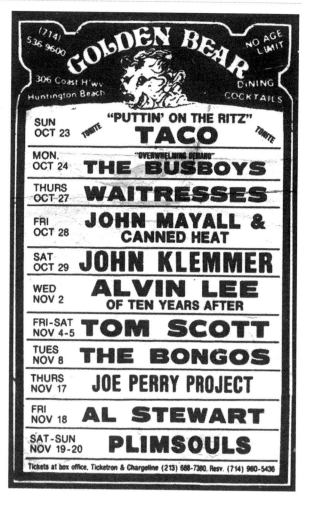

November 20
The Troubadour
Las Vegas, NV
Promoter: Michael Schivo Presents

November 21
After the Goldrush
Tempe, AZ
Promoter: Evening Star Presents
Other act(s): Swiss Banks
Set list: Train Kept A Rollin' / Something Else / 4 Guns West / Bang A Gong / Crossfire / Break Song / Red House / Women in Chains / Black Velvet Pants / Rockin' Train / Once a Rocker, Always a Rocker / Never Wanna Stop / Let the Music Do the Talking / Walk with Me Sally
Notes:
- An AUD recording circulates from this show.

December 1
Pollak Auditorium @ Monmouth College
West Long Branch, NJ
Promoter: Student Government Association / College Center Council / Residence Hall Association

December 2
The Living Room
Providence, RI

Other act(s): The Piccadilly Rogues

December 3 **TWO SHOWS
The Channel
Boston, MA
Promoter: in-house
Other act(s): The Fans (early), The Jackals, Damien Steel (late)

December 7
University of N.Y.
Alfred, NY

December 8
Riverboat
Rochester, NY

December 9
The Chance
Poughkeepsie, NY
Promoter: in-house
Other act(s): Kix

December 15
Casbah
Manchester, NH
Other act(s): Mirrors

December 16
My Father's Place
Roslyn, NY

December 17
J. Bee's Rock 3
Middletown, NY

December 18
Radio City
Scotia, NY

1984

January 25, 1984
E.U. Wurlitzer Music
Boston, MA
Notes:
- This was a Joe Pet drum clinic; however, the rest of the band were in attendance and performed a short set following the conclusion of Joe's demonstration.

January 27
Twilight Zone
New Haven, CT
Other act(s): Red Alert

January 28
Scotch 'n Sounds
Brockton, MA
Other act(s): Mike Viola Alliance

February 4
L'Amour
Brooklyn, NY

February 8
Annie's Saloon
Cincinnati, OH
Set list: Train Kept A Rollin' / King of Kings / 4 Guns West / Something Else / Crossfire / Bright Light Fright / The Mist is Rising / Red House / Break Song / Sweet Little Rock and Roller / Rockin' Train / Black Velvet Pants / Once a Rocker, Always a Rocker / Never Wanna Stop / Walk with Me Sally / Let the Music Do the Talking
Notes:
- An AUD recording circulates from this show.

February 9
McGuffy's
Dayton, OH
Other act(s): Illuzion

February 10
Harpo's
Detroit, MI

February 11
Tony's East
Toronto, ON, Canada

March 2
Penny Arcade
Rochester, NY

March 3
Gloversville, NY
Notes:
- MCA had a pressing plant in this town...

March 8
Mohawk Club

Shirley, MA

March 9
University of Southern Maine
Portland, ME
Other act(s): Ramones, David Johansen

March 10
Boston, MA
The Channel
Promoter: in-house
Other act(s): The Dream, The Citizens
Set list: Train Kept A Rollin' / Something Else / Bang A Gong / King of the Kings / 4 Guns West / Crossfire / Bright Light Fright / Break Song / The Mist is Rising / Red House / Sweet Little Rock 'N Roller / Rockin' Train / Black Velvet Pants / Once a Rocker, Always a Rocker / Never Wanna Stop / Let the Music Do the Talking
Notes:
- An AUD recording circulates from this show.

March 14 **NOON
Metro
Boston, MA
Other act(s): Til Tuesday
Notes:
- The WBCN 16th Birthday lunch

March 14 **EVENING
Blue Wall @ UMass
Amherst, MA

March 15
Roadhouse
Lynn, MA

March 16
Scotch 'n Sounds
Brockton, MA
Other act(s): New Man

March 23
Golden Bear
Huntington Beach, CA

March 24
Chuck Landis' Country Club
Reseda, CA
Promoter: in-house
Other act(s): Les Dudek, Changes

March 28
The Rodeo
La Jolla, CA
Set list: Train Kept A Rollin' / Something Else / 4 Guns West / Crossfire / King of the Kings / Bright Light Fright / Break Song / The Mist is Rising / Red House / Sweet Little Rock 'N Roller / Black Velvet Pants / Once a Rocker, Always a Rocker / Never Wanna Stop / Let the Music Do the Talking / No Substitute For Arrogance / Walk with Me Sally
Notes:
- An AUD recording circulates from this show.

March 29
Music Machine
West Los Angeles, CA
Other act(s): DC3

March 30
Keystone
Berkeley, CA
Promoter: in-house
Other act(s): Malice, Blind Illusion, Wizard

March 31
The Stone
San Francisco, CA
Promoter: in-house
Other act(s): Myth, Ambush

April 1
Keystone
Palo Alto, CA
Promoter: in-house
Other act(s): Hyts, Traveller
Notes:
- The final proper date in support of "Once A Rocker..."

April 28
Bayside Exposition Center
Boston, MA
Promoter: WBCN
Notes:
- The 1984 WBCN Rock 'N' Roll Expo '84 which ran over two days.

May 10 **AFTERNOON
Peabody High School
Peabody, MA
Notes:
- Final show with Joe Pet. Joey Kramer attends to become familiar with the band's set, in preparation for that night's show.

May 10 **EVENING
Hi-Lites
Leicester, MA
Notes:
- Joey Kramer simply fills in for the last three shows with Joe Pet having taken new paying opportunities...

May 11
Frolics
Salisbury Beach, MA
Notes:
- With Brad resuming his Project membership for the night, 60% of Aerosmith perform, 80% when Tyler joins the band for a few songs.
- An AUD recording circulates from this show.

May 12
Twilight Zone
New Haven, CT
Other act(s): Guardian
Set list: Train Kept A Rollin' / Something Else / 4 Guns West / Same Old Song and Dance / King of the Kings / Bright Light Fright / The Mist is Rising / Red House / Sweet Little Rock 'N Roller / I Ain't Got You / Rockin' Train / Black Velvet Pants / Once a Rocker, Always a Rocker / Never Wanna Stop / Let the Music Do the Talking
Notes:
- The final show of the initial lifespan of the Joe Perry Project due to the Aerosmith reunion. With the writing on the wall Mach and Danny had started working on a new project, the Wild Bunch, as soon as given the word that the end was nigh.
- An AUD recording circulates from this show.

(Cassettes... Superior packaging opportunities for the mid-1980s! Ask Mach?!)

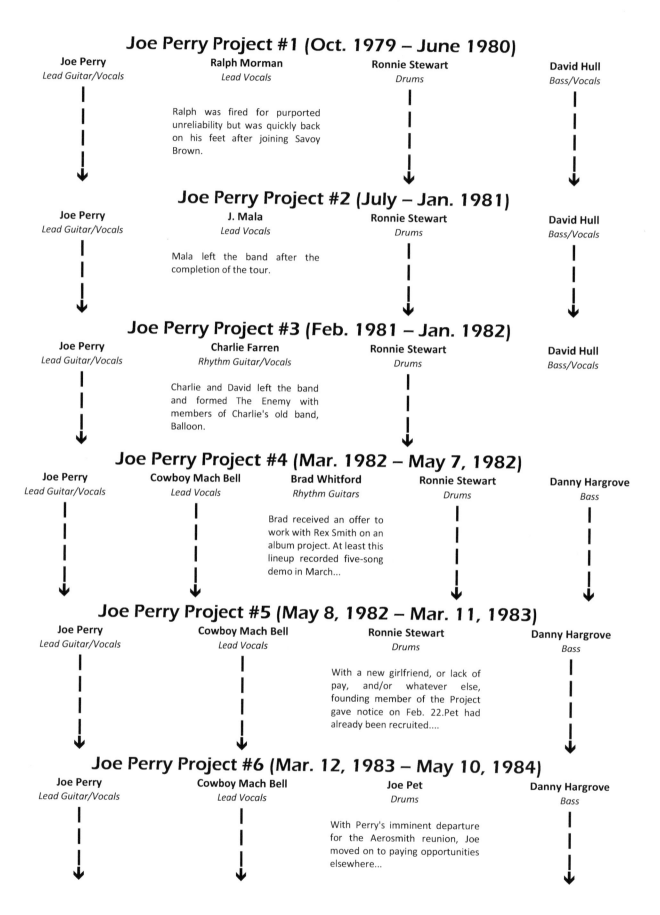

Joe Perry Project #7 (May 10–12, 1984)

Joe Perry
Lead Guitar/Vocals

Cowboy Mach Bell
Lead Vocals

Joey Kramer
Drums

Danny Hargrove
Bass

Cowboy and Danny start working on a new project, the Wild Bunch, before JPP ends. Kramer simply fills in for the last three shows...

Aerosmith #2 Again (May 1984 –)

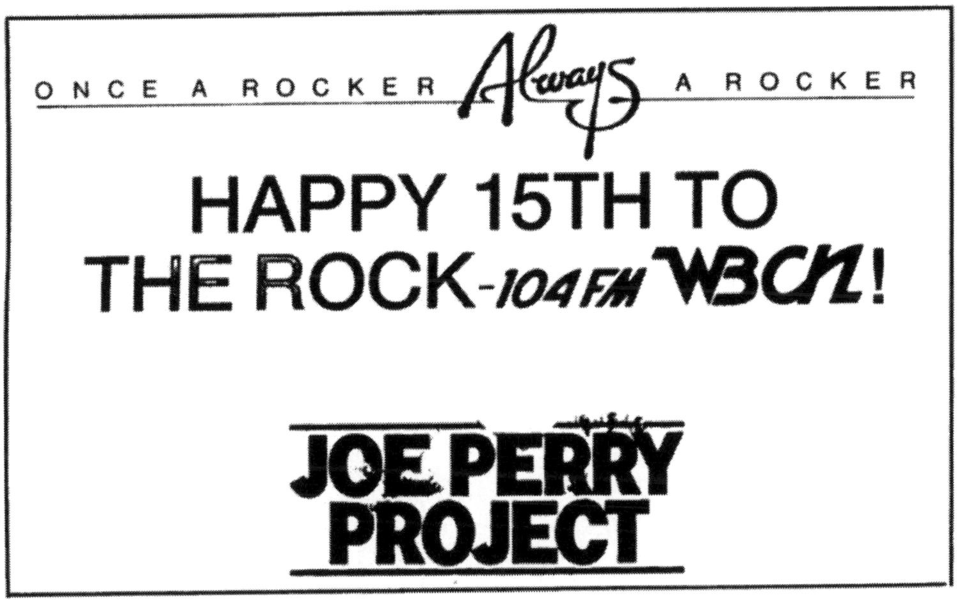

ONCE A ROCKER *Always* A ROCKER

HAPPY 15TH TO THE ROCK -104FM WBCN!

JOE PERRY PROJECT

520 | Aerosmith on Tour, 1973-85

1983 - Always a Rocker

1984 - Back in the Saddle

Steven Tyler: "We're the original. We're a from-the-heart rock 'n' roll band. We created a sound that was America's rock 'n' roll, America's Rolling Stones, America's whatever you want to call us. We play what the people want to hear. It was inevitable that we would get back together, and now we're ready to rock" (Chicago Tribune, 7/5/1984).

Perhaps it was inevitable that the MK. II version of Aerosmith would eventually reform, at least in terms of the band's personnel, if not in relation to their individual habits and behavior. The band members had never become estranged from each other past any point of no return. While there was certainly some sniping between Joe and Steven (and on occasion other band members) via the press, unlike their drugs habits, the level of bickering never spiraled out of control and ultimately that bitterness softened. The process of reformation was one built on cumulative baby steps, initially without any solid plan for a reunion. It was simply a matter of people who'd been in a band together for a decade reconnecting on a personal level. Band member paths also crossed on infrequent occasions; Steven and Brad had at least made an appearance at the debut show by the Project in Nov. 1979, though only Brad stayed for Joe's performance. Once Brad had also departed the band, even Jimmy, Tom, and Joey had started working on a side project, Renegade, as a proverbial night in the ruts for Aerosmith stretched into months of inactivity and stagnation. Not surprisingly, contact was sparse during the immediate aftermath of Joe's departure. The wounds from the fracture were all too fresh, and the interpersonal situation had been a festering mess for some time requiring a cooling off period. As Tom described it, "When Joe left, it wasn't a case of, 'OK, you guys, I'm leaving. See ya later.' Things within the band had gotten a little tense and it seemed best for him to leave. We all miss Joe Personally, but at the time it seemed best for him to do his thing" (Austin American-Statesman, 12/23/1982). There was more than enough dysfunction left within the band to deal with on the road and off. Both bands were also busy, with Aerosmith managing to finally complete "Night in the Ruts" and hit the road (sporadically) Nov. 1979–May 1980. Joe was equally focused on releasing his debut and hit the road with the project for most of 1980 to support it.

For Joe, two lead singers later, with his third working with him on the Project's second album, an unexpected reunion of sorts did take place... On February 28, 1981 he took to the stage with Cheap Trick during their set encores at the Boston Garden, for a performance of one of their regular closing songs, the Beatles' "Day Tripper." Minutes later Steven joined in for what was described as "a red-hot cover of the Stones' 'The Last Time'" (Boston Globe, 3/1/1981) and John Lennon's "Cold Turkey." Toxic twins musically in the same place at the same time, though not necessarily on the same wavelength... Neither apparently knew the other was there! Steven would be back on stage with Cheap Trick in 1982, for first of their two encores on August 27 at the Ritz in New York City. At that time, his condition was described in less than glowing terms in industry press: "Steve Tyler of Aerosmith joined Cheap Trick for the first of two encores, sharing vocal duties with Robin Zander on several numbers, including 'Day Tripper.' The Beatles tune brought out Rick Nielsen's best effort, played on a triangle guitar illustrated with the likenesses of the original fab four. The whole group seemed pleased as punch to share the stage with Tyler, a fellow protege of producer Jack Douglas. Unfortunately, Tyler on stage revealed only a faint glimmer of the great talent that sparks Aerosmith" (Billboard, 9/2/1982). In October, Steven Tyler and Rick Dufay visited with Joe backstage at his Bottom Line club appearance. It would be Steven's first interaction with Tim Collins with Tim giving Steven his phone number so that they could at least stay in touch. The lines of communication had at least been opened, if not always for the best.

The following month, Joe visited Aerosmith backstage at the second of their Centrum shows on November 16, and that interaction hadn't ended well for band or Joe. Even Brad was thankful to no longer be a part of the scene, despite the dire straits he was in financially. An additional visit, with the Project enjoying a night off nearby in Oakville, Ontario, allowed Joe to hang with the band backstage prior their show at Maple Leaf Gardens on Dec. 9. This time, a few drinks would be had, and Joe split before the band hit the stage. Getting the original members together at the same time and place took some doing, and there were hiccups along the way. One attempt took place New Year's Eve 1983/4, at the Centrum, following Aerosmith's latter part of 1983 hiatus. Unfortunately, when Steven mentioned that Joe and Brad might attend to local press, he hadn't told Joe, though also mentioned that he and Joe had been discussing getting back together for several months by that point. Joe commented, "It's absolutely not going to happen... Things didn't go so well. Steven didn't tell me they were going to record and videotape the show. I felt like I was going to get in the middle of something I had no control over. So, I said I was probably not going to do it, and that's how I left it" (Boston Herald, 12/31/1983). That Joey had been ill and replaced temporarily by Bobby Rondinelli also likely complicated matters, but at least Joe and Steven had continued talking in the background, even if other members of the band remained hesitant with the scars of past battles between the two and it took time for those members to come around to the idea.

Following their performance at the Orpheum in Boston, on February 14, 1984, Joe and Billie attended the band's after-show party at the Parker Hotel. While he hadn't been willing to watch Aerosmith perform, the social event was an opportunity for Joe to reconnect with people in Aerosmith's sphere in addition to seeing his former bandmates. This time, things went well between the participants and Joe left and was quickly reflecting on his situation: "The previous night's get-together had been nice, but I sensed that the animosity hadn't completely dissipated. Besides, Aerosmith was still being managed by Leber-Krebs, a situation I found intolerable... I was enjoying the freedom of being on my own and having a manager like Collins, who never pressured me to go back with Steven. Yet, I couldn't deny that it was good talking with Steven and the rest of the guys and enjoying the kind of rapport that we'd had in the early seventies" (Perry, Joe - "Rocks: My Life in and out of Aerosmith"). One thing that had changed were the significant others. In Steven's case, he was separated from Cyrinda, who was living in New Hampshire while he and new beau Teresa had become a solid couple. When introduced to Joe's new girlfriend, the pair actually got along. No Elyssa, no extraneous problems it seemed.

If Joe wasn't quite there yet, part of moving forward with Steven was laying the groundwork by properly introducing him to Tim Collins. The three met at Steven's hotel in New York City. If one takes Steven's word, then there's a multitude of factors that came into play for the reconstruction of Aerosmith. CBS had essentially cut Aerosmith off following the lackluster response to their album and wouldn't advance any further money until the band had some demos as proof of productivity and work. Having failed to recoup off an album that purportedly cost well over $1 million, they weren't in any rush to throw more money at a seemingly lost cause. And if it had been a struggle to get Steven writing for RIAHP, it was more difficult by late-1983. There were some riffs and ideas kicking around, notably "Written in Stone." They could barely tour either, to bring in revenue of note. Also important, for his inner muse, was the feeling he had on stage when performing with Rick Dufay and Jimmy Crespo. By his own admission, Crespo's similar stature and appearance to Joe's was a "fuck you" to him. That there was no question of Jimmy's chops or songwriting seems almost secondary. Jimmy was a pro and every bit qualified to that on that position in the band, as unenviable as it may have been. Jimmy was a talented guitarists and gifted songwriter, still when Steven was on stage and looking over towards his guitarist, it wasn't Joe there, nor was there the tension that had fueled so much of the band's creativity. And Wildman Rick, with his onstage antics, was diametrically polar opposite to the generally stolid Whitford, not that Steven much missed Brad. Steven's feelings about his original guitarists differed: "Brad won't be missed except I liked him; I liked the old squid. I miss Joe, too.

Somebody told them they could do it or maybe they told themselves that. Now I've heard Brad and Joe are playing local gigs together. It's a big shame they didn't get it together on a grander scale" (Pittsburgh Press, 11/24/1982). But even he couldn't deny that changes weren't impacting him. He later recalled, "We did alright. We still sold out concert halls. But sometimes — not very often, but sometimes — I could feel that the magic wasn't there, and I missed it. And when I would run into Joe and Brad, they didn't seem to be having too much fun, and it made me sad" (Chicago Tribune, 7/5/1984). Joey, perhaps, summarized the situation best: "Steven, Tom, and I tried to continue, and we really felt we were putting our best feet forward, recruiting as we did two guitar players. It wasn't until a little further down the road that I realized that it wasn't going to work. I enjoyed playing with Jimmy [Crespo]; he was a great guitar player. But it took a long time for it to dawn on me about the old pie syndrome: If you cut an apple pie into five slices, you can't take two out and replace them with two slices of blueberry pie. That's essentially what we tried to do, and it didn't work; it wasn't a whole pie. We really tried to make it work: Both Tom and I moved back to New York, we did a tour, and we did an album. But it just wasn't working" (Modern Drummer #105, 1988).

And those conflicting feelings possibly led Steven into a downward spiral trying to chemically compensate for that missing ingredient in his life. He recalled, "I went through a whole period of getting drunk and going to therapists to try and find out what was wrong. It took me more than three years to figure out that all I wanted to do was get out there and have the old magic back again" (Bangor Daily News, 8/4/1984). Unfortunately, he was in no state to bring the magic back. Steven's road has seen him bottoming out in mid-1983, leading to the cancellation of run of shows and his first real attempt at rehab which wrote of much of the second half of the year and left his bandmates twiddling their thumbs. The "Rock in a Hard Place" tour had started successfully enough in the arenas Aerosmith were accustomed to playing in, attended by the sorts of crowds to be expected after a lengthy layoff. Even in the face of an economic downturn, Aerosmith beat the odds, but all the odds don't stay in the gambler's favor for long and by mid-1983 venue sizes were shrinking in relation to attendances and the band was struggling to sell out theaters. The marquee value of seeing the band for the first time in several years quickly wore off for the ticket buying public, and Aerosmith had been superseded in the interim by a plethora of hot young bands with image appeal and musical dynamism. New album or not, they were dated and lumped in with other discarded acts who had enjoyed popularity in the 1970s. But if there was one catalyst that affected Steven, then it would be when word reached him that Joe was working with Alice Cooper. He was furious, offended, and the proverbial camel's back was snapped. If Joe's attempt to rediscover a level of success had had the passive-aggressive impact of causing Steven second thoughts about his own future, then Fortuna was indeed shining on all parties.

There seems to have been a continuing underlying frustration from Tom Hamilton. According to Joe, it was Tom who had blown up at him in the face of the Worcester fiasco in Nov. 1982, accusing him of harming the band and suggesting that it would be better for them all if he just stayed away (Perry, Joe - "Rocks: My Life in and out of Aerosmith"). Even though it was Cyrinda bringing the drugs that the toxic twins imbibed. The specter of Perry seemed to cast a long shadow... Tom recalled in mid-1984, "In the past couple of years we would be playing, and fans came up to us and say, 'Where's Joe Perry?' We understood the way they felt, but it was a little bit frustrating for us" (Rochester Democrat & Chronicle, 6/24/1984). It was almost a clear message that fans would never fully accept an Aerosmith with anything but the original lineup, even if those same fans continued to come to the shows. The spray-painted message on the wall of the Wherehouse in 1979 was proving understandably prophetic: "Come back Joe," indeed... The more lackadaisical Whitford had essentially dropped from the public eye in 1983. His issues and exit from the band had been far less complex than Joe's. Money and frustration of the situation had been the primary drivers. His problems had had names: "My main problem was with Joe and Stephen... It was insanity; there was no control whatsoever, with the two of them fighting all the time. When they resolved their problems, they resolved mine, too" (Detroit Free Press, 1/10/1985).

By early 1984, if Steven was concerned about "his" guitarist hooking up with Alice Cooper, then his guitarist was equally concerned about his own state of existence which drove the exploration of that possible collaboration. The Project was a drain on Perry, regardless of the performances and seemingly well-filled booking schedule. Another tour was lined up for late-January, but the band's recent album had bombed, and the efforts to keep touring were little more than an attempt to keep any money in to not drown under financial waterfall pouring down on him. The efforts required and weight of running a band was weighing him down, even with the benefit of Tim Collins' efforts as manager. It simply was the grind. Joe recalled, "I had a good time with the solo project. I enjoyed getting out and showing what I could do. But it was also really hard. The pressure was all on my shoulders" (Springfield Union, 1/4/1985). The constant pushing of WBCN cheerleader Mark Parenteau was critical in keeping alive the hope of getting Aerosmith back together. Mark was working on both Joe and Steven separately, primarily through Tim playing them off against one another and rebuilding a mutual appreciation society. Steven recalled, "Tim played the game all managers play — he'd tell me Joe was interested in getting the band back together, that he'd really missed playing with Aerosmith, blah-blah-blah, and they he'd go back to Joe and tell him I wanted more than anything to reunite the band, and that Joe was the essential element and without him, da-di-da-da-da — which was true, but it was all done through innuendo and manipulation" ("Does the Noise in My Head Bother You"). As Mark had purportedly told Tim, "You gotta put this band together. It's your mission from God" ("Walk This Way").

Cash flow had also dried up for the other members of Aerosmith as the band's fortunes declined. Both Tom and Joey had downsized their lifestyles, but the pressures remained and while Steven benefitted more as primary songwriter, even he faced challenges. But, according to Jimmy, he was burned out by the dysfunction within the band, and inability to get Steven to work on any musical ideas. When informed by David Krebs, Jimmy simply thought that it made sense given his awareness of the situation the band were in to bring the label back on side. Rick hadn't cared, he had his own things he wanted to do musically and saw that there simply wasn't that special connection within the band that there had once been. He pushed Steven, Tom, and Joey to get into the room with Joe to work things out. The guys in the Project seem to have been blissfully aware if anything was going on in the background in December 1983/January 1984. The private meeting announcement on Feb. 16 that Joe wanted to go back to Aerosmith took the Project members by surprise. Joe was simply out of options and only had that one gamble left to make. The same applied to the other band members. A reunion may have been nice from the perspective of going back to what had felt good in the past, but they were all drowning in money issues. Resurrecting Aerosmith was never going to be an easy proposition, and there was absolutely no guarantee that the effort was going to be successful. Like the steps that had gotten the band members back in the same room with a plan to get back in the saddle, the condition of the horse was if not questionable then unknown. Did that once proud thoroughbred have race wins in front of her, or did the glue factory await? Reunification wasn't a process that would be immediately completed, it too would be a project several years in the making; and then long afterwards an ongoing and uneasy process. The battles fought had left scars, both visible and some not, and with so much of the focus on Joe and Steven some wounds were not dealt with, acknowledged, or even known.

How viable the band was needed to be determined when the band reconvened at Tom's house and voted on reforming. Joe had one condition: No Leber-Krebs. They had, in his view, screwed him — and he'd end up suing to recoup unpaid back royalties they'd allegedly withheld from him, ultimately being awarded $192,270.58. Collins seems to have stayed in place mainly due to there being no other immediately obvious choice that any of the others could suggest as a replacement for him. Other than Joe Perry still being alive and having released one album, Tim hadn't exactly worked wonders for the Project who had continued to tour small scale venues mainly by road. But being his own boss had taught Joe one thing in particular: By putting so much of their business, both musical and personal, in the hands of Leber-Krebs and accountants — and not paying attention to the details and decisions themselves — they had lost any sense of reality, direction and control. And having ended up owing money to his management, it wasn't a situation he wanted to repeat. Joe was also adamant about how the band had to be: "We really had to redefine it all... It really resembled how it was when the band first got together. Everybody had a say. I was not going to let the band get back together if we were going to have the same old (problems) around. It was going to be like '72" (Orange County Register, 7/29/1993). Steven would ultimately realize that as large as Leber-Krebs had become that he felt that they were too busy to focus on the band and that they needed a new style of management. As the details for a reunion were finalized the Project finished up their scheduled dates, playing their final show of the tour at the Keystone in Palo Alto on April 1, though the agreement for Aerosmith to reconvene wasn't sealed until mid-April. Not that rumors hadn't already started circulating. However, the Project still played sporadic shows throughout New England through May 12, with Joey

Kramer playing drums at the final three dates. Joe didn't sound particularly upset about the demise of the Project. He'd later comment, "I had gotten my rocks off... I've always considered myself a songwriter and a guitar player, and I had a lot of stuff that I wanted to get off my chest, and I really enjoyed being the boss of my own project. But, as you can probably see by the turnover of members in my bands, there was a lot of talent, but the personalities didn't click. And the last Project was more a get-along-with-the-guys than the talent. So that's when I broke the Project up and I figured I'd try doing a little journeyman work — write with this one, work with that one, play on this one's album. In fact, I started to work with Alice Cooper, but that the same time, the calls (between Joe and Steve) were more frequent. Like, the blood was drying" (Creem, June 1986)

Crespo hit the road with Adam Bomb with a lineup that also included former members of Billy Idol's band (David Feit) and Riot (Sandy Slavin). The band was assembled by David Krebs around the young and talented Adam Brenner. They'd release their debut, "Fatal Attraction," via Geffen in May 1985, though starting at ground zero with a band was a bit of a shock to the system after being in an established act such as Aerosmith or having done the frustrating but exciting build work with Flame the previous decade. Dufay packed his bags and headed for London. He had a very strong sense of self and was comfortable with his musical identity. While things wouldn't work out for most of the decade, he'd return to the U.S. in 1989 and work with 1994's immensely talented vocalist, Karen Lawrence, before again doing his own thing. From the Project, drummer Joe Pet was a working musician and was in demand, quickly finding a new gig. Cowboy and Danny Hargrove had already started working on new ideas, which would become the Wild Bunch. Tim initially backed them and paid for a demo session and hooked them up with a booking agent. They'd slog for the next two years through many of the same venues they'd been performing at as members of the Project.

There were many factors that needed to be addressed before any Aerosmith reunion could take place. But from the highest level, it was simply a matter of success and by 1982 the fortunes of Aerosmith, collectively, and Joe Perry and Brad Whitford, individually, had declined to the point where some sort of drastic action was required. There was still a plethora of issues — interpersonal, personal, dynamic, and emotional — and the substance abuse. None of these could be fixed with one of "Dr. Nickadick's Magic Wishing Pills," and perhaps the larger issue was one of perception. By the early 1980s, bands like Aerosmith were seen as dinosaurs, past their sell-by-date by several years at least and laughing stocks for the drama and tabloid fodder which was often attached to their names. Collapsing on stage and cancelling concerts and tours were poor optics. It was a massive chasm from which to attempt to extricate themselves from. The plan was simple: The band had to prove to the concert bookers, industry, and themselves that they actually could go on tour, perform, and not die in the process. Secondary to survivability was that there would be enough of a paying audience interested enough to go and see the band. According to Perry, this is part of a plan to use the tour as both a proving ground for the reformed lineup and a way to spark revived interest in the group. Joe: "We want to get a groundswell going first... This is obviously not a major promotional tour; we're not even going west of the Mississippi" (Billboard, 6/23/1984).

Playing would, according to Brad prove the point about fan interest: "We figured the best way to find out how popular we were was to go out and start playing and see if we can turn heads still, find out if there's any interest out there... We've been surprised, absolutely; blown away was more like it" (Detroit Free Press, 1/10/1985). Playing a cat and mouse game with Leber-Krebs to protect box office receipts, the band had to build up a fund from which to start extricating themselves from their debt loads; and fight their former managers so that they could separate from the past and move forward. That process wouldn't be cheap, but they did manage to stay one step ahead of the debt collectors or process servers. Stripping off the levels of complexity that they'd slipped into over the natural course of their career, they were a streamlined and hungry operation. According to Joe, that mantra also slipped into the band's music: "Everything is back to basics now. We're here to entertain and give people the Aerosmith sound they want to hear. What excites me the most right now is that there's a whole new generation of kids out there who have heard the name, but they haven't heard the music" (Bangor Daily News, 8/4/1984). Prophetic words indeed, nearly five years after his departure, Aerosmith was finally going to let the music do the talking. But it wasn't easy, and the band's continuing partying ways nearly led to the tour being derailed during the first two-and-a-half-month leg.

Rehearsals for the tour started the day after the final Project show. Where the band had initially taken over a function room at the Glen Ellen Country Club for musical refamiliarization sessions, the soon moved to the Marquee Theater in Brockton for the more structured musical rehearsals. An important character entered the band's sphere at this time, before a single show had successfully been executed: Geffen's A&R guru, John Kalodner, flew into Boston to see the band. Even at that point, the band were looking further down the road and listening to the advice of what would be required to get labels and fans interested in them once again. As the musical landscape had shifted, Kalodner was a critical resource, particularly at a time when the band needed guidance from an industry guru for a new generation. John Kalodner: "It all comes down to the coolness factor. It's very hip to go see Aerosmith. I saw eight or nine dates on the tour, and it was all young kids there, and they knew the songs" (Billboard, 5/25/1985). And for Kalodner, music was all about the kids, the final A&R arbitrators, and their opinions and tastes, which he felt were more valuable than radio or statistics. "I only go by what kids talk about and feel," he told Billboard, "I don't think you can go by radio people and their trends. Art has to be made more with the kids in mind than with the media which delivers it" (Billboard, 5/25/1985). As a A&R executive, John felt that it was critical to be deeply involved in all aspects of an artist's creative career, even down to who the band would be touring with. Most importantly, John had a finger on the pulse of the youth and a rapport with them engendered in part by his manner and appearance, resulting in him being able to mine them for a trove of critical data to be if not exploited, then leveraged by his acts. Later he'd impressed by Aerosmith's ticket sales on the tour without benefit of an album.

The set list didn't change substantially from that performed at the last Crespo/Dufay Aerosmith show. A core of thirteen classics, were buttressed with additional songs such as "Bone to Bone" (recorded by both Aerosmith and the Project, "Rocks" powerhouses "Last Child" and "Get the Lead Out," and "Same Old Song and Dance." More surprising was the inclusion of "Lightning Strikes" and Perry favorite vocal spot "Red House" which also gave Brad an opportunity for soloing in the spotlight. Positively effusive reviews followed the band's first public performance at the Capitol Theater in Concord, NH, where the "Rock in a Hard Place" tour had kicked off 18 months earlier. A few days later the band hit the road for the "Back in the Saddle" tour with Orion the Hunter as opener. As the greatest hits blasted from the PA with a sonic reminder of the legendary power of the band, the "Greatest Hits" album benefitted from the new exposure. By mid-1984 the steady seller had been on Billboard's "Mid-Line Album" chart for over a year (it would remain firmly planted on that chart in 1985) but jumped to near the top of that chart. Columbia may have been cut out of the picture, but they still controlled the back-catalogue and leveraged the band's heightened exposure with their "Right Price" reissue campaign — which quickly resulted "Rocks" being certified 2x Platinum by the RIAA on October 19. The press, of course, was more concerned with the "would they" or "wouldn't they implode?" question that surrounded the effort.

The band hadn't magically cleaned up, and that was apparent for all to see at the band's July 14 show in Springfield, IL. Reportedly, Steve stumbled and fell off the stage after forgetting the lyrics to several songs, singing just two of the six songs performed. After scrambling back onstage there was an angry exchange with other band members resulting in the whole band leaving the stage after just 30-minutes. A publicist for the band suggested that he was simply sick, battling a case of the flu, and hadn't wanted to disappoint fans. According to press reports, "Tyler, 36, appeared intoxicated before he stumbled off the stage. Tyler, who was not injured in the fall, then got involved in a scuffle with fellow band members when he returned to the stage. After the remaining portion of the concert was cancelled, about 2,000 angry fans gathered outside of the convention hall" (UPI via Streator Times, 7/19/1984). When the promoter was unable to offer patrons refunds, or reschedule the show, a deal was worked out where fans could trade in their stubs for copies of the "Aerosmith's Greatest Hits" album. The records arrived at the PCCC in late August for distribution. For management and band, it was clear that there work to be done if the band were to truly become viable again. And work was certainly done during the downtime that kept the band off the road, September through early December.

Black 'N Blue drummer Pete Holmes provides the perfect external description of Aerosmith during the two legs of the tour: "We're playing with Aerosmith. So, to get to meet our childhood heroes was really something, but there was something off kilter. Everybody's really pretty nice, but Steven Tyler was a fucking prick — he was just a fucking asshole. Nobody could figure out, 'what the fuck?' All the other guys were super nice. They all had their separate dressing rooms, nobody talked to each other, [and] you never saw them hanging out. I mean a lot of bands have separate dressing rooms, but this was just evident that none of these guys liked each other. They were just getting fucked up. Tyler couldn't remember the songs let alone how to get to the fucking stage, the 120x50' stage... He couldn't figure out where that was, with all the lights and sound on it, 'God knows where that fucking thing went.' He would just blow it every night... For the most part it was just an embarrassment, but you know people loved it... We did about two months of that and then Geffen said, 'look these guys are a fucking joke. This is ridiculous, we're pulling you off.' So, they pulled them off the road. They pulled us off the road... Two months felt later we resumed, and the guys were totally straight, and they were fucking great! I mean Stephen Tyler was like a different guy... They all came back and were super cool" (Full in Bloom Podcast, 2018).

For the second leg, the set list was shaken up with more of the catalogue being represent through songs such as "S.O.S. (Too Bad)," "Movin' Out," "Adam's Apple," and "Seasons of Wither." The band also showed upstarts RATT how to do "Walkin' the Dog" the Aero-way. Most notable was the decision to bring "Let the Music Do the Talking" into the set. The song had yet to be rewritten to Steven became the fifth vocalist to sing it the way Joe wrote it. Brad expressed the newfound camaraderie: "We're having a great time, really enjoying it. It's like a fraternity. We're all in good shape now, so we can deal with everything better; touring, for instance, used to just be a test of 'How can I screw up my body now.' I think we've matured a bit, grown up. We'll have plenty of time to do what we want" (Detroit Free Press, 1/10/1985). It didn't mean there weren't problems or challenges, but perhaps the parties were simply better equipped to deal with some of them. And like night and day the second tour contributed to the rehabilitation of the band's image. By the time the tour ended in late-January, Aerosmith were closing in on the new record deal they needed, and ideas had started to be generated for a new foray into the studio. CBS released the "Metalmania" compilation in February, which included "Dream On" and the somewhat cynical selection of Joe Perry's "Let the Music Do the Talking." By that time, Aerosmith had signed a three-record deal, with Geffen having been victorious in a bidding war against Arista, and were ready to hit the studio for the next chapter in their story...

May 1984 **REHEARSALS
Glen Ellen Country Club
Millis, MA
Notes:
- Country club owner's son Michael J. Striar's had ties to Joe Perry, having financially backed him to the tune of $70,000 for the recording of "Once A Rocker" in 1983. The band conducted their initial rehearsals in one of the club's function rooms, nearly immediately following the final Project show on May 12, just getting to know one another musically again. The band were interviewed by the Boston Globe's Steve Morse at the club's 19th hole on June 1. Steven was clear in his thoughts about the reunion, "On our last tour the ticket sales went well, but the magic wasn't there. I can't put my finger on it, but when I look at Joe play now in rehearsals, I just get a feeling I haven't had in a while... I want to stress that they [Crespo & Dufay] weren't ousted because the sound was no good, but we just felt it was time to get the old band together" (Boston Globe, 6/2/1984). This sentiment would provide a recurring theme for interviews during the tour.

May / June **REHEARSALS
Marquee Theater
Brockton, MA
Notes:
- Even at this early stage, Geffen's A&R guru, John Kalodner, was already in the picture. He flew into Boston in May to see the band rehearse ("Walk this Way").

June **REHEARSALS
Cape Cod Coliseum
South Yarmouth, MA
Notes:
- As the band got Back in the Saddle, and the reunion was announced, their rehearsals scaled up accordingly. Stage rehearsals were conducted in Brockton while full production rehearsals were conducted at the Coliseum.

June 22
Capitol Theater
Concord, NH
Promoter: TFI Entertainment
Reported audience: (1,304 capacity)
Set list: Back in the Saddle / Mama Kin / Bone to Bone / Big Ten Inch Record / Three Mile Smile / Reefer Head Woman / Lord of the Thighs / No More No More / Last Child / Get the Lead Out / Red House / Lightning Strikes / Same Old Song and Dance / Dream On / Sweet Emotion / Walk this Way / Milk Cow Blues / Toys in the Attic / Train Kept A Rollin'
Notes:
- The initial 30-date tour featuring the reunited lineup was a viability test for the band and, in turn, it was hoped it would provide a spark that reignited interest in them. According to Joe Perry, "We want to get a groundswell going first... This is obviously not a major promotional tour; we're not even going west of the Mississippi" (Billboard, 6/23/1984). There were even plans for the band to film a video early during the tour, to get a song into rotation on MTV and other video channels.
- From a local review: "In their first gig since lead guitarist Joe Perry and rhythm guitarist Brad Whitford returned after a five-year absence, Aerosmith shook the rafters of the intimate, 1,300-seat Capitol Theater with a thunderous assault. Rather than having the stink of an over-the-hill gang slobbering through a mortgage concert, it had the sharp tang of a band going back to its steely, acid-blues roots with renewed commitment and drive. Both returning guitarists, Perry and Whitford, showed dramatic improvement from the old '70s days when Aerosmith cut a loud, snotty swath through stadiums around the country. Perry has perfected his traditional R & B/blues-based style and become more of an architect of guitar feedback than a coarse trench-digger. Whitford, meanwhile, is more authoritative and has added some smart experimental

touches to his rhythm work... Singer Steve Tyler, wearing a cutaway body suit of stitched-together T-shirts bearing the Aerosmith logo (a welcome-back theme created by Boston costume designer Francine Larnis), was his cocky, strutting self, booming out a blade-edged cross-section of tunes from all the band's albums.

Old favorites such as 'Back in the Saddle' and 'Reefer-Headed Woman' were bolstered by resurrected versions of 'Bone to Bone (Coney Island Whitefish Boy),' 'No More No More' (with Whitford added a striking third vocal harmony), 'Last Child,' 'Get the Lead Out' and a cosmic treatment of Jimi Hendrix' 'Red House,' in which Perry unleashed a torrent of brain-shredding bent notes and crashing transitions. The rhythm team of bassist Tom Hamilton and drummer Joey Kramer also played like men possessed, creating a throbbing wall of sound. With an excellent sound mix provided by a character named Night Bob (who also is returning to the band since the early days), Aerosmith climaxed their triumphant return with over-the-top slices of 'Lightning Strikes' (as the house lights were flipped on and off to simulate lightning), 'Dream On,' 'Sweet Emotion' and a crunching encore of 'Train Kept-a-Rollin'.' The band was clearly ready for the gig... it added up to a unanimous get-lost gesture to the cynics who've said they're washed up" (Boston Globe, 6/25/1984).
- An AUD recording circulates from this show.

June 23
Capitol Theater
Concord, NH
Promoter: TFI Entertainment
Reported audience: (1,304 capacity)
Notes:
- Tim Collins recalled: "That tour was pure guerrilla warfare. The band was still signed to Columbia, but no one at Columbia would speak to us. They would only speak to Leber-Krebs, who had a production contract for, like, seven more records. So, we just said, 'Fuck them. We're going to go on the road and get out of this contract'" (Rolling Stone #575). To protect the box office receipts from creditor's efforts to attach them, bogus corporation names would be created for each show. Aerosmith were desperate for money.

June 27
Cayuga County Fair Speedway
Weedsport, NY
Promoter: in-house
Other act(s): Orion the Hunter
Reported audience: (12,000 capacity)
Notes:
- Orion the Hunter included former Boston guitarist Barry Goudreau and Heart's Mike DeRosier, with Fran Cosmo and Bruce Smith.

June 28
Performing Arts Center
Saratoga Springs, NY
Promoter: in-house
Other act(s): Orion the Hunter
Reported audience: ~11,400 / 25,000 (45.6%)
Set list: Same as June 22
Notes:
- From a local review: "Aerosmith — once America's hard-rock heroes — made a moderately convincing comeback at SPAC last night... Their signature rang out loudly with 'Back in the Saddle Again' the claim behind the whole tour. Their thud-in-the-mud rhythm section bashed a slow to mid-temp blues shuffle under a snarl of linked-up guitars, and the high screams of Steve Tyler's vocals. Perry had described Aerosmith's music as 'very hard rock,' as distinct from heavy metal, 'with some finesse and some

class.' Little of either showed itself early, when out-of-focus sound mixing blurred the band into a dull, treble haze. The group sharpened up mid-set with some fairly authentic-sounding blues, derived from the Stones' model and fired by Perry's guitar. As a greatest hits performance, the concert more than satisfied Aerosmith fans, though their recording future remains unclear" (Schenectady Gazette, 6/29/1984).
- A below average AUD recording circulates from this show.

June 30
War Memorial
Rochester, NY
Promoter: John Scher
Other act(s): Orion the Hunter
Reported audience: 10,200 **SOLD-OUT
Reported gross: $115,821
Set list: Same as June 22
Notes:
- An average AUD recording circulates from this show.

July 2
Merriweather Post Pavilion
Columbia, MD
Promoter: in-house
Other act(s): Orion the Hunter
Reported audience: (14,000 capacity)
Set list: Same as June 22
Notes:
- From a local review: "It was 'The Same Old Song and Dance' for Aerosmith at Merriweather Post Pavilion Monday night. Together again for the first time since 1979, the original five members showed the same controlled delirium that propelled them to the top of the charts during the 1970s... The sizable audience was equally enthusiastic about the old tunes... The band always had a particular flair for the blues, and Mr. Tyler's fine harp playing has lost none of its bite. Likewise, Aerosmith has retained its unique stage presence. Call it self-consciously unselfconscious. The band wanders at will around the stage, often with backs turned to the audience. Mr. Tyler spits when he feels the urge. The one gimmick employed ad infinitum is giveaways. Drumsticks, hats, harps, vests — all are tossed out to the teeming throngs. Those hundreds standing in the rain at the rear caught no souvenirs, but they did get a chance to see the latest reincarnation of a durable rock institution" (Washington Times, 7/5/1984).
- An AUD recording circulates from this.

July 3
City Island
Harrisburg, PA
Promoter: Makoul Productions
Other act(s): Kix
Reported audience: (14,000 capacity)
Set list: Same as June 22
Notes:
- This outdoor concert venue had hosted shows with as many as 21,000 attendees (Grateful Dead). However, the capacity quoted is based on tickets made available for the Scorpions show on Aug. 25.
- An AUD recording circulates from this show.

July 5
Orange County Fairgrounds Speedway
Middletown, NY

Promoter: Glenn Donnelly
Other act(s): Orion the Hunter
Reported audience: (15,000 capacity)
Set list: Same as June 22
Notes:
- An AUD recording circulates from this stormy night show.

July 6
Scope
Norfolk, VA

Promoter: Whisper Concerts
Other act(s): Orion the Hunter
Reported audience: (13,800 capacity)
Set list: Same as June 22
Notes:
- From a local review: "Attending a rock concert at Scope can be a nerve-shattering experience. Besides the wretched acoustics, which transform musical notes into hellish noise, there's that omnipresent danger of having your head bashed in by something hurled your way. Or launched. At the Aerosmith concert Friday night, foot-long rockets (the real thing, left over from July 4,), [and] hundreds of firecrackers and assorted other bric-a-brac were among the objects that zoomed through the air... Which was somewhat grotesque, considering that the band's lead singer, Steven Tyler, had been severely injured when an M-80, hurled by a lunatic fan, exploded in his face during a concert on the group's last tour. Perhaps that was a grim sign that the band should call it quits. But the show, as they say, must go on. Unfortunately, in Aerosmith's case it is a dismal show. It wasn't simply that Aerosmith was lousy Friday night. Rather, the group was so bad the musicians seemed pathetic, even comical.

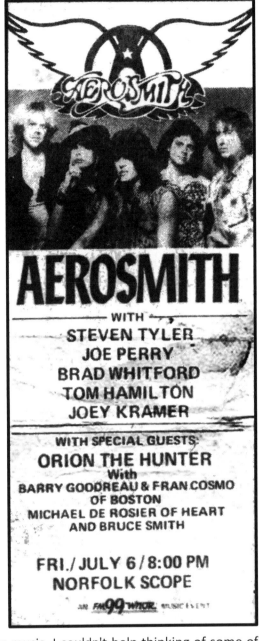

Watching Tyler and led guitarist Joe Perry lamely leap about on stage in their goony getups (Tyler in a flame-red kimono and hat) as the band churned out witless, repetitious, mind-numbing music, I couldn't help thinking of some of the comic book weirdos Spiderman used to encounter. Of course, Aerosmith is anything but funny to most of the group's fans, who screamed, roared, and held cigarette lighters aloft throughout the show. They were charmed by the band's rhythm section, powered by Brad Whitford (guitar) and Joey Kramer (drums), who nailed down the tempo with all the subtlety of a bunch of jackhammers and pneumatic drills. Nor did anyone appear even slightly upset that the lyrics were completely unintelligible. Such aesthetic considerations are trifling matters for Aerosmith fans. No, the fans, mostly teenagers, seemed intent on being part of a mass, a primal rite. The blood-curdling screams, the hypnotic rhythms, the sledgehammer attack — the more deafening the noise, the better" (Norfolk Daily Press, 7/9/1984).
- An incomplete AUD recording circulates from this show. It's missing the songs following Joey's drum solo.

July 8
Civic Center
Erie, PA

Promoter: Magic City Productions
Other act(s): Orion the Hunter
Reported audience: (7,300 reserved capacity)
Set list: Same as June 22

Notes:
- A below average AUD recording circulates from this show.

July 9
Kingswood Music Theatre
Vaughan, ON, Canada
Promoter: Nederlander and Associates
Reported audience: ~11,000 / 15,000 (73.33%)
Set list: Same as June 22
Notes:
- Tim Collins claimed in trade publications that $60,000 worth of tickets had been sold for this show in just two days without the benefit of any advertising (Billboard, 6/23/1984).
- From a local review: "Aerosmith is drawing near sell-out crowds on its current Back in the Saddle Tour. The song, which the band used to kick off its concert on Monday night at Kingswood Theatre, was from that 1976 album, Rocks. And given the attitude with which singer Steven Tyler, guitar hero Joe Perry and the rest of the crew took to their task, it was like going back to square one. Tyler, looking more than ever like Carly Simon from hell, was wearing his familiar second-hand dandy's rag-tag outfit: tailcoat, red fedora, legwarmers, tight black jeans and bits of scarves and dangling rags hanging from his legs. He spun, he screamed, he carried his microphone stand like a cross, and dangled a cigaret from his lips, which still look as though they've been on a course of steroids. The audience of about 11,000, mostly in its teens and early 20s, mostly male and long-haired, was easily the most vocal, combative, and rowdy that has come to any show all summer. These people loved everything and were standing on their seats from song one. This was living proof that no form of rock and roll ever dies; it just lies dormant for a while until the right record company overturns the rock it's lying under.

There's a definite pleasure in Aerosmith's sub-Rolling Stones, basic bash-it-out, slovenly, sexy, and stupid racket. And there are even a few songs, 'Dream On,' 'Sweet Emotion,' and 'Walk this Way,' which the whole crowd seemed to know well enough to sing along. The band is still among the loudest anywhere, but the music has little to do with the excesses of modern heavy metal. Joe Perry, a Jeff Beck stylist if ever there was one, was relatively subdued on Monday night, offering brief flashy solos only when required. Brad Whitford dominated on the more rocky, simple boogie numbers, which are the band's stock in trade. Essentially, though, it was Tyler's show, with the exception of a grandly staged drum solo by Joey Kramer, which was reasonably tasteful as drum solos go. But taste isn't the point. This isn't music for the heart, soul, or brain. As George Clinton said of funk, this music is purely cathartic, a kind of prune juice of the mind. It may not be pretty or fashionable, and it may not be for you, but it does the job" (Toronto Globe & Mail, 7/10/1984).
- An AUD recording circulates from this show.

July 11
Pine Knob Music Theater
Clarkston (Detroit), MI
Promoter: Pine Knob Music Corp.
Other act(s): Orion the Hunter
Reported audience: 15,775 / 15,920 (99.09%)
Notes:
- Two security guards were bitten by fans during the show...

July 12
Poplar Creek Music Theater
Hoffman Estates, IL
Promoter: in-house
Other act(s): Orion the Hunter

Reported audience: (12,000 capacity)
Set list: Back in the Saddle / Mama Kin / Bone to Bone / Big Ten Inch Record / Three Mile Smile / Reefer Head Woman / Lord of the Thighs / Last Child / Get the Lead Out / Lick and a Promise / Red House / Lightning Strikes / Same Old Song and Dance / Dream On / Sweet Emotion / Walk this Way / Milk Cow Blues / Toys in the Attic / Train Kept A Rollin'
Notes:
- An AUD recording circulates from this show.

July 14
Prairie Capital Convention Center
Springfield, IL
Promoter: Jam Productions
Other act(s): Orion the Hunter
Reported audience: ~6,200 / 8,000 (77.5%)
Notes:
- From a local review: "As soon as the concert began, Tyler began running around, bumping into things, sliding down his microphone stand to the floor and taking his socks off... Tyler also reportedly fell into a guitarist, slumped on amplifiers and knocked over an electric fan, almost sending it into the audience... Tyler's behavior didn't go over with the audience. It didn't go over with other band members, either. Members of the audience watched the bass guitarist knock Tyler down and exchange angry words and gestures. At one point, two band members used their guitars to pin Tyler to the stage. Stage workers then sat Tyler in a corner near the drums. When he got up, he fell into the barricade between the stage and the audience. While stage workers hauled Tyler off stage, the band played furiously in what turned out to be its final song" (State Journal-Register, 7/17/1984).

July 15
MetroCentre
Rockford, IL
Promoter: Contemporary / Pace Presentations
Other act(s): Orion the Hunter
Reported audience: (10,000 capacity)
Notes:
- The venue made a profit of $11,190 on this event.

July 17
Coliseum
Richfield, OH
Promoter: Belkin Productions
Other act(s): Orion the Hunter
Reported audience: ~8,000 / 10,200 (78.43%)
Notes:
- Geffen's John Kalodner attended this show to watch the band perform.

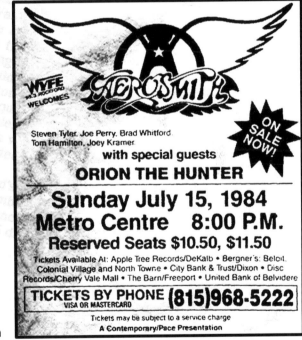

- From a local review: "Something like a miracle happened at Richfield Coliseum Tuesday night. Aerosmith, made up of hard rockers from Boston and one of the most popular bands of the mid-70s, played the kind of show they should have done in their heyday. And they were magnificent. This concert was a complete surprise... The group had run down to a point where it was embarrassing and had begun to lose its following. It seemed like a group of bad luck Charlies with show cancellations, accidents and allegedly too many ego problems and too much indulgence in the perks of the rock 'n' roll lifestyle. But the Coliseum theater was nearly full... The show itself was the real shocker... Aerosmith was funky, spirited, gutsy, [and] loose. Tyler has never seemed more comfortable on stage. He actually came to the edge of the stage at one point, handed his cup into the crowd, [and] shook a few hands. He didn't seem like the singer who once tried to keep his physical distance.

It's hard to believe that this group's members once tried to ignore each other on stage. There was constant movement and interplay between group members, lots of whispering and joking. Bassist Tom Hamilton, in particular, looked like he was having the time of his life. Besides showing some real enthusiasm, the group played a strong and satisfying program of its classic tunes... All were rendered with style and sometimes humor, as well as with Tyler's patented raunchiness... Tyler's sexual posing lacks the infantile meanness of Mötley Crüe's prattling. Guitarists Joe Perry and Brad Whitford, who have been working with their own groups, were better than ever now that they're back to playing decent material, and drummer Joey Kramer gave the band real muscle. It's odd to see a band with players in their mid-30s display the kind of rock 'n' roll power they never mustered while young. If the group still has some good tunes in it, it might have a second career waiting, and better than the first" (Plain Dealer, 7/19/1984).

July 18
Hara Arena
Dayton, OH
Promoter: Jam Productions
Other act(s): Orion the Hunter
Reported audience: (8,000 capacity)

July 20
Wendler Arena
Saginaw, MI
Promoter: Brass Ring Productions
Other act(s): Orion the Hunter
Reported audience: (7,200 capacity)

July 21
Castle Farms Music Theater
Charlevoix, MI
Promoter: Charlevoix Productions
Other act(s): Orion the Hunter
Reported audience: 7,546 /15,000 (50.31%)
Reported gross: $94,476
Set list: Back in the Saddle / Mama Kin / Bone to Bone / Big Ten Inch Record / Three Mile Smile / Reefer Head Woman / Lord of the Thighs / Last Child / Get the Lead Out / Lick and a Promise / Red House / Lightning Strikes / Same Old Song and Dance / Dream On / Sweet Emotion / Walk this Way / Milk Cow Blues / Toys in the Attic / Train Kept A Rollin'
Notes:
- An AUD recording circulates from this show. It's likely missing the final song.

July 23
Sports Arena
Toledo, OH
Promoter: Cellar Door Productions
Other act(s): Orion the Hunter
Reported audience: (7,500 capacity)
Set list: Same as July 21
Notes:
- From a local review: "As Aerosmith thundered onto the stage last night singing 'Back in the Saddle,' the regrouped band quickly proved it's not just an over-the-hill gang playing limp renditions of its former hits — some dating back a decade. Before a near sellout crowd at the Toledo Sports Arena. Aerosmith — the one-time king of the hard rock heap — showed how it can still muster that drive and commitment which was

once its trademark during the mid-70s... While Toledoans attending last night's concert had every right to be apprehensive, there was no sign of bickering or ill-will among band members. In fact, Perry and Tyler appeared more like two kids on the block who have been chums for years. Perry frequently toted his guitar over to Tyler's Side and helped him scream out a portion of the chorus. Despite all the uncertainties before the show, Aerosmith drew a crowd much larger than last month's Scorpions show at the Sports Arena. That's mindboggling because the Scorpions are one of the hotter hard rock offerings available today. The large crowd shrugged off the oppressive heat and greeted Aerosmith with an emotional charge that was reminiscent of the band's days of hard rock dominance.

But the trip down memory lane could become tiresome awfully quick, and it would behoove Aerosmith to use that renewed vivacity on stage and transform it onto vinyl. It would be the original band's first album in six years. Tyler's cocky stage antics and Perry's searing lead guitar made them the show's focal point. Of course, Tyler came equipped with his trademark colorful streamers dangling from his microphone stand as he strutted about the stage in Mick Jagger-like fashion. The band obviously had rehearsed diligently for this brief tour. At times, particularly during 'Walk this Way' and 'Lord of The Thighs,' I could swear this was the Aerosmith that I remember so well from a Cincinnati Riverfront Coliseum show in 1977, at the height of their career. The crowd reached a pandemonius level of enjoyment as Tyler screeched out the lyrics of 'Big Ten Inch Record,' from the band's 1975 platinum 'Toys in the Attic' LP, while making his customary vulgar gestures during this song. An unexpected twist found Tyler seated before a keyboard during the moody beginning of 'Dream On.' 'Sweet Emotion' and 'Train Kept-a-Rollin'' quickly followed as Aerosmith brought its reunion show to a tumultuous conclusion" (Toledo Blade, 7/24/1984).

- An AUD recording circulates from this show.

July 24
Five Flags Center
Dubuque, IA
Promoter: Jam Productions
Other act(s): Orion the Hunter
Reported audience: (6,700 capacity)

July 26
City Auditorium
Omaha, NE
Promoter:
Other act(s): Orion the Hunter
Reported audience: 3,698 / 10,000 (36.98%)
Notes:
- From a local review: "The idea behind the current Aerosmith reunion is to expose the new generation of fans to the hard rock that helped pave the way to its beloved heavy metal. But if the ill-attended concert at City Auditorium Arena Thursday is any indication, the Boston band is mostly attracting its old fans on the current tour... The flamboyant Tyler, 36, came out wearing a black tuxedo jacket, no shirt, [and] suspenders, black pants accented with scarves, a black fedora with long feather and an oversized pair of sunglasses. He quickly discarded all but the pants and the suspenders and more than once stooped to tie his shoes a probable occupational hazard with all his jumping around and screaming. For all his visual references to Mick Jagger, Tyler was hard-pressed to keep up the same energy. He was frequently seen panting away, taking a drink or toweling down in exhaustion long before his songs were over...

Perry, in gnarled long hair that frequently hung in his face, played Keith Richards to Tyler's Jagger, adding occasional harmony vocals, and playing most of the lead parts. For his limited success as a solo star, he took center spotlight only once Thursday to sing the old blues number 'Red House.' One got a funny feeling about the band coming back to play all these songs that were nearly all a decade old. Despite Tyler's prancing, the rest of the musicians played with the kind of enthusiasm found in factory workers who have returned to the plant after they've found they can't find any other jobs. In fact, I found the intact Aerosmith a whole lot less fun than the band with replacements that visited the winter before last. Of course, this band's performance can change drastically from night to night. Thursday just seemed especially sluggish and dull" (Omaha World-Herald, 7/27/1984).

July 27
Navy Island
St. Paul, MN

Promoter: Schon Productions
Other act(s): Orion the Hunter
Reported audience: ~7,000 / 15,000 (46.67%)
Set list: Same as July 21
Notes:
- Tickets were printed with July 26 date.
- An AUD recording circulates from this show.

July 29
Arena
St. Louis, MO

Promoter: Contemporary Productions
Other act(s): Orion the Hunter
Reported audience: 6,560 / 9,100 (72.09%)
Reported gross: $79,783
Notes:
- From a local review: "Just when you thought it was safe to go back into the concert halls, Aerosmith, the five-man band from Boston with a tendency for bringing out the animal in concert crowds, is on the loose again. In a summer already riddled with groups on the comeback trail, Aerosmith has apparently found a way to heal the rift that divided its personnel. Back in the Saddle again, for the first time since 1979, are all the original members: Lead singer Steve Tyler, lead guitarist Joe Perry, second guitarist Brad Whitford, bassist Tom Hamilton and drummer Joey Kramer. It was this newly re-formed (reformed?) lineup that took to the Arena stage Sunday night. Although there's little danger of them losing their reputation as rock's bad boys, Tyler and company now seem able to put together a show with a minimum of lewd and obnoxious behavior.

In contrast to last year's concert, on Sunday Tyler acted the saint. While he still instigated the stage rush and doused the front rows with water, there was none of the verbal abuse that characterized his previous performance. Instead, there was just plenty of hard rock, played in the aggressive blues-based style for which Aerosmith is known. Uniquely talented in the blues, Perry's true value to this band was evident as he reeled off solo after Jimi Hendrix-inspired solo, demonstrating his mastery of guitar special effects. Their personality and musical conflicts apparently resolved, Tyler and Perry looked like the tight songwriting team of the past as they collaborated on old favorites such as 'Dream On,' 'Walk this Way' and 'Sweet Emotion,' as well as material from the period of Perry's absence. With the present group making plans to record its first album in almost six years, it remains to be seen whether Tyler and Perry can work as well together writing new material as they did performing the old" (St. Louis Post-Dispatch, 7/31/1984).

July 30
Starlight Theater
Kansas City, MO

Other act(s): Orion the Hunter
Reported audience: ~7,200 / 7,958 (90.48%)
Notes:

- From a local review: "Time was when you could have added Aerosmith to the slag heap of rock burnouts. It had been shredded by critics as a cheap imitation of the Rolling Stones and personnel changes became almost annual events. No more, at least not for the barrage of incandescent music that captured the fantasy of 7,200 persons Monday night at Starlight Theatre. For those folks, at least, Aerosmith hit the bull's-eye... Leering amid the blinding glare of 36 airplane lights, Aerosmith's lead singer, Steve Tyler, kicked into a ferocious version of 'Back in the Saddle Again,' an almost over-powering tune that proved to be the anthem of the evening for this reunion tour that featured all five members of the original Aerosmith ensemble. From there it was a journey down memory lane as the band alternately broiled and toasted its most appetizing array of tunes. 'Bone to Bone,' 'Big Ten Inch,' 'Lord of the Thighs,' 'Dream On,' 'Sweet Emotion' and 'Walk this Way,' all emerged as if cast from the fiery musical forge for the first time. The audience responded in similar fashion, crowding the aisles, chairs, and shoulders of companions — fists raised in musical salute — from the first tune to the last, 90 minutes away. Mr. Tyler taunted, cheered, and urged them on all the way. Joe Perry, the band's original lead guitarist, and Mr. Tyler combined from the start to spark the evening's musical fireworks, mocking and literally spitting on their fans, while drummer Joey Kramer let fly with a seemingly constant barrage of drumsticks that kept the primarily youthful audience titillated and scrambling throughout the night. Despite the abandon of this reunion tour, the crowd was relatively contented. With the original ensemble again fueling its music, Aerosmith's somewhat smoldering reputation for live performance may be rekindled. Only time will tell whether this reunion will weather the musical storms ahead, or quickly — but never quietly —burn itself out" (Kansas City Star, 7/31/1984).

August 1
U.T.C. McKenzie Arena
Chattanooga, TN
Other act(s): Orion the Hunter
Reported audience: (10,240 GA capacity)

August 2
Coliseum
Roanoke, VA
Promoter: Whisper Concerts
Other act(s): Night Ranger
Reported audience: 6,179 / 9,000 (68.66%)
Reported gross: $78,107

August 4
The Centrum
Worcester, MA
Promoter: TFI Entertainment
Other act(s): Orion the Hunter
Reported audience: 20,441 / 23,030 (88.76%) **both nights
Reported gross: $242,692 **both nights
Set list: Back in the Saddle / Mama Kin / Bone to Bone / Big Ten Inch Record / Three Mile Smile / Reefer Head Woman / Lord of the Thighs / Last Child / Get the Lead Out / Red House / Lightning Strikes / Same Old Song and Dance / Dream On / Sweet Emotion / Walk this Way / Milk Cow Blues / Toys in the Attic / Train Kept A Rollin'
Notes:
- From a local review: "The skeptics were debating right up until showtime. Would singer Steve Tyler be able to finish without passing out? What shape would guitarist Joe Perry be in? Would there still be the hard-rock thunder of old, or would this be a long night with an over-the-hill band that didn't know when to quit? Those questions were on the lips of more than a few of Saturday's jampacked 13,500 fans, but Aerosmith silenced them with a booming display that was dramatic proof they're still a major league band. It was a night of making amends, for less than two years ago in this same hall, the unpredictable Tyler collapsed after just a few songs. And then only a couple of weeks ago, Tyler, who has been behaving much better on

this reunion tour, hit the headlines with a loopy performance in Springfield, Ill., causing the show to again be cut short. This time, however, it was all systems go, right down to the finale of hundreds of colored balloons released onto the crowd. Tyler was exceptional, keeping the crowd standing throughout with his lusty hard-rock shrieks and cries. He pranced, strutted, ran around, danced atop speakers and exhorted the fans with his outstretched arms, urging them to sing and shout to the rafters, which they did without hesitation in what was the noisiest, most ecstatic Centrum show in a long while.

Adding to the white-noise nirvana was the revived Joe Perry, who is looking so healthy these days he could be an aerobics instructor. Having kicked a drug problem and also now steering clear of alcohol, Perry played with astonishing fluidity and power. He got down and dirty on Jimi Hendrix' acid-blues, 'Red House,' fingered pretty arpeggios in the gripping ballad, 'Dream On,' and whomped out slashing, supersonic rhythms on the rockabilly of 'Milk Cow Boogie,' during which, with his shirt off and sweat pouring from his face, he raced around stage like a greyhound. The show focused on Aerosmith favorites (new songs will be recorded this fall), but they never sounded better. Macho anthems like 'Back in the Saddle,' 'Big 10' and 'Lord of the Thighs' quickened the pulse of the rowdy, boys-night-out crowd, but the elegantly moving 'Dream On' and 'Sweet Emotion' showed the band to be much more than hard-rock whores. It was the group's teamwork, however, that most impressed. Tyler and Perry were like blood brothers — always knowing where each other was and rushing together for wild vocal harmonies but they received plenty of help from the vastly improved guitarist, Brad Whitford (whose own leads sizzled as well), the cool, tireless bassist Tom and the brutishly forceful but skilled drummer Joey Kramer. The latter also offered a knockout drum solo, weaving rolls, bass kicks and elbow smashes, and standing up several times to check the crowd's reaction" (Boston Globe, 8/6/1984).
- A below average AUD recording circulates from this show.

August 5
The Centrum
Worcester, MA

Promoter: TFI Entertainment
Other act(s): Orion the Hunter
Reported audience: (11,000 capacity)
Set list: Same as Aug. 4
Notes:
- This second date was added due to popular demand.
- An AUD recording circulates from this show, though the show was purportedly professionally recorded.

August 8
Spectrum
Philadelphia, PA

Promoter: Electric Factory Concerts
Other act(s): Helix
Reported audience: 14,652 **SOLD-OUT
Reported gross: $171,635
Set list: Same as Aug. 4
Notes:
- An AUD recording circulates from this show.

August 10
Cumberland County Civic Center
Portland, ME

Promoter: FEI Entertainment
Other act(s): Orion The Hunter, Stompers
Reported audience: 9,500 **SOLD-OUT

Reported gross: $109,317
Notes:
- The Stompers were a fellow Boston band, but one that never broke out of the region though it had released two studio albums by this time. They had also shared bills with the Joe Perry Project in 1983. The band released their seven-song opening set from this show on their "White Lightning and Cold Cuts" album in 2015.

August 11
Le Forum de Montréal
Montreal, QC, Canada
Promoter: Donald K. Donald
Other act(s): Honeymoon Suite
Reported audience: (10,000 capacity)
Set list: Same as Aug. 4
Notes:
- By August 1, only 3,000 tickets had been sold for the concert. Fortunately, sales picked up and made for a respectable local showing. Unfortunately, a security guard was stabbed during this show.
- From a local review: "If you ever needed someone to start a riot, Steve Tyler would be an obvious choice. Tension ran a little high along the aisle separating the first-row seats and the stage as Tyler spent his time

baiting the crowd to come closer, while abusing the bewildered security guards. Luckily, no major incident occurred, and fun was had by all. The remnants of loyal Aerosmith supporters assembled at the Forum Saturday night to pay homage to a band many have idolized for the past 10 years. Even though Aerosmith played here last year, this time there was a difference: The five original members were Back in the Saddle again, delivering the aggressive, ear-shattering sound that had made them one of the most successful America hard-rock bands during the '70s. Flamboyant and wild but always in control, frontman Tyler plays the role of a rock 'n' roll animal to the hilt. This long-limbed scarecrow with Jagger facial figures flies around stage, his mike stand (with colorful ribbons attached) in hand, wailing, whining, and screeching as if there were no tomorrow.

Possessing a distinct and powerful voice, especially noticeable after guitarist Joe Perry sang Hendrix's 'Red House,' Tyler is a poseur at heart. He hangs from the speakers, does perfect flips, and constantly scratches his crotch, knowing that it's all just part of the game. The band's image was certainly more impressive than the sound, as the Forum proved to be its usual acoustical nightmare. From the outset it was hard distinguishing any of the instruments as they meshed into a single barrage of noise. For the most part the show was the Same Old Song and Dance routine. Aerosmith kicked off with 'Back in the Saddle' (no kidding!), and then played all the expected favorites during their 90-minute set... Visually, Aerosmith is a busy band, with each member around stage doing their bit for rock 'n roll. Guitarists Joe Perry and Brad Whitford play in classic — legs apart, torso leaned axeman stance backwards and lips pursed — as they engaged in double guitar onslaughts. Aerosmith drew a respectable crowd, though far from the expected turnout the promoters had hoped for on such a 'historic' occasion. Where the numbers lacked, fan appreciation and enthusiasm filled the space" (Montreal Gazette, 8/13/1984).
- A poor quality AUD recording circulates from this show.

August 13
Metro Center
Halifax, NS, Canada
Other act(s): Honeymoon Suite

Reported audience: (13,000 capacity)

August 14
Auditorium
Bangor, ME
Other act(s): Orion The Hunter, Stompers
Reported audience: (6,000 capacity)

August 19
Community Center Arena
Tucson, AZ
Promoter: Evening Star Productions
Other act(s): Black 'N Blue
Reported audience: ~6,000
Notes:
- Geffen signed act Black 'N Blue had released their self-titled debut album at the beginning of the month. Guitarist Tommy Thayer later became a member of KISS and was part of the band when they toured with Aerosmith in 2003. Black 'N Blue had a minor success with "Hold On to 18." They included a cover of "Same Old Song and Dance" as a bonus track on the Japanese release of their Bruce Fairbairn produced "Without Love" CD in 1985.
- From a local review: "On one hand, there is more to Aerosmith than just five dirty old men who want to keep on acting like teenagers. On the other hand, there isn't much more... Last night Aerosmith played the Community Center Arena for a relatively small crowd of approximately 4,500. If Aerosmith would come back in six months, it could probably sell out the place. There is no denying the band's appeal, regardless of its prurient interests. Several times Tyler had to caution the audience down in front to stop pushing and punching. The band's 90-minute set was filled with an animal urgency infinitely more sensual than anything the newer hard rock bands have done. The music, culled from the band's 14-year history, also has a softer edge than the often mechanical and compulsive sounding songs of newer groups... None of the songs for the new album were played last night. That was an Aerosmith retrospective, with Tyler observing the occasion by wearing a battered black costume full of gaping holes and ragged edges. By show's end he had stripped off everything but the tight pants and a pair of black suspenders.

Aerosmith has always been preoccupied with the themes of needing intimate companionship and feeling confined by authority. Raging not only against the night, but also against the day, week, and month. Tyler manages to make sleazy sex seem like the answer to everything. Wielding his microphone stand as both love object and phallic symbol, he prances and preens, pouting all the while. At his best, he combines the worst elements of Mick Jagger and Jim Morrison. Because Aerosmith doesn't use the extravagant makeup, costumes, or hair styles of new groups such as Mötley Crüe, Aerosmith seems more real. And consequently, more sinister. The audience sensed this on some subconscious level, for an unusually large number of objects were thrown onstage. Most of these were wadded up paper cups, it looked like. There were also a few baseball caps and a couple of larger, though equally harmless, items. For the band's part, drummer Joey Kramer kept flinging drumsticks into the crowd. Toss in a few mashed potatoes and the whole scene would have looked like something from the film 'Animal House'" (Tucson Citizen, 8/20/1984).

August 20
Veterans Memorial Coliseum
Phoenix, AZ
Promoter: Evening Star Productions
Other act(s): Black 'N Blue
Reported audience: 8,246 / 16,700 (49.38%)
Reported gross: $100,226
Set list: Same as Aug. 4
Notes:

- An AUD recording circulates from this show.

August 22
Golden Hall
San Diego, CA

Other act(s): Rough Cutt
Reported audience: ~3,000 / 3,200 (93.75%)
Set list: Same as Aug. 4
Notes:
- Jimmy Crespo later partnered with Paul Shortino in Paul Shortino's The Cutt and was included on the "Sacred Place" album released in 2002. Jack Douglas produced Rough Cutt's second album, "Wants You!" in 1986.
- From a local review: "A regrouped, presumably reformed Aerosmith is back, visiting its stormy '70s rock upon old loyalists and younger headbangers. Touring without benefit of a new album or, worse, without an MTV video, the band does have its original lineup intact for the first time since 1979... Aerosmith performs with the polish and passion of men who've learned their lessons well. Lead singer Steven Tyler commands as the prancing, Jaggering jester — scarves streaming, his voice shrill yet rebel-soulful—while guitarist Joe Perry is the lucid, fast-fingered flash point, sparring with guitarist Brad Whitford as bassist Tom Hamilton and drummer Joey Kramer thunder skillfully. None of this was lost on the more than 3,000 who packed Golden Hall here Wednesday night. They stood on chairs, rapt and responsive, from start to finish, as Aerosmith delivered its fierce, sardonic anthems... Aerosmith may have trouble withstanding its inner turbulence, but so far its best music is standing the test of time" (Los Angeles Times, 8/24/1984).
- An AUD recording circulates from this show.

August 23 **CANCELLED
Pacific Amphitheater
Costa Mesa, CA

Promoter: Parc Presentations
Notes:
- This show was cancelled and replaced with the San Bernardino date.

August 25
Greek Theatre
Los Angeles, CA

Promoter: Nederlander and Associates
Other act(s): Black 'N Blue
Reported audience: 5,870 **SOLD-OUT
Set list: Same as Aug. 4
Notes:
- From a mainstream review: "The 'Back in the Saddle' tour reunites the original lineup of this mid-'70s hard rock quintet... While the players may have looked as if they were exhumed for their comeback, they have lost none of their musical ferocity. The first of two sold-out nights at the Greek boasted an audience both too young to have bought Aerosmith albums when they came out, and so enthusiastic that the first sight greeting new arrivals was a human blockade of terrified security guards and at least one fan being carried out feet first. Aerosmith is a progenitor of all that metaloid music so popular today, and the kids remember their heroes... Steven Tyler — looking like he hasn't seen sunlight or eaten a balanced meal since 1979 — added harmonica breaks as guitarists Perry and Whitford traded off lead licks. Whitford, the less heralded of the two, turned out to be the better player. Still, it was Perry who was given a solo turn to cover Hendrix's 'Red House,' a song he introduced by saying his 'bitch' has been 'giving him a hard time...'

While Perry took the spotlight, Tyler went backstage to have his hair blow-dried, returning with the strongest segment of the show: 'Dream On,' Aerosmith's equivalent to 'Stairway to Heaven,' followed by 'Sweet Emotion' and 'Walk this Way.' The latter proved for the umpteenth time this night that the real

strength of Aerosmith is Tom Hamilton, who invents bass licks you can build a whole song around. Perry ended 'Sweet Emotion' by smashing his guitar into an amp (original move, Pete — err, Joe), and Kramer followed 'Walk this Way' with a drum solo he concluded by flinging the last of his sticks into the teeming crowd and beating the skins with his fists, feet, and face. The audience ate it up. 'Toys in the Attic' wrapped the set, with Tyler waving his scarf-emblazoned mike stand like a weapon, and the encore was 'Train Kept A Rollin'.' The evening was time in a bottle, a quick visit to 1977 more interesting as theatre than rock 'n' roll" (Billboard, 9/8/1984).
- A full AUD recording of this show circulates. There's a few tape speed issues, but it's reasonably clear.

August 26
Greek Theatre
Los Angeles, CA
Promoter: Nederlander and Associates
Other act(s): Black 'N Blue
Reported audience: 5,870 **SOLD-OUT
Set list: Same as Aug. 4
Notes:
- From a local review: "With the possible exception of Mick Jagger, Aerosmith has managed to outlive all the rock groups and performers they so shamelessly 'borrowed' from when they hit the big time in the '70s, which in a way makes irrelevant that particular complaint about this bunch of Boston head-bangers. That very survival, interrupted for a time when guitarist Joe Perry split for a solo career, also tends to soften yet another complaint: this band wasn't really all that good to start with, even within the limited qualitative confines of the hard rock genre. Reunited for the appropriately entitled 'Back in the Saddle' tour, the quintet still isn't very good, but they're certainly no worse, and in some ways, they're in considerably better shape. Greek Theatre show didn't showcase a bit of new material, although the group is now without a label and might have thought about providing a taste or two of new stuff for the various A&R reps spotted in the house that night. But for the capacity house of fans on hand — ranging in age from those clearly old enough to remember the original outfit, to those too young to do so — that was obviously just fine. While the phenomenon is frequently observed in other, softer musical genres, it's hard to remember when a heavy metal crowd has sung along with the band, word for word, every tune. These were loyal, loyal fans. Fanciers of guitar solos, drum solos, guitar-smashings, drumstick tossings, guitar pick tossings, and lead singer sex games could have 'sung' along on those parts as well. This band serves up these elements in ways which even the most retrogressive of 1980s heavy metal squads have retired. But somehow, Aerosmith seems charming doing them. The 90-minute turn, played at somewhat lower volume than desirable because of the outdoor locale, made the kids happy" (Variety, 9/5/1984).
- An AUD recording circulates from this date, though omits half of "Milk Cow Blues" and "Toys in the Attic."

August 28
Orange Pavilion
San Bernardino, CA
Promoter: Parc Presentations
Other act(s): Black 'N Blue
Reported audience: (6,000 capacity)
Set list: Same as Aug. 4
Notes:
- An AUD recording circulates from this show.

August 29
Civic Auditorium
Bakersfield, CA
Promoter: GMS Productions
Reported audience: (10,400 capacity)
Set list: Same as Aug. 4

Notes:
- An AUD recording circulates from this show.

August 31
Coliseum Arena
Oakland, CA

Promoter: Bill Graham Presents
Other act(s): Black 'N Blue
Reported audience: ~8,000 / 13,500 (59.26%)
Set list: Same as Aug. 4

Notes:
- From a local review: "Aerosmith's 1984 tour is called their Back in the Saddle '84 Tour, but from the opening number Friday night at the Oakland Coliseum lead singer Steve Tyler and the boys sounded more as though they had one foot in the stirrup and were hanging on for dear life. Tyler was, in fact, hanging onto his mike stand like a one-legged man to his crutch during Back in the Saddle, and for the rest of the evening moved slowly and awkwardly, appearing to be keeping his center of gravity as low as possible to avoid falling over. The same could not be said for the band and their music, which sounded so mushed down it had nowhere to fall. The sound was a major problem during the 90-minute concert, the brittle distortion obscuring the twin guitar filigrees of recently returned guitarists Joe Perry and Brad Whitford and smearing the band's dynamics... The sound was so bad that some of those very familiar songs remained unrecognizable after they were well along, and the ragged playing didn't help. The tour's title generally refers to the return of the band to its original, mid-'70s line-up, and more specifically to the return of guitarist Joe Perry, who left in 1979 to slog it out on the Bay area club scene.

Perry's rendition of Jimi Hendrix' slow blues, 'Red House,' on which he took an extended solo and a halting lead vocal, mostly proved why his solo career has gone nowhere. Still, the break from singer Tyler's imitation of a teenage alcoholic was a relief. Tyler, who looks something like an anorexic Carly Simon with matted hair, seems to have taken the rock 'n' roll party ethic too seriously. The results have been on stage (and, reportedly, offstage) fist fights, aborted concerts and a commercial nosedive after some very successful records in the mid-'70s. This tour seems unlikely to repair any of the damage done, the group coming off as a throwback rather than a viable, creative unit, although they did strike sparks several times, recalling their former fire. After all, at their best these guys had, and still have, a funky fluidity and bluesy soulfulness that few contemporary hard rock bands can muster. The group stuck close to older songs such... and funky rockers such as 'Big Ten-Inch Record' and 'Walk this Way,' as well as the top-10 ballad 'Dream On' and the rock anthem 'Toys in the Attic.' The conservative song choices were a good idea, for the group's recent material is sub-standard. And their standards were for a time pretty high: All of the songs mentioned here are solid, well-crafted and exciting rock and deserve better treatment than they got Friday night. Although most in the two-thirds capacity audience of about 8,000 cheered their approval, some dissented, judging by the number of shoes, shirts and rolls of toilet paper hurled at the band" (Sacramento Bee, 9/3/1984).
- Pro-shot video circulates from this show. Joe knocks Steven in the head with his guitar during a scorching version of "Milk Cow Blues," and then runs about the stage knocking over Steve microphone stand.

December 7
Tingley Coliseum
Albuquerque, NM

Promoter: Feyline Presents
Other act(s): Black 'N Blue, Stone Fury
Reported audience: 5,100 / 7,422 (68.72%)
Reported gross: $89,683
Set list: Back in the Saddle / Bone to Bone / S.O.S. (Too Bad) / Lord of the Thighs / Three Mile Smile / Reefer Head Woman / Movin' Out / Adam's Apple / Last Child / Walkin' the Dog / Let the Music Do the Talking /

Red House / Seasons of Wither / Dream On / Sweet Emotion / Walk this Way / Same Old Song and Dance / Toys in the Attic / Rats in the Cellar
Notes:
- MCA signed band Stone Fury included future Kingdom Come vocalist Lenny Wolf, who recalled, "I was wearing a ridiculous pink sparkling shirt with a golden butterfly on my chest. I don't know what pill made me do that — I'm still embarrassed! I do remember the big screen in the middle of the huge hall, which said: 'Welcome Stone Fury!' Getting my first 'big hello' from a great USA audience. Nice! Think it was Texas. Never thought I would start in America" (Full in Bloom, 8/6/2011).
- Steven suggested that the band went to extremes to get through the tour: "On this last tour, we looked at each other and promised that we'd both take Antabuse just for the tour. I'd fallen off the stage, going back to my old tricks again" (Spin, 9/1985).
- An AUD recording circulates from this show. Debut of "Let the Music do the Talking," though not yet rewritten in parts.

December 8
County Coliseum
El Paso, TX

Promoter: Feyline Presents / Jam Productions
Other act(s): Black 'N Blue, Stone Fury
Reported audience: 5,961 / 8,000 (74.51%)
Reported gross: $74,320

December 10
Memorial Coliseum
Corpus Christi, TX

Other act(s): Black 'N Blue, Stone Fury
Reported audience: (6,000 capacity)
Set list: Back in the Saddle / Bone to Bone / S.O.S. (Too Bad) / Lord of the Thighs / Three Mile Smile / Reefer Head Woman / Movin' Out / Adam's Apple / Last Child / Walkin' the Dog / Let the Music Do the Talking / Red House / Seasons of Wither / Dream On / Sweet Emotion / Walk this Way / Same Old Song and Dance / Rats in the Cellar / Toys in the Attic / Train Kept A Rollin'
Notes:
- An AUD recording circulates from this show. Steven would sometimes play some chords that sound similar to the beginning of "Darkness" prior to "Dream On."

December 11
Convention Center Arena
San Antonio, TX

Other act(s): Black 'N Blue, Stone Fury
Reported audience: (8,000 capacity)
Notes:
- Guitarist Dick Wagner attended this show with his sons and was a guest backstage. He recalled, "I was backstage saying 'Hello' to the guys, and Steven Tyler goes over in front of all of these people and puts his arm around me and says, 'this is the guy that sold us three-million records. It was the first time they had ever admitted that I had something to do with it. And of course, in front of my sons... it was very special that way. So, I've always held a soft spot for Steven Tyler in my heart. That was such a nice thing to do. He didn't have to do it, it was already non-credited for years" ("Not Only Women Bleed" / Bleedstreet, 8/9/2012).

December 13
Reunion Arena
Dallas, TX

Promoter: Pace Concerts
Other act(s): Black 'N Blue, Stone Fury
Reported audience: (14,939 capacity)
Set list: Rats in the Cellar / Bone to Bone / S.O.S. (Too Bad) / Lord of the Thighs / Three Mile Smile / Reefer Head Woman / Movin' Out / Adam's Apple / Last Child / Walkin' the Dog / Let the Music Do the Talking / Red House / Seasons of Wither / Dream On / Sweet Emotion / Walk this Way / Same Old Song and Dance / Toys in the Attic / Train Kept A Rollin'
Notes:
- An AUD recording circulates from this show as does some pro-shot footage. The presumed last song is not captured on tape.

December 14
The Summit
Houston, TX

Promoter: Pace Concerts
Other act(s): Black 'N Blue, Stone Fury
Reported audience: (14,950 capacity)

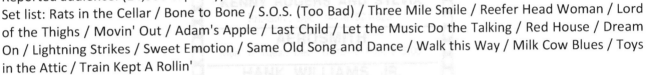

Set list: Rats in the Cellar / Bone to Bone / S.O.S. (Too Bad) / Three Mile Smile / Reefer Head Woman / Lord of the Thighs / Movin' Out / Adam's Apple / Last Child / Let the Music Do the Talking / Red House / Dream On / Lightning Strikes / Sweet Emotion / Same Old Song and Dance / Walk this Way / Milk Cow Blues / Toys in the Attic / Train Kept A Rollin'
Notes:
- Pro-shot video footage circulates from this show.

December 17
Sunrise Musical Theater
Ft. Lauderdale, FL

Promoter: Cellar Door Productions
Other act(s): Black 'N Blue
Reported audience: (4,000 capacity)

December 18
Sunrise Musical Theater
Ft. Lauderdale, FL

Promoter: Cellar Door Productions
Other act(s): Black 'N Blue
Reported audience: (4,000 capacity)
Set list: Rats in the Cellar / Back in the Saddle / Bone to Bone / Lord of the Thighs / Three Mile Smile / Reefer Head Woman / Movin' Out / Last Child / Walkin' the Dog / Let the Music Do the Talking / Red House / Lightning Strikes / Dream On / Sweet Emotion / Same Old Song and Dance / Walk this Way / Milk Cow Blues / Toys in the Attic / Train Kept A Rollin'
Notes:
- An AUD recording circulates from this show.

December 20
Orange County Civic Center
Orlando, FL

Promoter: Beach Club Concerts
Other act(s): Black 'N Blue
Reported audience: 4,254 / 5,800 (73.35%)
Reported gross: $50,637

Set list: Rats in the Cellar / Bone to Bone / Lord of the Thighs / Three Mile Smile / Reefer Head Woman / Movin' Out / Last Child / Walkin' the Dog / Let the Music Do the Talking / Red House / Lightning Strikes / Dream On / Sweet Emotion / Walk this Way / Same Old Song and Dance / Milk Cow Blues / Toys in the Attic / Train Kept A Rollin'
Notes:
- An AUD recording circulates from this show.

December 21
Bayfront Center
St. Petersburg, FL

Promoter: Beach Club Concerts
Other act(s): Black 'N Blue
Reported audience: ~8,300 **SOLD-OUT
Set list: Rats in the Cellar / Back in the Saddle / Bone to Bone / Lord of the Thighs / Three Mile

Smile / Reefer Head Woman / Movin' Out / Last Child / Walkin' the Dog / Let the Music Do the Talking / Red House / Dream On / Lightning Strikes / Sweet Emotion / Same Old Song and Dance / Walk this Way / Toys in the Attic / Train Kept A Rollin'
Notes:
- The last show with Black 'N Blue opening. The band's partied together afterwards.
- From a local review: "In terms of performance, the Bayfront show was uneven, especially when it came to the band's classics. Aerosmith is a band resplendent in rough edges and this concert had plenty of them, intentional and not. Some of the songs — like 'Dream On' and the set closing 'Toys in the Attic' lacked an emotional punch and sometimes were played out of key. Others — 'Sweet Emotion,' 'Back in the Saddle' and the encore 'Train Kept A-Rollin'' were set apart by more penetrating guitars that cut through the smoke-filled arena. The only 'new' song the band offered was a cover of 'Let the Music Do the Talking,' which originally appeared on an album by the Joe Perry Project. It had more melody than the average Aerosmith song and will be recorded by the band on its next record. 'Walk this Way' is easily Aerosmith's greatest tune, and it commanded the most enthusiasm from both the group and the fans. Something about the lyrics 'Walk this Way, talk this way' — and that fabulous interchange when Tyler screams '... just gimme a kiss like this ...' and Perry tears off that familiar guitar riff puts 'Walk this Way' head and shoulders above anything Twisted Sister or Iron Maiden will ever create" (Tampa Bay Times, 12/24/1984).
- An AUD recording of this show exists.

December 26
Civic Center
Glen Falls, NY

Promoter: Frank J. Russo
Other act(s): David Johansen
Reported audience: 4,941 / 8,100 (61%)
Notes:
- Longtime friend David Johansen had then recently released his first studio album in four years, the dance-rock urban "Sweet Revenge." He would be advertised on more opening bills than he actually appeared at. While he might not have been compatible with Aerosmith's audience at the time, the rock-rap hybrid "King of Babylon" may have been a portent of things to come...
- From a local review: "The some 5,000 (they yelled like 7,000) who waited to punch the air Wednesday night inside the Glens Falls Civic Center, who waited to see if Perry and guitarist Brad Whitford had really come home sweet home from their respective seasons of wither, wondered: Do they still have it? Is this the real Aerosmith? ... Tyler, Perry, and Company came out pounding. 'Rats in the Cellar' set the old and familiar Aerosmith pace and theatrics that shook the building during the 14-song, 1 1/2-hour show. A puffy-lipped

Tyler, dressed in gaudy red leotards and a flashy cape, twirled himself and the microphone, did little Indian dances grabbing the air with his hands, pranced, danced, and sassily teased the crowd like a controlled Mick Jagger, every nook of the center throbbing. A healthy-looking Perry laid back near the drums to Tyler's left, the man in black from head to boot to guitar, playing those longed-for choppy rhythms, stepping up occasionally to wail out a lick or sing into Tyler's mike, a seemingly animate version of Keith Richards. By the third song, 'Big Ten Inch Record,' it was apparent: they were playing tight, they sounded real good, [and] they were really enjoying it.

Tyler played the harmonica and tossed it into the crowd; Whitford jammed on his once-downplayed guitar with a rejuvenated power and grace. Some of the newer stuff was tossed in, including the catchy 'Three Mile Smile,' 'When the Lightning Strikes,' one of the few Aerosmith songs to appear on MTV, and even 'Let the Music Do the Talkin',' recorded by Perry during his absence. But the evening was by every nuance the Aerosmith songs everybody had banged their beer cans against road signs to during the last decade. As Tyler sat down to the piano to play 'Dream On,' which may have led the way for ballad-rockers like Lynyrd Skynyrd's 'Free Bird,' the crowd roared before the first ebony and ivory was touched. 'Lord of the Thighs,' 'Walk this Way,' and Sweet Emotion' manifested the same anticipation, the same wild response. Perry, quick and powerful as ever, pumped out the Hendrix blues tune 'Red House,' perhaps in an attempt to show the purists he could still play with the best of them, while Kramer, who tossed drumsticks into the crowd all night, beat out a 10-minute sole shortly after. After a somewhat sped-up version of 'Train Kept a Rollin'' during the encore, the only disappointments were songs left out, like 'Back in the Saddle'" (Glens Falls Post Star, 12/28/1984).

December 27
Civic Center
Providence, RI

Promoter: Frank J. Russo
Other act(s): David Johansen
Reported audience: 13,028 **SOLD-OUT
Reported gross: $153,151
Set list: Rats in the Cellar / Back in the Saddle / Bone to Bone / Big Ten Inch Record / Three Mile Smile / Reefer Head Woman / Lord of the Thighs / Movin' Out / Last Child / Let the Music Do the Talking / Red House / Dream On / Lightning Strikes / Sweet Emotion / Same Old Song and Dance / Walk this Way / Milk Cow Blues / Toys in the Attic / Train Kept A Rollin'
Notes:
- Numerous fans were stranded following the show, due to a heavy snowstorm that hit the area.
- An AUD recording circulates from this show.

December 29
Coliseum
New Haven, CT

Promoter: Cross Country Concerts
Other act(s): David Johansen
Reported audience: 9,945 **SOLD-OUT
Reported gross: $120,882

December 30
Orpheum Theater
Boston, MA

Promoter: Tea Party Concerts
Other act(s): Poison Dollys, Lenny Clarke
Reported audience: 2,800 **SOLD-OUT
Reported gross: $89,958 **both nights

Set list: Same as Dec. 27
Notes:
- The Poison Dollys were an all-female hard rock band from Long Island. They'd release their sole album in 1985. One of the songs on that album, "Love Is for Suckers," was later re-recorded by Dee Snider as the title track for that band's 1987 album.
- From a local review: "But, in late 1984, 11 years after the rock anthem 'Dream On' catapulted them to stardom, Perry and rhythm ace Brad Whitford have signed back on, and Aerosmith is playing with the hungry intensity of the old days, to when the band had to scrounge for rent money. The Bad Boys are back. Last night, before the first of two sold-out Orpheum crowds, the hard-rock quintet delivered a pulsating, let-it-all-out set that should silence all grumblers... Aerosmith got dirty right away, bashing through 'Rats in the Cellar' and 'Back in the Saddle' as fist-waving fans saluted their rejuvenated heroes. While the show included sharp, raunchy renditions of the band's long list of hits... it didn't stop there. Aerosmith spiced its repertoire with tighter, tastier solos and threw in the little-performed gem 'Movin' Out,' the first song Perry and lead vocalist Steven Tyler ever wrote together. Perry, who had released three strong albums during his sabbatical from Aerosmith, got a chance to flex his guitar hand with his best solo cooker, 'Let the Music Do the Talking' and some old blues passages borrowed from Jimi Hendrix.

Maybe it was enthusiasm of the homecoming crowd or the rebirth of the band, but last night's individual performances were among the strongest in years. Tyler, who has had his share of off nights in the past, was on this time around. A rock-and-roll vagabond dressed in pearl-green sequins and scarves, Tyler strutted the stage with his six-foot microphone stand with a furor and slapped hands along the way. His voice was back, too. Years of abuse had begun to rob Tyler of the screeches that made Aerosmith famous, but after last night it's clear he's in full power again. Perry seemed glad to be back, with no evidence of past scrapes with Tyler. Instead, the pair combined for sharp, tight harmonies in the solo Perry tune and played off each other well all night... The sold-out audience gave the locals a hero's welcome and the Bad Boys paid it back. In spades" (Lowell Sun, 12/31/1984).
- From another local review: "Aerosmith, the hometown boys who set hard rock on its ear 10 years ago, had their work cut out Sunday night at the stuffed Orpheum Theater. It had been five years since the band gigged here in their original lineup, and the crowd primed for the first of two sellout nights was howling for former glory. The goods were delivered with an atomic roar. Make no mistake, Aerosmith had this boys'-night-out crowd in the palms of their hands from the first crashing downbeat. Vocalist Steve Tyler, dressed in an androgynous satin-and-lace confection and sporting sunglasses you could drive through plutonium with, was born to hog a stage, and he took charge early, easily shrieking through 'Back in the Saddle' while lead guitarist Joe Perry snapped off tingling guitar fills. The 90-minute, revved-up blast showcased Aerosmith doing what they do better than any current hard rock outfit: strapping a rocket onto rock's essential blues roots...

But the 19-song set was by no means all Tyler and Perry's show. Second guitarist Brad Whitford stepped out for some pretty fantastic leads during the lean Jimi Hendrix classic 'Red House,' while resolute bassist Tom Hamilton and muscleman drummer Joey Kramer formed a steady intestine-grinding underpinning... To be sure, the band played it safe by sticking to can't-lose favorites and it was a little disappointing that they didn't whet the appetite of the crowd for their forthcoming album by offering some new tunes. But Aerosmith proved they still had a few tricks up their sleeves with the descent of a miniature spaceship of lights during Kramer's solo. It's hard to consider Aerosmith a 'reformed' band in the traditional sense, because that word reeks of quick-bucks hucksterism. The revived Aerosmith is young again, fresh, and forceful and back up to full steam. As the crowd of heavy-metal maniacs wandered into the chilly night, it seemed that an old friend had come storming home" (Boston Herald, 1/1/1984).
- An AUD recording circulates from this show.

December 31
Orpheum Theater
Boston, MA
Promoter: Tea Party Concerts
Other act(s): Poison Dollys, Lenny Clarke

Reported audience: 2,800 **SOLD-OUT
Set list: Rats in the Cellar / Back in the Saddle / Bone to Bone / Big Ten Inch Record / Three Mile Smile / Reefer Head Woman / Lord of the Thighs / Movin' Out / Last Child / Let the Music Do the Talking / Red House / Dream On / Lightning Strikes / Sweet Emotion / Same Old Song and Dance / Walk this Way / Milk Cow Blues / Toys in the Attic / Auld Lang Syne / Train Kept A Rollin'
Notes:
- Following this show Tim Collins decides that he has to get clean, in order to get the band members to also clean up their acts.
- Lenny recalled opening for Aerosmith on Jimmy Kimmel Live in July 2019: "I opened for Aerosmith; I didn't know who they were because I was into disco. You know, if you could dance, you could get laid. And I could dance! These guys would come see me, and the fact that I didn't know who they were made them love me even more. So, they invited me to open for them. I go to the theater, and I'm going in with the people and they're saying, 'there's a comedian on tonight. We're gonna kick his ass!' And I'm like, 'Oh, this doesn't sound very good...' I went on, they had runway lights, and I couldn't even see, and they're throwing bottles and then someone hit me in the nuts with a milk dud and brought me to my knees. Standing ovation! And Steven Tyler pulled me through the curtains, gave me a couple of grand, and said 'Come back tomorrow night...' Then they asked me to go to Japan with them."
- Pro-shot VID and SBD audio circulate from this show. The recordings of several songs were released on "Classics Live II" in June 1987: "Back in the Saddle, " "Walk this Way, " "Movin' Out, " "Same Old Song and Dance, " "Last Child, " and "Toys in the Attic."

1985

January 2, 1985
Veterans Memorial Arena
Binghamton, NY
Promoter: Jack Utsick Presents
Other act(s): David Johansen
Reported audience: ~4,500 / 7,200 (62.5%)
Reported gross: $59,719
Set list: Rats in the Cellar / Bone to Bone / Big Ten Inch Record / Three Mile Smile / Reefer Head Woman / Lord of the Thighs / Movin' Out / Last Child / Let the Music Do the Talking / Red House / Dream On / Lightning Strikes / Sweet Emotion / Same Old Song and Dance / Walk this Way / Milk Cow Blues / Toys in the Attic / Train Kept A Rollin'
Notes:
- From a local review: "Rock 'n' roll fans were treated to a couple hours of darn good music last night when the double bill of Aerosmith and David Johansen played at the Broome County Veterans Memorial Arena... Aerosmith must be commended for hitting the road without having a new album on the charts, as hit songs are crucial for pulling in crowds. Their Arena concert did not sell out, but you wouldn't have known it by the way the band played. Throughout their one hour, 40-minute set, which included 'Dream On' and 'Walk this Way.' Aerosmith was sharp, tight, and hard-hitting. Shifting back and forth between blues and pop, their songs' effectiveness was due more to dynamics and melody than mere volume. And what the songs may

have lacked in originality, the band made up for with chops. Lead vocalist Steven Tyler demonstrated that he still possesses good range with his screamer's voice, and he also threw in some fine blues harp and piano playing. He's also a pretty good dancer" (Binghamton Press & Sun Bulletin, 1/3/1985).
- A poor AUD recording circulates from this show.

January 3
Hersheypark Arena
Hershey, PA
Promoter: Makoul Productions
Other act(s): David Johansen
Reported audience: (9,062 reserved capacity)
Set list: Same as Jan. 2
Notes:
- An AUD recording circulates from this show that's presumably missing the encores.

January 4
Stabler Arena @ Lehigh University
Bethlehem, PA
Promoter: Makoul Productions
Other act(s): Poison Dollys
Reported audience: (6,000 capacity)
Notes:
- From a local review: "The black curtain rose, and Aerosmith blasted into 'Rats in the Cellar.' Five years after having gone their separate ways, the band members didn't look a day older or move a bit slower on stage. And the near sellout crowd at Stabler Arena, Bethlehem, Friday night, was as enthusiastic as fans from a few years back, too. They were on their feet after the third song, when lead vocalist Steve Tyler invited everyone down to the front of the stage to get a closer look. Tyler, wearing tight, white satiny pants and a matching white coat with tails, adopted his usual stage presence, complete with multicolored rags hanging from his microphone stand. Prancing about in his Jagger-esque fashion and doing some very suggestive stunts with the mike stand, Tyler was as dynamic as ever. Sounding more heavy metal than on its last tour, Aerosmith still is unique enough to be set apart from the many metal bands which have followed in its wake. The Steve Tyler-Joe Perry combination provides a special bond for the band (lead guitarist Perry has rejoined the band after a solo career). The group's song lyrics are also rooted in the '60s and '70s, rather than being characterized by the bland repetitiveness found in many metal acts of the '80s.

The audience went wild when Tyler played harmonica. On 'Movin' Out,' Tyler proved he could still hit those high screams and screeches raunchy, sexy voice, also showed the Aerosmith sound to be intact. Perry took the spotlight for his version of Jimi Hendrix's 'Red House,' presented underneath, of course, red lights. Ending the show was a 10-minute drum solo by Joey Kramer who

tossed drumsticks into the crowd during the evening. At the end of his solo, the crowd cheered for more. Kramer obliged and a few seconds later, the band also emerged. For the encore, it was the hit, 'Train Kept A Rollin',' a grand finale to the group's 'Back in the Saddle' tour. Judging from the age of the crowd, the concert was a kind of high school reunion for the audience, as well as for Aerosmith. The Boston-based band provided a one-hour 35-minute show of high-energy rock, proving it can still rock with the best of them" (Allentown Morning Call, 1/8/1985).

January 6
Civic Center
Springfield, MA
Promoter: Cross Country Concerts
Other act(s): Poison Dollys
Reported audience: 10,102 **SOLD-OUT
Reported gross: $129,576
Notes:
- David Johansen was noted as the opener in some ads.

January 7
Civic Center
Baltimore, MD
Promoter: First Class Promotions
Other act(s): Poison Dollys
Reported audience: 7,962 / 13,500 (58.98%)
Reported gross: $97,486
Set list: Same as Dec. 27
Notes:
- An AUD recording circulates from this show.

January 9
Holiday Star Theatre
Merrillville, IN
Promoter: in-house
Other act(s): Shuddup & Drive
Reported audience: (3,324 capacity)
Reported gross: $95,000 **both nights

January 11
Holiday Star Theatre
Merrillville, IN
Promoter: in-house
Other act(s): Shuddup & Drive
Reported audience: 3,324 **SOLD-OUT
Set list: Rats in the Cellar / Bone to Bone / Big Ten Inch Record / Three Mile Smile / Reefer Head Woman / Lord of the Thighs / Movin' Out / Adam's Apple / Last Child / Let the Music Do the Talking / Red House / Dream On / Sweet Emotion / Same Old Song and Dance / Walk this Way / Milk Cow Blues / Toys in the Attic / Train Kept A Rollin'
Notes:
- An AUD recording circulates from this show.

January 12
Joe Louis Arena
Detroit, MI

Promoter: Brass Ring Productions
Other act(s): Autograph
Reported audience: 14,854 **SOLD-OUT
Reported gross: $200,529
Set list: Same as Dec. 27
Notes:
- Autograph would only tour with Aerosmith for a short period but enjoyed the experience and felt that they received good exposure. They had already opened for Van Halen and had just released their debut album, "Sign in Please," in Oct. 1985. It included one of their best-known songs, "Turn Up the Radio," which enjoyed heavy rotation on MTV.
- A partial AUD recording circulates from this show.

January 14
L. C. Walker Arena
Muskegon, MI

Promoter: Charlevoix Productions
Other act(s): Autograph
Reported audience: (7,000 capacity)
Set list: Rats in the Cellar / Bone to Bone / Big Ten Inch Record / Three Mile Smile / Reefer Head Woman / Lord of the Thighs / Movin' Out / Last Child / Back in the Saddle / Lightning Strikes / Sweet Emotion / Same Old Song and Dance / Milk Cow Blues / Toys in the Attic / Train Kept A Rollin'
Notes:
- A partial AUD recording circulates from this show. It's missing the final two songs.

January 15
Rupp Arena
Lexington, KY

Promoter: Future Entertainment / Belkin Productions
Other act(s): Autograph
Reported audience: ~4,000 / 9,250 (43.24%)
Set list: Rats in the Cellar / Bone to Bone / Big Ten Inch Record / Three Mile Smile / Reefer Head Woman / Lord of the Thighs / Movin' Out / Adam's Apple / Last Child / Let the Music Do the Talking / Red House / Dream On / Lightning Strikes / Sweet Emotion / Same Old Song and Dance / Walk this Way / Milk Cow Blues / Toys in the Attic / Train Kept A Rollin'
Notes:
- From a local review: "Some things never change, and as far as rock music is concerned, Aerosmith is one of them. The Boston-based quintet started off as a cocky, earsplitting, goofy rock outfit, and last night at Rupp Arena its members showed they were all that and more as a crowd of 4,000 cheered them on... The original lineup opened last night with 'Rats in the Cellar,' from their 1976 album, 'Rocks,' which is still their finest effort. Almost at once, vocalist Steven Tyler, donning a white tuxedo, was off and running in scattered circles around the stage. Tyler remains one of the oddest frontmen for a rock band anywhere. At one point during the show, he would do somersaults or wave the microphone stand in the air as though it were a baton. At other times he would stalk slowly to a corner of the stage, bend over, and slam his hands on his ears as if he had a migraine (or maybe it was just a subtle hint for the sound crew). Antics like that, few of which were initiated by the music, reflected the uneven nature of the first half of the concert. Hits such as 'Last Child' just seemed to lumber along, and even Perry was holding himself in check, allowing Whitford the bulk of the soloing.

But when Tyler left the stage to allow Perry to solo and sing lead on, of all things, a cover of 'Red House,' Perry began cranking it out. While his vocals are pretty flat and thin, Perry made a very convincing statement of his instrumental abilities. When Tyler returned, the band finally kicked into place, ushering in hit after hit from their mid-'70s heyday. It was during this segment that one really had to be amazed at just how popular Aerosmith was for a few years, and how many FM hits they chalked up in such a short time.

Oddly enough, the band was at its tightest on 'Lightning Strikes,' which was pulled from 1982's Rock and a Hard Place, the only album recorded without Perry and Whitford. The song still has a direct, spontaneous feel to it that was lacking a bit in some of the older songs. The remainder of the show was pretty sloppy, and the sound mix was a mess, with Tyler's vocals fading in and out of most songs. During the encore of 'Train Kept a Rollin',' the only winner above the mix was Perry's feedback-laden guitar" (Lexington Herald-Leader, 1/16/1985).
- An AUD recording circulates from this show.

January 17
S.I.U. Arena
Carbondale, IL
Promoter: SIU Arena Promotions
Other act(s): Autograph
Reported audience: (10,816 reserved capacity)

January 18
Ohio Center
Columbus, OH
Promoter: Sunshine Promotions
Other act(s): Autograph
Reported audience: 7,218 **SOLD-OUT
Reported gross: $87,862
Notes:
- The "Back in the Saddle" tour was a success by any measure. The band had grossed $5 million and no one in the band had died.

1984 - Back in the Saddle

Epilogue

The strength of the "Back in the Saddle" tour should not be underestimated. The band had proven that they could still pull in an audience and had enough of a foundation from which to build from. More critically, the band had not imploded again, and none of them or any crew members had died. The issues the band were facing were massive with legal challenges, debts, continued substance issues, and the omnipresent interpersonal conflicts remaining. But with a record deal in the offing, the band had their proverbial foot back in the industry's door and half a chance to move the train down the tracks towards a new destination unknown. Joe and Brad, following their extracurricular slog and years in the wilderness, knew firsthand the void that awaited on the other side if they failed. Steven knew that alternative recipes had not made his cake taste better than the original. As Tim Collins may have put it, "there were no problems, only solutions." Those words were not the empty pontifications of an overly optimistic fool, or the vapid delusions of lunatic. He believed in the mantra. He believed in the band; certainly, with an overabundance of confidence that could alternatively described as delusion, arrogance, or unwavering faith. Ultimately, though, he would be proven right. Getting the band back into the studio was the next step. Even with a six-record deal with Geffen in hand, the resulting album missed on multiple levels.

There's no denying that "Done with Mirror's" production is lacking the fire that earlier studio creations emitted. It lacked energy, excitement, and feels unfinished and muddied akin to the toxic haze that still enveloped the band. It was also rushed, and there wasn't the time to sit down and truly approach the craft and taking the material to its very finest form — even if that meant discarding the ideas that weren't developing appropriately. Even in 1985 other producers had been considered for the project: Bruce Fairbairn, a successful contemporary producer, was ironically rejected on the basis that his work with acts such as Loverboy or Bon Jovi trended towards the "too pop" side of the spectrum; regardless of the quality of his work and the success with those band's and their resultant product. Ted Templeman was tied to the upper echelons of the industry, had worked with the challenging Van Halen, and had been responsible for the stunning Montrose debut in 1973. His resume was impressive. Also considered, but falling outside of the timing of the album, was the use of outside writers. Steven had met one Desmond Child in 1982, and by the time "Done with Mirrors" was being written, Desmond what showing his value with contributions to many contemporary and legacy acts across a very broad spectrum of styles and genres. The timing was again everything.

The reasons for the lackluster response to "Done with Mirrors" are both complex and simple, but the resulting product was another step in the right direction and gave the band another opportunity to tour and to continue to rebuild their reputation. For a new emerging group of fans, the band was looked at as the thing living legends are made off. The glorious stories of their misspent youth became magnified. After the commercial disappointment of "Done with Mirrors," things could so easily have fallen apart, or even worse, the band could have settled for a middling level of mediocrity as a legacy act. But in life, it is not only the strongest who survive, but the luckiest. If the band were lucky in the 70's, with the commercial lifeline the successes of catalogue singles provided them, then Rick Rubin's brilliance at pairing urban hip-hoppers Run DMC with the essentially washed up Toxic Twins was nothing short of a cosmic exclamation. In terms of getting some of the parties on board, it was literally a coup. These two vastly different musical worlds collided, but from the at times uncomfortable union both parties benefitted immensely. Aerosmith was catapulted back into the mainstream, or at least into a parallel universe where they finally kissed their past goodbye with a rebirth of sorts that served as a cleansing of the band's collective soul. In essence the event marked the birth of a new band, which is a story for elsewhere...

The scope of this work has been deliberately limited to that of the original CBS/Columbia era. Following the conclusion of the "Back in a Saddle" tour in early 1985 the band underwent a period of metamorphosis from which something beautiful, but a creature changed, emerged. But the CBS/Columbia era did not simply end, and there are the several catalogue releases that will be discussed, albeit briefly, in closing. Should it ever emerge, Vol. 2 of "Aerosmith On Tour" would span the "Done with Mirrors" tour through ???...

The Columbia Years (Cont)
Ex Post Facto...

While Aerosmith had signed with Geffen in 1985, Columbia continued to release archival material from the band's classic period. What follows is the discography including that material ...

1986 - Classics Live!

U.S. Release Details:
CBS/Columbia C/FC/CT/CK-40329 (Apr. 7, 1986)
CBS/Columbia CT/CK-57369 (Sep. 7, 1993 — 20-bit SBM digital remaster)

Tracks:
A1. Train Kept A Rollin'
(3:23) — Tiny Bradshaw / Lois Mann / Howard Kay
A2. Kings and Queens
(4:39) — Tom Hamilton / Joey Kramer / Steven Tyler / Brad Whitford / Jack Douglas
A3. Sweet Emotion
(5:07) — Steven Tyler / Tom Hamilton
A4. Dream On •
(5:08) — Steven Tyler

B1. Mama Kin
(3:42) — Steven Tyler
B2. Three Mile Smile / Reefer Head Woman
(4:53) — Steven Tyler / Joe Perry // Lester Melrose / Joseph Bennett / Willie Gillum
B3. Lord of the Thighs
(6:42) — Steven Tyler
B4. Major Barbra
(4:00) — Steven Tyler

Album Details:
Executive producers: David Krebs and Steve Leber. Produced by Paul O'Neill, except B4 produced by Paul O'Neill & Tony Bongiovi; Engineered by James Ball, Grey Russell and Thom Panuzio assisted by Teddy Treewella, Paul Special, and Carol Cariefro. Tracks A1, B1-B3 recorded live at the Orpheum Theatre, Boston, MA, Feb. 14, 1984; Track A2 recorded live at the Music Hall, Boston, MA, Mar. 28, 1978; Track A3 recorded live at the Civic Center, Huntington, WV, Dec. 12, 1982; Track A4 recorded live at the Capital Centre, Largo, MD, Nov. 9, 1978; Track B4 different to the "Unreleased Alternative Version" released on Pandora's Box in 1991; though the differences sound more like some doubled vocals, different mixing, and lack of the harmonica solo than being a completely different take. Notable overdubs: A2 (3:13, solo intro). Work on the album was conducted at Clover Recorders in Hollywood, CA.

Brad Whitford: "We think it's nice that our name is being kept in lights and stuff, but we didn't have anything to do with the release. There are a couple of things on in we're not real happy about, but if people enjoy it, fine. If they don't, all we can say is we're sorry. We had nothing to do with it" (Indianapolis News, 5/16/1986). The band had been invited to participate, but with the litigation against Leber-Krebs they never responded. Steven concurred, "I'd be more than glad to put out a 'Classics Live' album as long as I'm consulted. Had we been, we would have made different choices" (Boston Globe, 5/23/1986). Krebs, on the other hand, felt that "Bootleg" sounded dated and fans were looking for an undated-sounding live release. Steven was more than slightly agitated by the album, commenting, "They could have at least waited until we died" (Allentown Morning Call, 4/12/1986).

Players:
◦ Steven Tyler — vocals

- Joe Perry — guitars on A2, A4, and B4
- Brad Whitford — guitars on A2, A4, and B4
- Tom Hamilton — bass
- Joey Kramer — drums
- Jimmy Crespo — guitars on A1, A3, and B1-B3
- Rick Dufay — guitars on A1, A3, and B1-B3

Chart Action:
Chart Peak (USA): #84 (6/14/1986) with 12 weeks on the Billboard charts. The album also reached #71 on Cashbox (5/17/1986) during a 20-week run. Other countries: N/A.

04/26/86	05/03/86	05/10/86	05/17/86	05/24/86	05/31/86	06/07/86
123	113	100	98	95	91	86
06/14/86	06/21/86	06/28/86	07/05/86	07/12/86	07/19/86	
** 84 **	106	135	153	175	X	

RIAA/Sales:
Certified Gold by the RIAA on Jul. 22, 1991 and Platinum on Feb. 26, 2001. During the SoundScan era, the album had sold 524,771 copies between 1991 and 2007.

Supporting Singles:
• A compilation clip video for "Dream On," directed by Marty Callner for Cream Cheese Productions, was distributed in July 1986, in addition to a promotional 12" single featuring the song (Columbia CAS-2333).

1987 - Classics Live II

U.S. Release Details:
CBS/Columbia C/FC/CT/CK-40855 (June 29, 1987)
CBS/Columbia CT/CK-57370 (Sep. 7, 1993 — 20-bit SBM digital remaster)

Tracks:
A1. Back in the Saddle
(4:39) — Steven Tyler / Joe Perry
A2. Walk This Way
(4:22) — Steven Tyler / Joe Perry
A3. Movin' Out
(5:45) — Steven Tyler / Joe Perry
A4. Draw the Line
(5:05) — Steven Tyler / Joe Perry

B1. Same Old Song and Dance
(5:23) — Steven Tyler / Joe Perry
B2. Last Child
(3:44) — Steven Tyler / Brad Whitford
B3. Let the Music Do the Talking
(5:47) — Joe Perry
B4. Toys in the Attic
(4:05) — Steven Tyler / Joe Perry

Album Details:
Executive producers: David Krebs and Steve Leber. Produced by Paul O'Neill and Aerosmith; Engineered by James Ball assisted by Jim Henehan. Mixed by Paul O'Neil and James Ball at the Record Plant, New York City. Mastered at Sterling Sound by Jack Skinner. Tracks A1-A3, B1, B2 & B4 recorded live at the Orpheum Theatre, Boston, MA, Dec. 31, 1984, by the WCBH Mobile Audio Facility, engineered by Steve Colby; Track A4 recorded live at the Ontario Speedway, Ontario, CA, Mar. 18, 1978 during the California Jam II, by the Record Plant (LA) Remote, engineered by Jay Messina; Track B3 recorded live at the Centrum, Worcester, MA, Mar. 12, 1986 by Sam Kooper and Bob Demuth. Much of the "Done with Mirrors" show was broadcast as a Westwood One radio show the week of June 23, 1986. Three other songs from the show ("She's on Fire," "The Hop," and "My Fist Your Face") had also been released on the "Specially-Priced Limited-Edition Live Maxi-Single" for "Darkness" in 1986 via Geffen. When reissued in 1993, the numeric "2" in the title was changed to Roman "II."

Chart Action:
This album did not chart on the Billboard Top-200. From a trade review: "On the heels of group's hit collaboration with Run-D.M.C., 'Walk This Way,' and (as usual) in advance of the group's new Geffen release comes second set of concert shots, mostly from '84 dates. Hot enough, but mainly for the devoted" (Billboard, 7/11/1987).

RIAA/Sales:
Certified Gold by the RIAA on Oct. 28, 1994. During the SoundScan era, the album had sold 434,130 copies between 1991 and 2007.

Supporting Singles:
- There were no singles issued in support of this compilation.

Both "Classics Live!" and "Classics Live! II" were combined as "Classics Live! Complete" (SONY/Columbia 487351-2) in certain markets in 1998.

1987 - Video Scrapbook

U.S. Release Details:
CBS/Fox Video 5529 (Oct. 19, 1987)
CBS/Fox Video 5229-80 (1990 — Laserdisc)

Tracks:
01. Toys in the Attic
(3:45) — Steven Tyler / Joe Perry
02. Same Old Song and Dance
(3:53) — Steven Tyler / Joe Perry
03. Chip Away the Stone
(3:43) — Richard Supa
04. Draw the Line
(4:47) — Steven Tyler / Joe Perry
05. Dream On
(4:42) — Steven Tyler
06. Sweet Emotion
(4:43) — Steven Tyler / Tom Hamilton
07. Chiquita
(4:25) — Steven Tyler / Joe Perry
08. Lightning Strikes
(4:26) — Richard Supa
09. Walk this Way
(3:35) — Steven Tyler / Joe Perry
10. Adam's Apple
(4:34) — Steven Tyler
11. Train Kept A Rollin'
(9:49) — Tiny Bradshaw / Lois Mann / Howard Kay
12. S.O.S. (Too Bad)
(2:39) — Steven Tyler

Release Details:
Executive producers: David Krebs, Steve Leber, and Tim Collins. Directed by Hart Perry; Produced by David Krebs and Steve Leber; Edited by Bill Davis; Track 5 directed by Marty Callner; Tracks 7 & 8 directed by Arnold Levine; Track 12 plays in background to release credits. This package features an introduction to "Dream On" by Steve Tyler filmed specifically for the video, plus home video footage provided by Tom Hamilton, Steven Tyler, and Brad Whitford. Tracks 1, 2, 6, 9-12 were recorded live at the Silverdome in Pontiac, MI, May 8, 1976; Tracks 7 & 8 promotional videos from 1979 and 1982, respectively; Crowd shots in track 03 and track 05 from the California Jam II, Ontario Motor Speedway, CA (1978); Track 03 filmed live at the Capital Center, Largo, MD (1978); Some additional live footage from Cleveland Stadium, Cleveland, OH (1977).

Chart Action:
Chart Peak (USA): #2 (5/14/1988) with 49 weeks on the Billboard Music Videocassette charts. Other countries: N.A.

11/21/87	11/28/87	12/05/87	12/12/88	12/19/87	12/26/87	01/09/88
13	13	5	8	8	8	5
01/16/88	01/23/88	01/30/88	02/06/88	02/13/88	02/20/88	02/27/88
8	8	10	10	10	10	7
03/05/88	03/12/88	03/19/88	03/26/88	04/02/88	04/09/88	04/16/88
7	9	9	8	8	8	8
04/23/88	04/30/88	05/07/88	**05/14/88**	05/21/88	05/28/88	06/04/88
7	7	7	**2**	5	5	10
06/11/88	06/18/88	06/25/88	07/02/88	07/09/88	07/16/88	07/23/88
10	11	11	12	12	16	16
07/30/88	08/06/88	08/13/88	08/20/88	08/27/88	09/03/88	09/10/88
9	9	10	10	6	6	5
09/17/88	09/24/88	10/01/88	10/08/88	10/15/88	10/22/88	10/29/88
5	6	6	10	10	?	X

RIAA/Sales:

Certified Gold by the RIAA on Feb. 17, 1988 for sales of 50,000 copies. This title was originally only released on VHS video cassette though a Laserdisc version later followed. To date, this title has not been reissued in the U.S. on DVD.

1988 - Gems

U.S. Release Details:
CBS/Columbia FC/FCT/CK- 44487 (Nov. 15, 1988)
CBS/Columbia CT/CK-57371 (Sep. 7, 1993 — 20-bit SBM digital remaster)

Tracks:
A1. Rats in the Cellar
(4:03) — Joe Perry / Steven Tyler
A2. Lick and a Promise
(3:03) — Joe Perry / Steven Tyler
A3. Chip Away the Stone •
(3:59) — Richard Supa
A4. No Suprize
(4:24) — Joe Perry / Steven Tyler
A5. Mama Kin
(4:24) — Steven Tyler
A6. Adam's Apple
(4:31) — Steven Tyler

B1. Nobody's Fault
(4:16) — Brad Whitford / Steven Tyler
B2. Round and Round
(5:00) — Brad Whitford / Steven. Tyler
B3. Critical Mass
(4:51) — Jack Douglas / Steven Tyler
B4. Lord of the Thighs
(4:14) — Steven Tyler
B5. Jailbait
(4:35) — Jimmy Crespo / Steven Tyler
B6. Train Kept A Rollin'
(5:44) — Tiny Bradshaw / Lois Mann / Howard Kay

Album Details:
Executive producers: David Krebs and Steve Leber. Previously unreleased track A3 produced by Jack Douglas who had remixed it at Island Media in New York City using a Synclavier for sonic enhancements (to target it at album-oriented rock). The track was engineered by Heny Haid. From a trade review: "From a band that already has three live best-of albums under its studded belt, a second greatest-hits collection may seem excessive" (Billboard, 12/3/1988) ... Especially at a time when "Greatest Hits" had then recently been certified 4X Platinum by the RIAA (11/21/1988).

Chart Action:
Chart Peak (USA): #133 (1/7/1989) with 11 weeks on the Billboard charts. The album also reached #139 on Cashbox (12/24/1988) during a 12-week run. Other countries: N/A.

12/10/88	12/17/88	12/24/88	12/31/88	01/07/89	01/14/89	01/21/89
164	140	138	138	** 133 **	144	154
01/28/89	02/04/89	02/11/89	02/18/89	02/25/89		
155	152	170	189	X		

RIAA/Sales:
Certified Gold by the RIAA on Aug. 16, 1996. During the SoundScan era, the album had sold 434,130 copies between 1991 and 2007.

Supporting Singles:

• "Chip Away the Stone" was released backed with "S.O.S. (Too Bad)" (CBS/Columbia 38/38T-08536). It reached #13 (1/14/1989) during 12 weeks on Billboard's Album Rock Tracks chart and was accompanied by a Hart Perry directed video, which went on the air in early Jan. 1989. It also charted for one week in Cashbox's mainstream Top-100 singles chart at #93.

11/26/88	12/03/88	12/10/88	12/17/88	12/24/88	12/31/88	01/07/89
34	23	15	15	15	15	16
01/14/89	01/21/89	01/28/89	02/04/89	02/11/89	02/18/89	
** 13 **	14	22	39	47	X	

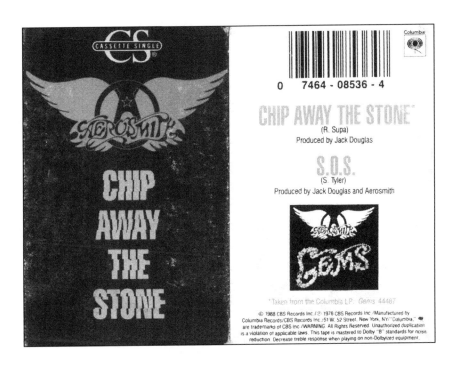

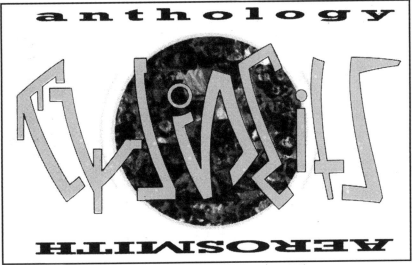

(U.K. licensed "Anthology" Cassette/LP, 1988)

1989 - Live! Texxas Jam '78

U.S. Release Details:
CBS Music Video Enterprises 19V-49013 (Apr. 25, 1989)
CBS/Fox Video 5229-80 (1990 — Laserdisc)

Tracks:
01. Rats in the Cellar
(3:43) — Steven Tyler / Joe Perry
02. Seasons of Wither
(4:15) — Steven Tyler
03. I Wanna Know Why
(3:10) — Steven Tyler / Joe Perry
04. Walkin' the Dog
(3:20) — Rufus Thomas
05. Walk this Way
(3:38) — Steven Tyler / Joe Perry
06. Lick and a Promise
(3:01) — Steven Tyler / Joe Perry
07. Get the Lead Out
(3:51) — Steven Tyler / Joe Perry
08. Draw the Line
(3:12) — Steven Tyler / Joe Perry
09. Sweet Emotion
(4:47) — Steven Tyler / Tom Hamilton
10. Same Old Song and Dance
(5:03) — Steven Tyler / Joe Perry
11. Milk Cow Blues
(5:23) — Kokomo Arnold
12. Toys in the Attic
(2:45) — Steven Tyler / Joe Perry
13. Lord of the Thighs
(1:08) — Steven Tyler

Release Details:
Executive producers: Deborah Newman and Jerry Durkin. Produced by David Krebs and Steve Leber. Directed by Hart Perry. Audio mixed by Jack Douglas. Filmed live at the Texxas World Music Festival at the Cotton Bowl in Dallas, TX on July 1, 1978. Ted Nugent guests on track 11. Track 13 plays over the credits, though the audio from it, track 03 and "Big Ten Inch Record" were released on "Pandora's Box" in 1994. Tom Hamilton recalled, "Texxas Jam. I look at the taps of me onstage — what I was, how I played — and I cringe. All I hear is the cocaine. Lots of cocaine, which gave us a tendency to play too fast. It was fucked, because when we put the band together, we worked so hard to learn to cook, to get that magical feel" ("Walk this Way"). The full audio version of track 13 was later released on "Pandora's Box," and some international product (along with "Big Ten-Inch Record).

From a trade review: "Aerosmith's spectacular 'Permanent Vacation' comeback began with their blistering set at the 1987 Texxas Jam, so a concert video of the band's 1978 performance there seems only appropriate. It also seems to be yet another case of Aerosmith's ex-label capitalizing on its former signees' current success. 'Texxas Jam' follows two fairly recent greatest-hits live albums, 'Classics Live I' and 'Classics Live II,' and another longform video of early concert clips, 'Aerosmith Video Scrapbook' (which has five songs in common with the current one). 'Scrapbook,' however, relied primarily on backstage footage as its between-song filler, while 'Texxas' utilizes your basic stadium shots (roadies at work, aerial pans of the crowd, fans rocking out, etc.). Perhaps coincidentally, it competes with a video of newer material, 'Aerosmith 3x5,' from the band's current label, Geffen" (Billboard, 6/17/1989).

Chart Action:
Chart Peak (USA): #13 (5/27/1989) during seven weeks on the Billboard Top Music Videocassettes chart. Other countries: N.A.

05/27/89	06/03/89	06/10/89	06/17/89	06/24/89	07/01/89	07/08/89
** 13 **	13	16	16	17	17	20

RIAA/Sales:
Certified Gold by the RIAA on Sept. 22, 1989. This title was originally only released on VHS video cassette though a Laserdisc version later followed. To date, this title has not been reissued in the U.S. on DVD. During the SoundScan era, the album had sold 28,055 copies between 1991 and 2007.

1991 - Pandora's Box

U.S. Release Details:
Columbia/SMEI C3T/C3K-46209 (Nov. 15, 1991)
Columbia/SMEI C3K-67995 (Mar. 18, 1997 — Jumbo jewel case packaging)
Columbia/SMEI C3K-86567 (Apr. 6, 2002 — Digi-book packaging)

Tracks:
Disc 1:
1-01. When I Needed You (The Chain Reaction, 1966)
(2:34) — Steven Tallarico / Don Solomon / Peter Stahl
1-02. Make It (w/ lead in, 1972)
(3:45) — Steven Tyler
1-03. Movin' Out (Alt. Version, 1972)
(5:42) — Steven Tyler / Joe Perry
1-04. One Way Street
(6:59) — Steven Tyler
1-05. On the Road Again (Outtake, 1972)
(3:36) — John Sebastian
1-06. Mama Kin
(4:25) — Steven Tyler
1-07. Same Old Song and Dance
(3:53) — Steven Tyler / Joe Perry
1-08. Train Kept A Rollin'
(5:33) — Tiny Bradshaw / Howard Kay / Lois Mann
1-09. Seasons of Wither
(5:39) — Steven Tyler
1-10. Write Me a Letter (Live, 1976)
(4:18) — Steven Tyler
1-11. Dream On
(4:25) — Steven Tyler
1-12. Pandora's Box
(5:42) — Steven Tyler / Joey Kramer
1-13. Rattlesnake Shake (Radio Live, 1973)
(10:28) — Peter Green
1-14. Walkin' the Dog (Radio Live, 1973)
(3:13) — Rufus Thomas
1-15. Lord of the Thighs (Live, 1978)
(7:13) — Steven Tyler

Disc 2:
2-01. Toys in the Attic
(3:05) — Steven Tyler / Joe Perry
2-02. Round and Round
(5:02) — Steven Tyler / Brad Whitford
2-03. Krawhitham (Outtake, 1977)
(3:59) — Joey Kramer / Brad Whitford / Tom Hamilton
2-04. You See Me Crying
(5:12) — Steven Tyler / Don Solomon
2-05. Sweet Emotion (Remix) •
(4:34) — Steven Tyler / Tom Hamilton
2-06. No More No More
(4:33) — Steven Tyler / Joe Perry
2-07. Walk this Way
(3:40) Steven Tyler / Joe Perry
2-08. I Wanna Know Why (Live, 1978)
(3:04) — Steven Tyler / Joe Perry
2-09. Big Ten Inch Record (Live, 1978)
(4:01) — Fred Weismantel
2-10. Rats in the Cellar
(4:06) — Steven Tyler / Joe Perry
2-11. Last Child (Remix)
(3:52) — Steven Tyler / Brad Whitford
2-12. All Your Love (Outtake, 1977)
(5:27) — Otis Rush
2-13. Soul Saver (Outtake, 1975)
(0:53) — Steven Tyler / Brad Whitford
2-14. Nobody's Fault
(4:22) — Steven Tyler / Brad Whitford
2-15. Lick and a Promise
(3:05) — Steven Tyler / Joe Perry
2-16. Adam's Apple (Live, 1977)
(4:48) — Steven Tyler

2-17. Draw the Line (Remix)
(3:43) — Steven Tyler / Joe Perry

2-18. Critical Mass
(4:51) — Steven Tyler / Tom Hamilton / Jack Douglas

Disc 3:

3-01. Kings and Queens (Live, 1978)
(5:33) — Steven Tyler / Tom Hamilton / Brad Whitford / Joey Kramer / Jack Douglas

3-02. Milk Cow Blues
(4:15) — Kokomo Arnold

3-03. I Live in Connecticut (Outtake, 1979)
(0:56) — Steven Tyler / Joe Perry

3-04. Three Mile Smile
(3:45) — Steven Tyler / Joe Perry

3-05. Let it Slide (Outtake, 1979)
(2:55) — Steven Tyler / Joe Perry

3-06. Cheese Cake
(4:16) — Steven Tyler / Joe Perry

3-07. Bone to Bone (Coney Island White Fish Boy)
(3:01) — Steven Tyler / Joe Perry

3-08. No Surprize
(4:27) — Steven Tyler / Joe Perry

3-09. Come Together
(3:46) — John Lennon / Paul McCartney

3-10. Downtown Charlie (Outtake, 1979)
(2:34) — Aerosmith

3-11. Sharpshooter (The Whitford / St. Holmes Band, 1981)
(5:32) — Brad Whitford / Derek St. Holmes

3-12. Shit House Shuffle (Outtake, 1979)
(0:36) — Joe Perry

3-13. South Station Blues (The Joe Perry Project, 1981)
(4:11) — Joe Perry

3-14. Riff & Roll (Outtake, 1982)
(3:18) — Steven Tyler / Jimmy Crespo

3-15. Jailbait
(4:40) — Steven Tyler / Jimmy Crespo

3-16. Major Barbara (Alt. Version)
(5:06) — Tyler

3-17. Chip Away the Stone (Alt. Version)
(4:07) — Richard Supa

3-18. Helter Skelter (Outtake, 1975)
(3:16) — John Lennon / Paul McCartney

3-19. Back in the Saddle
(4:49) — Steven Tyler / Joe Perry

3-20. Circle Jerk (Outtake, 1977)
(3:44) — Brad Whitford

Album Details:

Executive producers: David Krebs, Steven Leber; Produced by Don DeVito; Liner notes by David Wild. "Pandora's Box" was the comprehensive 3 volume collection of 52 songs that included 20 previously unreleased recordings plus a 64-page booklet chock full of details and band member commentary. Originally issued as in a long-box, a shrunken digi-book edition was also released in some markets. Steven recorded vocal overdubs in Studio B at Sound Techniques Inc., Boston, MA, with engineer Vic Anesini and producer Don DeVito. From a trade review: The "collection covers the seminal years of one of America's finest rock bands. The real joy is not the hits that you know by heart, but the amazing amount of unreleased tunes or alternate takes, including a song by Steven Tyler's first band... All of it is lovingly annotated in a classy 70-page booklet that lists the players on each track and includes marvelous recollections (or lack thereof, depending on the year and their sobriety level) by the band members" (Billboard, 11/23/1991). Promotional tie-ins included the band appearing on an episode of Fox Broadcasting Co.'s "The Simpsons," on Nov. 21. The album was reissued in a jumbo CD case, rather long box, to allow for easier display of the product in music store record bins.

Disc 1 details: Track 1 Produced by Richard Gottehrer and arranged and conducted by Dexter Foote. An alternate version previously released as the B-side of the first Chain Reaction 7" single (Date 2-1538) released in December 1966. While credited solely to Tyler, an amended copyright registration from Jan. 1992 is detailed above. Where the 1:58 single edit faded during the second solo the full outro is preserved, as is the reel reference at the beginning of the song; Track 2 features the lead-in riff (possibly edited out for the album), but otherwise is the same as the 1972 studio version; Track 3 an alternative 1972 version that features extended break section and outro motif; Track 5 an unreleased outtake from the 1972 Aerosmith sessions originally recorded by the Lovin' Spoonful for their "Do You Believe In Magic" (1965) album; Track 10 recorded live at the Boston Garden, Nov. 1976; Tracks 13 & 14 previously unreleased live versions recorded at Counterpart Studios in Cincinnati, OH on Sept. 26, 1973 for a radio broadcast; Track 15 previously unreleased live version recorded at the Texxas Jam, Cotton Bowl, Dallas, TX, July 1, 1978; Tracks 4, 6-9, & 11-12 are original album versions.

Disc 2 details: Tracks 3 & 12 recorded at the Cenacle in Armonk, NY, May 1977; Tracks 5, 11 & 17 are 1991 remixed versions of songs by David Thoener. The remix of "Sweet Emotion" has negligible changes, mainly noticeable in the crispness of the drums and a phasing effect added following the break. The remix of "Last Child" simply restores the additional guitar outro section originally lost due to the fade-out start of the album version. As a result, it adds 35-seconds to the duration. The remix of "Draw the Line" extends the break section adding 17-seconds to the duration; Tracks 8-9 previously unreleased live version recorded at the Texxas Jam, Cotton Bowl, Dallas, TX, July 1, 1978; Track 13 recorded at Record Plant Studios in New York City, NY, February 1975; Track 16 recorded live in Indianapolis, IN, July 4, 1977; Tracks 1-2, 4-7, 10, 14-15, & 18 are original album versions.

Disc 3 details: Track 1 recorded live in Boston, MA, Mar. 28, 1978. Previously released on "Classics Live," though more of the song's intro is present on this version (as is an artifact of a "whoo" at the end of the track not present on the WBCN broadcast bootleg); Tracks 3, 5, 10 & 12 unreleased outtakes from the "Night in the Ruts" sessions, 1978/9; Track 9 recorded at the Record Plant, 1978; Track 11 originally released on the Whitford / St. Holmes Band album in 1981; Track 13 originally released on the Joe Perry Project "I've Got the Rock 'n' Rolls Again" album in 1981; Track 14 an outtake from the "Rock in a Hard Place" sessions, 1982; Track 16 an alternative version to that previously released on "Classics Live;" Track 17 an alternative version to that previously released on "Gems;" Track 18 recorded at Great Northern Recording Studios, Boston, MA, 1975; Unlisted track 20 details later attributed to the "Draw the Lines" sessions, 1977; Tracks 2, 4, 6-9, 15 & 19 are original album versions.

Chart Action:
Chart Peak (USA): #45 (1/4/1992) with 9 weeks on the Billboard Top-200 album charts. Other countries: AUS #14; GER #52; HOL #41; SWZ #21.

12/07/91	12/14/91	12/21/91	12/28/91	01/04/92	01/11/92	01/18/92
80	64	48	48	** 45 **	56	97
01/25/92	02/01/92	02/08/92				
152	189	X				

RIAA/Sales:
Certified Gold by the RIAA on Jan. 14, 1992 and Platinum on Aug. 16, 1996. During the SoundScan era, the album had sold 444,425 copies between 1991 and 2007 (with 337,000 selling by the time of the release of the "Box of Fire" bonus disc in 1994).

Supporting Singles:
• "Helter Skelter" was issued promotionally and charted for five weeks on Billboard's Album Rock Tracks chart reaching #21.

11/16/91	11/23/91	11/30/91	12/07/91	12/14/91	12/14/91	
** 21 **	X	40	38	41	X	

• "Sweet Emotion" (Remix) was released commercially, backed with "Subway" and "Circle Jerk" (CBS/Columbia 38T-74101), as a cassingle. It reached #36 during 17-weeks on Billboard's Album Rock Tracks chart, supported with a video directed by Marty Callner. Other countries: UK #74.

12/07/91	12/14/91	12/21/91	12/28/91	01/04/92	01/11/92	01/18/92
** 36 **	42	39	39	38	45	43
01/25/92	02/01/92	02/08/92	02/15/92	02/22/92	02/29/92	03/07/92
46	41	44	46	48	41	40
03/14/92	03/21/92	03/28/92	04/04/92			
46	45	46	X			

A promotional sampler, the "Big Ten-Inch Sampler," was issued in 1991 featuring 10 tracks from the box set. A commercial release, "Pandora's Toys" was issued in select international markets in 1994 featuring a selection of 12 tracks from the box.

1994 - Box of Fire

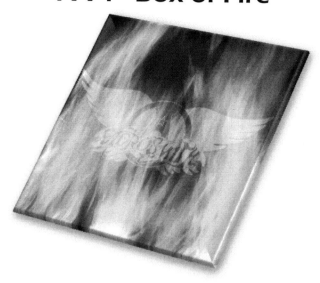

U.S. Release Details:
Columbia/SMEI CXK-66687 (Nov. 22, 1994)

Tracks:
01. Sweet Emotion (Remix)
(4:38) — Steven Tyler / Tom Hamilton
02. Rockin' Pneumonia and the Boogie Woogie Flu
(2:54) — Huey "Piano" Smith
03. Subway (Outtake, 1977)
(3:44) — Brad Whitford, Tom Hamilton, Joey Kramer
04. Circle Jerk (Outtake, 1977)
(3:44) — Brad Whitford
05. Dream On (Orchestral)
(5:44) — Steven Tyler

Album Details:
Initially scheduled for release on Nov. 8. As the first release under the 1991 $25 million SONY/Columbia deal, "Box of Fire" was a collection including all the 12 CBS albums issued 1973-88. It was released around a few weeks after "Big Ones" came out on Geffen and at the same time as the "Woodstock '94" album which included two cuts from the band's performance. The set came with a 5-track bonus CD. Tracks 1 & 4 had previously been released on "Pandora's Box," in the case of the latter track in an uncredited form as the unlisted disc 3 track 20 bonus (though without the "Hey now! Ain't you glad you stayed" introduction). It and the preceding track are finally attributed to the 1977 "Draw the Lines" sessions, both having served as B-sides for the box and later "Pandora's Toys" releases. Track 2 originally released on the DefJam issued soundtrack for the "Less than Zero" movie soundtrack in 1987. Recorded and mixed by Andy Wallace. Track 5 was a special orchestral version recorded for MTV's 10th Anniversary Special in 1991 and included on the "Last Action Hero" movie soundtrack. It was originally recorded with Michael Kamen at the Wang Center in Boston, MA, on Oct. 13, 1991 and broadcast on MTV on Nov. 27. The first 25,000 copies were intended to be individually numbered and contain a special Aero-Hologram sticker.

Chart Action:
This collection did not chart.

RIAA/Sales:
Certified Gold by the RIAA on Jan. 19, 1995. The "Box of Fire" collection was incongruously issued a year after the catalog 20-bit remasters had been released individually, but Columbia hoped that the $119.98 suggested pricing, plus packaging and bonus disc, would be enticing. SoundScan figures indicate that it had sold 59,158 copies by 2007.

RIAA Certifications

RIAA certifications (which cover the U.S. only) paint an interesting picture of the band: Prior to Dec. 31, 1983, the band only had officially certified sales of 5,500,000 copies of the 1973–82 catalog (even though some titles had clearly sold more than the number they were certified for due to varying circumstances). There is one major reason for this seeming inconsistency between trade magazine/PR hype and RIAA certifications — official RIAA multiplatinum certifications acknowledging album sales higher than 1 million units didn't exist until Oct. 1984 (over a year after the mid-line PC/PCT catalog reissue).

In 1976 the creation of a new sales certification had been a result of the numerous informal, or in-house, awards that were being created by labels and third parties to recognize the successes of artists. The RIAA hoped to bring some degree our legitimacy, control, and consistency to the process. And the first album to be awarded platinum certification? The Eagles' "Their Greatest Hits 1971–1975" on Feb. 24, 1976 (it had been released a week earlier). Unfortunately, for albums such as "Aerosmith," "Get Your Wings," and "Toys in the Attic," the new certification applied only to new releases AFTER Jan. 1, 1976 and did not apply to earlier releases.

Album	Date	Certification
Aerosmith	9/11/1975	500,000
Get Your Wings	4/18/1975	500,000
Toys In The Attic	8/11/1975	500,000
Rocks	5/21/1976	500,000
Rocks	7/9/1976	1,000,000
Draw The Line	12/9/1977	500,000
Draw The Line	12/13/1977	1,000,000
Live Bootleg	10/31/1978	500,000
Live Bootleg	12/26/1978	1,000,000
Night In The Ruts	3/13/1980	500,000
Greatest Hits	3/3/1981	500,000
Rocks	10/19/1984	2,000,000

Unlike the platinum award certification, the multi-platinum certification was retroactive, and many record labels jumped on the opportunity to leverage the new PR opportunities the new certification allowed. Five albums received the first multi-platinum awards on Oct. 12, 1984: Three Olivia Newton-John albums, plus her collaboration with ELO for the "Xanadu" soundtrack, and the Oak Ridge Boys. Of course, the timing was convenient for the timing of the "Back in the Saddle" reunion tour! However, a caveat: albums weren't automatically updated to any new certification level. A record company was responsible for making the request and participating in the requisite audit process. At that time only "Rocks" received recertification. Thus, **for the period this book covers**, Aerosmith's official catalog certification status was less impressive than it later became...

Following the reunion tour, though the end of 1986, the cumulative sales of the same catalog albums jumped to 14,500,000 certified copies when Columbia submitted the albums for recertification. By then, a further studio album and the Run D.M.C. collaboration had cemented the band's reformation. Particularly in 1986 the impact on sales of that unexpected collaboration success, and mid-line priced back-catalogue reissue campaigns as collections were refreshed with more convenient cassettes, saw an increase in sales. Of course, jumping forward to mid-2020, that 1973–82 core catalog stands at 32,500,000+ RIAA certified copies, illustrating the benefit of the increased exposure garnered during Geffen years — mega commercially successful albums from "Permanent Vacation" onwards — and the band's sustained mainstream popularity/visibility. The train certainly kept on a rollin' ...

Acknowledgements

Special thanks must be given to the following people for the time or assistance they generously gave me during this project! Not all are listed... In no particular order:

Bruce Kulick
Robert Lawson
Stephen Paley
Eric Singer
Tommy Thayer
Mike Gandia
Mark Prado
Andy Moyen
Chris Hoffman
Steven Emspak
BC Kagan (Photographs on pages ...)
Ken Sharp
Richard Galbraith (Photographs on pages ...)
BJ Kahuna
Bruce Botnick
Corey Nowlin
Tony Mann
Cowboy Mach Bell

Acknowledgements

Made in the USA
Columbia, SC
31 March 2021